The World of Digital Typesetting

John W. Seybold

© 1984 by John W. Seybold

All rights reserved. No part of this book may be reproduced in any form or by any means without permission in writing from the publisher.

10 9 8 7 6 5 4 3 2 1

Printed in the United States of America

Seybold Publications, Inc.
PO Box 644
Media, PA 19063

ISBN: 0-918514-08-8

John W. Seybold, the author of this book, began to work in the field of computerized composition in 1963, when he founded the world's first computer-composition service bureau, a company which he named ROCAPPI, an acronym standing for *Research on Computer Applications in the Printing and Publishing Industry*. This picture, taken in 1970 to serve as the cover for his first book on computer typesetting, shows Mr. Seybold standing in front of the company's Fototronic CRT typesetter, holding samples of text material output in complete pages on an RCA 301 computer, based upon software which Mr. Seybold and his associates defined and developed.

Mr. Seybold began his professional career as an economist, specializing in the field of industrial relations. During World War II he served as Wage Stabilization Director for the Third Region of the National War Labor Board. From 1946 until 1970 he also served as an impartial labor arbitrator, on panels of the American Arbitration Association and as a member of the National Academy of Arbitrators.

Mr. Seybold also worked in the field of industrial relations on behalf of the Philadelphia Printing Industry from 1946 until 1960, and is the author of *The Philadelphia Printing Industry: A Case Study in Industry-wide Collective Bargaining* (University of Pennsylvania Press).

Since 1970 Mr. Seybold has served as principal consultant for The Seybold Consulting Group, and as editor and publisher for Seybold Publications, Inc., whose products include *The Seybold Report on Publishing Systems*. His children, Jonathan, Andrew and Patricia, are also involved in consulting, writing, lecturing, conducting seminars and publishing activities, along with a staff of writers and consultants working in various offices of the two Seybold companies in the United States and abroad.

Table of Contents

Introduction

Chapter 1 *From Dawn to Mergenthaler*

Chapter 2 *The Typewriter*

Chapter 3 *The Handsetting of Type*

Chapter 4 *The Linecasting Machine*

Chapter 5 *Monotype Composition*

Chapter 6 *The Advent of TTS*

Chapter 7 *The Photocomposition Era Begins*

Chapter 8 *Second-Generation Solutions*

Chapter 9 *Third-Generation Typesetters*

Chapter 10 *Basic Computer Concepts*

Chapter 11 *Programs and Programming*

Chapter 12 *The System Environment*

Chapter 13 *The Composition Process*

Chapter 14 *Hyphenation Examined*

Chapter 15 *Input, Verification, Corrections*

Chapter 16 *Video Terminals for Composition*

Chapter 17 *Pagination and "Area Composition"*

Chapter 18 *File Management and Copy Flow*

Chapter 19 *Composition and Word Processing*

Chapter 20	*Data Base Typesetting*	317
Chapter 21	*The "Typesetting" of Art*	334
Chapter 22	*Looking Forward and Back*	358
Chapter 23	*Raster Image Processing*	374
Chapter 24	*Computer-Aided Editing*	399
Chapter 25	*Managing the Technology*	412
Index		419
Index of Illustrations		426

Introduction

THIS BOOK IS WRITTEN for what we hope will be a broad public: for writers, for editors, for traditional typesetters and printers, for entrepreneurs, for publishers contemplating the installation or improvement of a system for editorial input or for content and copy editing, for teachers and students of journalism and printing, and—of course—for those who purchase the services of compositors and need to know more ways of relating to their suppliers.

There is something here, too, for people who are concerned with the tasks of documentation and the preparation of manuals, for in-plant publishers and printers, and for information scientists who are custodians and builders of data banks or are data bank users.

In fact, it seems that there are very few persons in our society, either producers or consumers, who do not need to be kept abreast of all facets of "publishing." For example, the differences between publishers who print and those who distribute information *electronically* is not very great, and these activities are becoming more and more similar as time goes on.

To provide useful information and insights for readers so diverse in their backgrounds, experiences, and in their understanding of one another's tasks and tools, it will be necessary to take very little for granted and to build a foundation upon which an appreciation of the implications of these new technologies may be cultivated. To assist in this task there is a brief general discussion at the outset of the book about the evolution of writing and printing.

But our overall assignment is particularly difficult because of terminological limitations. There is no one label which adequately describes the area of our subject matter. For example, some readers might consider that our principal topic has to do with pre-press activity. But this term is simultaneously too narrow and too broad. It is too narrow because pre-press functions are not normally understood to embrace writing and editorial tasks. It is too broad since it embraces other operations, having to do with imposition, the processing of film, and the making of printing plates, which are only incidentally within the scope of this book—although each day their relevance becomes more evident.

And we must also pay some attention to the preparation of information which possibly will never be produced on a *printing* press, although it will indeed be *published* by means of some kind of imaging engine.

To some degree the term *word processing* might be used to describe the kind of activity we are concerned with, since this is a term which implies some participation by the writer himself, and, by inference, could be construed to encompass all subsequent operations up to the point of plate making and printing. But that term has, perhaps unfortunately, been pre-empted to describe certain activities which are less germane to printing and publishing than they are to the typing of letters and documents, proposals and forms, briefs and specifications. And these office-related functions are not necessarily carried forward with the thought of publication in mind. Nevertheless, we shall find that the needs and tools of word processing and office automation are similar in many respects to those we shall be considering. Indeed, we have prepared a separate chapter which deals with the interrelationships between word processing and publishing.

Our attention will be focused particularly upon the editorial and typesetting interface. An *interface* is the relationship between two or more entities, the manner in which they transact business (*i.e.*, communicate) with each other. Obviously our purpose is to strengthen and deepen all such interfaces, including the relationships between technical people and creative people, typesetting craftsmen and data processing experts, scientists and artists.

But as the reader will have observed, we have had little more success in explaining what our area of interest *is not* than what it *is*. We shall let the matter rest for the moment and hope that the reader will discover his own term for the subject at hand and perhaps determine the boundaries which this term embraces. As with many areas of technology, it is often some years before it is possible to explain what it is that we "have," what it means or portends, and how it can be used. New intellectual disciplines emerge; the practitioners lead the way while scholars follow afterward, seeking to provide a coherent account of what has taken place and why. In the meantime we shall have to suffer with some degree of imprecision, and there is inevitably some fuzziness when it comes to staking out explicitly the boundaries of our inquiry. The fact is that at this point we simply do not know where all of this is leading.

The impact upon the quality of writing

FOR EXAMPLE, one speculation that we have decided not to entertain has to do with the possible impact of new writing and editing technology upon the nature—and especially the quality—of creative writing. On one hand, it may be contended that if the process of recording one's thoughts becomes much more simple, thus facilitating spontaneity, the written product will be more slapdash in character—more poorly organized and perhaps less cogently phrased—because the author will not have had to labor so much at his writing task. On the other hand, it has been suggested that the facility with which changes within the manuscript can be made—massive deletions accomplished and entire paragraphs moved from place to place—

Introduction

should make it possible for the writer to do a better job. It has been argued that the typewriter itself has not promoted great writing and that computers will only make things worse. Authors, it is said, should in effect be obliged to scratch out their immortal lines with a quill pen. Some critics have implied that we would all be better off if written matter were tooled into marble so that the writer would pass on to posterity only the essence of his wisdom and inspiration.

It may be true that the *means* available to the writer do affect—for better or for worse—the quality and quantity of his work. But writing habits are so highly individualized that it would be dangerous, if not absurd, to hazard any generalizations about the impact of these new tools of the trade upon the subject matter itself. All that we can say with certainty is that the time interval between the conception of the idea and its appearance in print can now be dramatically reduced; what is written may be more pertinent to our times and more useful to help shape the future course of history.

But it may also be true that the relationship between *words* and *pictures* will gradually tend to change, and this may imply subtle differences in ways of imparting information. Already we place much more emphasis upon graphics because they are now easier to intermix with text in printed matter than formerly, and also because in non-print media they have been found to be so effective. In the new world of digital typesetting an even more profound evolution is taking place, which tends to make the distinction between letters and pictures more arbitrary than before.

On the whole, however, we have sought to restrain our impulse to draw broad generalizations about the impact of technology upon the quality of information, writing or imaging. But we cannot so readily ignore the concern that some editors and writers have expressed that they may well have less time to do their proper job if a large proportion of their day has to be devoted to the creation of *input* that is automatically fed into *the system*, by means of the *capture of keystrokes*. This concern will cause us to examine the extent to which the author or the editor is in fact inhibited, or whether he may not be liberated by the new technology. Moreover, the burden of accuracy and stylistic consistency may not be so onerous for the future as it has been in the past since there are certain kinds of functions of an editorial nature which computers can perform unobtrusively, and publishers and editors may come to appreciate the assistance so rendered.

But we are obviously flirting with the intriguing peripheral aspects of our topic before we have come to grips with its substance. We have injected considerations which relate to the effects of the new technology upon the people and upon the quality of their endeavors in order to underscore two caveats which we should be careful to remember. One is that we must not be overwhelmed by the technology itself, simply because it is there. And second, as a corollary, *people* should be the masters. But while technology should be the servant, the opportunities afforded by technology cannot be ignored. To some people, in some situations, a new way of looking at and of doing many things will emerge. Some will bury their heads in the sand; others will gallop into the fray only to be hoisted upon their own petards. The rest of us, more sensibly, will no doubt try to strike a happy medium.

The absence of a logical evolution

ONE FURTHER observation seems appropriate before we plunge into our subject, and this is that the technological changes we shall be discussing did not occur logically from a "system's" point of view. These changes started at the bottom and are working their way to the top. To express it even more colloquially, they began downstream and are moving upstream. Consequently, we are obliged to consider the subject matter somewhat in the order in which things came about, rather than to represent these events as if they comprised a rational, total solution. And so we shall begin with tracing the threads of the story very much (but not entirely) in the sequence in which the events occurred.

This is not the first effort we have made at writing this account. Our initial version of this text appeared in 1971, and three other books, under varying titles,[1] have appeared as revisions, more or less at three- to four-year intervals. No sooner does the book appear in print than it is out of date. This has been a source of some considerable dismay on the part of the author, but neither time nor economics have permitted more frequent revisions. And when the revisions occur, as with this edition, we cannot forbear the inclusion of a fair amount of historical material for fear that the way in which this whole thing has happened and is happening will otherwise get lost to posterity.

Nevertheless, the story must be continually updated and we shall try to make arrangements for successive versions to continue to appear, to comprise an ongoing record of what is not an insignificant train of events. One wishes that such an account had been available at the time of Gutenberg and in the centuries immediately thereafter.

By way of acknowledgment, we must also mention that an alternative record does indeed exist, but it is now too vast to tell the story succinctly. That record consists of thirteen volumes (for the most part of 24 issues each) of *The Seybold Report on Publishing Systems,* as well as five years' worth of issues of *The Seybold Report on Office Systems,* and another several years of *The Seybold Report on Professional Computing.* Obviously we have borrowed liberally from our findings in these publications and wish to express our appreciation to all of the members of the Seybold organization for their dedication and devotion as well as their insights.

---

1. *The Primer for Computer Composition*, GCCA, Printing Industries of America, 1971; *Fundamentals of Modern Composition*, Seybold Publications, 1977; and *Fundamentals of Modern Photocomposition*, Seybold Publications, 1979.

I wish to express my appreciation to the members of the extended family of Seybold Publications, Inc. for their loyalty, interest and affection. Above all I want to thank them for their willingness to assume responsibilities I should have been discharging while working on this book. Also, a special acknowledgment to Betsy Breakell for the artwork and Anne Marie Schultheis for her editorial support.

JWS

1

From Dawn to Mergenthaler

WE DO NOT KNOW when man first began to write. One can imagine that messages were scratched into the soil, or blazes were made on rocks and trees for a variety of reasons, many tens of thousands of years ago. Tools with some form of markings on them (perhaps symbols identifying ownership) have been found from the paleolithic or stone age period going back more than 100,000 years. Pictographs or drawings, such as in the caves of Lascaux in France, portray events of more than 16,000 years ago. But the oldest specimens of *writing* are thought to date from about 6000 B.C. Perhaps earlier civilizations wrote on many kinds of materials that did not survive. A stone relief from an Egyptian tomb dating from the twenty-seventh century B.C. shows scribes at work writing on rolls of papyrus, and there are clay tablets from Babylonia and Assyria and elsewhere in the Near East which have been identified as belonging to an era approximately 1900 years before the birth of Christ. These were marked with a stylus while still soft, and subsequently baked so that they became brick-like in substance.

Originally writing consisted of pictographs. But at some point in history they began to represent not only physical objects, but concepts (ideographs) as well. Hence a picture of an ear might be used to convey the meaning of hearing; an eye, seeing; a sun, the passage of a day.

In many countries, as in China, ideographic writing, where symbols stand for objects and ideas rather than sounds, still prevails even today. One student of the alphabet has commented that "a fairly diligent Chinese student is an adult before he has acquired a facility in reading and writing equivalent to that of a fairly diligent child of twelve in a country with an alphabetic system of writing. Especially in this highly technical modern age, the Chinese find themselves handicapped with a cumbersome system of writing. Only in recent years has the Chinese government authorized and undertaken to introduce a system of simplified and phonetic spelling."[1]

But in other countries, especially in the western world, sometime in the period between 4000 and 800 B.C., in an evolutionary development which was said to have taken over a thousand years,[2] pictographs ceased to stand for *things* or *ideas* and began to represent *sounds*. When this development began to occur, writing, as we think of it in our society, came into being. It then became possible to pass on to posterity the accumulated wisdom of the ages. This may well have been the most important event in the history of our civilization.

1. Douglas C. McMurtrie, *The Book*, Covici-Friede, New York, 1937, p. 4.

2. Otto F. Ege, "The Story of the Alphabet," in *Books and Printing*, World Publishing Company, New York, 1951, p. 5.

Origins in Phoenicia

IT APPEARS that our alphabet is derived from the Phoenician, via Greece and Rome. There is evidence that the Phoenician alphabet came directly or indirectly from Egypt, although the route is said to be difficult to trace. A non-pictographic or non-ideographic alphabet was used by the Phoenicians (noted Mediterranean traders) as early as eight or nine centuries B.C. and the Greeks had apparently picked it up at least by the eighth century B.C. Whatever pictographic connotation these symbols may have conveyed had disappeared by that time. There existed a true "alphabet" representing sounds which, in turn, could be combined into words.

The Phoenician alphabet was not only the precursor of both the Roman and Cyrillic alphabets but evidently also profoundly influenced the Hebrew, Arabic, Indian, Javanese, Tibetan and Coptic.[1]

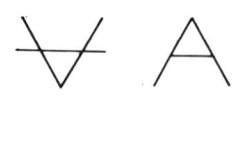

Since the Greeks were only interested in the sound value, they probably did not notice, as one writer points out:
"that A, for instance, had even been a picture of the head of an ox and that it was now drawn upside down, and that the Phoenician name 'aleph' meant ox, and that they mispronounced the sound in calling it *alpha*."[2]

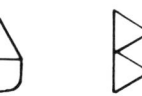

Similarly, the letter B was an abstraction of a symbol for a house. This was a square with a triangle sitting on top, representing a roof. The term "beth" (*Bethel*—house of God; *Bethlehem*—house of bread) was changed to *beta* and hence we get the words for our "alphabet."

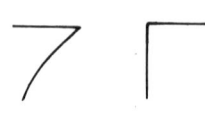

The letter C was derived from a picture of the neck of a camel ("ghemel") which became *gamma*, and D came from a representation of a door ("daleth"), probably of a tent, and daleth became the Greek *delta*.

The Phoenician alphabet consisted of 22 pictures. These the Greeks also used, but changed in appearance and name.

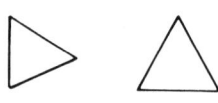

Eighteen of these were passed on to the Romans, probably about 400 B.C. And Otto F. Ege[3] tells us that most of our present 26 letters came from the Roman civilization of about 50 B.C. These are:

A B C D E F H I K L M N O P S T V V Y Z.
(One of the two V's became the letter U.)

Small (lower case) letters evolved during the period from 300 to 800 A.D., along with G and W. J came even later.

The writing materials

THE OLDEST PAPYRUS ROLLS date from about 3500 B.C. This reed was obviously an essential or even vital plant for the Egyptians. Tender shoots were used for food, roots for fuel, fibers for ropes, stalks for thatching and light water craft, and for writing material the reeds were split, then laid vertically on a wet surface and saturated

---

1. Otto F. Ege, *Ibid*, p. 14.

2. *Ibid*, p. 5.

3. *Ibid*, p. 4.

with a gummy substance. Then a similar procedure was applied in the horizontal direction. When the material dried it was polished.

Until papyrus became scarce, only the smooth side was used. Sheets were about twelve by sixteen inches in dimension, but they were pasted end to end in order to make up a roll which usually contained 20 such sheets.

Characters were drawn in columns, from right to left, and each line generally contained about 38 such characters.

It has been said that in the second century B.C. the King of Pergamum in Asia Minor, in an area now in the Caicus valley of Turkey, had a falling out with the Egyptians and that the latter imposed an embargo upon the shipment of papyrus. The use of skins (previously attempted in earlier civilizations) was therefore resumed, and the processes of splitting, tanning and bleaching were significantly improved, so that not only did this substance replace papyrus in Pergamum but throughout the western world. The name "parchment" was derived from Pergamum.

Writing tools

WRITING on a tablet consisted of gouging into wet clay with a stylus. Obviously this led to the use of sharp, angular lines. This writing is called "cuneiform" from the Latin *cuneus,* or "wedge." But writing on papyrus could be done with a reed pen. In fact, the scribes used two such pens—one for red ink derived from iron oxide, and the other for black ink derived from lampblack. Both were mixed with a watery solution of vegetable gum.

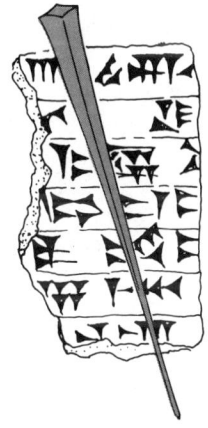

Clay tablet and stylus

The reed was soft and somewhat frayed, providing a brush, so that writing onto papyrus was much like painting. When parchment superseded papyrus the quill took the place of the reed and the character of the writing, as well as the shape of the alphabet, changed.

The Greeks also made use of wooden tablets with character symbols gouged into the surface. Frequently two or more such tablets were bound together. Sometimes the tablets were coated with wax so that temporary notations, as for business transactions, could be recorded and subsequently erased by smoothing out the wax surface. The Romans also made use of waxed tablets of ivory or wood, covered with a blackened wax. But parchment proved to be the prevailing medium wherever a permanent record was desired, and this remained the case until paper came to Europe centuries later.

Paper was actually invented in China in the beginning of the second century A.D. Previously silk had been used but proved to be too expensive. Ts'ai Lun was the inventor, during the Hun Dynasty. As a consequence, pure rag paper was used in China not later than 137 A.D. McMurtrie tells us that its migration can be traced to Europe as follows: Kashmir in the sixth century, Samarkand in 751, Bagdad in 793, Egypt perhaps around 900, Morocco about 1100 and, as a result of the Moorish invasion of Spain, mills were erected in Jativa, in that country, about 1150. The earliest paper mill in "Christendom" was built in Fabriano, Italy about 1270 and one was constructed in

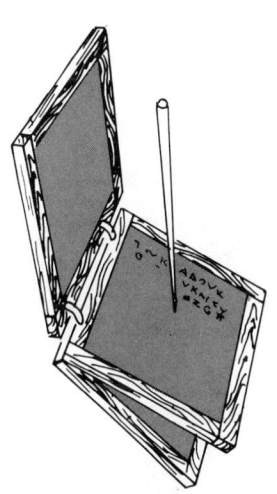

Wooden tablets coated with wax

Germany at Nuremberg in 1390, but not until 1494 was one built in England. Paper was first manufactured in America in 1690.

We are also told that paper was banned or discouraged by the official church because of its alleged Moslem or Jewish origin. Parchment, however, continued to enjoy its status for public documents and, indeed, is still used for the graduate's "sheepskin" even today.

Parchment of course was expensive, although it proved to be very durable. It was not until the printing press came into widespread use that paper began to supplant parchment.

We must now turn to the invention of printing.

Book reproduction prior to printing

BOOKS began to take the place of parchment rolls sometime in the fourth century A.D. The term *codex* was used to describe a collection of parchment sheets bound together. Sheets were folded, making each such sheet into what we would now term a "signature" of four pages (two sheets two sides). These sheets would be fastened together along their folds. These manuscripts (*libri* or *codices manu scripti*)—that is, "books written by hand" had to be so written since there was no other method of reproduction, and such copying took place, for the most part, in monasteries and other similar places. The manner in which such activities were carried on is described by McMurtrie in the following terms:

> The monastic scribe worked about six hours daily. He received his parchment in sections, each sheet separate but folded and arranged in the order in which it should appear in the book as finally bound. After the decision as to the style and size of the writing to be used, the limits of the written page were ruled in with "blind" marginal lines, the parchment being held in place with awls. In addition to the lines limiting the margins, guide lines for the individual lines of writing were ruled upon the parchment with a blunt instrument which made a little furrow in the material. Inasmuch as parchment has two distinct sides, a quarternion, or signature, was arranged so that each two facing pages had the same character—that is, both were hair side or both were flesh side.
>
> After the scribe had finished his quarternion, or group of four sheets in eight leaves, his work was proofread in comparison with the original by a second person, and the sheets were then sent to the rubricator, who inserted titles, headlines, chapter or other initials, notes, and the like. If the book was to be illustrated, the sheets next went to the illuminator. After he had completed his work on the volume, it was ready to be bound.[1]

McMurtrie also tells us that the greatest development of the art of creating manuscript books took place in Ireland, in the sixth through eighth centuries, during which time books of great originality in terms of design were produced, such as the "Book of Kells."

In most cases the manuscripts so copied were derived from other manuscripts created under similar circumstances, perhaps centuries previously. Monasteries created their own libraries. For example, by

---

1. McMurtrie, *op. cit.*, p. 78.

From Dawn to Mergenthaler

the end of the fourteenth century 186 monastic libraries in England cooperated to provide a registry of all the books they held. Universities began to arise in close connection with these church institutions, and in the thirteenth century such institutions existed in Paris, Padua and Bologna. In Paris, an ecclesiastic by the name of Robert de Sorbona was instrumental in the establishment of the university. It is still called the Sorbonne.

As universities began to thrive, a "book trade" developed. Book dealers, or *stationarii* hired scribes to prepare copies of manuscripts which were rented to students who, in turn, made their own copies of the ones they required for further reference or wished to keep in their own collection. Books available in university collections were usually chained to a desk.

There were, of course, book collections by the royalty. In 1373 the French royal library, founded by Charles V, contained 1,000 volumes. It represented the beginning of the Bibliotheque Nationale. Later on, prominent tradesmen also became book collectors.

The printing of books and documents

EVIDENTLY THE FIRST *reproductions* were made by man from images carved on flat stone. These were *intaglio* representations and would have required the use of an inky substance to be deposited in the indentations and thus drawn into the paper by capillary attraction. By the ninth century A.D. raised images on wooden blocks were used for printing in China. A similar process for printing on cloth was developed in Europe, apparently quite independently. Books printed from blocks of wood are called *xylographic books*, and these apparently came into being in the early fourteenth century. One such, issued in 1461, ("The Bible Pauperum") contained both text and illustrations.

The blocks of wood were inked, paper or parchment was laid against them, and manual pressure was exerted on a leather backing material. The inky impression on paper was so heavy that it was evidently impossible to print on both sides of the page.[1]

During this period there was also reproduction by copperplate engravings, and metal blocks cut to print in relief were likewise used. The engravers and carvers of such blocks were goldsmiths. Most plates evidently showed the images and letters in white on a black background, but there were also some plates showing black-line designs on a white background.

Similar techniques, involving wood and metal, were used for the production of playing cards in the fourteenth and fifteenth centuries.

It is obvious that such methods of producing books or other literary materials was extremely time consuming. And as the demand for books grew it became evident that a better method of printing was required. It was, of course, the invention of movable type which made such printing possible and, so far as we know, the development of this process by Johann Gutenberg apparently occurred quite independently of similar inventions in the orient perhaps some four hundred years earlier.

1. See McMurtrie, *op. cit.*, pp. 114-122.

The beginning of the printing process is often associated with the period of the Renaissance. McMurtrie comments that:

> If there had been a darkness covering Europe before, it was the darkness of a fog rather than of night, and the fog was now lifting. It was under just such circumstances that there existed in an extraordinary degree a social need for printing to help dispel that fog. It would be difficult to name any invention at any time for which the world was more eagerly ready.[1]

The Renaissance may be said to have originated in the fourteenth century in Italy. Economic and social conditions were favorable there. There was extensive trade with other areas due to Italy's geographic location. There were also extensive urban populations in the powerful city states, providing an opportunity for the exchange of ideas and the development of art and literature. Dante, Boccaccio and Petrarch were writing in the language of the people instead of in the language of scholars and the church. At the same time, the rise of the Turks threatened to cut off access to the orient and attention turned toward exploration to the west, by sea routes.

Among the many autonomous principalities in Germany, in particular, goldsmiths were at work, possessing the kinds of skills necessary for the processing of metal.

Johann Gensfleisch (who took his mother's maiden name of Gutenberg as was apparently the custom there and then) was born in Mainz about 1397. A dispute relating to his guild caused him to move to Strasbourgh in 1428. There he worked with a goldsmith named Hans Duenne and by 1436 he was involved in a project pertaining to printing. In 1438 he had obtained a printing press made to his specifications by Konrad Saspoch. But by 1448 he had returned to Mainz and had borrowed money from a relative there. In 1450 he borrowed yet more money, this time from Johann Fust, a prosperous merchant, and he increased his obligation to Fust two years later. Fust subsequently sued for repayment and sometime thereafter Fust and his son-in-law, Peter Schöffer, apparently took over some or all of Gutenberg's printing equipment. In 1465 Gutenberg accepted an appointment as a servant and courtier to the Archbishop of Mainz. He died sometime before 1468.

Little information is available as to Gutenberg's activities during the period from 1444 to 1453, but it was during these years that he evidently concentrated his attention upon his invention. The first dated piece of printing preserved today comes from 1454 (a year that can be remembered conveniently since it was one year after the fall of Constantinople to the Turks). The mental association occurs because that particular piece of printed matter consisted of a papal indulgence which was produced in quantity by Gutenberg's press to raise money for a campaign against the Turks. A leaflet ascribed to his press, produced during the same period, was entitled "A Warning to Christendom against the Turks." The famous 42-line Bible was completed not later than 1456. A 36-line Bible was set on new types designed by Gutenberg around 1460.

---

1. McMurtrie, *op. cit.*, p. 126.

From Dawn to Mergenthaler

It should be noted that there are claims that others, particularly from Holland, Italy and France, may have developed similar printing techniques during the same period. But on the whole the experts credit Gutenberg with having put together the means to establish the viable printing process which has contributed so much to the western world. It consisted of a method of designing, casting and molding type, arranging it into lines and pages, and taking numerous impressions from those pages.

The nature of the invention

THE TYPE developed by Gutenberg was not unlike that used for many centuries thereafter and that is still used today for the hand setting of composed material. Since Gutenberg had been trained as a goldsmith he was familiar with tools and techniques for metal working. Perhaps his employees had similar training and experience.

To be able to cast types a matrix or mold is required. To create such a mold it is necessary to develop a punch, containing the letter to be impressed upon the matrix. Such punches had been made before and were used to stamp identifying marks upon the work created by the craftsmen or their workshop.

But it was obviously more difficult to create a punch strong enough to imprint its image upon a piece of metal capable, itself, of serving as a matrix to receive molten metal. And the task of creating such a punch for every letter of the alphabet, in every desired size, was indeed formidable.

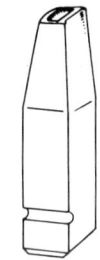
Punch containing character image used to create mold.

The punch cutter first prepared his punch stock, which was, even in those days, made of steel. The piece would have been several inches in length, with a face large enough to contain the letter of a desired size. The punch cutter would then proceed to remove the metal from the end of this stock, leaving only that which was to print. This was done by the use of files, rasps, gravers, planers, hammers and chisels or other similar tools. He would work from a precise drawing of the character to be created, holding the stock in a vise and using a "loop" or magnifying glass to guide the hand and enable the eye to study the effects of each stroke or blow. A proof of the image could be taken at any point by bringing the punch close to the flame of an alcohol lamp, causing the face of the punch to sweat. When the punch was plunged into the flame it acquired a coating of lamp black from which an image could be pressed upon paper.

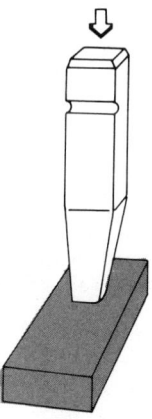
Impression from punch forms image for mold.

When the punch was completed, planed and squared, it was positioned against a somewhat softer metal and struck with a hammer to deliver the necessary imprint or matrix which served as the mold. Brass or copper was used for this purpose, copper being preferred since, being a softer metal, it was less damaging to the punch. A number of matrices could be created by the same punch, although there might be some deterioration in the quality of the image after successive blows had been struck and imprints taken.[1]

1. For a description of this process see Warren Chappell, *A Short History of the Printed Word*, Nonpareil Books, Boston, 1980, pp. 38-51.

Mold of character image for casting.

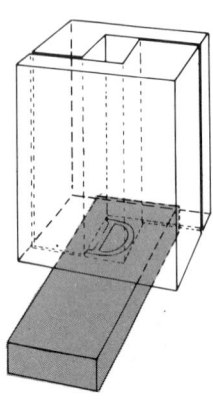

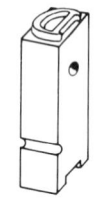

Type cast from image punched onto mold.

The copper matrix or mat would then be hardened as much as possible through an annealing process. Then the type would be cast. A box would be created by placing together two halves, each L-shaped so that when assembled they would form an empty box the size and length of the desired piece of type.

The matrix would be placed face up at the bottom end and held tightly against the mold by a spring. Molten metal, consisting of lead, antimony and bismuth, would be poured into the mold. The mold would then be disassembled, the type removed, inspected and dressed. A piece of type was thus cast.

The font that was used in the 42-line Bible of Gutenberg contained at least 290 characters. Gutenberg attempted to imitate the appearance of handwritten manuscripts where certain combinations of characters were drawn as one. These are called "ligatures." Subsequently many of these ligatures were abandoned in favor of the use of individual characters.[1]

History tells us that Gutenberg was involved in litigation with his financial backers. If it were not for this fact perhaps we would have even less information about his activities. It seems probable that in settlement or partial settlement of the claims against him he was forced to surrender some or all of his punches and matrices, permitting his backers, Fust and Schöffer, to "go into the printing business."

Gutenberg thus presented us with the gift of movable type. No longer would it be necessary for scribes to hand-copy manuscripts or for individuals to labor over the carving of wooden blocks or to scratch characters upon a copper plate. The task of typesetting was nevertheless laborious since it involved the hand assembly of individual types in their proper sequence and, after the printing process had been completed, the redistribution of that type into type cases for subsequent use on another job or another portion of the same job. The distribution as well as the setting was time-consuming work. And if the decision were made to save the "forms"—that is, the types in sequence ready for printing—then more type would need to be cast and prepared by hand for other work the printing office would wish to undertake. At this stage the distinctions between typesetter, printer and publisher were, of course, quite blurred for the printer was indeed the publisher unless, as in the case of papal indulgences, the job undertaken was "commercial" in nature.

The printing process

THE OTHER ASPECT of the Gutenberg invention was the development of a printing press. Until Gutenberg's time printing from raised surfaces, as from wooden blocks or metal plates, was done by applying ink to the image, laying a sheet of paper or vellum on top, perhaps applying some backing such as a leather pad, and then rubbing the sheet against the block with a frotton—a pad of cloth stuffed with wool. But it was natural to think of using a wine press as a device for

1. Chappell, *op. cit.*, p. 52.

From Dawn to Mergenthaler

providing the impression. Based upon this principle, Gutenberg apparently conceived of the design which was executed for him by cabinetmaker Saspoch. A heavy iron plate or platen is lowered against the printing form from the force exerted on a screw drive by the pulling of a handle in a horizontal direction. The bed of the press holds the form, which is made up of pages which have been locked into a metal frame, or *chase,* with the blank spaces filled with wooden blocks, known as *furniture,* and the metal type, held tightly because of the insertion of wooden or metal wedges called *quoins.*

The bed of the press can be moved in under the platen. Attached to the bed is a frame, called the *tympan,* onto which a sheet of paper can be stretched and attached. The tympan provides backing between the platen and the paper and it is possible to increase the packing in certain areas to adjust for variations in the height of the type. This is called an *overlay.* If you put packing under a portion of the form, thus providing an *underlay,* you may also improve the quality of the impression. The process is called *makeready*.

The actual equipment used by Gutenberg was not preserved. Mainz was raided and pillaged in the "Bishop's War" of 1462. This quite possibly caused the printers who were then employed there to migrate elsewhere, thus disseminating information about this technology. Damage to Gutenberg's workshop may also have been due to the machinations of scribes and illuminators who "wielded sufficient political power to have duplication of their works interdicted, except when done by hand."[1] Thus the environment was not necessarily conducive to the survival of a printing establishment.

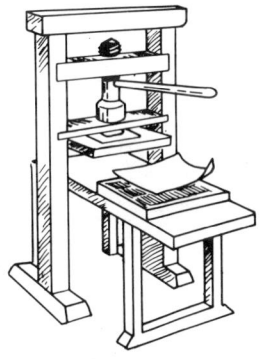

The original printing press was derived from a wine press.

The growth of printing

FUST AND SCHÖFFER were Gutenberg's successors. Gutenberg may have had his own rival printing establishment for a few years. But as early as 1461 there were presses in Strasbourg and Bamberg. In 1462 a press was established in Subiaco, near Rome. The next year there was one in Venice and in 1470 three German printers were invited to set up at the Sorbonne in Paris. By 1473 there was a printer in Ulm. By 1470 there were fourteen cities with printing facilities. By 1480 there were more than 100, of which 47 were located in Italy. Nicholas Jenson, born in France, where he evidently served as a mint-master, is said to have studied with Gutenberg for three years. Subsequently he moved to Venice and later to Rome. He was not only a book printer, but also a famous type designer. William Caxton, writer and translator, printed the first book in English in 1475, at Bruges, in Belgium. He returned to England in 1476 and set up a shop near Westminster Abbey called "At the Sign of the Red Pale."

Books printed between the time of Gutenberg and 1500 are called *The Incunabula*, meaning products derived from the cradle of printing.[2]

According to Chappell, by the year 1500 there were more than 1,100 shops in 200 cities, and they had produced some 12 million books in 35,000 different editions![3]

1. Chappell, *op. cit.*, p. 67.

2. *Ibid*, p. 57.

3. *Ibid*, p. 84.

Moving on to the sixteenth century, developments that are particularly relevant include the fact that a metal screw replaced wood in providing the power action for the printing press. Printing spread to ten more countries, including Mexico (in 1534). The first printing of Martin Luther's New Testament, with illustrations by Cranach, was completed in 1522. Woodcutting began to be used extensively for illustrations to appear along with type, most notably by Albrecht Dürer. Italic type was introduced, and type designers such as Claude Garamond, Robert Granjon and Christophe Plantin made their contributions to the state of the art. Jacob Sabon, a French punch cutter, opened the first independent type foundry in Germany.

By the end of the sixteenth century Queen Elizabeth was on the throne in England, and William Shakespeare's plays were not only being performed but were appearing in print.

The interplay of printing and popular culture

BY THE BEGINNING of the seventeenth century books and printing were very much a part of the cultural heritage. And it became clearer than ever before that the printing press was a powerful tool which could unseat governments or at least create political unrest. Restricting printing establishments was a widespread practice which was not solely introduced (although the pretensions were there) to protect calligraphers and illuminators. In England, for example, the number of print shops and foundries was limited by decree, and the same was true for the American colonies.

Although tracts and broadsides were printed and distributed from time to time, the *Avisa Relation oder Zeitung* of Strasbourg was the first newspaper. It appeared in 1609. Papers began to be introduced in other countries, especially in Holland, and there many clandestine publications intended for distribution in countries such as France, were written and printed. The Stephen Day press was established (the first in the American colonies) in Cambridge, Massachussetts in 1638. The *Bay Psalm Book* was published in 1640. The first American newspaper appeared in 1690. In that year the Governor and Council of Massachussetts passed an ordinance prohibiting "any person or persons to set forth anything in Print without License first obtained."[1] However, on the positive side, Frederick III, Elector of Brandenburg, required that printers of books deposit two free copies in the state's library as a means of preservation and dissemination of knowledge.

A newsletter in manuscript form was undertaken by John Campbell, a Boston postmaster who was in a position to pick up news from post riders and ship captains. In 1704 this paper began to appear in print. His successor founded the *Boston Gazette* which later served to rally the cause of American patriots. James Franklin was the first printer of the *Gazette*. His brother and apprentice, Benjamin Franklin, established the *Philadelphia Gazette* in 1729. The first magazine in the colonies appeared in 1741. Newspapers were begun in many colonial cities during the mid-eighteenth century. At about this same time

---

1. *Ibid*, p. 139

From Dawn to Mergenthaler

the stress portions of printing presses began to be made of iron, and by 1800 an all-iron press was in use.[1] Wood engravings were now widely published along with text. The first steam-driven power press was developed by Friedrich Koenig in Suhl, Germany. A "double press" with two cylinders was installed at *The Times* in London in 1814. It produced 1,100 broadside sheets per hour.

By the beginning of the nineteenth century the Fourdrinier paper-making machine was developed. Its purpose was to manufacture paper in rolls, and ultimately this made possible high-speed printing press production on rotary rather than sheet-fed presses. The other necessary ingredient came about when the *stereotype* method of producing curved printing plates was perfected so that forms containing type and other images could be mounted on circular printing cylinders. The first rotary printing presses were brought into use in the year 1865.

Aloys Senefelder had developed the concept of lithography, printing in a planographic fashion from stones in 1803, and this process was particularly appropriate for the printing of music and posters, as well as other types of illustrations produced by lithographic artists. Mechanical presses for the lithographic process were developed by mid-century, but it was not until the beginning of the twentieth century that offset lithography[2] was developed, and it was perhaps well into the 1940s before offset printing from metal plates produced consistent results for even moderate-length press runs.

Our brief account of the evolution of printing and typesetting technology thus brings us to the latter part of the nineteenth century. The next major change in the state of the arts occurred with the introduction of machine typesetting. This was brought about by the invention of the Linotype machine by Ottmar Mergenthaler, and also the Monotype, by Albert Lanston. These developments will be discussed in Chapters 4 and 5.

The role of the publisher

CHURCHES AND OTHER religious groups, governments, royal families, universities and wealthy merchants performed the functions of publishers and librarians until the time of Gutenberg. Thereafter the *printer* began to play his part and, as we have seen, this often involved a variety of activities. He served as his own punch cutter and type designer. He did his own typesetting. He also printed and probably bound the books that he produced. But beyond this he often served as the publisher, although this duty may have resulted from a commission such as that received by Robert Barker for the King James Bible.

The "press," as it was usually called, also handled the distribution of the product. Frequently the owner of the press decided what he wished to publish, and he may even have made arrangements to undertake the translation of a classic document written some centuries earlier in another language, or to publish some important contemporary work.

1. *Ibid*, p. 163.

2. Offset lithography differs from direct lithography in that the image is first transferred from the printing plate to a rubber cylinder and in turn offset onto the printing paper.

As time passed some degree of specialization crept in. Initially the owner of the press developed his own fonts and often his own type designs. Then foundries came into being, offering to sell matrices or even types to others. Book sellers became middlemen between the press and the ultimate consumer. This became a cause of concern to the printers who saw that their roles were beginning to change.

> The booksellers being growen the greater and wealthier member have nowe many of the best Copies and keepe no printing houses, neither beare any charge of letter, or other furniture but onlie paye for workmanship ...(with) the artifice printer growing every daye more and more unable to provide letter and other furniture, requests for good worke, or to give maytenaunce to any such learned correctours as are behoovefull.[1]

So commented Christopher Barker in 1582. Booksellers themselves became publishers and publishers became booksellers. And among the craftsmen, not only were type designers and foundries separated from the presses, but in many instances there developed a similar separation between typesetters and printers, as well as between printers and binders. Other trade specialties came into being, such as electrotyping, stereotyping and photoengraving. In some instances the typesetting and printing functions remained with the publisher, and under his control, as is the case with most newspapers and some magazines. It has been less true with book and journal publishers.

In any event, over the centuries an arms' length relationship tended to develop between writer, publisher, typesetter and printer. What we are witnessing today is a change in that relationship which may bring us full circle to the days of the sixteenth century presses. Certainly this is a very strong possibility.

As the evolution of typesetting technology is presented in this book, the reader will wish to pause to reflect, from time to time, on the manner in which the various changes discussed tend to affect the entire process of writing, publishing and retaining the published store of knowledge for convenient and effective use, and the consequences that such access may imply for the course of civilization.

But there is another strand to be considered, and this has to do with the development of a writing machine—the typewriter. At first glance it might appear that the consideration of this event and its effects upon our social and intellectual structure are not entirely relevant. Further reflection may indicate that this is not the case. Moreover, there are insights into the processes of composition which can be derived from a closer examination of the functions which the typewriter performs. Thus the next chapter deals with the typewriter.

---

1. *Encyclopaedia Britannica,* 1969 ed., Vol. 18, p. 841.

2

The Typewriter

PERHAPS it may be difficult for us to visualize a world in which typewriters did not exist. They may seem a bit old-fashioned now, since they are being challenged by word processing devices, but they have been so much a part of our life and times for so many years that one wonders how people got along before they existed. They are important not simply because of their usefulness in providing a method of writing which is more legible than the pen, but because they facilitate the process of *copying*.

Techniques for providing even a single copy of a handwritten document were cumbersome and generally unsatisfactory. For example, in the middle of the nineteenth century a business executive:

> ...either wrote his own letters in longhand in pen and ink, or summoned a young man to take shorthand dictation and transcribe, later, in longhand. At the end of the day, the office boys took all the originals and, by wetting them with evil-smelling felt cloths and then pressing the damp letters against the pages of a book, made one copy of each for the record.[1]

It was also possible to insert a crude form of carbon paper between the letter or manuscript and a second sheet, but this was evidently not a common practice. Had it been an easy task to make such a copy, Carlyle would not have had to recreate and rewrite his manuscript of *The French Revolution* when it was accidentally burned by someone in the household of John Stuart Mill. Surely there would have been a copy available!

After the introduction of the typewriter, the use of carbon paper soon followed, as well as stencils and duplicating machines which made it possible for small offices to take over their own internal publishing requirements.

Origins of the typewriter

BACK IN 1714 Queen Anne granted a Royal Letter of Patent to one Henry Mill, protecting for a fourteen year period his invention of "an artificial machine or method for the impressing or transcribing of letters singly or progressively one after another, as in writing, whereby all writings whatsoever may be engrossed in paper or parchment so neat and exact as not to be distinguished from print. . . ."[2]

Evidently Mill's idea, whatever it may have been, didn't work out. Nor did any other proposed solution, whether or not it found its way to a patent office. And evidently the first American inventor of a

1. Bruce Bliven, Jr., *The Wonderful Writing Machine*, Random House, New York, 1954, p. 6.

2. *Ibid*, p. 24.

typewriter, William Austin Burt, failed in his efforts to market either his device or the idea behind it, although he did obtain a patent in 1829.

Many similar patent applications were subsequently filed on the same idea by others. Many patents were granted. Christopher Latham Sholes of Milwaukee, who was "the fifty-second man to invent the typewriter,"[1] received his patent in 1867. Various models were subsequently developed by Sholes and some of his associates, but it wasn't until an arrangement was made with Philo Remington in 1873 that the product began to become practical. Remington agreed to manufacture 1,000 typewriters in his factory which was at that time making guns, sewing machines and farm machinery. Consequently, the first commercial device was called a "Remington."[2]

The first models of the typewriter provided only an all-upper-case alphabet. The use of lower-case characters, and a "shift" to differentiate them, first appeared in 1878.

Mark Twain (Samuel Clemens) was among the first purchasers of the Remington.

> Tom Sawyer appeared in 1876 and, according to Twain's autobiography, the manuscript was typed before it was submitted to a publisher. The Herkimer County (New York) Historical Society, however, believes that Twain made a slip; that he confused *Tom Sawyer* with *Life on the Mississippi* (1883). In any case, Twain was the first author in history to turn in a typewritten book manuscript, starting a double-spaced, one-side-of-the-page trend that has pleased editors ever since.[3]

Other inventors jumped onto the bandwagon and other models appeared—Hammond, Underwood, Royal and Smith being among them. "By 1910 . . . there were two million typewriters in use in the United States and about one-third of them were operated by young ladies gainfully employed for the purpose. The number of patents issued . . . was well past the 2,600 mark, and most of the large-circulation magazines would no longer read unsolicited manuscripts in pen and ink."[4]

The keyboard arrangement

THE TYPEWRITER KEYBOARD was arranged as logically as possible by Sholes and his associates. But the logic was not based upon efficiency from the standpoint of the operator. Blivens points out that "as Sholes struggled through one model after another he constantly changed the keyboard order, trying to avoid certain collisions and jamming that cropped up."[5] The left hand has to do more than half of the stroking. The most frequently used keys are not accessed by the index fingers, and the little finger of the left hand not only has to cover the letter a, but also the shift lock (and, for many years, the back space key).

Despite the drawback of the keyboard arrangement the number of people who have "mastered" the keyboard, or who are at least capable of operating a typewriter moderately well, must represent a

1. Bliven, p. 42.
2. *Ibid*, p. 56.
3. *Ibid*, p.62.
4. *Ibid*, p. 102.
5. *Ibid*, p. 143.

The Typewriter

significant portion of the American population. As of 1953 there were 23,000 schools, including high schools, teaching typing, "and there are seven hundred thousand practice typewriters used for four periods a day, on the average."[1]

In this chapter there have been frequent quotations from a book written by Bruce Bliven, Jr. which appeared in 1954. The book was published before electric typewriters became common and well before the IBM Selectric typewriter was introduced in 1961.

The Selectric substituted for the striking bars of the conventional typewriter a typing "element" popularly called a "golf ball" because of its shape and general appearance. The carriage of the typewriter no longer moved from side to side to make room for succeeding characters. Instead, the platen which holds and advances the paper, remains in a fixed position. It is the printing mechanism which moves across the page.

But the popularity of the Selectric was not due primarily to the improved "action" or responsiveness of the device. Perhaps more important was its ability to substitute one type face for another by replacing the typing element.

For a variety of reasons, it caught the public favor and became the typical office typing machine, although the less expensive, striking bar devices continued to be sold for home and portable use. It is estimated that there are more than 35 million typewriters in offices in the United States, that more than two million (most of them of the Selectric variety) are produced each year, and that the rate of growth has now slowed down to something on the order of two percent per year. These figures, obtained in mid-1983 from several trade association sources, do not include portable typewriters, since very little statistical information appears to be available on these machines.

While it may now be presumed that the heyday of the typewriter is over, the machine will not disappear in a matter of a few years. It continues to perform useful functions in offices and homes, even though for many applications it has been replaced by various types of word processors.

During the first eighty or so years of this century, typewriters, used in conjunction with carbon paper, produced a simple although not entirely trouble-free method of providing modest numbers of multiple copies of documents—for distribution to others and for filing purposes. In addition, it is of course possible to type directly on paper plate Multilith masters which can then be mounted on relatively low-cost duplicating machines in order to provide an inexpensive method of "publishing" when only a few hundred copies are required.

With the advent of the photocopying process in the early 1960s, copying machines began to be introduced in offices and many other public places. It is true, of course, that such devices are able to reproduce handwritten documents as well as those which have been typewritten, but it is probable that the overwhelming proportion of such duplicated documents are from typewritten or printed originals. Carbon paper, although less expensive than the photocopy, became

1. *Ibid*, p. 140.

significantly less popular for office use since it coped poorly with the matter of erasures or strikeovers. Under any circumstances the need to make erasures or to "white out" is messy and frustrating.

Because typewriting is so commonplace, and typewriters are so widespread in use, it is only natural for us to think about the typewriter when we want to put our thoughts down "in writing" for others to consider. As we shall see, the typewriter has become the model or standard which has most profoundly influenced virtually all forms of input and even of editing and telecommunications. It is possible that over the years to come we shall free ourselves from this model. (Some people today consider it rather a "tyranny" than a "standard," since it is or has been so limited in its capabilities—at least as we perceive today what they might be or become.)

Whatever one's view of the typewriter may be, we need to take a closer look in order to understand more clearly what it is, what it does, and how it influences our thinking about communication, printing and the processes related to publishing activity.

The "concepts" behind the typewriter

WHETHER OR NOT the typewriter was invented and developed with these concepts in mind, there are certain functions and notions that the typewriter implies that need to be made explicit.

The first of these is that the typewriter is—or at least until now has always been—a *direct entry machine*—that is, that the person doing the typing is engaged in both input and output functions.[1] Striking its keys activates a mechanism to cause the image of a symbol, letter or character to be printed on a sheet or roll of paper. Over the last century, and until very recently, this relationship between input and output has not benefited by being "buffered." When you strike a key, the character prints. You may have struck the wrong key. If so, you will have printed the wrong character. Thus, this form of direct entry does not imply any storage capability, either for the purpose of making corrections or for subsequent editing—both of which are possible, of course, on a word processor.

It must be said, however, that modern typewriters are now beginning to incorporate some of these word-processing-like features. The first step, introduced by the Correcting Selectric, made it possible for the user to strike a special key which would backspace so that when the wrong character was again struck, it would be "lifted" from the paper, and the desired character could then be typed in. This, of course, was solely a mechanical solution. Not even one keystroke was temporarily retained in any sort of "memory" for subsequent erasure. Later, "electronic" typewriters permitted the user to activate a key which could move back several characters—perhaps a half dozen or so—and, "remembering" what those characters were, cause them to disappear by this same "lifting process." ("Lifting" involves either strikeover with a white substance or the use of a chemical which pulls the black ink out of the paper or a combination of both.) Then the desired words or replacement characters can be struck in their places.

---

1. These terms will be considered in some depth throughout this book. The reader may wish to examine the index for specific references.

The Typewriter

It is perhaps best for the moment to ignore these recent improvements to the functionality of the typewriter. This is not to suggest that they are inconsequential, but the fact is that they have been developed in response to the new opportunities and challenges presented by the word processing devices themselves. These, of course, contain microprocessors, memory and logic—opening up new possibilities.

Such possibilities are most exciting when there is a complete separation between input and output. When you input you may not get a "hard copy" at all—certainly not on a keystroke-by-keystroke basis. Instead, you see a "soft copy" on a video display screen. Later you can obtain a hard copy if you want one—created by a printer which is not a typewriter at all, although in a way it might be considered as the back end of a typewriter, just as the keyboard might be regarded as its front end.

Escapement. The earlier typewriters were built so that the *carriage*, containing the platen, moved across in front of the print location. When each character or space is tapped the carriage moves by the width of that space so that the next character will not overprint on top of the preceding one. The amount of escapement in almost all typewriters is based upon either ten characters to the inch (in order to lay down a character of a size called "pica") or twelve characters to the inch (for the smaller characters of the "elite" size). The machine is so constructed that you select either one size type (and escapement) or the other. The escapement is mechanical in character, being activated by the use of gears and rachets, and cannot be changed after the machine has been built except of course, if it were to be rebuilt. In either case, the amount of escapement is always the same for every character or space. The carriage moves in monospaced increments based upon one-tenth or one-twelfth of an inch.

With the electrically-powered Selectric typewriter, on the other hand, it is the *typing element* which provides the escapement. It moves across the paper incrementally, at monospaced intervals based either upon elite or pica escapement.

However, later models of the IBM Selectric provided the user with the ability to set an adjustment which would permit the user to shift the machine between pica and elite escapement. The mechanism for moving the typing element, while mechanical, is controlled by a cable which, in turn, is regulated by a stepping motor. That motor can receive electrical instructions based upon either the pica or the elite escapement distance. Changes in escapement can be made even within the same document, although the margin alignments may not be precisely the same due to the different unit of measurement which then applies. In either case, however, the escapement is still monospaced.[1]

A few typewriters were designed to provide for some degree of *proportionality* in character laydown or escapement. The IBM Executive typewriter is of this kind. In this instance it is the carriage which "escapes." (Striking bars are used rather than a typing element.) It is electrically powered, but the movement of the platen in response to a

1. See examples on pp. 22-23.

AAAAAAAA
BBBBBBBB
IIIIIIII
JJJJJJJJ
KKKKKKKK
LLLLLLLL
aaaaaaaa
bbbbbbbb
cccccccc
dddddddd
eeeeeeee
iiiiiiii
jjjjjjjj

This is an IBM Executive Typewriter with proportionally spaced characters.

keystroke is mechanical, and the machine is so constructed that the amount of escapement is determined by which keys the operator strikes. Consequently, the escapement is activated according to a *unit system* which varies between two units of width per character and five units. The letter i is two units wide. The letter W is five units wide. Most characters are three units in width. The value of the unit depends upon whether the typewriter uses elite or pica type. The common lower-case characters, which are three units in width, can be laid down on the basis of either ten or twelve to the inch. Consequently, for an elite typewriter a unit is equal to 1/36″ and for a pica typewriter it equals 1/30th of an inch. Since the type face alphabets used are designed to be proportional, if these same characters were laid down on a monospaced basis the result would be unpleasing and difficult to read.

Vertical depth. Paper is invariably mounted on a roller which serves as the platen or backing to provide a firm, smooth surface against which an impression of type can be made. At the conclusion of each typed line the roller advances in increments which are almost invariably six to the inch. For some purposes typewriter gears are available which provide five lines to the inch. A half-line advance is usually possible as well, to permit the positioning of footnote call-out references and other symbols typed above or below the base line of the text itself. When so used, such characters are called *superiors* if above the base line, and *inferiors* if below it, or the terms *subscripts* and *superscripts* may be used.

Paper width. Typewriters may offer a choice of paper width acceptance. All will accommodate the standard 8½″ paper. Most will take a turnpage size of 11″. Some are built for the preparation of tables and charts which require a greater width, such as 13″ or even more. It is inevitable that the line width, which we shall hereafter call *measure*, must be somewhat less, to allow at least a minimum side margin.

Type faces. Typewriters with striking bars are of course made with "relief" (raised) character images. Most manufacturers offer several type faces to choose from in both pica or elite sizes. But once you have purchased the machine you have available only one style, whether it be script or some form of roman or sans serif.[1]

However, on Selectric typewriters and others of the non-striking bar variety, it is usually possible to replace the typing element at will and thus to be able to type a document which presents more than one type face or style. Changing such typing elements is relatively simple, requiring less than a minute to accomplish. Thus the user can intermix roman, italic and bold type if it is deemed worth the effort to do so. Obviously such a typewriter offers a great deal more typographic flexibility, and for any particular task the user may select a typing element offering a face which is appropriate for his or her requirement. He or she may also change from one face to another even to print just one word in italic.

---

1. The term "roman" is usually applied to a type face which is neither italic nor bold, and which is not sans serif. Sans serif means a type face without serifs. Serifs are the fine lines finishing off the vertical strokes of characters.

The Typewriter

The shift condition. On virtually all typewriters built during the last century each key that is struck (except for the spacebar and certain "function" keys such as backspace or tab) will produce two characters. When you strike the key bearing the symbol A you will get either a capital or a lower-case letter a, depending upon its shift status. There is also usually a shift lock which will keep the typewriter in upper shift until you unlock it.

It would be possible, of course, to design a typewriter which would offer more than one set of characters. There could be a "supershift" which could offer access either to other type faces or an alternative selection of characters and symbols, although there is obviously a limit to the number of images which can be positioned upon striking bars or upon a relatively small and highly mobile typing element.

The shift required to bring these additional characters into play was initially accomplished by mechanical means. Depressing the shift key changed the relative position of the platen with respect to the typewriter's striking bars so that two characters could be embossed upon each such bar. However, in a given shift position, only one character could impact the ribbon and deposit its image upon the paper. This was done either by raising the platen when the shift key was engaged, or dropping the entire typing "basket."

No such large and time-consuming mechanical motion is necessary for Selectric models or others with striking characters arranged on some sort of cylinder or wheel. All lower-case characters are on one side of the Selectric typing element, for example, and the depression of the shift key merely rotates that element 180° so that its other half is in a striking position.

We are quite accustomed to working with shift keys. This typing function seems to come as second nature so far as the upper- and lower-case letters of the alphabet are concerned. It is more awkward, however, when we want to get at characters which occupy positions above punctuation marks and numbers on the top row of keys.

Obviously the selection and location of the symbols over the numbers is largely arbitrary. And for the period and comma on the bottom row of keys it has seemed better not to provide alternate characters at all because of the nuisance of having to shift in order to access marks so frequently used. It is more tolerable to have to engage the shift if it is a matter of accessing either a colon or a semi-colon.

Character repertoire. If you purchase a typewriter with characters and symbols engraved, embossed or punched onto the striking bars, you are restricted not only to the type design you have chosen but also to the selection of the characters themselves. At the time you select the machine the dealer may be able to offer you one which gives you some choice of characters in a few positions. But it is impractical to make such machines too versatile. The available characters are chosen to provide as much universality as possible and at the same time to offer as many different characters as possible, even to the point where the user may be required to strike a lower case l (ell) in place of the number 1 (one).

The Remington is illustrative of the striking bar models of non-electric typewriters popular until the middle of the twentieth century.
An inked ribbon holder and a take-up reel were of course mounted on the spindles shown. There was no automatic carriage return. The lever on the left advanced the roller and permitted manual return of the carriage.

In the early 1980s electric typewriters "went electronic" and began to offer the ability to store repetitive phrases in memory and to perform automatic erasure of the last few keystrokes. The character repertoire remained basically the same as on the Selectric typewriters. The typing element can be replaced and alternate styles and pitches can be mounted.

Electrified versions of the striking bar typewriter are, of course, still available. The manual carriage return has now been replaced by the automatic return key shown on the right of the keyboard.

The Typewriter

At the moment the golf ball in our typewriter is called "Bookface Acad 72" and it is a "10-pitch" typewriter type face. This means that it will lay down ten characters to the inch if your typewriter is properly adjusted. (There is a lever on this model which gives us a choice of ten or twelve pitch.)

We have just reset this lever so that, with the same type face, we are now laying down twelve characters per inch. By changing the escapement setting we have not reduced the width of the characters, but we have reduced their side bearings.

It may be that you find the twelve-pitch setting more to your liking. You may or may not find words with the characters closer together to be more legible or readable. But this may also depend upon the type face design.

Here is another type face, called "Courier 12." It was in fact designed to be used at twelve pitch. It is interesting to note, too, that the weight of the type appears somewhat different from the Bookface font we used above. (For the moment we are using the word font to mean type face, but this is not entirely accurate.)

When we set the typewriter back to the 10-pitch setting, using a type face that was designed to be used for 12-pitch, the side bearings are wider. They are really too wide for the type design and the words almost seem to fall apart, becoming harder to read.

The World of Digital Typesetting

About 1968 the original, proportional-spacing IBM Executive Boldface I typewriter was outfitted with a special yoke to accommodate hanger keys for Greek letters and math symbols. This strike-on system was developed to produce *Physical Review Letters* and later was extended to the *Physical Review* itself—both publications of the American Physical Society. The system was also adopted by the American Institute of Physics for its publications. Several hundreds of thousands of journal pages were so produced.

Many extra characters were available and could be mounted on the yoke as required. (See below.)

The Typewriter

In the early 1970s the approach illustrated on the facing page was improved upon. An entire "fan" of special characters could be manually lowered as needed, but they would retract themselves automatically. Additional keys from the box holders shown to the left could be mounted as required. A sample from one of the *AIP* publications, produced in this manner, is also shown.

Integrations over $\vec{r}$ and t give Dirac delta functions of the form $(2\pi)^3 \delta^2[\vec{\eta} \mp (\vec{\xi} - \vec{k}_\perp)]\delta[\omega \mp (\Omega - \omega_0)]$. Then we can immediately integrate over $\vec{\eta}$ and ω to obtain [we include the z dependence of Eq. (4a)]

$$\bar{w}(\vec{\xi}, \Omega; z) = ik_z[\tilde{\alpha}(\vec{\xi} - \vec{k}_\perp, \Omega - \omega_0) + \tilde{\alpha}(\vec{k}_\perp, -\vec{\xi}, \omega_0) - \Omega)]$$
$$\times \exp(i\xi_z z). \tag{7}$$

Some considerable standardization of keyboard layout has developed over the years. The usual arrangement in the United States is the "qwerty" keyboard arrangement—so called because of the location of the six left-hand alphabetic characters on the top row of "alpha" characters, just below the numerals. But except for the letters of the alphabet (the alpha characters) there is less uniformity, although there tends to be a limited number of variations, depending upon the particular market served. A number sign (#) might give way to a "dagger" (†) and an "at" sign (@) might surrender its position to a "bullet" (●). Since the repertoire of characters is always limited there is no good solution—only a "least worst" compromise.

But where there is a replaceable typing element it is possible, of course, to provide not only alternate typeface designs, such as a script for a roman face, but to offer an *extended character set*. The problem then arises as to how to identify and locate these symbols on the keytops to be struck. If you decide that you need a Greek alpha, for example, would you get it by striking the a key (thus giving up the accessibility of the "a" itself) or would you perhaps position it where the percent sign (%) is normally located, possibly on the theory that the type of work which would require an alpha would not require the use of a percent sign. If so, how would you remember what key to strike? And would you be willing to give up the opportunity to gain a large number of new characters in order to preserve some of the regular ones where they are normally located? These are some of the human engineering problems and trade-offs encountered. While there seems to be no practical limit to the number of characters and symbols one might desire to print, most users will be quite happy with a subset which is selected to meet their needs. But what is suitable for one environment may not be applicable to another. Certain character and keyboard arrangements are commonly offered but many different arrangements can be had by special order.

The selection of characters comprising the repertoire on the typewriter may also be termed its *character store* since these are then the only characters which will be available. If, however, you keep several different typing elements handy, so that one could be substituted for another in order to get at a particular character which would otherwise not be available, you could say that the typing element which was mounted constituted your "on-line" character storage, and that the other typing elements constituted your "off-line" storage.

Even with striking bar typewriters you can sometimes have on-line and off-line character storage. For the typing of mathematical and scientific papers there are typewriters available which have removable striking bars. If you desire a particular character you may be able to detach a certain bar and mount another one instead. And for the use of an occasional special character you can sometimes purchase "clip-on" letters which can be mounted on any or selective striking bars, on top of the regular character.

Keyboard layout. Another aspect of the character repertoire problem has to do with the manner in which the symbols in the on-line

The Typewriter

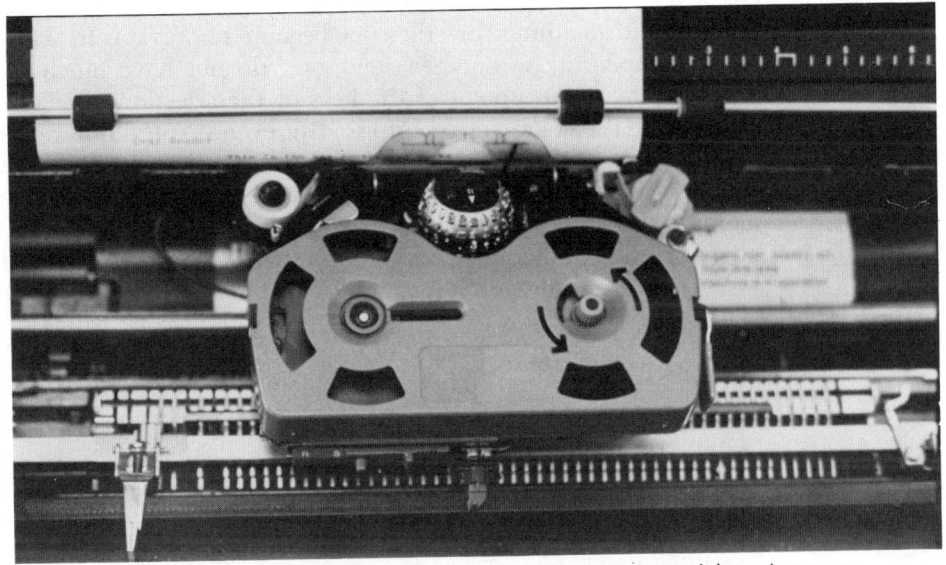

The IBM Selectric II typing element, with ribbon, and special erasing tape, moves across the platen.

This is the standard Selectric keyboard which has gained almost universal acceptance for keyboard arrangement in English-speaking North America.

What characters can we type on our Selectric typewriter? Obviously this will depend upon the <u>character repertoire</u> of the golf ball typing element. Here are the characters available to us with the Bookface typing element.

```
Third row, upper case:  ASDFGHJKL:"
           lower case:  asdfghjkl;'

Bottom row, upper case: ZXCVBNM,.?
            lower case: zxcvbnm,./

Top row, upper case:  !@#$%¢&*()_+
         lower case:  1234567890-=

Second row, upper case: QWERTYUIOP¼
            lower case: qwertyuiop½
```

character store are activated or accessed. This is where human engineering and planning for efficiency become important. In many instances, especially with typewriters, you do not have much choice either of the arrangement of the keys or the selection of characters available in the character repertoire. But even if you did have such a choice, there remains the problem of productivity and efficiency. If you were a manager of a typing operation with specialized requirements, would you be better off if you were to design a special keyboard arrangement appropriate for your class of work, but one which would require some period of training (even for experienced typists) before they became accustomed to it? Or would it be better to live with a less ideal environment because of the cost of training and the turnover of personnel? This is a problem that has perplexed many managers and owners in the typesetting industry for many years and no doubt will continue to do so.

Character selection. In addition to the matter of choosing the appropriate on-line store of characters and determining the manner in which the keys to access this store are to be struck by the user, there is another aspect to character selection. This has to do with *the manner in which the device itself manages to fetch the character and bring it into operation* or otherwise produce the image of that character on the page at the right time and place. Let us assume that the device has in its possession a certain limited collection of character images, which we will call a "font." What procedure will that device use in order to pick from its store the particular character which is desired? When one looks at a typewriter it would appear to be self-evident that the selection of a character from the on-line character store is merely a matter of striking the indicated key top. This is certainly the case when it comes to striking bar typewriters. But with a Selectric typewriter, for example, the relationship between the key struck and character accessed is somewhat more complex.

The Selectric typewriter does indeed preserve the relationship between key and desired character. But the problem remains as to the mechanism by which the Selectric will in fact access the desired character. The actual process of isolating one character from a collection of characters, and producing that character upon demand, turns out to be quite complex. We will have occasion to explore a number of different solutions to this particular problem as we discuss phototypesetting devices.

It may be of interest, however, to study the mechanism which is used on the Selectric typewriter. Note that the typing element does not spin. It merely rotates in either direction. Note also that the angle of the typing element changes according to the character struck. And for capital letters the opposite side of the sphere is brought into play. Contrast this mechanical method of character selection with that used on a computer line printer of the drum or chain variety. In these cases character selection occurs when the desired character in a constantly rotating character store comes into alignment with the indicated print position and the character is "picked off"—that is, struck or impacted at that point. There are many other ways that characters can be chosen from the character store and arranged in the desired sequence on a page. Solutions to this challenge are one of the major themes in this book.

Line-ending decisions. The person using the typewriter makes his own "line-ending" decisions. The ordinary typewriter does not contain "logic" to decide where to terminate lines. On the other hand, a line of infinite length cannot be printed or typed. Consequently, at some point on the line the user decides where to "return the carriage." On the old-fashioned, non-electric typewriter this meant pushing a lever on the right-hand side of the moving platen which advanced the paper either one or two lines while one simultaneously pushed the carriage back to its original position at the left-hand side of the page. On striking bar typewriters which are electrically driven the same thing occurs when you press the "carriage return" key. With Selectric or similar typewriters, the typing element automatically moves back to the beginning of the line when the "carriage return" is activated. You are warned to think about terminating the line by the sounding of a bell.

Normally you will terminate the line at the end of a word. You may, however, choose to hyphenate the word if you want your right-hand margins to appear relatively even. It is not possible to create aligned right-hand margins without a great deal of effort. This can only be done by retyping, as illustrated on the next page.

Page-ending decisions. There is no signal to inform you when you are about to reach the end of a page. You can judge by the length of the sheet which has already been typed. If you proceed too far you will lose control of the sheet and the alignment of the last line will suffer. Nevertheless, at some point you must make an end-of-page decision, and you may wish to avoid illogical page breaks. For example, you would not normally end the page with a subhead which pertains to material beginning on the next page.

The making of end-of-line and end-of-page decisions represents two of the judgments which have to do with the aesthetics of "composition." Some of the concerns people have with respect to the appearance of the typewritten page would of course relate to the selection of the *type*face, the length of the average line (*the measure*), and consequently the width and position of left- and right-hand margins. You would also think about whether the document should be single- or double-spaced, whether chapter or subject titles are centered (as best this can be achieved), whether paragraphs should be indented, and if they should also be separated from the preceding text by extra space. Some of the aspects of composition, as they pertain to typesetting, are discussed in the next chapter. However, it should be obvious to the reader that typewriter composition offers a limited range of options and presents relatively few challenges, because of the monospaced nature of the type used. For example, one of the more complex problems encountered when "true type" is used is to be able to "set" tables ("tabular composition"). Where tables consist of numbers, the proper alignment of the information in the table is made easier by virtue of the fact that, generally, all digits are given the same character width. Even so, to achieve *decimal alignment* requires some effort, and it is of course more difficult to center legends, captions or headings above the appropriate columns.

The treatment of white space. But perhaps the most significant difference between type composition and typewriter composition has to do with the treatment of "white space." With a typewriter you can lay down a character any place on a page. It may require a little effort to space out to the desired position and to move the platen back and forth to find the appropriate page depth. But you have no obligation to fill in all of the white space that you have skipped or to otherwise account for it. In our discussion of hot metal typesetting in the next two chapters, you will observe that it is not possible, when dealing with traditional "hot metal" typesetting, simply to place characters anywhere you choose without filling in all other areas in the page either with type or furniture. And when it comes to photocomposition or even word processing machines, some procedures must be used to instruct the device how to reach the point where the character laydown is to occur—by counting, in one fashion or another, all of the vertical and horizontal space which precedes that location.

```
This is a paragraph ofxx
text to be justified and
then the same text isxxx
retyped to align bothxxx
margins.
```

```
This  is a  paragraph of
text to be justified and
then  the  same  text is
retyped  to  align  both
margins.
```

The Typewriter

Raised type versus alternative imaging techniques. Characters and symbols which are stored on a typewriter are represented by raised images. The printing which appears on the typewritten page is created when such an image strikes an inked ribbon and leaves its impression on a sheet of paper. In a similar fashion, "hot metal" type creates its impressions from raised images which also carry ink. When these raised types are locked into a "chase," mounted onto a printing press and inked, the process of printing is known as "letterpress."

The raised images of the typewriter striking bars or typing element could also be used to create a "master." The impact of these raised characters upon a mimeograph stencil can cut through the stencil so that ink, contained in a reservoir behind the stencil when it is mounted on a mimeograph machine, can be squeezed through and permitted to come into contact with paper. This is a "planographic" process. The printing image is neither raised (letterpress or relief) or indented (intaglio or gravure).

You can also mount a "paper plate" on the typewriter platen. The typed image on this plate can be transferred to paper by means of the "duplicating process," which is a form of lithography.

Printing by the duplicating process (or other forms of lithography) as well as printing by means of stencil, would be considered printing from planographic images. In other words, the image is somehow transferred to the final "reader page" from a surface which is neither raised, nor etched *into* a plate or cylinder. The chemical properties of ink and water are used to cause the typed portions of the printing plate to retain ink while other portions repel it.

While in the preceding four paragraphs we have considered the capabilities of the typewriter to produce a product which could be used for printing, the typewriter's principal function is to produce single documents and not to print out multiple copies for widespread distribution, as is the case with a printing press. On the other hand, these documents can serve as "camera-ready copy" for the printing press, or as "masters" for the office photocopying machine.

However, one of the prospects which will be raised from time to time in this book is that the distinction between the process which creates only one copy of a page, and the process which can create many copies for wider distribution, will not be so clearly defined in the future. In other words, the relationship between the typewriter and the "printing press" is changing—as indeed all things seem to be changing in the graphic arts industry.

But let us now return to a more detailed consideration of the characteristics of printers' type in order to acquire the necessary background for a discussion of the evolution of the typesetting process.

3

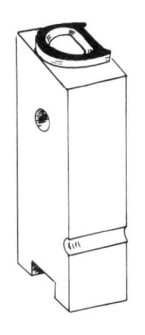

The Handsetting of Type

FROM THE TIME of Gutenberg until the time of Mergenthaler's Linotype[1] and Lanston's Monotype,[2] there was no practical way to "set type" by machine. And even after machines were invented and were applied to composition tasks in the last quarter of the nineteenth century, handsetting of type persisted for many classes of work. Even today it is practiced, and one hopes that the skills and attention which good handsetting from metal types require will continue to be preserved, if only as a hobby for those who take delight in the aesthetic opportunities it offers and the pleasure derived from it.

But the lessons of handsetting are important, whatever typesetting techniques may be put to use, and the traditions of handsetting will always remain a part of our typographic heritage. We must indeed start from this base if we are going to have an understanding of where we are today and where we will be going in the future.

The movable type which Gutenberg invented consisted of individual pieces of metal cast from matrices which, in turn, were created from punches. The types[3] themselves are very precisely cast to a height of .918″ or 23.328 mm and this is known as "type-high."[4]

The type image or *type face* consists of the raised shape of the letter or symbol to be printed. This image is inked for printing. Each type character must be cleanly cast and cleanly designed so that it does not trap ink, and a good impression is achieved by providing sufficient height between the face itself and the counter on which it appears to sit. The corners of the counter and indeed the entire bar or unit of metal must be square and well-machined so that pieces can fit snugly together. If type were not so designed it could never be "locked up."

Since each type character must be contained within a rectangle, it is difficult for the compositor to arrange certain letter combinations aesthetically. Consider, for example, the relationship between a capital V and a capital A. In the margin you will see what these two characters look like side by side if they "sit" within their own rectangles. In hot metal, if you want a closer fit between two characters you have only two courses to follow. One would be to saw off portions of the type body, as illustrated, to bring the letters closer together. The other is to design character combinations as one piece. These become "ligatures," "digraphs,"[5] or "logotypes." Ligatures consist of two or more characters created as one, as is the case with the *fl* and the *ffl*, or the *ct* in some French type faces. "Logos" include characters which

---

1. See Chapter 4.

2. See Chapter 5.

3. We use the word "type" to mean a type face or type style or any kind of type generically. But the word also means an individual piece of type, just as *types* means a group of individual pieces of type.

4. Type-high in France is 23.567 mm and in Russia it is 25.102 mm.

5. Digraphs consist of combinations of letters or letters and punctuation where one matrix is used to contain both images designed as one entity.

[30]

The Handsetting of Type

may be fitted close together or may even overlap, or they may consist of several letters which are separate and distinct but are incorporated into one piece of type or engraving, as might be the case with a distinctive "company logo."

When our discussion moves from metal composition to photocomposition we will see that in the phototypesetting process there is greater flexibility with respect to the positioning of characters. These characters need no longer occupy fixed spaces determined by the shapes of their metal bodies. We will also learn that even in hot metal composition the Monotype process makes it possible to cast type characters on a larger or smaller body and thus to provide different kinds of overall character spacing, although this technique could not be used to achieve the kind of *kerning*[1] which is possible once we have freed ourselves from the limitations of hot metal.

But despite these "limitations," type designed to be set by hand, with each character occupying its little cell, represents an extremely high level of artistic achievement and inventors of new processes still seek to emulate the results of hot metal setting as closely as possible.

In the handsetting of type, then, the area of the counter upon which the character "sits" is called the *body*. It must be of a sufficient size to contain the letter or symbol and the necessary side bearings which properly separate one letter from another. These are the *shoulders* of the type.

Hot metal hand composition

THE HAND COMPOSITOR first selected the type cases containing the type characters he would be using on a particular job and positioned them in front of him. Originally there were two cases. The upper case contained capital letters, and the lower case contained the small letters. Later, one case was arranged with space for both. The letters or types within the case (usually called *sorts*) were all of one size and style (such as Baskerville Roman, 10 point). A number of sorts for each character were contained in each compartment. Theoretically, there should be enough lower case e's, for example, to set the job at hand. It should be obvious, however, that in Gutenberg's day, and for several centuries thereafter, the typesetter's supply of "foundry" type was limited and it was possible for him to process only a relatively small number of pages at one time. Nor would it have been possible to save the type for a re-run at some later period. He needed it for other jobs or for the continuation of the same job.

Distribution of type was as much a part of the typesetting business as *composition* itself.

Setting the lines. The fundamental task of hand typesetting is the assembly of the types. Each individual character or symbol is picked by hand from the case and placed into a composing stick. When a take of perhaps a half dozen lines has been assembled it is carefully removed from the stick and deposited into the galley—an oblong metal tray with an edge around it about a half-inch high.

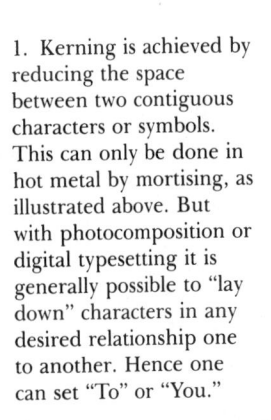

1. Kerning is achieved by reducing the space between two contiguous characters or symbols. This can only be done in hot metal by mortising, as illustrated above. But with photocomposition or digital typesetting it is generally possible to "lay down" characters in any desired relationship one to another. Hence one can set "To" or "You."

When a galley of type has been composed it is inked, a sheet of proof paper is placed over the top and one or several proofs may be pulled. The type is then cleaned and corrections are made. Individual types set in error are removed and the correct types are substituted. When the corrected galley has been proofed in the same manner it then awaits the page make-up process.

Since the assembled type will ultimately be locked up into a chase for printing, it must be set tightly or else it will work loose. This means that all short lines, such as paragraph endings, must be quadded out, or filled with quads and other fixed spaces of nontypesetting height. It also means that all lines must be *justified*.

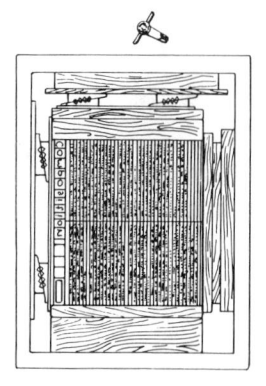

Hot metal type must be locked up in a chase and all empty spaces must be filled with quads or furniture.

What is justification? This term has two meanings in the typesetting industry. In its most common use it means setting type so that there are even right-hand margins. In its more general sense it merely means that all lines must be tightly filled to a given measure with either printing types or nonprinting spaces. Since type characters vary in their width and words vary in their length, the customary method of composing a line has been for the craftsman to assemble as many characters and words as will appear to fit within the measure. The measure is determined by setting the bracket of the composing stick at the desired width. When the compositor approaches the end of the line he has a "line-ending decision" to make. Is there room to fit another word in the line he is setting? If not, how much space remains which has to be accounted for in order to make the line sufficiently tight? How can that space be used up?

One possibility would be simply to add that amount of space at the end of the line, and thus to set it ragged. However, the more common solution, ever since the time of Gutenberg, has been to *justify* the line in the sense of distributing the extra space *evenly between the words* within that line. If the measure is very narrow, and there are only three words on the line, then there would only be two interword spaces available, and all of the extra space at the end of the line would have to be assigned to these two spaces, in equal amounts. In this fashion the line would be *spaced out*.

However, it might have been possible to add yet another word to the line in question if the space between the existing words were reduced. By removing the existing interword spaces and substituting smaller increments of space one might be able to make room for the next word in the manuscript, especially if it is a short word. Consequently, if you replaced larger spaces with smaller ones you would be justifying by *spacing in*.

The hand compositor learns to look ahead and develops a "feel" for how many words are likely to fit in the measure. He can thus space the line tightly from the beginning, with the expectation that he will justify by spacing out—adding extra spaces. Or he may set the line loosely with the expectation that he will may find it possible to add another word. The probability is that he would insert an en space between words since this value (representing, in many instances, the average width of a lower-case character) provides about the amount

The Handsetting of Type

of space that the eye would like to see between words in order to tell them apart. But it would be a very rare case if by so doing he managed to justify the line, setting it as tightly as it indeed must be set—without having to go back and add or subtract spaces not just at one location but with painstaking care to equalize spaces between all words so that there are no disconcerting spaces in the flow of the text.

Quite often the compositor can find no satisfactory solution. There is insufficient room to add another word—perhaps the next word is too big. The space between words will be unacceptably large if he has to space out. What can he then do?[1]

- He could *letterspace* by adding spaces between letters in all of the words as well as between the words themselves. He would have to add very small spacing increments. This would be time consuming and difficult. Moreover, the effect of letterspacing is usually disconcerting and unattractive.

- He could go back several lines and try to reset them with larger or smaller interword spaces, hoping that he could squeeze something up into the preceding line or carry something down from the preceding line, and thus resolve his problem. This solution is even more time consuming and it would mean that if he had already achieved the best justification he could contrive for those particular lines, he would have to compromise that solution simply to avoid an impossible problem at his current position.

- Usually his only other alternative, and generally the one which is most acceptable, is to *divide* (hyphenate) the "straddle" word—that is, the word which is too large to fit in its entirety.

Thus the hand compositor must know or be able to find out quickly *where* or *if* any given word may be hyphenated acceptably. There is always, of course, the possibility that the word may not be hyphenable, or—if it is—that the first portion of the word may still be too large to fit. Nevertheless, the compositor must somehow find an acceptable solution, even if it might mean resetting and respacing a number of lines of text. This must be done so that the types will be tight enough that they will not work loose in the printing process.

Hand composition and page make-up

MOST PAGES contain a mixture of different sizes of type. Footnotes and subheads, text or body copy, and running heads and folios (page numbers) may call for different point sizes and perhaps different type faces. An even greater variety of faces and sizes will be used for the setting of advertising material. But whatever is composed has to be set in rectangular blocks which, in turn, can be locked up in a form. And, as we have mentioned, all lines must be quadded out or filled with nonprinting fixed spaces. As much attention has to be given to the areas of the page which do not contain printed matter as to the type areas themselves.

Heads, to be centered over a block of text, also require the same treatment—the adjustment of solid spaces to fill in the necessary blanks, and the careful calculation of the amount of space required to

1. Options for solving justification problems are greater with today's technology since very fine increments of spacing exist, permitting positive (or negative) letterspacing that may be barely discernible.

achieve the desired result, so that the printed text would indeed be positioned in the precise center of the text area.

In the setting of hand type there is no means to precalculate the length of words. No common denominator exists which permits the adding of width values of the assembled characters, subtracting this sum from a given figure for the total line measure in order to obtain a difference which could then be divided between the nonprinting areas on either side of the head or text block. The handsetting of type is very much a trial-and-error procedure. As we shall see, the Linotype process of machine composition greatly simplifies the justification of lines. And Monotype goes even further by introducing standards of measurement and calculation procedures which can be applied to the assembly of characters and words.

Picas and points

TYPE COMES IN SIZES designated in terms of points. In the United States, until 1886, various sizes of type were less than precise, and names were used to designate them. But in that year the American Point System was adopted.[1] Type is now described in terms of *points* and *picas*. The decision was made that 83 picas should be equal to 35 centimeters, and it turns out that this means there are, fairly precisely, six picas to an inch. A pica, in turn, is divided into twelve points.

Manufacturers of hot metal typesetting equipment deviated somewhat in their implementation of this standard, and the point came to have a value of either 0.01383″ (Monotype) or 0.014″ (Linotype). It will be convenient to take the value of a point as .01388″ since when we divide one inch by 72 the quotient is 1.388888....

In considering the sizing of type we generally think in terms of its height. But there are, of course, two dimensions to be concerned with. We use the terms *set size* or *set width* to describe the horizontal space that the type metal takes up. We use the term *point size* to describe the height of the type—that is, the vertical length of the rectangle the type face sits on.

The height of the character will vary from one type design to another. Type characters are designed to appear to "sit" on an implied base line which leads the eye across the page. But if you look at the individual characters carefully, you will observe that some of them go below this optical base line. Letters which are curved, such as a lower-case e or o will drop slightly below that line, and of course there are other characters with descenders which drop well below the line. Notice also that lower case letters tend to have a height which is perhaps two-thirds that of capital letters (although this will of course depend upon the design of the face). We use the term *x-height*[2] to describe the height of a lower-case character which has neither descender nor ascender. Just as the descender drops below the x-height of a lower-case character, and thus below the optical base line, so the ascender rises above the x-height. Looking at the characters in the margin you will note that the ascenders and descenders are clearly identifiable.

1. Outside of the English-speaking community the French Didot system is widely used (Didot-Berthold in Germany). Twelve didot points equal a cicero and the body is about one-twelfth larger than that in the United States.

2. *Z-height* is also used in this context.

The Handsetting of Type

It should be evident, then, that the point size of type cannot be determined merely by measuring the height of an individual character, even a capital letter. For those letters, (such as the letter M) which sit on the base line, allowance must be made for the space required below the base line to accommodate descenders. In general, the height of upper-case letters will represent from 60 to 66% of the point size, in order to allow for descenders and also for clearance between successive lines of type. (Just as there are side bearings to keep letters from touching one another, so in hot metal type design there is an allowance represented by the shoulders of the counter to provide the necessary clearance.)

It follows from this discussion that point size is, in a sense, an abstract concept which relates to the amount of vertical white space necessary to accommodate the distance from the lowest descender to the highest ascender, plus clearance above and below the letter.

Leading. Before we complete our effort to clarify the definitions of points, picas and others printers' measurements, we will have to muddy the waters still further. Suppose you want to determine the point size of the text of a given sample of typeset matter. Can you measure the distance from the top of one ascender to the bottom of the descender of an adjoining character and find out what the point size of the type is? Probably not. The scale is usually too small, and most often you can't find two such characters close enough together to get a good measurement.

What, then, if you attempt to measure the distance from the base line of one line of type to the base line of the succeeding line? Here again, distances are usually too small to permit a definitive measurement. If you take a pica gauge and lay it along this text, for example, so that the beginning marker is at the base of the first line of this paragraph, and then count down ten lines, you should get a reading of 120 points, or precisely ten picas. This is because we are setting this text on twelve point "leading." In other words, we are setting "ten on twelve."

The term *leading* (pronounced "ledding") is derived from the practice of inserting strips of lead between lines of type, when composed by hand, to space them out so that they will be farther apart. Your eye will have trouble picking up the next line on fairly wide measure material if it is set "solid." *Solid setting* means setting with no leading or extra white space between the lines and hence the practice of separating the lines by inserting strips of lead, or "leading" between the lines when you do not want to set solid. While foundry type is generally manufactured to the true point size, in the expectation that the compositor will insert the extra strips of lead to provide the desired white space between lines, typesetting machines have the ability to cast, say, a ten point character on a twelve point "slug," thus building the lead into the body height—but not the width—of the character itself.

In whatever manner the "leading" is added, it should be obvious that *measuring the distance between lines will not tell you what the point size of the type is*. It will only tell you what the leading is. You would need to be something of an an expert to look at type—even measure it—and be absolutely certain what the point size is. This is especially true today, since, as we shall discover, the appearance and dimensionality of photocomposed type, or other forms of digitally created type, do not necessarily correspond closely with the appearance of hot metal type, whether created in a foundry or from a linecasting machine such as a Linotype.

While we are on the subject of leading, let us provide you with several examples, showing how this particular type looks when the same point size is set to different leadings. We are using a ten point type face for the body copy in this book. On page 37 you will see the same text set to other leadings. In order for you to judge what happens to the ascenders and descenders as you change the leading, we are including several lines consisting of alternating characters with descenders and ascenders. Thus you will not only be able to judge whether, for the 26 pica measure of this text, two points of leading (*i.e.*, 10 on 12) is sufficient or too much, but also how much less leading you can permit before the characters begin to touch or overlap one another.

The sizing of type

NOW WE MUST return to the problem of type measurement. We have learned that the size of type cannot readily be determined by examining the characters themselves, and certainly cannot be ascertained definitely by measuring the distance between lines of text unless we have already been told (or can figure out by the way the ascenders touch the descenders) that the text is set solid.

While we may have trouble identifying a given point size, there are obvious differences from one size to another. Type sizes range from very tiny characters, perhaps three or four points "high," to very large sizes—perhaps 72 points, or, as much as 96 or 128 points in the case of large banner headlines in newspapers.

Text type tends to range from nine points, generally used for newspaper stories, to twelve or thirteen points for books. Ten or eleven point type is very readable, especially when leaded. Large-print books for the nearsighted are usually set in 18 point type.

If you turn to page 38, you will also see samples of this same type face set in different point sizes so that you can get a feel for the readability and compactness of various sizes of type. These samples are set by photocomposition and from one character master image only. Later you will understand that this means that they will not necessarily correspond with hot metal faces.

Unlike the samples you will see on page 38, type faces for hot metal are usually redesigned for each point size or, more likely, for each range of point sizes. This is infrequently the case for photocomposition, but when different artwork is created for different point sizes, ascenders and descenders tend to become more pronounced,

(Text continued on page 39)

The Handsetting of Type

This is a sample paragraph presented so that you can see how this leading looks. Now we will follow up with samples set with other amounts of leading, but always using the same ten point type face. Following are two lines which show lots of ascenders and descenders.
qqqqq ggggg yyyyy qqqqq ggggg yyyyy qqqqq ggggg yyyyy qqqqq ddddd bbbbb hhhhh kkkkk lllll ddddd bbbbb hhhhh kkkkk lllll ddddd

This is a sample paragraph presented so that you can see how this leading looks. Now we will follow up with samples set with other amounts of leading, but always using the same ten point type face. Following are two lines which show lots of ascenders and descenders.
qqqqq ggggg yyyyy qqqqq ggggg yyyyy qqqqq ggggg yyyyy qqqqq ddddd bbbbb hhhhh kkkkk lllll ddddd bbbbb hhhhh kkkkk lllll ddddd

This is a sample paragraph presented so that you can see how this leading looks. Now we will follow up with samples set with other amounts of leading, but always using the same ten point type face. Following are two lines which show lots of ascenders and descenders.
qqqqq ggggg yyyyy qqqqq ggggg yyyyy qqqqq ggggg yyyyy qqqqq ddddd bbbbb hhhhh kkkkk lllll ddddd bbbbb hhhhh kkkkk lllll ddddd

This is a sample paragraph presented so that you can see how this leading looks. Now we will follow up with samples set with other amounts of leading, but always using the same ten point type face. Following are two lines which show lots of ascenders and descenders.
qqqqq ggggg yyyyy qqqqq ggggg yyyyy qqqqq ggggg yyyyy qqqqq ddddd bbbbb hhhhh kkkkk lllll ddddd bbbbb hhhhh kkkkk lllll ddddd

This is a sample paragraph presented so that you can see how this leading looks. Now we will follow up with samples set with other amounts of leading, but always using the same ten point type face. Following are two lines which show lots of ascenders and descenders.
qqqqq ggggg yyyyy qqqqq ggggg yyyyy qqqqq ggggg yyyyy qqqqq ddddd bbbbb hhhhh kkkkk lllll ddddd bbbbb hhhhh kkkkk lllll ddddd

This is a sample paragraph presented so that you can see how this leading looks. Now we will follow up with samples set with other amounts of leading, but always using the same ten point type face. Following are two lines which show lots of ascenders and descenders.
qqqqq ggggg yyyyy qqqqq ggggg yyyyy qqqqq ggggg yyyyy qqqqq ddddd bbbbb hhhhh kkkkk lllll ddddd bbbbb hhhhh kkkkk lllll ddddd

This is a sample paragraph presented so that you can see how this leading looks. Now we will follow up with samples set with other amounts of leading, but always using the same ten point type face. Following are two lines which show lots of ascenders and descenders.
qqqqq ggggg yyyyy qqqqq ggggg yyyyy qqqqq ggggg yyyyy qqqqq ddddd bbbbb hhhhh kkkkk lllll ddddd bbbbb hhhhh kkkkk lllll ddddd

In the above samples the first paragraph has been set 10 on 12. The second is 10 on 11½. The third is 10 on 11. The fourth is 10 on 10½. The fifth is 10 on 10, or solid setting. Note that the type design does not lend itself to solid setting. The sixth is 10 on 9½ and the last, or seventh, is 10 on 9 point leading.

Here is an example of six point type in the basic design of our text. We are setting it six point solid. We think this type looks somewhat smaller than conventional hot metal six point type, which means that because it was designed to look its best at around ten points the *x-height* is probably a little too small at six, and the ascenders and descenders too large, proportionately. Note that this face does not lend itself to solid setting.

As we move to seven points the type probably more closely resembles a true hot metal design for six point type.

In eight points the type grows even more like its hot metal counterpart, or so it seems to us. Obviously a great deal of individual judgment enters into one's evaluation of type, which is highly personal at best.

At nine points the face looks like this. You can also see that fewer characters fit on a line. As we said, nine points is a common size for use in newspapers, but it is quite often leaded to 9½.

The typesetting device we are using to set this book offers the capability of providing any desired type face in half point increments. We could have set any of the above samples in more sizes, therefore, but here is 9½ on 9½ leading just to illustrate the capability.

Now we are back to the point size used in this book, except that here we are setting it solid on ten points. As you will have noticed on the examples on the preceding page, type designed for photocomposition, even though it emulates hot metal, does not need to have the shoulders which hot metal type necessarily requires. Hence, there is a greater possibility for descenders and ascenders to meet or even overprint.

For a measure this narrow, 12 points is too large a type face. But we have chosen to set this 12 on 13.

And here is 14 on 15 leading. The higher you go in point size the more leading is helpful.

This is 18 points set across 21 picas.

This line is set in 24 points.

This is 27 points

Here is 30 points.

And here is 36.

This is 48 points.

This is 72.

The Handsetting of Type

and the x-height becomes proportionally smaller as the type increases in size. Moreover, the side bearings or white spaces between (non-letterspaced) characters become smaller and smaller in relation to the size of the individual character.

Character width measurements. So far we have discussed only the character's vertical height—that is, the distance from the bottom of the descender (and its shoulder) to the top of the ascender (and its shoulder). We have not considered the *width* of the type characters.

Until the invention of the Monotype hot metal typesetting machine in the latter part of the nineteenth century, there was no need for any particular standard of measurement with respect to character widths. Fixed spaces did have definite values, however, and were based upon the em space[1]—which was the same as the point size. In other words, for a font of twelve point type you would be provided with em spaces or "em quads" twelve points wide as well as twelve points high.

There is an awkward problem, however, that we must at least acknowledge at this point. That is that nowadays, and as a matter of fact ever since the invention of the Monotype system, it has been true that the "set" of type is not necessarily the same as its point size. It is possible to design type which is ten-points high but otherwise set as if it were nine-points wide, and in that case the em would have a value of nine points. It is also possible to change the sidebearings of type so that a ten-point character sets as if it were on a nine-point body. And finally, with modern typesetting devices, it is also possible to distort type images so that a type face designed to be set a certain width can in fact be made to appear wider (extended) or narrower.

En spaces are one-half of the width of the em. Thus for a "normal" twelve point type face the en space is twelve-points high by six-points wide. Figures (numbers), which must be of uniform width in order to be aligned in columns, are usually designed to the en width, although they can be assigned some other value, in which instance a font of type will also contain a fixed space known as a "figure space."

Vertical and horizontal justification. For purposes of determining how deep to set a page, one can add lines of type and varying amounts of "furniture" or leading, until the allotted space is full, just as one adds type characters and spaces until the line has been "justified." But with machine-oriented systems of composition (excepting always the Linotype process) one wants and needs some method of *counting* the accumulated width and depth of the type matter that is being composed.

While steps in this direction were taken by the Monotype system, a full understanding of the manner in which counting could be used to facilitate the vertical and horizontal justifications process did not come until the advent of photocomposition, and, more particularly, the computer era. Much of this book will be devoted to these developments and their implications.

---

1. An em space is often called a "mutt" and an en space is called a "nut" to avoid misunderstanding when verbal instructions are relayed.

Other fixed spaces which were commonly used for hot metal typesetting were the "3-em" space, which is really one-third of an em (or, in our illustration, four points wide for a twelve point face), a "4-em" (one-fourth em) space, which for twelve points would be three points wide, and a "5-em" space or one-fifth of an em.

You will note that these fixed space values are not absolute, but *relative to the point size under consideration*. Fixed spaces in today's vocabulary generally consist of ems, ens, figure spaces, or "thin" spaces which can take on any value one wishes to assign. One no longer hears about "3-em" or "4-em" spaces.

4

The Linecasting Machine

FROM THE TURN OF THE CENTURY and until about 1970, most composition was produced, at least in the United States, by the use of linecasting machines, although some quantity of type—ever decreasing even prior to the advent of photocomposition—was set by Monotype.

Ottmar Mergenthaler's Linotype was first introduced in the mid-1880s, the patent having been granted in 1886. Mergenthaler was not the only person to develop an automatic typesetting device. A chronological listing of "Typesetting Machines and Ancillary Equipment, 1822–1925" appears in *The Journal of Typographic Research* for July 1967, and it includes 173 such devices! Of these, 57 preceded Mergenthaler's patents. The list begins in 1822 with two inventions by Dr. William Church (an American who had settled in Birmingham, England). The tempo of developing technology is interesting in itself, with other patents granted in 1838, 1840, 1843, 1840, 1843, 1846 (2), 1849, 1850, 1853, 1854 (4), 1855, 1856, 1857 (3), 1859, 1860, 1862 (2), 1866, 1867, 1869, 1870, 1871 (2), 1872, 1873 (2), 1873 (2), 1874, 1875, 1876, 1877, 1878, 1880, 1883, and 1884.

But this was by no means the end of the road. In addition to the Lanston Monotype invention in 1887, there were many others—more than one hundred—most of which never truly became products and were never, in fact, used in a production environment.

All of this effort clearly demonstrates the old adage that necessity is the mother of invention. People were not happy with the methods of setting type which preceded the Linotype and the Monotype, and they still tried, even after the introduction of these products, to come up with better solutions.

It was Linotype and Monotype that survived, plus the Intertype linecasters which came along after the basic Mergenthaler patent had expired. Nowadays, when people talk about "Linotype" or the "Linotype process" they often use the term in a generic sense to embrace Intertype as well, since the principles of the Intertype machine were virtually identical.

At this point we shall devote our attention to the linecaster. The Mergenthaler Linotype Company sold approximately 74,000 such typesetters from 1893 through 1968. Between 1893 and 1900 almost 4,500 were delivered, which averaged approximately 645 per year. From 1901 through 1906 shipments increased to more than 800 yearly, and from 1907 through 1916 approximately a thousand a year were delivered. The rate of shipments went up to more than 1700 per

The Linecasting Machine

year from 1917 through 1922, and then fell to about 1,100 yearly until 1927. In three years, 1927 through 1929, they averaged 1,666 per year, dropped off to 710 between 1930 and 1936, moved up to 833 from 1937 to 1942, declined to 782 between 1943 and 1948, moved back up to 1,250 per year in the 1949-1952 period, and then averaged only 510 per year from 1953 through 1959. However, in the meantime, Mergenthaler's popular "Comet" was released (for which statistics were kept separately), and from 1951 through 1958 something like 330 Comets were delivered each year.

Mergenthaler's sales do not tell the entire story. Intertype began to sell in 1913 and by 1957 had distributed some 27,000 units. This figure rose to a total of about 38,000 by the late 1960s. In fact, Intertype's sales from 1950 on seem to have equalled or exceeded those of Mergenthaler. In 1956, for example, Intertype shipped 1,150 units.

Thus it may be seen that from the period of the invention of the linecaster until the time when they were no longer made in the United States (say about 1970), more than 100,000 linecasters were sold within the U.S. and Canada, or, in some cases, shipped abroad from U.S. factories. Even allowing for obsolescence, surely more than 35,000 linecasters stood on composing room floors in the U.S. in the late 1960s, available to be used in production.

From the year 1886, when the first Linotype was installed in *The New York Tribune*, until 1893, and on even until about 1900, there was a gradual accommodation to the new technology. A skilled hand compositor was said to be able to compose about 2,000 characters per hour, and the average output of the Linotype was estimated at about 6,000 letters. But perhaps even more important was the fact that the task of "distribution of type"—so frequently associated with hand composition—was no longer required. Moreover, the Linotype's circulating matrix provided an ever-ready source for new type images, and the slugs of type cast from the assembled matrices, after their use for printing, were recycled via the "hell box" into the melting pot. Furthermore, if you needed to keep the "standing type" for possible subsequent reuse, the only cost of doing so was the equivalent cost of the value of the metal, plus the storage space involved.

There were other advantages to linecasting besides the ease of setting and the avoidance of distribution. Lines as slugs were easier to handle, and blocks of type were less likely to "pi"—that is, to become mixed up. Justification was much simpler—and this accounts for a great deal of the increase in the amount of composition set per person—since the spacing in and spacing out techniques for justification and tight setting necessary in hand composition were totally eliminated. No longer did you have to substitute, experimentally, smaller or larger fixed spaces between words (such as the three-em, four-em, or five-em) until the line was tight enough but not too tight, and the spacing between words was more or less evenly distributed. Variable spaces, created by spacebands, took the place of fixed spaces of varying widths, and all the operator had to do was to *bring the line within justification range*. The actual justification was in fact accomplished by spaceband expansion.

1. *The Journal of Typographic Research*, Vol. 1, No. 3, July 1967, 245-274. Article by Richard E. Huss, published at that time by The Press of Western Reserve University, Cleveland, Ohio. See also Huss's book on this subject, *The Development of Printers' Mechanical Typesetting Methods, 1822-1925*, University of Virginia Press, 1973.

Principles of the linecaster

PERHAPS THE BEST WAY to summarize the major features of the linecasting machine is to quote from Mergenthaler's *Linotype Machine Principles*—the official manual—copyrighted 1940.

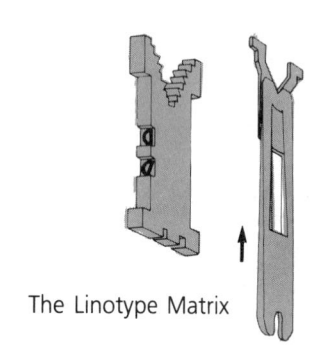

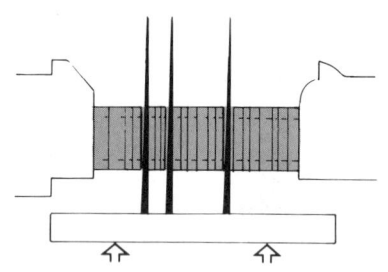

The Linotype is not a type-setting machine. No types are used in it. It composes with matrices—small brass units having characters indented in the edges—hence the name "matrix." These matrices are assembled into justified lines. From the matrix line the Linotype automatically casts a solid bar, or line, of type. This bar is known as the Linotype slug. It is ready for use when it leaves the machine.

The Linotype has four major divisions:

1. The Magazines which contain the matrices.—They represent type cases. Because every matrix circulates automatically back to its place in the magazine as soon as it has served in a line of composition, a font of matrices is small in number as compared with a font of type. A magazine is so compact and light that the operator can handle it without exertion, and produce a variety of composition simply by changing magazines.

2. The Keyboard and its related parts.—This controls the release of matrices from the magazine in the order in which the characters are desired. The Linotype operator, from his seat at the keyboard, has complete control of every function of the machine. His duties are limited merely to operating the keyboard keys—justification and distribution are mechanically automatic.

3. The Casting Mechanism.—The division of the machine makes the Linotype-equipped printer his own type founder. The justified line of matrices is presented automatically to the casting mechanism, molten type metal is forced into the indented characters on the edges of the matrices, and the cast line, a single unit with a new typeface, is delivered to galley on the machine, precisely trimmed and ready to go into the form.

4. The Distributing Mechanism.—When a line of matrices has served for casting the line of type, it is lifted automatically and carried to the top of the magazines, where, by a simple though ingenious system, each matrix is delivered to its proper place in the magazine and is ready to serve again. Thus, in the Linotype-equipped shop, there is no distribution of type.

The four elements which stand out with respect to the Linotype, are, to our way of thinking:

- That it is a keyboard-oriented machine.
- That it uses spacebands to perform justification.
- That it generates lines as solid slugs.
- That individual type characters are cast from intaglio images positioned on the edges of matrices which are automatically called into

The Linecasting Machine

position when the key is struck and are automatically dispatched back to the proper magazine channel after the matrix has served its purpose—ready to be used again.

The linecasting production process

WE SHALL DESCRIBE the activity as though it no longer exists. As of this writing there are still some linotype machines in use, but this account will be written in the past tense since what took place in linotype shops is no longer typical of the typesetting process.

Manuscript was received in the composing room where it was "copy cut" according to the type faces, sizes and measures of type to be composed. Usually the manuscript was marked by the copy editor with symbols to indicate the desired measure, faces and spacing, but in some instances markup was left to the discretion of the composing room mark-up man or copy cutter. It must be remembered that a Linotype machine could compose only to one measure without a manual adjustment of the pre-set vise jaws. Lines of up to 30 picas could be cast on all machines, and some were built to accommodate lines of up to 42 picas. Machines requiring a still wider measure could sometimes create "butted" slugs, which meant in effect that two lines could be composed and laid side by side in an interlocking fashion.

But within the width limits of the particular machine a manual adjustment was made to the vise jaws, thus defining the length of the line to be composed.

On a typical linecaster, one magazine of 91 channels was available at one time. Such a magazine weighed between 50 and 60 pounds when filled with matrices. One magazine contained one font of type of a particular point size (from four to 60 points, with text machines usually setting up to 18 points). Since duplexed matrices were generally used, it was thus possible to compose roman and italic or roman and bold, setting to a certain measure in a certain point size, without the need to change magazines or to reset fixed jaws. Some linecasters had "mixing" capabilities. Mixers had multiple distributors so that circulating matrices could be returned to the appropriate magazines. Other models might permit the mounting of several magazines simultaneously, although only one could be used at a time. There were also models which offered side or auxiliary magazines to enhance the available character repertoire.

Copy cutting. Generally speaking, then, several operators would be involved in the production of one job, depending upon the type faces, sizes and measures required. If a book were being set, consisting of body text, footnotes, extract and some display material,[1] the manuscript would either be cut into sections or routed from one operator to another so that each could key relevant portions. Sometimes several machines were set up with identical magazines so that more than one operator could compose text matter on the same job at the same time. Nevertheless, except in the newspaper industry, where most of

(Text continued on page 46)

1. Extract may be defined as a block of text set to a smaller point size and possibly indented somewhat from the standard measure in order to set off an extended quotation from some other source. Display material consists of large type used for attention-getting headlines.

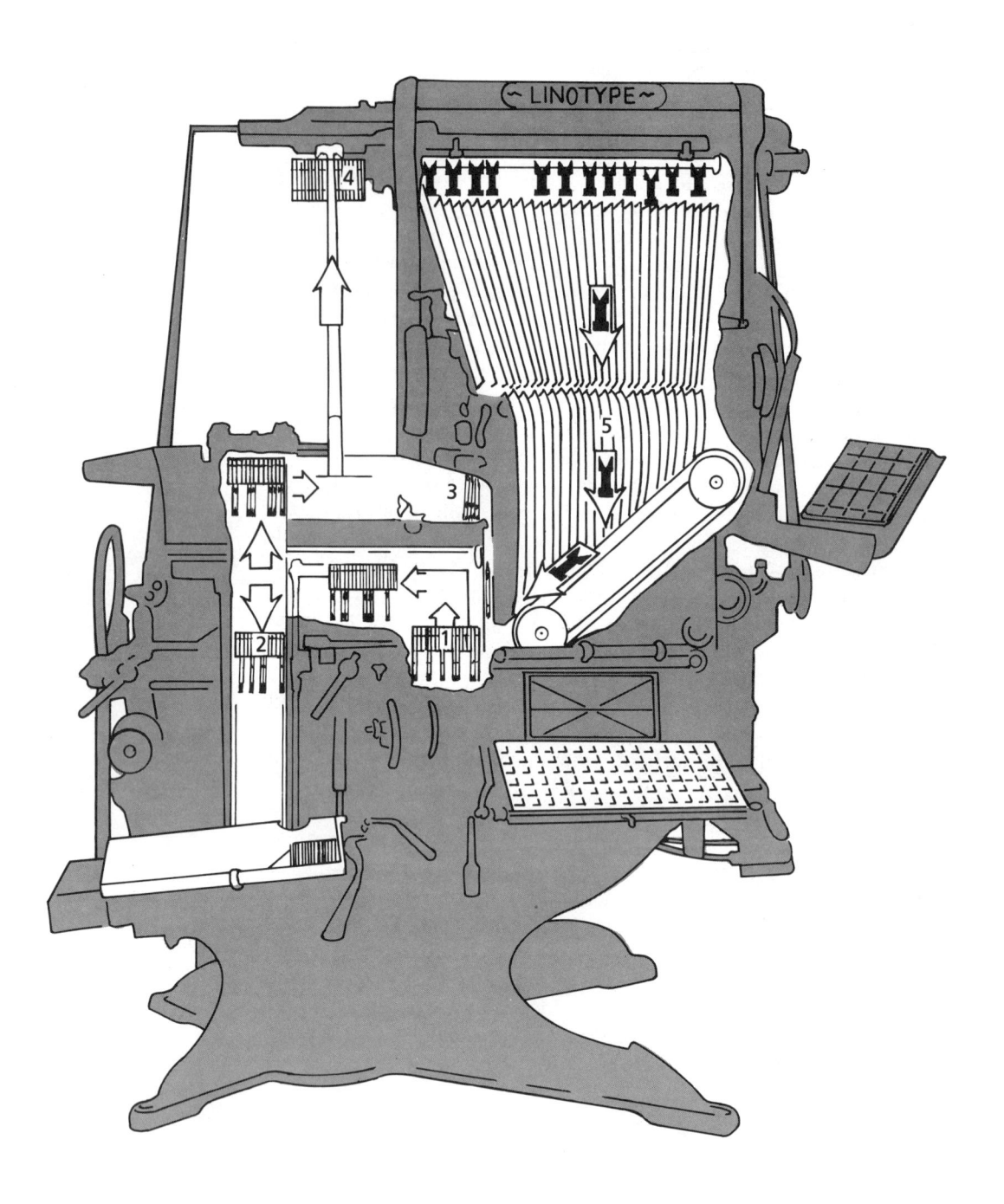

Lines of matrices and spacebands are collected in the assembly area (1) and then are transferred to the casting area (2). After the slugs have been cast and delivered to the galley in the front of the linecaster, the matrices and spacebands are redistributed: spacebands at the upper left (3), and matrices in the magazine (4). Each matrix occupies its own channel within the magazine and descends to the assembly area when the character's key has been struck (5).

The Linecasting Machine

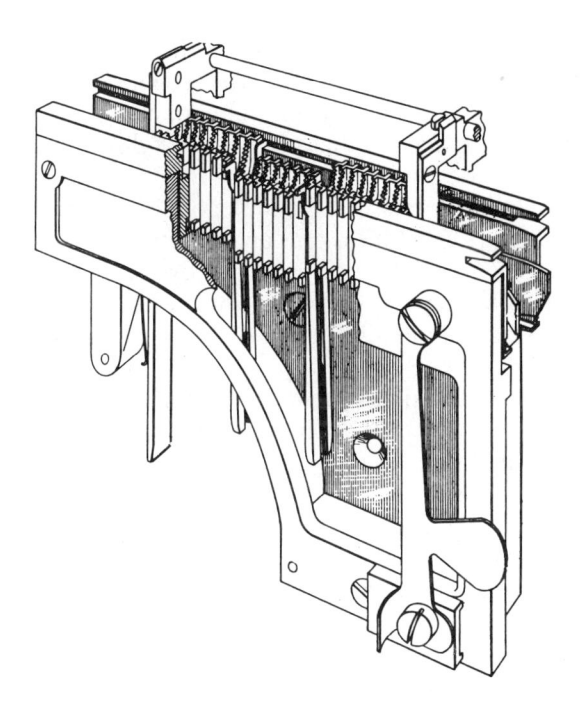

View of the delivery channel with a portion of the channel cut away to show the matrices and spacebands in different positions. The channel is simply a passageway for the matrices and spacebands in the same position in which they are received from the assembling elevator. The sectional views at the upper right show how the matrices and spacebands are supported while passing through the delivery channel.

At right: Perspective diagram of the assembling mechanism of the Linotype. **1** is the keybutton; **2**, keylever; **3** is the key weight, called the keyboard bar; **4**, the trigger; **5**, keyboard cam; **6**, keyboard rod or key reed; **7**, keyboard stop cam pin; **8**, keyboard cam yoke; **9**, matrix on assembler belt; **10**, magazine; **11**, matrix; **12**, matrix delivery belt; **13**, assembling elevator; **14**, spaceband buffer finger; **15**, escapement lever.

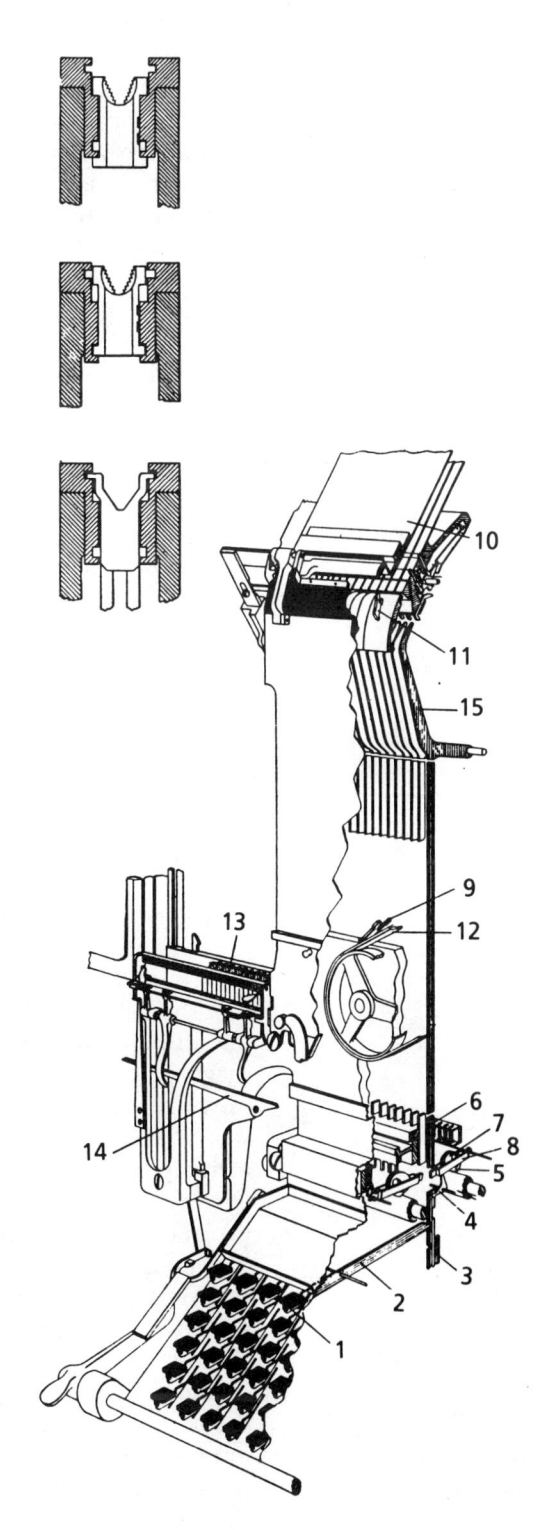

the copy consisted of news text or ad "agate"[1] to be set to a given face, size and measure, the number of persons who could share the task of composing the same job at the same time was generally quite limited. Matrices and magazines were expensive. So were the linecasters themselves. No owner wanted to pay for idle equipment. Consequently, the effective management of men and machines in hot metal shops was complicated, and one of the factors that often slowed down production on a given job was the problem of the lack of availability (within the shop) of the required fonts. For example, one shop might have one or two wide-measure machines, one or two "mixers," and three or four 30-pica models. It might also own only two magazines containing ten-point Times Roman, two of ten-point Caledonia, and one with eight-point Times, and perhaps one or two magazines with a particular size and face of display text.

While some operators were capable of setting complicated text, others could not be trusted to compose difficult material. The reader can readily understand that the task of supervision and scheduling was indeed complicated—more so, of course, in a trade shop performing a wide variety of jobs than in a production shop associated with a newspaper, where experience developed a routine and where work flow was predictable from day to day.

The work flow. The linecaster operator composed type slugs which were then placed in galleys. Proofs were pulled, often by an apprentice or a proofpress boy. Each galley was identified, and the type was laid out sequentially—although for proofing purposes it often was not yet assembled into its final order. In other words, it might have been necessary to proofread all of the extract material assembled into one galley, footnotes from another, text from a third, and display from still a fourth. On the other hand, the various elements might have been combined in their proper order by hand compositors or "bank men" before galley proofs were pulled.

Errors were marked by proofreaders with their own special annotations, and it was then necessary to compose corrections. This meant that the galleys had to go back to operators—not necessarily the same operators—but often!—who sat at machines on which the proper magazines were currently mounted, adjusted to set to the proper measure. It often happened, of course, that the setting of corrections was delayed until machines or operators could be freed up from other assignments. But finally the necessary slugs were reset. Sometimes corrections required setting not merely the line that contained the error, but on down to the end of the paragraph, since the substitution of even one letter for another could occasionally result in the rejustification of a line which, in turn, could have an impact upon the next, and so on until the change worked itself out or the paragraph came to an end.

Usually these corrections were proofread before they were incorporated into the text, and, of course, new errors could crop up—often in text that had been correctly set the first time but which had to be reset as part of paragraphs or takes in which errors had been found.

---

1. Agate is a term generally used in the newspaper industry for 5½ point type or for blocks of such type used to set classified ads.

The Linecasting Machine

Thus, corrections were made to corrections, and these again required proofreading.

Finally the proofreaders were satisfied and the corrected matter was put together with the original uncorrected text. This meant removing some line slugs and substituting others. There was, of course, the possibility that the wrong slugs might be removed or replaced, or that the galley itself might be tipped and a number of lines thrown out of sequence. Therefore another excursion into the proofreading department was in order to verify that the corrections had been inserted into the proper positions and no new errors had inadvertently been created.

Then, if not before, came the time to assemble all of the various typographic ingredients—the extract, the display, the footnotes—as much as possible in the proper order. This permitted new galley proofs to be pulled, which might again go to the proofroom and then, finally, in the case of outside work, back to the customer.

The job was not yet "into pages." Perhaps the publisher or editor already had some approximate idea of the length of his job. Perhaps the initial manuscript had been written to some copyfitting formula. Perhaps it was typed with a predetermined number of lines per page and characters per line, in the belief that, when set in type, a certain result in terms of column depth, number of pages, or even the number of signatures[1] could be predicted. Nevertheless it was still certain that pagination problems would present themselves.

But at this point it was now easier to see more precisely what the length of the material would be—not to the exact number of lines, of course, because page make-up poses its own problems. Editing might therefore be necessary to achieve better fit. The publisher or editor might discover the unfortunate fact that some operators set "tighter" than others, and projections as to the length of the material might have been thown off as a result.

It was also likely that the editor—or, more probably, the author—would introduce further changes—for he, too, would see the galleys, and indeed in the case of a book or an article, he would have been looking forward to the moment when his words became memorialized into type. As we all know, the trauma of seeing now in type what you have written cannot help but induce a fervent desire for last-minute changes: a word here or there, the turning of a more felicitous phrase, a degree more precision, a *bit* more emphasis, an aside that did not occur to the author before but now as he looks at his work with "new eyes" strikes him as being singularly apt, and the addition of a few facts that arrived on the scene after he dispatched the manuscript to the editor. All of these produce "author's alterations" and might well require a substantial amount of resetting.

We shall not trace the process of introducing these changes, of proofreading and incorporating them, of dividing galleys into pages, inserting running heads and folios, positioning illustrations, resetting lines to reference the illustrations, assembling the book, and then waiting until the index could be created, read and corrected. Obviously the process went on and on.

---

1. A signature consists of a group of pages which are printed on two sides of the same sheet of paper, or on two sides of a given length of paper cut from a continuous web or roll. Signatures usually consist of 4, 8, 16, 32 or 64 pages and are usually consecutive.

This, then, was the procedure that evolved over the years. Most of these work habits, customs and procedures were determined or conditioned by the technology of the linecasting machine. Some of them, of course, antedated the Linotype.

We will have occasion later in this book to see how many of these steps can be eliminated or greatly simplified through the use of more modern technology. Much more material can of course be composed sequentially. Type faces can be mixed, line lengths can be changed. Display, extract, and even footnotes can be composed as encountered. White space can be assigned for illustrations. And when corrections are required, one machine is likely to have available, at one time, all of the fonts, sizes and capabilities desired. Moreover, generally speaking, the quality of the composition—that is, the justification of the lines themselves—may be entirely operator-independent.

New processes present problems, of course. The publisher-customer has been familiar with old ways, just as the typesetting supplier has been. Sometimes it is easier for new users to adopt new procedures than for old users to change. Nevertheless, today linecasting has become a rarity and we are now concerned with the implications of still more doses of new technology upon the techniques of writing, editing and typesetting which have emerged over the past twenty years or so. While new patterns of work flow—from author to final product—have taken shape in many specific situations, especially in the area of newspapers and news magazines, at this writing the world is still trying to come to grips with the ways in which new techniques can be applied advantageously, and what this will mean in terms of specialization, the acquisition of new skills, and the relationships between those who play some part in the publishing process.

Other peculiarities induced by the linecaster

TYPE IS COMPOSED by circulating matrices. It was not rare for matrices from the wrong font to find their way into a particular magazine. Moreover, with circulating matrices (and therefore with a number of replications of the same matrix stored in a given channel so that there would always be a character on hand ready to fall into the assembler) it was possible that some of these mats would become defective. Thus it might happen that certain individual letters—but not all of them—might become imperfect or out of alignment. Moreover, mats might fall into the assembly area out of sequence, so that there could be machine-generated errors as well as those created by operators.

Another common problem was the failure of the man on the "bank," who was charged with the responsibility of removing slugs which were incorrectly set, or had been revised, to remove the proper ones or to substitute the intended slugs in an improper sequence or location. While the hot metal compositor was accustomed to reading his type upside down and backward, wherever human intervention is required or permitted there is always the possibility of human error, and with typesetting it appears that such is indeed the case!

The role of the Linotype operator

THE LINOTYPE MACHINE owed very little to the typewriter. Its keyboard layout was in many respects much more logical, but it soon became apparent that the journeyman operator had no desire to learn the typewriter keyboard and the office secretary, on the other hand, had no opportunity to sit at a Linotype. The keyboard "feel" was also completely different. There was, therefore, little affinity between these two devices and to characterize the duties of a Linotype operator as akin to "typing" would have been construed as a derogatory remark, belittling the skill of the journeyman.

While the operator no longer had the need to engage in the intricate "spacing in" and "spacing out" functions of the hand compositor, it was still his obligation to make "end-of-line" decisions. He watched the matrices and spacebands as they accumulated in the assembler and determined when the line was sufficiently full to cast. It was necessary for him to judge whether the unfilled space remaining between the jaws was less than the expansion capacity of the spacebands within the line. This would depend, of course, upon the number of spacebands within that particular line, bearing in mind that the only justification possible was achieved by *spacing out* from the minimum spaceband position, with the maximum expansion being roughly three times the value of the band's narrowest position.

When he judged that the line was as full as he could make it the operator would press a lever or handle which would cause the spacebands to be driven upward between the words until they forced the matrices as far apart as was possible, given the position of the jaws. This was called "sending-in the line." At that point the slug would be cast, the matrices and spacebands—no longer required—would be returned to their storage areas through automatic distribution, and the operator would continue with the next line during this machine cycle. Thus three lines were "in the works" at all times—one being composed, a second being cast into a slug and the matrices of the third being distributed back into the magazine channels.

No counting logic was required, either on the part of man or machine. Matrices were not designed to any particular unit of measurement, but it was customary for each matrix to provide two images, one of which represented the roman or normal text mold and the other was usually the same letter in either italic or bold. Thus, whatever the width of the roman character, the *duplexed* letter had to be the same width since the thickness of the matrix, when assembled between the jaws of the linecaster, determined the width of the character. To cause the duplexed letter to be cast within the line instead of the character in the roman or text font, the operator moved a lever called a "rail" which affected the position of that particular matrix.

The linecasting process, unlike Monotype (to be discussed in the next chapter), was based upon the notion of the single operator. Striking the keys represented the manner of selecting the desired character. The operator also made the end-of-line decision. The keyboarding process was continually interrupted by this and the delays which it entailed. Nevertheless, it was Ottmar Mergenthaler whose invention of the Linotype definitely determined the manner in which type was set for more than fifty years throughout the entire western world. He was a German emigrant (a watchmaker by trade) who came to the United States in 1872. In 1876 he left Washington D.C., where he had been employed to inspect and repair clocks, moved to Baltimore, and spent the next eight years on his invention. Thereafter he played an important role in the subsequent improvement of the device as a founder of the Mergenthaler Linotype Company. That company survived on its own for many years and then became part of the Eltra Corporation. Eltra was acquired by the Allied Corporation. In 1983 the decision was reached by Allied to move the corporate headquarters from Long Island back to Germany where the highly successful European subsidiary, Linotype GmbH was well established. However, Mergenthaler no longer manufactures the Linotype machine. Its products are now based upon electronic devices and make extensive use of photographic techniques and principles that will be discussed in subsequent chapters.

5

Monotype Composition

THE MONOTYPE METHOD of composition was patented in 1887, and was first exhibited in 1889. Tolbert Lanston (1844–1913) was the inventor of the process. A sergeant in the U.S. Army during the War Between the States, he subsequently became a civil service clerk in the U.S. Patent Office. Although he took a law degree in his spare time, he devoted his leisure to "gadgetry," inventing an adjustable horseshoe, a mail bag lock and an adding machine. When he saw the Hollerith Tabulator, presumably at the Census Bureau,[1] the idea occurred to him to develop a typesetting machine driven by coded paper tape.

After the prototype was displayed at the Columbian Exposition in Chicago, production of the first 50 machines was begun under contract with the Philadelphia firm of Sellers & Co.

Originally, the Monotype "caster" was a die stamping device which reproduced single types from cold strips of type-high lead, with a character repertoire, in terms of the stamping case, of 225 characters. Shortly thereafter it was modified to become a metal caster, with a font of only 132 matrices.

Four of these machines were shipped to England, and during the Atlantic crossing two of Lanston's associates met up with the Earl of Dunraven, who formed a syndicate virtually on the spot to purchase (for one million dollars) British rights to the patent. This development solved the American company's financial crisis and provided money for further development. Thus a Lanston Monotype Company was founded in England in 1897.

The British company manufactured component parts, including molds and matrices. It also marketed the product throughout the world, outside of North and South America, but it did not make keyboards or casters until after World War I. Meanwhile, many improvements were introduced into the design of the machine: a justification wedge was added and the matrix case was restored to its full character set of 225 positions.

The British company established its principal "works" at Salfords, about twenty miles south of London. The company began to make significant strides after World War I. During that war its facilities were devoted to the manufacture of machine gun components, but in 1922 work was commenced on the actual fabrication at Salfords of complete keyboards and casters. In 1927 the British company began to market products exclusively made in the U.K., and these were sold around the world, except in the Americas.

1. See our discussion of the Hollerith card in our treatment of computers in Chapter 10.

[51]

From that point on the paths of the American and British companies diverged increasingly. There was no common ownership of shares, no centralization of decision-making. Monotype (Ltd.) began its important work in the field of "typecutting" following the appointment of Stanley Morison as typographical advisor in 1922.

World War II again converted the Salfords Works into a munitions factory. When the war was over the company was literally overwhelmed by the demand for its products. This was not at all the case in the United States with Lanston, where linecasting had already made much greater inroads. The decline of the American company was already obvious in the mid-1950s and in the 1960s it was absorbed by other financial interests and then ultimately it was discontinued.

This brief bit of history has been included to make it clear that Monotype is now a British company, and that the principal market for its hot metal productions has long been international. The flexibility of the Monotype system readily lends itself to the setting of foreign languages—even, with casting machine modifications, Arabic and Hebrew.

Principles of operation

IT IS WORTH spending time to understand the Monotype system because it represents the first application of *counting logic* to the typesetting industry. As we have already observed, there is no need for the compositor to know anything specific about the widths of the various

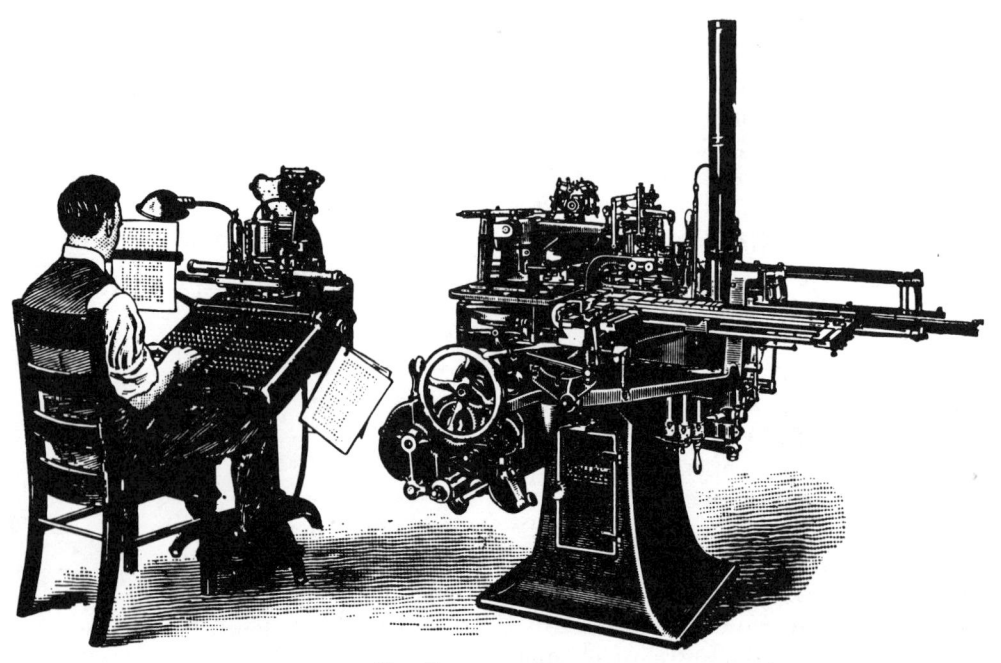

THE COMPLETE MONOTYPE

Monotype Composition

proportionally spaced characters so long as the physical assembly of the types themselves is done manually (as with hand composition) or by the operator himself observing the process of line filling which takes place in the assembly of the linecaster. But the separation of the keyboard from the casting machine in the Monotype system made it necessary to provide the keyboarder with a counting mechanism. This brought about the adoption of a "relative unit" system, and a mechanical means whereby a counting device is incremented with each keystroke to show how much of the line remains.

The keyboard. It was the function of the keyboard to perforate holes in a paper ribbon which was subsequently mounted onto the casting machine in order to "drive" it. Combinations of holes in the tape indicated which character positions were desired, or, more precisely, which locations in the matrix case were to be accessed during the casting operation.[1] It was also the function of the keyboard to increment the "Unit Wheel" and to provide a pointer to a cumulated total width value count, thus enabling the operator to key, at the end of each line, the value of the interword space for that particular line. Since the paper ribbon was read backwards by the casting machine, the interword space widths were the first fact that the machine encountered, and these values were thus used for the spaces for the line in question.

The width of the individual character was "known" by the mechanics of the keyboard itself. A keybar associated with a particular key incremented the Unit Wheel—a gear with 162 teeth. When the key was struck a pawl lifted to engage the wheel, causing it to revolve in a counterclockwise direction until as many of its teeth had passed the pawl as there were units in the character struck. Thus as the operator continued across the line the counting mechanism added width units and signaled as the line approached the indicated measure. The measure to be set was determined by the length of the unit rack wheel track.

Whenever the spacebar was struck a justifying space counter was incremented and this caused the pointer on the counting mechanism to rise to a different level, indicating a different set of values and thus providing information as to the number of ems and units of an em to be input by the operator at the end of the line.

Depressing a character or space key also caused a punch, activated by compressed air, to rise and perforate a hole in the paper ribbon. The location of these perforations across the ribbon determined the characters which the casting machine would manufacture.

Since different fonts might have different width values for the various characters in the font, it was always necessary to be certain that the keyboard was set up for the particular font or matrix case to be used for a given "take." This involved a relatively simple exchange of keybank components.

The casting machine. The caster was controlled by the paper ribbon which is mounted in its air tower. The perforations in this ribbon

---

1. Later models, called the "Monomatics," used different principles for reporting on width values and perforating the paper ribbon.

The discussion of the Monotype system has been written in the past tense as if models of this device were no longer manufactured or in use. As of this writing they are indeed still widely in use in various parts of the world, and some units are still being manufactured, although they are used less and less nowadays in industrialized nations.

serve as a valve to permit compressed air to regulate the movements of the casting machine, causing it to bring the matrix for the character to be cast over the mold and thus into casting position, and to draw back the mold blade the proper amount to make the type body the width required for the character to be cast.

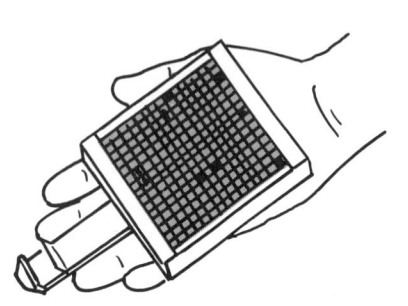

The matrix and the matrix case. Later versions of the Monotype offered a larger matrix case, but for many years the case consisted of a 15 × 15 arrangement of characters—a total of 225 in all, of which 13 were fixed spaces.[1] Individual character matrices could be assembled within the case as desired by the user, but the arrangement needed to correspond to his keyboard layout. The cellular matrices were slipped into the teeth of "combs" which held the characters firmly, and these combs were then assembled into the case.

Characters were arranged within the case so that their widths corresponded to their location. In other words, all characters slotted into the same comb had to have the same widths. A common or "standard" arrangement is shown in the diagram on page 58, with one row for each unit size, from five to eighteen inclusive, except that there were three nine-unit rows, three ten-unit rows, and the sixteen- and seventeen-unit sizes were not required. For offices specializing in tabular work the keyboard and mat case were often adjusted to provide four nine-unit rows.

Two holes punched across a horizontal row of tape indicated the character to be cast, although in some cases one hole or no hole conveyed the desired instruction. A punch in the horizontal direction, from A to N, would cause the mat case to move backward or forward (with no punch necessary for the column O). A punch in rows 1 to 14 moved the mat case to the left or right. (No punch was required for row 15.) Consequently, the em space shown at the lower right-hand corner required no holes at all in the tape.

Perforations at the beginning of the line as read by the casting machine (really the end of the line since the tape is read from back to front) contained the justification information and caused the machine to position its justifying wedges in such a manner that the justifying spaces in that line would be of the size required to justify it.

In addition, a "normal wedge" moved with the mat case in order to control the character set size. It regulated the distance that the mold blade was pulled back before the type was cast. A different normal wedge was required for each different set size of type.

The Matrix Case

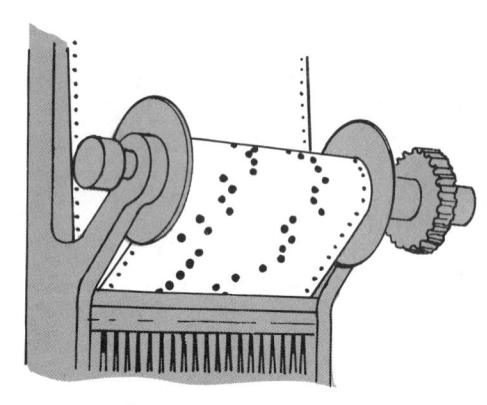

The roll of paper ribbon on the keyboard

1. Subsequently, the mat case was increased. In 1925 a 15 × 17 matrix case was introduced. In 1963 a unit shift feature was developed which virtually made the matrix widths independent of their unit row value. The unit shift arrangement provided for a 16 × 17 matrix case.

Implications of the Monotype system

IT IS INTERESTING to read literature supplied by the Lanston Monotype Company in the year 1916 because it underscores the virtues of the system at the same time that it seeks to "sell" its capabilities in an environment still (at least in part) dominated by the hand compositor—but nevertheless in a setting in which the linecaster had made substantial inroads.

> Composing-Room Efficiency can be obtained only by keeping clearly in mind this fact: The composing-room of a printing plant is a great deal more than a place in which to operate composing machines: it is a department maintained to produce complete pages locked-up in chases ready for printing, or electrotyping, or stereotyping.
>
> Now, in the production of complete pages, the work of the hand compositor is quite as essential as the work of the composing machine operator, because no composing machine ever devised can eliminate the hand compositor; his work is essential for making ready for the chases the machine-set matter and also for setting by hand the display matter used with the machine product.
>
> Therefore it is not possible to obtain composing room efficiency if the machinery used in the composing room fails to provide for the needs of the compositor.
>
> The Monotype is the only composing machine that recognizes the existence of the hand compositor. It is not built upon the impossible theory that the compositor can be driven from the printing industry; instead, it provides the means for increasing his efficiency and making his work highly profitable to his employer.
>
> Not only does the Monotype furnish a product that the compositor can correct and alter without the help of the machine operator, but also, since it is a complete type foundry, it supplies the compositor with all the equipment he requires to work efficiently—type, space material, rules, leads and slugs.

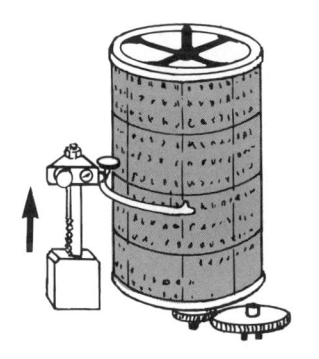

The Justifying Scale

The Lanston manual goes on to claim that the Monotype is the simplest and fastest composing machine—"a machine so free from mechanical limitations that it handles the most intricate composition as easily as straight matter"—and that the system gives much lower cost *for complete pages* "than is possible with any other composing machine," and that the product "is superior in quality to any other process of composition—hand or machine."

The Lanston Company also stressed the advantage of separating the keyboard from the caster:

> The Monotype, two machines in one, is both a type caster and a composing machine; it is the only machine that delivers new type in justified lines in ordinary galleys; it is the only mechanical means for producing printing surfaces far superior to hand-set foundry type, the only composing machine that handles straight

and intricate matter with equal facility. Its product is corrected and made-up the same as foundry type, it forces no changes in composing-room methods, it requires no special rules, saws or other paraphrenalia; it is built upon the principle that the printer knows best what he needs, and it gives him the type he has always used instead of "something just as good."

Composition is separated from casting by the Monotype System quite as distinctly as in the days of foundry type. The type foundry was separated from the composing room; the compositor who uses the Monotype Keyboard gives no more thought to typemaking than does the compositor who sets by hand type bought from a foundry. The Keyboard is as simple, as easy to learn, and as easy to operate as a typewriter, its Key arrangement is the same as any universal typewriter, and no machine has a lighter or more elastic touch. . . . The Casting Machine produces every character and space struck by the Keyboard operator when he perforated the ribbon, and the arrangement of these characters and the justification of the lines are exactly as he made them; in short, the ribbon controls the Casting Machine just as the paper roll on a pianola controls a piano. Thus, although the Keyboard operator can direct every movement of the Casting Machine, the two machines are absolutely independent; they may be located together, or apart, as desired, for any ribbon will control any Casting Machine at any place or at any time. A ribbon may be saved and used again for a repeat order, or, for matter that duplicates, as many casts as are desired may be made from the same ribbon.

The advantages of this separation cannot be overestimated. This is an age of specialization and the Monotype applies to the composing room this principle that has made American manufacturing pre-eminent. The Keyboard operator does not have to be a compositor, a mechanic, and a metallurgist combined. Removed from the fumes and dirt of casting he gives all of his attention to the work for which he is best fitted—composition.

The simplicity of the Keyboard is worthy of special comment: it has been called a "cross between a punch and an adding machine"—certainly it could not have been described more briefly . . . depressing a key does more than perforate the ribbon; it automatically registers the width struck and adds this amount to the sum of the width of the characters previously struck.

Lanston also stresses the flexibility of the Monotype: "the ease with which it handles the most intricate matter," including multilevel math, or "built-up equations." But the flexibility of the machine in terms of its character repertoire needs also to be considered. A skilled Monotype operator can arrange both his keyboard and his mat case so that they will afford him the specific characters he requires. It is even possible to use "double matrices"—that is, characters twice as high as "normal" letters. The matrix extends beyond the body on which the character is cast. To provide for this overhang, allowance must be made in the line or lines above the one in which the larger characters appear. Quads and spaces equivalent to the width of the larger characters must be set in the appropriate position.

The character repertoire

AS WE HAVE SEEN, the user can arrange whatever selection of characters he desires in his mat case, so long as he achieves a proper allocation of set widths. In other words, he must fill his mat case and if he has three nine-unit rows he must therefore include in that repertoire 45 characters of that particular width. Most commonly, the 225 characters in the mat case provide for roman, italic, and small caps, as well as ligatures and dipthongs. An alternative arrangement substitutes a bold face for the italic, and it is possible to substitute accented characters for certain of the "signs" which are less frequently used.

On the next page we illustrate the manner in which the keyboard layout and the mat case relate to one another, by selecting one of the many possible common arrangements.

The concept of "set"

THE MONOTYPE EM is given a value of 18 units, and in the normal instance these 18 units are equal to the point size of the type face in question. In other words, if one were casting 18 point type the em space would be 18 points wide and each unit would have a value of $1/18$ of an em. If the type matrices were nine point characters then one unit would be equal to one-half point. If the type matrices were six point characters then one unit, or $1/18$ of an em would have a value of one-third of a point.

In the creation of the type face the designer would have decided which characters should be given widths of $4/18$, which of $5/18$, which of $6/18$ of an em, and so forth.

However, it is also possible to require the Monotype system to compose and justify type to a different set width than that for which the type face was initially designed. By using different sizes of normal wedges, type faces may be cast on wider bodies. Below, we reproduce illustrations of a group of related type faces designed for eight point, eight and one-half set. But these faces can also be "opened up" and are shown in three other versions, each one-quarter set wider than the previous one. It is of course necessary to change the justifying scale to correspond with the desired normal wedge.

Eight-point faces—eight-and-one-half-set
A NEW IDEA in machinery has been embodied in the latest construction of the MONOTYPE, for, like "elastic" book cases, modern filing cabinets and composing-room furniture, **the Monotype is built up of units** which may be combined to suit the needs of each individual printing office.

Same eight-point faces—nine-set
A NEW IDEA in machinery has been embodied in the latest construction of the MONOTYPE, for, like "elastic" book cases, modern filing cabinets and composing-room furniture, **the Monotype is built up of units** which may be combined to suit the needs of each individual printing office.

Same eight-point faces—eight-and-three-quarters-set
A NEW IDEA in machinery has been embodied in the latest construction of the MONOTYPE, for, like "elastic" book cases, modern filing cabinets and composing-room furniture, **the Monotype is built up of units** which may be combined to suit the needs of each individual printing office.

Same eight-point faces—nine-and-one-quarter-set
A NEW IDEA in machinery has been embodied in the latest construction of the MONOTYPE, for, like "elastic" book cases, modern filing cabinets and composing-room furniture, **the Monotype is built up of units** which may be combined to suit the needs of each individual printing office.

The World of Digital Typesetting

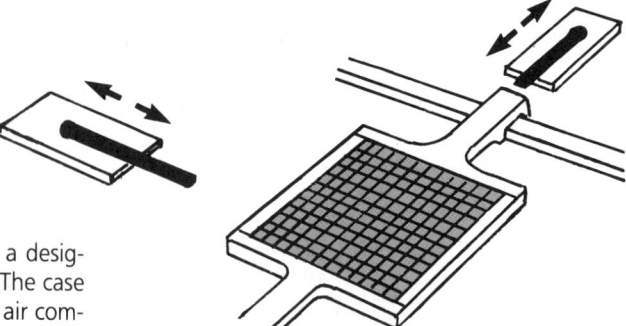

Each character matrix is positioned in a designated location within the matrix case. The case is then moved into casting position by air compression, according to a paper-tape signal.

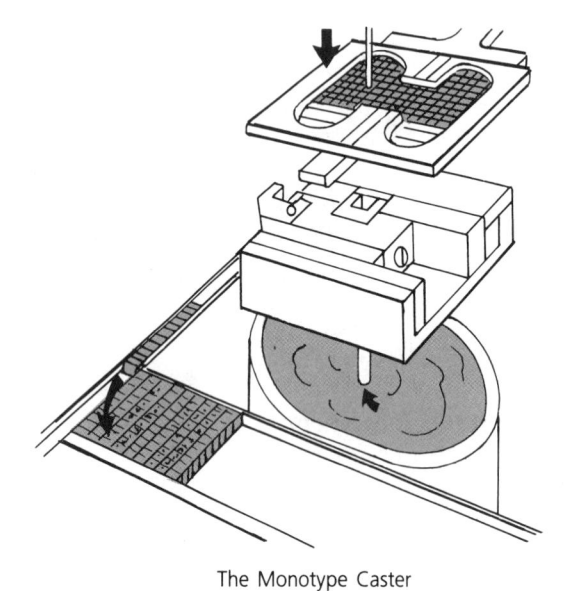

The proper matrix is selected by means of paper-tape signals from the paper-tape reader and the desired matrix is positioned over the mold. Metal is then squirted in to permit the character to be cast.

The Monotype Caster

The unit value as shown in the left-hand column corresponds with the character location in the matrix, as designated by row and column.

Unit Value	Row	A	B	C	D	E	F	G	H	I	J	K	L	M	N	O	Row
5	1	∎	∎	*l*	*t*	'	.	,	∎	l	i	]	[	'	∎	1
6	2	*j*	*f*	*i*	!	:	;	-	j	f	I	!	:	;	∎	∎	2
7	3	*c*	*r*	*s*	*e*	)	(	'	'	r	s	t	J	ʋ	°	z	3
8	4	‡	*q*	*	*b*	*g*	*o*	?	I	z	c	e	z	s	†	?	4
9	5	*I*	∎	9	7	5	3	1	0	.	9	7	5	3	1	0	5
9	6	C	∎	8	6	4	2	§	–	$	8	6	4	2	∎	6
9	7	*x*	*k*	*y*	*d*	*h*	*a*	*x*	J	g	o	a	P	F	L	T	7
10	8	A	*fi*	*u*	*n*	.	S	v	y	p	u	n	Q	B	O	E	8
10	9	D	∎	*fl*	*p*	fl	fi	q	k	b	h	d	v	Y	G	R	9
11	10	H	&	*J*	*S*	*œ*	*æ*	*ff*	∎	Z	∎	ff	X	U	K	N	10
12	11	*O*	*L*	*C*	*F*	*w*	*£*	*æ*	L	P	F	¶	M	Z	Q	G	11
13	12	*E*	*&*	*Q*	*V*	*C*	B	T	O	E	A	w	P	T	R	B	12
14	13	*D*	*A*	*Y*	*ffl*	*ffi*	*m*	*œ*	Y	U	G	R	Œ	Æ	w	V	13
15	14	*K*	*N*	*H*	ffl	ffi	X	D	N	K	H	m	&	fb	X	U	14
18	15	Œ	Æ	¾	¼	½	W	M	—	.	M	W	%	Œ	Æ	∎	15
Unit Value	Row	A	B	C	D	E	F	G	H	I	J	K	L	M	N	O	Row

Effect on type design

THE MONOTYPE SYSTEM—although it required relating all type characters to a common base of 18—did not in fact impose unreasonable restraints upon type designers, and the ability to position characters in various matrix locations (so that they could take on the width values assigned to that row) made it possible to exercise a great deal of freedom in giving shape and proportion to individual characters. Moreover, unlike the linecaster, which commonly "duplexed" bold and roman, or roman and italic, these faces could now take on widths more appropriate to their characteristics—the italic characters a little narrower than their roman counterparts and the bold characters usually a little wider.

But to deviate from a "standard" layout meant "reprogramming" (if that word can be so used) the keyboard. To do this you had to change keybanks and keybars and mount the proper justifying scale. If the only change you wanted to make was to set a different point size you had only to replace the justifying scale. But a different mat case layout would require replacement of keyboards and perhaps also the keybanks as well. Despite the contention that the keyboard is as easy to use as a typewriter, it is evident that the price one had to pay for "flexibility" in character repertoire was that the operator who moved from one layout to another had to concentrate to remember that certain key positions had been reassigned. Thus a change from one layout to another was not a trivial undertaking, although it could easily be accomplished by experts.

Remember, too, that when setting on the Monotype keyboard there was no "hard copy"—nor no "soft copy" either. In other words, there was no feedback, either in the form of an instant inked impression or some kind of screen display as to the actual character activated. All that you would be able to see would be one or two holes punched in the paper ribbon, which meant only that a certain position on the mat case had been addressed.

What Monotype taught us

ONE THING we must conclude from the Monotype experience is that typesetting devices must serve a wide variety of needs. The Monotype solution, developed at a time when the link between cause and effect (keystroke and character actually cast) was achieved by means which were primarily mechanical rather than electronic, illustrates that human ingenuity has not been substantially limited by the necessity of devising solutions so mechanically complex. On the other hand, today's methods are not nearly so cumbersome, and are often so unobtrusive (*i.e.*, "transparent to the user") that we may not appreciate the complexities involved, and the intricacies of the electronic solutions. Many people have had to think all of these same problems through, taking into consideration every conceivable variable, in order to arrive at a "general purpose" answer.

6

The Advent of TTS

IN THE EARLY 1930s a new method of setting type on linecasters was introduced. This is a method known as *TTS*. The initials stand for "teletypesetting," a technology developed to send impulses over a telegraph or telephone line for the purpose of permitting type to be set at remote locations. The inventor of the teletypesetter system was Walter Morey whose background included work as a composing room superintendent and as a Monotype salesman. He began his experiments in the 1920s in Newark, N.J., and later received financial backing from Frank Gannett, a newspaper publisher in Rochester, N.Y. who founded the Gannett newspaper chain.

Morey's invention came to fruition in the early 1930s, but was hardly used until after World War II. The most practical application for TTS was what we call the "wire services." These are news-gathering agencies such as UPI (United Press International) and AP (Associated Press). At that time reporters would phone or otherwise relay their stories to a central news bureau. Here the stories were keyboarded, edited, channeled for distribution according to interest and category of news, and transmitted over the teletype to local newspapers. There they were received on teletype "printers." Local editors could read and garner information from these reports, rewriting what was relevant to them, or sending them on to the composing room to be typeset in their entirety as received.

Morey visualized the possibility that stories could be transmitted in justified form and could be received not only as "hard copy printout" but also as punched paper tape capable of activating a linecaster. Tape from stories selected for publication would thus be available for setting *without the necessity of rekeyboarding.*

The wire services were slow to begin the transmission of pre-justified stories, keyed and justified at the transmitting end. There were many obstacles in the way, such as the absence of a uniform typographical format on the part of the newspapers (especially column widths and type faces), their uncertainty about whether or not they wished to use the wire service stories more or less intact, and union objections to the elimination of local keyboarding. Nevertheless, in 1951 both AP and UPI did begin the transmission of such material. They were encouraged to do so in part because a certain number of newspapers, particularly in the south (notably in North Carolina and Arkansas), were using TTS input internally and were therefore equipped to receive it.

The "internal" use of TTS

THE FACT IS, therefore, that from 1932 until the 1950s TTS hardly caught on, and when it did it was primarily employed not as a consequence of teletype transmission but for whatever advantages it offered for purely local or internal production. Perhaps the major exception was in the case of Time, Inc. There, for some years beginning in the 1940s, text matter keyboarded in Time's editorial offices in New York was transmitted to several locations (notably Chicago and Philadelphia) where the signals were recorded by paper tape punch and the tape, in turn, was mounted on linecasters. But by the late 1950s this practice of multiple transmission and setting was discontinued as air travel became quicker and more reliable. Electrotype shells were flown from Chicago to Philadelphia and elsewhere. TTS transmission continued to be used between the editorial offices in New York and the plant of the printer (R. R. Donnelley) in Chicago.

TTS is a method which is, however, more suited to straight text than for the setting of complex work, and at least initially, it could only be applied in situations in which typesetting with unit-count fonts was acceptable. As we have already explained,[1] linecasting fonts were not designed with any unit-counting system in mind. The operator made his own end-of-line decisions on the basis of his visual judgment. But if the keyboard is to be separated from the caster so that the keyboarder can no longer see the matrices fall into the assembler, then some method of counting is essential so that he can determine where to place his line-ending decisions.

To use TTS initially it was necessary to develop a method of counting at the keyboard, and this led to the creation of so-called "unit-cut" or "unit-count" fonts. Modifications of existing artwork of type masters were drawn for the Linotype which, following the example of Monotype, began to make use of the unit system. But unlike Monotype, where a given character could vary in width from one font to another, there was initially no such flexibility with respect to type designed for the linecaster. And so, regardless of type face or style, each character had to be redesigned to take on an appearance that could be represented by an assigned universal width. A Times Roman lower case a had to have the same unit value as a Spartan, Trade Gothic or Corona a of the same point size. Moreover, the character repertoire itself was more or less standardized. Hence a standard perforator (tape-perforating keyboard) could be employed. Every newspaper receiving wire service data would set it in an 11-pica measure, in nine-point type of whatever unit-count face was chosen. Later, other unitized but nonuniform faces could be used.

The TTS keyboard

LIKE THE MONOTYPE keyboard, the original TTS Standard Perforator performed two basic functions—it punched coded holes in paper tape and it provided a counting mechanism. Pressure on the

1. See p. 49.

keys activated selector bars. These made electrical contacts which sent signals to the solenoids in the punch mechanism. The same selector bars provided information to a "squirrel cage" which rotated according to the unit count of the character. This rotation caused a pointer or scale to move. (In earlier models, affectionately known in the trade as the Fairchild *Brownies*, the scale was fixed and the pointers moved.) One pointer, on the left of the scale, indicated the increasing accumulation of character widths, while two other pointers on the right indicated the amount of space taken up by the spacebands as calculated, and their minimum and maximum values. When the left pointer found itself within the area which measured the difference between minimum and maximum interword space expansion, the operator knew he was within justification range and could release the line by striking the return and elevate keys.

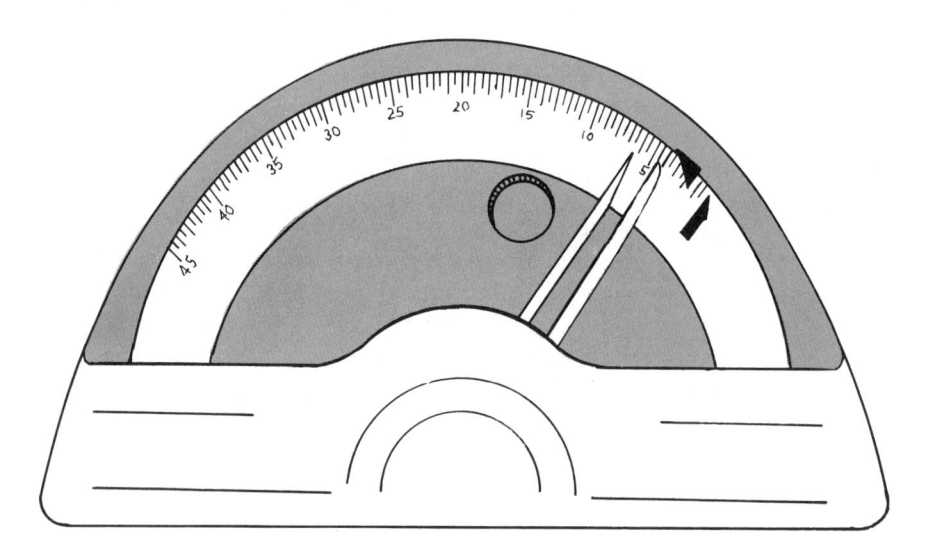

Subsequently, the multiface perforator was introduced. This device included a counting magazine consisting of a series of blades which were contacted by the selector bars and which in turn activated the squirrel cage. The movement of the squirrel cage and its pointers was determined by the location of the blades in the counting magazine which designated character widths.

The multiface perforator was based upon a 32 unit-to-the-em system. A separate counting magazine had to be inserted for each change of type face. The brass width values of the linecaster matrices were rounded off to the nearest $\frac{1}{32}$ of an em. For example, a nine-point em should measure .1243" and thus the $\frac{1}{32}$ of a nine-point em would equal .0038812". In order to assign unit values to type not designed with this in mind, the brass width of each character would have to be measured by a micrometer. If a lower case a "miked" at .063", and you divided this figure by .0038812 you would derive 16.23 units, which would then be rounded off to 16 relative units.

The Advent of TTS 63

These rounding errors, being plus or minus .00194" (in our illustration) would tend to cancel each other out. But if they did not do so—giving consideration to the frequent use of certain characters which might be over as opposed to others which might be under—you could be over or under by as much as .05" in an 11-pica line. This might—in relatively rare instances—cause a line to be set either too tightly or too loosely to cast properly.

The Multiface Perforator had a removable counting magazine which was inserted in the slot at the right. The machine logic "consulted" the width values "read" from these electrical contacts.

A typical TTS keyboard. The "shift" key had to be used before a capital letter, with "unshift" whenever it was necessary to return to lower case.

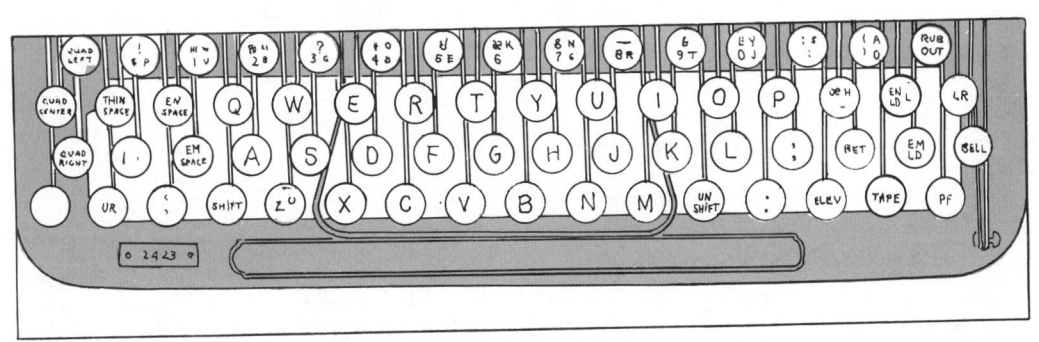

Nevertheless, so far as we know, hot metal type was never redesigned for multiface TTS operation on the basis of the 32-unit system, although type was designed for unit-count operations. As we have indicated, in the 1950s the wire services did begin to transmit prejustified tapes—and the transmission of stock market data also occurred. More and more newspapers therefore converted to unit-count designs so that they could avoid rekeyboarding.

On the other hand, some book and commercial shops made fairly extensive use of multiface perforators. The principal advantage appears to have been the higher productivity of the TTS keyboard operator as compared with the linecaster operator at his machine. Even after allowance is made for the fact that a "monitor" (linecasting machine operator) would be required for every two, three, or perhaps four tape-driven linecasters, total keystrokes produced divided by total man hours, seem in general to have increased. And in some cases acute labor shortages were alleviated since TTS keyboards could be operated by persons with typing skills (plus some additional training) who did not need to serve a formal four- or six-year apprenticeship. And by adding more keyboards on the "day side," it was possible to keep linecasting machines busy on the "night end" and even on the "lobster shift" without the need to pay night differentials, and without the problem of recruiting additional personnel for night work.

Let us turn our attention to the manner in which the linecaster was driven by TTS tape. Characteristically, this tape is (or was) "read" by the "fingers" of a mechanical paper tape reader, which sensed the presence or absence of holes in the paper tape and conveyed electrical signals to an adaptor keyboard, under which an "operating unit" depressed the keys that released the matrices. The same operating unit also controlled the "rail" in the assembling elevator (to access the alternate duplexed font of italic or bold) and caused the elevator to rise in order to cast the line and to redistribute the matrices. Subsequently, the operating unit was enhanced to be able to handle the functions of an "automatic quadder" which filled out short lines at the end of paragraphs with the necessary fixed spaces.

Later models of linecasters, beginning about 1959, such as the Intertype Monarch and the Linotype Elektron, were built to read paper tape without the need for an adaptor keyboard or operating unit. Such machines were capable of casting from ten to fifteen newspaper lines per minute, although the latter figure was seldom achieved. Twelve lines per minute is the equivalent of approximately six characters per second (whereas a Monotype caster could not quite achieve a speed of three characters per second.).

The paper-tape coding

THE SIX-LEVEL CODE which drives the linecaster was developed by Walter Morey, inventor of the TTS system, as an adaptation of the five-level code which had been used in message transmission over telegraph and telephone lines. As the reader no doubt knows, telegraphers originally used the Morse code, consisting of dots and dashes

The Advent of TTS

(*circa* 1840). Several subsequent inventions sought to devise a method of semiautomatic transmission, one of which was the Wheatstone Automatic Telegraph. Professor Charles Wheatstone developed a centered sprocket tape which recorded a dot by punching a hole on one side of the sprocket feed and a dash by punching a hole first on one side and then (in the next position) on the opposite side.

Because each letter consisted of different combinations of dots and dashes—some more lengthy than others—a blank sprocket position separated the characters.

Subsequently, Émile Baudot (1845–1903), a French engineer who pioneered long-distance telegraphic installations (as from Paris to Vienna), developed a five-level code which was produced by a "chord" keyboard consisting of five keys. The signal from combinations of these five keys was picked up serially—that is, each of the five components (present or absent) was transmitted in sequence, preceded and followed by a start and stop signal. (The normal operating speed of this method was considered 30 words per minute, and this led to our use of the term "baud" to describe serial transmission speeds.)

A. C. Booth developed a more conventional typewriter-like keyboard which also produced the Baudot code, but now as a *frame* across a paper tape. A subsequent variation produced in 1901 called the *Murray* code (known in the U.S. as the Baudot code) made use of an advanced sprocket hole to indicate the direction of the paper tape. (*See illustration on page 68.*)

The Murray code affords a combination of 32 possibilities (assuming "no holes" to be one such). The 26 alphabetic characters and a space were supplemented by a carriage return and "line feed." The other two codes were used to signal a shift from letters to figures and back to letters again. The figure mode included some punctuation marks as well as the ten digits. Obviously there were no lower-case alphabetic characters.

The basic principle behind the assignment of holes across the tape was that the wear on the tape punch should be minimized. Hence, what were taken to be the most frequently used characters were represented by the fewest holes. The letters e and t, as well as space, required only one hole each, and s, h, r, d, and l needed but two. Morey thus created a whole new series of codes, since the addition of the sixth level (actually called row 0) added 32 new possibilities. These were used for the most part to meet typesetting requirements—quad left, right and center, em, en, thin and add-thin spaces, upper rail and lower rail. Also the letters and figures concept gave way to the upper case and lower case. The figures and special characters were thus assigned to sixth level (row 0) positions in a shift or unshift mode.

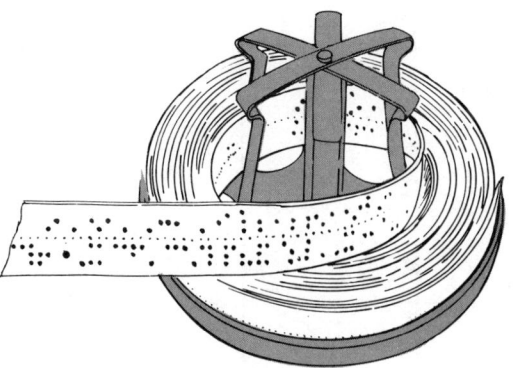

Paper tape from a TTS keyboard ready to be fed into the linecasting machine's paper-tape reader.

Table I—The Morey (TTS) Adaptation of Murray-Baudot Coding

Murray			TTS		
	Letters Mode	Figures Mode		Downshift Mode	Upshift Mode
11 000	A	hyphen	011 000	a	A
10 011	B	?	010 011	b	B
01 110	C	:	001 110	c	C
10 010	D	$	010 010	d	D
10 000	E	3	010 000	e	E
10 110	F	! or *	010 110	f	F
01 011	G	& or *	001 011	g	G
00 101	H	★	001 101	h	H
01 100	I	8	001 100	i	I
11 010	J	Bell	011 010	j	J
11 110	K	)	011 110	k	K
01 001	L	(	001 001	l	L
00 111	M	.	000 111	m	M
00 110	N	,	000 111	n	N
00 011	O	9	000 011	o	O
01 101	P	0	001 011	p	P
11 101	Q	1	011 101	q	Q
01 010	R	4	001 010	r	R
10 100	S	apos.	010 100	s	S
00 001	T	5	000 001	t	T
11 100	U	7	011 100	u	U
01 111	V	=	001 111	v	V
11 001	W	2	011 001	w	W
10 111	X	/	010 111	x	X
10 101	Y	6	010 101	y	Y
10 001	Z	+	010 001	z	Z
00 010	carriage	return	000 010	carriage	return
01 000	line	feed	001 000	line	feed
11 111	Letters	Letters	011 111	Unshift	Unshift
11 011	Figures	Figures	011 011	Shift	Shift
00 100	Space	Space	000 100	Space	Space
			100 000	Thin space	Thin space
			110 000	3	?
			101 000	lower	magazine
			111 000	|	!
			100 100	Add thin	Add thin
			110 100	Em space	Em space
			101 100	8	—
			111 100	7	&
			100 010	'	'
			110 010	-	@
			101 010	4	*
			111 010	Bell	Bell
			100 110	,	,
			110 110	Quad left	Quad left
			101 110	En space	En space
			101 101	0	?
			111 101	En ldr.	En ldr.
			100 011	9	option
			110 011	Upper rail	Upper rail
			101 011	;	:
			111 011	Lower rail	Lower rail
			100 111	.	.
			110 111	1	⅛
			101 111	Quad cent.	Quad cent.
			111 111	Rub out	Rub out

The Advent of TTS

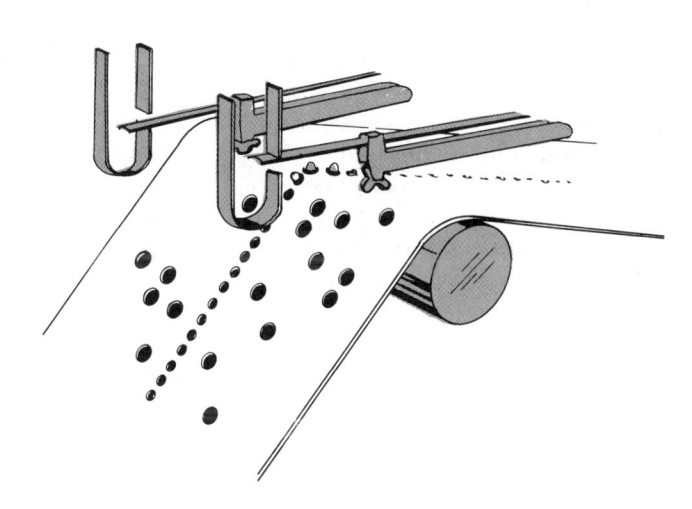

While TTS keyboards punched their own tape, a paper-tape punch was often used for computer typesetting where line-ending decisions were made by the computer, and paper tape was output to drive linecaster machines (and later, phototypesetting devices).

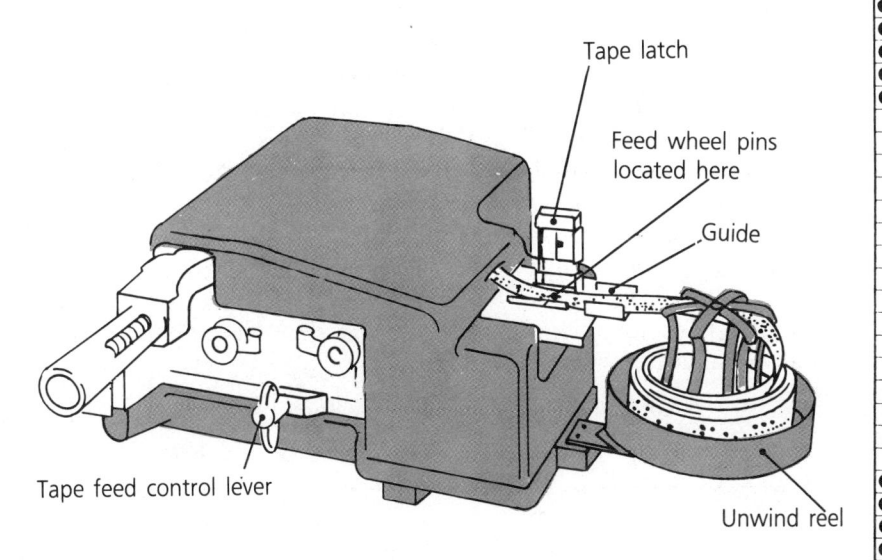

Tally Model 625 Paper-Tape Reader. Such readers were either electronic or photomechanical. Here photo diodes sense the presence or absence of light from a source above the transport mechanism. The sprocket holes are either "advanced," so they align with the edge of the perforations, or are centered.

The Teletypesetter
6-level code (TTS)

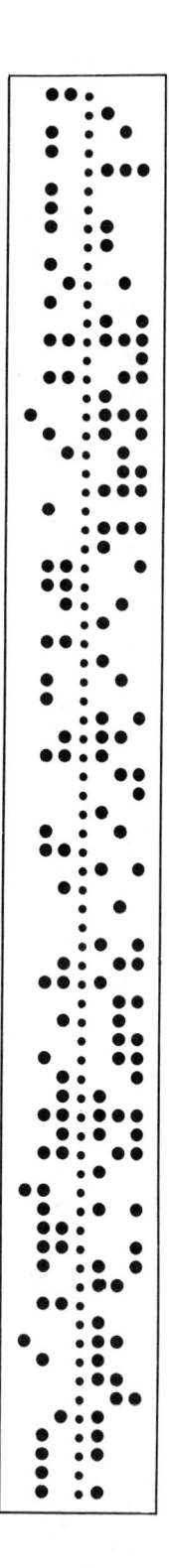

Analysis of TTS code assignments

SIX-LEVEL TTS PAPER TAPE carries its information in frames of 64 available codes. Some of these have the capability of changing the meaning or application of subsequent codes. For example, a shift code indicates that until further notice, that is, until an unshift code is encountered, all subsequent codes are to be interpreted as referring to characters or functions normally associated with the shift position. In like manner, an *upper rail* code means that, until further notice, all subsequent codes relating to characters will be set in the upper rail (*e.g.,* italic) mode.

Similarly, there is a code which can be used to indicate that, until further notice, all matrices desired should be accessed from the *lower magazine* as opposed to the *upper magazine*. In this way, given a Linotype "mixer" it is possible to access a wider range of type faces. There is, of course, a similar code to return to the upper magazine.

In addition, there are codes to access type characters which are the same whether they are found in upper case, lower case, upper rail, lower rail, upper magazine or lower magazine. This would be true, for example, of such formatting codes as quad center, quad left or quad right. There are also a few codes, such as the period, the comma, and the em or en "leader" which represent the same characters whether in upper or lower case.

In general out of the 64 available codes about 40 of them are mode-related—that is, they will change their meaning according to the pre-existing signals or flags. Other codes consist of the flags themselves or nonmode-related commands, as well as symbols that may be valid across certain of the modes.

It is also possible to provide for different combinations of characters or symbols in the upper rail as opposed to the lower rail, thus getting more mileage from the limited number of channels and rail positions. The table below shows how the character repertoire was usually enhanced for book work.

Lower Rail		Upper Rail	
Downshift	*Upshift*	*Downshift*	*Upshift*
0	fl	J	Y
1	ffi	V	W
2	?	C	?
3		D	O
4	ff	E	L
5	æ	F	K
6	&	G	N
7	—	R	—
8	fi	T	option
9	fl	J	Y
|	!	P	option
;	:	;	S
)	(	Q	A
-	œ	-	H

The use of a precedence code or mode determiner

AN EXAMINATION of these code conventions illustrates the manner in which one set of codes can do double duty. With the Murray-Baudot five-level code, for example, there are two modes which are represented by the same combination of holes and no holes on paper tape. The person doing the keyboarding will indicate by a *precedence code* or *flag* which mode he intends. This means that of the 32 available code combinations in the five-level code structure, one code must be reserved to signal the *entering* of one mode and another must be reserved to signal *departure* from that mode and hence entrance into an alternate, or perhaps default mode. One of these two modes represents the alphabet and the second is designated for figures and other miscellaneous characters. If the second or alternate mode is not signaled, perhaps it may be assumed that a basic default mode will govern.

The precedence code injects into the text stream an "until further notice" condition. In other words, the new mode governs until the decoder (the teleprinter, for example) is told otherwise. This makes it important, in processing or reading the paper tape, to observe the *sequential nature* of the input stream, for if you moved about at random, using only a portion of the incoming tape rather than starting from its beginning, the decoder would not know what mode would govern.

Thus, in a sense, the precedence code becomes a switch and when it is encountered an alternate set of symbols is substituted. To use computer terms—which will become more familiar to us later—we might say that the precedence code causes a program to "branch" or acts otherwise to direct the use of a different set of *translate tables*—that is, the use of some method of substituting one set of symbols or meanings for another. We might also say that we substituted one *overlay* of characters for another, within the same code structure.

The six-level TTS code offers 64 combinations of holes and no holes (as opposed to the Murray-Baudot 32). In this case, however, we encounter two different kinds of precedence codes. One differentiates upper-case characters from lower-case characters. You will observe that the code combination of holes for a lower case *a* and an upper case *A* are precisely the same. (Make a mental note that this is *not* true for seven-level or eight-level ASCII.[1]) The decoder can only know which of the two symbols is intended by the use of a precedence code which states that "until further notice I intend you to use only upper-case characters." This is precisely what happens on a typewriter when you press the shift lock. YOU WILL REMAIN WITH CAPITAL LETTERS UNTIL YOU turn off the condition. When you unlock the shift lock you are creating (figuratively) an unshift or downshift code.

While, on the conventional (non-Selectric) typewriter the upper- and lower-case characters are not only on the same key but on the same striking bar, on a linecasting machine the lower case *a* and the

1. See Chapter 15.

upper case A, while accessed by the same key, are not on the same matrix since the width of the capital letter is greater than the brass width of the lower case character. On the Selectric "golf ball" typewriter, on the other hand, the character locations have a different relationship, being opposite one another on the typing element.

The reader will recall that the upper case condition is more confused in the numbers row. On a typewriter, the shift symbols above the numbers are more or less arbitrarily assigned, although there now is some degree of standardization. But for the TTS-driven linecaster the assignment of these codes often depended upon the nature of the character set required—whether for book or job work, for example—since in the former case SMALL CAPS and ligatures might be desired, and other possible symbols might have to be sacrificed, such as the "one-piece" fractions (⅛, ¼, ⅜, ½, ⅝, ⅞, ⅓, ⅔).

Beyond the shift condition, however, TTS required yet another set of precedence codes. This had to do with a shift from lower to upper rail.

In the lower-rail position you would generally set type in a roman face. In the upper-rail position you would generally set either an italic or a bold face type. When the TTS encoder read a flag sending the machine into upper rail, it would remain there until further notice, casting letters from the alternate type face—"duplexed" so that the lower-case roman a corresponds in width with the lower-case italic or bold **a**.

In this instance, then, the code does in fact cause the linecaster to access the same matrix. The A and the **A** are paired together, and the a and the **a** are also duplexed and paired together.

Now we can see that of the 64 available codes, two have been preempted to indicate shift and unshift and two to indicate upper and lower rail. Thus these codes open up parallel tracks: those codes generally used to describe characters (as opposed to functions) now have four alternate meanings depending upon their mode. The same code can mean: a, **a**, A, **A** or alternately a, *a*, A, *A*.

As an exercise, let us suppose that we represent each code as a capital letter in order to convey the impression that the code itself is neutral with respect to modes. And let us represent an upshift as [C] for capital and a downshift as [S] for small letter, bearing in mind that the [C] and [S] codes are really only one character and one keystroke each. In like manner, let us represent the basic face as [L] for lower rail and [U] for upper rail. To underscore the fact that codes representing letters are the same whatever the case or rail condition, we shall present them as capital letters:

[L][C]T[S]HIS IS THE WAY THE TEXT STREAM WOULD LOOK. [U][C]N[S]OW WE HAVE SHIFTED INTO ITALIC.[L]

This is the way the text stream would look. *Now we have shifted into italic.* Or:

[L][C]R[S]OMAN. [U][C]I[S]TALIC.—That is, Roman. *Italic.*

Again, to clarify the location of the characters:
[L][C]A [S]A[U][C]A[S]A.
A   a   **A**   *a*

These are on the same matrix.   These are on the same matrix.

Unhappily, the situation does not end here. The reader will remember that two other codes may also be appropriated to introduce still another condition: upper magazine and lower magazine. This presumes a linecaster which is a mixer and which can, upon signal, automatically shift from one magazine to another, thus permitting 91 alternate channels, each containing two-character matrices (91 each in the upper-rail and lower-rail modes).

Let us suppose that the alternate magazine offers bold and bold italic, and let us use [LM] to represent the code for the basic or lower magazine and [UM] to represent the alternate magazine. Hence we can now have:

[LM][L]R[S]oman. [U][L]*I*[S]*talic.* [UM][L][C]**B**[L]**old**. [L]*B*[S]*old* [L]*I*[S]*talic.*

We may now see that there are in fact eight different conditions available to us under TTS hot metal coding: four fonts with an upper- and lower-case mode available to each. They are:

Basic Magazine	**Alternate Magazine**
Lower Rail	*Lower Rail*
Upper case	Upper case
Lower case	Lower case
Upper Rail	*Upper Rail*
Upper case	Upper case
Lower case	Lower case

TTS input consisted of justified lines, with the operator making line-ending decisions based upon the keyboard's counting logic. As we shall see, the TTS keyboard, slightly modified and simplified, could also be used for the production of unjustified running text for subsequent computer processing. Hence this technology provides a bridge between hot metal and computer typesetting.

7

The Photocomposition Era Begins

IN THE YEAR 1946, two events of significance marked the beginning of the era of photocomposition. One was the first field testing of the Intertype Fotosetter, and the second was an agreement between the Lithomat Company and two Frenchmen (Higonnet and Moyroud) which led to the development of the Photon typesetter.

The Intertype Fotosetter was first exhibited in the year 1950. It, as well as the Monophoto (which came along shortly thereafter) are what are called "first-generation" phototypesetters. By this it is meant that, although they expose type images on photographic film or paper rather than to cast type or slugs from molten metal, they do not differ substantially in their basic design from their hot metal progenitors. On the other hand, the Photon typesetter, which was developed at about the same time, was a true "second-generation" machine because it did not in any sense resemble a hot metal caster, being based upon entirely new electro-mechanical principles.

Why photocomposition?

THE NEED for a photocomposition device was readily apparent. There had already occurred a shift in the printing process so that an increasing proportion of all printing, at least on the continent of Europe and in North America, was produced by offset or lithography instead of by letterpress. While letterpress requires printing from raised type, or from stereotype or electrotype plates formed from an impression of raised type, offset—being a planographic process—requires exposure of the plate from a photographic negative or positive[1] and the use of raised type for typesetting was therefore a liability. In fact, elaborate techniques had been devised to provide either the equivalent of a photographic positive from metal by printing "reproduction" (or "repro") proofs directly on a transparent carrier, or by rubbing the type form with carbon black, then burnishing the surface, and photographing the form itself. This latter process was known as "Brightype."

In addition, in the late 1950s, raised printing plates created by photographic means began to appear (e.g., magnesium or acetate "etched" plates, or photopolymer plates such as DuPont's Dycril). This technology set into motion a flurry of experimentation which—while it did not deter the growth of offset printing—made its own contribution toward the ultimate obsolescence of hot metal typesetting for many if not most applications.

---

1. Whether a negative or positive is desired for offset platemaking depends upon whether the offset plate is intended to be "negative working" or "positive working." With a negative working plate, that part of the coating which is *not* exposed to light is soluble in the developer, whereas with a positive working plate the coating which *is* exposed to light becomes soluble.

The Photocomposition Era Begins

Among other factors contributing to the growth of offset was the great expense of producing letterpress engravings for the reproduction of pictures (both line drawings and halftones). The offset process eliminates completely the need to etch illustrations into zinc and copper plates, to mount these plates on wood blocks, and to lock these blocks into a metal form for imposition or platemaking. And even before the advent of photocomposition, display heads were being composed by such devices as Filmotype, Fototype, Hadego, Typro and other photo-lettering machines. These served the same general purpose as did the Ludlow process of casting display slugs from hand-set matrices. But of course for letterpress they required that cuts be made to provide the required raised image.

The (Harris) Intertype Fotosetter

SINCE INTERTYPE was subsequently acquired by Harris—becoming first the Harris-Intertype Company and then later on the Harris Corporation—we shall associate the name Harris with the product in our discussion even though there was at the time of the Fotosetter's introduction no such connection. The Fotosetter development began toward the end of World War II, and the first units were tested as early as 1946 in the U.S. Government Printing Office. However, the device was not shown to the general public until the year 1950 at the first major printing exhibition to occur in the United States following World War II.

The Fotosetter was a keyboard-operated machine strongly resembling the linecaster, its hot metal counterpart. It utilized the slug-casting machine principle of the keyboard cam-release, and the hot metal technique for the assembly of matrices as well as for their distribution back into the magazine. But the actual act of casting was replaced by the substitution of a camera and by the introduction of a somewhat different principle to achieve spacing and line justification.

The matrix which contained the photographic image was shaped precisely like hot metal circulating matrices, including the teeth and notches which guided the matrix back into its proper channel. The thicknesses of the brass matrices, as with a hot metal mat, determined the amount of space each character was permitted to occupy within a line, but the process worked in a different fashion. As will be noted from the illustration on the next page, the images are stationary as they are photographed, but the film itself, including the elaborate mechanism for supporting the film cassette, moved after each image was photographed by an amount corresponding to the width of the matrix. An interesting departure in the machine design was the absence of spacebands.

Any one of eight prefocused lenses could be inserted (with appropriate adjustments in the carriage-movement mechanism) and two sizes of Fotomats (8 and 12 point) made it possible to offer selected settings between 6 and 36 points. Other lenses could be obtained to set 4, 5 and 30 points.

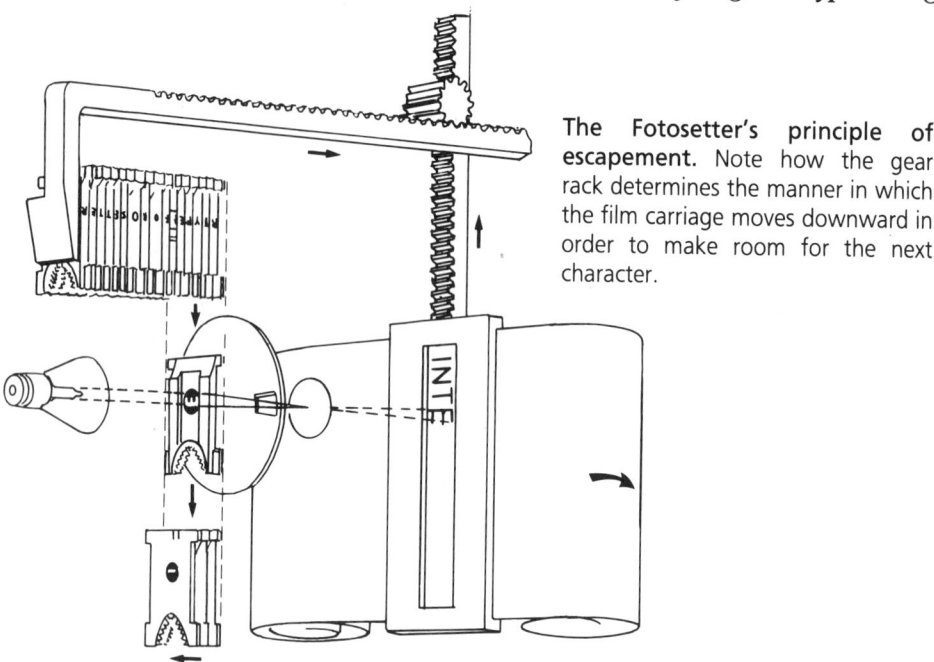

The Fotosetter's principle of escapement. Note how the gear rack determines the manner in which the film carriage moves downward in order to make room for the next character.

Justification. There were no spacebands. Blank mats of a given uniform width were assembled when spaces were called for. Then the camera mechanism measured the height of the pile of Fotomats after the line had been assembled, and the difference between the height of the pile and the desired line length was automatically distributed throughout the line. Thus the line was justified only by means of *letterspacing*—that is, assigning an equal amount of the leftover space to each character in the line, including interword spaces. Later models of the machine eliminated this deficiency and offered a capability of adding extra space only between words. A Fotomatic model was also developed to be driven by TTS punched paper tape. A turret lens system offering eight sizes was also a feature of the Fotomatic, although size changes could only be accomplished by a manual movement of a dial and not by tape command. However, the Fotomatic did not make the impact upon the market which had been anticipated since, by the time it was offered for sale, there were other (second-generation) typesetters available on the marketplace.

The Monophoto

THE OTHER FIRST-GENERATION phototypesetter was the Monophoto, which was originally developed by British Monotype's George Westover as the Rotophoto in 1949, but it lateremerged in 1955 as the Monophoto. It was based upon the same principles as the Monotype and hence it, too, is a first-generation machine.

The keyboard unit prepared a paper ribbon justified at the keyboard in much the same manner as with the hot metal Monotype process. This ribbon—not to be confused with the narrower ¾-inch

The Photocomposition Era Begins

TTS tape—then drove the camera unit which originally contained a 15 × 17 mat case containing, of course, photo mats. This mat case moved vertically and horizontally in the same fashion as with the Monotype caster in order to position the desired character at the location where—instead of providing a mold for casting—it furnished an image to be photographed. A single lens, which operated more or less on a zoom principle, sized the image within a range of six to 24 points, although manual adjustment was required to secure the desired magnification. Several different sizes of photo matrices were available.[1]

The film, although it was advanced in front of the camera for the setting of each successive line, did not, like the Fotosetter, move horizontally across the line on a character-by-character basis. Instead, after the image was twice deflected through a set of "folded mirrors" it was again bounced off a larger set of such mirrors which stepped sideward in such fashion as to lay down each character across the measure according to its indicated width. That width was of course ascertained from the character's location in the mat case in the same manner as with the Monotype caster. From this knowledge of the character's width the data were provided which governed the movement of the final set of mirrors much as it governed the spacing wedges of the Monotype casting machine.

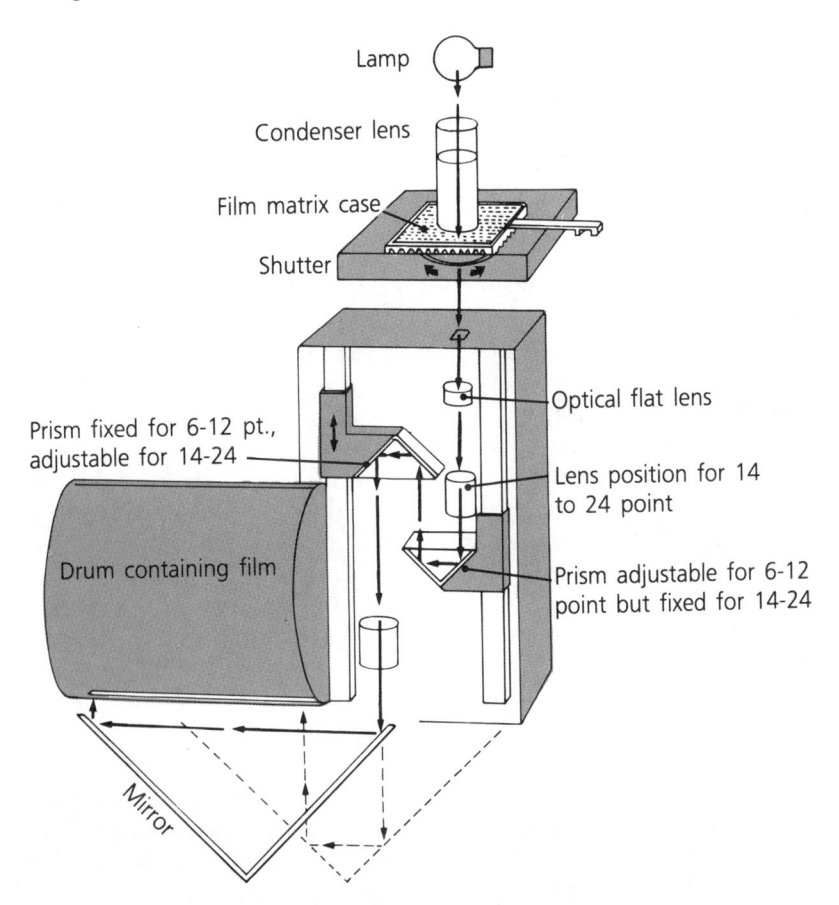

[1]. In 1965 the Mark 3 version was introduced offering an increased running speed and improved justification. In 1967 the Mark 4 increased the matrix case to 340 characters and spaces, and in 1969 the Mark 5 Monophoto filmsetter appeared, offering a much greater flexibility of film feed for variations in interlinear spacing. At some point in this evolution it would be appropriate to consider the Monophoto no longer a "first-generation" device.

The quality of the image of the Monotype was superb, but the speed of the phototypesetter did not represent any significant improvement over its hot metal counterpart.

The ATF typesetter

THERE WAS PERHAPS one other first-generation typesetter, if we consider such machines as having been derived from the design of a typesetting machine originally intended for a traditional purpose. American Type Founders introduced a "system" in the early 1960's which was based upon the principles of the Friden Justowriter Recorder and Reproducer units.

The term "system" may be appropriate since this approach involved two units in the same sense that the original Monotype approach was also a "system" and that TTS-tape-driven linecasting represented a system.

Whereas the other two devices we have termed as first-generation typesetters were based quite precisely upon hot metal designs, the ATF typesetter found its origins in an approach which was adapted from the typewriter, but which had the capability of setting and justifying proportionally spaced strike-on type—namely the Friden Justowriter.

It may be appropriate to digress for a moment to describe the background out of which the Justowriter emerged. In the year 1948 a wave of composing room strikes occurred in the United States. The primary reason was the passage of the Taft-Hartley Act, and the reaction to the new law by the International Typographical Union, a labor organization which represented a very substantial number of typesetting craftsmen (known as printers) in the United States and Canada.

In the summer of 1947 that Union's convention initiated a strategy recommended by its president, Woodruff Randolph, that reserved to its members the right to strike, automatically terminating their labor contracts, if employers sought, by the hiring of non-union members, to comply with the mandatory provisions of the Taft-Hartley Act which outlawed so-called closed shops.

Not since 1921 had there been such a wave of strikes, and the effect of these dislocations—in some instances the strikes lasted as long as six months—strengthened the resolve of employers (particularly in the newspapers) to decrease their dependency upon the skills of their typographical union members. Moreover, many newspapers experimented with substitute processes during the period of the strike, and these processes were, perforce, strike-on or typewriter-like solutions.

The Justowriter emerged in response to this expressed need, although as a matter of fact it never did make any inroads in the unionized sector of the industry. However, it found its way into the small weekly newspaper field, and became the principal means by which such newspapers were typeset in the period of the late 1950s through the 1960s. All newspapers, except the large metropolitan dailies,

The Photocomposition Era Begins

were increasingly shifting their printing arrangements from web or sheet-fed letterpress to web offset.

The strike-on methods of composition which were developed during this period made use of such machines as the Coxhead Composing Machine DS-J, the VariTyper, the Fairchild Lithotype Composer and the IBM Electric Executive Typewriter, but the Justowriter led all the rest in terms of sales and general acceptance for run-of-the-mill strike-on composition.

The Justowriter consisted of two machines: a Recorder and a Reproducer. The Recorder produced a preliminary hard copy or typed sheet of paper as well as a perforated paper tape. Operators made their own end-of-line decisions when a light indicated that the text was now within justification range. Width values were ascertained by assigning to the characters one of four set widths, from two to five relative units. Hence, a Justowriter type font was a unit-count font in the sense that all like characters—whatever the type face design—had a uniform width. Moreover, the Reproducer was capable of setting only one size of type—that machined onto its striking bars. When the operator terminated the line, keying the justification code, this code (when encountered by the paper-tape reader on the Reproducer unit after the same paper tape was mounted thereon) told the Reproducer the amount of interword space escapement needed in order to justify the line.

More than 19,000 Justowriter units were sold between 1951 and 1970—the year when the decision was made to no longer manufacture them. But, in addition, more than 1,100 machine chassis were sold to American Typefounders for modification into phototypesetters.

ATF kept the input unit (the Recorder) much as it was, but modified the Reproducer so that, in place of the platen, a film carrier was mounted. And in place of the striking bars a rotating disk was positioned along with a light source. When the paper tape called for a particular character, the disk rotated forward to that location, stopped, and the light source then exposed the character. Next the carriage containing the photographic paper cassette moved over by the character width.

The disk offered 168 characters, consisting of two duplexed[1] fonts of 84 characters each. Body sizes (on different disks) ranged from 5 to 14 points.

Many shops, especially newspapers, got their first exposure to photocomposition through these ATF B-8s.

ATF B-8 Recorder Unit

ATF B-8 Reproducer Unit

1. Duplexed fonts consist of two type faces (usually of the same family) but differing in appearance, as with roman and italic or roman and bold, but with the same width values for identical characters in each font. Thus they are paired in the same manner as with the linecaster matrix.

The Photon 200

WE TURN NOW to what was truly the first second-generation typesetter—the Photon 200. This machine was developed in the late 1940s and was brought to the United States in the conceptual stage by the French inventors Louis Moyroud and René Higonnet.

According to legend, these two engineers had been doing research on the timing of airplane propellers by the use of high-speed strobe lights.[1] They prepared a report describing their studies, and in their search for a typesettting supplier for this article they visited various composing rooms and printing plants and were appalled by the awkwardness and inconvenience of the typesetting methods they were exposed to. They began to think how convenient some sort of photocomposition device would be, and their background and experience naturally led them to consider some sort of a spinning disk containing photographic images with a high-speed electronic timing mechanism to keep track of each image as it went spinning by. When the desired character passed the strobe light source, a flash would be triggered, thus exposing the character "on the fly." Escapement was to be provided by a prism or mirror arrangement that would advance across the film of paper, moving the distance of the width of each character as it was exposed.

One could write a book simply about the trials and tribulations of Photon and its products. A company called Lithomat came to an arrangement with the inventors in 1946 and subsequently changed its name to Photon. It sought financing from influential backers in the printing and publishing industry. It was first conceived as a quasi-nonprofit venture, but after it had exhausted its initial infusion of capital the company was restructured as a publicly held corporation.

The first operating prototype (1948) is at the museum of printing in Lyon, France, and the early model of what was to become the Photon 200 (a machine called Petunia and built in 1951) is at the Gutenberg museum of printing in Mainz, West Germany.

The Photon 200 consisted of a keyboard unit, a second unit called the "relay rack," and the output unit—all of which worked together in the manner of a direct-entry typesetter. The operator composed lines, obtaining a character countdown for justification purposes. As his line-ending decisions were made, the electronic information was passed on to the output unit for typesetting. A typewriter was used as the keyboard, and it produced hard copy during the keyboarding process. However, it generated and sent signals to the relay rack and received in turn a display of the countdown of line length remainder as well as indicators of point size, leading and selected font. When the line was composed and released it was set on the output portion of the photo unit. This box contained the film transport and a revolving disk with 16 fonts—each font occupying one-half of one of eight concentric circles of type masters. A lens turret with twelve lenses provided for selected point sizes, generally from four to 72 points.

---

1. Strobe refers to stroboscopic—a high-intensity, short-duration light source which can enable the camera to take a picture of an image in motion as if in a state of rest.

The Photocomposition Era Begins 79

The Photon 200 Admaster. You will note that this is a keyboard-oriented machine, with an elaborate panel of controls on the right to specify line length, leading, font, sizing, and other conditions.

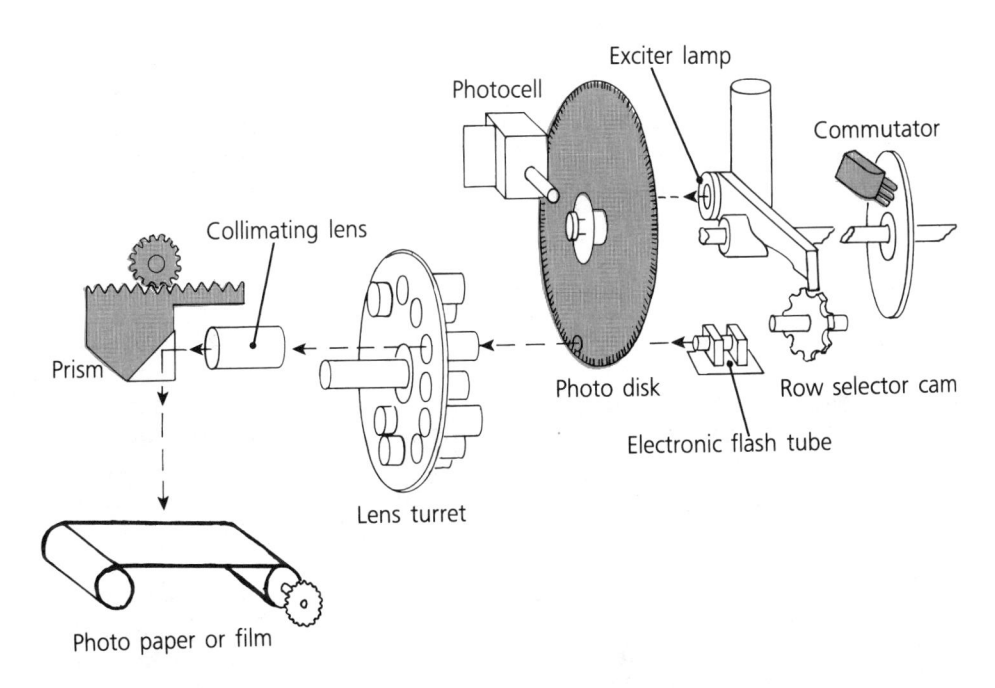

Optical principles of the Photon 200. The photo disk, containing 16 fonts in eight rows, is mounted on the spindle, and rotates continuously at a constant speed. Pulses from the exciter lamp enable the photocell to keep track of the timing slits on the edge of the photo disk so that the electronic flash tube will be triggered to expose the desired character. The negative image of this character (described as "the window") will pass through a sizing lens, a collimating lens, and be deflected by the prism onto the photofilm or paper. The prism "escapes" after each character has been exposed in order to lay down the next character image at the desired location, determined by the width of the preceding character.

The relay rack provided the computations and housed the width cards needed for each of the various fonts. It then furnished the output unit with the information which it required as to the row and font to access, the character to flash, the lens to position and the width to escape for each character and for each interword space.

Photon subsequently separated the keyboarding or input function from the output unit so that a direct connection between the two units was no longer required. Instead, paper tape was perforated and passed on to the paper-tape reader in the output unit. The models so driven were the Photon 260, the 513, the 540 and the 560. All used the same spinning disk output device. Each required paper-tape input of prejustified lines. However, the 513 contained the logic to look up its own width values from cards plugged into the unit itself. The 540 and the 560 models, on the other hand, required that width values be provided directly on the paper tape along with the character codes. This meant that more frames[1] of information had to be provided for each character by the paper-tape punch, and decoded by circuitry behind the paper-tape reader. First the character was identified by its position on the disk, and then one or more additional frames indicated what the width of the character was meant to be. The same was true of spacing codes: a space was called for and the width of the desired space was also stated.

Initially the Photon operated on a 24-unit-to-the-em system but the company then changed to a 36-unit system. Later models (all paper-tape driven) added still more capabilities providing, for example, access to characters from either of two spinning disks. There was also a one-half sizing lens which dropped in front of the lens turret, thus offering a total of 23 sizes from the same type masters.

The Mergenthaler Linofilm

OBVIOUSLY IT WILL NOT BE possible to discuss each second, third, or even fourth-generation typesetting machine that has been introduced into the market since alternatives to hot metal typesetting became feasible. More and more of these devices continue to enter the market, with ever-lower prices and increased speed and versatility. Moreover, as we shall see the distinction between a typesetter and other kinds of computer output devices is becoming more and more blurred. However, we should make mention of at least the next machine to reach the marketplace after the Photon was introduced. This was a second-generation device called the Linofilm, and it was produced by the Mergenthaler Linotype Company in response to the Intertype and Photon achievements.

Mergenthaler had been caught short when Intertype came to the 1950 exhibit with the Fotosetter, and Photon's prototype device was also well known. But back in the early 1940s Mergenthaler had done some experimental research with a cathode ray tube typesetter and had abandoned the project as untimely—as indeed it was. In this same period, Eastman Kodak carried on similar research, as did RCA,

---

1. A frame consists of a row of holes across the paper tape. Normally a character can be expressed by a frame of six or eight holes. If width values are also to be carried, a second and perhaps a third frame would be required.

The Photocomposition Era Begins

but these were strictly laboratory experiments. However, for the 1950 show, Mergenthaler displayed a mock-up of a phototypesetter it had never built and wasn't at all sure it would in fact produce, largely to sample opinion on the subject of photocomposition. The reaction was evidently sufficiently positive since they set about building a machine which was available for field testing purposes in 1956 and was available for sale and use shortly thereafter.

The Linofilm separated the keyboard from the photo unit. Much like the Photon station (which was originally not so separated), the keyboard provided a continuous countdown as character widths were computed, and it also offered typewriter hard copy. Width cards to match the width values of the 18 fonts or grids that were to be mounted in the output or typesetting unit were positioned in the keyboard, and these were consulted by the keyboard's logic. Changes from one grid to another were indicated by the use of supplementary buttons and switches on the keyboard.

The output unit contained a grid basket in which were seated 18 grids—each of 88 characters—and the desired grid was selected for immediate use somewhat in the same manner as a victrola record might be retrieved for play by a juke box. In other words, the grid turret revolved, and the desired grid was tipped out and held in place in front of the light source. A series of shutters masked out all characters except for the one that was to be exposed. This character was

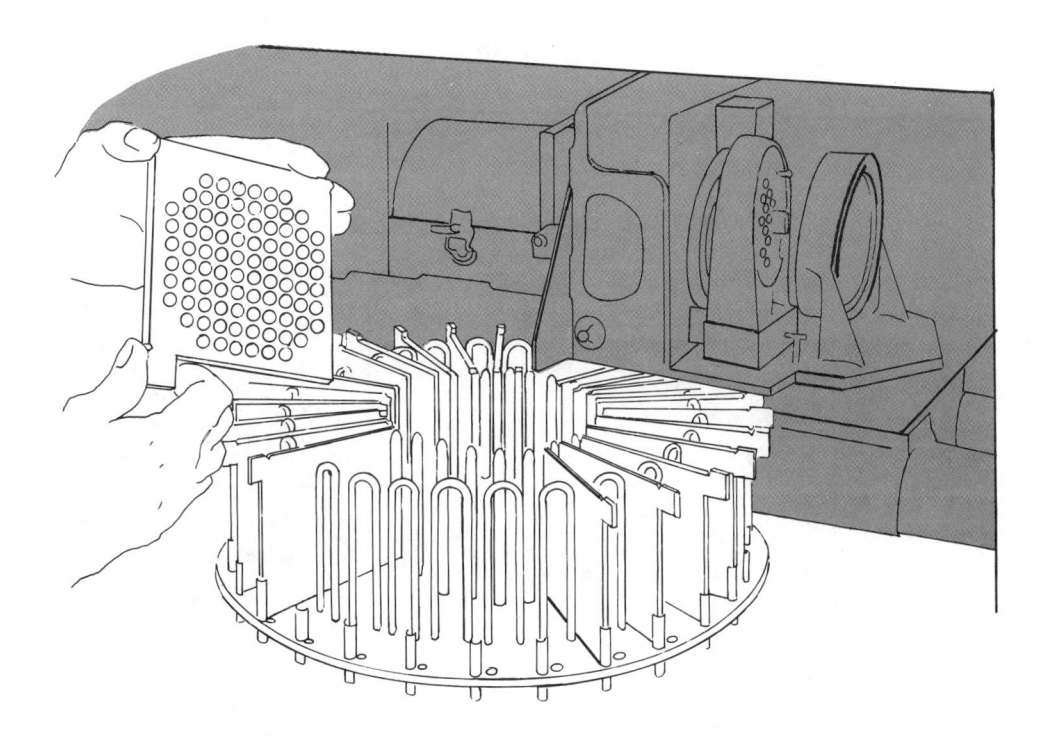

Eighteen grids are being positioned in the rotating grid basket.

then sized through a zoom lens system, and a traversing mirror directed the character onto the film plane. Thus the character image was stationary when photographed, and the quality of the image on photographic paper or lithographic film was superb.

In general, grids of three different master sizes were offered: A-range fonts were suited for text sizes. B-range fonts were intended for display setting in the spread from 12 through 18 points, and C-range fonts were used for sizes from 18 through 36 points, although smaller and larger sizes could also be made available.

Because of the zoom lens method of character enlargement, different sizes of characters could not be aligned on the same optical base line. But the use of different size masters (in order to produce larger or smaller images through the same lens system) nevertheless made it possible to select type masters more suitable for the intended size ranges, with proportions more pleasing to the eye than is usually the case if one master image is to be enlarged or reduced over an extended range of point sizes.

The Linofilm output unit was completely a slave. It was driven from 15-level paper tape, considerably wider than the usual six to eight-level tapes used by most other machines (except, of course, for the Monotype with its 31-level paper ribbon).

Fifteen levels of data were indeed required by the Mergenthaler unit in order to convey the information about the character to be selected from the grid as well as to provide information about the width of each character. However, it was the output unit which calculated the amount of space to be inserted between words for justification purposes. The basic character widths were read from the paper tape by the first of two paper-tape readers. The second paper-tape reader then deciphered the character calls and processed the information on a character-by-character basis, using the interword spacing values which, in the meantime, had been assigned to that line by the electronic logic in the back end or photo-unit.

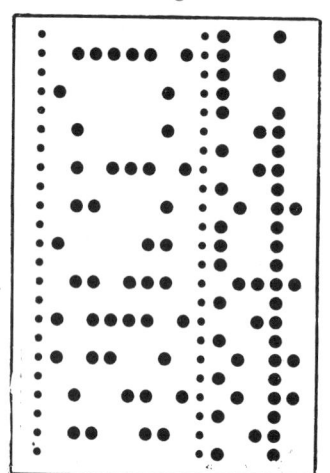

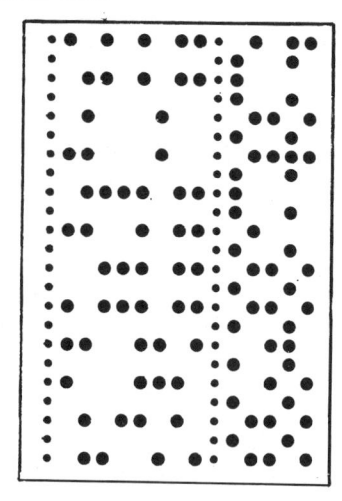

Linofilm 15-level tape. In order to clarify the coding each character has been separated by the code for an em space. Character coding also includes character width values.

Summary

WE HAVE PRESENTED this historical approach to the development of phototypesetters in order to pave the way for a discussion of more general principles. These principles must be understood in order for us to trace the subsequent evolution of such devices and so that the reader can more readily grasp the significance and direction of the dramatic evolution which was afoot. Consequently the next chapter will deal on a more theoretical level with the alternatives and trade-offs which were available to engineers and market strategists when they considered the appropriate design for a new second-generation device.

Just as Gutenberg sought to imitate the qualities of the medieval manuscript, so did the designers of photocomposition equipment seek to provide output which could be compared favorably with hot metal typesetting—especially such machine typesetters as the linecaster or perhaps even the Monotype. They did not consider what might follow from the introduction of these new methods. Neither they nor the publishing industry stopped to think about the way in which new technology might change the entire process of manuscript creation, editing, typesetting and publishing. No one would have understood that profound changes might be set into motion by the application of new techniques. In fact, for many years after these devices came into being the industry sought to imitate and preserve the entire sequence of steps which had grown up around hot metal typesetting. Even today—more than a generation later—we are struggling to discover appropriate ways to take advantage of the machines and techniques which modern electronics make possible.

8

Second-Generation Solutions

THE TWO DEVICES discussed toward the end of the preceding chapter were merely the first in a long series of second-generation phototypesetters. The Photon 200 and the Mergenthaler Linofilm were the earliest entries but many more were to come. Perhaps many more will yet follow, although it would appear now that with today's technology there are faster, better and less expensive ways of accomplishing the same ends. In fact, the evolution of these machines over the past twenty years is a testimony to the ingenuity of the human mind and its ability to contrive alternative approaches to identical or quite similar problems. The trend to be observed is that, with a few exceptions, each succeeding device has offered less mechanical complexity, greater reliability, and a greater reliance upon the contribution of electronic components.

It would not be useful to describe each such machine and the sequence in which it was introduced to the marketplace. It should be more instructive to consider instead the fundamental problems and principles underlying all such devices, and to weigh the merits of the approaches which have so far been taken.

All of these second-generation machines have in common the fact that their purpose is to project images of photographic masters onto photosensitive film or paper for the purpose of setting text as well as a mixture of display type faces. They differ from first-generation machines in that they were originally designed for their intended purpose, rather than adapted from hot metal or strike-on predecessors. They differ from third- or fourth-generation machines in that the type images are indeed generated directly from photographic masters, by the process of directing a light source through a series of negative images of the desired characters and symbols.

It is important to understand the contribution of these machines— how they work and what some of the design trade-offs have been. By studying them and their evolution we learn much about what can be done through the use of such technology and what is implied in terms of the performance characteristics of such devices.

Here are the six principles which we shall consider:
- How characters are stored.
- How characters are selected.
- How characters are exposed.
- How characters are sized.
- How characters are laid down (the escapement process).
- How justification takes place.

Character storage

WE HAVE ALREADY SEEN that the Photon 200 stored its repertoire of characters and type masters on a revolving disk. This was also true of the earlier, first-generation ATF photosetters, although in the latter case the disk was arrested in order to expose each character in the absence of motion, whereas with the Photon the disk continued to revolve at a relatively high speed so that the light exposure had to be very rapid indeed.

On the other hand, the Linofilm stored its character type masters on a series of grids, just as was the case with the first-generation Monophoto. A grid remains stationary during exposure, although the process of selection requires illuminating only one character at a time or masking out all of the others.

Characters must of course be placed very carefully on the grid, disk or other carrier so that they will not present problems of vertical or horizontal misalignment. The master size of the artwork from which the character is chosen is customarily not the size of the image stored on film within the machine.

A determination is first made as to what the "true" master size should be. For example, if the type is supposed to look its best as a text face, a master drawn to look well at say ten points may be selected. This master will then be enlarged many times so that it can be touched up and perfected by hand. Then it will be photographed to the size required by the typesetting machine's optical system design—the size at which the character will appear on the disk or grid. That size may be ten points, or five points, or even two and one-half points, or some other appropriate size. In other words, the machine design may be such that to set on a "one-for-one" basis (*i.e.,* an original ten-point master for ten-point type), a magnification factor of 2:1 may be contemplated. In such a case the film master on grid or disk would turn out to be five points.

Whatever the stored master size may be, it will be mounted or otherwise presented on the carrier—a grid, a disk, or film strips to be affixed to a rotating drum. In general, these characters will be arranged in fonts and the font may vary in repertoire from as few as perhaps 84 or 88 characters to as many as perhaps 120 or so. Usually—but not always—more than one font is available on the typesetting machine at one time.

The manner of storing fonts—*i.e.,* whether on a grid, disk, drum, cylinder or otherwise—is determined by the method by which the desired character is to be selected from within the font or from among an array of characters comprising more than one font.

Character selection

THERE APPEAR TO BE two basic principles for character selection, although both principles may be at work more or less simultaneously. One is to position a particular character over the light source (or the light source over a particular character) and to flash the light at that time. The other is to expose all or a number of characters and to mask out the images of all except the one that is intended. It is possible, for example, as with the Linofilm, to illuminate the entire grid, and then to mask out every character except one. It is possible to move the individual character in front of the light source, as with the Monophoto. With the ATF B-8 a disk was rotated and then halted in place at the time of flashing, and with the Photon 200 the character was exposed "on the fly" by careful timing of the flash. Let us look more carefully at a few examples.

Consider the illustration of the Photon 713. There were two light sources located within the spinning drum. One exposed simultaneously all four characters in the same drum position for the upper four fonts. The other exposed four characters for the lower four fonts. Thus the first step in the selection of the character was to determine its drum position. Next was to determine whether the desired character was to be found among the upper four fonts or the lower four. If the former, the upper xenon flash would be triggered. If the latter, the lower. In either case, one character in each of four fonts was simultaneously exposed. But there was a shutter which moved up and down behind the row of characters to mask out all rows except one in the upper matrix of four fonts and one in the lower matrix of four fonts. (*See illustration.*) Thus we can see that character selection occurs both by moving certain characters into an exposure position—in this instance while they are revolving at a constant and relatively high speed—and also by masking out the unwanted characters that would also be exposed from that position.

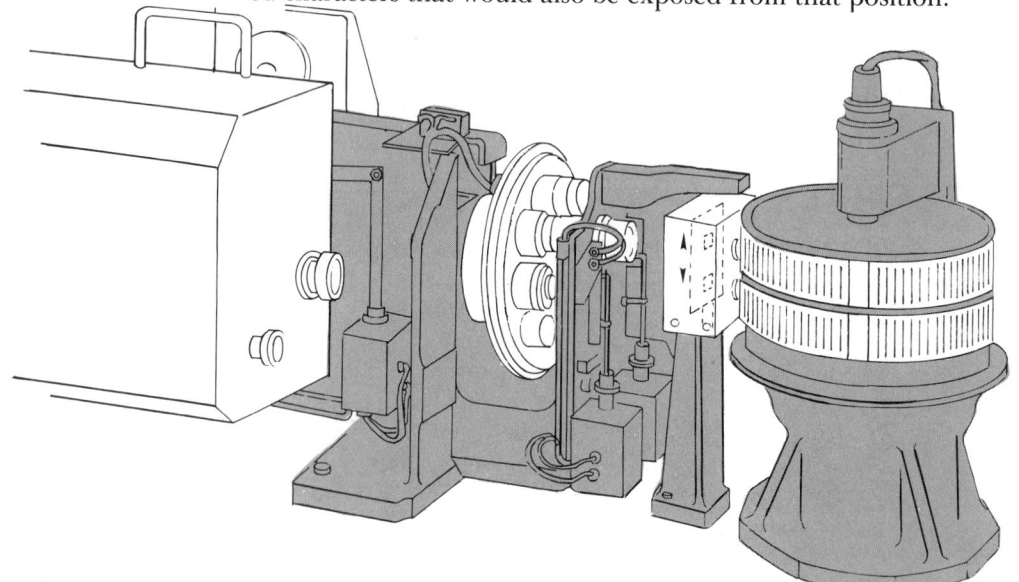

An interior view of the Photon 713. On the right is the font drum onto which are mounted two filmstrips, each with four fonts. Wires attached to the xenon flash units can be seen rising out of the center of the drum. These units are located inside the drum itself. Immediately to the left is the shutter which masks out the unwanted characters. Next comes the revolving turret, into which are mounted eight sizing lenses. At the top left is the film or paper cassette which contains both exposed and unexposed material.

Second-Generation Solutions

There were various drawbacks to this technique. The first was that the strobe did not quite manage to arrest the character in its revolving motion, and a slight blur could be discerned, which made the exposed image somewhat less sharp than it should have been. Secondly, it was important for the intensity of the two flash sources to be equal or unwanted variations in the "weight" of character images might result when fonts were mixed on the same job. The third deficiency was perhaps the most serious of all. The shutter that masked the unwanted characters had to move up and down at a relatively high speed. If it failed to position itself accurately the character could be "clipped" so that some portion—usually a piece of a descender—might be missing on the exposed output.

It should be noted, as well, that the eight characters positioned for exposure at a given time on the drum were not precisely on the same optical path. A set of prisms or mirrors was used to direct the image to the appropriate position to be "caught" by the magnifying lens on the lens turret. The turret, of course, rotated to provide for different sizes. Timing, which was initially provided within the Photon by electrical relays, and later by electronic "logic circuit boards," was of course very critical and had to make allowance not only for the speed of the revolving drum, and the random sequence on the drum of the characters to be flashed, but also the delay introduced by the time it took to move the lens turret from one position to another. On the drum there was of course an initializing position or "zero" location from which all character positions had to be calculated. The letter "a" might be in the eleventh position after the zero location, but it would not follow that a character would or could be flashed every time the drum revolved. When a delay was introduced by a lens turret movement then the counting process would be re-initialized. Other delays were caused by the escapement mechanism and also by the film advance after the setting of a line was completed. There was also the possibility of a computational delay before the system "knew" precisely where the escapement mechanism was to be positioned at the time a given character was to be exposed and a certain amount of time was required to recharge the strobe.

One of the most curious and ingenious methods of character selection devised during the early days of "second-generation" typesetters was that of the Photon 900 or "ZIP"—the first high-speed machine, capable of laying down characters at a rate in excess of 600 characters per second. This machine normally contained three large grids of 88 characters each, providing a total of 264 characters (representing several different fonts of type). There was a xenon flash tube *behind every single character*, so that the desired character was selected merely by flashing *one particular lamp*. However, in order to bring that character into the proper optical path, a reciprocating lens would catch the image and direct it through a pair of reflecting surfaces, catching the light rays and straightening them out so that they could be passed on to the lens system and to the photographic paper.

The principles involved are illustrated and explained on the next page. One of the drawbacks to this technique was the problem of maintaining the same exposure density for each character, taking into account the variations in the flash elements themselves and the disparity in terms of their location and the number of times, from a given position, that the character image was bounced back and forth. Note from the diagram that the escapement mechanism was provided by the movement of a relatively large mass consisting of a reciprocating lens and two relatively large and heavy glass plates. The image had to be caught by the lens from whatever position it (the lens) occupied as it moved back and forth across the film plane.

At the time of this invention it was not practical to have a large number of light sources in a small space, such as behind each row of characters on one font master disk. Later it became possible to conduct light by way of fiber optic tubes from one light source to a specific character location or to different rows or rings of a revolving disk, thus avoiding the necessity of providing alternate light sources or having to move different fonts into position by mechanical means.

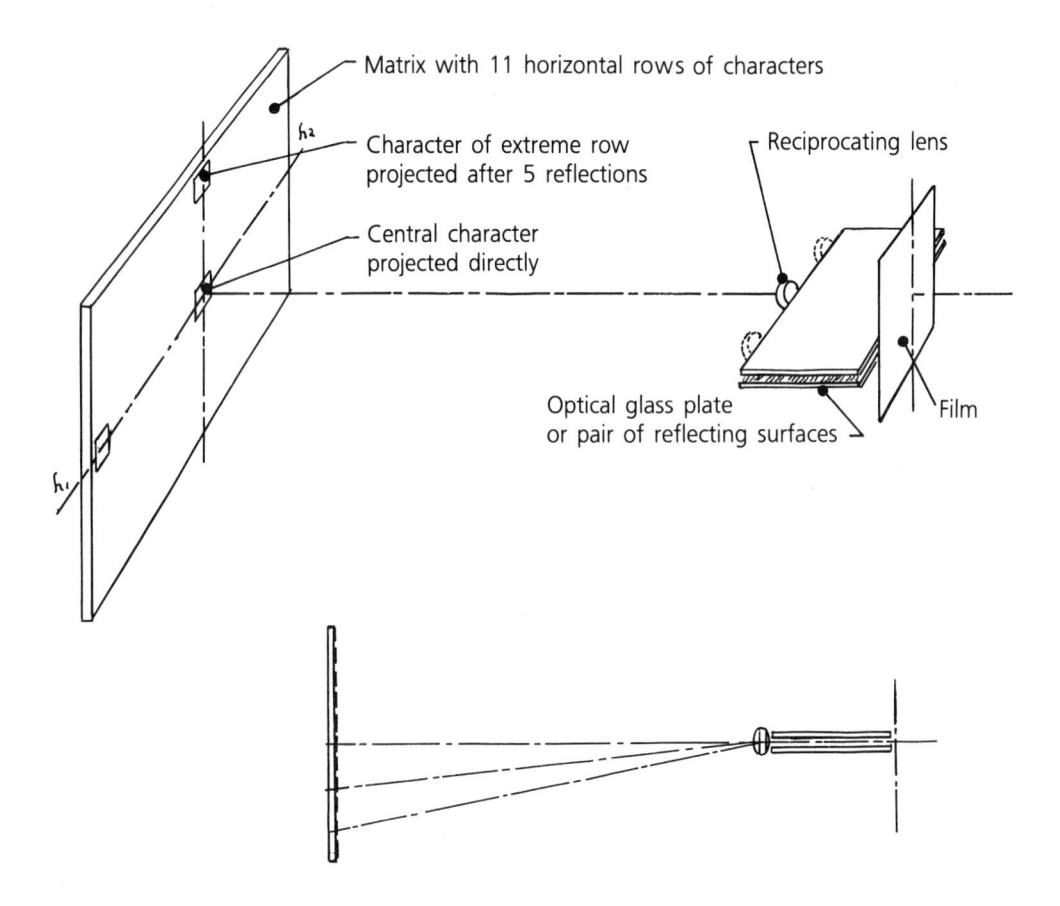

The Photon ZIP. Imagine an array of light sources, one behind each character, in each of the 11 horizontal rows of characters. Notice how the reciprocating lens plates align the images at the level of the film plane.

Second-Generation Solutions

We have by no means exhausted the techniques used for character selection. Those which involve the fewest moving parts are usually the most successful. If characters are to be masked by shutters, the shutters may tend to stick or to clip off portions of images, and a time interval is required for the movement of the shutter. If the entire disk must be shifted (as to position a different font row in front of the light source) vibrations may be induced, causing the machine to jiggle and to produce a less perfect representation. For example, it was necessary to program a blank character—a "null"—immediately after a row change on a Photon 513 to give the machine a chance to "settle" after a disk movement had taken place!

By whatever method the character is to be selected, the choice must be made between exposing images on the fly and exposing images that are in a stationary position at the moment they are called for. Many people believe that exposing characters while they are in motion produces images which are not as sharp and as well defined as would be the case if the character master is held stationary in front of the light source while being photographed. But there are also other considerations which may be more significant from the standpoint of the quality of the image. The design of the type itself, the quality of the lenses, the critical timing of the flash if the image is indeed in motion, and the accuracy of the character lay down are all at least equally important.

Some fonts contained on a rotating disk or drum are so mounted that an error in the timing of the flash could result in irregular alignment with respect to the base line. On the other hand, character spacing would be adversely affected by improper flash timing in those instances in which the images spin by in a horizontal direction.

Various approaches to the storage and selection of characters are depicted in the accompanying illustrative matter. The reader may note, for example, the simplicity of the early Compugraphic machines, as shown on the 2961 model,[1] and the complexity of the Mergenthaler Linofilm Quick[2] and the Mergenthaler V-I-P.[3]

The following is a summary of some of the principal methods of character selection:

1. Devices which illuminate all characters simultaneously, masking all but one. (This is most likely to be the technique employed where characters are stored on a stationary grid (*e.g.*, Linofilm, Linofilm Quick). But the Photon ZIP showed us that multiple light sources are not necessarily inconsistent with the grid approach.

2. Devices where only the selected character is illuminated, and that character is stationary when exposed. This is the technique used not only by the ATF B-8 and the Monophoto, but also by the Mergenthaler V-I-P which was extremely popular in the mid-1970s. It involved the use of an oscillating drum or drums which would move in either direction, following the shortest path to reach the next desired character.

3. Devices in which only the selected character is illuminated by the use of a fast flash which picks off the image from a constantly

[1]. See the drum depicted on p. 90.

[2]. See the illustration on p. 91.

[3]. See the illustration on the bottom of p. 98.

rotating disk or drum, where the disk shifts in position in order to expose the desired font, or where a different light source may be used to select characters from one or more alternate fonts.

4. There are also devices in which more than one character is illuminated—but not all of them. Those illuminated but not desired are masked out.

Patent problems. In evaluating various solutions to the problem of the design of phototypesetters the reader must be aware that some solutions were made necessary because competitors' patents may have precluded the adoption of what would appear to have been a logical answer to a specific problem. For example, the Photon patent on the use of a revolving disk, with timing slits and a flash to pick off the character, was a case in point. Other manufacturers wishing to utilize this technique were obliged to pay royalties in order to do so, or found themselves involved in litigation.

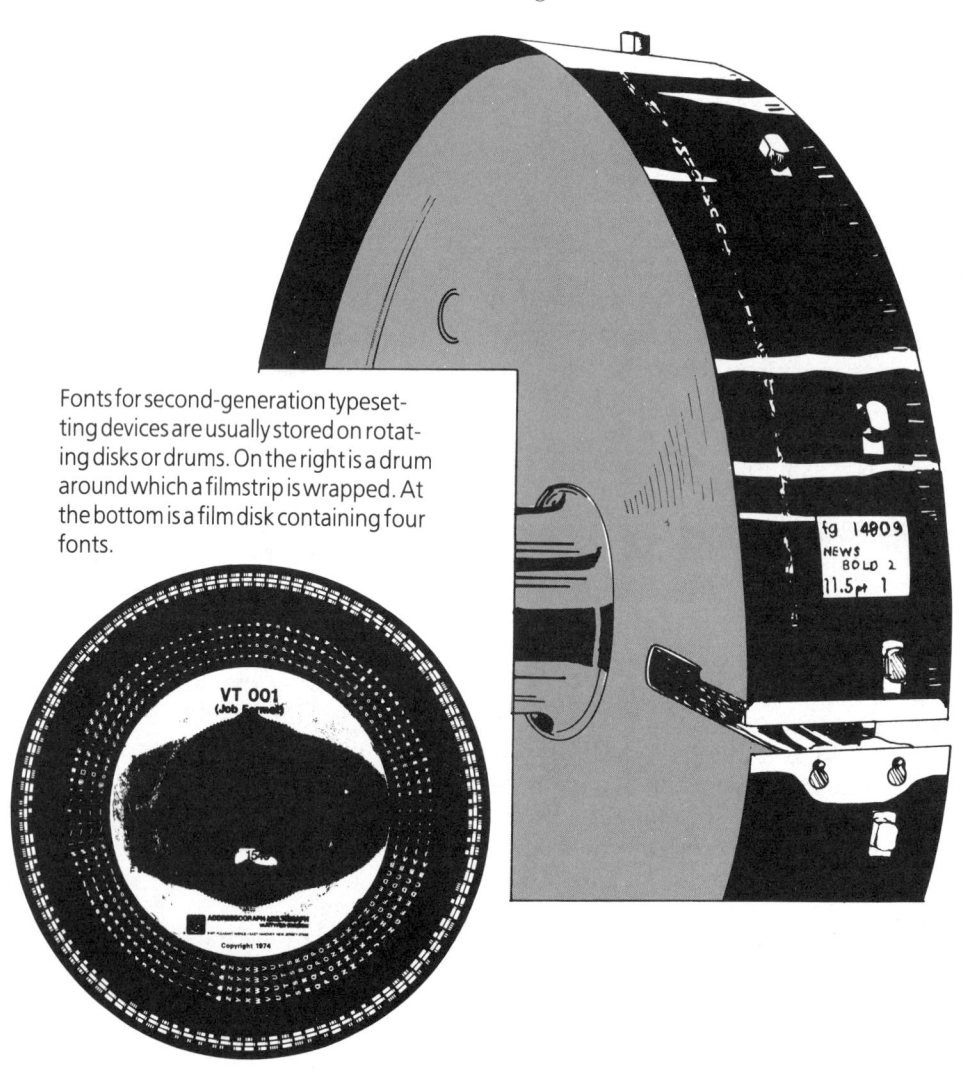

Fonts for second-generation typesetting devices are usually stored on rotating disks or drums. On the right is a drum around which a filmstrip is wrapped. At the bottom is a film disk containing four fonts.

Second-Generation Solutions

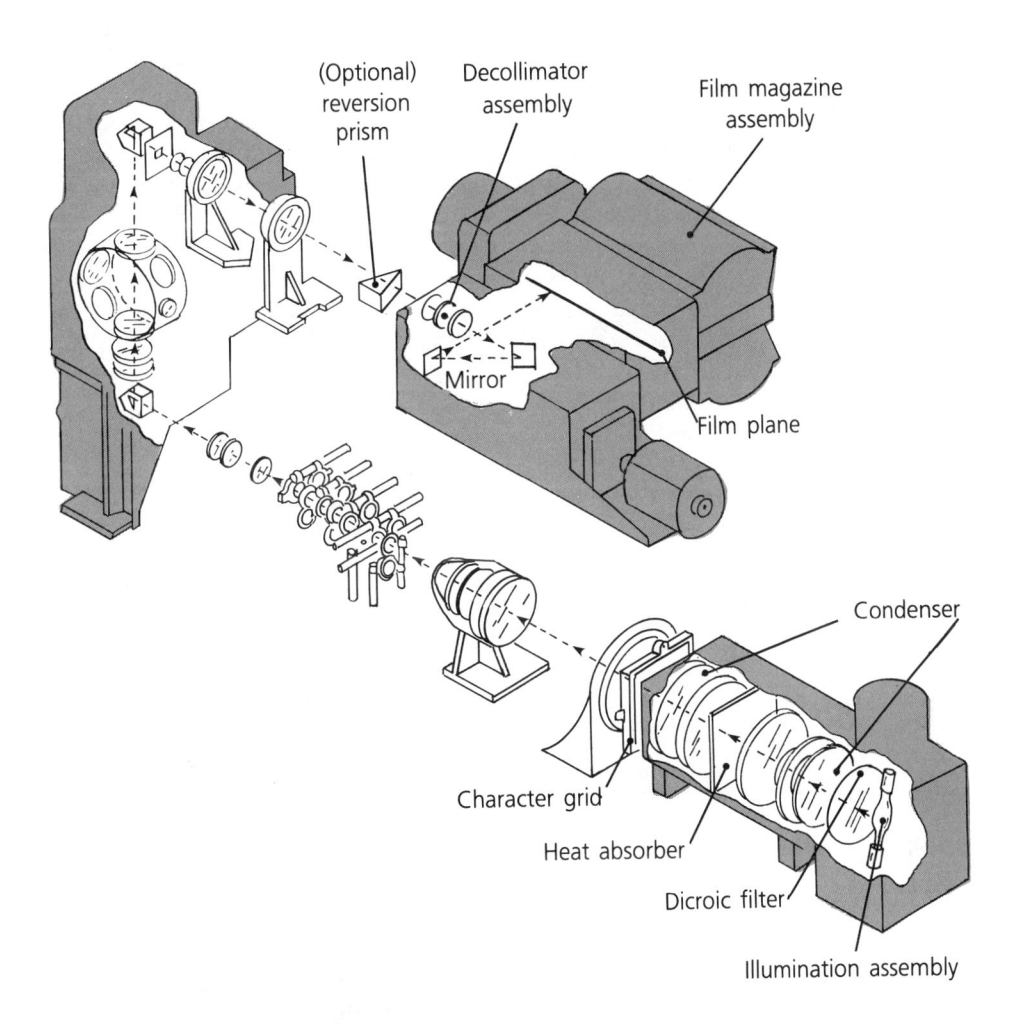

The Linofilm Quick character selection and optical system was certainly the most elaborate and most mechanical of all the photomechanical typesetters. Characters are contained in a grid. All are illuminated simultaneously. The images are then blacked out except for one. This was deflected until it reached a collimating lens. Then a moving mirror positioned it on the film plane.

How characters are exposed

THE TWO BASIC WAYS of exposing characters have already been mentioned: from a stationary or from a moving position. If a grid is used the character is always stationary, although the grid may move between exposures (as was the case with the original first-generation Monophoto). We have also seen that when a grid is used either the individual character desired may be illuminated or all or a group of characters may be exposed and all but one masked off. Some systems using grids may not require a high-intensity short-duration light source, and such systems may be able to make use of slower-exposure lithographic films because, as a rule, these systems operate at much slower setting speeds (perhaps less than ten characters per second).

For the most part, however, second-generation typesetters have tended to operate at somewhat higher setting speeds—from forty or fifty to several hundred characters per second, and although the flash is fairly intense it is of such short duration that the film or paper emulsion must be quite fast. Special "chemistry" is often required to develop thse high-speed films or papers.

How characters are sized

IN SOME CASES, characters are not "sized" at all. They derive their size exclusively from the image on the film strip or grid. This does not mean that the image is not enlarged. The character may be stored and exposed as a smaller image than that which appears on the film or paper. But the lens system magnifies at only one ratio. On a one-lens Compugraphic 2961, for example, the lens enlarged at a ratio of 1.2X.

If you wanted to set a particular size, you had to mount the appropriately sized filmstrip. You changed the filmstrip and not the lens. Thus one possibility exists that characters will derive their sizes from the dimensions of the stored master and not at all from the lens system. It is even possible to offer more than one size master on the same filmstrip or disk. For example, the Compugraphic 4961 offered four fonts, two of which might be of a different size. The Harris Fototronic 600 offered six fonts, each of which could be of a different size, and yet all were contained on the same disk.

Obviously, machines which do *not* do their sizing through lens systems offer less typographic flexibility than those which permit you to enlarge or reduce from one master size. The former are often intended for such straight matter as newspapers or periodical composition, and if you require much mixing you would need to do a great deal of hand stripping or assembly of pieces of exposed film or paper. Moreover, if you wanted sizes other than those which comprised the current "dressing" of masters, it was necessary to stop the machine in order to mount other filmstrips. (And with some such typesetters you could not even change the filmstrip without exposing the output and spoiling the work!)

Second-Generation Solutions

On the other hand, it has been possible for such machines—even relatively inexpensive ones—to offer a high-quality type image since each size can be designed to different proportions than all other sizes. More attention can be given to the design, focus and alignment of the lens system, as well as its quality. Only one—and not an entire set—of lenses is required, and it can be mounted more or less permanently. An example of such a machine is the Alphatype AlphaSette which was widely used by advertising typographers in the 1960s and into the 1970s.

There were also instances in which a single-lens, single-size system was used but where other sizes could be obtained by making manual changes in the lens. Either you would unscrew one lens and mount another in its place, or you might throw a lever or rotate a turret by hand to position a different lens and thus obtain a second size of type. For example, the Compugraphic CompuWriter Jr. offered a 1.2X and a 2.4X lens system. Hence if you mounted an eight-point filmstrip you could set eight point type, or you could open the machine, blank out one lens and uncover the other, and set 16-point type. If you mounted a 10-point master you could obtain either 10- or 20-point type. But the sizing required manual intervention.

Happily, however, most second-generation phototypesetter models offered the ability to size type automatically—without having to stop the machine in order to make manual adjustments. Signals to alter the type size might be initiated directly from a keyboard, recorded on and conveyed from paper or magnetic tape, or from an on-line computer. This generally means, then, that one font master can be "sized" over a range which might vary from perhaps six to 72 points. It does not imply, however, that all sizes within this range are available. Perhaps eight different lenses could be provided, mounted on a lens turret. The choice of the specific eight sizes within the six to 72-point range might be selected by the user when he purchased his machine. A "16 × 16" typesetter is one which offers 16 fonts in 16 different sizes. However, eight of those sizes could be multiples of the other eight, determined by the automatic superimposition of a second lens on top of the other sizing lens.

The alternative to the lens turret is the use of "zoom lens sizing." In such a case a lens or lens system is automatically racked into a different position, closer to or further away from the type master image location, just as a movie or slide projector may project a smaller or larger picture according to its distance from the screen, or alternatively, with some such projectors, the relationship between two lens elements may be altered.

It is also possible to change *both the size of the master and the sizing of the lens*. For example, the original Mergenthaler Linofilm offered "A," "B," and "C"-range masters and the same thing was subsequently true with certain models of the Mergenthaler V-I-P. On the V-I-P an "A" range font could produce ten different sizes within the range of six to 24 points, and by mounting a "B" range font the six point lens setting produced an 18-point image with the larger font master, and the 24-point setting produced a 72-point image.

When a zoom lens system is used it may or may not offer a wide range of sizing options. For example, as noted above, the V-I-P provided only ten sizes from 6 to 24 points. It is possible to design such a machine to provide more "way stations" within the minimum-maximum range. A Varityper Comp/Set, for example, with a normal range from 5½ to 74 points, is able to set 70 different sizes: 5½, 6, 7, 8, 8½, 9 and every point size thereafter up to 74 except for 55 points (the two-digit command for that size would conflict with the command for 5½).

Lens turrets. Lens turrets, on the other hand, have offered only a certain number of sizing alternatives, and in theory at least, they have been less flexible than the zoom lens approach, although a secondary lens system might also be superimposed upon the first range of sizes.

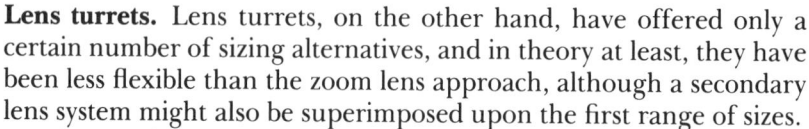

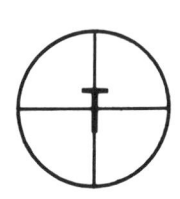

One problem that sometimes arises when a zoom lens is used to increase the size of type is the difficulty of maintaining the base alignment of the characters imaged on the machine. This problem is most likely to arise if several different point sizes are set within the same line. If characters are simply enlarged then they tend to position themselves around their optical center and not on their base line. Consequently some technique for displacing larger characters to assure base alignment may be required—or, more commonly, the zoom lens system used will be so designed that it positions the character in an upper quadrant of the lens rather than in its center. (This principle is illustrated in the margin.) In order to allow sufficient clearance, the person creating the input for the typesetter needs to know what the largest type character will be that he wishes to set within the line, but he should not be required to compensate for possible variations in base line positioning.

Normally we have only to change the defined point size, as is illustrated on the line below:

ABCDEFGHIJKLMNOPQ

Selection of sizes. Where separate sizing lenses have been provided, the user might or might not be able to select the specific point sizes he desires. Even if the vendor can offer him his choice it is often difficult to decide which ones would most often be required.

In some instances it has even been possible to purchase anamorphic lenses on special order, which without changing the height of the character, will squeeze type widths, making the face more condensed and thus fitting more such characters into the line.

One other observation may be made with respect to the sizing of characters from a given master. When you increase or decrease the size of the image you may alter the intensity (or density) of that image. It may be necessary to effect a change in the lens aperture to compensate for this problem, or to add filters to certain lenses in order to reduce the apparent blackness of the image at certain sizes. Alternatively, some typesetters were programmed to double or triple

Second-Generation Solutions

flash in order to provide more light for larger point sizes where the degree of magnification was so great that the character might otherwise appear to be "washed out." It seems to be true, also, that the larger sizes should look blacker; but it is equally true that very small point sizes—such as six point— seem too light, and some of the serifs tend to disappear.

<small>Although this book is not being typeset on a second-generation photosetter the same generalization probably applies to the third-generation Mergenthaler 202 which is being used here for setting, where the same type master (even though a digital one) may be used for the entire range of sizes, as is the case in this instance.</small>

Compare the above with the same type in 18 points.

Some machines do indeed attempt to compensate for these variations in boldness. On a second-generation device the flash intensity may be changed as the zoom lens moves back to set larger sizes. Hence more illumination is provided because the lens becomes faster. Other models open up the lens for larger point sizes by means of a mechanical shutter contrivance. Students of optics will recall, however, that the depth of focus suffers as the lens aperture is enlarged, and sharpness of the image may be less assured. Third-generation digital typesetters do not pose the same problems, although there are other constraints which we shall in due course consider.

Character escapement

AT THE OUTSET we drew an analogy to a typewriter and pointed out that with the conventional striking bar typewriter the platen moves by the width of each (monospaced) character after its key has been struck. If the typewriter is designed to set at ten characters to the inch, the platen moves to the left by one-tenth of an inch, and the gear track is machined to make this possible. Consequently, escapement is provided by the movement of the platen and the paper—you could consider this the "film plane"—and the image is always generated at the same position relative to the font store of the striking keys.

On the other hand, we recalled that the IBM Selectric typewriter handles its problem of escapement quite differently. The platen does not move at all. It remains fixed (so far as its horizontal direction is concerned) but the typing element moves from left to right—again one-tenth or one-twelfth of an inch at a time.

These are two different principles of escapement or character lay down. In one case the film plane moves. In the other case, the "image carrier" moves. In both cases the movement is nonproportional—*i.e.*, in a monospaced fashion.

With second-generation phototypesetters the physical act of escapement may be handled in different ways. What are the alternatives? Basically there are three and of these perhaps the third is the most interesting.

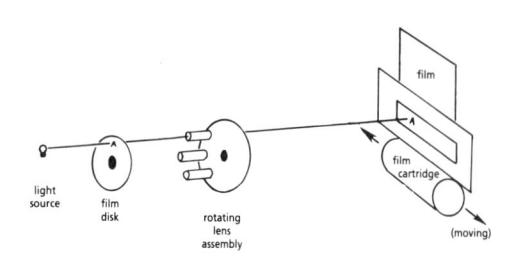

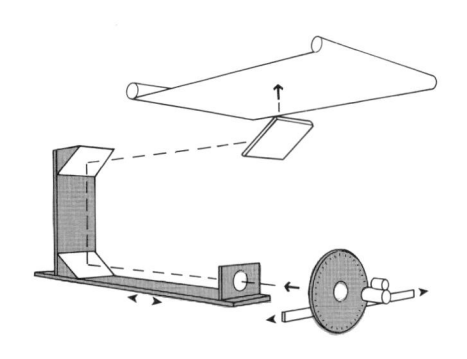

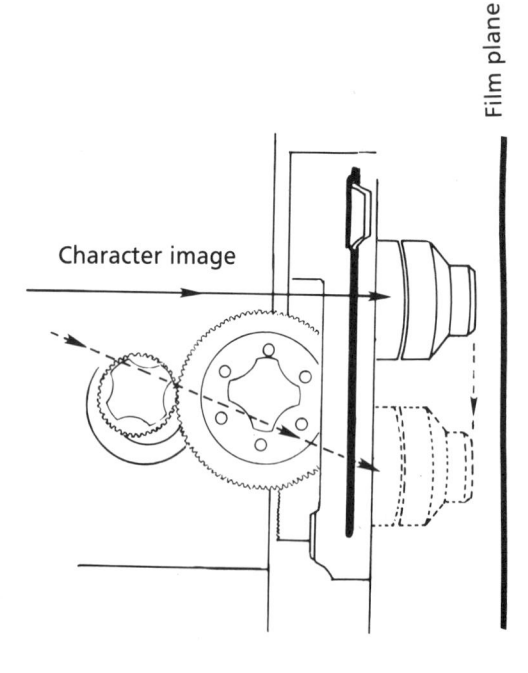

1. The *film carriage* (comparable to the typewriter platen) could move horizontally, the image thus projected being from the same position. This involves the movement of a large mass, since the film or paper take-up cassette is part of the film carriage. The Compugraphic ACM 9000, the ATF B-8, and the Fototronic Fotosetter worked in this fashion, except that the Fotosetter carriage motion was vertical rather than horizontal.

2. The *imaging mechanism* can move across the film plane. (The analogy would be to the Selectric typewriter.) This would require that the entire disk assembly mechanism and the light source would step across the film plane, character by character, flashing each image, moving the necessary width and then returning for the next line as the film is advanced. A stationary wide-angle lens "catches" the image from whatever angle it is generated. The AM 725 (shown at the left in the diagram) worked in this fashion.

3. Most common of all is for both the imaging portion of the machine and the film plane to remain stationary while something "in between" causes the character images to position themselves appropriately.
- It could be the lens itself which steps across in front of the film plane, as with the Compugraphic 4961 shown in the margin. Wide angle lenses do have the property of picking up the image of the flashed character and transferring it onto the film plane.
- Or the lens can remain stationary and the image as projected from the lens can be deflected by prism, mirror or similar device. This involves the least mechanical motion.

Most of the displacement techniques are of the third category. The image location at the time of exposure is constant, as is the film plane. The projected image is displaced by means of a stepping mirror or prism which deflects successive pictures of character images as shown on the next page. Simply explained, a mirror is positioned at a 45° angle so that the image which is projected is deflected (usually by 90°) onto the film plane. Then the mirror, which is seated on a track and which is moved along a track by a set

Second-Generation Solutions

of matching gears driven by a stepping motor, backs up the required amount and receives the next character flash. Alternatively, the motion could be controlled by cable, while the mirror or prism moves along a rod or similar support. The stepping motor controls the distance of each incremental move according to the width value of the character. Either the displacement mirror moves first, by the width of the next character and then that character is exposed, or the character is exposed and then an escapement occurs equal to that value.

For example, if the character were four-eighteenths of a six-point em in width, then the distance the mirror would have to move before (or after) exposing the character would be that amount necessary to move the character image .018496″. Or, this value could be rounded off to the nearest ten-thousandths of an inch, such as .0185″. In general, the stepping arrangements are such that while the "backward" movement of the character laydown is accomplished in very tiny increments, at the end of the line there is a very rapid return of the mirror or prism (the forward movement) so as to coincide with the film advance and to minimize the "dead time" before the next line may be typeset. However, it is possible for such devices to be so constructed so they can lay down characters in either direction—both left to right and right to left.

The moving prism or mirror technique was first employed by the Photon 200, and it was retained in the design of the subsequent Photon products until the Pacesetter line appeared in the early 1970s. At that time Photon developed a technique to reduce the total travel distance necessary in order to set a line. This is called *optical leverage*. The diagram below illustrates the principle.

Note the twin or folded mirrors. The image is bounced against the first and then the second mirror before it is directed toward the film plane. The mirror therefore travels only one-half of the required distance, but the effect is as if it had moved the entire distance because the angle at which the light bounces between mirrors changes constantly. As the mirror moves to the left, the spot of light strikes a point further from the center on the surface of the first mirror, is reflected to a point further from the center on the second mirror, and hence moves twice as far as the movementment of the mirror assembly. Note, too—and we shall return to this later—that in this case the image is sized after the displacement occurs.

To set a 20-pica line, for example, a mirror movement of only ten picas would be required, and a carriage return of only the smaller distance would be necessary as well.

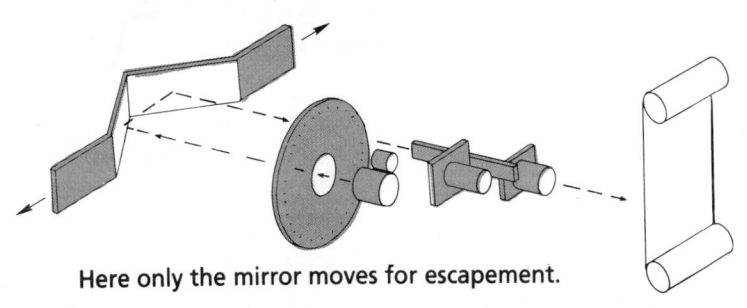

Here only the mirror moves for escapement.

The World of Digital Typesetting

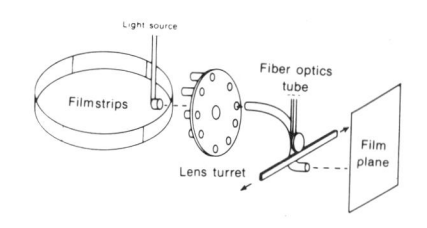

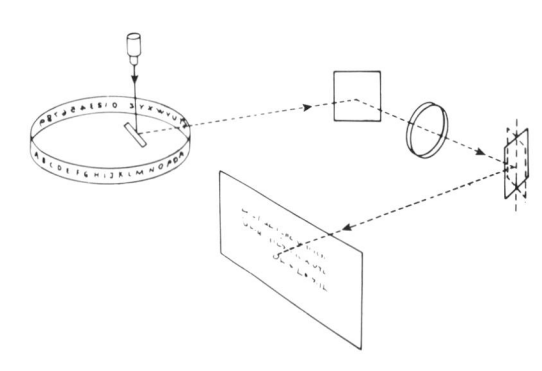

Fiber optics bundle. Another method of character displacement is to employ a fiber optics "bundle" to carry the sized image from the lens turret to the film plane. Such a bundle has the property of conveying patterns of light in such fashion that there is no need for a sight-line optical path.

Rotating mirror. Yet another method of character lay down involves no actual stepping out along a rack or track, but merely a change in the angle of a mirror which "sprays" characters across the setting line. Reference to the accompanying diagram illustrates the principle involved. The picture of the image is projected against the surface of a mirror and bounced off the mirror through the lens system and onto the photographic film or paper. To achieve escapement nothing moves except for the mirror, which must change its angle (after exposure of each character) by a very fine increment, on a character-by-character basis, in order to lay down each character in succession from left to right across the film plane. Several typesetting devices have made use of this principle.

There is a serious problem of character or image distortion which must be dealt with when escapement is handled in this fashion. If you were to imagine holding a mirror, bouncing a light from a fixed source onto the mirror, and then rotating the mirror so that the spot of light would move across the surface of the wall (the film plane), you would notice two imaging problems. First, the focus of the image

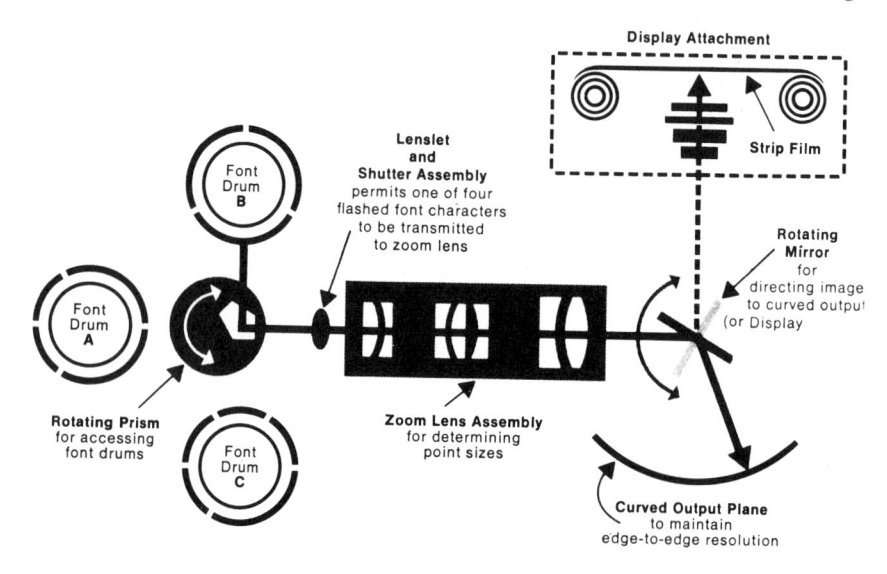

Second-Generation Solutions

against the wall will change. The distance from the mirror to the ends of the hypothetical line of type will be greater than the distance from the mirror at the center of the line. Consequently, if the image is in focus at the center of the wall, it will be out of focus as you move away from the center. The second problem is that the shape of the image will tend to be elongated on the sides. If it is a circle in the center, it will be an oblong on the outside edges of the arc of travel.

To some extent the out-of-focus problem can be compensated for. How badly out of focus the image would be at the edges if it were in focus in the center would depend upon the depth of field of the lens system—which is, of course, the distance that an image tends to remain in focus. By projecting the image a considerable distance, using mirrors to bounce it around inside a cabinet, one can obtain a greater depth of field. Another approach makes use of a "field flattener" lens to bend the light rays so that they remain in constant focus. A third approach is to form the film paper into an arc, so that the distance from the mirror to any position on the arc is always precisely the same, as with the Mergenthaler V-I-P.

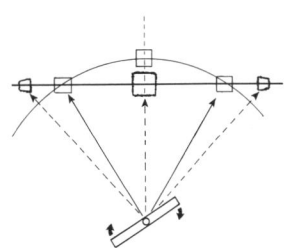

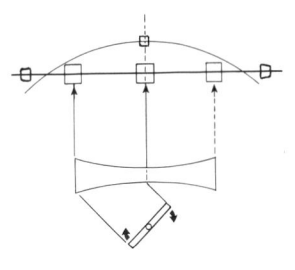

Escapement before or after sizing

ONE OF THE MOST popular second-generation phototypesetting devices in the 1970s was the Photon Pacesetter.[1] A somewhat detailed description of this device will indicate one manner in which character selection, sizing and escapement problems were resolved. As we mentioned earlier in this chapter, a folded mirror approach made it possible for the device to reduce by half the amount of escapement travel required. To further reduce the escapement complexities the design engineers decided to perform image sizing after escapement instead of beforehand. This meant that the calculations involved only had to do with the amount of escapement required by the master character image rather than its various sizes.

It happened that the master images on the Pacesetter disk were five points high, although they were often drawn from ten-point masters. Due to the principle of optical leverage, in order to escape by the width of one five-point em it is only necessary for the mirror system to move two and one-half points, even though you are setting a ten-point character, or more specifically, a character the width of a ten-point em. Since character magnification takes place after escapement it is only necessary for the mirror system to move by two and one-half points, thereby reducing the amount of motion by four times.

Consider the more extreme example: even if a 72-point character the size of an em were to be laid down, only two and one-half points of escapement would be required. To set an entire 45-pica line of 72 point characters would require a total movement of only 18¾ points!

Another advantage to this method of escapement is that it simplifies the arithmetic. It is not necessary, then, to multiply the width values of individual characters times their point size.

The principles of operation f the Pacesetter are made clear in the schematic appearing in the middle of the next page. Note that

---

1. The company changed hands several times. The Photon Pacesetter became the Dymo Pacesetter and, later on, the Itek Pacesetter.

there are four xenon flash light sources, and that the light from each is directed to a specific row by means of a fiber optics bundle or light tube. The character, once exposed, is bounced against twin mirrors which minimize the escapement distance according to the principle of optical leverage. Note also that the escapement takes place before the images are sized.

The lens turret shown here could offer a total of 16 sizes, but focusing and sizing are accomplished in part by locating the lenses at different distances from the mirror assembly. This allowed, among other things, for the larger field of vision required by the system.

Any of four disks (each containing four fonts) could be rotated into position between the flash lamps and the escapement chassis.

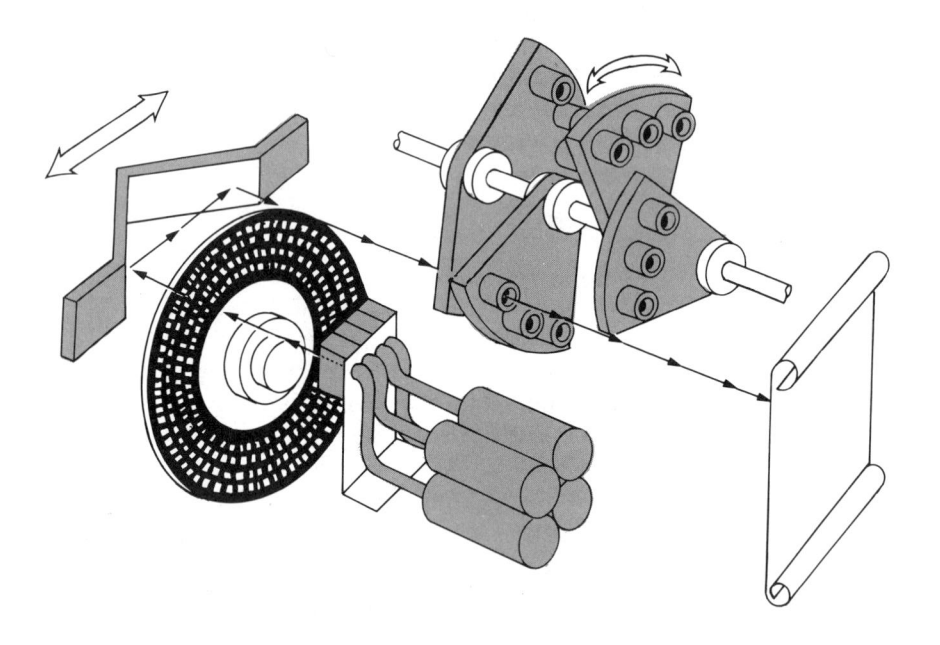

For the most part, however, second-generation typesetters size *before* they escape, and so the amount of escapement must be calculated in relation to the desired point size. However, escapement must always be executed in *absolute* terms and must be expressed in some increment of a fraction of an inch or centimeter. Escapement values are derived by mutiplying the unit value of a character by the point size in question, and because it is usually possible to intermix point sizes within the same line a rounding error often occurs, even when the ultimate escapement is reduced to a displacement as fine as one ten-thousandth of an inch. The electronic logic of the machine must not lose sight of this rounding error and when the totals are cumulated and add up to too much or too little, some compensating adjustment must take place.

But how does the typesetter know in the first place how much to escape on a character-by-character basis? This brings us to the next topic which has to do with the technique for imparting to the typesetter a knowledge of width values.

Escapement values

IN THE BEGINNING of this chapter we indicated that we would discuss the principle of escapement as one of the major concepts relevant to an understanding of the photocomposition and digital typesetting process. The preceding pages have explained the way in which the physical act of escapement takes place within second-generation phototypesetting devices—the movement of platen, film store, character store, lens, or some other kind of lay down device. But the other half of the problem is to figure out a way to tell the typesetter what the character widths are that must determine the computation of these values. Then (perhaps) these will be converted from relative to absolute terms. Here are some of the typical solutions to the problem of relaying width value information to the typesetter:

Predetermined hard-wired values. There have been a few typesetting machines for which the escapement was restricted to a minimum number of alternatives, and these were "hard wired" into the machine. This was true, for example, of the Justowriter and also one of the earliest models introduced by Compugraphic, the 2970. Character widths for these machines varied only from two to six units, much like an IBM Executive typewriter. A lower case a would always have the same value, regardless of the font. It would be a relative value, depending upon the point size, but that value, regardless of whether the type face was a pseudo-Times Roman or pseudo-Helvetica, would be four units.

Unit-count fonts. There were also a few machines which used only *unit-count* or *unit-cut* fonts with widths used in the justification of newspaper wire-service tapes. Since all fonts have the same widths (even though there are finer increments and more variations between characters than is the case with Justowriter fonts), the font width tables can be wired into the logic of the typesetter. There need be no "table look-up" and no "plug board." Several early machines—the ExecuWriter and CompuWriter Jr. by Compugraphic, and the CompStar 190 by Star Parts, were of this kind. Despite the homogeneity of width values for given characters in all type faces, some of these faces nevertheless appeared quite varied and attractive.

Unitized fonts. Other typesetters use true unitized fonts, and by this is meant type faces each of which may be designed differently in terms of character widths (although some faces may in fact be duplexed or triplexed so as to simplify the storage of width values). These type faces will be designed to a relative unit system and the unit count is most likely to be either 18, 36 or 54 units to the em, although there are some machines that use a different kind of common denominator. For example, the Harris second-generation typesetters used an absolute value which they termed a "piclet" and which was equal to one-tenth of a point or $1/170''$. Subsequently they introduced a "triclet" which divided piclets into thirds. But the critical point is not so much how the type is designed and to what base, but rather how the width values are stored or described in electronic logic.

For example, suppose you devised a system which allowed only four combinations of "bits"[1] to describe character widths. It would thus seem that such widths could be expressed as variables ranging from 0 through 15, since four bits offer only this many combinations. On the other hand, if you determined that no character or space could be smaller than $3/18$ of an em, you could simply add three units to the expressed values to make a scale ranging from 3 to 18 and this could be considered an 18-unit system since one character's width could vary from another by as little as $1/18$ of an em, providing that no width fell below $3/18$. In like manner, a five-bit method of storing character widths would give you 0 to 31 different possibilities, and by adding six units you could express character differences in increments as small as one out of 36, within a range of 6 to 36.

One must ask, then, $1/36$ of what? Presumably no one is going to set type in a one-point size, and yet it still may be convenient to work in absolute units, such as points, rather than relative units (particularly if you want to mix different point sizes within the same line). Consequently you may elect to go through the arithmetic calculation of multiplying all relative width values by the point size in order to come up with a common absolute denominator, the lowest theoretical value of which is $1/18$, $1/36$, $1/54$ or $1/72$ of $1/72$ of an inch (the latter being the size of a one-point em).

On the other hand, there are some typesetters which offer the ability to set type in half point increments—especially for the 5½ and 8½ point sizes. And there are also typesetters which offer the opportunity to size type in one-tenth point increments, which would suggest that the finest increment in which a type character's width might be expressed could be $1/100$ of $1/10$ of $1/72$ of an inch!

Width value storage. But for our purposes the most relevant point is how the widths—whatever they are—can be conveniently stored within the typesetter, or fed to the typesetter, so that it can take this information and make whatever additional calculations it may need in order to figure out how far to move a prism, rotate a mirror, shift a carriage, advance a fiber optics tube, or move the film plane itself. And again we return to the fact that the machine must either use predetermined width values or else it must have some means of referencing them. One approach is for the typesetter to be told what each width value is when it encounters the code calling for a particular character. This may be done in one of two ways: the machine can read the width value from the font disk itself, or it can be provided with the character width information along with the character code on the input stream. For certain later model machines the character width may be derived from the stroking pattern which makes up the character itself. (More about this later.)

---

1. Bits are the on/off elements which comprise a computer "word." See Chapter 14.

Except for the more primitive second-generation machines which have used unit-count fonts whose width values are generated mechanically, the typesetting device must somehow come into possession of character width information. One method of telling the typesetter what width values to use is to provide for the insertion of one or more plug boards which connect with its electronic circuitry. When the codes for a certain character and font are encountered, an electrical circuit is directed to a certain location on a plug board where it picks up, for example, certain relay signals to cause the stepping motor to rotate a certain number of revolutions. The necessary calculation would be made within the device itself to multiply these width signals by the desired point size.

Plug boards were widely used in the early days of phototypesetting, especially for low-cost entries. The input program or counting keyboards had to produce results which agreed with those stored values so that the line ending decisions which had been made would in fact be implemented by the typesetter.

Alternate methods of storing width values

STARTING WITH THE PHOTON 713 in or about 1968, small computer memories were built into typesetting devices so that they could store the width values required for a given machine "dressing." Hence when a code was encountered which called for a certain font and character, its position could be ascertained and its width values imparted from a "look-up table." When the machine was dressed with the desired fonts, widths were loaded into memory at the same time, usually from paper tape. A diagnostic panel was provided to assure the operator that the values were "read in" properly. In fact, even with the 713, you could also load a table to determine the code configuration to be used to describe each machine function and to identify each character position. This was the "program tape."

Storing width values on the film disk. Character width values can also be stored on the type disk or filmstrip itself. This was one of the earliest methods of storing widths, in the case of the mid-1960's Fototronic 1200. Photodiodes were used to decipher various combinations of bars and non-bars (transparent areas) in order to ascertain from these configurations what the individual character widths were. Later, an alternate approach was developed by certain manufacturers whereby all width values are "read" from the disk at one time and stored into memory when the machine is primed.

The "slave" typesetter. This term is often used to describe a typesetting device which must be instructed in every particular by the input job tape. It would describe not only the individual characters to be read and set, but also the width or amount of escapement for each character or space. Most typesetters, however, are not necessarily slaves in the complete sense. They may have some other way of knowing what width values are associated with the character input stream. The original Linofilm phototypesetter read 15-channel tape created by the operator on the keyboard console. This tape conveyed character widths as well as character and font identification information. Later, a three-frame six-level tape provided the same data. Early Photons (models 530, 540 and 560) also required a multiframe tape for the same purpose.

Once the width values are known to the machine, then the mechanics of escapement can be accomplished. This may involve moving a mirror, advancing a prism along a rack, or otherwise displacing the image onto the film plane.

The justification function

MOST OF THE EARLY typesetters also needed to be told the value of the interword spaces which had to be inserted in order to make lines justify. Even if they knew the width values of characters and could lay down such characters with the necessary amount of escapement, they did not necessarily know the value assigned to interword spaces. Hence, at the keyboard level computations were made which provided this information, much as with the original Monotype, except that the operator was no longer obliged to key in the needed data at the end of each line. In this connection several possibilities were available to the designer of phototypesetting devices.

- A counting keyboard could provide precise information as to the value of each interword space.
- A counting keyboard could provide information as to the total value of all interword spaces (or the excess over an established minimum value), and perhaps also the number of interword spaces, so that the typesetting device could make its own calculations.
- The keyboard could merely provide information as to the point at which the line ending would occur, and expect the typesetter to add up all width values, count the number of interword spaces, ascertain the "deficit" that had to be made up, and distribute this deficit among the available interword spaces or perhaps even between characters, if letterspacing were necessary and permitted.
- There are also some phototypesetters which cannot make their own calculations. These "slave" typesetters have to be told by the input keyboard (or computer system) just how much space to allow for each spaceband. But quite early in the history of the development of photocomposition it became obvious that phototypesetters should be able to accept and to process tape directly from TTS keyboards to drive linecasting machines in a TTS mode. Linecasting machines could, of course, justify lines that had already been specified as being within justification range, by virtue of the mechanical feature of spaceband expansion. Thus it was deemed necessary to design phototypesetting machines which could somehow produce the same results—that is, to compute the value required to be inserted between words in order to cause a line to justify after it had been brought within justification range.

With respect to this problem—of how to teach the machine to justify—the earliest solution was a mechanical one, namely that incorporated into the design of the first-generation Fotosetter.[1]

But there were soon to be more sophisticated solutions to the problem of justification by building some sort of justification *logic* into the machine itself. When speaking of justifying logic in this sense we do not mean logic which counts character widths *in order to make end-of-line decisions*, but rather logic to *implement end-of-line decisions that have already been made* by the operator on his counting keyboard. But as we shall see, phototypesetters frequently contain another kind of justification logic which permits them to make their own end-of-line decisions.

In order for the typesetting device to compute the values needed for interword spaces when such information is not provided within the input stream, the typesetter must look up the character widths and decrement them from a counter which establishes overall line length. It must also count the number of spacebands (variable spaces) within a line, and ascertain the deficit to be divided among the spacebands. We shall discuss this function further in our consideration of the justification process in Chapter 14. But it should be evident that some fairly sophisticated and very rapid arithmetic calculations are required before each line of type can be typeset. The entire line must be processed before the first spaceband code is "escaped," and hence before the first character in the line can be typeset.

In one case this was accomplished by giving the typesetter two paper-tape readers. One read the tape until it encountered a line-ending code. While its logic worked on the problem the paper tape was passed over to another reader for character information and subsequent exposure.

A second approach was to read the paper tape until an end-of-line signal was encountered, set the spaceband widths, and then back up the tape to the previous end-of-line code, and reread the tape on a character-by-character basis for processing through the actual character lay down and setting procedure.

The most common method, however, was to read the line into a *buffer* which stored the codes for the entire line, and then for the machine's electronic logic to examine the information in that buffer, first to make the necessary interword space calculations and subsequently to set type. In the meantime a new line could be read into that or an alternate buffer.

Initially, these interword space calculations were made by what we call "hard-wired" logic. But after a few years most phototypesetters of the second-generation variety came to have some sort of minicomputer or electronic "controller" to serve as typesetting "controllers" and also to perform other functions. As typesetting "controllers" they kept track of character positions on the revolving disk or drum. Also, they triggered the xenon flash to expose characters at the appropriate time, and they conveyed information on how far to escape after exposing the character. Finally, they informed the film advance mechanism when and by how much to move the photo-

1. See pp. 73-74.

graphic film or paper in order to compose the next line. And, as noted, they also computed the justification information and implemented it.

As we shall see in the next section of this chapter, these small computers can perform other functions as well. They can actually make the end-of-line decisions and even determine where and how to break words in order to achieve better justification. They can also simplify the keyboarding and typesetting process by storing formats or character strings which may be used frequently, and thus achieve quite complex typesetting results, such as arranging material into tabular formats.

Evaluating second-generation typesetters

A TYPESETTING MACHINE must be selected with a specific purpose, with the expectation that it will function in a particular kind of environment. Initially second-generation phototypesetters were sold as a "system." An installation consisted of one or more counting keyboards which produced paper tape. In most instances this tape was produced on counting keyboards where the operator made his own end-of-line decisions. The paper tape so generated was then mounted in the paper-tape reader of the typesetting device and it set the type. The typesetting machine did not contain any counting logic or any "front-end intelligence" except, perhaps, to achieve justification of lines that had already been brought within justification range, and perhaps to be able to respond to certain combinations of codes which would induce it to respond to some somewhat more complex commands, as for the setting of tables or indents.

However, subsequent developments permitted the typesetting device to make its own line-ending decisions, so that the paper tape fed into the machine consisted of a string of "endless text"[1] but with codes signalling paragraph endings and other typographical conditions. The "intelligence" of the "front-end" of the typesetter—which was a small computer—formatted the text and performed the line justification process. Still later, vendors began to supply to the market "direct entry" typesetting devices, which consisted of a single unit with both keyboard and film-imaging capability. In this case it would be difficult to say whether the counting logic resided in the "front end" or the "back end." However, such devices are of three types: they will make the end-of-line decisions for the operator; they will require the operator to terminate the lines; or they will operate in either environment.

Since we have not yet discussed how computers perform the processes and tasks of justification it is perhaps premature to presume sufficient knowledge on the part of the reader to understand just how these processes take place. Nevertheless, since we are now considering second-generation phototypesetting machines we shall present some information indicating some of the features such machines possess—each machine in a manner somewhat different from its competitors. The reader may prefer to return to this discussion after he

---

1. Sometimes called "idiot tape" in the trade. The French expression is "tape à kilometre" or "tape by the mile."

has read five or six of the following chapters and has acquired sufficient grounding in the basic principles of computer composition to be able to understand more precisely what these features mean and how they work.

However, a comparison chart which would seek to enumerate machine characteristics to aid the potential purchaser in making a purchase decision would surely consider the following points:

What is the speed of the machine? Each manufacturer is likely to make a claim for the speed of his typesetting machine when it is setting "straight" matter. In all cases the output speed of the phototypesetter is specified in terms of the number of nine-point, eleven-pica newspaper lines the machine can set in one minute. It may not be assumed, however, that the relative speeds reported would be relevant outside of the newspaper straight matter context. Even for straight matter, some machines lay down characters faster than others, but lead or film advance more slowly (or *vice versa*). Consequently, a linear relationship does not exist for wider measures. Moreover, font changes, size changes, and additional film advance (leading) will take more time on some machines than on others, and will usually require some additional time on all machines. Two machines with the same claimed output speed on straight newspaper copy may perform quite differently on more complicated material. The only way to gauge throughput accurately is to take copy considered to be typical of the kind of work the user expects to do and to set it and time it on the machines he may be considering. The purchaser should bear in mind that he may be able to optimize speed by customizing the font and lens arrangements or even, in some cases, combining different sizes on the same film carrier.

Some machines obtain higher speeds by reducing the number of characters available, in order to provide character redundancy and to flash more characters during one or more revolutions of the spinning disk or drum. When it is possible to run these machines in two modes of operation (one with fewer characters and higher speeds) both speed ratings and both sets of character complements need to be specified.

Flexibility. The versatility of the typesetter (apart from its speed) is a function of the characteristics discussed in the paragraphs below and represented by italicized lead-in topics.

Number of characters. This is the number of individual character image masters available on the machine at one time. On most most machines (but not all by any means) there is at least some time loss when you mix or select characters from different fonts. And, as stated above, the number of characters may be reduced if a higher running speed option is elected.

Number of sizes. This is the number of lenses or lens positions. Sizing is accomplished by rotating different lenses into position, or by a zoom lens arrangement. A time loss is involved in either case.

Some machines allow the user to mount larger or smaller sized font masters and thus to produce a greater range of point sizes from the same lens complement. This, however, may tend to reduce the number of different character masters on the machine (as in the case of the "B" fonts on the Mergenthaler V-I-P). Therefore only the number of sizes it is possible to produce from one character master should be considered, and not the total number of sizes possible with different size font masters in combinations with different lenses or lens positions. If manual intervention is required to change lens size to get a size other than that provided by a given master/lens relationship, the number of sizes thus obtainable need to be distinguished.

Number of characters times number of sizes. This is a calculation obtained by multiplying the total number of individual characters available on the machine by the number of sizes in which each character may be produced. This calculation is useful because it provides at least a rough index of typographic flexibility. If manual intervention is required to change lens sizes, the statistic thus computed needs to be differentiated from the total otherwise available.

An illustration of such a calculation may be of interest. Let us suppose that the typesetting machine is the Itek (erstwhile Dymo, Photon) Pacesetter Model 1616, which means that it offers 16 fonts and 16 sizes. If run at the speed of 90 lines per minute, the device offers a total of 1,792 character masters or a total of 28,672 characters × sizes. To run at the speed of 150 lines per minute, character images are duplicated and thus only 896 different images are provided, making for a total of 14,336 characters × sizes.

This is obviously a tremendous capability—both in terms of speed and versatility—if one makes a comparison with hot metal typesetting devices, but some third-generation (CRT) typesetting machines can offer on-line character × size combinations in the millions.

Size range. This information indicates the largest character size which can be set and the smallest. But it does not mean that every size or fractional size within this range is available. One would need to know the number of sizes as well.

Fonts. The number of different font masters will indicate how many fonts can be mounted on the machine at one time, whether they are disks, grids or filmstrips. The higher the number of font masters the greater the flexibility of the machine. One needs to consider, however, the number of characters within a font since these vary from machine to machine.

It does not follow, however, that each of these fonts can be replaced individually. For example, from four to sixteen fonts may be provided on a single disk, and the user is consequently limited with respect to the machine dressing. Suppose the user wished to set some jobs with Times Roman and Helvetica and other jobs with Baskerville and Helvetica. He might need to purchase two disks, both containing Helvetica.

Machine characteristics. Naturally there are limitations having to do with the way the machine is built. How wide a measure can it set? How much material can it output on a given run or take? These are some of the facts one needs to know. Certain of these characteristics are itemized under italic lead-in headings in the following paragraphs.

Maximum line length. This is the widest measure the machine is capable of setting. However, certain machines cannot set their widest measure in all point sizes and may not necessarily obtain left-hand alignment of certain sizes with certain others.

Maximum take length is the maximum length of photo material which can be exposed before the operator must remove the cassette from and/or load new material into the machine. Most of the typesetters use roll film or paper, and in these cases the length of the maximum take is dictated by the capacity of the output or take-up cassette which generally has less capacity than that of the supply box or cassette. Some machines use only sheet film which is, of course, limited in size.

Input tape formats. For many years second-generation phototypesetters were operated primarily from punched paper tape. Now many of them are operated on line to a computer or from a floppy diskette. There have been various kinds of paper-tape formats, tape widths and sprocketing arrangements. It was necessary, as a rule, to purchase a keyboard with a paper-tape punch which was configured to drive the particular typesetter you operated. Some typesetting machines read only 6-level TTS-coded paper tape. Others could be programmed to read different input code structures. Still others could be programmed to read 7- or 8-level paper tape in different code configurations.

Font-width increments. Each typesetting machine measures character widths in certain increments—usually fractions of an em of whatever point size is being set, although, as indicated above, there were some manufacturers with an "absolute" unit system.

In general, the larger the number of increments used to describe character widths the more aesthetically pleasing the typeset output should be. The crudest designs for proportionally spaced type were the Justowriter fonts of days gone by. The next step up was represented by "unit count" fonts. Virtually all typesetting machines now use "unitized" fonts, and in this case the number of units per em can be taken as an indication of better quality type design. Unit measurements for second-generation machines may run from 18 units to 36, to 54, or perhaps even higher. In some cases, however, the finer increments are misleading. It is possible to have a 36-unit scheme merely by using fonts designed for 18 units and multiplying each increment by two. On the other hand, even in such a case interword and intraword spacing for justification purposes may be more flexible and produce more pleasing results.

Finest leading increment tells us the smallest amount of "film advance" the typesetter can put out. Most machines provide leading in one-half point increments, thus enabling you to set, say, 10 on 11½ leading. But for spacing-out purposes, as when you may wish to "vertically justify" a page by distributing very fine increments of extra space between lines, the half-point leading capability is extremely restrictive, virtually prohibiting this kind of spacing, since it would be too gross. Here one-tenth point leading would be useful, or one-fourth point at the least.

Reverse leading is a very useful feature. It indicates whether the machine can back up the film or paper to permit the setting of a second column alongside the first, or otherwise to perform more complex setting and facilitate the composition of entire pages.

Functions under tape control. These are the functions that can be performed by remote commands embedded in the input stream. If the functions could not be performed under tape control it would be necessary for the operator of the typesetter to reset certain dials or switches, or even to open up the machine and make changes internally. Change in *line length*, change in *point size*, and change in *leading* are such functions, as well, of course, as change in *type face*, which may usually be assumed.

Wire service input. In the past it was often considered useful to be able to feed paper tape generated by the wire services directly into the typesetting machine. This could be handled in one of two modes: either to honor the line-ending decisions which the tape already contained, or to *strip out* these line endings so that the typesetting machine could make its own line endings for setting to a different measure or in a different type face.

Justification. Over the years many second-generation typesetting devices were built so that they could take over the function of making line-ending decisions and could thus accept "idiot tape" or could strip out decisions already made, in the case of the wire services, and substitute new line-ending decisions. *Hyphenless justification* offered one such possibility. This means that the machine can break lines but can do so only without trying to break (hyphenate) words. *Logic hyphenation* might also be provided, which means that the typesetter has also been programmed to hyphenate at least some words by the use of a logic routine. Sometimes logic hyphenation is enhanced by the addition of a small *exception word dictionary*, which would be consulted by the program before (and instead of) applying its word-breaking logic.

There are of course many subtleties involved in the process of justification and it is for this reason that this book devotes an entire chapter to the subject, as well as yet another to the subject of hyphenation, and still a third on the problems and tasks of inputting generally into a typesetting system. However, it may be stated at this point that some typesetting devices that are capable of performing the justification task (from endless tape or raw text input) usually include the ability to handle left, right and center *indents* and also to be able to format some simple kinds of *tabular material*.

Front-end intelligence. A typesetting device which can make "its own" line-ending decisions is said to have its own "front-end" intelligence, and it is of course useful, when buying a typesetting device, to find out as much as possible about what specific features it may offer—such as the ability to provide *automatic white space reduction* for larger point sizes, *tabs* for tabular setting, and *stored formats*.

Direct-input devices

THE ORIGINAL FIRST-GENERATION Fotosetter was a direct-input machine, although the first-generation Monophoto was not. The distinction arises out of the fact that the keyboard in the Monophoto is separated from the photo unit itself, just as with Monotype the keyboard was separated from the caster.

Some of the early second-generation devices, such as the Photon 200, were direct input machines, capable of outputting only at the speed of the keyboarder. But even in the early evolution of phototypesetting it became apparent that it would be better to separate keyboarding and typesetting so that the typesetting devices could be freed up to operate faster than a person could strike keys, even if not making line-ending decisions. An excellent typist may be able to type 60 words a minute, which might represent perhaps 300 characters. A typesetting device may be able to set that many characters in a second's time. Thus more than one keyboarder is needed to keep the output device busy, and keyboards could be manufactured more cheaply than the entire keyboard-typesetting unit.

However, by the mid-1970s this trend was somewhat reversed. As component costs were reduced and typesetting machines became more electronic and less mechanical, many direct-input or direct-entry devices (the terms mean the same thing) were introduced at quite low prices. But again, after this happened, emphasis was placed upon making it possible for even these machines to accept external input (most frequently via floppy disk), and even to permit the simultaneous processing of two jobs—one in the background (*i.e.*, typesetting a job which had already been keyboarded) and another in the foreground (*i.e.*, keyboarding a new job at the same time, or correcting a job which had already been keyboarded)—and storing the input onto a floppy disk so that it could subsequently be typeset. And as microcomputers were developed and their prices dropped, the distinction between machines used for *word processing* and those used for *typesetting* began to become less and less distinct.

But we are ahead of our story. All of these issues must be considered in some logical order when we have laid the proper background. Let us continue with our account of the evolution of the typesetting machines, and turn to *third-generation* devices.

9

Third-Generation Typesetters

THE CONCEPT of applying generations to typesetters was probably borrowed from the computer industry, and in that instance it is presumed that each generation introduces an entirely new technology. The first generation of computers made use of vacuum tubes. The second generation introduced transistors and solid state concepts. The third generation involved the use of monolithic integrated circuitry and semi-conductors. And after that, things began to happen so fast that it was no longer helpful to think in terms of generations. We talk instead about mainframe solutions and mini- and microcomputers, personal and professional computers, desk-top and lap-top versions and various kinds of architectures and networks. Similarly, after third-generation typesetters were around for a while a wide variety of other approaches began to appear that are much more difficult to categorize. This chapter will be concerned only with the third-generation approach, however, and a discussion of subsequent technologies will be delayed until later in the book. (See especially Chapters 21 and 23.)

First-generation phototypesetters were adapted from hot metal models (or impact typewriters) and worked as nearly as possible on the basis of the same principles. A second-generation machine was one which was especially conceived and designed to set type by photomechanical means. *A third-generation typesetter is one which does not in fact expose type directly from photographic masters but reproduces them electronically on the face of a cathode ray tube (like a TV screen).* The images thus created are in turn photographed (either the same size or enlarged or reduced by means of a lens system) directly from the screen. If this seems a roundabout way of setting type, there are nevertheless significant advantages. One of them is that the image on the screen can be manipulated electronically in a variety of interesting ways. Another is setting speed. A third is the absence of mechanical parts and motions which present maintenance and reliability problems.

We shall learn that there have been two basic categories of CRT typesetters. One derives its character images by scanning a photographic master which is stored on grids, much in the same manner as with a second-generation device. But at the same time that it scans, it paints that image on the face of a cathode ray tube, stroke by stroke. And as each stroke is painted, the light from this stroke passes through a lens and thence onto photographic film or paper, thus exposing not a character at a time, but a stroke or slice of the character at a time.

Third-Generation Typesetters

Hence the character store is photographic even if the image is not exposed on the film by the conventional means of shining a light through it.

This first approach is no longer used, but in the early days of third-generation devices it was quite common. The alternative, and now much more common, approach is not to store the character as a photographic image, but rather as a digital representation. It is true, of course, that most characters are scanned in order to be converted into digital form. But the scanning process takes place only once, in an entirely different operation in order to create the information for subsequent storage within the typesetter, whereas with the first approach each character is scanned on the fly as it is typeset and must be rescanned each time it appears even if this occurs many times within the same line of text.

Both of these basic types of CRT typesetters—those with photographically stored character masters and those with digitally stored character masters—will meet the definition of a third-generation typesetter as one which generates characters on the face of a CRT as strokes or dot patterns.

What is a cathode ray tube?

THE ILLUSTRATION below indicates the manner in which the cathode ray tube works. Such a tube contains a cathode which emits a stream of negatively charged particles of electrons. These electrons are subjected to high-voltage acceleration in an electron gun and this action creates a beam of charged particles which is capable of being concentrated or deflected, either by electrostatics or magnetics. A grid pulse controls the emission of electrons. Anodes within the tube focus the beam. Deflection is caused by changes in the potential across the horizontal and vertical electrostatic plates or by deflection coils that create right-angled magnetic fields.

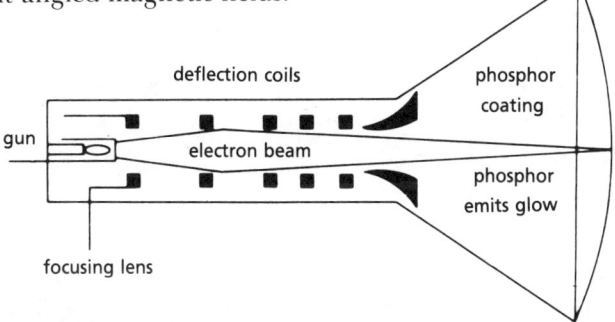

Functional diagram of a cathode ray tube as used for character generation in a CRT typesetter.

There is a phosphor coating on the inside of the face of the tube, and the electron beam, when it strikes this coating, excites the phosphor causing it to glow. If the phosphor coating is very fine and the beam is closely focused, a very tiny and quite brilliant dot can be created. If the beam is moved vertically, by deflection, then a series of dots, resulting in a vertical line, will be formed. How long the line will be visible on the face of the tube will depend upon the "latency" of the image—the "decay" time of the phosphor. For some applications, where the same image has to remain for a period of time, the image is refreshed at perhaps 60 cycles per second by recycling the same bombardment of electrons. But for typesetting purposes, a low degree of latency is desired, and the initial image must be sufficiently brilliant to photograph well. In fact, it is the individual dots, or, at most, strokes, which are "captured" and not the entire character at one time.

Such tubes generally fall into two classifications: one is like a TV tube which is so designed that the beam will sweep the tube in a predetermined fashion, thus creating a network of horizontal lines in a "raster scan" pattern, very close together. The other type of CRT tube will direct its beam in a random manner, in order to "draw" on the face of the tube, depending upon the emission and deflection signals it receives. It is this latter type of tube which is to be found in the third-generation phototypesetter.

Distortion. Since the beam has to travel further to reach the edges of the tube, the beam is somewhat more diffused (out of focus) when it arrives. Also, because of the angle at which it strikes, there will be an additional spreading of the dot into an oval shape. Hence characters produced anywhere other than in the center of the tube are subject to some degree of distortion unless there is a correction factor introduced into the electronic circuitry, causing more or less deflection and changing of focus patterns. But applications involving high-quality reproduction nevertheless seek to avoid the use of the outer perimeters of the tube, especially the use of the far corners. The distortion around the corners is called pin-cushion distortion.

Compensating circuitry is therefore built into the electronics to correct for distortion in all models of CRT typesetters. The larger the area of the tube used, the more expensive it must be and the more difficult to build. In the 1960s, Columbia Broadcasting Laboratories was involved with Mergenthaler in the design and construction of the Linotron 1010 because the full-page feature of that device required an unusually large CRT of exceptional quality, and it was this technology that the laboratory could contribute.

The Linotron 505

WHILE THE FIRST third-generation photocomposition device was either the Linotron 1010 or the VideoComp 820 (depending upon whether the historian goes by date conceived or date delivered), it is more logical to begin our discussion with a description of the Linotron 505 since its operating principles are closer to second-generation machines.

The original 505 was developed by Peter Purdy and Ronald McIntosh—two Englishmen whose work was financed by K.S. Paul. Their development effort began in the year 1963. The initial concept of the machine was not unlike that of the (later) Photon Zip[1] in that

---

1. See pp. 88-89.

Third-Generation Typesetters

256 flash tubes were to be employed for the purpose of character selection. But as the months went by the product definition changed. They decided instead to *scan* photographic images, at first planning to use 64 indexing tubes, each of which would be able to scan four characters. Finally the machine's basic structure emerged and a prototype was revealed at the DRUPA show in June 1967, many pounds and several years off target.

That prototype, capable of setting only in sizes up to 14 points, was installed at the Portmouth (England) *Evening News* in February 1968. But Mergenthaler, the American typesetting manufacturer and vendor, reached an agreement to acquire the company and its machine, at, or immediately following, the DRUPA show. However, the Mergenthaler/K.S. Paul agreement was conditioned upon the British company's ability to extend the maximum point size to 28. This was in fact accomplished although it made necessary the revamping of the entire optical system. The new machine was ready, then, to be unveiled at PRINT 68 by Mergenthaler as the Linotron 505 (one half as powerful as the 1010 which was being build for the U.S. Government Printing Office).

The 505 represented a distinctive approach to CRT phototypesetter design. Perhaps the two most important facts to remember about the machine are that it uses photographic grids as a character storage medium, and that is uses a traveling lens system to lay down characters—or, more precisely, the vertical strokes that go to make up these characters.

The use of the traveling lens eliminated the problem of distortion correction on the face of the CRT. Only one vertical stroke or slice of the character was generated and reflected onto a traveling mirror or prism, which deflected that stroke onto the photographic film or paper. Unlike second-generation machines, where the entire character would be positioned by a traveling mirror or prism, here the escapement took place one stroke at a time. As each stroke was generated a light-sensing raster read the position of that stroke and called for the scanning beam to transmit another. A succeeding vertical slice was then generated. The mirror traveled across the line at a constant speed, calling for consecutive vertical strokes—650 times for each inch of travel in the coarser resolution, or 1300 times for each inch in the finer resolution.

Characters were stored as photographic masters on four grids, each of which contained 238 images. In addition, a separate "pi plaque" of 64 characters was provided.

Each of the four grids consisted of an array of 16 sections. Directly in front of this grid were 16 lenses, and in front of them was a character selection scanning tube or CRT, which was capable of "indexing" a particular location on the tube—that is, generating raster strokes which were picked up by all the lenses in such fashion that a particular character location was scanned on each of the 16 grid sections. However, behind the grid there were sixteen photomultipliers, only one of which would be turned on, so that only one character would be scanned and stroked. This stroking information would then be conveyed to the output tube which, in turn, would generate comparable strokes, each of which would be laid down by the traveling mirror. Between the mirror and the film plane there was a lens which reduced the stroke image at a ratio of 9.5:1, thus enhancing the quality of the output. Later models of the 505 substituted a tiny traveling CRT output tube for the traveling mirror, but the principle of selecting and scanning and transmitting character information on a stroke-by-stroke basis to a traveling stroke lay down device remained.

Despite the fact that there were lenses in this system, the sizing was nevertheless electronic in character. In other words, the length of the stroke on the output tube and the number of strokes per character determined the size of the output character. At the resolution of 1300 lines per inch, for example, a character 36 points wide would consist of 650 vertical strokes, whereas a character 18 points wide would consist of 325 vertical strokes. Electronic circuitry would know the desired size of the character and consequently how many slices of that character would have to be scanned.

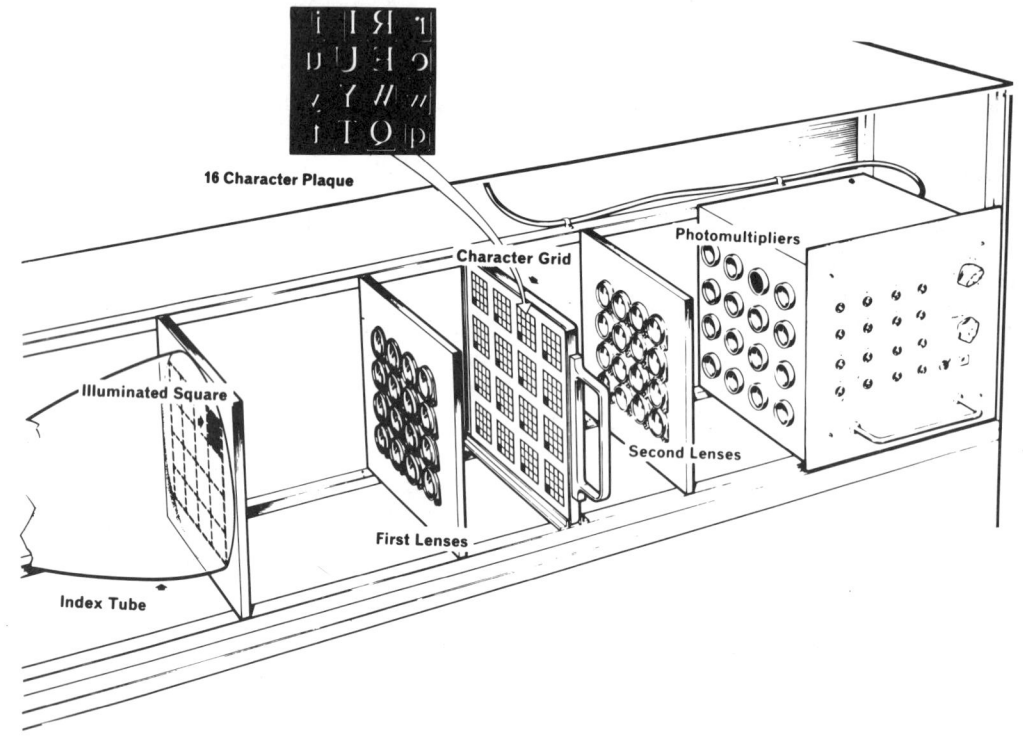

Character images are stored on a grid which contains 16 plaques, each in turn consisting of photographic masters for 16 characters (although only 238 characters are represented in all). In front of this grid, to the left in the diagram shown above, is mounted an index or scanning cathode ray tube. Sixteen lenses focus the face of this tube onto each of the 16 grid plaques. Sixteen additional lenses behind the grid focus each of the 16 grid plaques onto one of the 16 separate photomultipliers. The face of the index CRT is divided into imaginary squares. To scan a character on the grid, the 505 will generate a series of scan lines in one of these square areas on the tube. These raster lines are projected through "first lenses"—all 16 of them—in order to stroke one character from each of the 16 photomasters on the grid. These strokes all pass through a second group of lenses, but only one character is then selected for transmission to the printout tube, because only one photomultiplier is activated.

Third-Generation Typesetters

What the 505 achieved. By way of character store, 238 typographic characters were available in each grid. Four such grids could be mounted. New grids could be replaced by manual insertion. All characters on one grid were instantly available. A grid windmill could shift any one of these grids into position, but required 2.8 seconds in the worst case. Hence there was some time delay, causing the moving carriage, for character or stroke lay down, to return to the beginning of the line whenever a grid change took place, and to move out again to the location where it had been when the command was received. There were also pi plaques of 64 characters each that were accessible without time delay.

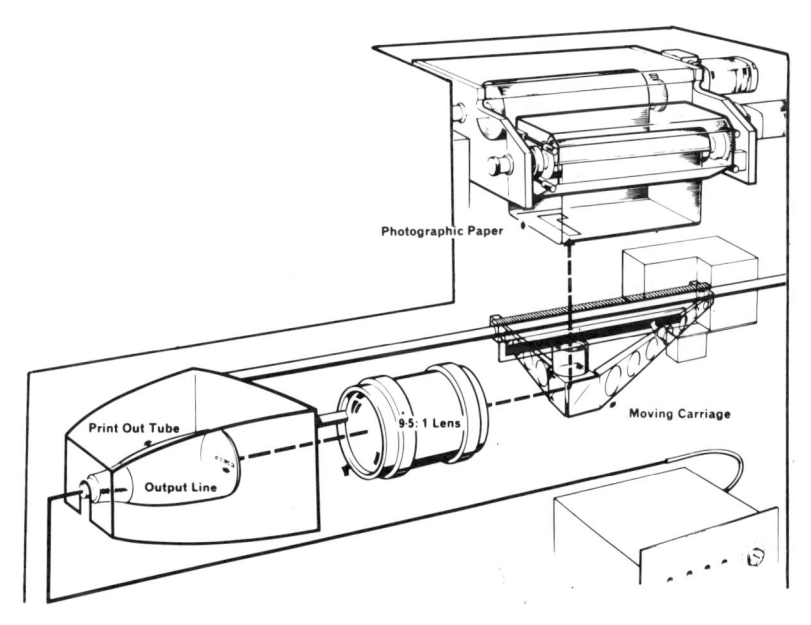

The heart of the printout end of the photo unit is a carriage which travels along a rail underneath the photo media to be exposed. On the rail is a fine-line grid with a calibration line every 1/18th point (making approximately 1300 per inch). Every calibration line, or every alternate calibration line, depending upon whether the 505 is being run in high or standard resolution, causes the carriage to send back a signal which calls for the next stroke. A scan stroke is then generated on the index CRT and the CRT beam on the output tube shown in the diagram above is deflected in "synch" with the scanning stroke. When the photomultiplier behind the character to be set senses the light from the scanning beam *(see preceding diagram)* it signals the beam on the output to turn on. When it no longer senses light from the scanning beam it signals the beam on the output tube to turn itself off. The character image is thus transmitted to the photographic film or paper in a stroke-by-stroke fashion as the carriage moves across the measure.

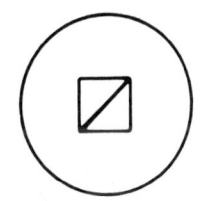

Electronic manipulation—slanting. It was possible to cause the output stroke on the printout tube to be generated slantwise at a 12° angle (8° in Germany by their preference) through electronic means. In other words, the single stroke generated by a single scan of the index tube appears in the CRT "window" in the manner illustrated in the margin. This, of course, produces an obliqued roman rather than *afi*

a true italic, and true italic characters could also be stored as photographic masters on grids. But where an artificial italic or obliqued font would serve, as is often the case with sans serif type, the repertoire of the machine was thus extended by electronic manipulation.

Electronic manipulation—changing point sizes. It was also possible to change point sizes, in the manner previously discussed, by lengthening the stroke on the output tube. A choice of 15 type sizes was thus available, and a wide-range version of the machine offered the possibility of creating a stroke four times longer, making it possible to obtain 22 different point sizes (if we discount those which were duplicated). In other words, the basic machine could set 4,5,6,7,8,9,10, 11,12,14,18,20,24 and 28 points. The 4× option would convert the 4-point size into 16 points, the 5 points into 20 (which would be a duplication of the standard 20 points), but no type could be generated above 72 points.

Electronic manipulation—changing base lines. Another electronic character manipulation feature was the ability to raise or lower the base line (still within the CRT window) in six steps without the need to move the film forward or to reverse it. Such deflection made it possible to create, from any typographic image, a superior, a superior to a superior, an inferior, or an inferior to an inferior. Later even greater flexibility was added, making it possible to raise or lower any character in one-half point increments, within the "window."

Electronic manipulation—changing set sizes. As with most other CRT typesetters, the 505 was able to treat character height and width as two independent variables. For example, photographic masters could be scanned as if they were twelve points high and six points wide, or vice versa. Thus you could set an 8-point character as if it were 9, 10 or 12 points wide, or a 12-point character as if it were 8, 9, or 10 points wide, *etc.* This capability proved to be extremely useful for newspaper applications, especially for display headlines.

Resolution

THE 505 WAS BUILT to offer a resolution of either 650 or 1300 (actually 1296) scan lines per inch. As previously stated, the resolution is determined by the frequency with which the moving carriage calls for a new scan line.

CRT typesetters which generate their images by scanning photographic masters invariably lay down character strokes at a constant resolution. In this case, as we have mentioned, the resolution is either 650 or 1300. On the other hand, many CRT typesetters which generate their characters from digitally stored masters rather than photographic images, vary the resolution or number of strokes per inch in order to achieve different character widths to correspond with changes in point size. On the whole, it would appear to be advantageous to try to maintain the same resolution regardless of point size, but in actual practice a variation in resolution is not as important as it would at first seem since there are methods of compensating for the variations in character density which might otherwise result. For example, if standard resolution were 1000 lines per inch and an increase in point size meant changing the resolution to 800 lines per inch, it is possible to increase voltage somewhat, creating a slightly larger and brighter dot, to help fill in the character image.

Speed

THE SPEED of the 505 is first of all a function of character resolution. At 650 lines per inch (when not using the 4× feature) you would be able to set 160 twelve-pica lines per minute regardless of point size, assuming no grid changes or other slow functions. If, however, you had two grid changes per line, from grid #1 to grid #3 and back again, speed would be reduced by 2.8 seconds per line, plus the time it would take to rescan the portion of the line already set, which would mean that under such (unlikely) circumstances, throughput would be reduced to about 20 lines per minute.

Quality of the image

IMAGES CREATED by the scanning of photographic masters on the fly will generally not be as clean as images of comparable resolution generated from digitized masters. This is because when you scan a straight line precisely along its edge you will get random effects. On one occasion the scanning beam will sense an image and on another it will not. This tends to create "burrs" and "notches" in the character outline, but such deviations are usually not nearly so substantial as deviations attributable to the variations from casting identical characters from the circulating matrices of the linecaster.

The Linotron 303

THE "WINDMILL" ARRANGEMENT for providing additional font masters, although it substantially enhanced the character repertoire of the 505, slowed it down considerably. Consequently, in 1974 the company announced the 303 which replaced the 238 character grids with smaller grids of 144 characters each, but provided either 22 or eleven such grids within a rotating container, reducing grid change times very significantly. But by the time the 303 reached the market interest had clearly shifted away from CRT devices with photographic masters to machines which kept all of their fonts on line in a digital form. Mergenthaler itself introduced digital machines.

The Compugraphic Videosetter

THE VIDEOSETTER was first demonstrated in 1973. Thus ten years had elapsed from the first Purdy-McIntosh effort that gave rise to the Linotron 505. And compared with the 505, the Videosetter represented some startling innovations. These resulted in a product price which broke away from the established CRT pattern as dramatically as Compugraphic's introduction of the 2961 and 4961 models of second-generation typesetters in 1968 broke away from the then established prices of similar devices. At a time when no other CRT typesetter was available at a price under $100,000, Compugraphic announced the Videosetter I at $32,950 and subsequently reduced the price of an improved product to $21,950!

Initially, the Videosetter was a very limited machine in terms of its character repertoire, maximum point size and setting measure. Only 106 characters were available at one time, only certain sizes up to 36 points could be generated, and a line no wider than 27 picas could be set. This was clearly intended to be a machine for the newspaper industry, and especially for the composition of single-column measures along with two-column display ads. Subsequently, however, some of these limitations were overcome.

Principles of character generation. The accompanying diagram should make the principles of the machine quite clear. A grid containing 106 characters is mounted below a light-diffusing lens so that all 106 characters are simultaneously illuminated, and the entire grid image is reduced by a ratio of 2:1 and brought into focus on the face of an *image dissector* tube. It is this tube which provides the key to the system. The scanning beam of the image dissector is able to select from the grid pattern one character and to scan that particular character and transmit its features despite its minute size. The image on

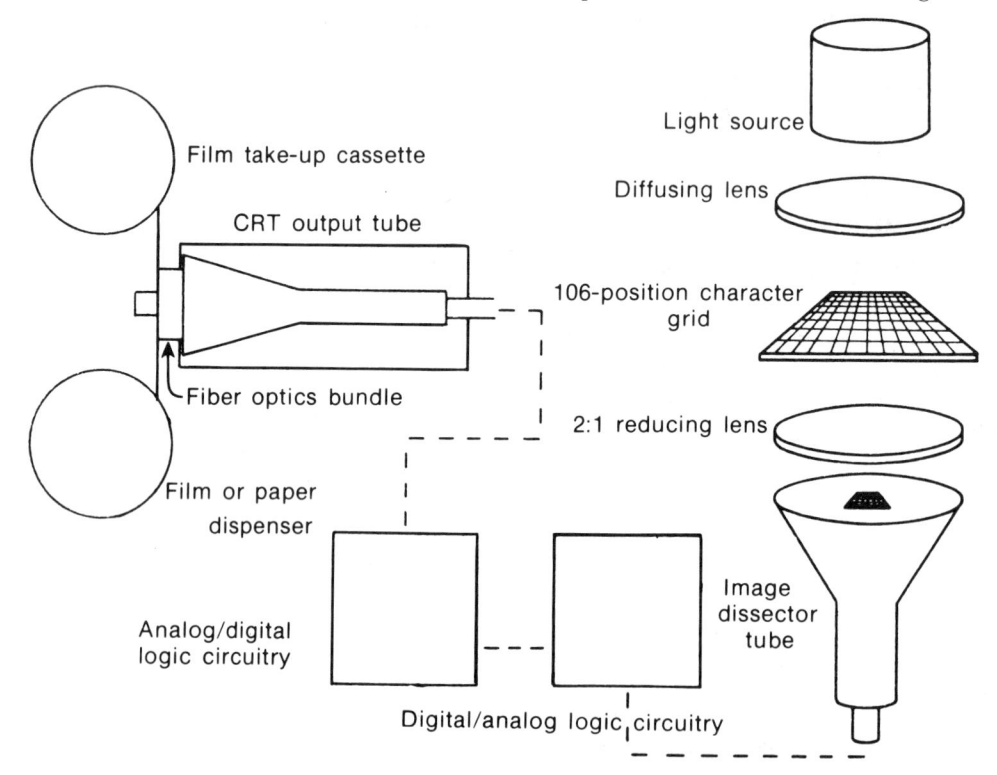

Third-Generation Typesetters

the grid itself represents a 12-point master size. It is reduced through the focusing lens to six points. Nevertheless, the character is scanned or swept by the scanning beam at a frequency which provides a resolution on the film plane of 1,300 lines per inch. The signals which are read during the scanning process are used to turn a writing beam on and off on the output tube. But the length of the stroke on the output tube is a function of the size of the character desired to be typeset, just as the number of times the character is scanned on the image dissector is also a function of the desired character width.

And just as the logic of the image dissector circuitry must know what character to scan, so the logic of the CRT character generator must know where, on its tube, to lay the character down. This process is relatively simple since the characters are generated in consecutive order.

Compugraphic could have created larger characters than 36 points and longer lines than 27 picas had it chosen to interpose a lens between the output tube and the photographic material. Instead, it elected to use a CRT tube with a *fiber optic face plate*. In this fashion it saved the cost of a high-quality lens. A fiber optic face plate consists of a bundle of fiber optic tubes which are bonded to the face of a CRT character generator. The photographic paper comes into physical contact with the outside ends of the fiber optics bundle, while the inside ends, which are coated with phosphor, are mounted directly into the tube itself so that they can be excited by the electron gun.

The Videosetter grid. If we examine the grid layout shown above, certain other features of the machine immediately become obvious. Note how the most common characters are positioned in the center of the grid where the scanning capabilities of the image dissector will provide the best results and the minimum amount of beam deflection will be required in order to access these images. Note also that there are no characters to be found in those areas where distortion is most troublesome and those closest to the corners are characters where distortion would matter the least. Nevertheless, it is important for the tubes—both the image dissector and the character generator—to contain appropriate circuitry to correct for distortion, and this is done not by dividing the tubes into segments for correction purposes, but by devising one hard-wired map (with adjustable controls) to regulate beam deflection and dot intensity to compensate for the inherent limitations of any such CRT device.

When the grid is mounted in the machine the machine is primed. When the machine is activated, the image dissector reads the encoded width values for each character and stores them in its memory. Thereafter these width values are no longer accessed or scanned by the image dissector, for now the machine knows what each character's value is. You will note that Compugraphic used an 18-unit system. There are white squares out of a black bar wherever there is a value to be read. Here the bar on the left has a maximum of white space. Reading from the top you get 8+4+2+1 which equals 15. Compugraphic added three units to all such values, making the first total 18. The second bar shows 8+1 (plus 3, of course) and the third shows 4+1.

Electronic manipulation. The Videosetter could reproduce only 106 characters, and these were sized as if they were 5, 6, 7, 8, 9, 10, 12, 14, 18, 24, 30 or 36 points. But other electronic games were also possible. The original machine offered the ability to stroke a character vertically at one point size on the output tube, while reading its width horizontally at another size, thus achieving the ability to expand or condense the appearance of the type face. In addition, characters could be obliqued to simulate italics or emboldened to simulate a bold face.

Subsequently Compugraphic enlarged its Videosetter line, offering several models, of which the Videosetter Universal was the most flexible. This machine provided for the mounting of eight grids and it output onto an eight-inch instead of a five-inch tube, thus making it possible to set a 45-pica line length and to generate characters up to 72 points. With so many different grids on-line users were less inclined to take recourse to the emboldening or even the slanting of obliquing options. They could now mount character images which were already designed as true italic or true bold faces.

The spot size on the face of the output tube, and hence on the film or paper, was approximately one mil (one one-thousandth of an inch). The 1,300 line-per-inch resolution allowed for sufficient, but not excessive, dot overlap. The speed of the machine was approximately 45 column inches per minute, which was equivalent to 360 11-point lines of 9-point type per minute.

Other photographic master machines

FOR THE SAKE of completeness, we should mention that one of the very early third-generation typesetters was designed by Mergenthaler for the U.S. Government Printing Office. This machine was known as

Third-Generation Typesetters

the 1010. Only five such machines were ever built, and the first of these was accepted for delivery in September, 1967. Like the 505, characters were generated on the face of the CRT from scanned photographic masters. A four-inch square grid, containing 255 characters was positioned so that its store of characters could be scanned. A windmill-like arrangement permitted shifting from one grid to any of the three alternate grids. Characters were not scanned by a flying spot but a very sophisticated and expensive solution was developed whereby a "cloudlet" of electrons was swept over a stationary aperture causing an analog signal to turn the current on and off. This signal was then used to generate the character image on the face of the CRT.

The 1010 output tube was a "full face" character generator, which meant that the machine set a page at a time, and then moved the film or paper in order to compose the next page. The face of the tube therefore had to be large enough to contain the entire page ($8\frac{1}{4} \times 10\frac{1}{2}$) as enlarged 2:1. This made for a very expensive tube, with complex correction circuitry.

Another CRT using photographic masters was the Crosfield Magnaset, which arranged them in rows around a rotating drum, and when a character was desired by the output module that particular character would be scanned and electronically recreated on the face of the CRT character generator. The purpose behind this design was to eliminate the delay in setting occasioned by the necessary grid movements of the Linotron 505. However, by the time it was nearly perfected (1973-74) the digital font storage method had grown in popularity and acceptance and this project was therefore abandoned.

The digital machines

WE SHALL NOW discuss the CRT typesetters which do not derive their character patterns from the on-line scanning of photographic masters. That is to say, the desired characters, while they initially may have been scanned by some device for the purpose of digitizing them, are not stored photographically, but rather in some form which provides stroking information. Thus some kind of digital representation of each character is stored on line and accessed whenever the characters are desired.

Therefore it is not the output characteristics of the digital machines which tend to make them unique; it is the use of digital character storage. A font of characters, or a subset of a font, or even an individual character, is brought up into the memory of the CRT typesetter on call. Such fonts are now customarily stored on a moving-head disk which is a peripheral to the typesetter, although with some of the very early machines fonts were loaded into the memory of the typesetter from magnetic tape, one font at a time, as part of the text stream.

Generally speaking, a character consists of a series of vertical strokes (just as if it had been scanned) and these strokes are painted on the output tube from the bottom of the character to the top. Hence, if one wanted to describe a character one has only to record a series of start/stop points which indicate where the electron beam character generator is to be turned on and off. The beam circuitry would continue to sweep the aperture of the tube in regular strokes (but not in a raster pattern since the beam can be deflected both vertically and horizontally by signal). The deflection circuitry generally moves evenly across the tube's aperture, especially when painting a particular character. When that character has been completed deflection electronics will position the beam where the next character to be set is to be located. But the electronic bombardment occurs only when the gun is turned on to spray the electrons which will excite the phosphor coating on the inside of the tube. Thus, what is significant here is the signal to turn the beam on and off during the course of the deflected stroking movement. Since the timing of the beam movement is known, a signal to start the beam stroke, to hold it on for the equivalent of four (hypothetical) vertical cells, to turn it off for three more, to turn it back on again for two, and then to turn it off and wait for the next starting point, one stroke to the right in order to begin another sweep, would permit the generation of a light pattern to comprise a vertical slice of the desired character.

If we consider the task of generating a ten-point character true size, and if we wish to create this character with a resolution of 720 strokes to the inch, and since there are 72 points to the inch, a ten-point solid em would consist of 100 strokes. Also since it would be a square, the depth of the stroke would also consist of 100 picture elements ("pixels"). A lower case a—if it were one half of an em in width—would therefore consist of somewhat less than 50 vertical strokes, allowing for the character's side bearings. It appears to be most convenient to express character widths in terms of a 100-unit-to-the-em system. Thus our lower case a would have a width of 50 relative units and an absolute value of five points at true master size.

If the average character were, in fact, an en in width—which is likely—and the master were ten points, then 50 vertical slices would be sufficient to describe that character. But the number of times the beam would have to be turned on and off during the stroking cycle could be quite considerable. Perhaps the worst case would be the "at" sign for, as you can see in the margin, there would be a number of locations where the starting and stopping points for beam exposure would have to be specified. A more typical case might be represented by the letter d shown on the next page. To simplify the illustration this character has been drawn, rather roughly, on a scale of 50 strokes to the em rather than 100, and the locations for turning the beam on and off are also shown, with the horizontal indication of on/off locations indicated by numbers 0 through 49.

An inspection of this crude character makes one wonder how it is possible to create satisfactory graphic images from a grid pattern or dots or strokes. A slight dot overlap is helpful to give the character a better shape, and the finer the stroking pattern the better the representation will be. To illustrate this point we have also shown the letter D as it would appear in type and as it looks as digitized artwork. Diagonals are obviously more difficult to represent than vertical lines,

Third-Generation Typesetters

125

Right: The capital letter D is shown in its digitized form (from Autologic), with the master size also shown.

Below: The lower-case B with its starting and stopping points defined below it.

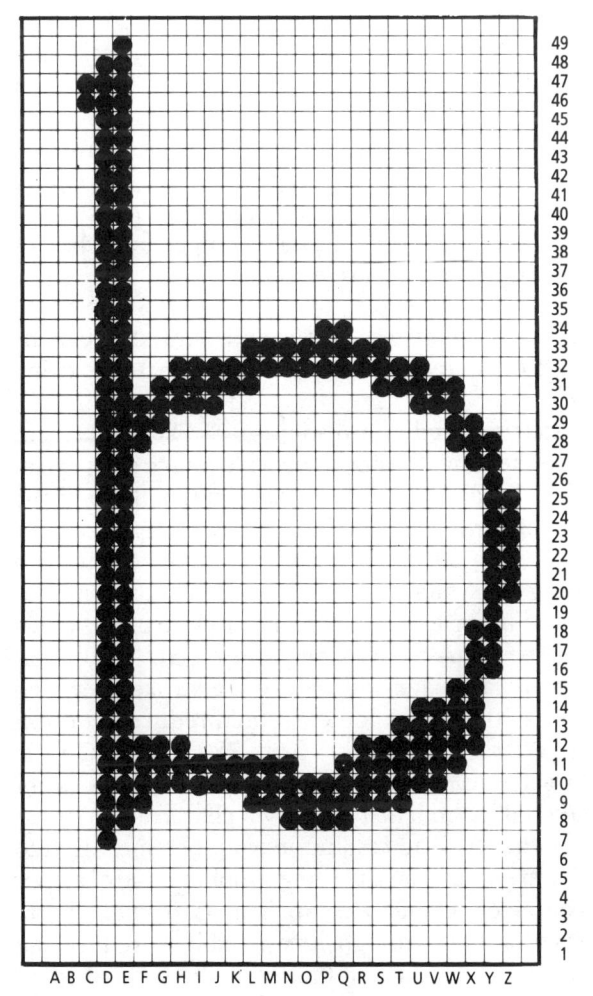

```
A B C D E F G H I J K L M N O P Q R S T U V W X Y Z
46 7  8  9 10 10 10 10 9  9  8  8  8  8  9  9  9 10 10 11 12 16 20
47 49 48 12 12 12 11 11 11 11 11 11 10 10 11 12 12 13 14 14 15 18 28 25

         28 29 30 30 30 31 31 31 32 32 32 32 32 31 31 30 30 28 27
         30 31 32 32 32 32 33 33 33 33 34 34 33 33 32 32 31 31 29
```

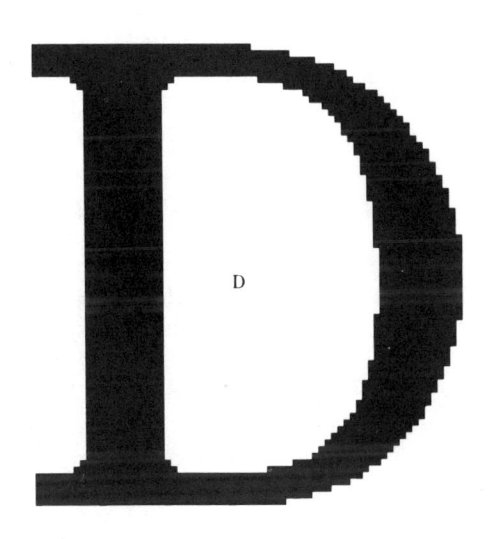

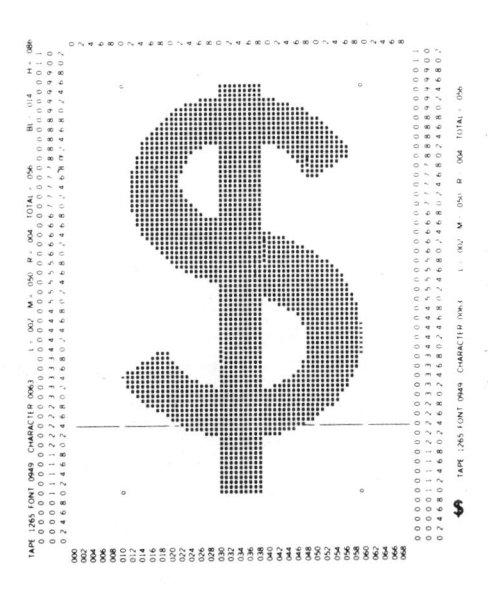

Above: A graphical representation of a dollar sign as digitized by Autologic. The start and stop points and positions of each stroke may be ascertained by the coding. The latter does not correspond, however, with Autologic's stroke encoding storage technique, but is purely for analysis in editing.

and graceful curves may be hardest of all, particularly if they are subtle. It is for this reason that CRT type is most successful when it has been edited. The mere digitization of artwork usually (but not invariably) leads to inconsistent and less-than-satisfactory results, just as the scanning of photographic images usually produces character shapes which are not as clean and well-formed as those which have been digitized first and then edited. One reason this is so is because the scanning of the edge of a vertical line often results in a ragged appearance as the scanning beam becomes confused. Another reason is that a typographic editor who is an expert in type design can add dots or take them away in order to create a particular illusion or effect, thus simulating the features of the type face he seeks to emulate.

The coding we have illustrated for the letter b represents starting and stopping points for every portion of every stroke. To store digitized information for a single character by this means—or a similar means called "run length encoding"which sets forth the number of contiguous black or white cells—usually requires several hundred memory locations (even for a ten-point master). To bring in a single font to store within the memory of the typesetter might require 20,000 bytes of information. As we shall see, larger font masters require a great deal more storage, and hence data compaction schemes are sometimes used or other methods are developed.

Electronic sizing. Once the digitized character is stored it can be used to generate a range of character sizes and shapes. First the sizing itself:

If a ten-point master is stored at a resolution of 720 strokes per inch, it is possible to use the same master to provide image sizes up to, perhaps 15 or 16-point characters. This is done by lengthening the strokes and spacing them farther apart. In order to compensate for the greater distance between strokes the dot size may be enlarged somewhat, by increasing the voltage going to the electron gun and causing it to emit a more intense bombardment of electronics. However, the resolution of the character has been impaired. A 50% enlargement of the same digital image will reduce the strokes per inch from 720 to 540, just as a 100% enlargement would reduce the number of strokes per inch (not per character) from 720 to 360. On the other hand, if the character size were reduced so that the same number of strokes occupied half as much space (say a character intended for a five-point setting), the stroking resolution would be increased to 1,440 lines per inch. There would be the same number of strokes per character but each character would take up half its former width. Under these circumstances, even though it is possible to reduce the dot size somewhat and to decrease the intensity of the spot, at some point there would be too much dot overlap and the character would tend to become fuzzy. In general—depending of course upon the chosen master-size resolution, the size of the spot and the extent of any character magnification—satisfactory type can be produced by enlarging the image as much as 40% to 60% and by reducing it as much as 20% to 40%. Thus, a 10-point master could produce acceptable type within a range of from 6 to 16 points. A 20-point master could produce acceptable type within a range of 16 to 32 points, and a 40-point master could produce good type from perhaps 30 to 64 points. An 80-point master could generate satisfactory images varying in size from perhaps 48 to 128 points. It should be noted that the larger the master size the greater the number of point sizes it can encompass. There are ten point sizes between 6 and 16, but there are 80 point sizes between 48 and 128.

Consequently, to produce a full range of sizes it is necessary, generally speaking, to store perhaps four different master sizes when digital characters are generated by stored stroking information. These masters may be designed to have different characteristics so that they more closely resemble their hot metal counterparts. For the larger masters one would expect smaller x-heights, larger descenders, and serifs to be more graceful and proportionately smaller. But for every increase in master size the digital font storage requirements are likewise increased. Since there would be twice as many strokes in a 20-point master as in a 10-point master, there would be twice as much digital information.

The RCA VideoComp. The first such digital third-generation CRT typesetter was the VideoComp, or perhaps more exactly, the Hell Digiset from which the VideoComp was derived. (At the same time a company called Alphanumeric was developing the APS-2.)

Dr. -Ing Rudolf Hell was a manufacturer of electronic components and devices in Kiel, West Germany. In 1964 he was approached by telephone company interests to ascertain whether he could produce a machine that would compose telephone directory galleys on 70 mm film. This led to a discussion with other potential customers and in these explorations the concept of the Digiset emerged—specifically, the product known as the Digiset 50T1, subsequently sold in the United States as the VideoComp 820.

Dr. Hell made his plans known in a speech at an international industry exhibition in 1965, and at that time a laboratory model had been built which set type on 70 mm film. Presentations were made, slides were shown, and in February 1966 a prototype of the 50T1 was shown at the Hannover fair. Just shortly before this, Dr. Hell, in a visit to the States, described the project to RCA at about the time that RCA's newly formed Graphic Systems Division was getting off the ground. RCA itself was researching the same type of product.

An arrangement was therefore made by RCA to market the Digiset 50T1 as the VideoComp 820. Shortly thereafter RCA began to press for a more sophisticated version, and the 50T2 came into being. This product was marketed in the U.S. as either the VideoComp 830 or 840, or later, as the 800-series VideoComp with various options. Hell supplied only the back end of the 50T2, and it continued to produce its own hard-wired front end for the European market. However, RCA used a small computer (the 1600) to serve as a front end controller for the U.S. market.

Hell delivered a total of 89 Digisets to RCA from 1967 through 1971. These consisted either of 820s or the output end of the 50T2. At one time, during RCA's venture into the typesetter business, there were possibly about 46 VideoComps in the field. Information International, Incorporated (also known as III or Triple-I) subsequently took over the VideoComp project when RCA decided to abandon it. III continued to service and to sell the 800-series machines and then developed its own model which it called the 570.[1] In the meantime, Hell went its own way and has manufactured and marketed a series of its own including the 40T1, the 40T2, the 40T3 and a lower-cost 20T2. In the interest of brevity we shall discuss only the basic principles underlying the VideoComp products, with particular emphasis upon the features which seem to us significant to indicate the march of technology in the typesetting area.

The RCA VideoComp 820. The first machine to be introduced was quite limited in the measure to which it could set. The typesetting aperture, when reduced by a sizing lens to approximately three-fourths of its original dimensions, permitted a line 32.5 picas in length by 56 points. Size ranges from 4 to 24 points (except for 11 points) could be set, with no half point sizes. Size range I provided 4, 5, 6, 7, 8, 9, 10 and 12 point images with stroking resolutions of 300 to 900 per inch. Size range II offered 8, 10, 12, 14, 6, 18, 20 and 24 points, again within the 300 to 900 resolution range. Horizontal sizes of characters could be determined independently of vertical sizes, but both had to be within the same size range. Characters could be obliqued by command, with the normal angle of 15 degrees. The machine would film advance in a forward direction only.

Optimum performance from both the 820 and the computer used to drive it could be achieved only if all fonts required would fit into memory at one time. It was possible to fit four fonts of size range I, two of II, or two of I plus one of II.

In the typical installation, fonts would be stored on disk as part of a computer composition program. When the magnetic tape to drive the VideoComp was prepared the first fonts required for the job would be pulled off the disk pack and written onto the front of the tape. Thereafter, the input tape would contain text interspersed with font stroke information for such font changes as were required. Reloading the memory of the VideoComp would take a little over one second of time on computer and typesetter. Consequently, throughput setting speed would be profoundly influenced by the number of times new fonts or font replacements would have to be read into memory. Optimum output speeds assuming no font changes could run as high as 600 characters per second.

This device was sold, with magnetic tape reader, for $236,500 in the late 1960s.

The RCA VideoComp 830. The 830 used a finer resolution CRT, enlarging the image (2:1) rather than reducing it. This made it possible to set a measure 68 picas wide by 96 points tall, providing a line

1. Subsequently it also introduced the InfoSet 400, a lower-priced, wide-measure machine intended primarily for newspaper applications.

Third-Generation Typesetters

length of nearly 70 picas—wide enough to set a five column telephone directory.

Five master point sizes were offered, each one setting a portion of the entire range, from 4 points to 96. Some half point sizes were available and characters could be set in any combination of point and set size within a given size range. Leading was offered only in a forward direction in increments of one-thirty-second of a point, taking into consideration base line deflection as well as leading pure and simple. Resolution generally ran from 400 to 900 lines per inch. A micro-image optional attachment could be purchased to set 35 mm microfilm.

Speed on the 830 depended upon the nature of the fonts, but with Type I fonts (of superior resolution), setting speeds would typically exceed 1,000 characters per second. Delays were encountered in font loading, as on the 820, but greater flexibility was offered with respect to font storage so that font subsets, rather than the entire font, could be loaded into memory.

The purchase price of the 830 was $337,975, obviously not a typical trade compositor's tool. An 840 model helped to solve the font storage problem by providing an on-line disk to the typesetter's 1600 minicomputer so that fonts no longer had to be loaded along with the text stream.

The Autologic APS-2 and APS-3. The Alphanumeric Photocomposition System (APS) was developed by Alphanumeric, Inc., a Long Island-based company which is no longer in business. The original APS-2 typesetter was developed by the company for its own use in a service bureau setting. The machine was redesigned as the APS-3, and was also marketed for a while by IBM as its 2680. Like most of the other CRT devices, the APS-3/2680 did not use the entire face of the tube, but rather a narrow horizontal aperture across its middle. But to maximize setting speed the machine composed type on the CRT *uphill within the aperture* at the same rate that the film advanced. This eliminated the need for a delay while film or paper was advanced under normal operating conditions.

The principal difference in its method of character selection from the VideoComp was that Alphanumeric used a separate master character for each type size, rather than electronically enlarging or reducing from a few size ranges. The normal resolution was 800 lines per inch. Sizes from 4 to 18 points were offered, with no half-point sizes, and fonts were stored on a disk or drum for relatively fast access. Alphanumeric secured a patent on a method of font compression so that fonts stored on disk could be recorded in a relatively compact manner.[1] The key to this method of font compression was to describe only the manner in which a succeeding stroke differed from the one that went before. A typical 10-point character thus might require only about 80 bytes of information. Hence more fonts could be stored in the memory of the typesetter at one time.

The machine offered a maximum line length of 50 picas with a maximum point size of 18 points. Dot size was 1¼ mil with lens

1. Alphanumeric's "Schwartz" patent covered the description of digitized characters by recording starting and stopping points in a manner such as run-length encoding. Their "Manber" patent covered a technique for reducing the amount of information which needed to be stored.

magnification from CRT to film plane of 2:1. In the normal mode with 800 line-per-inch resolution, optimum setting speeds averaged about 2,000 characters per second at eight points.

Perhaps 20 APS-3 machines were manufactured to be sold at $385,000 each. A half dozen found their way into Alphanumeric service centers. Most of the others—if sold at all—were shipped abroad, principally to Japan. The APS-3 is primarily of interest because it was the predecessor of the APS-4 and APS-5 machines which we shall discuss shortly.

The Fototronic CRT. The Harris Corporation (then Harris-Intertype) entered the CRT market in 1968 when it introduced the Fototronic CRT. A basic machine cost $350,000, with a 512-character font storage memory on a revolving drum, with a larger drum capable of storing twice as many characters.

Some 18 machines were manufactured and sold between 1969 and 1973. Two features were particularly interesting. First, characters were not created by vertical stroking—possibly to get around the Alphanumeric patent. Instead they were painted by a more or less random movement of the CRT writing beam. Each character consisted of a set of patches of dots, and each patch had a common base line reference point. Three, four or more patches would comprise the entire character. When the character was called for, the typesetter could access a certain track on the revolving drum with a fixed read head for each track on the drum. That read head would pull off the first available patch or segment of the character and continue to read in these segments and to paint them on the output device until the entire character had been created. In general, depending upon the character's size and the number of dots it comprised, one character, in segments, could be stored at least twice on a track in order to minimize access time.

Again, characters were stored for distinct size ranges and could be sized, obliqued and expanded or condensed electronically. The normal resolution for the master fonts was 720 lines per inch. The lens magnification factor (from CRT to film plane) was 1:1, making for a relatively sharp image, even with a dot size of 2.5 mils.

The machine could set type in sizes from 3 to 28 points in one-half point increments. Electronic obliquing was also provided at a 20° angle. Forward or reverse leading was available in increments of one-tenth point, making this the most flexible machine, capable of setting the highest quality type of any such device on the market prior to the early 1970s. A shifting film carriage was available as an option, extending the maximum settting width from 51 picas to 69.[1]

1. RCA also made one CRT typesetter with a shifting film carriage. It was called the 822X and was sold to Time, Inc. for full-page composition of *Time* pages at the plant of a Chicago printer.

The Autologic APS-4 and APS-5. In late 1970 Photon announced that it would market a new CRT phototypesetter to be developed by Autologic, Inc., then a subsidiary of Alphanumeric. The specifications quoted for the machine sounded completely competitive with the VideoComp and the Fototronic CRT but the price, on the other hand, was to be competitive with the Linotron 505. That machine

Third-Generation Typesetters

reached the market as the Photon 7000 in 1971. The arrangement between Autologic and Photon subsequently collapsed and the device became the APS-4.

Alphanumeric had run out of money trying to operate typesetting service bureaus. A small company it had acquired in California, called Autologic, was able to survive on its own and inherited the Alphanumeric patents. The engineering work which led to the APS-4 was done by Autologic itself, but there are certain similarities between the APS-3 (and even more with the APS-2) and the APS-4.

As with most other CRT typesetters, type is generated a line at a time across the face of a high-resolution CRT and focused onto moving photographic film or paper. Fonts are digitally coded and are stored on a moving head disk. A font change is effected simply by calling the appropriate digital coding from disk into the memory of the typesetter's minicomputer controller. Unlike the Alphanumeric machines which required a separate master for each size, the APS-4 adopted the sizing conventions of the VideoComp, but offered many more combinations. In fact, type can be sized in one-tenth point increments so that it is possible to set a character 8.7 points high by 9.3 set wide, or 63.8 points high by 52.9 points wide. In addition, obliquing is possible to the user's specifications, which may be changed upon command, and may be implemented as a left or right slant in increments of one-tenth degree from -45° to +45°.

The APS-4 uses a typesetting window 4¼ inches wide by one-half inch tall on the face of a 5-inch tube. This is generally enlarged 2.2 times to provide a 57-pica aperture. The APS-4 sold for $125,000 with 16K of memory and a 500 character-per-second paper tape reader. With magnetic tape input and 32K words of memory the price was $146,000. A 100-pica machine was subsequently developed, consisting of two overlapping output tubes. It cost $210,000 with magnetic tape input.

The Autologic APS-5. In the fall of 1975 Autologic began making shipments of a new CRT typesetter priced at under $80,000. It involved a significant redesign of the APS-4, although the two machines are quite similar in basic concept. The principal differences are that the optical bed in the "5" is mounted vertically rather than horizontally, helping to make the "5" more compact than the "4." The "5" uses analog circuitry for correction of distortion across the tube, while the "4" uses a digital technique. At the time of this writing (1983) the "5" is still available as a 57-pica machine, using a 2.2 enlarging lens or 70 picas using a 2.6 lens.

A "5U" version could be upgraded to a 100-pica machine. The APS 5/100 uses a 10" tube rather than a 5" one, with a 2X enlarging lens to set a full 100-pica width.

The APS-5 is offered with a nonremovable 2.5 million character disk with optional 10 million and 100 million character storage disks. It offers only one oblique angle rather than 900—namely 12.5°.

Four font masters are required to cover the entire size range. On the 57-pica machine a 10-point master covers 5 through 12.5 points the 20-point master covers 10 through 25 points, the 40-point master covers 20 through 50 points, and the 80-point master covers 40 through 80 points.

The output writing dot is approximately 1.4 mils at the master size. Stroking spacing at master size is 720 lines per inch and characters are also divided into 720-per-inch segments in the vertical direction. As type is scaled, stroking resolution may vary from 1,440 lines per inch down to 600 lines per inch. Because font master size ranges overlap, it is never necessary to use a resolution of less than 720 lines per inch up to 80-point type.

Output speed is limited to 500 cps when reading from paper tape, but when running on line to a host computer or from magnetic tape input speed will be approximately 2,000 newspaper lines per minute.

It is interesting to consider—given Autologic's font compaction techniques—how many fonts can be stored in memory at one time, and how many can be stored on one 2.5 million byte disk. (Bear in mind that additional or larger disks can also be configured.) The following table indicates the number of characters which will fit into the core memory if the memory is 16K or 32K and would thus be accessible without any time loss:

		16K	32K
Techno Medium	Size range 1	341	1,024
	2	222	668
	3	107	321
	4	57	173
Times Roman	Size range 1	263	789
	2	160	481
	3	80	240
	4	52	157

In the instances in which an entire font will not fit into memory at one time (*e.g.*, a large-sized master font with a 16K machine memory), the font will automatically be segmented and loaded into memory in pieces as needed.

As to disk storage, if every font is required in all four master sizes, at least 30 100-character fonts may be stored on one 2.5 million byte disk. But since some fonts are used for text only and some for display, many more text fonts can be stored. In text sizes they take up much less room.

A double-disk configuration would store at least 35 additional fonts in all four size ranges. If only size range 1 masters were stored, a double-disk system would accommodate at least 600 different fonts.

The reader should remember that a font can produce a large number of point sizes and variations of point and set sizes. If one wished to duplicate such a library of magazines for a linecasting machine one would require literally hundreds of thousands of such magazines.

Third-Generation Typesetters

The MGD Metro-set. The CRT typesetter introduced by the Information Products Division of MGD (Miehle-Goss Dexter, a division of North American Rockwell) was relatively short-lived. It was a highly successful device but the company decided not to continue to offer products directed toward photocomposition applications and discontinued manufacture of the Metro-set and other similar products, selling its customer base and "know-how" to Information International. There would be no need to mention this product at all except for the fact that it differed from other CRT typesetters on the market in one very interesting respect. While characters were generated by vertical strokes, as with the VideoComps and APS models, these strokes were not stored as digital starting and stopping points. What was stored on disk was a description of the character outline, made up of descriptors of outline segments—an idea borrowed from a company named Seaco which manufactured several prototype CRT typesetters but went bankrupt prior to MGD's entry into the field.

When these outlines were called from disk to the typesetter, specially configured hardware studied the outline of the character (much as if it were scanning it) and then generated a stroking pattern for the desired size. This meant that, unlike most other digital CRT typesetters, MGD would set type at any size (within the range of 5 to 72 points) from the same master and without varying the resolution of the character in terms of strokes per inch, just as was the case with CRT typesetters using photographic masters for font storage.

Three resolution modes were offered: one of 744 lines per inch and a second at 1488 lpi. In addition, a low-resolution proof mode was provided, with a stroke density of 496 lpi. In all modes, the resolution in the vertical direction was a constant 1,024 dots per inch.

To set type from a given font master, the Metro-set would call up from disk the digital coding which would describe that font and load it directly into one of the two 4K memory banks in the stroking processor. Metro-set fonts could contain up to 126 characters and there were almost no fonts which could be completely contained in 4K of core memory. Depending upon the complexity of the font, between 50 and 100 character masters would fit into memory at one time. Thus a portion of the memory bank was reserved for so-called "transient" characters. The Metro-set would look ahead into the input text stream in order to load the coding for these characters from disk into core before they were required. The Metro-set was the first machine to use look-ahead logic for this purpose. Subsequently, other manufacturers (notably Harris and Mergenthaler) applied the same principles and Compugraphic applied a similar concept to its Videosetter Universal.

The Metro-set used a large 11"-diameter output tube with a fiber optics face plate. No magnification or reduction in stroke size could be achieved. The image was always set at the same size at which it was generated on the tube.

Another interesting feature of the machine was that it would set as many lines of type as would fit within the one-inch aperture before advancing the film.

Other CRT typesetters. As we have seen, during a period of less than ten years, the price of a high-speed cathode ray tube digital typesetter dropped from more than $300,000 to less than $100,000. All this occurred during a period of time when the general price level of other things was increasing dramatically. And the benefits of modern electronics continue to offer ever lower prices.

These and other manufacturers introduced yet other products. There was the Harris Fotronic 7400, which was introduced in 1976, a 100-pica version called the 7600, and a subsequently redesigned machine called the 7500. There was the Mergenthaler Linotron 606 and the 404, and finally the Linotron 202 was introduced in 1978. This machine was offered on the market for well less than $50,000 so that lower-speed second-generation machines and higher-speed CRT typesetters actually overlapped in terms of price. The 202, for example, was intended as a replacement for Mergenthaler's V-I-P second-generation machine and it did indeed make significant inroads into the same market—namely the quality trade typesetter.

The speed of the 202 was considerably less than that of the APS-4 or the APS-5 which succeeded it. It was not nearly as great as that of the APS-Micro-5, a $57,000 entry of Autologic with a rated setting speed of 1,000 newspaper lines per minute. The 202 is rated at approximately 450 lines per minute—about the same as the Compugraphic (photographic master) Videosetter, and from one-third to one-sixth the speed of an APS-5, a Linotron 606 or the later model VideoComp, the 570.

The 202 also made use of outline fonts with the same masters for a wide range of sizes, and it too used a fiber optics face plate.

Yet another interesting entry was the Alphatype CRS typesetter, which was introduced in 1977. Oddly enough this was intended to be quite a slow-speed CRT typesetter, offering an unusually compact character resolution. In some respects it was similar to the Linotron 505 or 303 since escapement was provided by mechanical movement—in this case the movement of a travelling lens which stepped across the film plane as each vertical stroke of the character was generated. The stroke size (generated at a very large scale on a very inexpensive TV tube) was reduced by a lens in the ratio of 30:1, thus affording the incredible resolution or stroke spacing of 5,000 strokes per inch. Adjacent strokes overlap by approximately one-third. The spot size on the film plane is approximately one-third of a mil. Stated output speed is 50 newspaper lines per minute in sizes not larger than twelve points. Discrete master sizes for each point size are loaded.

Compugraphic introduced its 8600 CRT typesetter (speed 860 lines per minute) in order to offer a digital machine to replace its earlier third-generation photographic master product, the Videosetter. This typesetter was intended to compete with the Linotron 202 in the under-$50,000 price range. Yet a cheaper model, setting at 150 lines per minute, is represented by the 8400 at a price under $30,000.

At the upper end of the scale, the III VideoComp 570 carries a price tag of more than $188,000. It is a "full-face" typesetter. Instead of stroking within an aperture, it sets type over the entire face of

Third-Generation Typesetters

the CRT tube so that it is not necessary to advance the film or paper until an entire page has been composed, and to lay down several columns of type on the same page it is not necessary for the machine to reverse lead in order to reposition the film or paper for the setting of a third column (or to sort the text so that all columns can be composed across the face of the tube). Instead, type can be laid down at any location on a page simply by moving the stroking beam from one place to another.

The VideoComp 570 has also been used to typeset pictures as well as type characters. This capability will be discussed at some length in Chapter 21.

"Direct-input" CRT phototypesetters

WE HAVE SEEN that third-generation typesetters have experienced dramatic price reductions. At the same time they have become increasingly reliable and the quality of the type image they can set has made dramatic improvements. But the time has also come when the principles that underlie these machines can also be applied in an entirely different market—namely the very low cost personal typesetters or direct-entry machines.

When typesetting devices are extremely expensive it is, of course, necessary to seek to produce a considerable volume of work from the same device so that it can pay its way on a per-page basis. This means, of course, that the input to such a device must be derived from the keyboarding efforts of a large number of persons, or the device must be used to set and reset files of text which have been accumulated over a period of time and are maintained to be updated and revised (as with telephone directories).

But when it is possible to manufacture such machines at significantly lower prices it is economically feasible to use them in a setting on which they may only require the output of one or a few persons. Of course, one may argue that there is no need for applying the esoteric technology of a CRT machine to an environment where the quality and quantity of type required may be produced quite satisfactorily by a second-generation typesetter of the photomechanical variety.

But the fact is that CRT typesetters are much more flexible. They can offer a much wider variety of type sizes on line at any time. They can manipulate the type electronically. And they may prove to be much more trouble-free than second-generation machines.

So we have indeed seen, especially since 1980, the application of this same third-generation technology to low-priced units which may even be intended simply to keep up with the output of a single keyboarder, or perhaps two or three. By 1983 the Mergenthaler CRTronic and the AM Varityper 6400 were beginning to be widely used. The CRTronic, for example, stores digital fonts in the form of character outlines on a floppy disk and this outline information is loaded into the memory of the machine when the font is called for by the text. The outline is converted into stroking and sizing information and the character is actually typeset by the movement of a tiny CRT tube across the film plane. Thus there is the mechanical motion of the second-generation typesetter so far as character (or more precisely stroke) lay down is concerned. Mechanical motion of a very similar nature took place in the Linotron 303, except that this was a much more expensive machine, and it digitized its images "on the fly" from photographic masters. However, the stroke lay down of the newer machines with digital masters can often be quite sophisticated. It may even be possible, in some instances, to set strokes representing several lines of characters as the tube passes across the film, just as several lines of type might be set within the same aperture of a larger CRT tube before film or paper advance takes place.

For example, on the CRTronic, the moving tube (*see illustration*) can stroke characters in two lines at once in all sizes up to 14 points so long as the leading between lines does not exceed 14 points. This means that each stroke in these smaller point sizes actually paints out a portion of two characters as the tube moves "boustrophedonically," that is forward and backward "as the ox ploughs." On the other hand, to set characters above 54 points (up to the maximum of 72 points) the images are segmented and overlapped.

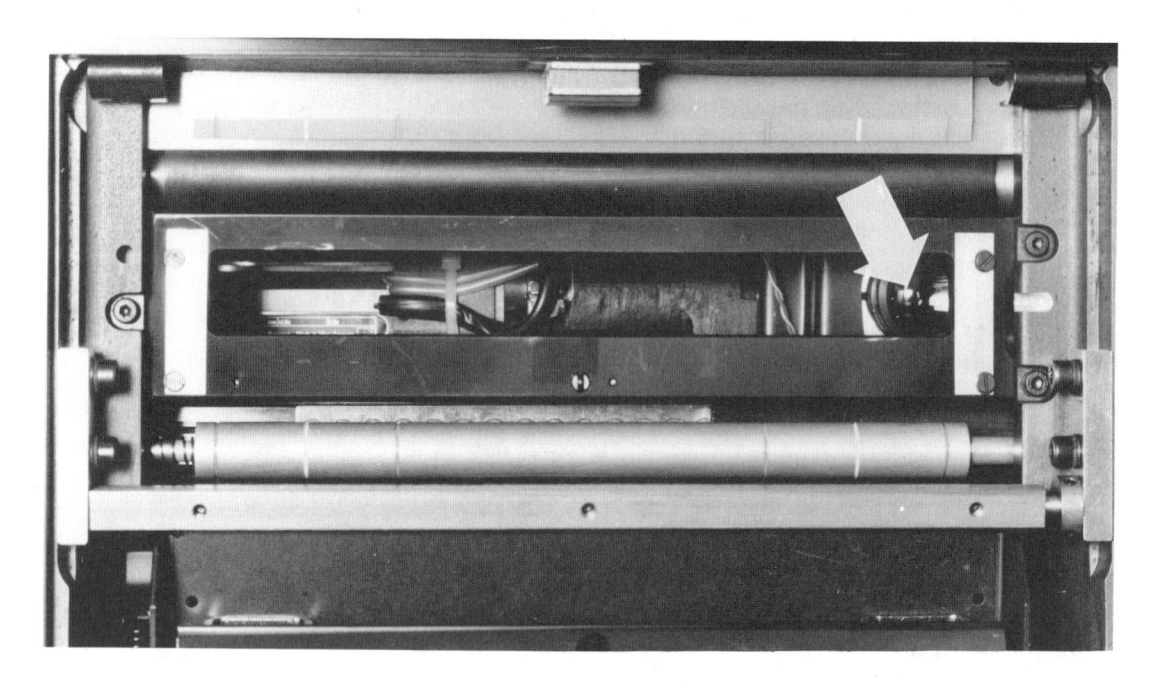

The Mergenthaler Linotype CRTronic. The arrow indicates the small cathode ray tube which moves back and forth across the film plane, laying down character strokes as it moves in either direction. The photographic paper moves in front of the aperture and is advanced in increments which can be as small as one-tenth of a point. Reverse leading is also provided. The machine has the capability, from the same digitized masters, of sizing characters in one-tenth point increments and to vary set size from 50% of the point size to 200%, with the ability to slant each master size. At the time of its introduction (1979 in Germany, 1980 in the U.S.) it offered the greatest versatility of any direct-entry typesetting machine. Character resolution is 1,270 lines per inch. Yet the entire machine (typesetter and keyboard) fits on a desk top.

Third-Generation Typesetters *137*

More to come? It will be evident to the reader that vendors have shown no lack of imagination in designing new third-generation typesetters. There is no reason to expect that other similar machines—with different combinations of features—will not be introduced in the future. Prices continue to fall due to the continued impact of new technology.

Fourth-generation technology

ALL OF THE TYPESETTERS we have described as third generation are CRT machines. You will recall that some of them store their type images photographically and some digitally. Some of the machines require a moving part to sweep the strokes across the film plane. Most do not. Some (the VideoComp 570 and certain models of the Hell Digiset) offer a full-face capability, while the others set type within an aperture of the tube. Some of the latter move the paper or film continuously across the face of the tube while the paper is advancing ("dynamic leading"). For the most part those machines that compose within an aperture offer reverse leading to permit the setting of multicolumn material, but this feature would not be necessary on a full-face machine where the beam can be directed to the area where the next block of text is to be positioned.

Some machines magnify or reduce the image between the CRT tube and the film plane. Others use a fiber optics face plate which transfers the same-size image from CRT tube to film.

Some machines also offer a microfilm or microfiche option so that the image generated on the surface of the tube can be written out as full pages in the very tiny size which micro-imaging devices require. And some CRT typesetters make it possible for the user to digitize and reproduce not only type but line drawings or halftones. (See Chapter 21.)

But we have not exhausted the possibilities in the design of typesetters by any means. It is possible for a laser platemaker to be a typesetter. It is possible for an office copying machine to generate its own type. It is possible, at least in theory, for an electronic camera to set type. Most of these devices make use of laser technology and most of them function in a raster scan mode. For present purposes all we need to know about the laser is that it is capable of generating a very fine and very intense spot of light. It is possible to interrupt this light source so that the light emissions can be pulsed or timed to coincide with some other event. It is also possible to deflect the light from a mirrored surface and to rotate that mirror so that the light beam will sweep a given area. Within certain limits it is also possible to deflect the laser beam in a vertical as well as a horizontal direction.[1]

On the other hand, the Monotype Lasercomp which will be discussed in Chapter 23,[2] uses a raster scan technology but is able to lay down not individual characters which are made up of slices or dots on a character-by-character basis, but a horizontal slice of an entire page, so that no single character is formed until all the dots or pixels in the same line or row are also laid down.

1. This was true, for example, of the Dymo DLC 1000, which used a laser to stroke characters in much the same fashion as with CRT typesetters. This device was developed, exhibited, but then withdrawn from the market during a period of company reorganization.

2. See especially pp. 386*ff.*

As composition programs, including page make-up, become more and more sophisticated, and as computer memories become larger and cheaper, it becomes increasingly possible to hold in memory a "bit map" of all the tiny dots or spots that a laser (or conceivably an ink jet) would be called upon to lay down during one sweep across the page. While this technology seems very complex, it is likely that this method of setting type will be used increasingly, and there are similarities between the Lasercomp, the ECRM Autokon electronic camera, and the EOCOM laser platemaker.

Yet other technologies are available. Some we know about; others we do not. For example, in 1983 the Itek company introduced the Digitek which forms characters by sweeping a small (12-point high) write-head made up of 128 optical fibers, each of a diameter of two thousandths of an inch. The other end of each fiber is attached to a very tiny light-emitting diode (LED).

Whether this device belongs to a fifth generation of typesetters or, because of the mechanical motion involved, might better be described as a third and one-half generation machine could be a moot point. For the moment, at least, it seems as though the concept of new generations is no longer useful and that post-third generation will suffice.

The Itek Digitek is also a direct-entry typesetter, and while it is made up of two boxes, it too is a desk-top device. This is the LED fiber optics machine (Itek calls it an "LFO") which is described above.

10

Basic Computer Concepts

COMPUTERS began to impact society immediately after World War II, although at first the apparent impact was minimal. As they have gone through various stages—from large, vacuum-tube monstrosities that occupied entire rooms to tiny desk top or even portable microprocessors—they have profoundly affected the way we live and conduct our businesses—and even the way we think about society and its problems.

Obviously this book is not the place to chronicle the history and development of computers or to discuss their sociological consequences. We must assume that the reader is either reasonably familiar with what computers are and can do, or will make it his business to acquire a sufficient understanding to follow our exposition. But for those whose exposure to computers has been minimal or nonexistent (if indeed there are any such among our readers), we will offer some background detail in order to provide a common vocabulary for subsequent discussions. However, many of you who have worked with and/or used computers or engaged in programming activity, will find it sufficient simply to thumb through this chapter.

There are very few inventions throughout the history of the world that have had or will have the impact of the modern computer. In point of fact, even the science of mathematics—or more precisely of numbers—is itself of more recent origin than many of us may have imagined. Positional notation—such as the decimal system—apparently was first developed by the Babylonians about 3000 B.C., but was subsequently lost to posterity. The Mayans, around 200 A.D., developed what is said to have been a comparable concept, but it too had no impact upon our civilization. The Hindus, on the other hand, made substantial contributions to algebra during the period from 500 to 1200 A.D.

It was the Arabs in the ninth century who developed decimal notation, yet it was not until the twelfth century that roman numerals began to be superseded by Arabic numbers in Europe. We are told that the Arabic system was in general use for scientific purposes by 1400, although "no Arabic numerals are to be found in English parish registers or Manor Court rolls before the sixteenth century."[1] The multiplication table was still a mystery to most educated people even in the seventeenth century!

Mechanical calculating devices, as distinguished from the ancient abacus, came into being in the seventeenth century. Until the middle of the twentieth century gears were employed to provide a method of

1. See the discussion in *Electronic Computers* by S. H. Hollingdale and G.C. Toothill, Penguin Books, 1965, especially p. 15.

"carrying" from one row of numbers to another. The developing of a "setting" counter and a "result" counter made the mechanical process of addition possible.

Blaise Pascal (1623-1662), the French philosopher and mathematician, is generally given credit for the development of the first mechanical calculating machine. This was essentially an adding and subtracting tool. Multiplication could be carried forward only as repeated steps in addition. Leibnitz (1646-1716), the German mathematician, contributed to the ability to mechanize multiplication. For every addition a counter clocked the result, and division was derived similarly from the process of subtraction.

But writers reporting about modern computers generally start their history with Charles Babbage (1792-1871). It was in 1812 that he conceived the notion of computing and printing tables of mathematical functions through the construction of a Difference Engine. Unfortunately his machine was never completed, although several such devices subsequently were made. Babbage turned his attention to the idea of building an Analytical Engine which was to be a universal computer rather than a mere device for the solution of polynomials. In other words, Babbage's first concept was a special-purpose computer, and his second was to be a general-purpose instrument.

Those were the days in which inventiveness revolved largely around the capacity to devise intricate mechanical machines. Babbage's task was therefore to contrive ways of storing information in the form of gear movements and ratios. Each gear with ten teeth could in turn drive a second gear that would advance only one position when the first gear completed its entire rotation, and so on through each succeeding gear sequence. But to avoid the problem of setting the gears initially by hand, Babbage thought he might be able to use a system something like the one that Joseph Marie Jacquard (1752-1834) had developed for the weaving industry.

Jacquard had contrived a system of activating rods which would in turn lift warp threads so that the weaver's shuttle could pass underneath them. Each of a set of cards would be brought into contact with a set of rods in such fashion that in those instances in which the card contained no holes, the rods would be pushed into an alternate position.

Babbage conceived of the idea of using somewhat similar cards to serve two purposes: to handle the *input* data and to store the results—*output* or *interim output*.

Babbage continued to work on this project until his death in 1871. The problem was not with his conception. It was merely that the device conceived was too complex mechanically to provide sufficient accuracy and reliability. It was Augusta Ada, Countess of Lovelace (1815-1852), the only child of Lord and Lady Byron—a philosopher and mathematician in her own right—who undertook to create a chronicle of the Babbage project and who contributed substantially to its conceptual implications.

Our attention next focuses on Herman Hollerith, an employee of the U.S. Bureau of the Census, who took the Jacquard punched-card concept and applied it to the recording of such census data as could be answered by yes and no questions, or by grouping data into categories. By 1890 he had several machines in operation. It is believed, as we have already suggested, that his concepts influenced Tolbert Lanston in the development of the Monotype system.[1]

The tab card era

BY THE YEAR 1910 Hollerith tab card systems were beginning to be used quite widely, and until the advent of the modern digital computer, tabulating systems handled the bulk of the world's mechanized data processing applications. It is significant to note that by that time the tabulating process, with its use of punched cards, had turned to electrical circuits—unlike the rods employed by Jacquard, the gears of Babbage, or the columns of compressed air utilized by Lanston. When a punched card was fed into one of the several machines developed to perform various types of calculating and related tasks, electrical contacts were made. The reading of a hole in a column was accomplished by an electrical brush coming into contact with a metal roller.

Among the tasks to be performed was the sorting of alphabetic lists. Generally this was accomplished by reading information from only one of the 80 columns at one time. Thirteen alternative vertical holes are available in each column, and thirteen pockets could be provided for sorting purposes. A plug board could alter the electrical circuits so that not all thirteen alternatives needed to be selected, and some deselecting could also occur.

Once the first column was examined and cards assigned to bins in accordance with the value of the figure in the first column, a similar processing run could take place for all the cards which had been sorted into the first bin in order to subsort these and to arrange them in a secondary sequence. Then all of the cards with common letters or digits in the first two columns could be sorted with respect to the information provided in the third column, etc.

Many other functions could be performed by tabulating equipment, such as addition, subtraction, multiplication, and even printing (*e.g.*, checks or tables of results). Also, these tasks could be performed at what seemed to be relatively high speeds, since such cards could be read at the rate of several hundred per minute, and various types of calculations or functions could be carried forward at comparable speeds. Cards thus provided the initial input, and results could also be recorded automatically on similar cards. Moreover, information could be printed on a tabulating or printing unit which worked very much like an upper-case typewriter.

And so between the period of World War I and World War II the tabulating machine came into its own. But it was no doubt World War II that provided the impetus for the first truly electronic calculator. This invention is generally credited to J.P. Eckert and J.W. Mauchly, of the Moore School of Electrical Engineering at the University of Pennsylvania, although a British professor, Alan Turing, an

1. See Chapter 5, pp. 51-52.

American zoologist, Norbert Wiener, and Howard H. Aiken, also had done prior pioneering work which culminated in the 1938 model of the Automatic Sequence Controlled Calculator of the Mathematical Institute of Harvard University.

The Eckert-Mauchly *ENIAC*—Electronic Numerical Integrator and Calculator—was intended to assist in the computation of missile trajectories. Eniac differed from its predecessors in that it performed all of its functions by means of electronics, except for the tasks of reading or punching cards. Eniac contained 18,000 vacuum tubes! It was not a binary, but rather a decimal, machine. A special circuit was developed which kept track of pulses and "carried" a digit when the tenth pulse was received.

However, Eniac was a special-purpose computer. Each program had to be loaded into the machine by wiring the required functions.

Eniac was in operation by 1945, and in 1946 John Von Neumann came to the fore in presenting more clearly the analogy between the performance of *logical functions* and those which had to do with mathematical or arithmetic calculations. It quickly became apparent that binary systems were both more reliable and easier to design than decimal systems, and were better able to perform logical tasks. Finally, during the 1950s, and particularly during the 1960s, cheaper, faster, and more dependable circuits were constructed which no longer required the use of vacuum tubes, but could use the newly-invented transistors in the first place, and, somewhat later, silicon chip technology.

Two problems, apart from cost, plagued the vacuum tube technology. One was the problem of reliability. It was simply impossible to depend upon 18,000 or more such tubes to work as they were supposed to function, all at the same time. The second problem was the amount of heat generated, which had disastrous effects upon other electrical components.

Transistors, happily, were developed just at the critical time. They generate very little heat, take up little space, last hundreds of times longer than vacuum tubes, and can therefore be configured into more elaborate systems, capable of performing functions more rapidly. Transistors are "semi-conductors" consisting mainly of a crystalline substance such as silicon and germanium, into which certain impurities are introduced. Two negative-type semi-conductors are generally separated by a positive wafer. These three substances are usually sealed in plastic, with a wire leading from each segment. The wires are connected to an electric circuit, and if the electronic components of the segments are properly designed, a small current flowing between the emitter (one n-type element), the base (a p-element), and the collector (another n-element) produces a current amplification.

The transistor was the product of a joint effort of John Bardeen, Walter H. Brattain, and William Shockley (all of whom later shared a Nobel prize). It was announced by the Bell laboratories in 1948. A transistor has no filament, requires no warm-up, and generates little heat. Transistors can be mounted on small boards and connected

Basic Computer Concepts

together by wire wrapping or by printed circuits. These boards or panels can be mounted vertically and side by side within a small area. Individual boards can easily be replaced.

It was not until the mid-'50s and the early '60s that transistor technology took over. In the later 1960s and early 1970s, LSI (large-scale integrated circuits) of MOS (metal oxide silicon) chips introduced another dramatic change, since just as one small circuit board (say of postcard size) could replace a large cabinet of vacuum tubes, so one chip the size of a pinhead can replace several hundred or more circuit boards.

The use of Boolean logic

GEORGE BOOLE, English mathematician and logician (1815-1864) was a relatively obscure professor at Queen's College in Cork, Ireland, and published *An Investigation of the Laws of Thought* in 1854 as well as some works on calculus and differential equations. Boole sought to apply mathematical principles to logical thought and was therefore one of the founders of *symbolic logic*. He developed a set of concepts perhaps more basic than the Aristotelian propositions (*e.g.*, syllogisms) and certainly more valid for the analysis of problems and the pursuit of inductive reasoning processes. Most of the logical propositions that are currently related to the computer's electronic circuitry and much of the programming logic which utilizes this circuitry, derive from Boole's work and from his propositions. These can be stated in terms of electronic circuitry design or as logical statements. Improvements in methodology were contributed by Augustus De Morgan (a contemporary of Boole's), John Stuart Mill, Lord Bertrand Russell, and Alfred North Whitehead.

Logical propositions lie at the heart of the computer's electronic circuitry. To be sure, there are many tasks which are procedural in nature: the reading in of data, the output of information, and even the performance of arithmetic functions. But there must be an underlying set of logical principles which can determine whether certain things are alike or different. You can't, of course, add apples and oranges, but you can count up the number of pieces of fruit on the table. We can therefore handle information constructively if we are painstakingly aware of the respects in which things are similar and in which they are different from each other. Thus we may find it necessary to talk about "people" (living or dead?), and also males and females, girls and boys (how defined?), as well as persons with other characteristics, such as education, experience, income, attitudes and innumerable other variables—all of which relate, somehow, to classes which serve to include or to exclude for whatever analytical purposes we may have in mind.

Such logical tasks may be performed quite simply by electronic circuitry. It is not our intention to provide an exhaustive account of principles of computer circuitry any more than it is to provide a dissertation on symbolic logic. Our intent is merely to give the reader some feeling for the nature of the concepts that are relevant.

Some electronic circuits

WHAT ARE the functions which computers are able to perform? Their tasks and capabilities are many and varied, and yet the essential processes are made up of a relatively small number of logical components. Basically, the ingredients consist of "and-gates," "or-gates," "negators," and "flip-flops."

These are, in substance, Boolean concepts which have electronic circuitry counterparts. Let us consider several of them.

A "gate" is what its name implies: some things enter and some things leave. But not everything which seeks to enter may be permitted to pass through. In the case of an "and-gate" only those things can leave which meet *all* of the relevant tests. There must be more than one such test. There may be two. There may be more than two.

Let us consider the "and-gate" which requires the presence of two conditions. We may say that only those things are "true" which satisfy both conditions. Visualize a light bulb which is connected to a battery with two switches wired in series. The light will only turn on (truth!) if both switches are closed. If either switch remains open the light cannot be illuminated. Hence "a" and "b" must both be true.

On the other hand, the "or-gate" could be like a light bulb in a circuit so wired that *either* of two switches, *or both*, will turn on the light. You can pass through the gate if you are either male or female. Both males and females may pass through the gate.

A "negator," on the other hand, has the simple property of turning whatever exists into its opposite, assuming that there is a true opposite—and the opposite may even be everything that isn't one specific thing. If a negative charge of electricity is sensed, it will be converted into a positive charge instead.

A "flip-flop" has the property of changing the state so that *either* one condition is true *or* an alternative obtains. Whereas a "negator" transforms one thing into another, a "flip-flop" selects one thing *rather than* the other, and what it selects is not necessarily the opposite. It simply leads us down a different path.

Without belaboring the point, it should be clear that quite complex logical decisions can be made electronically. For example, if we want to indicate a six-level code as one of 64 possible conditions to be recognized from a TTS tape, the logical diagram would look something like the following:

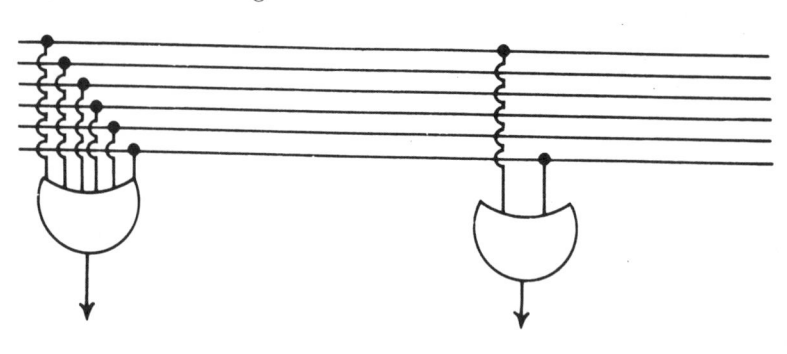

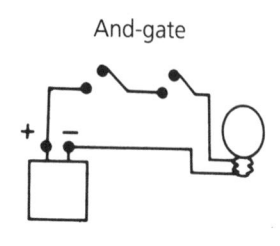

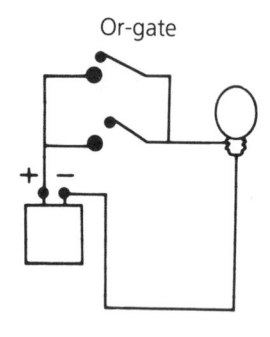

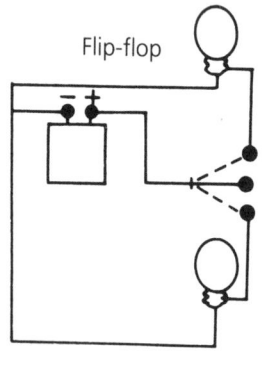

Basic Computer Concepts

On the preceding page are only two of the logical circuits necessary to pick out certain combinations of six bits. The first set of connections, on the left, presumes an "and-gate" which would require the presence of inputs from all six circuits (0 through 5). The second diagram, on the right, shows an "and-gate" which need only detect input from 0 and 5. A similar gating arrangement must be provided for every possible combination (63 in this instance). However, fewer different gates could be provided if successive gates were applied.

The structure of a computer

NOW LET US consider the structure of the computer itself. A computer may be said to be made up of five components:
1. One or more input devices.
2. Communicating channels.
3. A "mainframe" or "central processing unit" (CPU).
4. A "memory."
5. One or more output devices.

Increasingly, however, we will encounter other peripherals—that is, units which are added on to the computer system and somehow interfaced (or connected) to the computer in order to perform additional functions or to provide additional resources. A supplementary store of data may need to be consulted. A work area may need to be provided where tentative results may be stored for later reference. Methods of communicating may be desired for users who are located remotely.

Later on we shall discuss input and output at greater length. For the moment let us merely suppose that input can come (among other sources) from punched cards, from punched paper tape, from connecting keyboards, or from scanning and sensing devices.

Output can be directed toward a printer (usually called an on-line printer), or a console typewriter. Punched cards and magnetic tape can also serve for output purposes. Output sometimes consists merely of signals that some other mechanism such as the keyboard of a terminal, a paper tape punch, or in the case of "process control" devices, a milling machine, grinder or planer.

Communicating channels. At this point we wish to direct our attention to the communicating channels which connect the main frame or CPU to the input and output devices, and often link memory to the CPU itself. These channels or *buses* are also used to connect other peripheral devices which serve as a temporary store for data, such as magnetic tape drives or disks.

A channel not only *transmits* the flow of data, but also regulates and controls this flow so that it is synchronized with other operations. When a peripheral device is ready to transmit, the channel controller will be signaled. It will then accept the data or a manageable slice of it, often in a fashion which permits the virtually simultaneous transmission of other data in an overlapping manner. Information which is received as input may be accepted in an "asynchronous" mode which means that it comes more or less without warning and certainly not on any prearranged or clocked schedule, or it may be "synchronous" which means that the information is expected, and is clocked so that its processing corresponds to the operating speed or cycle time of the computer or of some of its components.

There are often two kinds of channels: multiplexor channels and selector channels. A multiplexor is used for slow peripheral equipment and breaks the channel down into what could be thought of as a number of subchannels. Data may be transmitted in tiny, encapsulated elements, in some order or sequence, from different devices, and are assigned work or storage areas which in effect permit the assembling and processing of data from one unique source, relating to one unique task, without regard to the fact that other information has been intermingled during the course of transmission. An example from the telephone industry is the ability to transmit many different conversations over the same wire at the same time without any user being bothered by, or even aware of, the fact that others are sharing the same line. Information which is received on a multiplexor channel may also be received in a "bit serial" fashion, rather than "parallel"—which means that it is received a bit at a time and, before processing, must be reconstructed into an array of bits which are to be analyzed simultaneously.

A selector channel, on the other hand, generally conveys information from only one source at a time in what is called a "burst" mode—which is a very rapid infusion of data which fully occupies the capacity of that high-speed channel for the period of time of the particular transmission.

To make it possible for channels to be used in these two ways, and especially to be capable of accepting several different kinds of assignments, such as to transmit data from input device to CPU on one occasion and from CPU to output device on another, there are controllers which operate in conjunction with the CPU to accept and process data in multiplexor and burst modes. Controllers vastly enhance the efficiency of the mainframe since the latter can be commanded to work on tasks already in hand rather than to wait until new data may be transmitted. Similarly, the processing of new information need not be delayed until the old has been disposed of (as output) since the CPU can continue to perform available work. In other words, the mainframe is not so likely to be "input bound" (tied up) and it can spend its time doing computations, rather than having to wait for input or output devices to perform their tasks.

The tasks we are speaking of may relate to other jobs if the computer is working in a "time-shared" or "multiprocessing" environment. Or they may simply have to do with the performance of a variety of different functions associated with the same job or task.

Channels and their controllers also provide the mainframe with certain other services: they will interrupt an operation to inform the CPU that an error condition exists or that the input has been terminated. They will also perform certain "storage protect" functions which prohibit the inadvertent destruction of stored information by

Basic Computer Concepts

preventing data from being written on top of useful tables, program areas, etc. "Read only" features exist which permit data to be picked up from a given location, but nothing new may be written to that location.

Another common type of computer architecture involves the use of the Unibus structure which is found in certain of Digital Equipment Corporation's PDP-11 minicomputers. In this case all computer system components and peripherals connect to and communicate with each other on a single high-speed bus known as the Unibus. With bidirectional and asynchronous communications on the Unibus, devices can send, receive and exchange data independently without processor intervention. Device communications on the Unibus are interlocked. For each command issued by a "master" device, a response signal is received from a "slave," completing the data transfer. Device-to-device communication is independent of the physical bus length and the response times of master and slave devices. Moreover, interfaces to the Unibus are not time-dependent. Input/output devices are nevertheless given the highest priority by a "bus arbitrator" and may request "bus mastership" and may "steal" bus and memory cycles during instruction operations. The processor resumes operation immediately after the memory transfer. Multiple devices can operate simultaneously at maximum direct memory access (DMA) rates by stealing bus cycles.

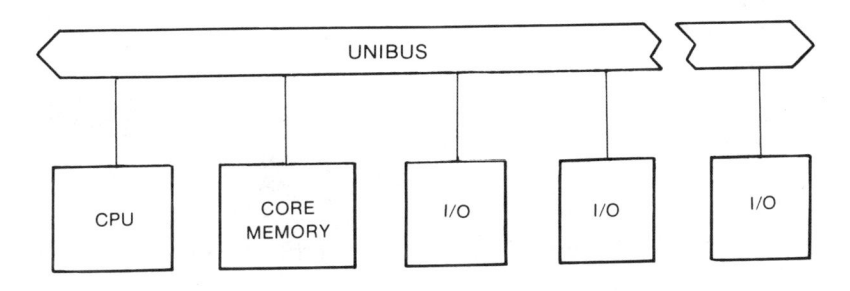

PDP-11/34 system simplifed block diagram

It may be seen, then, that there are various ways in which the mainframe may be related to its peripherals, and that the task of controlling many diverse operations is quite complex.

The mainframe or CPU

THE CENTRAL PROCESSOR generally has these elements:

1. A control unit
2. A storage unit
3. An arithmetic and logic unit
4. A set of registers

The control unit. This unit interfaces with the channels and their controllers, and it also coordinates the various functions within the mainframe itself. Control is partly "hardware" (wired instructions built into the computer), partly "software" (programs), and it can also be partly "firmware"—*i.e.*, programmed instructions which change the logic paths of the machine as they might otherwise be hard-wired, and usually stored permanently in nonvolatile memory, such as PROM (programmable read-only memory). It will not be necessary for our present purposes to discuss the intricacies of *control*. But it should be obvious that ability to execute commands and to keep track of data is essential to the functioning of the computer.

Storage. Data coming into the central processor needs to be put somewhere until it is processed, and then arranged in a store somewhere until it can be presented as output. Data (including the programs themselves) will be pigeonholed into "locations" which have "addresses" so that the information can be found when needed.

Data elements are stored in *memory* (or on disk, drum or tape) in the form of bits, bytes and words. A bit is the presence or absence of an event which can generate an electric pulse—whether the event is a hole in a paper tape or a positively or negatively charged minuscule doughnut-shaped piece of ferrite or by a fuse or electrical conductor which either permits passage of a current or does not.

In a sense, a bit is a switch, which is always in an on or off position, and it can be interrogated in order to find out which condition governs. Since we can only consider two conditions, we can describe bits as either 0 or 1, no or yes, true or false. Two bits taken together can describe four conditions:

$$00$$
$$01$$
$$10$$
$$11$$

In like manner, three bits can describe eight conditions:

000	100
001	101
010	110
011	111

Five bits can describe 32, six bits can describe 64, seven bits can describe 128, and eight bits can describe 256 different conditions.

Six-, seven-, or eight-bit bytes are or have been used most frequently to describe letters of the alphabet and other related symbols—especially in typesetting. But most people prefer to use the term byte to describe a string of eight bits.

The manner in which characters are stored in memory is a function of the size of the word or string of bits hitched together at one address and generally manipulated at one time (moved from one place to another, as from memory to a register). In the IBM 370-series computers, four bytes make up one word, and two bytes are

Basic Computer Concepts

considered a half word. But we often hear the term 16-bit words used to describe the manner in which memory is constituted. One might say, for example, that a certain mini- or microcomputer has 64K words representing a 128-byte machine, since two eight-bit bytes make up a 16-bit word.

For purposes of doing arithmetic, a four-bit byte may be sufficient. If we wish to deal only with decimal numbers we have need only for 0 through 9, plus a few control characters which should stand for functions like "end of message" or "end of record." But for the treatment of alphanumeric data (numbers plus letters), six or more bits in a byte are better. If we are not concerned with upper- and lower-case characters—and if our character set or character repertoire need not be extensive—a six-bit byte will be ample. We would only need:

```
26 letters
10 numbers
10 punctuation marks (approximately), and
 6 or so control codes
___
52
```

Therefore all of the most commonly desired characters could be described with six bits, and a computer printout with a print chain of 64 characters would be adequate.

By the use of a precedence code for upshift characters and another to signal a return to lower case (assigning other symbols to the number codes in upper case), a six-bit code structure—as in TTS—is sufficient, although an eight-bit byte offers greater latitude.

Using six-bits and a computer with a six-bit word we can visualize computer storage as consisting of memory which looks something like this:

Location	Bit Configuration
0	0 0 0 1 1 0
1	0 0 0 1 0 0
2	0 0 0 1 0 1
3	0 0 0 1 1 1

This could represent the number 6457, beginning at memory location 0.

And to handle text as well as numbers, if we wished to store the word "word" beginning in location 0, that portion of memory might look like this: (In this instance we are using TTS codes to describe the letters we wish to store. The internal language of the computer might well be ASCII, which, although made up of seven- or eight-level codes, resembles TTS for the six right-most bits.)

Location	Bit Configuration	Character
1	0 1 1 0 0 1	W
2	0 0 0 0 1 1	O
3	0 0 1 0 1 0	R
4	0 1 0 0 1 0	D

The concept of parity. Often, for purposes of assuring machine and transmission accuracy, an added bit is provided for in memory, and it may also be present on the paper tape, magnetic tape or disk platter which transmits information to and from the computer. This extra bit serves as a check to determine if the device which writes out or reads the codes is functioning properly. It is called a "parity check bit." Wiring and logic are added to the computer to cause it to count the number of "1" bits in a byte. If this number is odd, an additional "1" bit will be added to make it even (or *vice versa* if the object is to provide an *odd* parity check bit).

Parity Bit	Other Bits in Byte	Without Parity
1	0 0 0 0 0 1	odd
0	1 0 0 0 0 1	even
1	1 1 0 0 1 0	odd
0	1 1 0 0 1 1	even

A parity check means that the memory must always be configured to accommodate one additional bit for purposes of error checking, even though the parity bit is ignored for other purposes.

Other methods of parity checking may be used, such as a longitudinal parity check whereby all of the bits in a certain vertical row (for a given block of data) are counted and checked to determine whether the total is odd or even. Then a check byte is written at the end of each block, corresponding to the composite finding for all of the rows.

What is a convenient byte size?

IN A LATER chapter we will discuss special problems of typographic representation, storage and information transfer which arise from our typesetting and editing requirements. At this point we need say no more about the manner in which characters are stored and described other than to indicate that seven-bit bytes plus parity, making eight, or eight bits with or without an additional parity bit, are used much more frequently than are six.

Eight bits provides 256 distinct code combinations. The code structure which eight bits affords is often called hexadecimal although this term more properly describes a particular method of notation based upon the eight-bit byte coding structure. Hexadecimal means that the numbering system most convenient to this code structure is not based upon a set of ten, but rather upon a set of sixteen. A numerical set is a concept which relates to the number of units which can be described by a single digit (occupying only one row) when used for counting purposes. Sets are new math concepts well understood by young people but not so easily grasped by adults who learned their arithmetic twenty or more years ago. Perhaps we should digress briefly to talk about sets and particularly the hexadecimal and octal sets. But first let us consider the concept of binary notation.

Basic Computer Concepts

Binary. A binary set is made up of only two numbers: 0 and 1, and yet it is possible to count to infinity with such a system. The problem, nevertheless, remains one of describing the numbers you are counting. In pure binary arithmetic the only numbers you have available to work with are zero, one, ten, eleven, one hundred, one hundred and one, one hundred and ten, one hundred and eleven, one thousand, one thousand and one, and so forth. It might be difficult to follow the statement that I have 101 fingers on one hand and that the sum of fingers on both hands is 1010, and so it is easier to use binary notation, but to think in terms of a more inclusive set, such as decimal, octal, or even hexadecimal. Here we have a string of binary numbers with their decimal equivalents:

Binary	Decimal	Binary	Decimal
0	0	110	6
1	1	111	7
10	2	1000	8
11	3	1001	9
100	4	1010	10
101	5	1011	11

It may be observed that in a binary set:

$$1 = 2^0 \text{ or } 1$$
$$10 = 2^1 \text{ or } 2$$
$$100 = 2^2 \text{ or } 4$$
$$1000 = 2^3 \text{ or } 8$$
$$10000 = 2^4 \text{ or } 16$$
$$100000 = 2^5 \text{ or } 32$$

The binary set is made up of only two numbers, 0 and 1, but it can be used to express decimal concepts. The table we have shown above setting forth binary and decimal numbers illustrates this. On the other hand, an "octal" set would consist of only eight numbers, from 0 through 7. Here is the relationship between octal and decimal:

Octal	Decimal	Octal	Decimal
0	0	11	9
1	1	12	10
2	2	13	11
3	3	14	12
4	4	15	13
5	5	16	14
6	6	17	15
7	7	20	16
10	8	21	17

But an octal set can be described in binary numbers as well as in the arabic numbering system that we are accustomed to. If the six-bit binary codes are considered as two parts it is easier to describe them in octal terms, calling the first three binary bits one number, and the second three a second number or, more precisely, a second digit.

Binary Codes	Octal	Decimal
000 000	0	0
000 001	1	1
000 010	2	2
000 011	3	3
000 100	4	4
000 101	5	5
000 110	6	6
000 111	7	7
001 000	10	8
001 001	11	9
001 010	12	10

Looking at the codes as shown above, it is easy to see that:

000 000	is an octal 00.
000 100	is an octal 04.
001 001	is an octal 11.
011 100	is an octal 34.

This is a very convenient arrangement, since we can then create a "table look-up" arrangement which appears like this:

	0	1	2	3	4	5	6	7
0	0	1	2	3	4	5	6	7
1	8	9	A	B	C	D	E	F
2	G	H	I	J	K	L	M	N
3	O	P	Q	R	S	T	U	V
4	W	X	Y	Z	!	.	+	"
5	%	¢	&	*	(	)	-	—
6	.	,	?	/	'	,	$	
7								

The vertical row of numbers outside the block represents the first digit of a two-digit octal number. The horizontal row on top of the block represents the second digit. Thus an octal 11 is a 9 and an octal 40 is a W.

The characters shown in the above grid have been assigned arbitrarily, and not all of the codes have been used up, but it will be noted that we have made our decimal 8 an octal 10 and the letter T is an octal 35.

The hexadecimal system

THE SAME PRINCIPLE is involved in the hexadecimal system, except that our number set, instead of consisting of eight digits, 0 through 7, consists of sixteen, 0 through F. In other words, the set counts out as 0, 1, 2, 3, 4, 5, 6, 7, 8, 9, A, B, C, D, E, and F.

The table at the top of the next page clarifies this concept somewhat. The fact remains that translating a number from decimal to hexadecimal is not easily done in one's head. Reference tables are generally provided for this purpose.

Basic Computer Concepts

Decimal	Hexadecimal
9	9
10	A
11	B
12	C
13	D
14	E
15	F
16	10
17	11

And so on, until we reach:

25	19
26	1A
27	1B
28	1C
29	1D
30	1E

Then 31 becomes 1F and 32 is a hexadecimal 20.

When these concepts are understood we can then discuss binary coded hexadecimal (BCD), which looks like this:

0000 is a hexadecimal 0
1001 is a hexadecimal 9
1010 is a hexadecimal A (which is a number)
1011 is a hexadecimal B
1100 is a C
1101 is a D
1110 is an E
1111 is an F

And just as three bits can enable us to count 0 through 7, so four bits can count from 0 through 15, and the number 16, in decimal set brings in the second or left-hand, group of four bits:

0001 0000 is a hexadecimal 10, although a decimal 16
0001 0001 is a hexadecimal 11 and a decimal 17
0001 0110 is a hexadecimal 16. What is its decimal value?
0001 1111 is a hexadecimal 1F
0010 0000 is a hexadecimal 20
0010 1111 is a hexadecimal 2F
0011 0000 is a hex 30 (decimal 48)
1111 1111 is a hex FF (decimal 255)

Because of the difficulty of thinking in hexadecimal some people prefer to stay with octal. In this case they divide the groupings of the eight-bit byte into the following array:

00 000 000

Thus we can describe the bit combinations in octal terms, bearing in mind that the left-hand grouping could never equal more than 3:

11 111 111 would give us octal 377, which is a decimal 255, and which of course remains hex FF if we group the bits into two arrays of four.

Returning to the hexadecimal concept, a translate table can be prepared which shows two hexadecimal characters as coordinates. In this case, the leftmost digit is usually shown at the top, and the rightmost digit at the left side.

	0	1	2	3	4	5	6	7	8	9	A	B	C	D	E	F
0	0	g	w	M	:	]										
1	1	h	x	N	;											
2	2	i	y	O	'											
3	3	j	z	P	'											
4	4	k	A	Q	-											
5	5	l	B	R	—											
6	6	m	C	S	(											
7	7	n	D	T	)											
8	8	o	E	U	$											
9	9	p	F	V	%											
A	a	q	G	W	¢											
B	b	r	H	X	&											
C	c	s	I	Y	*											
D	d	t	J	Z	@											
E	e	u	K	.	#											
F	f	v	L	,	[											

The characters we have shown in the above matrix are again arbitrarily assigned and this assignment does not accord with any code structure in common usage. The reader may be interested to study two different code structures which are commonly employed for information transfer. One is called EBCDIC (pronounced "Ebsa-dick") which stands for Extended Binary Coded Decimal Interchange Code, and the other is USASCII ("Yousaskey") or ASCII ("Askey") which stands for United States of America Standard Code for Information Interchange. We have chosen to show (on the next page) both EBCDIC and ASCII eight-bit or hex codes on one diagram. Displaying them in this fashion does not emphasize sufficiently the number of blank spaces (unused code assignments), although some of them are taken up with information-handling codes rather than information-content codes.

It may be seen, then, that the modern general-purpose computer, being by its very nature a binary device, processes data as strings of bits which are organized into bytes and words, and that people have devised several (actually many!) code configurations for the purpose of representing computer instructions and alphanumeric informa-

Basic Computer Concepts

tion. Data will be brought into the computer as a string of bits, it will be processed as bits, arrayed in some combination using programs expressed as bits, and it will be stored and output in the same manner. During the production or processing cycle various translations of bit streams or bytes may take place since the input coding structure, the internal coding conventions, and the output coding requirements may all differ.

EBCDIC and USASCII Coding

Left half of byte in hexadecimal coding

		0	1	2	3	4	5	6	7	8	9	A	B	C	D	E	F
		0000	0001	0010	0011	0100	0101	0110	0111	1000	1001	1010	1011	1100	1101	1110	1111
0	0000			Sp	0	Sp @	& P	-	p					{	}		0
1	0001			|	1	A	Q	/ a	q	a	j	~		A	J		1
2	0010			"	2	B	R	b	r	b	k	s		B	K	S	2
3	0011			#	3	C	S	c	s	c	l	t		C	L	T	3
4	0100			$	4	D	T	d	t	d	m	u		D	M	U	4
5	0101			%	5	E	U	e	u	e	n	v		E	N	V	5
6	0110	LC		&	UC 6	F	V	f	v	f	o	w		F	O	W	6
7	0111	Del		,	7	G	W	g	w	g	p	x		G	P	X	7
8	1000		Can Can	(	8	H	X	h	x	h	q	y		H	Q	Y	8
9	1001			)	9	I	Y	i	\ y	i	r	z		I	R	Z	9
A	1010			*	:	¢ J	! Z	j	: z								
B	1011			+	;	. K	$ [	, k	# {								
C	1100			,	<	< L	* \	% l	@								
D	1101	CR CR		-	=	(M	)]	- m	' }								
E	1110			.	>	+ N	;	> n	= ~								
F	1111			/	?	| O	-	? o	" Del								

Right half of byte in hexadecimal coding

In the chart above, characters in EBCDIC are in the top portion of the box. Characters in 8-level ASCII are in the lower portion. Hence, "A" is 1100 0001 in EBCDIC and 0100 0001 in ASCII, but lower case a is 1000 0001 in EBCDIC and 0110 0001 in ASCII. SP=Space, LC=Lower Case, Del=Delete, Can=Cancel, UC=Upper Case, CR=Carriage Return.

Computer speeds

ONE OF THE MOST interesting facts about a computer is the speed with which it can process information. We have already suggested that a computer may be limited in its processing speed by slow input or output devices—and this is all the more reason for processing several jobs simultaneously while waiting for input to come in or for output to be disposed of. But the cycle time of the computer itself can be extremely fast, and thus even if the basic tasks a computer performs are repetitive and often exceedingly complex, they can be done very quickly and the computer has made possible the performance of lengthy and complicated calculations which could not otherwise have been performed even within many lifetimes.

Computer speeds are generally described in terms of cycle time—which is the time required to move one word of data from one location to another, as from one place in core (memory) to a register, or from a register to another location in memory. Remember that a word can be the length of several characters. A 16-bit word machine can simultaneously describe two eight-bit characters. An IBM 370 word can contain four eight-bit characters.

Often instructions take up a computer word, and hence cycle time may relate to the length of time it would require a computer to fetch (but not to execute) the instruction.

Only a few years ago we were impressed that computers could execute such a cycle in a certain number of milliseconds. Thus, a nine-millisecond cycle time would mean that a computer could move a word in .009 seconds. This is a little less than one one-hundredth of a second. Thus a hundred such operations could be performed each second. But now computer speeds have moved into the microsecond and nanosecond range. Just as a millisecond is a thousandth of a second, a microsecond is a thousandth of a thousandth of a second. So with a speed of six milliseconds a computer could perform 166,666 operations in a second! And now we speak of even inexpensive personal microcomputers which handle 16-bit words in the nanosecond range, which is a thousandth of a microsecond.

Suppose you ran one job and only one through a computer that operated at a speed of 800 nanoseconds, and suppose that the input from this job consisted of reading in one character at a time from a paper tape, on a paper-tape reader that operated at 1000 characters per second. Of course there would be other tasks to be performed, but if only one cycle were required to bring this information from paper tape to a computer register, then the computing power to be used for this operation would require only one out of every 12,500 available cycles. It would be as if you were to spend one second on a task and then wait for the assignment of another task (to occupy only one second) for three and one-half hours. If the basic task you were expected to perform were one which required an hour, then your next assignment would be a year and a half later, and if it took a day, you would only have to perform this duty once during your entire

Basic Computer Concepts

working life span. These examples are suggested to dramatize the potential productivity of the computer and the problem of its effective utilization.

The instruction set

WE HAVE ESTABLISHED the fact that a computer can perform certain input/output operations (generally called I/O) utilizing its channels and controllers, and that it can also store data in its memory in binary form. But how does the central processing unit manipulate the data? These are the functions which are performed by the use of its arithmetic and logic unit, with the assistance of its registers, storage capabilities and controllers. What are the arithmetic and logical functions the CPU can perform? These are a function of the machine's *instruction set*.

Different makes and models of computers have different instruction sets depending upon their design characteristics and the applications for which they are intended. An instruction is called an operation and it is expressed by an "op" code. The command tells the computer what to do and where to do it, where to get the data and where to put it. Operations may be *declarative*, which defines the element to be worked with, and *imperative*, which then orders that something specific be done with that element. What is to be done and the circumstances under which it is to be performed are set forth in what are called *arguments*. There may be imperative commands of an arithmetic nature (add, subtract, multiply or divide), or of a logical nature (do this if this and that are true; do this until you have done so a certain number of times or until something else—which is specified—occurs). There are also imperative commands of a manipulative nature—move this right or left, fill it with zeros, pack or unpack the data, translate it, align the decimal points, etc. Or, read in a block of information from magnetic tape; print out a block of information on a line printer.

Here are some common imperative commmands, set forth in a simplified version of a possible instruction set:

Add	Execute	Start
AND	Load	Store
Branch	Move	Subtract
Compare	Multiply	Test
Convert	OR	Translate
Divide	Pack	Unpack
Exclusive OR	Read	Write
	Shift	

These instructions (and others which are more specific) are effected by "machine language" commands contained in an "object program," but they are executed by the arithmetic and logic unit, assisted when necessary by channels and controllers and peripheral devices. The wiring of the unit can permit it to perform certain tasks very fast, as we have already seen. The principle behind binary addition, for example, is that:

$$0 + 0 = 0$$
$$0 + 1 = 1$$
$$1 + 0 = 1$$
$$1 + 1 = 10$$

Instructions are executed electronically by invoking the use of certain circuits which are able to perform logical functions in the manner we have already discussed. It is also possible for the computer to be microprogrammed—which means that many of the instructions can consist of software subroutines which perform functions similar to those which are hard-wired or even more complex instructions. Furthermore, computers can be programmed to perform multiprocessing functions, which means that one program can be interrupted and another can take its place. In this case the contents of the first program's registers will somehow be stored so that when that program is resumed (a millisecond later, perhaps!) it will have its own data to work with and its own links to indicate what the conditions were when the task was interrupted.

The use of registers

REGISTERS ARE DEVICES for storing one or more words in order to facilitate arithmetic, logical or manipulative operations, such as the address of the next instruction, a counter of the number of operations already performed, a check to ascertain the existence or non-existence of a certain condition, or a quantity or constant to be used in making certain calculations. Data movement operations from one register to another may be much faster than from memory back to memory or from memory to register. In other words, there may be a direct transfer of information from one memory location to another.

Computer peripherals

EARLIER IN THIS CHAPTER we alluded to input and output devices. These are among the computer peripherals or related operating units which comprise the computer system. In typesetting applications one or more paper-tape readers may have been connected to the mainframe. Now it is more likely that on-line input and editing terminals will be so connected, or that data will be read in from off-line terminals with their own floppy disks. Data may also be transferred from remote sites via modem and telephone lines. Thus we have the possibility of off-line or on-line input. The computer in question may be capable of multiprocessing or, if it is a personal computer or microprocessor, it may be able to perform only one job or task at a time. Still, even the small personal computers are usually capable of performing certain multitask operations, such as to read in and store one task on disk, to process a second, and to output (as to a printer) yet a third.

And so we may have on-line or off-line keyboards as input devices. There may also be OCR (Optical Character Recognition) input. Some computers can accommodate magnetic cassette readers which

Basic Computer Concepts

can take the output of word processing equipment. Many more have developed the possibility of reading (directly or indirectly) input from floppy disks. Magnetic tape stations can serve for both input and output, as well as for interim storage. The magnetic tape input may have been generated on another computer system.

Computers will also have one or more disk drives. These disks provide a place to store programs, to store other relevant data which must be accessed or brought into memory from time to time, and to provide additional working space—a "scratch pad" for interim steps in the processing cycle. Such disks are generally "fixed head" or "moving head" in nature. The former generally offer faster access time since there is a read/write head for each track on the disk. Moving head disks have only one read/write head for each disk platter surface, and the arm on which these heads are mounted will move from one track to another in order to access the piece of information or data required.

There are removable disk packs, and nonremovable "Winchester" disks. There are also floppy disks or diskettes. Some systems make use of magnetic drums. All of these provide *random access* to a supplementary store of data, whereas information stored on a magnetic tape requires a sequential search of the tape until the desired data have been found. Because of the randomness of disk-stored data, an index must be maintained to indicate where the desired information may be found. That index may be on the disk itself or it may be kept in memory, but it must be constantly updated, so that a record of the disk, track and sector of the track, will be associated with the name or number of a particular file.

Output devices. A paper-tape punch may be an output device. Output can also be transmitted on-line to a cable-connected typesetter, thus eliminating the need to handle paper tape. Data can also be output to magnetic tapes, floppy disks, or removable disks. Obviously a printer or plotter[1] is an output device, and a video terminal can serve both for input and output purposes. Much information is never output except to video terminals, as may be true, for example, of the flight information made available to local travel agencies, or data on train arrivals and departures.

Summary

DATA ARE BROUGHT IN for processing by various input devices. Programs must also be fed into the computer to direct a sequence of logical operations. It is the CPU or mainframe that performs the logical and arithmetic operations, utilizing peripheral input and output devices and external storage media as well as memory, so that the various commands can be executed.

Channels and controllers help keep track of traffic and try to assure the efficient use of the compute power of the mainframe. This power is determined by the size and speed of the computer and also the variety of instructions it has been wired to execute.

---

1. A plotter works like a printer but is able to draw pictures instead of characters.

There is an increasing tendency for "distributive processing" to take place, which means that "intelligence" is located not only in large mainframe devices, but also in terminals or terminal controllers which serve as subsystems and perform certain tasks which the mainframe will delegate or perhaps "download." Computer architecture also permits the use, on a "local area network" of terminals (workstations) which are intelligent and which perform functions quite independently of any external computer control, except perhaps for the assistance of a "file server" which provides storage for the system and is able to route data from one workstation to another.

Computer design is changing rapidly. More and more power is available—in terms of processing cycles per second, additional memory, and even data storage. Many of the tasks previously performed on large and very expensive computing devices can now be performed on small and inexpensive ones. It may be necessary to adapt or rewrite or totally redesign the software, modifying it according to the requirements and possibilities of the computer's operating system. The relationship between computer hardware and software is indeed very intimate. We must turn now to a consideration of programming and software.

11

Programs and Programming

PROGRAMMING is a very complex subject. All that we can hope to accomplish is to give the reader an impression of the processes and procedures involved and to make him or her aware of the implications of what is known as the hardware-software interface—that is, the way in which programs interact with the computer to provided desired solutions in specific applications.

In general, there are two ways to approach the creation of a program. One way is to assume that a particular computer with a given configuration of equipment is available: how should *it* be programmed for the desired application? The other approach would be to define the problem and then to determine what combination of hardware and software would best meet the user's needs. The latter implies a system's overview and it assumes that the application is big enough to justify the installation of the ideal system. For the most part, programmers are handed assignments to perform on a given configuration of equipment. Systems analysts are asked to recommend the best overall solution, in terms both of hardware and software. However, the term systems analyst is being used increasingly to describe those who are responsible for the design of major software undertakings, even on a given hardware system. Junior programmers are sometimes called coders since their function is to follow a flow chart or other carefully mapped-out procedures.

Perhaps we should propose a third approach to the creation of a program, and that is to seek to write one which is "device-independent" or "portable" so that it will on run various kinds of equipment. For example, now that personal and professional computers are popular, programs are often written so that they will run on various models or products in the market place. Such programs may be said to be "CP/M compatible," for example, if they will run on any eight-bit microprocessor which will accept the CP/M operating system (provided always, of course, that the floppy disk which contains the program is also hardware compatible with the particular micro). Or they may be "IBM PC compatible," so that they can be run on either that popular model of microcomputer (which, at the time of this writing, is rapidly becoming a de facto standard for a certain category of machines), or on IBM PC "workalikes."

But for the moment, as a starter, let us consider only programming itself, more or less independently of any hardware implications. It is customary for the programmer to start out with a precise definition of the assignment, as well as an identification of its component elements, which is usually accomplished by flow charting the steps which will have to be taken.

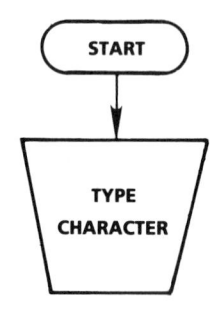

The reader will quickly discover that the flow chart is a most valuable tool, and if one can make one's self think like a computer he or she will gain new insights into many problems and will improve his or her ability to analyze assignments and reduce them to manageable proportions. In many situations where the installation of a computer has been contemplated, potential users have discovered that the discipline required for computer programming—namely, to break the task down into its relevant elements—produces results which are valuable in and of themselves and may even obviate the need for the computer system.

In order to illustrate how a flow chart may be prepared and what use it may be put to, we shall take as an example the task of typing a finished paper from an author's manuscript. We shall assume that the paper will be typed manually, but that the steps to be taken would be precisely those that a computer might be asked to follow. We will find, in fact, that the computer will be called upon the make the same decisions that an individual would make, although he or she generally makes them subconsciously, just as one walks without thinking: "Now I will advance my left foot; now I will shift my weight from my right foot to my left foot; now I will advance my right foot; when I advance my left foot I will swing my right hand backward to provide balance and momentum."

If the reader will study carefully the flow chart on the next page (and he may find errors in it or wish to enlarge upon it), he will see that it consists of several different routines, which may be described as follows:

- Start job and set up counters.
- A page numbering routine.
- A line-counting routine which ejects the page when there is no longer any room on the page for additional lines.
- A word reading and typing routine, which continues to read and type words until all words have been read, and which types words character by character until the next word will not fit in the line, in which case it is placed on the following line.
- A letter verification routine.

These routines are interlocked. In a sense the program works as follows:

Start job: number page (except perhaps a separate routine for chapter "sinkage" and page numbering on first page of manuscript). Go down to where the first line of copy should appear. Read a word. Determine if the word will fit within the line. Type the word, verifying each letter. (If the letter is incorrectly typed, backspace, rub it out, retype the correct letter. Verify that it is correct, and if not, repeat the verification routine.)

Programs and Programming

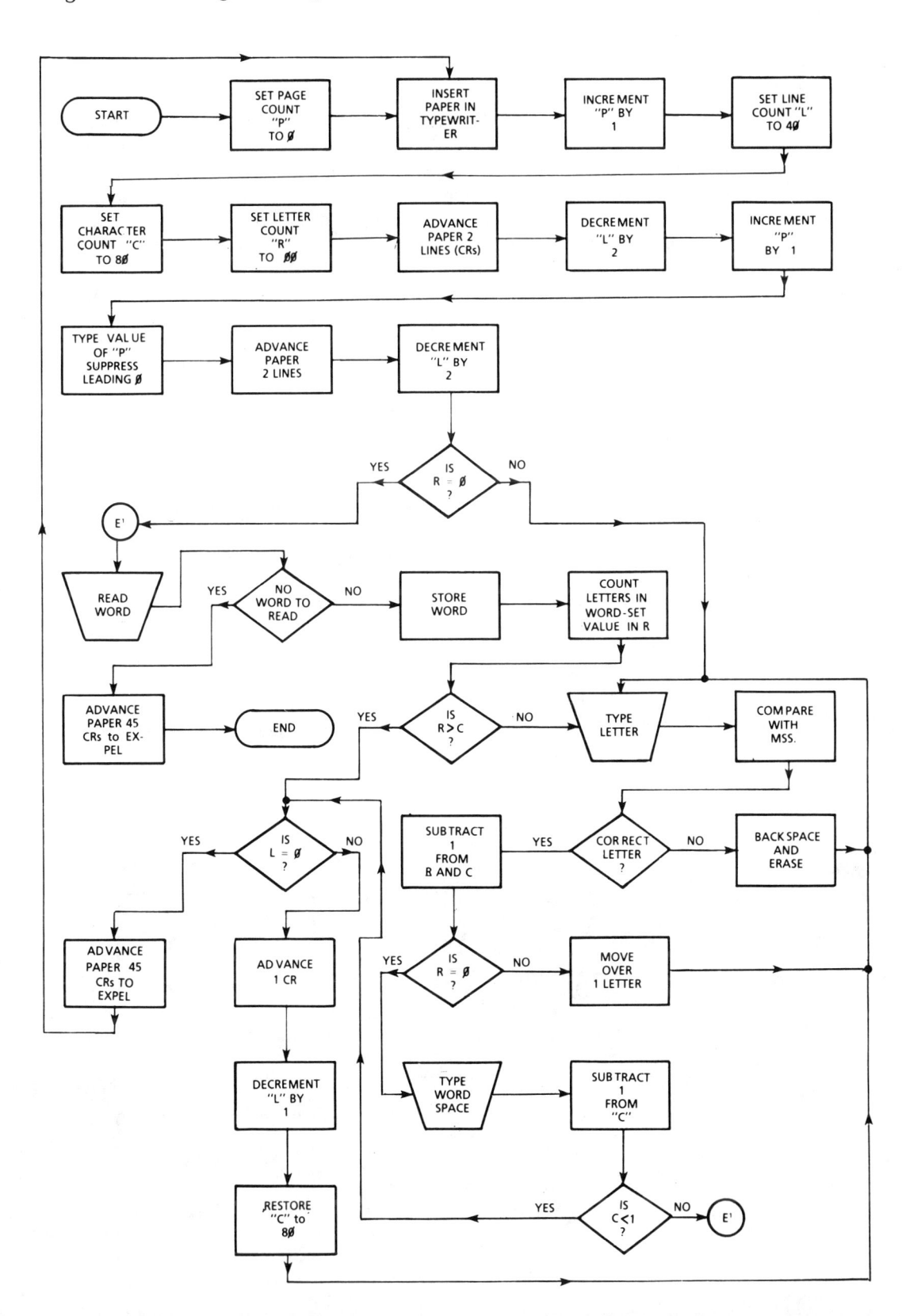

When the word is finished, verify the word (use verification routine to correct if necessary). Read another word. Determine whether or not that word will also fit on the same line. Determine that if it does not fit on that line that there is room for another line on the page. If the word fits, type it, using letter verification subroutine. If the word does not fit on the line, use line advance routine which involves carriage return and paper advance.

Determine now (for example) that there isn't room on the line for a new word. Determine also that there isn't room on the page for a new line. Eject the page. Feed in another sheet. Start a new page. Number the page, etc.

The reader may be confused with the evident complexity of the flow chart shown on the preceding page and it may therefore be easier to start with something just a little simpler. Instead of starting at the beginning of our program, therefore, let us consider for the moment the typing of an individual character. The shape of the first box (a keystone shape) will suggest that this is an input or output function. In this case type character may be assumed to be an input function (although obviously it happens to be both).

Now suppose we imagine that a person types a particular character and then looks at it and asks: "Is this the correct character?" If he or she finds that it is not, let us assume that the solution can be found in backspacing, somehow rubbing out the character and then typing the correct one. Then the typist must check again to see if it is correct.

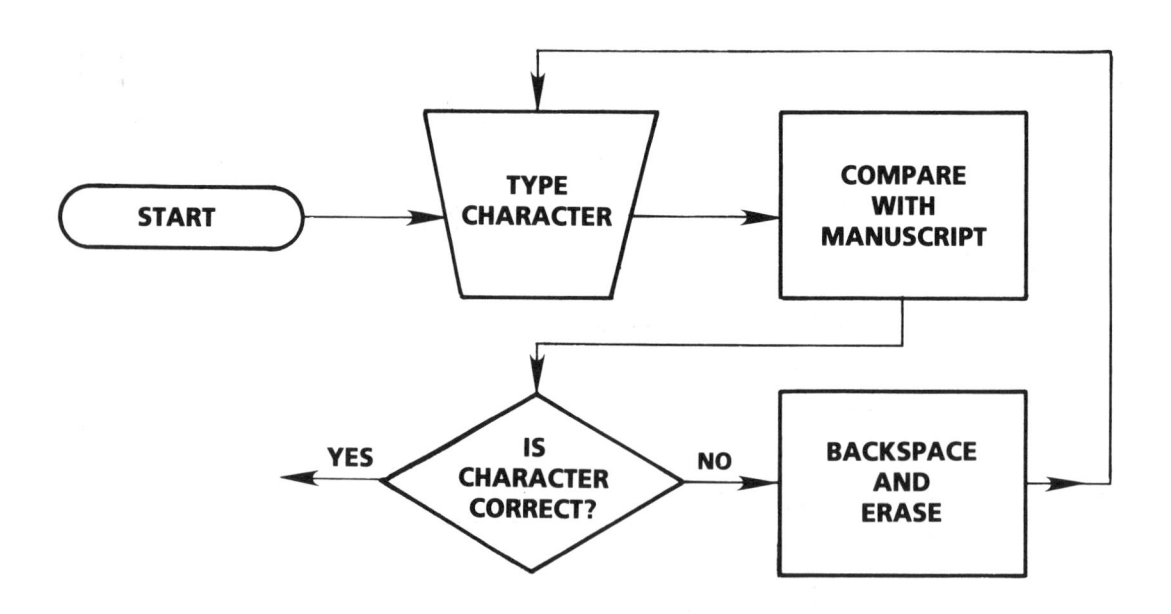

Programs and Programming

You will notice that the "compare" function leads to a decision. In flow charting, decisions are indicated by a diamond, whereas a rectangle indicates some kind of machine processing activity other than input/output or decision-making. You will also notice that we have diagramed a "loop." As long as the wrong character is keyboarded and detected the loop persists. If the correct character is struck and verified, there is a "branch" away from the loop. In a sense, then, this loop could be called a subroutine.

Suppose we have a counter ("R") to indicate the length of the word we are typing, and another counter ("C") to indicate the length of the line. Whenever the correct character has been typed the line length counter will be reduced (decremented) by one, and so will the word-character count for the individual word ("R"). When the word-character counter is at zero the word has been typed and a word space is needed (and that value has also to be subtracted from the line). Until the word-character counter equals zero additional characters in the word will be typed, and this makes another loop. We branch away from this loop when the word-character counter shows a value of less than one. (It could be either zero or minus one since the space after the word at the end of the line is not significant for this project as defined.) In either event, at the conclusion of the word we would go to the "new line" routine.

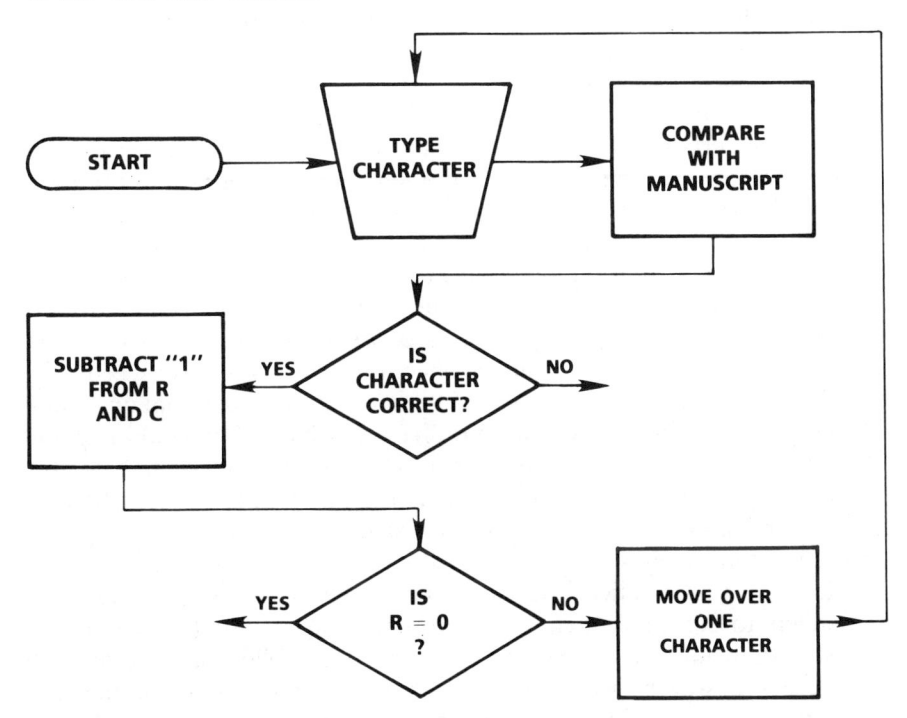

Of course the word may be too large to fit within the line. What then should be done?

We need not belabor our illustration any further. The reader may wish to try a flow chart of his own on some specific task, such as backing a car out of the garage:

Do I have the keys to the car?
(Go to "*Get Key*" routine if answer is "no.")
Is garage door open?
("*Open Garage Door*" routine if answer is "no.")
Open car door.
Get in.
Insert key.
Press starter.
Is car an automatic or a manual?
(*Branch*, alternatively, to one or the other. Assume automatic here.)
Put gear in reverse.
Depress accelerator.

Other subroutines may be relevant. For example, should there not be a routine to inquire if the gear is in neutral before pressing starter? What about releasing the hand brake? Some people would insist that the first steps after entering the car would be to fasten the seat belt, adjust rear-view mirror, *etc*. But did the reader notice one very significant omission? Our flow chart does not include a very necessary instruction: close the car door!

Flow charting may be carried on at a very detailed level or on a very general level. Once a particular routine has been thought through, thereafter it may be sufficient merely to describe that routine within one rectangle, even though it contains many branches and several loops of its own.

One very important aspect of flow charting is to check continually to be certain of appropriate conditions. For example, it is easier to include an instruction to see if the line counter will permit the next word to be typed even if we know that we have just gone to a new line and the word most surely would fit. This enables us to use the same loop or subroutine for all words in the line, and it will not require us to devise a separate routine for the first or first several such words. And it will also bring to light the rare case where we define the line as being exceedingly short and we encounter a word that is exceedingly long. What would we do, then, if we find that the word contains more characters than the line length we have specified? This could happen either because we have mistakenly specified the line length as too short (perhaps we have misplaced a decimal point in our parameters) or some abnormality has been associated with the word. (Perhaps we have inadvertently dropped a word space, or we have incorporated a lengthy mathematical equation into the text.) Or, perhaps we have failed to recognize that the boundaries of a word (by definition) should include an em dash to take care of the following condition: "I agree—however," where (lacking a hyphenation routine and not recognizing an em dash as a "break point") we may have to split the linked word arbitrarily.

We can see, then, that our flow chart must consider every possibility, even the absurd or unlikely ones. We come upon the general principle of programming, that we must anticipate every conceivable contingency. We must learn to visualize the conditions we are likely to encounter, and we must ask ourselves to consider every possible condition, even for applications that we do not presently have in mind, but for which some day we might wish to use the same routine.

From the flow chart to the coding

ONCE WE HAVE DEVELOPED satisfactory flow charts we need to reduce our concept or plan of action to a specific computer program. This may be done merely by coding if our charts are specific enough. But if we have left open many questions and choices, then an experienced programmer or systems analyst—much more qualified than a coder—will of course be required. How does the program get written?

Ultimately our program must be reduced to machine language coding: commands that will instruct a specific computer in the performance of its tasks. If we wish, we can write our original program in machine language, although this is not done very frequently. When you write in machine language you have to keep track of every single location of every element you are working with. If you read in a data element and decide to store it temporarily in location 1000, then you must remember that that is where it is, and you cannot use this location for any other purpose. You must also plan your program so that all of your instructions are sequential. For example, if all instructions take one word, your first instruction might begin in location 1001. If you wanted to add a subroutine between the first and second instructions you would have to renumber and reassign all of the subsequent instructions—which might be very many.

Consequently, you are not likely to write programs in machine language. The closest you would come to machine language would be assembly language. Here you will use many of the same instructions and codes, but they will be somewhat less specific—especially since you will not designate memory locations but give a name to the area in question. An assembler program will later be run against your subject program, and it will assign specific memory locations to your instructions and data areas. When you modify your program these locations and areas will be reassigned as needed in the next assembly. The computer manufacturer will supply you with an assembler which will take your subject program and create an object program in machine language. Each time you reassemble it you will get a new object program.

Your assembly language program will not be generally "portable." It will be written in a language which can be understood only by the assembler designed for the particular make of computer. If you want a more "portable" language you will want to write in a "compiler" language, such as FORTRAN, COBOL, ALGOL, or perhaps BASIC. Chances are that you will select "C" and write under the UNIX operating system for one of the new microprocessors such as the Motorola 68000.

The computer manufacturer or some software house will provide you with the compiler which will translate the programs you write in FORTRAN, for example, into machine language for your computer. Your subject program will be compiled into an object program in machine language, and recompiled as necessary whenever you wish to revise it.

When you use these higher level languages for your programs you are also able to pick up many existing subroutines for certain basic functions. Programming is usually much simpler, quicker and trouble-free. You do not need to debug routines which have already been perfected by others, especially for I/O functions. On the other hand, the routines others have written may not do precisely what it is that you want to do, and you may have to achieve the desired results by more roundabout procedures. Specifically, for typesetting applications, compiler programs are usually not efficient, if they will work at all. Such programs are generally intended for the solution of problems in business, economics, mathematics or science, rather than for the purpose of character-by-character processing usually required for typesetting and text editing. Thus the kind of programming generally taught in colleges and universities, and which is intended to help a businessman or scientist gain access to a computer to perform occasional tasks, just as he might sometimes need the services of an adding machine or calculator, may not be very helpful where production programs are needed which must be quick, efficient, and reliable for the processing of varied input.

However, in the past several years some composition programs have been developed in compiler languages—or mostly in compiler languges, with some patches in assembly—which seem to be quite efficient. Better compilers are presently being written, and new computers offer faster cycle times and more memory so that if the object program happens to be somewhat slower this may prove not to be too consequential. Nevertheless, even today the largest proportion of composition programs are still written in assembler. The use of "C" and even PASCAL is changing this, and in any event there is always a trade-off between the efficiency and productivity of the program on the one hand and the number of man-years of effort required to write it, on the other.

Loading the program

WHEN A PROGRAM has been written and debugged so that it is available for use in a production environment, it will generally be stored in its machine language format, and it will not be necessary to recompile it or reassemble it each time it is to be used. The stored program may be kept on magnetic tape or on punched cards, or it may remain on disk. When it is to be run, that program, or a relevant portion of it, is called into memory, sometimes by operator intervention and sometimes by a terminal command from the user. The program sets up its own registers and establishes whatever conditions are needed and checks to see if the desired pieces of peripheral equipment are ready and available. It then accesses the first instruction, executes it, and moves automatically either to the next sequential

Programs and Programming 169

instruction, or, if there is a branch or conditional transfer, the program contains the address of the location of the next sequence of instructions. Hence the program is "in charge," and the operator's function (if everything turns out as it is supposed to) is merely to service the requirements of the computer—such as to put on or take off magnetic tapes or floppy diskettes.

If the program "hangs," a logging printer will usually enter a record of this fact or the operator is otherwise notified. This is not inevitably the case. Sometimes a program can get into a loop, from which it can never extricate itself, and the operator must be aware of probable running times and other expected conditions so that he can diagnose problems if they seem to occur. If something goes wrong he can abort the run or try to recover, and usually will be instructed to take a "memory dump" and readings of registers so that the programmer can try to find the source of the difficulty at his convenience.

Operator diagnosis or intervention is not likely to be very helpful where multiprogramming or multiprocessing takes place. This occurs when the same computer is able to run several different jobs more or less simultaneously. Multiprogramming describes a condition in which each user's program works within a partition of memory, and time-sharing describes a condition under which various users share the same sections of memory in successive, very brief, slices of time. Under either of these conditions or combinations of both, all programs run under an operating system and the operator's attention is directed primarily to the requirements of the system rather than the peculiarities or shortcomings of individual programs. It must generally be assumed, therefore, that all successful computer programs must be trouble-free, and they must anticipate all conditions to which they might be exposed. They must also be designed to provide recovery points so that a job which aborts need not be started again at the very beginning. Diagnostic features can and should be built into the programs as well as ways of keeping track of the status of jobs.

Documentation

FLOW CHARTS provide the basic clue to an understanding of the program, but a more detailed explanation is essential, and such documentation can be provided by the programmer as he does his coding. Explanatory comments may accompany his array of instructions, and these in themselves, if produced conscientiously, may be sufficient to enable another programmer to understand what the first has tried to do.

Above all else, documentation should be intelligible for the people who need to access it. It must take into account the institutional framework within which the program is to run. The next chapter looks more closely at that framework.

12

The System Environment

IN CHAPTER FOUR, beginning on page 40, we have made some preliminary observations about the typesetting production process as it emerged over the more than fifty years that the linecasting machine dominated the setting of type. That process also had much in common with what had previously prevailed under handsetting.

When new technology comes into being old habits are not quickly set aside. It takes some time before new institutional arrangements can shape themselves in such fashion that the advantages of new technology can be optimized. But the relationship is even more profound. Given the potential thrust of new technology, how can the systems themselves respond to possibilities and needs that cannot yet be understood or articulated? A system is more than a mere collection of pieces of hardware, or even of hardware and software. It is also a collection of people and procedures, services, support facilities, customs, expectations, and perhaps even legal arrangements. It represents the way things get done.

Thus it is that typesetting devices have to be understood and evaluated as part of such a system in which printing has—at least until now—been considered as the ultimate end product. The need for additional end products could of course affect the validity of the system, and obviously the viability of the system depends upon the manner in which the components fit together. For example, if the printed product must be produced by letterpress, photocomposition has offered a less logical typesetting solution than hot metal, since in the latter case printing can be done from the type itself (in short-run work) or from plates made from molds taken from the type (in long-run work). Hot metal is still a popular process for very long-run pocket books which are printed from rubber plates, since such plates can be molded from the images of raised type.

The system must also take into account the work flow—the total organization of production from the time the manuscript is received until the printed output has been delivered. The intensive time span for critical production must also be considered. One typesetting system may be good in one application but not in another depending, for example, upon whether the customer needs to inspect the product at intervals as it is being created, and whether or not he will revise it substantially while it is in an interim stage.

The system also has to take into account the typographical ingredients themselves—the variety of type faces and sizes, the format

The System Environment

requirements, the amount of illustrative matter, *etc*. A method which is entirely appropriate and necessary for the production of scholarly treatises in advanced mathematics may be completely inappropriate for setting newspapers or business forms.

Moreover, there is increasing emphasis on the development of systems which include the author or writer (as well as the editor) in the "loop." Where this is possible the system clearly goes beyond typesetting and becomes at least an editorial system if not—as with some newspapers—an electronic newsroom.

In view of the complexity of the problem, how can we discuss typesetting and composition systems, in this digital world of ours, in an intelligent and reasonably comprehensive manner? Obviously we shall have to approach the topic by a consideration of prototypes or models. Our generalizations will be relevant only for the set of assumptions that the model implies.

Varieties of composition

BOOKWORK IS NOT the only category of composition that one needs to consider. There is work which pertains to magazines, scholarly journals and scientific publications, advertising typography, financial typesetting, general job work (which includes brochures and catalogs as well as letterheads, billing forms, business cards and the like), business forms, newspapers, even music publishing. While it was true that typesetting was originally performed by the publishers—who were, in fact, principally type designers, typesetters and printers and perhaps only incidentally publishers, a separation of functions began to appear even during the renaissance period, and this separation was enhanced significantly by the introduction of hot metal machine composition. But since the advent of photocomposition this trend has been markedly reversed. Many publishers have again installed their own composition capability, and as the editing process becomes more intimately related to the composition process this trend becomes even more marked.

An interesting case study may be derived from a report prepared by the managing editor of *The Farm Journal*, in 1970. At that time the editor, Jerry A. Carlson, was considering whether there might not be better ways to produce a magazine such as his.[1]

> Tracing a typical article in *Farm Journal* will give a fair indication of the amount of editing that goes into a story before it reaches print. Glenn Lorang, one of *Farm Journal's* field editors, phones in from Spokane, Washington, suggesting a one-page feature on farmers who are starting their own grain-hauling fleet of trucks to bypass the railroad's high shipping rates. The managing editor assigns the story, and for several days the reporter fills notebooks with quotes and facts. He roughs out a manuscript on his office typewriter. The preliminary draft is composed of copy paper taped or glued together, paragraphs circled and marked "insert at A below," heavy pencil tracks throughout. Without going to the trouble of an actual word count he can only guess as to its total length. Next morning his

1. *Magazine Writing and Computer Video Terminals*, an unpublished document in the author's possession.

secretary retypes the article. Glenn checks it for typographical errors and mails the corrected manuscript to *Farm Journal* headquarters in Philadelphia. It arrives in the managing editor's office three days later. The final character layout specifies room for 80 lines averaging 52 characters. That is about 70 lines shorter than the original manuscript, so it will need severe cutting to fit. It also needs other editing, so several sections must be rewritten. The rewritten version then goes to a secretary who types a clean copy. This copy, done in five carbons, receives further minor pencil editing and typographical markup. Finally, it is ready to be sent to the printer. Fortunately, the airline pouch service out of Philadelphia is not delayed and the story arrives in the Chicago printing plant the next morning. The foreman of the plant's composing room carries the copy to the Linotype section about 120 feet away. The article then waits its turn at the Linotype work center for about three hours, then the Linotype foreman hands it to a Linotype operator. The operator keyboards the text in galley form.

The lead galley is carried to a proof press, several copies run off, and then the type itself is assigned a rack location to be stored while the galley proof awaits its turn in the proofreading room.

A proofreader matches the galley with original copy and marks typesetting errors on the galley proof. New corrections are set for the galley, which is then sent to the composing room section. The composing foreman parcels out the correction work to a specialist. This "comp" first inserts the galley corrections in proper position, then begins fitting the type into page form to match the artist's specifications. It takes about an hour to compose the page. With a final hammering down of type and locking of quoins, he shouts for a proof boy to run several white proofs at the nearby hand press. The proofboy is somewhere else, so the comp, with appropriate descriptive phrases, runs off the page proofs by himself.

Later, the comp foreman hand-carries this proof and others 200 feet to the proofreading room. The proofreader marks all the errors she finds on the proof, then copies by hand all the changes again on a duplicate proof, since one copy will be going out to the customer and another retained at the plant as back-up.

Now signed proofs and increasingly smudged, dog-eared copy is sent back to the composing room foreman, who removes one signed proof, puts it in the air express pouch for delivery to the authors, and piles the remaining material on a shelf. The pouch containing the proof will be 800 miles away in Philadelphia next morning, if the messenger service works well between airports on both ends, if the planes are on schedule, and if the airline people do not bury the pouch in an unknown storage igloo under tons of other air freight.

The editor, busy getting three other stories into shape for sending to the printer, sees correcting the proof as an unpleasant chore which can be delayed until the last minute. That time arrives quickly, and the editor's pencil comes down on the carefully typeset and corrected proof. Six lines too long! But he deletes a couple of words in each of three paragraphs, pulling up three hangers and shortening the article by three lines. One sentence that is not essential occurs at the top of a long paragraph. Cutting it would mean resetting the entire paragraph. A more essential sentence near the end of a paragraph could be dropped without very much expensive resetting. He elects for editorial integrity and deletes the expensive-to-cut sentence. That is two more lines out. Here is another possible hanger to cut: If he deletes these two words, will that two-word hanger come up to the line above? He measures with hash marks on a slip of paper as a ruler. Maybe it will fit, if the lino sets it right.

Again, the pouch courier service willing, the proofs travel between Philadelphia and Chicago. The composing-room foreman checks over the editor's proofreading corrections, watching for any proofreader's queries the editor may have missed. He brackets in red ink the lines that will have to be reset—in this case about 10 percent of the story—and carries the proof to the lino section. Corrected slugs again await a composing specialist, who inserts them and cleans up the page for proofing. The proofreader again goes over this hopefully final proof—now on yellow paper instead of white—and if all is well, the page will be ready to send to the foundry for press plate making.

By now, the final yellow "foundry" proof has arrived in Philadelphia. Somehow, this yellow color stimulates an editorial scrutiny that the white proof could not. It is a last chance to fix an oversight before the presses roll. In this case there were no errors or changes of heart after the plate was made. Many articles are not so clean and fortunate, which means a second plate must be made—a "Number Two" that usually costs the publisher roughly twice as much because of foundry overtime charges.

Perhaps one proof out of five also goes through a "revise" stage, where the corrections are so heavy an editor cannot count lines and achieve a fitted page the first time. In a big, efficient job shop where every customer waits his turn, that can add a day of time before foundry plates are made. A substantial share of an editor's time—perhaps 30 to 50 percent—will be spent with such mechanical copy fitting and related processing chores.

The author-publisher typesetting relationship

IN TERMS OF RELATIONSHIPS between author, publisher and compositor, we have been witnessing and are continuing to witness a complete restructuring of responsibilities. We shall find that there are different concepts of what the functionality of a composition program should be. One approach implies that the manuscript not be sent to typesetting until it is perfect and all of the specifications have been determined, including the necessary coding for totally automated processing. An alternative affords the greatest possible opportunity for author, editor, and designer, wherever located, to interact at any time during the writing and composing process. And obviously there are many solutions or approaches that fall in between these extremes.

The first concept, alluded to in the paragraph above, is "batch" processing. Although there could be considerable interaction during the initial writing process, once it has been completed the file would be sent to composition as a "batch" job, to be composed and paginated and typeset with no possibility for review. If it is faulty in some respect, either it would have to be done all over again, with changes being made to the text input and the control codes which it contains, or—if one is lucky—certain portions of it only might be pulled from the file and reprocessed.

Awkward as this approach may seem, it is perhaps the best approach to be taken for certain types of work which are relatively standardized and repetitive in nature and devoid of design complexities.

On the other hand, newspapers and weekly news magazines now operate systems which offer a high degree of interaction. In fact, it has become customary to look at these publishing systems as indicative of what might be more generally applicable.

A modern newspaper system

WHILE AUTOMATION of the editing and composition processes was long delayed in newspapers because of the hot metal orientation of at least the largest of them, this condition changed dramatically beginning about 1974. In part the change became possible because the relationship between the editorial process and composition activity is relatively well defined and homogeneous throughout the industry—which is rarely the case with other segments of publishing. In larger part, perhaps, it is because writers are captive in the sense that they generally work in the same building, so that their keystrokes can easily be captured and they can also be subjected to some small degree of procedural discipline. But for whatever reason, including economic pressures and the size of the market to potential vendors, a system concept has gradually emerged within the newspaper industry—a concept which may even be extended to include many related business functions, as well as those having to do with the storage and retrieval of information from the newspaper's library or morgue.

Today's newspaper is thoroughly committed to the use of the video display terminal (VDT) for initial input of reporters' copy. The reporter sits at the terminal much as he or she would at a typewriter, cradling the telephone to the ear, and taking notes of interviews, building up a scratch pad of information which can be referenced at his or her convenience. This is filed within the reporter's "queue" and can be accessed on the screen in a matter of a split second simply by typing the appropriate command.

Then the reporter begins to construct the story. He may revise it as he types, and he can use the terminal to manipulate text by moving paragraphs, searching for key works, or making "global changes" in terminology if this seems indicated.

When satisfied with his story he can "route" it to his supervising editor. This is done "by the system"—usually by his merely pressing the "send" key. The name of the story will then appear upon the editor's directory, with an indication of the approximate story length and the name of the writer. By positioning his "cursor" at that location within the directory and pressing the "get" or "fetch" key the editor will bring that story immediately to his screen. He is able to "scroll" through this "file" and make whatever changes he desires, even incorporating side comments which are not themselves a part of

The System Environment

the story and also indicating changes made within the story in such fashion that they are distinguishable from the original draft.

He can then send the story to be "hyphenated and justified" (or composed) to whatever measure and point size he wishes. For typical stories he need enter no formatting information. For others he may designate, with a few keystrokes, what the size of the head or type or column width should be.

With many systems the story will come back (almost instantaneously) and appear on his screen so that he can review its precise size and appearance. He can then send off the story to someone else for further review, editing or comment, or he can command that it be typeset or held for full-page setting. In the latter case, the "file" will be queued for the on-line typesetter and will very shortly appear either as a galley to be stripped into position on the indicated page, or on the totally composed page itself.

As an alternative, the story might next flow to a make-up man[1] who would indicate the position of the story, working with a video tube on which a diagrammatic representation of a particular newspaper page is displayed. When satisfied with the general appearance and fit of the entire page the page editor can then command that the entire page be composed, including, in some instances, all of the photographs and other artwork intended for publication on that page.

While all this is going on other editors are scanning through wire service listings, already stored on disk as they flow in from the various news agencies, deciding which stories to use, calling them up and editing them, or even combining two stories (from different sources) by making a side-by-side comparison on their "split" screen. These stories, when so selected and composed, would in turn be routed to page make-up or directly to composition.

And in another area of the newspaper, ad takers sit in front of VDTs entering classified ads as they are dictated over the telephone. Their screens capture these ads, perform credit checks against the persons placing the ads, and direct the ads to be sorted or sequenced for those days on which they are to appear (taking into consideration "skip dates" and various regional editions). When a command is given to "dump" the day's classified ads they will be typeset at once, at very high speeds, often in complete pages and in the proper sequence. Billing information will also be generated by the program.

Magazine systems. Front-end editorial systems in the magazine industry have many of the same features. In fact, certain magazines such as *U.S. News & World Report* led the way in this automation process. In these magazines, when the pages are completed they are transmitted by satellite or microwave from the editorial office to not one but a number of printing plants where the final, fully paginated typesetting takes place and printing plates are made so that the period between the closing time of the last few pages and the appearance of final bound copies of magazines, ready for mailing or newsstand delivery, is merely a matter of an hour or so.

---

1. Throughout this account, to avoid repetition of pronouns, the use of the male gender is intended to include the female as well. The modern newspaper employs men and women in comparable job slots, often in equal proportion.

Even more far-reaching changes are in process. Just as writers now use terminals as editorial tools, so are there terminals or workstations for designers, where the artwork and layout instructions are created. In addition, sizing information for reproducing photos and graphics can be captured and communicated to those directly concerned. Thus a writer may receive an assignment to fill a particular hole on a page, and as he types in his story it will be formatted precisely to occupy that space.

What a contrast between the kind of relationship described by Carlson and that within the modern newspaper or magazine! And how much of this technology can rub off or be relevant for other applications, such as book publishing?

The experiences of the present writer may be of some interest in this connection. As publisher of three newsletters having to do with publishing, office systems and professional computing technology he is able to review all of the material being prepared by writers and editors scattered across the United States and in England as well. He and others in the publishing office can make changes and comments and reroute the text back to the original writers for their comments. They in turn can make further changes.

Editors at still other locations review the same copy. Proofreading also takes place at the workstation and, of course, copy-fitting as well. No paper is used in the process until galleys are typeset for inspection, or perhaps the copy goes directly into page make-up, which is also performed on the terminals. These pages are then picked up by the printer as "camera-ready" copy.

The writers and editors, wherever located geographically, are in constant communication with one another, using their same terminals for sending and receiving messages, and are thus kept aware of what others in the organization are doing and thinking about.

Once these newsletters are completed the same text is transmitted to an on-line time-sharing service so that they can be accessed and searched by readers and researchers virtually anyplace in the world.

The technology which once was only affordable by newspaper and large magazine publishers is now appropriate, at some scale, but with comparable capabilities, for virtually every kind of publishing endeavor.

But we now need to examine more carefully just what the processes are which must take place.

13

The Composition Process

IN SUCCEEDING CHAPTERS we will be dealing with the functions of composition and the composition cycle, so far as computer programs are concerned. We shall not be immediately concerned about that portion of the composition process which constitutes input, nor shall we consider the problems posed by final output to the typesetter. At this point our only interest in the typesetter has to do with its front-end intelligence if or when it is used as a computer to perform various software tasks. For convenience in our exposition, then, we shall assume that these various software functions will in fact, take place within a "stand-alone" computer—that is, one which is not buried in a keyboard, or an editing terminal, or in a typesetter, or in any other device (such as an optical character reader or an ad markup or page layout terminal). In point of fact, of course, many or most of these composition functions could indeed be performed in one place while certain others could be done elsewhere. Increasingly many or most of the functions will be capable of being run on home personal or professional computers.

The first such computer program that the author was involved with was written for an RCA 301 computer beginning in 1963. Its input was punched paper tape in an "idiot" or "uncounted" format, which entered the computer by means of a 300 character-per-second paper-tape reader. There was no disk store on the system and so interim versions of the file were written to magnetic tape, and the programs also resided on mag tape (there were two tape drives). The computer in question consisted of 20K of six-bit words—that is, 20,480 bytes of six-bits each. At present the writer has, for his own personal use at home, an IBM PC XT with the equivalent of 500K of eight-bit words, two floppy disks capable of storing 360,000 bytes each, and a 10-Mb Winchester hard disk.

The RCA computer, with tape drive, paper-tape reader and punch, and an on-line printer, cost approximately $350,000. The IBM PC XT cost about $8,000.

There was no operating system for the RCA. We had to write our own. For the IBM PC there are several such available—all very powerful. The programming language we used for the RCA was assembler. Today one would explore the possibility of using "C" or a "C" derivative, and might even map out certain of the routines to test out the logic in BASIC, or would perhaps install a Digital Equipment VAX to write the software and then "port" it to the professional computer, which is really an "intelligent workstation."

The point is that if powerful composition programs could have been written in 1963 for a so-called "mainframe" computer, they certainly can be written today to run within a workstation, or can be buried in almost any piece of processing equipment. However, for purposes of the following analysis, we shall assume that the program will run in a "dedicated," free-standing CPU.

Program modules

THE MAIN CATEGORIES of composition software have to do with:

- *Justification*—which is a broad term for arranging text horizontally across the line. It is concerned not only with running text, but also with the composition of "display."
- *Hyphenation*—which is a subset of justification, concerned exclusively with the question of how words should be divided ("split"), when necessary, in order to achieve better justification.
- *Pagination*—or other methods of composing text vertically as well as horizontally, so that text is properly spaced out to fill a page and appropriately divided into pages.
- *Editing and corrections*—which are directed to the elimination of input errors, or to resolving problems created during the composition or pagination processes, or to improving the final product by introducing changes and "author's alterations" after the initial text has been input into the system.
- *Operating and file management systems*—These vital supporting programs become increasingly important as video-terminal systems become more common and more useful.

Because editing and corrections may take place at various stages in the composition process, much of what we shall have to say on these particular subjects will be scattered through the remainder of the book. Of course it is possible to visualize a program in which corrections and composition are indeed overlapping functions so that as soon as a correction or change is introduced it is reflected in a composed piece of text which can be viewed by the writer. This is indeed the case with many word processing programs. The term sometimes used for this kind of implementation is called "WYSIWYG" (pronounced "wizziwig") which means "what you see is what you get." The ideal "wysiwyg" implementation would show the true type faces and sizes in a "soft" version, as on a TV monitor and would feed back this information in "real time" to the writer or operator.

On a word processor, intended to drive a monospaced printer with only one size of type, if the line length is confined to a page size of 8½"×11" such a capability is not too difficult to implement, although some "scrolling" of text may be required. Obviously the task is more difficult for proportionally spaced type in many hundreds of type faces and sizes for all kinds of applications. But there are nevertheless programs and systems addressing this problem.

The Composition Process

But our first task will be to consider justification. Despite the fact that we really want to consider the program in the context of a batch run, as performed by the CPU, we shall first describe it as performed on a "direct-input" typesetter which has a counting keyboard, because virtually all of the essential operations will immediately become clear.

We shall use as an example a VariTyper Comp/Set or Comp/Edit and assume that it is being used simultaneously for input and composition, although in fact these two operations can be performed separately. In other words, we shall look at the typesetting function as performed in a counting mode. One will note that there is some resemblance to what it was that a linotype or monotype operator actually performed in the hot metal days, or what was done on a TTS-counting keyboard.

In this instance the operator mounts the desired font disks and hits the "reset" button which causes the device to read and store the set width values for the individual characters as they are represented on the film disks by bar codes. In some models not all of the width values are stored—in the interest of saving "memory"—but most of them are. The others are read on the fly when they are requested.

The operator must then fill in the blanks at the top of the screen. He indicates the desired point size, the line length in points and picas, the "primary" leading to be associated with each line, the "secondary" leading which may be used from time to time. He knows that he has

This is a representation of the Comp/Set screen showing two lines. The first has already been set. Notice the small marker within the word "complete" indicating the point at which (given the 11-unit interword space maximum) the line began to be within justification range. For the second line of text, which has yet to be typeset, the beginning point of justification follows the word "is." These lines are exceptionally long since they are to be set in six-point type across a 45-pica measure.

mounted a total of 16 fonts—four each on four disks—that will be designated as A1 through D4. He also indicates whether he wishes the machine to make its own end-of-line decisions if it can do so, or whether the operator wishes to make them.

The operator also indicates the minimum acceptable interword space value (unless this is determined for him by a default table which he is at liberty to change). Let us suppose we are on an 18-unit-to-the-em system and that we set this minimum interword space at 4 units. The maximum interword space value we shall set at 12. And we shall assign a letterspacing value of zero since we generally prefer not to permit extra spaces to be added between letters within words.

Now we find ourselves in font C1, size 11 on 13 leading, for example, with 4 to 12 as the interword space expansion potential.[1] After we have keyed in a line length of 32 picas, the machine computes that there are 629 units in the line and displays this under "LR" for line remainder, at the top of the screen. It derives this calculation in the following manner: in 32 picas there are 384 points. Dividing the point size by 11 yields 34.9 11-point ems. Multiplying 34.9 by 18 units per em should produce about 628.2 units, but it is rounded off to 629.

As we key across the line in the manual mode (where we have to make our own end-of-line decisions) the counter will display decremented character widths. When we reach the first point at which the line is within justification range, based upon our definition of the maximum acceptable interword space—in our case 12 units—a beep will sound and a blinking symbol will appear at that location on the screen. But we can continue to key, watching the countdown, which shows us how many relative units remain in the line. When we see that we cannot fit another word into the line, we can strike the "return" key. The line will be terminated and the machine will proceed to justify the line as it typesets it (flashing characters onto the photographic paper) or as it writes it onto disk for subsequent typesetting. This happens at the same time that we continue to key the next line.

When the computer processes. Substantially the same thing happens when a stand-alone computer performs the processing of input which does not contain end-of-line decisions. In most such programs the countdown assigns the minimum interword space to the spaceband value and continues across the line until it has been overset. Then it backs off to the end of the preceding word. If that word falls within the justification range the program then terminates the line.

A better solution would be to compute the desired interword space value and then, when the computer encounters a "straddle" word which would go below that value if included but exceed it if excluded, would make its decision based upon which determination is the "least bad." In other words, if we had indicated a preference for nine units as the optimum, then if to include the straddle word would lower all interword spaces to four units, but to exclude it would be to raise them to eleven, it would probably choose the latter as closer to the optimum.

1. The parameters we are now assuming differ from those in the picture on page 179.

The Composition Process

To perform this routine the computer is instructed to accept what amounts to a continuous stream of data, although if the input were from magnetic tape or disk it would be "blocked" so that there is a gap or flag after a certain number of codes have been recorded. The codes that will be read and processed are of two kinds: instructions to the computer and text material. The first category consists primarily of "tags" which identify typographic situations or conditions, such as paragraph endings or the beginning and ending of display heads. It is the function of the program to be able to distinguish between such flags, tags or signals (which are intended to activate certain processing routines). The balance of the input is, of course, the text matter that the instructions relate to. (There may also be a few system codes such as "end of file.")

Usually the first block of information to be processed has to do with setting up the job. Perhaps there will be a job title or an operator number or some other type of identification. This is useful for record-keeping purposes, but it may also be a key element in determining what the typographic conditions for that file should be, for the "parameters" for the job may not be included in the first few blocks of codes, but contained in a separate "style file" which may be accessed by the program. In such a case the codes within the job itself identify typographic situations in a somewhat generic sense, and they take on specific meaning according to the interpretation of the style file. If the style file is redefined then the parameters, and hence the appearance of the job, will be different.

However it is arranged, immediately after the identifying material the program will look for line length, point size, and font and leading information. This may be expressed as one combined command in which this information is provided sequentially—as, for example [cc01,10,12,25p] for type face "1" to be set in 10 points on 12 leading across 25 picas. Or the commands could be given separately as [f1], [ps10], [tl12], [ll25p], for font one, point size ten, type leading 12 and a line length of 25 picas.

Notice that the program may require a "begin command" and an "end command" flag, which we have shown here as square brackets. Not all commands require both beginning and ending commands. Some programs will permit only one flag where there is no "argument"—in other words, where no variables are required, such as [rr for ragged right or perhaps [er for "end ragged."

As with our illustration of the Comp/Set, the first task of the computer software is to reduce the line length to units of measurement which will correspond to the set width values for the type characters to be fitted into the line. One could elect to express and compute type widths in terms of an absolute unit system (which is converted into millimeters or thousandths of an inch), or even perhaps in tenths of a point. (A six-point em would consist of 60 units, and a 12-point em would consist of 120 units.) We might, if we preferred, adopt a relative unit system so that an em of whatever size would be made up to 18, 36, 50, 60 or 100 units. In either case (relative or absolute unit values) there are special problems which will be encountered in the conversion of character widths to units, especially where different type sizes are intermixed within the same line. But most important of all, a good composition program would be written to be "output-device-independent"—which means that the relative unit system for *any* typesetter could be accepted by the same program, given proper setup instructions.

We shall revert to the implications of these counting procedures at a later point in this discussion. For the moment, however, we shall assume that we have established a line length (32 picas) and a point size (11 points) and a unit count based on 18 units to the em, using [f1] to indicate the roman text type face of, say, Baskerville. We shall imagine that the computer has now processed the parameter definition, has been instructed as to the desired interword space values or has used its own default parameters, has now read the first identifying blocks and then sent this much of the text stream into a work area of memory which we shall designate as area "A."

[cc1,11,13,32p]{em}This is the first portion of input into our typesetting program, and we are ready to begin processing the text {ql}.

(We have used {em} and {ql} to indicate the em space at the beginning of the paragraph and the quad left at its end. Normally we would be able to generate these codes with one keystroke and they would be carried on the input and within the computer as one code each.)

The initial calculation which the program must go through is to determine, just as with the Comp/Set, the number of 11-point ems which will fit into the 32-pica line length. Let us assume that the program reaches approximately the same conclusion, but it will be easier for our illustration to assume that it comes up with 630 relative units.

It will now be necessary to bring into computer memory one or more tables of width values. For the moment let us assume that we have somehow loaded into memory one table which establishes the width values for text type face "1" in which we are going to begin to set. Using an octal (six-bit) coding structure in order to keep our example simple, we may imagine a table which reveals that the code which represents an em (assume it is 010 000 or an octal 20) has a width value of 18 units. Consequently the program writes the code for an em space into another work area, "B," which corresponds to the output buffer, and decrements the line counter by 18. It goes on to the next character, which is a capital *T*. Since we have supposed a six-bit or six-level input system, the program learns of the fact that the *T* is an upper-case character by first encountering an upshift code. The program therefore goes to the upshift portion of the width table and learns that the capital letter *T* has a unit value of 12. It writes the *T* to the output buffer and decrements the counter by 12, so that it now stands at 600 units.

The table look-up procedure just described is more complicated than it appears on the surface. Actually, the em value of 18 or the *T*

The Composition Process

value of 12, which is stored in the table or tables, may best be represented by a single character. If we are dealing with an 18-unit system we may only need 18 characters to describe the various widths, and we could store in the "box" whatever symbols correspond to the octal numbers 111 000 through 010 001 to represent 1 through 18. Let us suppose that we have assigned for the first 18 codes the numbers 0 through 9, and the letters *A* through *H*. Thus the width of the em would be expressed by an *H*—which in this instance would be interpreted as 18—and the width of the *T* would be expressed as a *B*, which would mean 12.

The example which you will find on the next page illustrates the process at work. It will be noted that the program continued to loop through the cycle of moving characters into the output buffer and decrementing the counter until the counter went negative. Then it was necessary to reverse the procedure, adding character widths back on in the reverse order, up to and including the preceding spaceband. At that point, then, there is a tally of 37 relative units left over and there are 13 spacebands over which this surplus—it is usually called a deficit since it represents the amount by which the line is short—can be distributed. Dividing 37 by 13 spacebands yields something more than two units per spaceband and less than three. If the function of the program is merely to bring the line within justification range, then this line can be passed on for output (when the job is completed) with the knowledge that it will justify within the specified parameters. But if the program must "put out" the specific value required for each interword space, it would call for seven relative units instead of four for the first 11 interword spaces, and six units (instead of four) for the remaining interword spaces.[1]

But suppose that when the program "backed off" the last word because the counter overflowed, the counter remainder (divided by the number of spacebands still left in the line) produces a quotient greater than the indicated desired maximum interword space. The program would then call for the hyphenation routine in an effort to discover whether there is a portion of the "straddle" word that could be made to fit in the line. If, however, the word could not be hyphenated, the program would have to release the line as a "loose" line, leaving it to the discretion of the typesetting device (if it actually accomplished the final justification), or exercising the remaining parameters of the composition software in the computer (if it was charged with the distribution of the deficit) to decide how much, if any, of the excess interword space should be distributed between characters as letterspacing. In the latter event, another calculation might be required—that of determining the number of *characters* in the line, so that the finest possible increments of *intraword* spacing could be distributed.

This line has been set without any letterspacing.

This line has been set with some letterspacing.

---

[1] We are assuming that the spaceband, in the initial calculation, is given a value of its desired minimum, or four units.

Character	Character width	Line count remainder	Number of spacebands		Character	Character width	Line count remainder	Number of spacebands
		630					(298)	
Em	18	612			r	6	292	
T	12	600			s/b	4	288	9
h	10	590			t	6	282	
i	5	585			y	9	273	
s	9	576			p	10	263	
s/b	4	572	1		e	9	254	
i	5	567			s	9	245	
s	9	558			e	9	236	
s/b	4	554	2		t	6	230	
t	6	548			t	6	224	
h	10	538			i	5	219	
e	9	529			n	11	208	
s/b	4	525	3		g	11	197	
f	7	518			s/b	4	193	10
i	5	513			p	10	183	
r	6	507			r	6	177	
s	9	498			o	11	166	
t	6	492			g	11	155	
s/b	4	488	4		r	6	149	
p	10	478			a	10	139	
o	11	467			m	13	126	
r	6	461			s/b	4	122	11
t	6	455			a	10	112	
i	5	450			n	11	101	
o	11	439			d	9	92	
n	11	428			s/b	4	88	12
s/b	4	424	5		w	13	75	
o	11	413			e	9	66	
f	7	406			s/b	4	62	13
s/b	4	402	6		a	10	52	
i	5	397			r	6	46	
n	11	386			e	9	37	
p	10	376			s/b	4	33	14
u	10	366			r	6	27	
t	6	360			e	9	18	
s/b	4	356	7		a	10	8	
i	5	351			d	9	–1	
n	11	340						
t	6	334			d	9	8	
o	11	323			a	10	18	
s/b	4	319	8		e	9	27	
o	11	308			r	6	33	
u	10	298			s/b	4	37	13

Note the broken line. At this point the counter is overset, and the program then goes into an overset routine in order to get back to the nearest word ending just short of the overset condition. Of course, it must discard the spaceband in the process. In the above illustration we have not included a character counter within each line, which might be useful for calculating letterspacing if this is to be performed by the computer program rather than by the output typesetter. After determining the last complete word that will fit on the line, the program must ascertain whether the calculation falls within the allowable interword space maximum. If it does not, the hyphenation algorithm is called for. It is only after this routine has been performed that a character count would be relevant since at this point the final end-of-line decision has not yet been made.

It may be seen, then, that the logic of the justification program is not difficult. For the moment we are considering the hyphenation routine as a "black box" that is plugged into the system. In other words, it is completely independent of the logic of justification. Justification involves establishing a line count, reading in characters, keeping track of spacebands, decrementing the line counter, and determining when the counter goes negative. When this happens you back up to space out the line if this can be done. If it cannot be done, and the hyphenation routine provides a negative answer—*i.e., no hyphenation possible*—most existing programs that we are familiar with can offer no solution any better than to insert extra space (beyond the maximum limits defined) between the words in the line or between the characters in the word, or both.

But when type is set in hot metal by an expert and the operator encounters a loose line, he will discard the preceding line or lines and try to rework those lines so as to move a word or portion of a word up or down, in order to try to solve his problem in some other way. This solution can also be tackled by a computer program and there are a few programs which accomplish it. One approach is to retain perhaps ten lines in computer memory and to go back over those lines exploring alternate breaking points to avoid the excessively loose line. Another is to try to resolve the problem on a page-by-page basis in those instances in which a computer program tackles justification and pagination simultaneously.[1] A third would be some sort of post-processing routine to try to smooth out such problems.

Nevertheless, impossible situations will still arise. There is nothing you can do about a loose line at the beginning of a paragraph except to rewrite that portion of the text. But, in consolation, we may observe that some typesetting machines presently have the capability of distributing white space in such fine increments that so-called loose lines may cease to be offensive and may effectively be disguised.

Set width tables are vital

THE VITAL ROLE of set width tables should be apparent at once. Just as the justifying or counting keyboard has to access character widths so that the operator can make his own end-of-line decisions, so must the computer know the relevant width values. These must somehow be available to the computer, either because they reside in memory or can be brought into memory when they are needed.

If memory is restricted there may not be room to contain all of the tables that will be required for a particular job. (Some typesetters maintain 18 fonts or more on line and some jobs require that they all be used. Thus it may well be that many tables are necessary.) One factor that will influence the number of such tables that can be stored is the amount of room required for each table. If each point size needs to be described by its own table then many times more room will be required. It seems better to store one table for each font—at least within a given range of sizes—and to develop a formula which takes into account the point size or set size of the type called for in a

1. This is the approach taken by "TEX," the program written at Stanford University by Professor Donald Knuth.

particular job. It is also extremely important to find ways to compress the font information into a minimum of space.[1]

Moreover, since some of today's typesetting machines can create type in half point increments, the design of our system should consider the possibility that we may well want to set in 7½ or 8½ point sizes, and if we have a CRT typesetter we might want to create type in 6.8 or 11.2 set. It also seems desirable to express unit values in terms which permit them to be reduced to a common base without incurring rounding errors. In doing so we must still be able to relate them to the manner in which they were expressed by the type designer and also be able to represent them as required for all the phototypesetting devices that we may wish to access.

The common denominator in a relative unit system could be 18, 24, 36, 50, 54 or even 100 units to the em. Point sizes can be in half points or tenths of a point. The best system we have encountered accepts the desired value per em (say 100 units) and multiplies it by tenths of a point. This takes care of all possibilities except for those typesetters—fortunately very few at the moment—which can set characters in quarter-point increments. The trouble with our scheme is that it inevitably means we may have to add up very large numbers: 100 units to the em times 60 for a six-point em yields a count of 6,000 for only one em of space. But fortunately computers can usually cope with such large numbers.

In a six-level system, if we represent widths by single characters, we will be able to describe only 64 different width values, because six bits can only yield that many combinations. The chances are, however, that we would not need the first five- or six-unit values since they would be too low. So we could add perhaps five units to each value shown, and reach up to perhaps a 69-unit system. Nevertheless, a six-level system presents problems for the store of a sufficient range of values. An eight-bit code structure, yielding 256 different width combinations, is generally used and is probably sufficient. This value would, of course, be multiplied by the point or set size factor prior to the line length accumulation process.

Pages 188 and 189 provide a crude flow chart indicating some of the essential steps in the justification routine. The reader will note that we have branched to a "linend" subroutine where this is appropriate, as well as an "overflow" subroutine, but we have not shown the flow charting of the hyphenation logic, since that will be covered in the next chapter.

The underlying "justification" concept

IF WE THINK of the justification program as one that is designed merely to accept a string of text and arrange it into lines we will not fully appreciate the task that confronts us. Perhaps we moved too early into a discussion of justification, without sufficient attention to the fact that the underlying task is really one of *composition*, in which justification is only one aspect. Composition goes far beyond the arrangement of text into justified lines, or even its positioning within

---

1. Such tables may also store other kinds of information, such as kerning pair values.

made-up pages. Composition has to do with the aesthetic treatment of consecutive areas of white space upon which typographic and graphic images are to be superimposed. If we think of the task in this light our entire approach may well be different. We may be more concerned with the arrangement of *areas,* in terms of *x/y coordinates,* than with the formation of lines of text. Especially for typesetting devices like the Linotron 1010 or the VideoComp 570, or for any of the raster scan imaging machines we shall be discussing in Chapter 21—wherever the capability exists to produce images at any point on a two-dimensional surface, an area composition concept will be helpful. There are typesetting programs which start out with the premise that type is to be "poured" into areas or shapes with defined boundaries. But even if the immediate concern is with lines rather than areas, they must be capable of being arranged in some sort of frame, whether rectangular or free-form. What are some of these justification tasks that need to be performed?

Quadding

PERHAPS THE MOST OBVIOUS is "quadding" textual material—not just at the end of a paragraph of running text, but for single lines that stand by themselves. Such lines are not in fact justified from left margin to right margin, but it is still necessary for the program to go through the motions of counting the relative width of characters to make sure that they will fit within the line, and perhaps to pass this information on to the output typesetter. The quad codes (left, right and center) are used to signal the existence of a collection of words that are intended to be positioned within a single line, either flushed to the left, or to the right, or centered, with equal space on either side.

The quadding signal most often comes at the end of the line in question, although there are some programs which indicate that the text which follows is to be so positioned. In this case some kind of signal is required to identify the termination of the block of text.

If the composition program is interactive in nature, or if it is located in a counting keyboard, the person doing the input will know immediately whether or not the intended words will fit as visualized without flowing over to the next line. In the absence of such feedback there are rules which can be applied to the use of the quad left when it ends a running paragraph:
1. If the line almost fits its measure, space it out.
2. If the line falls short by a defined amount, use normal—not minimum—interword spacing.
3. If the line is very short, consisting of only a word or a portion of a word, consider the possibility of reprocessing the latter portion of the paragraph, if feasible, in order to pull it up.

But none of these rules would apply to the self-contained quadded line which happens not to fit within the assigned measure:

Borough Council Reinstates Westchester Police Chief

Borough Council Reinstates Westchester Police Chief

Sample Justification Routine

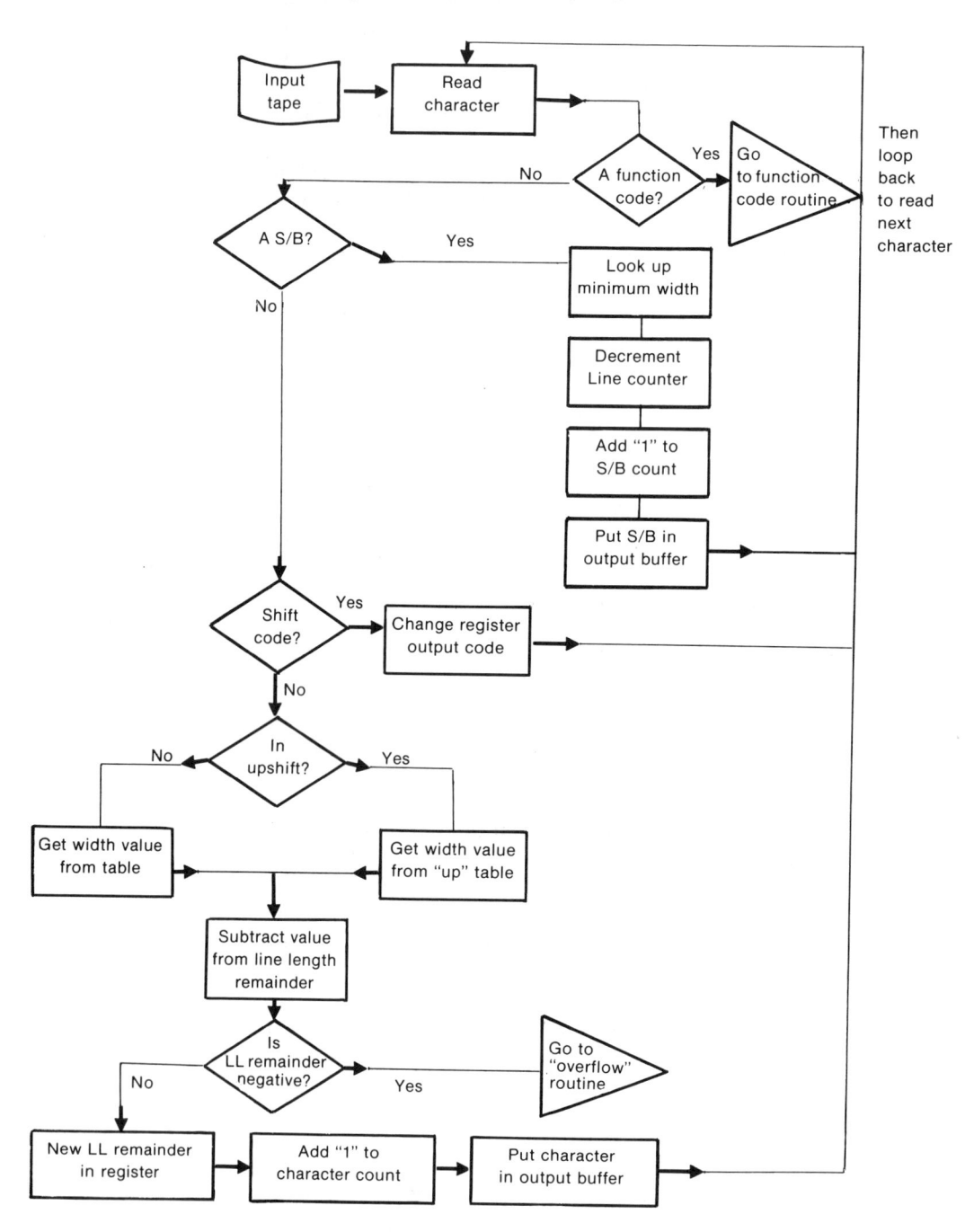

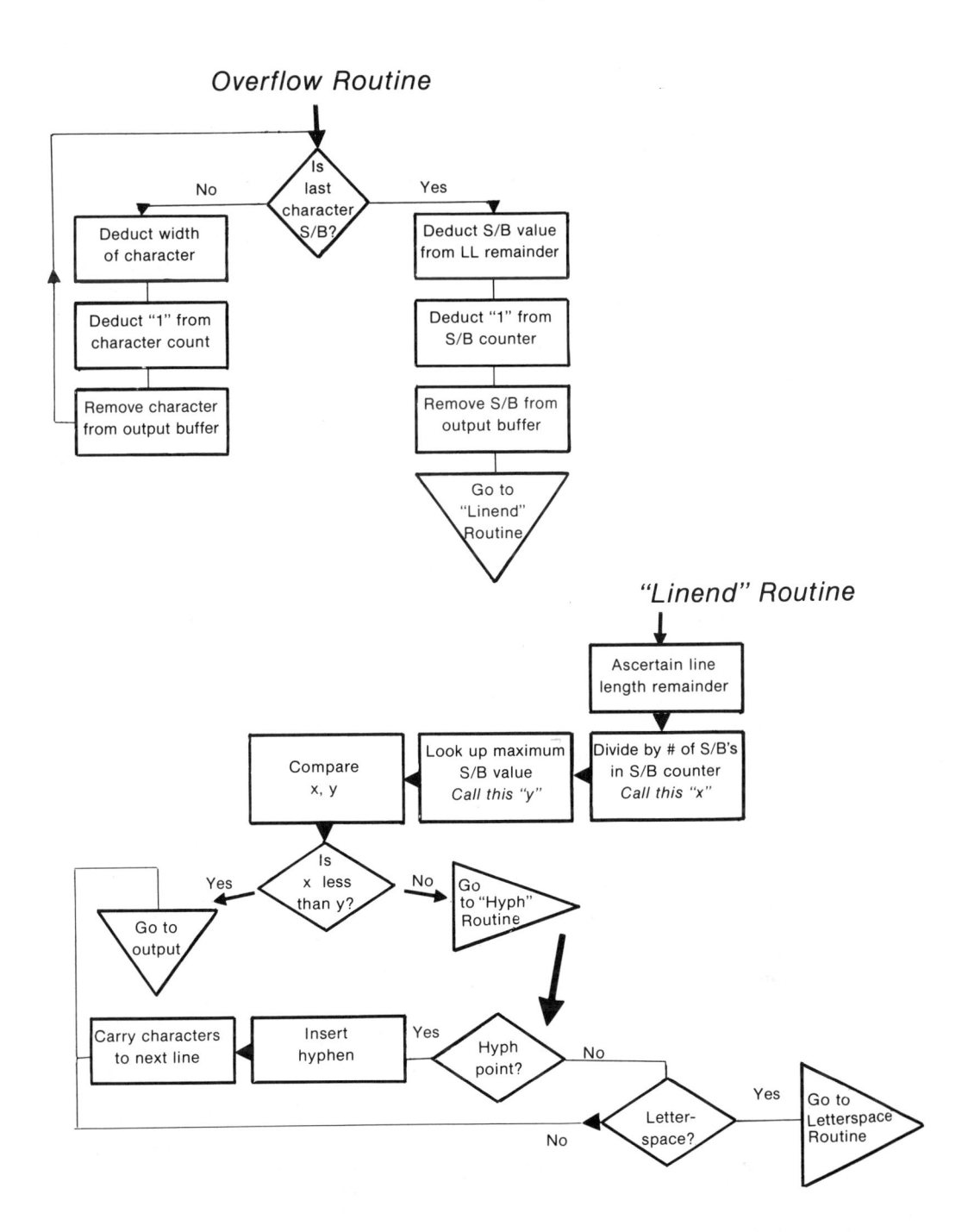

The Composition Process

Overflow Routine

- Is last character S/B?
  - **No** → Deduct width of character → Deduct "1" from character count → Remove character from output buffer → (loop back)
  - **Yes** → Deduct S/B value from LL remainder → Deduct "1" from S/B counter → Remove S/B from output buffer → Go to "Linend" Routine

"Linend" Routine

- Ascertain line length remainder
- Divide by # of S/B's in S/B counter — Call this "x"
- Look up maximum S/B value — Call this "y"
- Compare x, y
- Is x less than y?
  - **Yes** → Go to output
  - **No** → Go to "Hyph" Routine
- Hyph point?
  - **Yes** → Insert hyphen → Carry characters to next line
  - **No** → Letterspace?
    - **Yes** → Go to Letterspace Routine
    - **No** → (return)

There is no easy solution to the problem of head fitting without some form of interactivity, and indeed some composition programs offer a "partial processing" routine which permits the user to send to composition only a small block of text in order to see how it will fit. Even without a "wysiwyg" terminal, the normal VDT with monospaced characters will nevertheless show line breaks when the job (or a portion thereof) is called back to the screen after composition is performed.

The off-line keyboard operator or writer, producing unjustified input for a computer composition system, gets no such feedback. Perhaps the markup man can continue to count out width values or otherwise estimate them in some fashion, but this is laborious and inefficient. Fortunately nowadays one of the capabilities of composition programs is that they can be interactive and can provide, through the video display terminal, a "window" into what decisions the computer program proposes to make so that they can be overruled.

For example, with respect to the two headlines on the bottom of page 187, in order to make it possible for us to set the two headline illustrations side by side within the allotted spaces, it was necessary to experiment with the point size, finally determining that 15 points would fit within the allotted space, but not 16.

The problem of the self-contained quadded line comes to light not only in the setting of heads and other display material, but also in the setting of poetry or other types of lines, such as "listings" that may or may not "turn over." We therefore find it necessary to define—in the event the line does turn over—the conditions we would wish to have govern. Should hyphenation be permitted? Should the second line be indented, and if so, by how much? Are there places where the first line should not break, even without hyphenation? Should the first line be left ragged or should it be justified?

Consider some of the following examples:

When, in disgrace with fortune and men's
    eyes
I all alone beweep my outcast state,
And trouble deaf heaven with my bootless
    cries,
And look upon myself and curse my
    fate—

When, in disgrace with fortune and men's eyes

I all alone beweep my outcast state

And trouble deaf heaven with my bootless cries,

And look upon myself and curse my fate–

Smith, G. W. 1400 Mayfield . 565-2489
Society for Advancement of Barbershop Quartet Singing of America 5 Fifth Ave. 233-4600

Smith, G. W. 1400 Mayfield 565-2480
Society for Advancement of Barbershop Quartet Singing of America
5 Fifth Ave. 233-4600

Cooper, James Fenimore, The Last of the Mohicans, MacMillan, 1952

Cooper, James Fenimore, The Last of the
    Mohicans, MacMillan, 1952

Some of these problems may never be entirely resolvable in any kind of non-interactive program of computerized composition. The operator may need to get feedback in order to appraise the aesthetic

The Composition Process

consequences of his input. But for other kinds of work—including the listings in the examples above—a general rule can be formulated and programmed, such as to carry the runover line as a "hanging indent" and to set the first of several such lines in an entry in a ragged or flush left manner if justifying it would exceed the desired interword space.

In general, as the reader well knows, the quadding function embraces such format possibilities as:

Quadding left
Quadding center
Quadding right

Quadding left and right
Leadering from left.................................... to right
Leadering from left..to right
And generating rules ─────────────────────

In like manner, runover lines can be set with the succeeding line or lines flushed left.
In like manner, runover lines can be set with the succeeding line or lines flushed right.
In like manner, runover lines can be set with the succeeding line or lines quadded center.

Changes of measure and the use of indents

THE PROGRAM has to be able to cope with instructions to change line length. Such instructions are generally imbedded in the text. They may or may not occur at the beginning of the text or at the beginning of a paragraph within the text. In this instance we have given a command for the left indent to start at the beginning of the sixth line and to continue for six lines before it reverts to the normal measure. In this fashion we can set a "notch" which could be used in a newspaper column for a "mug shot" of the writer. Or it could be used to accommodate a "wraparound" for some other kind of illustration. Often this kind of command can be used in such fashion that matched left and right indents can occur in adjoining columns. It is also possible to vary the amount of indent from line to line by skewing it. This will be illustrated in the next paragraph.

Indentions are of various types. There is the indention of *specified duration*, which is to continue for a given number of lines or points and then is to be dropped. Or there is the indention of *indefinite duration* which is to be continued until a signal is given that (as of the next line) it should be eliminated. There must be a capability of handling left, right, or center indents, and to create hanging indents, and to calculate the amount of indention required to align with a string of characters whose total width the input operator doesn't know.

This latter function is often called "indent text." Here is an example of what we have in mind in the case of an "indent text command. You will note that
> this line begins where the previous one left off and that the indent continues until it has been canceled. Here we are going to input the command to cancel it and to return to the full measure.

The hanging indent is often used for listings and, as a matter of fact, you will find that it has been employed for all of the material set beginning on page 194.

It is also possible to nest one indent within another. First we will start off with a left indent and then we will nest another left indent inside of this, and then we will center an indent on the text immediately above. Now at the beginning of the next line the left indent
> begins and it will continue throughout this take. And at the beginning of the next line a second left indent will also take
>> effect and this too would continue either until we canceled it or until the end of a specified number of lines.
>>> This indent is not only centered on the preceding material but it is also calculated to terminate of its own accord when the paragraph has been ended, so that the text will then return to the condition which governed immediately before.
>> Now we have returned to the prior condition and in another line or so we will cancel all indents and return to the full measure.

This has now been done and all text should be set full measure. As you will see, a great many different effects can be achieved by using different combinations of indentions.

Ragged setting

SETTING TEXT in an unjustified or ragged manner is another very common aesthetic effect. The fact is that to set a column of text "ragged" and to make it visually pleasing is really quite difficult. It isn't just a matter of breaking lines in the usual way, but of substituting a normal but constant interword space value for variable interword spacing. The trick is to achieve a degree of raggedness which avoids any kind of obvious pattern and manages somehow to vary each line by at least an em (some would prefer two ems) from the preceding and following lines. There are some composition routines that have been especially written to achieve this. Some of the problems are illustrated on the next page. At the top of the next page on the left is a justified paragraph, while on the right it has been set ragged. The line endings differ primarily because the interword space value for ragged setting is always a constant while it is wider than the minimum of the range applied to justified settings.

The Composition Process

Here is an example of text which is being set "justified" with hyphenation being allowed. We shall then reset this same paragraph without permitting interword space expansion to take place. This is one form of ragged setting known as "ragged right." Then we will set the same material line for line, also ragged, but ragged left rather than ragged right, and finally, ragged center.

Here is an example of text which is being set "justified" with hyphenation being allowed. We shall then reset this same paragraph without permitting interword space expansion to take place. This is one form of ragged setting known as "ragged right." Then we will set the same material line for line, also ragged, but ragged left rather than ragged right, and finally, ragged center.[1]

There are special "ragged" setting programs which seek to assure that line lengths will vary by a certain value from those that precede or follow, and that variations between lines are not too repetitive, but are more or less randomized. Unless one has developed a very sophisticated program for ragged setting, it is better to set the material several times until the results are pleasing. Obviously this is not a very efficient solution. It is also generally necessary, as we have done here, to increase the width of the measure somewhat.

Here is an example of text which is being
set "justified" with hyphenation
being allowed. We shall then
reset this same paragraph without
permitting interword space
expansion to take place. This is one form
of ragged setting known as "ragged
right." Then we will set the same material
line for line, also ragged,
but ragged left rather than ragged right,
and finally, ragged center.

A typical command structure

TO GIVE the reader a more precise understanding of the nature and extent of the composition language and the typographical effects that the language is intended to achieve, we have listed all of the major commands of the IBM "Printext" software package, which in turn was patterned after one of the most widely copied composition programs known as the IBM 1130 FDP composition program. Most of these commands, or their equivalents, will be found in virtually all such composition programs at this time, especially those which are batch-processing oriented. However, we have made some editorial comments in italics.

1. The other versions are not in fact represented here.

AB—*(abbreviate).* To abbreviate a text string in an attempt to fit. Switch to caps and small caps from caps. Switch to caps and lower case. Drop vowels from end. Drop letters from end. *Not a common command. Not found in most software packages. Of marginal value.*

AE—*(alternate face until end).* To call for the alternate face for setting the remainder of the line only. *Here, again, this is not a common command. It was apparently devised to simplify certain kinds of input. The condition would not be encountered frequently.*

AF—*(alternate face).* To call for alternate face until further notice. *It is more usual to specify the desired type face rather than to designate an official "alternate."*

AG—*(allow ligature).* To indicate that individually entered characters are to be combined into ligatures. *This is a common feature of most good composition programs. It eliminates the need on the part of the operator to key ligatures, and permits him to change his mind about whether he wants ligatures or not, thus providing a text file which is more universally processible.*

AL—*(allow letterspace).* To indicate that from this point on letterspacing is allowed if the spacebands in the line would otherwise exceed the maximum defined width. *This command is common to virtually all typesetting programs.*

CA—*(change assembly).* To change face, using another "assembly" *(e.g., font disk)* until the end of the take or until further notice. *This is a somewhat unusual command. It presumes that the codes which designate a given font will now stand for another font, as on another disk or drum, and it arises out of the limitations of some typesetters. But it is unusual to change a font "dressing" in such cases during the course of a job.*

CC—*(change column).* To specify the column, or more precisely, the line length of measure to be used to set the following text. *This command or its equivalent is common to all typesetting programs, and it must be given at the beginning of every take (if not more frequently) unless "default" conditions are being observed or unless it is generated by "modes" which are associated with particular type faces.*

CF—*(change face).* To specify the face (font master) to be used for setting the following text. *Like the command immediately preceding, it is vital for all typesetting programs.*

CL—*(change leading).* To specify the amount of leading to be used to set the following text. *Again, this is a common command, always given unless a default condition is expected to prevail.*

CM—*(compare strings).* To compare the contents of two strings and to set a result. *This is an unusually sophisticated typesetting command not commonly found in composition programs. Its purpose is to permit the user to cause text to be set differently depending upon what conditions are encountered. Conditional commands of this character are found only in very complex software packages, although the same results may be achieved in other ways, especially if the program is "interactive."*

CO—*(comment).* To store information with text for later use, as for a user-provided post-processing program or to include information relevant for a subsequent operation. *Many composition programs offer the user the opportunity to put editorial comment or instructions within the text which the composition program will ignore and not typeset.*

CP—*(change point size).* To specify the point size to be used for the following text. *This is of course a vital command, always given at the beginning of a job, and frequently during the course of a job. The syntax of the command is usually something like [CP06] to change to six-point type.*

CS—*(change set size).* To indicate that the following text is to be set in a different set size, but same point size unless otherwise indicated. *Some programs assume the same set size as the indicated point size. When this command is given it requires the program to recalculate width values to the new set size, just as would be the case if a change in point size occurred.*

CT—*(change table).* To request a different keyboard or printer graphics table. *This assumes that there are various "overlays" of graphic symbols which can be substituted one for another, either on input or output, or on both. Such a condition could be implied rather than explicit.*

DE—*(do end).* To define the end of a series of commands that are controlled by a **DW** or **DI** command. *(See below.)*

DF—*(define function).* To specify data to a user-written routine to provide implementation for unique features of the device. *This type of command is becoming increasingly common. It provides for coding that is "passed through" the program without any need for processing, since it expects the output device to cope with it. It might be a signal for the CRT typesetter to draw a vertical rule of a certain depth at a certain location.*

The Composition Process

DI—*(do if)*. To conditionally execute a series of composition commands. *Again, this is a sophisticated and not-too-common command of more value in a "batch" environment than in an interactive one.*

DL—*(define leader)*. To define the character to be used for leader insertion. *While this command is quite common, it is also common to have the ability to define two such characters and to alternate them in a certain order, as with a dot and a dash.*

DM—*(define module)*. To indicate a job table that specifies a device module number to be used and/or an output setup number. *Many programs now make it possible, one way or another, to process text which is destined for one of several on-line typesetters.*

DO—*(define operator)*. To define the operator who input or edited a job so that statistics with respect to operator performance can be developed and credited to the operator. *This type of management control function is increasingly common as an "add-on" to composition software.*

DW—*(do while)*. To loop through a series of composition commands while the specific item is positive. *Again, this is a conditional command perhaps more appropriate for a batch program. It is not common in other software programs at this time. Of course the condition that governs must be specified by the command "argument."*

EF—*(end format)*. Specifies that the format statement is being defined in order to be terminated and stored. Also used to denote end of execution when format is called. *To understand this, the reader will have to refer to our discussion of "stored formats" which follows.*

EP—*(end paragraph)*. To specify that the present paragraph is to be immediately terminated. *A quad left code might do just as well, but it is possible to associate other conditions with the paragraph ending, such as an em indent to begin the next paragraph.*

ER—*(erase line)*. To prevent the current line from being output to a photocomposer or output device. *This command is not relevant for a composition program but is concerned with what to do with erroneous input. However, there are some other "conditional format" circumstances in which it might be used.*

ES—*(end of short)*. To separate short takes when it is desired to reset the system defaults before each part.

ET—*(end of take)*. To indicate that the current take is to be terminated.

EX—*(extract)*. To move data from an input record to a numbered string for data processing-related activities. *Not a common composition command.*

FA—*(font assignments)*. To specify the physical fonts available and their locations. *This is generally not part of a composition package but is rather a "pre-processor utility" routine to enable the software to address the desired font locations in order to access designated characters.*

FC—*(film cut)*. To cause film or paper to be cut by the output typesetter into a desired length or take.

FS—*(fixed space)*. To cause the immediate insertion of a fixed amount of space in a line. *The "argument" following the command will indicate the value of the fixed space, usually in relative units.*

GE—*(get at event)*. To indicate a format to be invoked when certain conditions occur, as if a "get format" command were issued. *This is another of the more sophisticated "if" commands not commonly included in run-of-the-mill composition programs.*

GF—*(get format)*. To call from disk or memory store a predefined format. *"Get format" and "use format" commands are basic to virtually all composition programs.*

GS—*(get string)*. To compose the contents of a string. *Similar to a "get format" except that the string could be text or a combination of text and format instructions.*

HO—*(homograph)*. To specify where hyphens are to appear in a word which is a homograph—that is, a word which hyphenates differently depending upon meaning. *A discretionary hyphen will accomplish the same result.*

HT—*(hyphenation test)*. To hyphenate a word or words and print out all the hyphenation points produced. *This is usually a feature of a "utility" program rather than the basic composition program itself.*

IF—*(indent first line)*. To specify the amount of left or right indention of the first line of all succeeding paragraphs *(ascertained by test following a quad left for example). This command obviates the need for keying an em or other indent at the beginning of each paragraph.*

IH—(*indent hang*). To specify the amount of left and/or right indention of all lines within a paragraph other than the first line. *The argument must of course indicate the value of the indent, as in ems and ens, picas and points, or even fractions of an inch or millimeter, depending upon the program.*

IL—(*indent left*). To specify an amount of left indention for a given vertical distance. *The duration of the indent may be indicated in the argument—as so many lines, or so much depth in points—or it may continue until canceled.*

IM—(*imbed take*). To switch the input stream to the referenced take and include it at this point. *Not a common composition feature since there are other ways to accomplish this.*

IN—(*indent*). To set indention values and cause indention. *More commonly a left, right, center or hanging indent is specified.*

IP—(*indent paragraph*). To specify the value of left and/or right indent for all the following lines in the current paragraph only.

IR—(*indent right*). To specify the amount of right indention for a given vertical distance or until further notice.

IT—(*indent take*). To specify the amount of left or right indention for all the following lines in the current take only.

IX—(*indent text*). To specify an amount of indention when the numeric value is unknown but the indention is based upon the positioning of the command within the line.

JU—(*justify line*). To terminate the current line at the present point and to seek to justify it whether or not it accords with normal justification procedures. *Usually called "force justify."*

LI—(*leader insert*). To specify the location of leaders for lines ended by a quad, from the point of the command or from a quad middle command, or also for tabbed lines.

LJ—(*line justify*). To specify that a line of type is to be set using one or more system-selected point sizes, so that the line fits within the column measure at the largest size possible.

MC—(*merge control*). To transfer program control between the format input stream and the normal input stream.

MT—(*measure text*). To output an undeterminable amount of space or to save the value of this space as a variable. *This is a most useful command to enable the user to ascertain how much space is taken up so that he can issue commands to reverse lead or to end a page. It approaches the pagination routines which will be discussed in a subsequent chapter.*

NF—(*normal face*). To signify that the normal or designated face is to be used from this point on until further notice. *It may save the operator the problem of finding out what the normal face is supposed to be. Not a common command.*

NS—(*non-space*). To request that the next character be set with a zero width so as to permit the positioning of a "floating accent."

OF—(*off switch*). To set the switches specified to the "off" position. *In this context, a switch is a routine to be invoked. This is not, properly speaking, a composition command, but part of a language subroutine.*

ON—(*on switch*). To set specified switch to "on."

PS—(*place string*). To clear and copy a single string or to concatenate multiple strings. *Again, not a common command, but more in the nature of a composition "language" for developing special subroutines.*

QC—(*quad center*). To indicate that the present line should be immediately terminated and quadded center.

QF—(*quad from middle*). To terminate a line in which leaders or white space will appear. Multiple leader insertions (**LI**) and/or white space (**WS**) may appear in the line. *In other programs it is sufficient to terminate the second half of the line with any quad code.*

QL—(*quad left*). To terminate the current line and quad it left.

QR—(*quad right*). To terminate the current line and quad it right.

RC—(*ragged center*). To produce ragged left and right margins.

RD—(*read record*). To open and read an external file. *Not a common command. Interactive video-oriented techniques provide various methods for getting at such files.*

The Composition Process

RL—*(ragged left)*. To produce a ragged left margin.

RN—*(repeat number)*. To set multiple copies of the same line. *Not a common command.*

RR—*(ragged right)*. To produce a ragged right margin.

SC—*(set conditional)*. To set a variable with one of three values depending on the sign or zero condition of a specified data field. *Not a common command, implying much more sophistication than many programs offer, but important for batch-oriented page make-up.*

SF—*(save format)*. To save text and/or commands on disk under the format number specified. *Most programs offer this capability, except that the saving can also be done in memory.*

SI—*(set item)*. To cause up to five digits, representing the integer value of an item, to be set in the input stream. *Unique to this particular program.*

SL—*(skew left)*. To create copy with skewed indent on the left side.

SN—*(slant)*. To specify to the output device that the text which follows is to be set in a slanted (obliqued) mode. *Usually a "pass through" command for CRT typesetters.*

SS—*(substring)*. To create a new string from a portion of another string. *More or less unique for this particular software.*

ST—*(save text)*. To place text into a format where everything else is standard. Used in conjunction with a *get at event* command, it allows the keying of copy in one sequence and setting it in another. *Unique to this particular software, although similar capabilities are usually provided in most good programs.*

SV—*(set variables)*. To set the values of variables to be used in later commands. *This feature is found in most advanced composition programs.*

TB—*(tab between)*. To specify the end of tabular material and cause the text to be centered between the next two available stops.

TC—*(tab center)*. To specify the end of tabular material and cause the center of the text to be placed at the next available stop.

TJ—*(tab jump)*. To specify a skip to the tab stop specified. *Not common.*

TL—*(tab left)*. To cause the word preceding the command to be tabbed flush left against the next tab stop. Or to indicate the beginning of the first text in a line which is going to be followed by a tab command.

TN—*(tab number)*. To set a specified number of equally spaced tab stops.

TP—*(tab proportion)*. To set tabs when the exact location is not known but the proportional distance between them is known. *As to equalize a given space between three columns.*

TR—*(tab right)*. To specify the end of tabular material and cause the text to be tabbed right flush against the next available tab stop.

TS—*(tab set)*. To set tabs at the points specified.

TW—*(tab width)*. To set tabs at the point specified in the first data field plus the widths specified in the following fields.

TX—*(tab text)*. To specify a tab point when the numeric amount is unknown.

UF—*(use format)*. To call from disk a previously defined format statement.

UN—*(unslant)*. To specify to the output device to set the following text in the normal mode.

VC—*(values for composition)*. To set one or more values to control aspects of composition. Column or line width. Width on the left side into which punctuation may be "hung." Width on the right side for the same purpose. Number of the desired hyphenation module. Number of the exception word dictionary to be used, or no dictionary. *While this particular approach differs from others, most of these capabilities exist in all good systems, including the "hung punctuation" provision.*

VH—*(values for hyphenation)*. To override temporarily the default hyphenation values in the job table.

VL—*(values for letterspacing)*. To change temporarily the default letterspacing to be applied.

VR—*(values for ragged copy)*. To override temporarily default values specified in the job table for ragged copy.

WS—*(white space)*. To cause available room in a line to be filled with white space.

XG—*(cancel ligatures)*. Ligatures should no longer be combined.

XH—*(cancel hyphenation)*. Hyphenation is no longer to be done.

XL—*(cancel letterspacing)*. Letterspacing is no longer to be done.

XR—*(cancel ragged)*. Return to normal margins, setting all lines flush left and right.

It can be seen that most of the above commands are "mnemonic"—that is, the "name" of the operator suggests its function to help the markup person or operator remember what the commands stand for. Even so, when there are so many commands it is impossible to remember them all, and some of them do not seem to be as mnemonically helpful as they might be.

During the course of the explanation of these commands we have alluded to the fact that many of them require "arguments"—that is, the number of lines an indent is to be observed, or the size of the type to be set, or the number or name of the type font must be specified as part of the command. Obviously many of these commands are quite complex, and they must be input quite precisely or else the program will ignore them or become confused and not know what to do. Thus an effort is made to simplify them. Unfortunately, this is not easy to do, and the best that can be achieved—as a rule—is to identify those which are used frequently and to be certain that they are marked properly and keyed and input correctly. Then be sure to store them away as formats which can be called out with one or two unique keystrokes that are easy to keyboard. Commands, unfortunately, are difficult to input exactly each time because they are not familiar words and do not come easily to the keyboarder's fingers. "String substitution" helps to overcome this problem, and one simple, unique string can be used to stand for not just one command but for several commands which are invariably used together. Hence most composition programs now offer the ability to substitute a simple string of codes for a more complex string. These can be stored away as formats. "Use format 01"—[UF01]—or some other kind of "string substitution" routine can be invoked. The unique combination of "$a" can be exploded into a very complex set of instructions, or a combination of instructions and text.

It is often troublesome to develop the proper codes to achieve desired results, but once they are debugged by testing and stored away, thereafter their use is quite trouble-free, and ordinary keyboarders can be taught to compose composition results which are quite complex.

Use of stored formats

STORED FORMATS are therefore the salvation of computerized photocomposition. Modern phototypesetters offer many capabilities, but to cause these machines (or the programs that drive them) to go through their paces and thus to enjoy all of their benefits is usually quite difficult. Hence, stored formats are called into use. Not only can such formats be exceptionally complex in and of themselves, but they can also call out other formats. In other words, stored formats can be "nested," and this is particularly useful if the program in some way limits the length of a given format. By tacking on to the end of that format still another format call you can get the benefit of a more complex statement of conditions. There are also formats which are called "merge" formats, and which contemplate that one will, at a

The Composition Process

given point, "exit" from the format and at a given signal, usually known as a "merge" call, return "control" to the next step within the format again. On the right is an example from the Digital Equipment Typeset-11 composition software manual. In this instance the commands are expressed differently, but they accomplish the same results. Within brackets a "combined command" is given. Thus "f2" means "font 2," "v36" means vertical leading of 36 points, and "c10.6" means a column width of 10 picas and six points. By studying this example you will see how the "at" sign (@) is used to return to the format (merge) again and again.

Need for diagnostics

ONE OF THE SECRETS of a good composition program is for the programmer to anticipate mistakes that users are likely to make. The program should be able somehow to ignore commands that do not make sense, but nevertheless to identify them as having been ignored. For example, if the input calls for a ten-pica indent to be set within a one-pica line length (not at all an unusual error), the program should either abort the balance of its processing, identifying the location of the error, or continue processing as best it can. This would depend upon whether the program is a batch or an interactive one.

Some of the most successful programs will first scan through the entire file for commands, prior to any processing, and will immediately identify most of those that do not make sense.

Summary

THE JUSTIFICATION PROCESS embraces a wide variety of composition routines, many of which are extremely detailed and all of which are meticulously conceived to achieve the same capabilities which a highly-skilled craftsman learned to give effect to in hot metal. With the use of these commands and the routines they call forth—branching from the character-by-character processing loop to the additional steps and complications implied by the composition language—high-quality composition can in fact be achieved with extraordinary efficiency.

But the kind of composition system required must be tailored to the environment in which it will be used, and the persons involved in its use must understand the processes that are intended to take place. We will return to a more detailed consideration of the "system environment" after we have considered the principles involved in three other important areas—hyphenation, editing and corrections, and pagination.

Font 2, 27 pt — **SHOES FOR SUMMER** — 36, 24

Font 6, 12 pt — Our Reg. 4" to 5" / 4 Days Only — 16, 12

Font 4, 72 pt — **2⁹⁵** — 72

Font 1, 8 pt — All brand new vinyls, in leading styles / and shades that are super. Sabots, / and T-straps! 5-9 — 20, 8, 8

|← 10.6 →|

1. Straight markup
   ```
   [f2p27v36c10.6]          SHOES FOR/c
   [v24]                       SUMMER/c
   [f6p12v16]                Our Reg. . . ./c
   [v12]                    4 Days Only/c
   [f4p72v72]                      2 95/c
   [f1p8v8va12]         All brand new . . . 5-9./1
   ```

2. Format definition
   The definition is written simply by copying everything over from straight markup except, in place of each block of text, enter a call point @ as follows:
   ```
   *DEPTAD1 = [f2p27v36c10.6]@
   /c[v24]@
   /c[f6p12v16]@
   /c[v12]@
   /c[f4p72v72]@
   /c[f1p8v8va12]@
   /1 =
   ```

3. Format use
   ```
   *DEPTAD1*SHOES FOR@SUMMER@
   Our Reg . . .@4 Days Only@2 95@
   All brand new . . . .@
   ```

14

Hyphenation Examined

A HYPHENATION ROUTINE is an essential part of a justification program. Without hyphenation, the quality of justification is unacceptable except perhaps in very wide measure composition. There are techniques for "hyphenless justification," but without some recourse to letterspacing the results are such that one might better consider ragged setting as a more pleasing alternative. (Even in ragged setting some hyphenation is desirable to conserve space and to provide for more flexibility in determining line endings.)

Here are two examples, in narrow measure, of hyphenless justification. The only difference between them lies in the presence or absence of letterspacing:

Justification and hyphenation go together. There is an intimate relationship between these two concepts. The greater the latitude afforded for spaceband expansion, the less frequently hyphenation is required. If there is very little allowance permitted for the expansion of spaces between words, then hyphenation must be performed very often. The first criterion for successful typesetting by computer composition, therefore, is to work out, for a given assignment—considering the desired measure, type face, point size and the presence or absence of large words—the proper assignment of minimum and maximum spaceband values.

Justification and hyphenation go together. There is an intimate relationship between these two concepts. The greater the latitude afforded for spaceband expansion, the less frequently hyphenation is required. If there is very little allowance permitted for the expansion of spaces between words, then hyphenation must be performed very often. The first criterion for successful typesetting by computer composition, therefore, is to work out, for a given assignment—considering the desired measure, type face, point size and the presence or absence of large words—the proper assignment of minimum and maximum spaceband values.

It seems clear enough that if margins are to be justified, hyphenation is an essential exercise in order to avoid awkward and unseemly intra- and interword spacing. To the extent, then, that valid hyphenation points cannot be discovered by the program, and no hyphenation occurs, the quality of justification suffers.

It is also evident that the frequency of hyphenation, within a given context, will be (among other things) a function of the amount of interword spaceband expansion which is specified. On the next page are two examples of the same text set with different parameters for interword spacing, resulting in more or less frequent hyphenation and successively looser setting, with obvious impact upon the quality of justification.

Justification and hyphenation go together. There is an intimate relationship between these two concepts. The greater the latitude afforded for spaceband expansion the less frequently hyphenation is required. If there is very little allowance permitted for the expansion, of spaces between words, then hyphenation must be performed very often. The first criterion for successful typesetting by computer composition, therefore, is to work out, for a given assignment—considering the desired measure, type face, point size and the presence or absence of large words—the proper assignment of minimum and maximum spaceband values.

Justification and hyphenation go together. There is an intimate relationship between these two concepts. The greater the latitude afforded for spaceband expansion, the less frequently hyphenation is required. If there is very little allowance permitted for the expansion of spaces between words, then hyphenation must be performed very often. The first criterion for successful typesetting by computer composition, therefore, is to work out, for a given assignment—considering the desired measure, type face, point size and the presence or absence of large words—the proper assignment of minimum and maximum spaceband values.

But the fact that the program calls for hyphenation does not assure that the words submitted to the hyphenation routine will in fact be divided. These are words which are encountered at the "fall-off" point—that is, where their inclusion is impossible, but their exclusion would necessitate overexpansion of the spacebands beyond the amount stipulated. The writer often uses the term "straddle words" to identify those so situated. Clearly not all straddle words can be hyphenated.

What constitutes a "word"?

THE FIRST QUESTION to be answered is what *is* a word for purposes of hyphenation? The first step must be to identify a certain string of characters as probably embracing a word, based upon their "delimiters"—that is, the unique characteristics surrounding the string. Obviously a spaceband on either side of the string would enable us to determine that there may be a word in between. But not only spacebands serve this function. For our purposes, a hyphen—as in a compound word—provides a similar delimiter, whether it occurs at the beginning or the end of the string (micro-organism and multi-purpose are examples). We might not want to hyphenate one of the components of a compound word string, but the component would be a word nonetheless. In like manner, an em dash, or an en or nut dash could serve as a delimiter—as you can see right at this point. ("Delimiter" and "as" are words in their own right.) A fixed space may also be considered a word delimiter—as with an em space at the beginning of a paragraph. A quad, such as a quad left, would serve as a delimiter at the end of a paragraph.

Another more troublesome delimiter may be the slash when it is preceded or followed by alpha characters. Hence *and/or* would be two words, rather than one. Often in scientific terminology one encounters similar expressions. Even in our own vocabulary we might choose to use an expression such as the "word-processing/typesetting interface."

"Cleaning up" the word

ONCE A POSSIBLE WORD has been identified, we must examine the string more carefully to make certain that it consists of mostly alpha characters. The hyphenation routine is only concerned with the 26 letters of the alphabet. (It is possible that accented characters will be treated differently in some foreign languages.) But in English, at least, all other symbols must temporarily be set aside. It may be, for example, that we are dealing with numbers. "There are 1,001 ways to approach this problem," one might say. But 1,001—although delimited by spaces—is not a hyphenable word. On the other hand, it may be permissible to split numbers, if they are long enough. If we write out a number string such as 1,000,000,000,000, it may be necessary to split it, being certain that we leave behind or carry forward at least three digits. But this string, when so analyzed, would not normally be referred to a hyphenation routine. Rather, it would go to a separate number-splitting routine.

Moreover, there are some combinations of words that should not be divided, even though they may be (or seem to be) separated by spaces. It may be convenient to use an en space to provide such separation, and not to identify it as a word delimiter. We have in mind the following situations: 345 mi., where "mi." belongs with the preceding number. Or 24 kg, or 55 B.C., or 6:45 p.m., or perhaps an expression such as "O Lord." When a nut space is so used and not regarded as a delimiter, the line will sometimes look rather strange, if that nut space happens to have a conspicuously wider or narrower value than other spaces within the line. Consequently, we have often advised composition systems designers to provide a unique character which does not serve as a delimiter, but is considered as a space in that it takes on the value of other spaces within a line.

Let us return, however, to the subject of "cleaning up" the word. If it is a word at the end of a sentence, allowance must be made for the fact that to the left of the next interword space or quad left there will be a period. But it could be something else. It could be any one of the following, and some or all of these conditions might apply with respect to words anywhere within a sentence:

computer."
hurry!
forever?
illustration.[1]
chart*

Or, there may be something at the beginning of the word, such as:

"However,
••Note
©reserved

And there can even be "garbage" in the middle of the word. This is invariably the case when the word contains an accent or a dipthong. But there may be coding to provide for a font shift, such as to give emphasis: "You must be mis*taken*!" It is even possible for the garbage to consist of alpha characters, such as an alphabetic footnote call-out reference.

Differentiation of capital letters

EVEN BEFORE going to a hyphenation routine, there are some programs that scan the cleaned-up word to see if it contains any uppercase characters. (We assume that if the word consisted of *all* uppercase letters it would hyphenate normally.) But if a capital letter occurs in the middle of a word, it may be permissible to split before this capital. This would most likely be the case with proper names, such as McLean, MacIntyre or MacKenzie. One occasionally encounters a duPont or a benZion, a vonBitter or a delaRue. There is, however, a rule never to divide proper names at all, but this is sometimes impossible.

How big a word must it be?

LET US ASSUME that we have identified a word string, and that we have cleaned up the word by removing all nonalpha characters, setting them aside since we know that they must be put back into the string and proper allowance be made for their widths. We must also remember, in our program, to be sure that if the divided word requires a hyphen, there will also be room to add the hyphen itself at the end of the line.

What we have left must obviously consist of more than two letters to permit division. Some routines permit the user to specify how many letters the word must contain before it is to be sent to the hyphenation algorithm. The accepted rule is that the word must contain no less than five letters, but there are some users who are willing to divide four-letter words, and perhaps there are some who would not want to split a word unless it contained six or more characters. Our own preference is the five-or-more letter combination, with the understanding that generally one would never "leave behind" fewer than two letters. Hence one would not hyphenate "a-gain"or "a-head" or "u-nion."

There is another rule, more honored in its breach, which suggests that not fewer than three letters should be carried forward. Therefore "may-be" should not be divided. This rule is valid for wide measure setting, but is hardly enforceable in either a newspaper or news magazine environment.

Vowel group analysis

NOW WE COME to the logic of the hyphenation algorithm itself. We have discovered the word, we have cleaned it up so that it is no longer a "dirty" word, and we have counted the characters in the clean word to see if there are at least five. All of these conditions have been met. It is time to go into the logic of the hyphenation routine.

Some programs first scan the word to satisfy themselves that there are at least two "vowel groups." Others prefer to do the vowel group analysis at the end of the routine to be certain that there is at least one vowel in the portion of the word left behind, and at least one vowel in the portion of the word carried forward. In the English language the vowels are *a, e, i, o* and *u*, and sometimes *y*! It is the y that is troublesome. The y in "yesterday" is not a vowel. The y in "merely" is. But it is the y's in the middle of the word that cause problems. Consider, for example, "dystrophy," "leapyear," "marrying" and "synonym."

Every vowel does not constitute a vowel group. "Through" and "straight" contain only one vowel group, so we can see that vowels must generally be separated by consonants to be considered as belonging to a different syllable. (Except for such words as "coerce," "reunion," "reinstate" and "cooperative.")

And not every vowel separated by a consonant can make the claim that it represents a distinct vowel group. There is the problem of the "silent e." The e is silent in "moose" or "proves," but not necessarily in "rages" and certainly not in "ragged," although it is considered silent in "proved." Most hyphenation routines that make use of a vowel group analysis—and all should, at some stage, if only to check the results—will assume that an e at the end of a word, unless preceded by an l is to be disregarded for purposes of vowel group analysis. And many routines will also apply the same rule if the letter e is the second-to-last character in the word, perhaps followed by an s or d, but not an r.

But perhaps the problem of determining the number of vowel groups is not mandatory—at least in the early stages of analysis. Perhaps this problem can be dealt with in a string analysis of alpha characters, so that at this point our only problem could be to determine if the word *may* be hyphenable. However, at some place in the routine this difficulty will be encountered and must be resolved.

What hyphenation programs do

IN GENERAL, hyphenation programs consist of one or both of two kinds of procedures. One is a *logical* approach. The other is a *dictionary*. Let us consider the logical solution first. As a rule such algorithms do not examine the entire word, but only inspect a portion of it. In fact, one of the most common algorithmic tests is to ascertain whether a hyphen may or may not be placed between the second and third of a string of four characters. The analysis may not begin at the back end of the word, or the front either, for that matter. The program may start with a group of four characters including the last two which, when added to the value of a hyphen, would barely fit on the line, and adding to the string the following two "fall-off" characters. If the word which straddles the fall-off point is "photographer" and the last two letters that could be included within the line are "gr," then there would appear to be no purpose in testing more than the two letters beyond the fall-off location. Hence, the first interrogation would be made of the tetrad:

photo(gr/ap)her

1. What are the possibilities of a hyphen occurring *before* "ap"? The answer might be that the chances are relatively high.
2. What are the possibilities of a hyphen occurring *between* "r" and "a"? Again, the possibilities might be good.
3. What are the possibilities of a hyphen occurring *after* "gr"? The answer would most certainly be negative.

The logic program, based upon an analysis of the English language, should be able to ascertain that no syllable can end with a "gr." Hence, even though the answer to the first two questions was not negative, the hyphen point fails to meet the test. Hence this hyphenation point would be rejected and the program would then shift one character to the left (since there would be no point in moving further to the right, where the word split would not fit in any event). Thus the program would look at:

phot(og/ra)pher

Here, presumably, we should get an affirmative answer to all three questions. This hyphenation point would be accepted. Note that the program would not examine the entire word. But even if it did, it would confine its attention only to each four-letter combination, and, at least in this example, the answers would provide more affirmative points than would be valid. If the analysis shifted one more character to the left and looked at:

pho(to/gr)apher

the answer would again be affirmative. While this solution would be valid for "photographic" it would not be proper for "photographer." Hence, a correct solution to this and many other word breaks would be a matter of chance, depending upon what particular combination of characters would fit within the line.

There are some hyphenation programs that start at the beginning of the word, rather than from the back end, and take the first hyphenation point that the routine encounters and verifies—stopping there without proceeding any further to determine whether or not another answer which provides for a tighter line might not be found. If the program is instructed to take the first acceptable hyphenation point "and run," it would certainly be better to work toward the front of the word from the fall-off point or just beyond it, rather than from the beginning of the word.

Although it requires more processing time, it seems better to have the program examine the entire word—even that portion which would not possibly fit—to feed to the justification program all answers (possible or impossible from the standpoint of fit), and let that program select the place which most nearly satisfies the justification needs of the particular line. In this connection some weight might be given to hyphen points that appear to be more favorable than others.

Statistics might be calculated as to the relative probability of a successful solution, perhaps in the following manner:

Tetrad	Probability	Tetrad	Probability
ph/er	90	to/gr	85
ap/he	70	ot/og	60
ra/ph	85	ho/to	80
gr/ap	0	ph/ot	60
og/ra	80		

In this case, the first three solutions would be discarded because they would not fit within the line. The highest probability solution remaining would be to/gr—which, unfortunately, would be wrong.

Where would such statistics come from? Many researchers in the field of hyphenation have input large dictionaries, along with their hyphen points, and have developed computer programs to study the probability of hyphens falling before or after certain letter combinations. One drawback to such research is that the raw data has often been unreliable. The input has consisted of too few words, words have not been weighted in accordance with the frequency of their use so that uncommon words have been given as much consideration as those used commonly and syllabification points have been used rather than genuine hyphenation positions. But even if these weaknesses had been corrected, we suspect that the statistics so generated would not produce results any better than those one could develop through the application of his or her own common sense.

Our illustration has already prejudiced our analysis against this hyphenation routine, but we chose a difficult example! If the answer is to be found by looking at only a portion of a word there is no assurance, other than coincidence, that the right answer will be achieved consistently. Of course there are certain sure-fire combinations, but these are unfortunately rather rare. For example, one can be fairly certain that:

a syllable will not end with:	*a syllable will not begin with*
bc, bd, bg, bj, bk, bm,	bb, bc, bd, bg, bh, bk, bm,
bn, bp, bq, br, bv, bw, bx	bn, bq, bs, bt, bs

If we take just these cases of consonants beginning with b (and our list should be extended to consider all consonants), we find that hyphen points after the first category and before the second could be prohibited. Note that this particular test is useful (if our empirical observations are correct) not for the purpose of finding a hyphen point, but for the purpose of rejecting one found by other techniques. We know of one program which makes all of its hyphenation judgments solely by an analysis of vowels and consonants without any regard to which specific ones they are. Once such a determination is made, a second check of the kind indicated here would be helpful.

In fact it is not very difficult to find acceptable syllable breaks by studying combinations of two or more consonants. There are certain problem combinations. Where two b's occur together the chances are greater that the hyphen would appear between them, but it could occur after. Where bbt occurs we can be certain that the hyphen

Hyphenation Examined

would follow the second b, as in Crabbtree, but where sth occurs the word could be masthead, asthenia, or asthma. The st combination is particularly difficult, as witness as/ter, cast/er and be/stir.

Hyphenation procedures are much more complicated in those cases in which we are dealing with a group of letters involving the occurrence of a single consonant with a vowel on either side. For example, consider bas/il, ba/silic, ba/sin and bas/inet. On the whole, there is probably only a 50% chance of being correct when dealing with an otherwise unidentified portion of a word containing a single consonant at the proposed hyphen point, such as:

  re/si   *re/side, res/i/dence*
  re/se   *re/serve, pres/ence*
  em/or   *fem/oral, de/moralize*

The accuracy of the algorithm may be enhanced somewhat by taking a five or six letter combination, such as:

    de/mor or *dem/ora*

but it is doubtful whether the inclusion of one or two additional characters in the diagnostic string will contribute significantly to the solution of the problem.

Word structure analysis

ANOTHER APPROACH to an algorithm involves a more substantive analysis of the structure of the word itself, aimed at identifying prefixes and suffixes as well as root words, and treating each component independently. As a general rule it is permissible to hyphenate after a prefix, such as *re* in reentry or restructure. Other examples might be *anti*, *dis*, or *mis*, *in*, or *un*, or perhaps *trans*. Suffixes such as *er*, *tion*, *sion*, *tious*, *ceous*, *able*, *able*, *ible*, *ness*, *ish*, *ate*, *ive* and *some* may likewise be acceptable post-hyphen syllables in many cases.

Looking first at the prefix possibilities, we may generalize that a hyphen may almost always be placed after *in* at the beginning of the word, but there are a few exceptions, such as inchworm, inkless, and innkeeper. The prefix *un* would give us trouble in union, unction, unicorn, unified, unison, united and universe. The prefix *dis* wouldn't work for dishwasher, and *mis* would cause difficulties with misogyny, and mishmash. *De* would bring trouble in the case of decalogue, debonair, debutante, decadence, and many others. As a prefix, *anti* would produce the wrong result for antiphony and antiquity. *Re* would be most unsuccessful. Witness reappear and reaper, react and ready, recognizance and recognize. *Inter* will present problems for internship or interior.

Looking at suffixes, there are *dream/er* and *boul/der*, *check/er* and *chat/ter*, *chas/er* and *Chau/cer*, *control/ler* and *poll/er*, *floun/der* and *bound/er*. Or consider *ca/pable* and *wash/able*, *commu/nism* and *social/ism*, *pa/tron/age* and *out/rage*, *consum/mate* and *elector/ate*, *admon/ish* and *bran/dish*. Clearly there are relatively few trouble-free suffixes. Probably *tion* and *some* and *ness* are the most consistent. The letters *ing* are unusually difficult, for we have such peculiarities as *let/ting* and *grat/ing*, *graspl/ing* and *shop/ping*, *stall/ing* and *appall/ing*, *whis/tling*, *whisper/ing* and *confer/ring*.

Many of these apparent contradictions are capable of resolution. An *ive* generally seems to be preceded by a consonant which is affixed to it (*res/tive*, *mo/tive*, and *pas/sive*), but logical algorithms to differentiate the rules to handle apparent inconsistencies may become very involved. The plain fact is that the English language permits the division of words in singularly arbitrary ways and the rules are not always susceptible to analysis on the basis of the facts at hand since they have something to do with the pronunciation of particular vowels, the derivation of the word, or its part of speech. The proofreader might know the rule that *ing* stands by itself when it follows a double consonant that exists in the root word (*pass/ing*), but that there is a division between double identical consonants when the root word does not contain both letters and the second is added as an aid to pronunciation (*let/ting*).

There are still other aberrations. There are differences between British word divisions and American (*pro/gress* and *prog/ress* for the noun; *pro/cess* and *proc/ess* for the verb). The British pay more attention to the derivation of the word (*demo/cracy* instead of *democ/racy*, *know/ledge* instead of *knowl/edge*). And even in the United States more emphasis upon word structure and less upon pronunciation is reflected in the word division principles of Webster's second edition as compared with Webster's third edition dictionary. In the latter, more and more popular as a guide in the United States, pronunciation tends to take over, so that the word becomes *concor/dant* instead of *concord/ant* and *depen/dence* instead of *depend/ence*.

Difficult as it is to program good word division, at least it does not present the complications of Swedish, where the rule is that certain letters must be repeated when a word is hyphenated. And so *glasstrut* (ice cream) becomes *glass/strut* when it must be split. A similar condition occurs in German.

But our description of the problem is not yet over. The rules distinguish syllabification points from hyphenation points. (The reader is warned that many dictionaries do not!) *The Chicago Manual of Style* specifies, for example, that word division should be made after a vowel "*unless by so doing, the division is not according to pronunciation. Where a vowel alone forms a syllable in the middle of a word, run it into the first line.*"[1] Hence *commemo/rate* is better than *commem/orate* and *physi/cal* is to be preferred to *phys/ical*. On the other hand, *ac/etate* is possibly marginally better than *ace/tate*, and *Bab/ylonia* might be preferred to *Baby/lonia* although neither is a very happy choice.

Where there are two vowels that are pronounced as separate syllables, they should be split—such as *initi/ative* rather than *initia/tive*. Furthermore, compound words should be split where possible so that their elements are kept together. *Ante/cedent* is preferred to *an/tecedent* and *homo/geneous* to *ho/mogeneous*. Where words are joined by hyphens already, one should avoid placing another hyphen if at all possible (*quasi-public*, not *quasi-pub/lic*).

One wonders whether any algorithm can do justice to the problem of hyphenation. There are homographs which generally hyphenate differently according to their meaning. Such words include:

---

1. *The Chicago Manual of Style*, 13th edition, University of Chicago Press, p. 165.

acerous, adept, agape, anchorite, arsenic, arundel, associate, baton, bunter, coster, crater, decameter, decanel, denier, desert, divers, dosser, draper, elipses, ergotism, ergotize, Eunice, evening, former, founder, fuller, gaffer, gainer, gaiter, genet, genial, gilder, graining, groper, grouser, halter, hinder, homer, hurter, impugnable, invalid, legate, limber, luster, master, minute, nestling, petit, periodic, pinky, planer, prayer, precedent, present, produce, progress, putter, putting, rafter, rebel, record, refuse, resume, *rosier, spiller, stater, stingy, stover, tamper, tenter* and *welter.*

Obviously nothing can be done about these homographs except to flag them when they are divided, or to instruct the keyboarder to insert a discretionary hyphen in case they should fall at the end of a line. Thus we could indicate that we wish to *re/cord* the *rec/ord* we made, or he got his just *de/serts* in the *des/ert*. A contextual analysis would obviously create too complicated an algorithm to include a mere hyphenation routine.

The exception word dictionary

IN VIEW of all the problems, it is not possible for a logical program to yield good hyphenation results if our criteria for such results take into account frequency, accuracy, throughput speed, and computer memory utilization.

The safest thing to do about a combination of letters which should break differently when they appear in different words is not to rely upon them at all. If the program rejects all such conditions its accuracy will be high while the frequency of word breaks would be very low. While too frequent hyphenation is undesirable (as perhaps with three or more lines in a row), infrequency can produce very loose and very tight lines, making reading difficult and the appearance of pages unattractive. Thus the program needs to be good enough to find the most valid hyphenation points in almost every hyphenable word. If it fails to do so, poor justification will rear its ugly head.

Accuracy is important not only because a bad hyphenation detracts from the authentic nature of the product, but also because to correct it requires the resetting of at least two lines and can even alter pagination in some cases.

One reaches a point, therefore, where further improvement in the logical aspects of the program, undertaken in the interest of greater frequency and accuracy, makes great demands upon throughput and memory, and it becomes expedient to try to deal with the complications of hyphenation by using an exception word dictionary to supplement the logical program. Unfortunately, it is generally true that those who, in the interest of economy, cut down on the space devoted to the hyphenation algorithm, for the same reasons cut down the size or availability of an exception word dictionary.

When such a dictionary is used the word which straddles the fall-off point is usually first sought out in the stored dictionary. If it can be found there, the possible hyphenation points are given. If it cannot be found, it is assumed that the word may be divided correctly according to the logical rules of the program.

One of the earliest routines for hyphenation was developed by Perry Publications of West Palm Beach, Florida, in 1962, for an RCA 301 computer. A large dictionary was stored in an optimized fashion on a magnetic tape which could be searched by "read forward" and "read reverse" instructions. The words on this dictionary were those which could not be broken correctly after the third, fifth, seventh or ninth character. Thus *sedentary* would not be found in such a dictionary, nor would *secretary*. Some words that did not follow the 3-5-7 routine might also not be considered exceptions if some other criterion kept the routine from doing any harm. For example, *cactus* divides after the third letter, and while it should not be divided after the fifth, the instruction that requires two or three letters to be carried over would prevent a hyphen except after the third character.

Since there were many exceptions, this simple logical program needed a big dictionary. If the logic were more elaborate, the dictionary could have been smaller, but the unfortunate implication of such a dictionary is that it almost always has to be searched before the logical rules can be implemented. Even if the algorithm is reliable enough to produce the desired result, the dictionary look-up procedure is usually not avoided. Another limitation is the assumption that if the word is not specified as an exception, then it must follow the rule. On the other hand, the word simply may not have been included—in ignorance, because it had not been encountered before, or for lack of room.

Exception words are usually stored in memory rather than on tape or disk because memory can be accessed more quickly and can be indexed, if necessary, for random access. Because of memory limitations not all exceptions can be stored, and newer programs are consequently making use of peripheral storage for this purpose. Whatever means may be used to store this dictionary, access time is exceedingly important, especially for those programs which run in an interactive mode. It may be less critical for programs which run in the background. Tape, which is inevitably sequential, is the slowest method of access. A fixed-head disk or drum arrangement would be ideal, but it is possible to make use of a conventional moving-head disk, especially if the program is "bright" enough to find something else to process while it is waiting the minute fraction of a second required to obtain the answer. In our own experience, a *total* dictionary, which is able to locate any word stored on disk with one disk "seek," is faster than any combination of logic and exception word storage. The price one pays for such a dictionary is that it does take up a great deal of disk storage. Generally one would require more than 100,000 words. If the average word consisted of ten characters (assuming words with less than five characters would not need to be stored and would not be hyphenated in any event), then as much as one million characters of disk storage would be necessary. However, there are interesting methods of data compression, such as not to use eight bits, or even six, to describe each of the 26 letters of the alphabet, and to use certain characters within the word for an address so that they may be assumed and hence not stored.

The other price one pays for the use of a large dictionary is the computer time required to add words to it. Some programs will permit such words to be added to the dictionary file when the system is "up" and performing composition activity for other users. Other programs require that dictionary updates be performed after hours by running a dictionary utility program in a dedicated environment. It might require perhaps 30 to 45 minutes to run a "hasher" program against the master dictionary file.

Nevertheless, the writer's strong preference is for the treatment of *all words* as exceptions—in other words, to rely upon the dictionary for the discovery of hyphenation points, and to use logic only when the word cannot be found in the master dictionary. The principal advantage gained is the assurance that the hyphenation decisions are correct according to the approved dictionary. If the dictionary stores only those words that are exceptions to the logic routine, the user has no way of knowing whether the hyphenation decision was made by logic or by dictionary look-up, and will be forced to check all hyphenation results in order to be assured that they are correct, for they may not have been included among the list of stored exception words, and thus were resolved improperly by the hyphenation routine.

It is much better, therefore, to look up all straddle words and, if the word is not found in the dictionary, to use logic. Also, flag the word to indicate that logic was in fact used. Thus only *those* words need to be checked, and they can then be added the next time the dictionary is updated.

The writer also prefers that words so stored should not only contain all hyphenation points but that these points should be ranked in order to indicate the best place for the word to be broken, from the standpoint of word meaning and general appearance. The line-ending routine may be able to select one point as opposed to another and still remain within justification range. The user can decide whether he would prefer the best and most consistent justification or to use better word breaks. This may be done by storing preference points more or less as follows: com(1)put(3)er, com(1)put(2(ers) and com-(1)put(3)er(2)i(1)za(2)tion.

Note that it will be necessary to store not only the basic word but also all of the variants of the word. This requires the development of a special dictionary since most dictionaries do not list such variants (follow, followed, following, follows, etc.).

The role of logic programs

WHILE LOW-END composition programs make extensive use of logic programs, sometimes supplemented by a very limited list of exception words, there is clearly a need for the use of logic solutions at all levels as part of a total approach on hyphenation. So that the reader may gain some understanding of what is involved in such a program we present, on the two following pages, a flow chart

HYPHENATION ALGORITHM

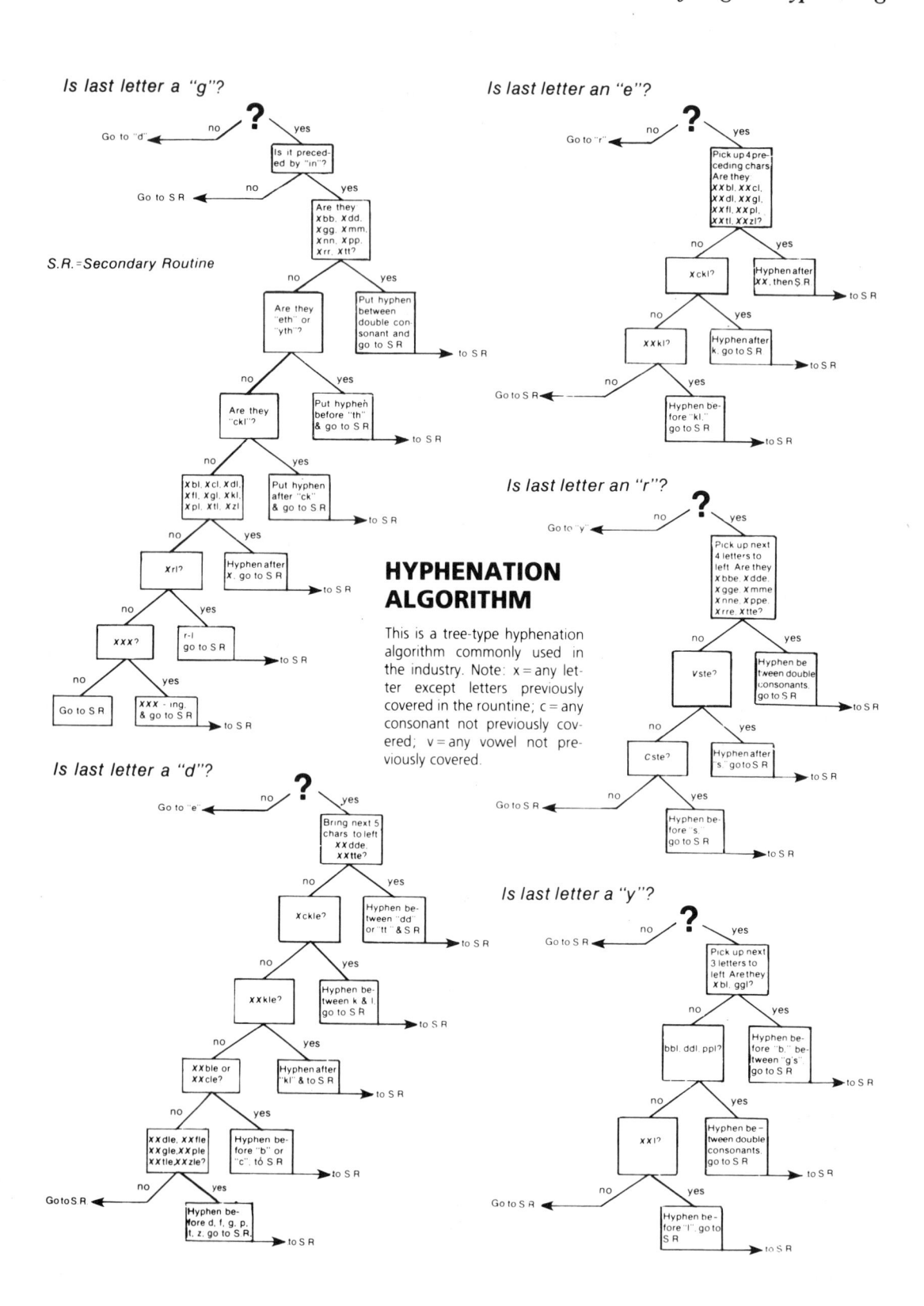

This is a tree-type hyphenation algorithm commonly used in the industry. Note: x = any letter except letters previously covered in the routine; c = any consonant not previously covered; v = any vowel not previously covered.

S.R. = Secondary Routine

Is last letter a "g"?

- no → Go to "d"
- yes → Is it preceded by "in"?
  - no → Go to S R
  - yes → Are they Xbb, Xdd, Xgg, Xmm, Xnn, Xpp, Xrr, Xtt?
    - yes → Put hyphen between double consonant and go to S R → to S R
    - no → Are they "eth" or "yth"?
      - yes → Put hyphen before "th" & go to S R → to S R
      - no → Are they "ckl"?
        - yes → Put hyphen after "ck" & go to S R → to S R
        - no → Xbl, Xcl, Xdl, Xfl, Xgl, Xkl, Xpl, Xtl, Xzl?
          - yes → Hyphen after X, go to S R → to S R
          - no → Xrl?
            - yes → r-l go to S R → to S R
            - no → XXX?
              - yes → XXX - ing, & go to S R → to S R
              - no → Go to S R

Is last letter a "d"?

- no → Go to "e"
- yes → Bring next 5 chars to left XXdde, XXtte?
  - yes → Hyphen between "dd" or "tt" & S R → to S R
  - no → Xckle?
    - yes → Hyphen between k & l, go to S R → to S R
    - no → XXkle?
      - yes → Hyphen after "kl" & to S R → to S R
      - no → XXble or XXcle?
        - yes → Hyphen before "b" or "c", to S R → to S R
        - no → XXdle, XXfle, XXgle, XXple, XXtle, XXzle?
          - yes → Hyphen before d, f, g, p, t, z, go to S.R. → to S R
          - no → Go to S R

Is last letter an "e"?

- no → Go to "r"
- yes → Pick up 4 preceding chars. Are they XXbl, XXcl, XXdl, XXgl, XXfl, XXpl, XXtl, XXzl?
  - yes → Hyphen after XX, then S R → to S R
  - no → Xckl?
    - yes → Hyphen after k, go to S R → to S R
    - no → XXkl?
      - yes → Hyphen before "kl", go to S R → to S R
      - no → Go to S R

Is last letter an "r"?

- no → Go to "y"
- yes → Pick up next 4 letters to left. Are they Xbbe, Xdde, Xgge, Xmme, Xnne, Xppe, Xrre, Xtte?
  - yes → Hyphen between double consonants, go to S R → to S R
  - no → Vste?
    - yes → Hyphen after "s", go to S R → to S R
    - no → Cste?
      - yes → Hyphen before "s", go to S R → to S R
      - no → Go to S R

Is last letter a "y"?

- no → Go to S R
- yes → Pick up next 3 letters to left. Are they Xbl, ggl?
  - yes → Hyphen before "b", between "g"s, go to S R → to S R
  - no → bbl, ddl, ppl?
    - yes → Hyphen before "b" between "g"s, go to S R → to S R
    - no → XXl?
      - yes → Hyphen between double consonants, go to S R → to S R
      - no → Hyphen before "l", go to S R → to S R

Hyphenation Examined

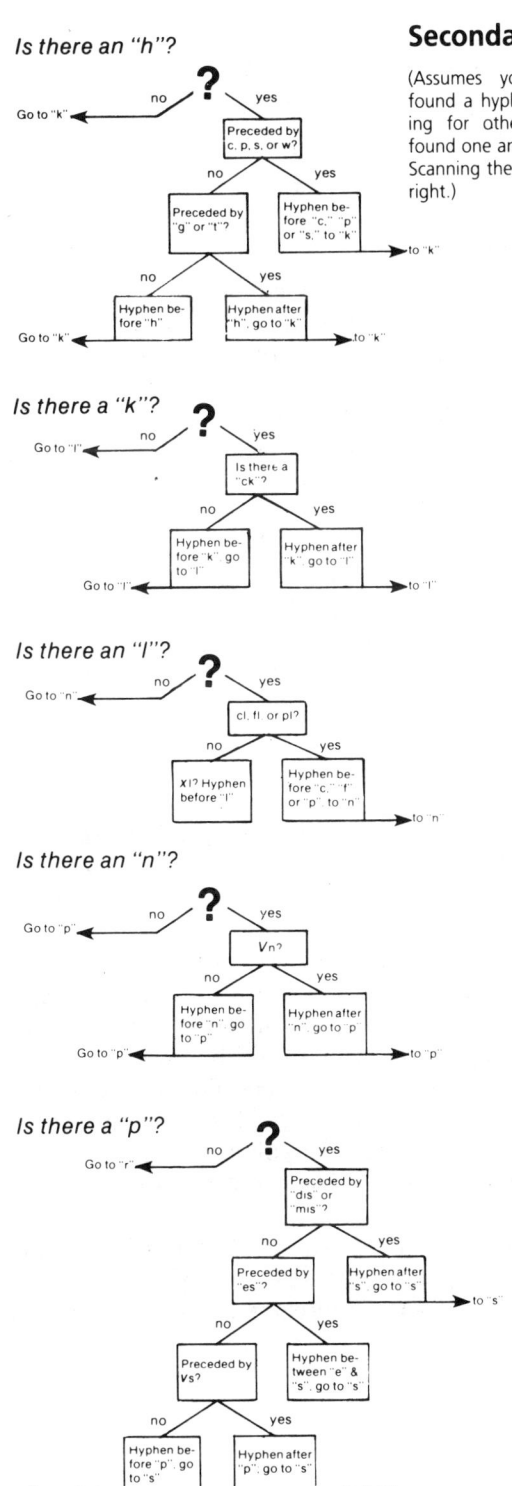

Secondary Routines

(Assumes you have already found a hyphen and are looking for others, or have not found one and are still looking. Scanning the word from left to right.)

Is there an "h"?

Is there a "k"?

Is there an "l"?

Is there an "n"?

Is there a "p"?

Is there an "s"?

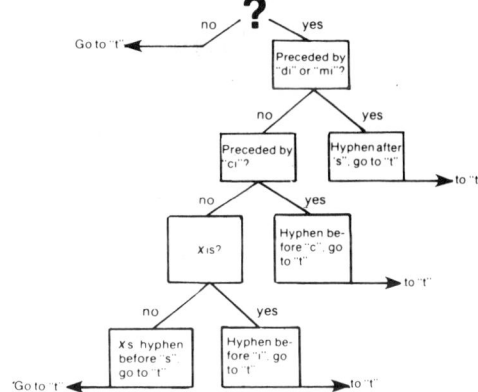

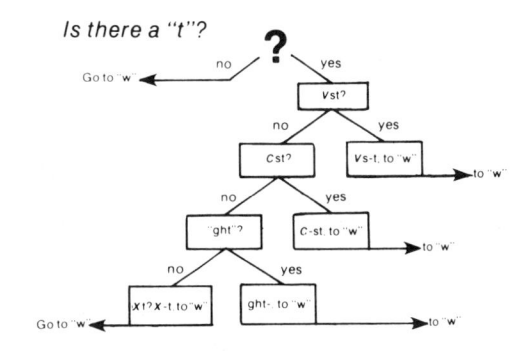

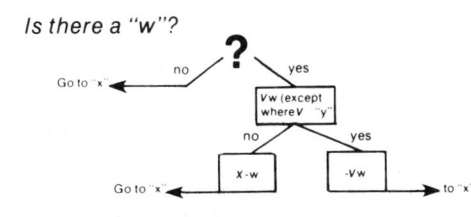

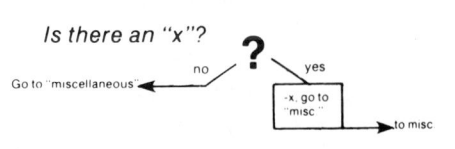

Is there a "t"?

Is there a "w"?

Is there an "x"?

Miscellaneous letter combinations within the word

vb,vc,vd,vf,vg,vm,vn,vs,vz: Hyphen before the v

cb,cc,cd,cf,cg,cm,cn,cs,cz: Hyphen between the two consonants

Note: c-r,v-r,vs-tr,c-str,ght-r,x-tr

or diagram of one such routine which is relatively simple to implement and produces results which are fairly acceptable from the standpoint both of accuracy and frequency. Obviously there are more elaborate and better routines, but if the logic program follows recourse to a "total dictionary" it is not necessary for the program to be exceptional. What is necessary is that words which are hyphenated by logic should be flagged as such.

Hyphenation verification

ANOTHER interesting approach, if a total dictionary is not used, is to cull out all of the words which have been divided, to keep track of their position in the text, and to print out the solutions developed by the hyphenation logic program. This not only serves as a check on the accuracy of the solution (and allows the user to locate the bad ones easily), but it can also call attention to problems with the routine that may be capable of rectification. One such routine automatically checked all hyphens against a stored dictionary, and endeavored to move characters up or down within prejustified lines, flagging only those which could not be so adjusted. Usually a bad word break is only off by one or at most two characters. But such an approach does not deal with the other half of the problem: the discovery of words that could and should have been divided, which were ducked by the algorithm.

Multiline justification solutions

THE BEST HYPHENATION program will still produce results which are less satisfactory than those achievable by a human, if the programmatic answer is made in the vacuum of a single line of text. What made the human operator's result better, in many cases, was his rejection of the line he had already composed. He then went back to reset the preceding line, bringing a small word down or up, or dividing a fall-off word from a preceding line in a different place to get better results in the line which followed. It would be possible for a computer to approach the problem in the same fashion, and to look at five or six lines at the same time. If it can succeed in doing this, and if it used a total dictionary with preferred hyphenation points, no human would be able to obtain comparable results in a consistent fashion.

And so, as we have seen, the hyphenation of text is indeed a complicated and fascinating subject. For scholars and programmers alike there will always be scope for further research and experimentation.

15

Input, Verification, Corrections

IN THE EARLY days of computerized composition, input was almost invariably prepared on punched paper tape, using off-line tape perforating keyboards of the non-counting variety. This tape was then fed into the computer by means of a paper-tape reader. There were, however, some alternate methods of input.

One such alternate method involved the use of punched cards, prepared on the usual type of data recording equipment. Character repertoire was seriously limited. All letters were in upper case and needed to be preceded by a special character to indicate an upshift and another for lower case. Very few special symbols were available unless the conventions to represent them were invented as combinations of other characters. However, the use of punched cards did offer the opportunity for proofreading and/or verification.

The hard copy image on the cards could be proofread and if mistakes were found a new card could be substituted for an old one. Each card would normally only contain 80 characters. Another method of checking the accuracy of the input was to use a key punch verifier. One operator punches the data onto a card. A stack of such cards is passed, along with the original manuscript, to another operator who works on a verifying punch. That person inserts the stack of cards into one hopper and a stack of blank cards into a second hopper. That operator then rekeys from the manuscript and the device makes a comparison on a keystroke-for-keystroke basis. If the original card is incorrect and the operator strikes the proper key, the keyboard locks so that the data cannot be entered until a determination as been made as to which data element is the correct one. Thus the card which emerges from the verifying punch is bound to be correct in all cases excepting the possibility that both operators might make identical errors.

Such a method of input was of course cumbersome and tedious, but it was and perhaps still is used for the entry of fielded text, for a textual data base, such as a telephone directory.

Certain "key-to-tape" or "key-to-disk" systems were also used. These consisted of small clusters of keyboards. A stream of data flowing from each operator was filed away with a tag identifying its source. At the end of the shift or at some other logical time the various data streams would be separated from one another and each such stream would be written to magnetic tape which could then be mounted on the mainframe computer used for composition processing.

Whether or not key-to-tape or key-to-disk techniques are used, it has sometimes been customary to employ two persons to key the same document and to input the two data streams simultaneously, so that a computer program can compare one with another and flag any inconsistencies in the input stream. This technique has been used often when the source of the data input is Korea, or Malta, or Jamaica, or some other location where wage rates are significantly below those prevailing in world publishing centers. This approach has been used for the keyboarding of large jobs, such as encyclopedias, if the time factor permits.

It is more likely today that input would be prepared either on a terminal which is on-line to a computer system, or in an off-line mode onto a diskette (floppy disk) which would then be mounted onto the computer system for the purpose of "dumping" the file or files. In all probability, any effort to verify the contents of the file would be performed after the file was resident on the computer system rather than before it was entered.

Proofreading or verifying the file

HISTORICALLY, the most common way of verifying the accuracy of the file was to obtain a printout of its contents, using an on-line printer. Such printers usually offer a limited character repertoire. Sometimes they can present text only in upper case. When this happens certain conventions are applied in an effort to distinguish between capital letters and lower-case ones. As can be seen from the example below, the proofreading of any such document leaves a great deal to be desired and would clearly be uneconomical in a competitive environment.

```
+#T&HIS IS A SIMULATION OF AN ALL-UPPER-
CASE PRINTOUT SUCH AS WAS FREQUENTLY
PROOFREAD DURING THE EARLIER DAYS OF
COMPUTER COMPOSITION.
```

Fortunately, upper- and lower-case printers are also more common today, and they generally produce output which resembles that generated on a typewriter. In fact, some of these printers are said to be able to present "correspondence quality" copy to the reader. In order to indicate changes of type face, such as italic and bold face, as well as roman text, conventions have been developed which rely primarily upon the use of underprinting or overprinting. Such a representation is shown below.

```
Some correspondence-quality printers
use emboldened text and underlined text
to indicate changes of type face.
```

There are two ways in which the proofreading and verification process might procede. Both may be used. One way is to provide a proof of output prior to the running of the composition pass ("h&j"). The purpose of proofreading or verifying at this stage is to make certain that the computer will in fact be able to process the input stream of text and commands. If the commands are incorrect the program might "hang" if it were not designed to anticipate all of the problems that might conceivably arise—such as an instruction to indent six picas in a measure which is defined as two picas in length, or to set six columns of tabular material within a format which only calls for four such columns.

To avoid any such difficulty it is common to write a special "diagnostic" program which may be run prior to composition, the specific purpose of which is to make certain that all commands are in fact accurate and are not mutually inconsistent. Often command strings err in that the operator has failed to include both delimiters, so there is no way for the program to determine what the command's "argument" consists of. Not all errors can be caught in this fashion, but perhaps most of them may be.

It would seem logical, if such a diagnostic program is offered, to provide a printout (prior to composition) of the text stream, along with the flagging of errors uncovered by the diagnostics. An alternative approach, when there are video terminals on the system, would be to permit an operator to call a file to the screen subsequent to the running of the diagnostics, and to search for the error flags.

Correcting the errors

HOW, THEN, would such errors be corrected? Two alternatives present themselves. One is to make the corrections in a "batch" mode. This generally involves keyboarding the corrections and asking the computer to apply this correction file against the initial input file. This was the common method of making such corrections in the 1960s and 1970s, but this technique still persists on large mainframe computers offering programs known as "line editors."

It was customary for the initial (unjustified) file to be broken by the computer and printed out as lines of arbitrary length such as 80 characters per line, but with "word wrap" so that words would not be broken between lines. No hyphenation was yet applied since such word breaks would be meaningless in terms of the final output.

These lines were then numbered, and the numbers appeared on the printout so that the reader could identify those which required correction.

A naive program would permit batch input of numbered lines to be substituted for the lines containing errors. A more sophisticated program would require only the identification of that portion of the line to be changed. For example:

        203 teh/ the
        209 Campell/ Campbell
        222 "No"/ "No,"
        228 "However, there/ "There

It should be observed that in the preceding illustration the line number is identified and then the word in error is carefully keyed, followed by the corrected version. Another approach, which the author of this book developed in 1963, used a line number and an interword space to describe the location of the text to be corrected.

> 203 0304 the—(*i.e., line 203 between the 3rd and 4th spaces*)
> 209 0304 Campbell
> 222 0001 "No,"
> 228 0002 "There

Some such programs did not use line numbers but required a search technique. It was necessary for the operator to key enough text surrounding the correction that it would be unique, and then to key the substitute phrase. This would of course necessitate keying a longer string and was always susceptible to the possibility that the string might not be unique. On the other hand, "global" substitutions could easily be made, such as to change every occurrence of "sceptic" with "skeptic."

Normally, corrections made by line number must be made sequentially since there is always the possibility that the line numbering will be thrown off by the changes entered. One program of this kind, known as "Datatext" and developed by IBM in the late 1960s, worked best if corrections were made from the back of the manuscript forward, so that any changes in line numbering would not affect the next (*i.e.,* earlier) entry.

When corrections are made interactively they may be applied by the person who is proofreading the document, or by someone whose task it is to enter changes indicated by a proofreader. In the latter case a printout of some kind is presumed. Changes desired are marked on the printout which is then handed to an operator. The operator calls the file to the video screen (VDT) and, starting at the beginning, locates each point where a correction is to be made. He or she may do this by line number if the program so permits, or by use of a search technique. Once the word or phrase is located he makes the change by using insertions and deletions, and proceeds to the next place where the need for a correction has been indicated.

The reader will observe that it would appear to make more sense for the person who discovers the error to make the correction at the time of the discovery. Then that person can verify the fact that the correction was indeed made properly rather than having to check it later. Consequently, in many establishments today the proofreading of hard copy has given way to the function of editing on a terminal. There may still be a conventional proofreading function after the material has been typeset.

The absence of true type

THERE IS always a risk when one proofreads or verifies a representation of the text rather than the text itself. This is so because it is often difficult to visualize the impact of the typographical commands

Input, Verification, Corrections

upon the text stream. If there is a command for indention which is buried within a text file, the person reading that file will not be able to judge what its effect will be upon the following text, and may not remember to look carefully to see if somewhere there is a corresponding command to go out of indent. The same would be true of commands to go into italic, or bold face, or to set ragged as opposed to justifying, and the problem exists in spades where tabular material must be verified.

Consequently, many production shops prefer to "go to type" and not to attempt to read until then—or to read in a somewhat cursory fashion on a video terminal and then read with meticulous care after the material has been typeset. This means, of course, that two typesettings must occur, but then, they almost invariably do in any event.

But there is a problem as to how the terminal operator will be able to identify or to discover the points where the corrections (now marked on typeset galleys) are to be located, and how to address them.

A more profound problem is posed with respect to whether or not the file from which the document was typeset can also be used for purposes of correction. This is because the file changes its form during the composition process—not merely with respect to line breaks and justification, but also in other ways. In order to understand this we must know something more about the composition process.

Before we turn to this subject, however, an observation needs to be made about what it is that the proofreader or the editor sees. If it is possible for the person reviewing the file to see "true type" or a simulated version thereof—and to see it prior to typesetting—the need for second, third or perhaps even fourth typesetting runs—as galleys or perhaps pages—could possibly be eliminated. Consequently there are several current efforts of considerable interest.

One such effort, of course, is to be able to show the "true type" or simulations of "true type" on the video screen so that one can distinguish between roman, bold and italic and also between one size of type and another. If one were able to do this, and to make corrections to this file, and to see the impact of these changes immediately—again in terms of true type—the process would be greatly simplified. But this is not easy to do, and, accordingly, there are various compromise approaches.

- One early approach, still extremely effective, is to show "modes" on the screen which can be used to represent either different type faces or different type sizes, or both, according to whatever conventions the "house" wishes to adopt on all jobs or on particular jobs, or on particular sections of particular jobs. This representation can be displayed with respect either to preliminary input which has not been "composed," or to input which has been formatted into galleys or perhaps even pages.

    This approach is illustrated on the screens shown at the top of the next page. It is possible to tell when one has changed from one type face to another. Two versions are depicted. One shows text which has not been composed. The other shows text which has been run through composition.

- Another method is to provide a preview of what the text will look like when it is typeset. This version cannot be corrected. It can only be inspected. If errors, especially errors of format, are

The Mergenthaler Linotype CRTronic preview terminal, called the Typeview, displays true images on the screen. The type face shown here is "Linotext." Files are first created and viewed on the CRTronic screen and then sent to the Typeview for previewing. The Typeview can store up to 16 fonts at a time using its megabyte of memory. Jobs can be shown in a variety of scaled enlargements. The box in this illustration uses rounded inside corners generated by the CRTronic, which also supports underlining of text ("Washington").

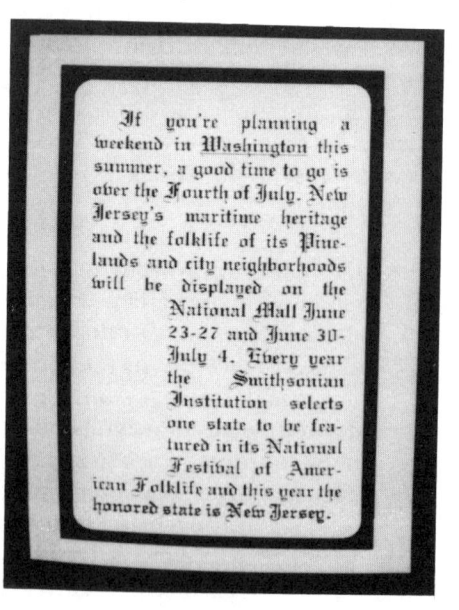

detected, one would return to an editable version of the file to make corrections, and then call up the preview version to see if the problem has been rectified. It should be obvious that this is not the best way to inspect for corrections having to do with keyboard errors, or so-called "typos," but it is very handy when it comes to checking for format or appearance. It is also a useful procedure for the debugging of formats prior to the input of the job. For example, one might want to experiment with various ways of arranging a complex table by entering representative portions, incorporating problem areas, before keyboarding the entire table.

- But, as indicated above, the approach which appears to represent the best of all possible worlds would be to be able to present the text, after composition, in hyphenated and justified form, with true or simulated type fonts in true sizes, and to be able to make corrections in real time and see that the corrections are properly incorporated and that they satisfactorily resolve any problems either of format or contents. This is obviously the most challenging of all programs because it implies the utmost in interactivity, and gives you a WYSIWYG (*what-you-see-is-what-you-get*) approach to the entire problem of composition. To be able to achieve this effect without having to reprocess more of the file than is changed by the correction represents perhaps the ideal goal. But it is not always easy for the program to know—given the serial nature of most input—what commands have preceded the instant block of text and what commands will follow subsequently.

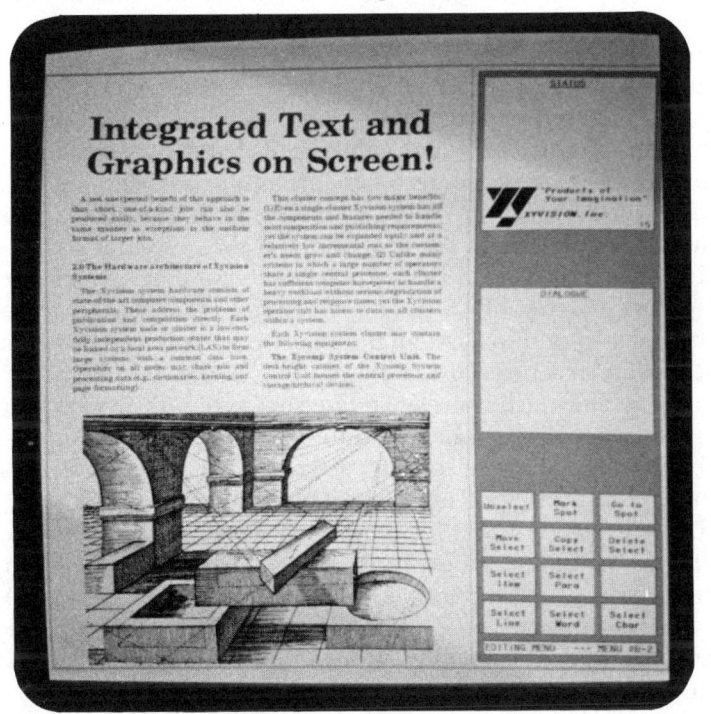

Relation between composition and corrections

IT SHOULD BE obvious that the relationship between the composition (h&j and perhaps pagination) programs and the effective use of editing and correction capabilities constitutes the essence of the problem of defining a satisfactory and productive system approach. There are indeed very powerful batch composition programs, capable of handling quite complex work, both in the galley mode, and even in terms of totally automatic page make-up. But such programs perform most reliably in a batch environment, and they assume that the input into the program must be perfect. Absent such perfection, the efficacy of the system begins to fall apart. Many such programs abort the task when errors are encountered or formatting inconsistencies cannot be resolved. The system design concepts may be such that it is necessary for the user to revert to the input file to make his changes, and then to try to reprocess the entire task again. Unless repetitive jobs of a highly uniform nature are to be produced by persons who become intimately familiar with the strengths and the limitations of such systems, the running of such programs can become a nightmare consisting of repeated efforts to wade through a seemingly impenetrable morass of pitfalls and obstacles. Let us examine the composition process more carefully to see why this is so.

The input programs. One must begin, of course, with the input process. Early computer typesetting programs often assumed that input would correspond with output so far as coding and character representation are concerned. For example, the program and system might take for granted that the input would be generated by TTS-keyboarded paper tape, with the same codes and methods we described in Chapter 6. The primary difference between input and output would be that the output contained end-of-line decisions inserted by the computer and perhaps some other formatting conventions, such as indents, which would involve the automatic generation of a fixed amount of white space at the beginning (or the end) of a line.

It is true that most of the early typesetters—even the phototypesetting devices—were TTS compatible, but it quickly became apparent that the composition system would do well not to assume a certain input coding structure, just as the output of the system should not assume a specific output-driver coding structure. Consequently, typesetting systems became somewhat more modularly designed, translating one or more input coding sets into an internal processing language, and translating again to an output-driver coding set.

But it is not sufficient for the interfaces between the input module and the main line program, on the one hand, and the main line program and the output module, on the other, to perform a code-for-code translation, as between TTS and ASCII. It is not even sufficient to perform a conversion, say, from six-level to eight-level coding, which might involve differentiating upper-case characters not by a precedence code (the "upshift") but by changing the bit pattern which distinguishes an "a" from an "A"—as by adding one higher-order bit to the same basic lower-level code. *Strings of codes* may be converted into a single code "going in" and a single code may be converted to a code string "going out"—or vice versa.

In order to resolve the perplexing problems of input compatibility one needs to be able to translate not only one code to another, but also one string of codes to another.

The keyboard. For every application there is, presumably, a best solution, but it will have to take into account factors of human convenience and habit as well as ideal theoretical conceptions. Although most coding conventions today are expressed in an eight-level byte, a keyboard with 256 keys, or even 128, may not be a good idea. If the keyboard layout bears no resemblance to any other keyboard, and its use require substantial retraining of writers and operators, that keyboard would certainly need to offer a demonstrably better solution to be worth the retraining effort.

On the other hand, it may be easier to use a keyboard with only ten keys, all of which rest immediately under the fingers (something on the order of a Stenotype), and to strike combinations of these ten keys, rather than to search for the proper key on a larger keyboard.

A good solution will be oriented toward the user's specific applications, and yet there should probably be some degree of commonality between all approaches: they need to be reducible conceptually to some basic structure which will facilitate data interchange.

Keyboard conventions. In order to achieve this objective we will need to reach some kind of agreement on conventions for typesetting and related information interchange. Conventions, we are reminded, need not be binding. Yet there are times when it is essential to be certain that we are understood.

Our need for conventions relates to two primary areas of information interchange. One has to do with the presentation of the character repertoire itself. The other is concerned with a definition and identification of typographic situations.

Character sets. Let us look first at the problem of the character repertoire. If we can agree to group certain characters into families or sets we can greatly simplify the problem of character access. For example, there are 44 keys on a typewriter, plus a space bar and certain function keys—backspace, shift, tab set, tab clear, tab and margin release or reset. If our typewriter is a Selectric, with a "golf ball" typing element, we can design our own golf ball and access any characters on that new golf ball if we know what key it is we need to strike. We might have a Greek typing element, and another for mathematics, and still another for foreign accents, and perhaps one with all kinds of interesting special characters we might need for scientific or logical representation. Suppose we worked out ten different golf ball elements. Apart from our preferences for type faces and type styles, we could probably cover most of our typographic needs merely by mounting successive golf balls as the occasion required. We would soon learn which character set was which, and which keys to strike to access the desired symbols. But if everyone designed his or her own character sets, with entirely different groupings of characters each positioned differently on the typing element, it would be tedious indeed to discover the characters we wanted to use. We would know neither which golf ball to mount nor which key to strike.

However, a computer can cope with this problem better than a mere human. For every user it would be necessary to input an elaborate translate table, especially made up for that one application, listing every one of perhaps 880 different characters, and identifying the particular golf ball and the particular position on that element for each such character. Since the character repertoire is open ended, the translate table routine would also have to have an infinite capacity for expansion.

But how much better it would be to agree on at least a half dozen families or groupings of characters that would mean the same for everybody, even if they did not accommodate each individual's needs quite as readily as his own special-purpose solution!

What is true on the input end may also be true on the output end. Each user may have a need for a slightly different character set, or at least one arrangement may be much more efficient for his requirements than another. If one is setting stock market quotations, one would want to make extensive use of fractions, with special symbols such as bullets and daggers. If setting legal statutes, one might prefer to give up a convenient location for fractions in favor of having the section mark, the paragraph symbol, and call-out references for footnotes. What is important is not merely which characters are available, but how conveniently they may be accessed. This is true both with respect to input and output.

Input keyboards can indeed be tailor-made, and so can output typesetting font arrangements. But customization is expensive. Yet a case can be advanced for what we may call "position keyboarding." By this we mean that we can simply number each key beginning at the upper left-hand corner, and let that number correspond with a position on the output device's font strip. Hence we would know that if we struck key 22, we would always access character number 22 on the output device (and if we had an interim proofing arrangement, such as an on-line printer, we would also want character 22 to correspond at that level as well).

An alternative to position keyboarding would be to provide computer look-up tables to stand between input and output and furnish the necessary directives to indicate the characters we intend, and to find them for us on the output machine. We can therefore devise a "pseudo-font" to use for input and internal processing, while on the output pass the program can "map" the characters we want to whatever location they might occupy on their filmstrips or within the digital memory of the typesetter. In fact, we could even economize in the disposition of our graphic images. Conceivably, for all fonts and character arrangements we might require the use of only one period, except perhaps to differentiate bold from roman type. On the input end we would of course assume the existence of a period on every keyboard layout.

This concept is not as far-fetched as might at first appear. There is an increasing tendency to arrange character and keyboard layouts so that the operator no longer has to worry as to whether there is a bullet in a particular font, or whether it is necessary to transfer from font 1 to font 3 in order to access a bullet. With only one bullet in his type library he can assume that there is indeed a bullet in every font and in every keyboard arrangement. (This is what we mean by a pseudo-font.) The actual location of characters on the output device can be determined by what is most efficient for that machine. It may require too much time for the typesetting device to effect a transfer from one type disc or filmstrip to another every time a period is required. It may even be helpful to have more than one "e" spinning around on the font, in order to accelerate the throughput of the typesetter. The task of the computer program would be to put out a generalized code for an "e," and the typesetting machine itself might be required to keep track of where the "e's" are located and flash the first one that came around.

In like manner, the assignment of characters to the input device or devices should be arranged to optimize input efficiency. This is not merely a function of locating keys and corresponding characters in positions where finger travel is minimized. It may prove to be most efficient to locate characters where people expect them to be. Thus, although a better keyboard arrangement can be developed—and several studies suggest that the Dvorak keytop assignments are substantially more efficient that the QWERTY—it is the reaction of the average user which will determine what keyboard arrangement and character assignments should be chosen for the input task.

For our part, we have come to the conclusion that conventional groupings of characters will probably work out best, but how large a group of characters should be assembled in one set is itself an interesting topic for speculation.

Definition of terms

AS AN AID to the establishment of input conventions, greater precision in our vocabulary would be helpful. Some years ago, Walter Jessell, of IBM's System Development Division in Boulder, Colorado, prepared a paper entitled *Extended Character Sets in Systems with Photoprinter Output*[1] and presented the following definitions:

Alphabet: A set of letters or other characters with which one or more languages are written.

Sign: A letter of an alphabet, a figure, or a symbol standing for one orthographic identity, independent of graphic appearance or size.

Text: A purposeful concatenation of signs.

Graphic: A representation (form, shape) of one sign (including space) contained in a font.

1. In a draft dated January 21, 1970.

Character: The basic unit of a font; a general term for both "sign" and "graphic," making no distinction between content and form.

Orthographic equivalents: Graphics of different design or size which would not alter the meaning conveyed by text (*e.g.*, a word) in which they are contained if they were substituted for each other. (**Antonym: Orthographic contrast**)

Font: A complete, purposeful assortment of characters for the composition of text in one alphabet, containing one and only one graphic for each sign. (The term **font** is deliberately restrictive to obtain unambiguous access to each member of the set from a single code, or through prefix conventions, from two codes. One font may include upper-case, lower-case, and small cap letters of the alphabet, in addition to figures and symbols.)

Font section: A program-addressable subset of one font, containing 191 or fewer encoded graphics, with optimally-ordered code assignments conforming to standard provisions. Not all fonts will contain all sections. Some sections may be common to several fonts.

Graphic escape code: A control character which, when preceding a sign code, causes that code to represent a different sign. A mnemonic relationship will usually exist between the original sign and that produced through graphic escape. (*E.g.*, Spanish open exclamation point = Graphic escape + Exclamation point.) A graphic escape code may be generated on an output device by a special function key, or by a key whose original function was given up.

This writer is not entirely in agreement with some of the suggestions that Mr. Jessel advances in his paper, but we find the terminology extremely helpful. For example, the letter a is a "sign," whether it is roman or bold or italic, in eight points or 18. On the other hand, a Times Roman eight-point a is a graphic. An italic *a* and a roman a are *orthographic equivalents*. Our major point of difference lies in the fact that we believe a font section should consist of any arbitrary number of characters (it could be called a font subset) smaller than a font, and the graphic escape code cannot, in our judgment, meaningfully and usefully be followed only by a single character. The mnemonic symbology must allow for greater variety, since the character must presumably be selected from an extension of a basic font section.

Actually, Mr. Jessel doesn't quite come up with the definition we feel to be vitally essential. Font section relates to a purposeful selection of particular graphics. What we need is a term which relates to a purposeful selection of a standard grouping of signs, which we shall call a *pseudofont*, or perhaps, more accurately, a *standard signset*, since font implies graphic characteristics, and the signs we have in mind would have orthographic universality.

Such a standard signset should consist of 256 or fewer signs. Since more signs than this are required to handle scientific, technical and foreign language settings, there must be alternate signsets, and the number of these must be considered to be infinite, since different arrangements of signs would be most efficient (at least for input purposes) for different classes of work. For example, one signset might consist of an arrangement of English, Greek and math. Other signset might present the Greek alphabet without either the English or the math.

There will always be some ambiguity in the presentation of signs. Is a superior number the same "sign" as a regular number, or is it merely a different "graphic"? We may worry less about the definition of a "sign" in this context that we would about the method of arranging the keyboard. For certain classes of input it will be most convenient to position superior (and possibly inferior) numbers on the keyboard. Alternatively, one could visualize an entire signset of inferiors and still another signset of superiors. The same thing could be true of inferiors to inferiors, superiors to superiors, superiors to inferiors, *etc.*

Ideally, we could conceive of four different arrangements of signs and graphics: one for input, in order to optimize the efficiency of input for a particular class of work; a second for output, in order to optimize the efficiency of the output device, given its own peculiar characteristics. A third arrangement of signsets might be adopted by the programmer or systems analyst in his effort to optimize the efficiency of his own software. A fourth signset would be developed for the purpose of information interchange. This would contemplate a standard signset, and a certain number of agreed-upon common variations from the standard to accommodate the treatment of scientific information interchange.

It would follow, most certainly, that the signset most useful for information interchange would not be the most efficient for purposes of input, output or internal programming.

There are profound problems involved in this entire area. No signset conventions have in fact been adopted, despite some efforts on the part of certain committees to reach agreement. EBCDIC and USASCII do not properly address the subject. When it is dealt with intelligently it will be clear that the differentiation between signs and graphics must be observed, and ultimately we should arrive at a convention which would enable us to compose all signsets in any available graphic design (with appropriate default arrangements to access alternative characters that might not be available in a selected type face). This would of necessity assume that the typesetting device at all times had access to its entire repertoire of graphic images, and thus it almost certainly would imply the use of at least a third-generation typesetter.

Some special considerations. One problem has to do with the representation of small caps. Some type fonts offer capitals, lower-case letters and small caps as well. The use of small caps needs to be specified at the time of input, and these characters need to be accessed on output. In the internal program, their width values need to be stored and accessed, and occasional words might have to be hyphenated. To fi

fl ff

ffi ffl

ß ç

á à â ä ã

Á À Â Ä Ã

göras på

Grâce

Œ œ

add small caps to a signset might be misleading, however. They are to be differentiated as graphics rather than as signs. This writer believes that the best way to handle them is to consider that, as signs, they do not differ from lower-case characters, and to create a special pseudo-font within the program which places small caps in the lower-case positions. The program does not, in fact, need to know that these are small caps rather than lower-case characters. The output program, of course, would have to access them.

Another area of difficulty has to do with ligatures. It would be unfortunate if the user were required to key ligatures as separate characters or signs. This would present a special problem to the hyphenation routine and would also make it necessary for the person performing the input to know whether or not a particular font did or did not offer ligatures. The better solution is not to include ligatures in the signset at all, but to rely upon the computer program to access ligatures wherever they are required (so that their width values would be stored in the character tables) and to output these characters in the driver program. Consequently, ligatures would not appear on the keyboard as signs, but only on the typeset output, as graphics.

Fractions may be treated in the same way. The operator would key 1/2 for one-half and the program would generate ½ as a one-piece or stand-up fraction (sometimes called an en fraction) and is thus available for the output device.

Accents, too, present special problems. Is an accented character a separate sign? It may be convenient to think of the accent itself as a sign, and the character below the accent as another sign. But accents are sometimes provided as one-piece characters, and at other times letters are created by the use of "floating" accents. In the latter case the program determines whether the width of the accent is greater or less than the width of the character, and puts out the wider width, centering each in relation to the other. In the case of an accent over a lower case i the program has to be "bright enough" to access a "dotless i" instead of a regular one, as in the word *Nîmes*. The program would also have to be able to associate bold accents with bold characters, italic ones with italic characters, *etc.*, and cap-high accents with capital letters. Witness Élève.

In Europe and French Canada some operators would prefer to have distinct keys for accented characters. In English-speaking countries it is usually easier to key either the accent and then the character, or vice versa. (Which of the two should come first is a matter of input convention that ought to be standardized but has not yet been.) As far as output is concerned, the program can either access a one-piece accented character or generate a floating accent over a conventional letter depending upon which solution is available. The operator should not be required to stop to think whether he requires an accent over a capital, a small cap or lower-case character because he knows the program will resolve that matter for him.

Another problem is posed by possible use of digraphs or dipthongs such as æ or Æ. These one-piece characters cannot be combined by the computer program since they occur only occasionally,

Input, Verification, Corrections

such as in *Ægean*, and they would, in all probability, confound the hyphenation program.

The reader may be interested in a keyboard layout which the author helped to develop for the National Geographic Society. This is particularly interesting because it poses most of the problems we have touched upon, only perhaps in an acute condition. There are the following accents: *acute, grave, breve, macron, umlaut, circumflex, cedilla, klicka, tilde, Polish hook, Polish slash, barred D (upper and lower case),* and some special Arabic reverse apostrophes, and single dots, lines or hooks under such characters as *s, t, h, e, d* and various others. In addition there are, of course, the reverse (opening) exclamation and question marks of Spanish, the chevron-like quotation marks for French, the lowered opening quotes for German, as well as a series of digraph combinations in caps, small, caps, lower case, and combinations thereof.

In this instance the keyboard offers a central keypad and two supplementary keypads, plus those used for editing and command codes. It was decided that all accents would be keyed as if they were floating accents with the exception of the barred O, L and D (upper and lower case). We had available to us a "supershift" mode as well as a shift mode. (The shift and supershift modes change the bit configurations.) One key can thus represent four characters. That key, when the shift or supershift—or shift *plus* supershift, are held down, will cause codes to be recorded in entirely different patterns.

We created a different signset layout for combinations of caps and small caps, and the small cap digraphs of AE and OE also appear on this alternate signset arrangement. In like manner, we agreed that the alternate signset layout would imply the use of "Oldstyle" (non-aligning) numerals rather than the more conventional base-aligning figures.

An Atex terminal keyboard layout as customized for the National Geographic Society.

The layout also contemplates the use of three different kinds of hyphens: a hyphen to be input for compound words; a discretionary hyphen to be input to assist the program, where necessary, in breaking words, or ordering that words not be broken (where the discretionary hyphen appears at the beginning of the word); and a machine hyphen. The latter is generated by the program when words are split. It is never input by the operator, but it is required to be on the keyboard in the event that the operator wishes to command the computer to institute a "global search" for every word hyphenated by the machine.

The use of the supplementary keypads may also be of interest. Here we departed from the notion that fractions should be created by the program and the common fractions do in fact have keys of their own. All others would be generated. Ligatures are of course not included since the program will create them where needed, and the kerning of characters is implemented by table look-up, although special typesetting commands can also be given for space-reducing effects.

Except as indicated, the alternate (SMALL CAP) signset arrangement duplicates the first or standard signset layout. Changes in point sizes and type faces are introduced by other keys, not shown.

This solution necessarily appears complicated because the problem it addresses is quite complicated and intricate. Nevertheless, every single one of these characters in the standard signset layout can be represented by a unique eight-bit code with enough codes left over to describe characters which need not appear as signs (*e.g.*, ligatures) and to give other instructions to the output device or devices.

It will be seen that we have tried to use the National Geographic keyboard layout to represent signs and not graphics. Other keys we have not shown would call for different modes or type faces, which would imply the graphic images. Similar commands could be used to signal the point sizes in which we were to compose the type. Even with these conventions, however, the keyboard is rather large, in terms of number of keys—larger than one might wish. A more conventional keyboard may be desired. Yet even that keyboard should have the potential to describe not only the signs we have placed on the National Geographic keyboard, but many more as well. It is for this reason that *escape* codes are often used. The escape symbol will signal the fact that the user wishes to shift to a different sign or a different graphic, or both. In a sense, the supershift key which is on the left of the National Geographic keyboard accomplishes this by enabling the keyboarder to access two additional code groupings (in the shift and unshift positions) so that every key can have four meanings. But even in this instance you are not escaping from the basic 256-level code configuration—there is still a unique code for every sign (although not for every graphic).

It is also possible to escape from the ASCII or EBCDIC representations themselves (or most of them) so that each code can stand for an entirely different signset—Cyrillic or Hebrew, chemical symbols, astronomical signs, representations of the four suits in the game of bridge, or whatever else one might require. If this is done, then the program must know whether or not to subject the code stream to the hyphenation program. Unless told, it may think that it is working with English language words when it is not in fact doing so. But the program could be so conceived that when one escapes to another signset (as one might for the French language, for example) a different hyphenation program (French logic hyphenation) could be invoked.

The role of the typewriter

FOR ENGLISH, and perhaps for many other languages, the typewriter will probably retain its role as a frame of reference for keyboard design. Although some—perhaps most—keyboards intended for use in connection with composition provide auxiliary keys, the typewriter can indeed be made to serve. For example, since the typewriter cannot express a fixed space value, input into a computer system can be translated to recognize that the combination "(em)" shall be translated as an em space, and "(en)" as an en space. In like manner "(ql)" can mean quad left, "(qc)" can stand for quad center and so forth. Even special characters can be described by mnemonics. One could use "(de)" for a degree symbol, "(da)" for a dagger, "(mu)" for a Greek letter *mu*. One would probably not use the open and closing parentheses as delimiters. One might prefer some combination of signs that would not normally occur in conjunction with one another, such as "mu."

It is obvious that more keystrokes are required to provide the full signset desired, and that still additional keystrokes will be necessary to state the typographic codes such as change font, change measure, etc., but these and all other commands—even to the most complex—can surely be described by some combintion of unique keystrokes, and translated by the input program. For a more detailed explanation of this subject, see our discussion of optical character recognition (OCR) below.

In other words, since the keyboard is limited, what is involved is recourse to a kind of "keyboard longhand" which requires a more roundabout way of indicating the desired signs and functions. (Just as "shorthand" expresses the ability to save keystrokes or characters and still convey essential meanings, here the effect is achieved by using *more* keystrokes or characters than those within the root meaning desired.) Whether this use of additional keystrokes is more efficient than a provision for extra keys may be debated, but the consensus seems to be that on the whole it may be better to use fewer keys which lie beneath the fingers than more keys whose locations cannot be memorized. On the other hand, will it be more difficult to remember the mnemonic combinations necessary as opposed to locating the special button which would conjure up the desired character or function? In any event one would quite possibly desire the flexibility of defining mnemonics for new uses rather than the rigidity of established key tops and key positions.

A happy compromise is offered by programmable keys which permit the user to assign whatever meanings (single codes or code combinations) he may choose for certain keyboard positions. These assignments can be operator-related or even job-related. If this cannot be done, mnemonic improvisation is available assuming that the input program can be designed to implement it. This would be possible by introducing, even at the beginning of a job, a table of special meanings to be observed for the application in question.

In point of fact, there are both programmed and programmable keys. The former make it possible for the user to output a string of preplanned codes selected by the manufacturer, with the use of only one keystroke, based upon storage of such character strokes in PROM (programmable read-only memory). But there are also "soft" keys which permit the user himself to program certain key positions and to store particular sequences of character strings for future use. As a general rule, such soft key meanings must be down loaded since information stored in RAM (random access memory) is usually not retained when the keyboard is turned off. There are even keyboards for which every key position is soft and capable of redefinition—thus offering as much flexibility as one might desire in customizing such a keyboard to one's own purposes.

Hard copy, soft copy, and "blind" keyboards

AT ONE TIME there were differences of opinion as to whether hard copy keyboards or "blind" keyboards were more efficient. The hard copy keyboards produced an output, as does a regular typewriter, either by activating striking bars or through the use of a typing element or "golf ball." Consequently, except for certain functions which could not be represented by typewriter keys,[1] the operator could tell when a mistake was made, and rub out the incorrect keystrokes. But it was argued that such keyboards were less efficient because the hard copy distracted the operator and the operator's rhythm was interrupted by the need to wait for the carriage return. Consequently, many favored the use of a blind keyboard which merely punched holes in paper tape and provided the operator with no visual feedback.

But soft copy keyboards soon came into being. These provided a representation of the character on a moving display (sometimes called a self-scan display), much like the manner in which the Times Square illuminated signboard carries the news. Such self-scan devices generally show either the last 32 or the last 64 characters keyed, and the best of such units will represent every single character or keystroke with an appropriate visual image. When these displays are used there is no delay for a carriage return, and if the operator is distracted by the visual representation (which we think unlikely), the display can be turned off.

The CRT full-screen display is of course much more popular today, along with cursor editing capabilities. Blind keyboards are seldom used, and self-scan devices are generally found only in portable keyboards intended for light use, as on an airplane.

---

1. For example, en, em, thin and figure spaces.

Over the last few years the emphasis has shifted so that one is less likely to consider the keyboard as a device for the input of manuscript copy by operators whose task it is to transform such pages into machine-readable input. Nevertheless, in many commercial shops the rekeyboarding of manuscripts will still take place. Whether these keyboards will be designed primarily for the purpose of producing typographic input or whether they will be adapted from word processing devices and from personal or professional computers remains to be seen. Increasingly, it is becoming possible for video terminals to be used for the keying of text for input into composition systems. It is to this issure which this chapter primarily is addressed.

Counting keyboards

WHILE MANY KEYBOARDS are used to create input either into a computer system (where the computer performs hyphenation and justification and makes end-of-line decisions), or directly to an "intelligent" typesetter (where the front-end intelligence of the typesetter makes such decisions) there was at one point some considerable demand for counting keyboards. Such keyboards needed to be capable of accepting tables of width values for the specific fonts to be set. Usually such width values were provided by preprogrammed read-only memories (ROMs). One such keyboard provided sockets so that up to 48 ROM chips, representing 48 fonts, could be plugged in at one time. Or an off-line "black box"[1] could be plugged into the keyboard, thus enabling it to access as many as 255 fonts stored on magnetic tape and read into RAMs (random-access memories).

For some years counting keyboards, initially producing output on paper tape and later onto floppy disks, were extremely popular, especially among the smaller but very numerous trade typesetters. The output of such keyboards already contained end-of-line decisions and served as input to various makes of primarily second-generation typesetting devices.

But within a few short years, it became possible to manufacture and sell direct-input typesetters for prices not much higher than the price of the keyboards themselves. And shortly after that it became possible to incorporate automatic line-ending logic and even simple hyphenation algorithms with small exception word dictionaries into these direct-input typesetting machines. Thus the use of counting keyboards as such has fallen off considerably, although we often find that operators may elect to do some of their input in a counting mode when the option exists of keying either in counting or noncounting modes.

Relation of input to function

WHEN INPUT IS PERFORMED in a production (as opposed to an editorial) environment it should be clear that a careful study must be made of the various input alternatives, with as much customization as possible in order to meet the requirements of the individual user,

1. The term black box is generally used to describe a special-purpose piece of hardware, often improvised inexpensively to meet a unique need.

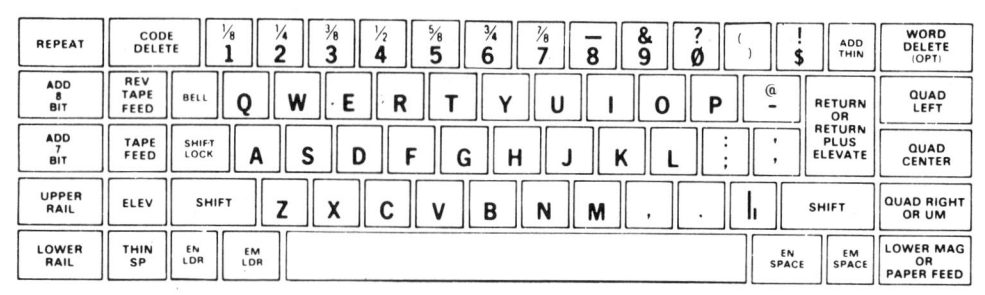

CIT-70 Keyboard Layout

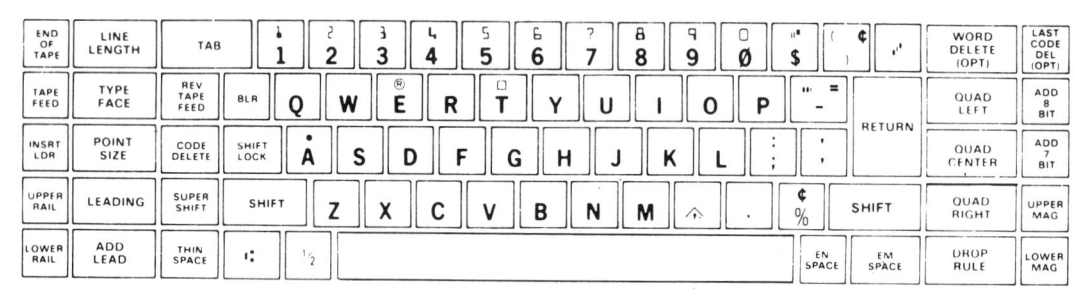

CIM-80 Panel and Typical Keyboard Layout

CIM-100 Panel and Typical Keyboard Layout

PCI-120

These paper-tape perforating keyboards were designed by Automix Keyboards, Inc. (AKI) in the 1970s, when AKI had a dominant role in the industry because of its proficiency as a keyboard supplier. But as the industry moved away from punching paper tape in favor of using video display terminals on line to a front-end system, AKI's market position was eroded and, near bankruptcy in 1979, the company was acquired by Atex, Inc. Under Atex, AKI was converted into a commercial system supplier offering equipment quite similar to the Atex product line. But when Atex, Inc. was acquired by Eastman Kodak in 1981, the overlapping of products was viewed as a liability and, in 1982, AKI as an entity ceased to exist.

Input, Verification, Corrections

given the output device, the system concepts and the kind of work he or she produces. But when input is generated by a writer who, unlike the newspaper journalist, is not linked to an editorial/composition system, a case can be made for the use of generic input which can be adapted for acceptance by any of a number of editing or composition systems. Some generic standards are beginning to evolve for this purpose. It is unlikely that they will meet every need since there are peculiarities encountered in the composition process. However, in many cases it is both quicker and more economical to convert such input rather than to rekey it. And where an established relationship can be created with a selected compositor of one's choice, or with one's own in-house facility, trial and error—aided by an analysis of the job's specific requirements—can produce a quite satisfactory and mutually advantageous relationship between author and typesetting supplier.

Optical character recognition

THERE IS, of course, another form of input into a typesetting system, and that is optical character recognition. It is appropriate to consider this subject in this chapter since this technique has offered an interesting way to accomplish several objectives at the same time.

- It offers a way to get input into a typesetting system without the need to rekey it.
- At the same time it provides hard copy which affords an opportunity for proofreading and the making of certain kinds of corrections even before the text enters the system.
- And some very interesting translate table functions are also often provided, helping to solve the problem of the limited character set of the typewriter and to offer an opportunity to insert needed format codes more or less surreptitiously.

For a brief period, optical character recognition (or OCR as we will hereafter term it) played an interesting role as a part of the composition systems approach. Experiments with OCR go back further than most people realize. Patents on an OCR device were filed by Hiram Goldberg in 1912. Considerable research was done both by Columbia Broadcasting System and the Radio Corporation of America during the 1930s and 1940s, largely as an outgrowth of work on television systems. In the late 1940s a company called Intelligent Machine Corporation began to work on a machine to read numeric information printed on credit card slips. The company's first commercial reader for this purpose reached the maraket in 1954.

It cannot truly be said that the world was waiting breathlessly for OCR readers. By 1970, 16 years after the first Intelligent Machines model appeared, there were only about 1,000 machines (of whatever make) in use worldwide, although the exact figure may depend upon a precise definition of what is meant by an OCR reader. By 1979 that figure had grown to well over 4,000, with more than one third being used in typesetting applications, and an increasing number being sold to augment word processing systems. But by 1983 OCR had pretty well shot its bolt so far as composition systems were concerned, although it was still used in certain specialized applications. However, it continued to play a somewhat decreasing role in the office—(*i.e.,* word processing environment).

Most of the machines installed in the 1970s were for purposes related to typesetting. In the early- to mid-1970s at least three times as many OCR readers were sold for graphic arts applications as for all other uses combined.

There was, indeed, a dramatic change in the use of such readers in the graphic arts field after 1970. The OCR reader was transformed from an expensive and esoteric device into a production tool. And, in the process, typesetting applications became the largest single market and the largest impetus for the renaissance of interest in OCR generally. Were it not for the changes which took place in 1970 and 1971, the subsequent proliferation of OCR would not have occurred.

The first scanner used specifically for typesetting input was a unit built by Recognition Equipment, Incorporated, and installed in 1965 at Perry Publications' newspaper plant in West Palm Beach, Florida. Two REI scanners were eventually used there to process both news copy for various Perry newspapers and for commercial work as well, until 1969, when John Perry lost interest in the newspaper business and sold his papers and scanners. Essentially, all that remains now of Perry's pioneering efforts is the "Perry" typewriter font, developed for use in West Palm Beach and modified slightly for the CompuScan reader. It is still one of the most widely used OCR fonts.

```
Clearly, the keyboarding of marked-up copy is
little different whether it is done on a typewriter
or a paper-tape perforator, except that a modern
paper-tape perforator has convenience keys and
functions that are not found on a typewriter.
```
The Perry font

Aside from the Perry installation, most efforts to use OCR input for typesetting during the 1960s were focused in one of two directions. First, there was the application of OCR essentially as an alternative to paper-tape perforators. Copy was retyped for OCR input, then fed into a scanner. The OCR readers for this purpose were generally large and expensive: the REI input, Control Data machines, IBM and Scan Data readers. The size and cost of these readers dictated either an exceptionally large volume of work or a service-bureau type of operation in which the costs of such expensive equipment would be distributed over a number of users.

The primary advantage of scanned input, according to its proponents, lay in the fact that typed input was faster and/or cheaper to produce than input created on paper-tape perforators—especially as

Input, Verification, Corrections

relatively untrained typists could be used, perhaps even in a cottage industry situation in which the typist is paid only for work produced and need not be paid at all if there is no work to perform.

More recent developments in both OCR readers and alternative technologies have changed the picture somewhat. Scanners are now far cheaper and much more powerful, but paper tape, magnetic tape, or more likely key-to-disk input keyboards and video terminals are also far more effective than they were. The merits of retyping copy specifically for OCR input are less heatedly debated today.

Scanning typeset documents. The second approach to OCR during the 1970s was to use OCR readers to scan copy which had already been typeset and printed. Many jobs which were kept in hot metal and updated year after year could be better handled as computer-stored data files. The problem has been that the "capture" of such jobs for computer processing required rekeyboarding and reproofreading of all of the text, which had been previously "stored" in metal. Other jobs, such as a Bible, a textbook or training manual, might already have been typeset and printed and the metal subsequently destroyed. In either case it would be quite useful to read material which had already been typeset and printed so that it could be converted into a form which is processable by a computer.

Naturally, reading typeset material requires a far more sophisticated device than does reading typewritten material. In the first place, the scanner has to cope with proportionally spaced rather than monospaced type. Secondly, it has to be able to read a variety of fonts—none of them designed with any thought of being scanned. In the third place, the quality of the printed output is often uneven or smudged, and the pages to be read are less susceptible to the use of an automatic transport or feeder mechanism.

Several OCR readers have been built for this purpose. Originally such devices were exceedingly expensive. They were omnifont readers which contained heuristic (self-learning) programs. In 1978 the less expensive Kurzweil reading machine was offered to the market, and its introduction did in fact revive interest in the reading of printed matter. This device also offers simulated voice output for the blind.

When presented with a new document and a new typeface which it has not encountered before, a scanner of this sort will stop and ask the operator to identify each new character it reads. In this way the operator will "teach" the scanner to recognize a new type face or a new version of an old type face.

But even with "omnifont" recognition logic and microfilm document transports to simplify the task of bringing the text to the scanner, the problems of reading already typeset material are formidable and (until the appearance of the Kurzweil product) devices with such capability have sold for several hundreds of thousands of dollars. On the whole there has been a greater interest within the graphic arts industry in the reading of material which was either previously typewritten or which is typed expressly for the purpose of being scanned.

As between these two situations, the latter is obviously the most trouble-free approach. If one is going to type text with the foreknowledge that it is to be read by the scanner, it is possible to select or design a typewriter face that is trouble free and to select paper and develop other procedures to optimize the success of the undertaking. This is indeed what happened in the graphic arts industry, and particularly the newspapers, during the early 1970s.

The first vendor of low-cost specialized OCR systems was a company called ECRM (possibly standing for Electronic Character Recognition Machine). This scanner was designed to be used in a newspaper environment. The thought was that material created would be captured at the source in machine-readable form, and thus there would be no need for rekeyboarding in the composing room. If it does not require rekeyboarding and if the scanning process is accurate, then it would not require proofreading or correcting either. It would also be possible to process copy much more quickly from reporter to final pages.

Copy to be so captured would be created on inexpensive typewriters. No expensive computer terminals would be needed, and anyone with basic typing skills would be able to produce satisfactory input.

The paper flow within a newspaper would be preserved. Editors would still work with the familiar typewritten copy rather than with unfamiliar devices such as video terminals.

But to achieve these objectives two other steps needed to be taken. If paper flow was to be maintained, then it should be possible for the editor to correct the manuscript, after it had been typed, as he had always done. And second, there had to be some way of including within or along with the manuscript the necessary typographic parameters to tell the computer how to compose the copy.

This latter requirement, in particular, imposed a new burden on the OCR reader since now, for the first time, it was not sufficient simply to read the characters on a page. The scanner also had to generate string explosions from "copy mark-up" commands. But what is even more difficult, the scanner had to be responsive to at least light editing changes—insertions, deletions, replacements and corrections.

Interest in the ECRM approach was evident immediately. Other manufacturers jumped in: CompuScan, Cognitronics, Graphic Systems, Bobst, Hendrix, Compugraphic, Dest and Taplin among them. In the first six years after the first ECRM production unit was delivered, at least 2,000 relatively low-cost graphic arts-oriented OCR readers were sold. Although the ECRM concept was the dominant one, not all OCR readers for the graphic arts industry were or are used in the same precise manner. Alternative concepts relating to the use of OCR gained currency.

OCR vs. on-line video terminals. At about the same time that ECRM was getting off the ground another approach to newspaper production was gaining impetus—that of capturing copy in machine-readable form by means of computer terminals, most frequently, video terminals—and then performing all subsequent editing and copy handling by means of video terminals on line to a central computer data base. Literally hundreds of such systems have now been implemented. Systems combining OCR (for input) and video terminals (for editing) have also been implemented. This approach, it has been claimed, offers some of the cost advantages of OCR input with the editing flexibility of video terminals.

OCR readers, particularly the newer, lower-priced models now selling from less than $10,000 to $35,000, have also found their way into commercial (non-newspaper) installations. Here they may be used in a quite different manner. By and large commercial typesetters do not create the material which they typeset. The commercial typesetter, then, must train his customers to create input for his OCR reader or must rekeyboard the material before it can be scanned. This represents an entirely different and less compelling set of economic conditions from those that have presented themselves in newspapers. Nevertheless there are circumstances under which OCR can play a role in the non-newspaper section of the graphic arts industry.

What is OCR? The initials OCR can stand for either optical *character* recognition or optical *code* recognition, with the distinction that *character readers* read "human readable" type fonts while *code readers* read a bar code image printed *below* the human-readable characters. Sometimes OBR is used to describe the latter devices. Except for recognition logic, code readers behave very much the same as character readers.

The function of OCR readers is to convert the alphanumeric information on typewritten documents into electronic bits and bytes. We almost said into "machine-readable" form, thinking of a magnetic tape or of paper tape, for example, as "machine readable." But because of OCR, the typewritten document itself *becomes* machine-readable.

An OCR device, whether it is reading codes or characters, consists of three basic elements: the paper transport, the reader or scanning mechanism itself, and the recognition logic. To these, the devices we will now discuss generally offer a fourth element, which we have termed "post-recognition logic."

Paper transport. The readers with which we are concerned are all page readers. That is, they will read standard $8\frac{1}{8}" \times 11"$ or $8\frac{1}{2}" \times 14"$ pages, and perhaps some other sizes as well. They are not document readers in the sense that they were designed to read post cards or department invoices.

The function of the paper transport is to select sheets in sequence from an input stack and to move them, one at a time, into the scanning area of the machine. This should be done without double feeding, since the material to be read usually needs to be written out and processed consecutively. Once scanned, the pages are removed and deposited in a bin. In some machines the paper transport may also serve the function of advancing the page to be read, one line at a time, in front of the read mechanism. In others it may also actually sweep the line of type to be scanned past the read head.

After the sheet has been read it will be deposited in the output bin. Most OCR readers have only one bin. A few have two bins, and the machine logic will direct to the second bin any sheets which have been rejected as unreadable or presenting reading problems.

The paper transport mechanism is one of the most difficult and costly aspects of scanner design, accounting for more than 50% of the cost of the unit and 80% of the trouble, and because it is the mechanical portion of a basically electronic package the transport mechanism is the portion least amenable to cost reduction.

The scanner. The central operating part of an OCR reader is the scanning mechanism for "data capture." The function of data capture is to reduce the image on the typewritten page to black and white patterns which can be analyzed by the recognition logic. This is usually done by measuring on a point-by-point basis the amount of light reflected from the surface of the paper. A common approach is to scan a line at a time with a single spot of light, recording the variations in the intensity of the reflected light as they are observed or detected in a series of closely spaced points across the line. One method of doing this is the "flying spot" scanner. A cathode ray tube generates the scanning beam and deflects it across the tube. This beam is in turn focused on the paper to be read. One or more photocells read the amount of light reflected on a point-by-point basic.

Another means of achieving the same end without the cathode ray tube and its attendant circuitry has been to flood the entire document with light yet read or sample the reflected light value of one small spot at a time. This is done by interposing a spinning disk between the document itself and the photocell which measures the intensity of the reflected light. The disk is perforated with a series of small holes. When these holes are arranged in a spiral pattern it is called a *Nipkow disk*. As the disk spins in front of the photocell, light from different points on the document being read passes through the holes in the disk. This technique has been widely used in the past. It is cheaper and slower than the flying spot scanner. However, it has been largely supplanted by the use of laser and multipoint scanners.

Laser scanners work on the principle of projecting a brilliant, coherent light[1] across a page, usually by means of a rotating or vibrating mirror. As the light passes along, a photocell measures its value as reflected at various points. Since a great many closely spaced readings are required, the laser beam will have to sweep across each line of copy 40 or more times to generate 40 or more slices of data which will be assembled by the recognition logic to build a digital picture of the line which has been scanned.

Because it is deflected into an arc on a flat piece of paper, the laser presents some of the same problems of geometric distortion as does a rotating mirror in a second-generation typesetter. Compensation in electronic circuitry or through the interposition of a field flattening lens may thus be used, or the scanning beam can be split in two, with one portion projected against a fine-line grating in order to

---

1. A coherent light has the property of maintaining a constant focus regardless of the distance from the light source to the object.

Input, Verification, Corrections

measure the position of the scanning beam with respect to the line being read.

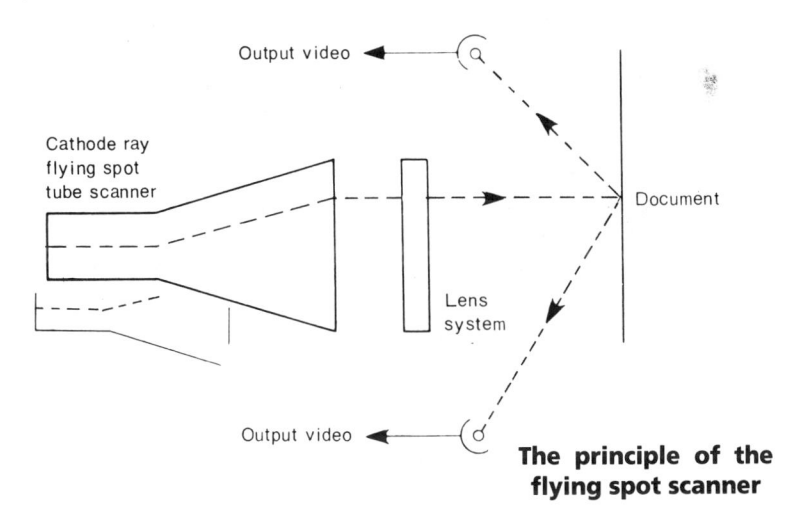

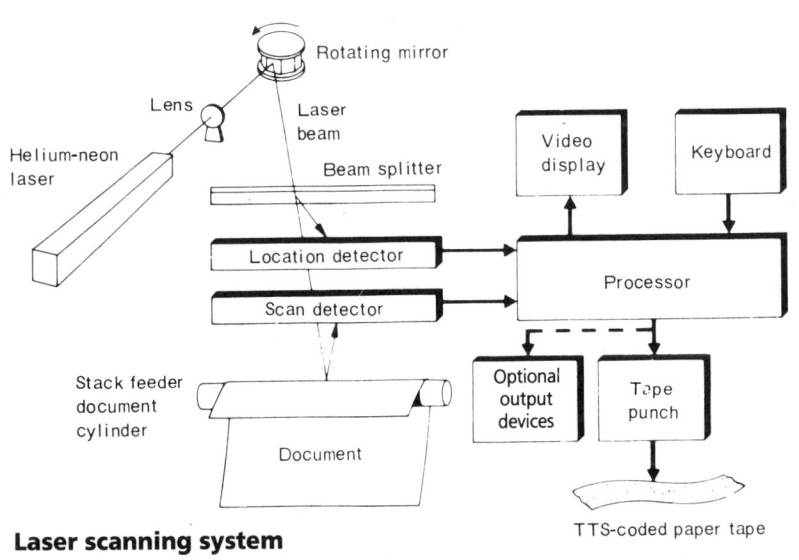

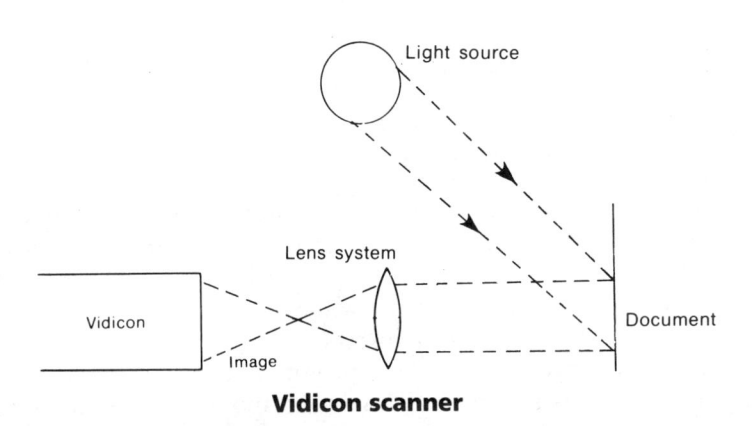

The principle of the flying spot scanner

Laser scanning system

Vidicon scanner

Yet another method is to project the image onto a vidicon tube. In this case, the beam of the vidicon scans out the patterns of black and white. However, a single such tube does not have enough resolution to scan an entire line of typewritten copy, so to eliminate the mechanical motion that would otherwise be required to move the scanning tube past the paper or to move the paper past the scanning tube, ECRM initially used six vidicon tubes.

It is also possible to move an array of photocells along the line, or to move the paper, line by line, in front of such an array, and to sample a whole series of points.

Once the black and white patterns that make up a line of type have been captured it is the task of the recognition logic to identify the characters. Reflected light levels picked up by the scanner are converted from analog (intensity) to digital patterns before being submitted to the recognition logic. This is done by matching the light values read against a "threshold" value: any amount of light above the threshold is read as white or blank paper, and any value below the threshold is read as black or part of a character image.

The first task, of course, is to identify the individual lines of data, and then to separate out, somehow, the individual characters within the line. All of the readers with which we are familiar scan one line at a time. However, so that the reader can accommodate slight skew and mispositioning of lines on a page, the area scanned is always greater than the height of one line. Most recognition techniques therefore require that there be at least one horizontal "row" of data—all blank—above and below each line of typed copy. In other words, a line is defined as being an area containing some black data which is bounded top and bottom by areas of all white.

These would be identified as *one* line of copy:

```
Here is one line of typewritten copy.
Here is another line typed with a skew.
```

These would be identified as *two* lines of copy:

```
This is one line of ↕copy.
This is another scannable line.
```

These would be identified as *one* line of copy:

```
This is one line of ↕copy.
This line could not be scanned.
```

The more room between descenders on one line and ascenders on the next, the more latitude there is for skew and for character cross-outs. Even more critical, the more room there is between lines, the more latitude we will have if we wish to make insertions between lines of typed copy. Frequently insertions are to be made after the page has been removed from the typewriter. It is all too easy when you put a page back into the machine to misposition the paper or to

Input, Verification, Corrections 243

skew it so that its base line, if projected toward infinity, would intersect with that of the original copy.

The amount of space between lines is a function of the design of the type font used, the setting of the line spacing ratchet on the typewriter, and the gear ratios of the ratchet itself. Most scanners require that single-spaced copy be typed at one-and-one-half-line spacing (four lines to the inch rather than the normal six). When the Perry font is used on the CompuScan readers, single-spaced copy may be typed at five lines to the inch.

Identifying characters. Once the logic has decided what constitutes a line, it must determine what constitutes a character within the line. Just as one assumes that a line must be bounded top and bottom by white space, so it is assumed that a character must be bounded on either side by white space. To insure that the OCR reader can identify individual characters even if the typewriter which produced the input copy is not perfectly adjusted, OCR fonts are designed with somewhat more white space between characters (larger side bearings) than is the case with most other typewriter fonts. Where a font not specifically designated for scanning has been adapted to this purpose (for example the IBM Courier 12), it is typed at a wider-than-normal spacing. (A 12-pitch typing element is mounted on a 10-pitch typewriter.)

```
This is a sample of IBM Courier 12, 8 pt.
type. We have taken a 12-pitch typing element
and mounted it on a 10-pitch typewriter.
```

Character recognition. Once the reader has isolated an individual character by its logic, it must decide what that character is. The logic to do this—the real recognition logic—is closely and jealously guarded by the various manufacturers. However, most of them use some combination of the following techniques:

- *Matrix matching.* The digital matrix which describes the character as seen by the scanner is matched against a series of matrices representing the character repertoire of the font being read until the closest match is found. This has now evolved into a reasonably complicated set of procedures whereby character stroke widths are normalized to predetermined values before matches are attempted. Moreover, this technique may be combined with some sort of "feature analysis," with the latter being used to divide characters into "classes," and fairly rough matrix matches being applied to help identify characters within each class.

- *Feature analysis.* Characters are classsified into categories by *stroke analysis geometric feature analysis* and *abstract feature analysis.* Geometric analysis looks at attributes such as corners, junctions and crossovers. Abstract analysis looks at density of blackness within the white space, the selection of short characters (lower case x's and z's, s's and a's), along with tall but narrow characters, or tall and wide characters with little mass on the left-hand side or on the right, such as an X, or a C or a K.

Whatever the technique or combination of techniques, most of the logic systems which have been developed make intensive use of table comparisons. In most OCR readers it is therefore possible to change the type font read by changing the recognition tables, although in some cases it may be necessary to modify the recognition logic as well.

Manual intervention. Frequently, logic recognition will step through a series of "levels" in its attempt to identify a character. One option which has been offered on OCR devices for a number of years has been a mode of operation in which the scanner will stop if it cannot identify a character after going through the first few logic steps, or if it cannot find a match for the character in question within preset error limits. The reader will then display for an operator a representation of the character which is causing the difficulty, along with some of the text which precedes it and follows it, or else it will enable the operator to look into the machine to see, by examining the original manuscript with a pointer poised at the location of the indecipherable character, just what the problem is. The operator then uses a keyboard attached to the device to signal the identity of the questionable character. In some systems the device will remember this identification in case the character appears again.

Naturally an OCR reader will be more accurate (that is, it will misread fewer chracters) when operating in the human-intervention mode. However, a reader running in this mode will produce more slowly and it will require more operator attention. Thus, manufacturers who offer this feature permit its use to be disabled.

Another possibility which is being used increasingly, is a kind of "after-the-fact" intervention. The OCR reader does not stop on a questionable character, but flags it. This information is passed on to the next step, and if that step involves the use of a video tube to display the text, then when the problem areas are displayed on the screen the doubtful or unidentifiable characters are presented as a blinking image or blob so that an operator, who may also be performing editing or composition functions, can determine what the appropriate character should be. Such an extra step on video terminals which would be used for editing the copy anyway is less time consuming than having the OCR device stop and wait for instructions.

Post-recognition logic. As we mentioned earlier, the ECRM concept involved the extensive use of what we have called "post-recognition" logic. Generally speaking, this logic performs one of three basic functions: code translating and formatting, editing (*i.e.*, making corrections), and "forms control."

Translation routines. The simplest form of post-recognition logic is the code translator. In its crudest form this logic simply outputs what has been read in whatever code structure the user desires. Quite commonly this is six-level TTS coding which requires that the routine

Input, Verification, Corrections

must insert shift and unshift codes into the data stream. Unfortunately the limited signset available on a typewriter is not sufficient to express the variety of typographic symbols and spaces, or the typographic command codes that even relatively simple typesetting applications may require. Hence the code translator rapidly evolves into a *string translator* as well.

A string translator will examine text which has been scanned and search for the occurrence of certain characters or strings of characters, and replace them with other single characters or with quite complex strings of characters.

A string may map several characters into one. In most of the readers sold to this industry, a "1/2" on the typewritten input will appear as a single character "½" on the output, and a "1/4" with be treated in the same manner. Moreover, since typewriters do not differentiate between opening and closing quotes, the scanning logic will take on this task. A double quote preceded by a space would be output as two opening quotation marks. A single quote preceded by a space would be output as a single opening quotation mark. A single quote preceded and followed by characters would be output as an apostrophe, and a double quote followed by a period or a space would be output as a closing double quotation mark.

A string translator may also convert one character into several characters. However, given the limited signset of the typewriter, it will be more likely to translate several manuscript characters into one typesetting character. Here are examples of some of the more standard conventions:

Two hyphens (--) will translate into an em dash (—).
One to four spaces will translate into a single interword space.
Five or more spaces at the beginning of a line will start a new paragraph.
More than four spaces in the middle of a line will signal the end of the line.
*EM or /// may stand for an em space.
*EN or // will stand for an en space.
TS or /+ will represent a thin space of a width value to be defined.

Such codes, and many others, can be redefined to meet user requirements. For example, ECRM also provided four "autostrings" and eight "autofunctions" for which the user could specify his own output coding by means of a "header sheet" or even by means of commands typed directly onto an input job.

	# ST =	start take
	# ET =	end take
	# PS =	start paragraph
	# NL =	new ad
Autostrings:	# SL =	slug line
	# F1 thru F4 =	call for four type faces
	# BF =	bold face
	# LF =	light face
Autofunctions:	# IF =	indent first line of paragraph

The accompanying examples show some of the standard string translations used by suppliers of OCR readers for graphic arts applications. But it is also common for the manufacturer to be able to accept header sheets for classes of jobs, or even for individual jobs. A user can define his own output translate table and coding structure—ASCII, EBCDIC, TTS or whatever he might like. He can also make up his own string translations for typesetting formats. One user even applies the string routines to insert discretionary hyphens in words that he knows would be hyphenated incorrectly, and to insert "minus value" commands between letter combinations that should be kerned. With enough memory in the OCR reader one can also use string substitution routines to "explode" keyboard shorthand routines, to make corrections to copy by "global" search and replace functions—for example, to change every occurrence of GPO to Government Printing Office—or even to do automatic proofreading for commonly misspelled words.

	CompuScan	ECRM	Cognitronics		CompuScan	ECRM	Cognitronics
Em space	///	*EM	⊬ms	Elevate	/e	*EL	⊬el
En space	//	*EN	⊬ns	Add thin		*AT	⊬at
Thin space	/+	*TS	⊬ts	Return		*RT	⊬re
Em leader	/..	*ML	⊬ml	Paper feed		*PF	
En leader	/.	*NL	⊬nl	Bell		*BL	⊬be
Quad left	/|	*QL	⊬ql	Force upshift	/Ss	*SH	
Quad right	/r	*QR	⊬qr	Force			
Quad center	/c	*QC	⊬qc	downshift	/Uu	*UN	
Lower rail	}	*LR	⊬lr	Vertical rule		*VR	
Upper rail	{	*UR	⊬ur	End p'graph	=		⊬ep

These represent typical implementations of means of accessing basic typographic command codes. The fact that entries are left blank on this table is of no consequence. These codes can be redefined to meet user requirements, and new definitions can be added. The table is presented for illustrative purposes only. The Cognitronics product was formerly marketed by MGD Information Systems and by Graphic Systems, Inc.

The purpose of translate routines. Why does a scanner for typesetting input need translate routines? We have implied several answers to this question in the foregoing discussion, but perhaps we should state them specifically:

1. Translate routines compensate for the limited character set available on a typewriter to make it possible to express such things as fractions, fixed white space codes, and typographic command functions.

2. Translate routines adapt the scanner output language to the requirements of a particular user's computer typesetting program.

3. Translate routines make input as simple as possible by reducing the need for typographic command codes. The beginning of a paragraph can be signaled by an indent of five or more spaces.

Input, Verification, Corrections

Single column text can be signaled by "*t." A 24-point head can be signaled by "*24." This makes it possible for classified ad and editorial personnel to prepare input for typesetting programs without having to learn specific typographic commands. It is doubtful that nearly as many OCR readers would have been sold to newspapers without these functions.

Of course one would not need an OCR reader to perform string translations and substitutions. One could perform the same functions in the computers of the typesetting system, or even, perhaps, in the front-end controller of a phototypesetter.

However, most customers for this type of equipment did not have an in-house programming staff for typesetting software. The OCR readers performed these functions because they had to perform them if they were to be sold as stand-alone units to feed into existing typesetting systems. When scanners were sold as part of a total system it was perhaps less consequential where the functions were performed.

Thus even less expensive OCR devices were developed to be sold as peripherals to typesetting systems, and these did not contain any of the post-recognition logic capabilities since they could be performed by the computer software in conjunction with the video terminal system itself.

However, during the relatively brief period of popularity of OCR in the newspaper industry, many users became familiar with string translation capabilities and thus gained new insights into the flexibility which actually lay behind the apparently intractable demands of computer typesetting machines and systems. Later on these same approaches were applied to the task of converting input from word processing machines so that it could be processed with comparable convenience by typesetting systems.

Editing or correction routines. The orginal thrust behind the use of OCR readers—in the newspaper industry in particular—was that reporters and classified ad takers could create their own input in OCR-readable form, correct their own errors as they were typing, and even make additional corrections after the paper had been removed from their typewriters. Each of these options will now be considered.

Corrections at the time of input. If the typist is aware of the fact that an error has been made, it can easily be corrected by typing in a symbol instructing the OCR device, during the reading process, to ignore certain characters or lines.

In the illustration on the following page a lozenge is used to effectuate three different kinds of changes. In the first instance the symbol is understood to instruct the scanning device to ignore the preceding character. In the second instance two lozenges are used to instruct the device to ignore the entire word (back to the preceding space). In the third case three lozenges are used to instruct the program to delete from memory all of the text it has read within that line up to the point where the lozenges appear.

```
Delete the preceding charr⌑acter.

Delete the preceding wrd⌑⌑word.

Delete the whole drn sntence⌑⌑⌑

Delete the sntnc⌑⌑⌑Delete the sentence
up to here.



I ti#yped the wrong cah##haracter.

Now I want to delete there###ree characters.
```

Another vendor uses the number sign (#) to indicate the number of characters to be deleted by the OCR reader logic.

It is possible in some cases to inform the OCR reader what the operative character to be used as a flag will be. Another variation permits the operator to use one symbol to indicate a character deletion and another to indicate a word deletion. In the latter instance each consecutive repeat of the word symbol signifies an additional consecutive word to be deleted. A repeat symbol is used for each word to insert one such symbol.

Thus when the typist senses or feels the making of a typing error, or changes his or her mind after typing a character or a word or even more, delete symbols can be used. Clearly these symbols can make it possible for even an inexpert typist to prepare copy for OCR input. On the other hand, such copy, if replete with such symbols, will be difficult to read or to edit prior to scanning.

Corrections subsequent to input. The delete symbol is not helpful in every case. It can be used only if you catch your error or change your mind at the time you make the error. Once you have typed well beyond that point it is too late. Here the cross-out is more effective. A strike-out or cross-out is a procedure by which a person draws a line through the letter or words he or she wishes to delete, thereby making it impossible for the scanner to recognize the character or word. The cross-outs must be made carefully, usually with a nylon-tipped, dark-colored pen. It may be performed either by the person who creates the copy or by someone who reviews it later. As a rule, vertical cross-outs are made to indicate the deletion of a single letter and horizontal cross-outs signal the desire to delete an entire word or series of words.

Input, Verification, Corrections 249

h**ø**oney   hone**ǿ**y   h**ǿ**oney

This cross-out would be acceptable to an MGD device but not to ECRM.

This cross-out would not be acceptable to any scanner because it intrudes into the space occupied by the following character.

This would be acceptable to ECRM, but not to MGD.

This is a ~~manual~~ deletion.

Insertions. It is also necessary to cope with insertions usually added by a reviewer or editor. Most OCR readers have been programmed to hold two lines of copy at one time in their buffer memories. Whenever the logic encounters a horizontal or a vertical cross-out it will jump to the end of the line on which the cross-out appears and search the next line for an insertion. If it encounters an insertion, it will replace the copy crossed out with the insert copy. If it does not, it will simply delete the crossed-out copy. To enable the scanner to identify copy to be inserted, a delimiter code must be placed before and after the insert. If there is more than one replacement in the line the program will process them in sequence. If there is a deletion on the same line as an insert, but preceding it, then a dummy insert of a "null" must be associated with the deletion so that the logic will not apply the replacement at the wrong location.

```
MGD and Graphic Systems {Bobst}: This is an xxx delimiter.
          + insert +

ECRM: This is an xxx delimiter.
        /insert/

CompuScan: This is an xxx delimiter.
  Δ insert Δ

ECRM:
    Here we are going to make deletions and substitutions.
        //         /substitutions/      /deletions./
```

The limitations of interline insertions. If we are to make interline insertions and replacements, the original copy must offer space to do so. This means that copy which is to be so corrected must be typed at twice the normal spacing (two lines to the inch rather than four) to allow room for inserts and replacements to be added between the lines. Moreover, the scanner must be instructed to look for insertions. Naturally, to run the scanner in this mode slows up the reading process. More importantly, this method requires that the person making corrections put the page back into the typewriter in order to type them, and it must be put in carefully to avoid skew.

These difficulties, along with jurisdictional considerations, led to a division of labor in some newspapers. Editors might mark corrections in ink which the scanner could not see, and typists or composing room personnel (depending upon the labor contracts prevailing) would actually make the cross-outs with a dark-colored pen and type in the replacements and insertions.

It should be obvious that these correction facilities were useful only for relatively straightforward and relatively light copy editing. There was insufficient space available to add more than a short phrase, and there was no way to transpose or rearrange blocks of copy. Several of the manufacturers devised ways to overcome these limitations:

- *Cut and paste.* One such concept was that editors could handle major revisions by cutting copy and scotch-taping it back together again. This was one of the reasons why the ECRM scanners would accept input sheets of virtually any length, and why they have been quite tolerant about variations in paper thickness. However, even so, the cut and paste processes needed to be done with some care.
- *Paragraph insertion.* CompuScan offered a paragraph insertion program for its scanners. This was a means of inserting more copy than could be typed between the lines on original input. The standard program would accept one or more inserts of up to 300 characters in total length. An expanded program would accept more inserts or larger inserts. The copy to be inserted had to be encountered prior to the point where it was to be used. Generally this meant that it would be typed on a separate sheet of paper inserted at the beginning of the job, or, if there were a number of inserts to be made, just before the page on which the insertion was to appear. The text of the insertion was stored in the memory of the scanner and then called out to be inserted when the appropriate code was encountered.

Type fonts for OCR input. The scanners just discussed have for the most part been designed to read only one typewriter font, or, at best, several such fonts, all of which are intended to be scanned. While the type characters are legible, they are not usually standard fonts. They usually consisted of specially designed typing elements for the IBM Selectric or similar devices. However, several manufacturers have more recently added to the repertoire of fonts which can be

Input, Verification, Corrections

scanned with a fairly high degree of accuracy. In all cases, however, best results are obtained if pages are typed with the expectation that they will be scanned. Scanning of manuscript pages not so prepared is quite a bit more difficult and usually requires a device such as those manufactured by companies such as Kurzweil, and they imply that the user must first teach the scanning device what to expect.

Thus it may not be assumed that "any old" typewriter can prepare input acceptable to the scanner. Moreover, the device must be maintained with great care. Often typewriter repair persons unfamiliar with the requirements of OCR are not capable of providing this level of maintenance.

The quality of paper is often extremely important, and some degree of training—not only in the conventions for insertions and deletions, but also in the spacing of material on the page—is required.

Shifting responsibility to the writer. The capture of keystrokes does imply that the writer is to be held accountable for the accuracy of his input, including grammar and spelling. While editorial changes can be made in the fashion described, if they are substantial the entire process breaks down. Some writers are unwilling to accept this responsibility or are unqualified to perform under it.

So far as accuracy of scanning input is concerned, when the material has been properly prepared and the OCR device is in proper adjustment, misreading is less likely to occur than would be the case, for example, with a paper-tape reader. One error in 10,000 characters read is claimed as a maximum by most manufacturers and some make even more extravagant claims. But it may not be assumed that those characters which are troublesome to the OCR device will invariably be flagged. Such flagging may be suppressed in the interest of speed. Moreover it is possible for the reader to guess (with a high degree of certainty) that the character is something other than it truly is, and not raise a question even in the flagging mode.

Samples of some commonly used OCR fonts

OCR-A	OCR-B	IBM Courier 12
1234567890-=	1234567890-=	1234567890-=
qwertyuiop■	qwertyuiop°	qwertyuiop]
asdfghjkl;'	asdfghjklñ;	asdfghjkl;'
zxcvbnm,./	zxcvbnm,.'	zxcvbnm,./
ABCDEFGHIJKLM	ABCDEFGHIJKLM	ABCDEFGHIJKLM
NOPQRSTUVWXYZ	NOPQRSTUVWXYZ	NOPQRSTUVWXYZ

The impact of OCR. As shall be indicated in the next chapter, other techniques for input and editing came into being because of the growth in power and popularity of video terminals. Today OCR is used primarily in the office environment for converting into machine-readable form certain documents and manuscripts which were generated in offices in which there are not enough word processors or other on-line terminals to go around. Occasionally it is used for situations in which there is a massive one-time need to enter large quantities of text into a computer in a relatively short period of time. But our attention shall now focus upon the contributions made to the input and editing process by the video terminal.

Let is be said, however, that many of the techniques which had to be developed to cope with the limited repertoire of the typewriter, such as the use of header sheets and translation tables, have made a lasting contribution to the publishing industry. What we learned by trying to cope with OCR and to make it effective in a publishing environment was extremely useful in that it provided a foundation to enable us to develop similar solutions in accepting input from typewriter-like devices in word-processing environments.

Our problem remains the same, however—how we can go about the process of providing a trouble-free flow of information in all directions: from writer to editor to publishing to consumer, and back again, and to accomplish this in such a way that no compromises need to be made either with respect to ultimate typographical appearance or the character repertoire and information content of the material.

The other related objective is, of course, to permit changes to be made easily at any time during the writing/editing/publishing/information-digesting process so that the enhancement of the product and its usefulness to society will not be arbitrarily constrained by the process itself.

16

Video Terminals for Composition

THE VIDEO TERMINAL clearly represents the single most important development in the field of computerized composition and text editing since the initial days of batch-oriented single-pass hyphenation and justification systems. The writer remembers very vividly how difficult it was to produce acceptable photocomposed output during the days when photocomposition was a "blind" process. The video terminal or CRT gave us our first window into this process. But it provides more than an opportunity to see: we now have the opportunity to review and to change, and to see the effects of the change. We can do this not only at one point in the process, but, if the system is properly designed, at virtually any stage. And now that we are moving into the world of digital typesetting—a world which implies greater fluidity and versatility with respect to the output of images of all kinds, both words and pictures—it is the VDT and its supporting hardware and software which plays the central role.

The technology may change. The screen may create its images by means of some still yet unknown technology, but from now on the individual at his workstation or desk will have a window which virtually permits him to reach out to touch and shape the end product he is designing or creating.

While video terminals were used in conjunction with computers as early as the 1950s, they made little headway in the graphic arts industry until the early 1970s. Today, most of the video terminals used in our industry have been specifically designed for text processing and typesetting applications, just as the OCR devices which caught on in the industry were also specifically engineered for these purposes. Tomorrow we will witness the use of workstations which are more generalized and ambidextrous. The same or similar terminals are now beginning to be applied in a wide variety of situations.

Ignoring a few early systems that demonstrated the feasibility of applying video terminals to text editing, our story really begins with the introduction of a stand-alone terminal developed by the Harris Corporation and first shown at the American Newspaper Publishers' Association Research Institute (ANPA/RI) exhibit in New Orleans in June 1970. The immediate acceptance of this terminal—called the "1100"—ushered in a new era not only for the newspaper industry, but for all practitioners or potential users in all aspects and facets of typesetting and related text processing—both in production and in editorial environments. Other manufacturers or suppliers soon began to develop more or less comparable terminals.

Indeed, one such supplier, Hendrix Electronics, brought a product to the same show. But the quality of the image and the functionality of the Harris product inaugurated the new era, spawning many imitations as well as inspiring subsequent improvements by Harris and others with respect to concept and design.

The 1100 was shown as a "paper tape in-paper tape out" editorial tool. In other words, the theory was that an editor would feed a paper tape into the machine, storing the contents of the file within the buffer memory of the terminal. This file would most likely be a wire service story which was to be edited to meet the interest of a local readership and the space requirements of the newspaper. The story, or portions of it, could be displayed on the screen and corrections and modifications could be effected randomly. It was possible to contain within the workstation's memory a story of average length, and when the editing process was completed a new paper tape would be punched out which could then be fed to the composition computer or directly to a typesetting machine that had the capability of doing its own justification.

The terminal also offered the new capability of *cursor editing*. In other words, by positioning a marker at a given location on the text one could insert material at that point or delete text already there.

Harris had not initially conceived of the 1100 as a production tool. It had visualized that the terminal would be used by editors to make changes in wire service stories received at the local newspaper level in the form of Teletype printout and paper tape. Twenty-five lines could be read in and edited at one time, with 50 characters across the screen, or 50 lines, each of 40 characters, could be presented in a two-column format. Hence enough information was available at one time to get the sense or flow of the story, but it was not possible to move text beyond the area of the terminal's buffer.

But what the industry saw in the 1100 at that time was not primarily related to editing. It was rather conceived as a better method of "tape perfecting" that was faster and easier than any of the existing precomputer[1] tape-merging devices. It was also more interactive[2] than the batch correcting and merging techniques offered by existing computer composition systems.

Within a year or two many similar terminals had come into being. Hendrix withdrew its 5102[3] offering and introduced the 5200. Mergenthaler marketed the CorRecTerm, and Omnitext came out with its 1500, which sold under the Mohrtext name, and subsequently as the Singer 8400. All of these were configured to receive their input from paper tape and, in turn, provide paper-tape output. They could be used for editing, for proofreading and correcting, or merely for the implementation of corrections already noted from reading printouts or preliminary typeset copy.

When used directly for proofreading, the purpose was to verify that the text had been keyed correctly, and, if not, to make necessary changes at the same time that the errors were detected. When used for correction implementation the purpose was to locate and correct those errors that had already been marked on a printout or galley.

---

1. That is, prior to the processing of the input for composition on the computer.

2. Operation was interactive only in the sense that the operator could see that the correction was in fact implemented.

3. Hendrix Electronics developed an editing terminal in 1969. A prototype of the terminal, which was called the 5102FD, was installed in the office of the Associated Press in New York City in 1969. Several other models were installed at various sites.

Video Terminals for Composition

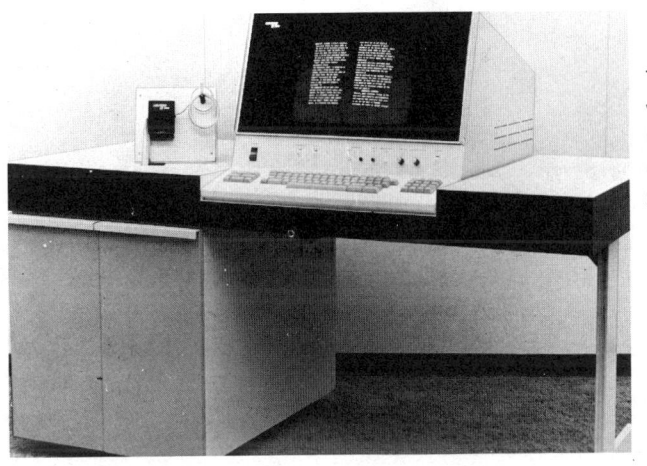

The Harris 1100 terminal, a hard-wired device which used paper tape as its I/O medium, was introduced in 1970. It displayed upper- and lower-case characters on the screen in single- or double-column format.

Right: The Hendrix 5200 terminal, a redesigned version of the 5102, was presented for the first time at the ANPA conference in Milwaukee in January 1971. It, too, used hard-wired logic and could perform the basic editing and correction functions found on the other contemporary terminals, e.g., overstrike, insert and delete. The 5200 operated either with paper-tape input and output or on-line to a computer system.

Left: Mergenthaler's CorRecTerm (note the emphasis on CRT) was also a hard-wired terminal which was released in 1971. It, too, offered single- and double-column display modes, and was a paper-tape oriented device.

Automix Keyboards (AKI) introduced its *Ultra*-series (top left) line of editing terminals in 1972. Each terminal had its own built-in microprocessor, a "computer-in-a-chip." The AKI terminals made use of either paper tape or magnetic cassettes for text storage and revision.

Later in the 1970s most terminals used in the publishing industry for writers and reporters were attached to a front-end minicomputer system. The Zentec ZMS 70 (center left) used micrcocomputer logic and even had floppy disks to provide off-line data storage.

As time progressed, personal computers became versatile enough to be used in a graphic arts context. Even the Apple IIc (bottom left) with a telecommunications interface could pass text to a composition system, although it has no composition capability of its own.

On the other end of the scale, very elaborate WYSIWYG terminals, such as that by Qubix (top right) handle both text and graphics.

Video Terminals for Composition

Basic components and functions

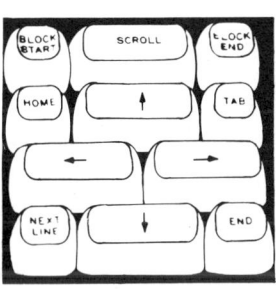

WE HAVE MADE use of the name "terminal," although a stand-alone device, such as these units started out to be, is not truly a "terminus" (that is, an adjunct to a system) in any on-line sense. It *is* an adjunct to a system in a production sense, of course. But because the VDT (video display terminal) resembled computer video terminals such as those found at airline counters for communicating with large computer network systems, the name terminal—at least in the graphic arts industry—has been associated with these stand-alone devices. These are called VDTs (for video—or visual—display terminals), and the British have more correctly labeled them as VDUs (video display units).

Typical grouping of cursor control keys. This particular key cluster forms part of the keyboard layout on the Omnitext 1500 terminal.

The terminal provides a keyboard and a video screen. On the keyboard will be found—alongside of the usual typewriter-like arrangement of key buttons—a set of *cursor control keys*. These are used to direct the cursor or pointer to move from line to line and from character to character on the screen, thus signaling a specific location—an individual character—within the text displayed. A position is thus identified where an operation may take place, such as to overstrike and thus substitute another character for the one occupying that particular location.

Some VDTs are so designed that the cursor will move automatically from one line to the next so long as you continue to hold down a sideways cursor direction key. Others are designed not to move off a given line, and you must consequently strike a cursor up arrow or down arrow in order to get the cursor to depart from one line and go on to the next.

Generally cursors move only vertically and horizontally, but there are some VDTs where you can cause the cursor to move diagonally, using a "track ball" which can be rotated, by means of a "mouse" or by depressing the "cursor right" and "cursor down" keys simultaneously.

And so we have, then, a keyboard with cursor controls capable of identifying a location within the buffer, and perhaps of scrolling lines up and down across the window of the screen to the extent permitted by the size of the buffer. There are also some terminals which use a mouse or a "joystick" in place of the keyboard cursor controls or in addition to them. This provides another method of moving the cursor around the screen.

As we have mentioned, the screen shows a display of characters across its face, either in a single or double-column format. The character set—unlike that of most computer video terminals—comprises both upper- and lower-case characters and also presents certain common typesetting symbols. The characters are "refreshed" so that they remain on display in a relatively flicker-free state until they are changed by a keyboard command or the unit is turned off. In the models which were used in the graphic arts industry in the early 1970s, the characters on the screen were input from a paper-tape reader, or by direct keyboarding from the unit itself.

The buffer is usually organized in what is called the efficient mode—which means that memory positions are assigned only where actual text is written, and not where end-of-line blanks are to appear. The "display screen" mode would require a position for the blanks as well.

The first VDTs which became available to the industry provided only a "screen-sized" buffer, although subsequently this buffer was optionally enlarged. By "screen-sized" we mean that the buffer contains only that number of characters which are displayable on the screen at one time. For example, if the unit is designed to display 25 lines of 80 characters each the buffer would consist of 2,000 character locations. But if a 4,000-character buffer is provided with a displayable area for only 2,000 locations, more room is available to edit text randomly, and, as we shall see, it is then possible to scroll text back and forth across the "window" of the tube.

Character images are generated on the tube by the use of integrated circuit chips, known as ROMs, or read-only memories. Each character identity code is communicated to the ROMs and translated into a dot pattern.[1] Where programmable character sets are offered, RAM replaces ROM so that the user can define his own character images and store them in random access memory.

Most characters are created by the use of dot matrix patterns, although a different kind of tube (which strokes characters or constructs them from vectors) could be used. The TV tube is most common, and its characteristic is that it functions in a "raster scan" mode. The electronic beam moves horizontally from left to right, writing a series of dots wherever required by the character matrices. Then the beam is shut off and redirected to the left of the screen, where it creates the next scan line of dots. This normally happens at the rate of 60 cycles per second, so that the entire image of each character is refreshed 60 times per second. There are a few video terminals where the raster scan occurs only on alternate scan lines each 1/60 of a second, which means that the first, third, and fifth lines would be refreshed (*etc.*) before the second, fourth and sixth horizontal lines are. This is known as "interlacing," and it is a method which fools the eye into thinking that the character image is more persistent than it really is.

The dot matrix out of which each character is formed usually consists of a monospaced area of, say, seven dots horizontally and perhaps nine lines vertically, with perhaps two blank scan lines between the text lines. At least a 7 × 9 dot matrix is necessary for an adequate display of upper- and lower-case characters, although it is also possible to "drop" the entire pattern of a 5 × 7 matrix by one or two horizontal lines, where there are characters with descenders, to create the effect of a 7 × 9 matrix.

Editing on the tube

ONE COMMON METHOD of operating a VDT is in the "overstrike" mode. This means that a character may be written from the keyboard

---

1. The description is of a TV-type video display. There are a few such terminals which use "storage tube" technology so that the screen does not require refreshing. There are, however, certain liabilities associated with this technology. There are also some editing VDTs which use a calligraphic or random-stroking, character-generating technique. There are also some that use LEDs (light emitting diodes) for a relatively crude presentation.

Video Terminals for Composition

at the cursor position, and if a character is already located at that position the new character overstrikes or takes the place of the old. If there is no character at that position, then you are adding onto the existing block of text. If there is a character already present, you are substituting one for another.

An alternative mode for input is the "insert" mode. In this mode the new character is inserted just before the cursor location and everything else in the line moves over. If the line is already full then the character at the end of the line "falls off" onto the next line.

In order to make it easier to read the text on the screen "word wrap" is generally implemented. This means that if a complete word does not fit at the end of the line the entire word is moved on down to the next line. If the "efficient" mode of storage is used and there are blank positions at the end of such lines, these are disregarded.

Delete. Just as "insert" is one of the most important editing capabilities, so is "delete." One or more delete keys is provided, along with other editing keys, and by striking that key at the cursor position the character on which it rests is automatically eliminated and all following characters move over one space to fill the void. In most systems this will also bring up characters from the next line (but only if there is enough room for the first word on the succeeding line to fit), again following the "word wrap" procedure.

Thus insertions and deletions can necessitate the reformatting of everything shown on the screen below the location of the change which has just been introduced. This activity generally takes place so quickly that it is not annoying. However, there are some terminals where the process of shifting characters and implementing word wrap is too slow, and shortcuts or compromises are taken.

One such compromise would be simply to shorten the line in question when you delete a character, and not to attempt to move characters from one line to another. Some systems will move characters upward when you delete, but will not reimplement "word wrap" unless you ask for it by pressing another key which in turn causes the data to be restructured, perhaps after a series of corrections has been made. (One system calls this key "Tidy.")

On many systems it is possible to delete not only a character, but a word or a line or a sentence—or perhaps even an entire paragraph by a definition of the element to be operated on. Of course the delete key generally has a "repeat" function (like the cursor keys) so that if you hold it down it will continue to swallow up characters as they move into the cursor position from the right. But it may be easier to strike another key captioned "delete word," or one called "delete line." These, too, can have repeat functions for rapid deletions.

For terminals with a "delete sentence" capability the logic of the terminal (or the external editing logic which supports the terminal) will search for periods within the text and will delete all text from one period to the next. Likewise, a delete paragraph command would delete material from one quad left code (ending a preceding paragraph) to the next.

In some cases, to make certain that you do not destroy text too easily, the delete word, line or paragraph functions may be divided into two parts. One is to define what it is that you intend to do, and then the second portion of the activity is to execute the command. In such systems you may define a word, define a line, or even define a sentence or paragraph, causing that element of text to blink or to be defined by an underline. Then you can depress the delete key, and whatever it is that you have defined will disappear from the screen and from the terminal buffer.[1]

It may be seen that the delete function is more demanding on system resources than the overstrike function since all text below the point of deletion is affected and may be required to move up. In like manner an insertion causes such text to move down. In the best terminals this restructing of text occurs instantaneously. It should be obvious that, with such rapid movement of characters, "ghosting" or very slow fading away of previous character images would be annoying. Hence the tubes generally offer a phosphor with a very low "persistence." If the tube is refreshed in 1/60 of a second, then whatever changes are indicated should be effected—at least for a single character—in that time span. Hence successive characters (or sometimes even entire words) can often be deleted in one-sixtieth of a second.

Inserting. The insertion function has already been referred to. This would require going from an overstrike into an insert mode. Usually there is an "insert" key. You go "into" insert, add the material you wish—whether one or more keystrokes—and then return to the "normal" overstrike mode again. However, there are many systems which assume that the insert mode is normal, although toggling back and forth between insert and overstrike is usually provided.

One annoying feature of some of the earlier editing terminals was that if you were in insert, and you made a mistake, thus needing to rub out or delete the character you had just inserted, you found yourself no longer in the insert mode, and had to go to the trouble of reminding the system that you were in fact engaged in the act of inserting. Most systems now make it possible to preserve the insert condition even while deleting.

Discussing such features as these for today's readers, most of whom are familiar with video terminal editing, may seem unnecessary. But the fact is that these capabilities, which we have all grown accustomed to on our word processors and our personal or professional workstations, were developed initially in the graphic arts industry and reflect the lessons learned in this setting. Sometimes these lessons have not been carried over as completely and logically as one might wish. Naturally the terminals which have been developed for text editing in a typesetting environment have tended to be somewhat more complex in nature since they have also sought to deal, at least to some extent, with composition formatting commands. But increasingly, as will be revealed by the thrust of our presentation in this and succeeding chapters, such requirements have tended to become more generic in nature and thus they have tended to intrude less and less

---

1. Many systems will "remember" the command which has just been executed so that if you change your mind it can be aborted and the condition which existed prior to that change can be restored. Most systems also make an effort to preserve the most recent file prior to the version currently being edited.

Video Terminals for Composition

upon that portion of the text-editing function which has to do with writing and editing for content rather than for form. Editing for typographic presentation will always remain somewhat more complex.

Other editing features

WE HAVE DESCRIBED the most common editing features—overstrike, delete and insert. There are usually others as well: *copy, move, save, get,* and even *search* and *replace.* But before we discuss these we must give a little more thought to the functional characteristics of the terminal itself.

Terminal architecture

OUR INITIAL DISCUSSION of terminals began with a description of the so-called "stand-alone" VDT. Input came from paper tape which was read in several paragraphs or a buffer-full at a time. Output went to the paper-tape punch in the same manner, preparing a new, "clean" tape which could then be mounted on the paper-tape reader of the phototypesetter or fed into a computer system. More recent models substitute one or more floppy disks, or even a hard disk of the "Winchester" variety,[1] for the paper-tape reader and punch.

With this terminal, the character-generating electronics, the refresher circuitry and the editing logic must all be built into the single device, and with disk storage some kind of "file management" operating system is also required. It is, as we said, a "stand-alone" unit.

But it is also possible to configure such a terminal in some other way. In fact, there may be a number of different approaches to terminal design. For example, you could have a cluster of two or more terminals. Each terminal may have its own floppy disk controller, but the character-generating and refreshing logic, as well as all of the editing and file management logic, could be provided by a supporting black box or built into just one of the terminals within the cluster, designated as a "master station."

Or, each terminal could have its own character generation and refresh capability, but borrow the file management and editing logic from the master station or black box.

Or, all files could reside on a common disk configuration shared by all users. It could well be more economical for several devices to share many of the same components, especially if they are located close to one another. It is also common, nowadays, for such devices to offer access to a common printer and perhaps a common telecommunications port.

The logic which performs the editing functions could be hardwired—that is, not programmable but built to perform the defined tasks. Or a mini- or microcomputer could be programmed to perform these functions and even—perhaps—the character generating and refreshing tasks. It has become more and more common to use programmable computers for these purposes, and consequently suppliers have found it possible to utilize the same computer for the performance of other functions as well.

---

1. Winchester disks consist of one or more small, nonremovable platters to prevent contamination. They are relatively inexpensive and generally store from 5 to 40 megabytes of data.

The counting keyboard/editing terminal

ONE SUCH APPLICATION contemplates that the same terminal could be used not just to correct material which has already been keyboarded, but for the initial keyboarding as well, and not merely for the keyboarding of unjustified text but to furnish counting logic so that the keyboarder can make appropriate end-of-line decisions. In other words, the terminal will store width values for the desired type faces, add up these values and signal when the operator has brought the line within justification range, and again to indicate when the line has been overset, so that the last word or portion thereof can be deleted.

On other occasions the terminal could be used to read in text already stored on disk, having been keyboarded elsewhere, simply for the editing of the unjustified text, or perhaps for the insertion of typographic commands.

Or, unjustified text could first be input or read in, and then corrected. Subsequently the counting logic could be applied to the incoming text, on a line-by-line basis, so that the corrected output would also now contain end-of-line decisions.

The next step in the evolution of the video terminal was to allow the operator to key or read in text in an automatic mode whereby those lines that would "fit" would be output with their end-of-line signals inserted by the logic of the VDT. For those lines that could not be justified, the cursor would position itself on the last character (within the overflowing word) which could be fitted into the line. The operator may then decide if and where to hyphenate the word in question, making a manual end-of-line decision and returning control to the automatic mode until another overset line is encountered.

And then simple hyphenation logic was built into some VDTs so that the process could be completely automatic. Unjustified input could be read and updated, and then it could be justified and hyphenated and prepared with the desired codes to drive a particular typesetter.

Moreover, to facilitate the process of making corrections, a "search" feature was built into the VDT so that the operator could work his way from one correction to the next, allowing the VDT to process intervening text without interruption, but requiring that it stop when it encountered a certain combination of consecutive characters or codes, to permit operator activity.

And finally, it was possible to build the output device—the typesetter itself—directly into the same box with the VDT, and even to share the same counting logic and other computing requirements. Thus the editing or correction terminal became a direct-entry typesetter, capable of inputting, correcting, composing and outputting the entire job.

To continue with the evolution, these direct-entry typesetters were and are sometimes equipped with other peripherals and capabilities, such as a telecommunications port so that input can be

Video Terminals for Composition

transmitted over telephone lines and stored directly on the disk of the workstation or cluster. Also, a correspondence-quality printer might be added so that the same system could be used for writing letters or to get a "dump" of a job in progress.

And in order to perform a variety of functions more or less simultaneously, the computational logic was enhanced so that it became possible to perform some tasks in the "foreground" and others in the "background." Thus the operator could input or edit one job while typesetting another.

To continue the evolution still further, other terminals could be interfaced to the workstation (making it a master workstation) so that they could share the same typesetter, the same printer, the same disk storage, and the same telecommunications capabilities. Thus what started out as a simple editing terminal ultimately became a complete composition system indistinguishable in functionality from other such systems except that it was perhaps based on microcomputer technology.

Our account of this evolution has been somewhat oversimplified. For example, it is not easy to use the same VDT simultaneously as a counting keyboard and as an editing terminal. It is not so difficult to use the VDT as one or the other. The problem arises if you wish to make a correction in a line which has already gone through the counting logic calculation. The relationship between *counting* and *editing* is and will always remain complex, just as the relationship between *batch* and *interactive* is complicated.

Nevertheless, with the advent of video terminals, the industry became more accustomed to the convenience of the soft copy display. Input keyboards began to look—and even to act—more like editing terminals. And even where video terminals are not used, we find that many input keyboards offer certain editing features. A small self-scan display may be provided, along with a search feature, so that previously prepared input may be read in, perfected, and written out. But generally speaking, only the VDT offers the kind of "buffer" within which corrections need not be made sequentially—and perhaps only then, as we have noted—if the counting or justifying process is not taking place simultaneously. It may be possible, however, to use the terminal first to key original material, second to correct it, and third to justify it, all on the same device but as three different processing steps.

The "move" function

RETURNING NOW to a discussion of editing features (and disregarding the possible use of the terminal for counting or assisting with end-of-line decisions), we can consider the "move" command as illustrative of still another editing capability.

It is often convenient to move text about on the screen. This is more likely to be desired when the terminal is used for editorial purposes—when a writer or editor is manipulating his own text, and perhaps creating it as he goes along, using the terminal for initial input. Even without a "move" command it is possible to move text—or to achieve the same results—by deleting material from one place and inserting it at another. The trouble with this is that one may not remember what it is that has been deleted. And obviously this procedure requires more effort. It is clearly more convenient to be able to "define" a particular word or phrase, a sentence, a paragraph or some other block of copy (which can be indicated by the use of a "begin block" and an "end block" marker). Then the cursor can be positioned at some other location and the defined text can be moved to the new location, whether it is to a position earlier in the text or further down the line, or even, conceivably into another file or a new file of its own.

If only a few words are to be moved, and if they are only to be moved a short distance, it may be possible to make such a move within the area of text displayed on the screen. But often one desires to move text to a location which lies outside the displayed area. This may be accomplished by forward or backward scrolling and is possible if the buffer is larger than the amount of text displayed at one time, or, alternatively, if there is convenient disk storage supported by the necessary text-handling programs.

For example, if the terminal buffer contains 10,000 characters, of which 2,000 can be displayed at once, it is usually possible to make moves within the entire 10,000 character buffer area, by scrolling. If the file is still larger, it is possible for the file handling program to use a floppy or hard disk as an additional scratch area.

The search function

THE SAME THING may be true of the "search" function. It may be possible to search through a buffer-full of text for the occurrence of certain words or other character combinations. It may be possible to issue a command to substitute one string for another—but this cannot be done except within the terminal buffer or work area unless the editing process is supported by a disk file-handling program.

Obviously the editing power of the terminal is much greater if it is possible for the VDT operator to scroll through a large quantity of text—rolling the text backward or forward on his screen, or searching through it, using the screen as a window which permits random-like access to any portion of the file in question, or even of several files.

The on-line VDT

WE SHOULD INQUIRE more carefully, then, about the relationship between the video display terminal and its support system, especially if all of that support is not to be found within the terminal itself, and access to a supporting computer (terminal control unit or mainframe or both), or at least a file handler, is provided.

We can then avoid an arm's-length relationship between the VDT and system. Scrolling can now be infinite rather than limited by the buffer. Perhaps even more than one file can be viewed at once (using a split screen or alternate screen approach) and text can even be defined and moved from one file to another. It can also be routed from one terminal to another.

What methods of connecting terminals to other devices are there? Below is a discussion of three of these methods.

"Bit-serial" information transfer. One common way to "interface" or connect a VDT to a computer system is to arrange for the text material to be transferred to and from the VDT by means of a "bit-serial" mode of transmission. What this means is that a bit stream is communicated from computer to terminal and back to computer again, and that these bits are arranged into bytes or words when they reach the terminal or when they are returned to the computer. Often such interfaces make use of a phone line, and the information is relayed as auditory signals. The speed of such transfer is described as the baud rate. At 2400 baud, 2,400 bits of information may be transferred in one second's time, and this is roughly equivalent to 240 characters, since up to 10 bits may be required to describe each character in a bit-serial transmission mode. To fill a 2,000 character buffer and video screen would thus require eight seconds of transmission time. To dispose of that information (sending it back, corrected, to the computer) and to get another 2,000 characters would thus require more than 16 seconds. If the buffer contained 4,000 characters, each transaction would take twice as long.

Paging. Usually, when you interface a terminal by bit-serial connection, you "page" text from disk to computer to VDT, and back again. A page is a terminal buffer-full or some portion thereof. If the editing logic is built into the terminal, then only that material within the page is subject to correction. And if you wish to access text buried deep in a file you may have to page through many bufferfulls—a very time-consuming process—to get at the text with which you wish to work.

One way to speed up this process is by using a higher baud rate, if it is available—such as 9,600 baud or even 19,200. At the later rate, a 2,000-character screen can be filled in about one second.

To avoid paging it is possible to program the computer so that some of the editing functions may be performed by computer logic rather than by terminal logic—especially the ability to "get at" or "get to" a particular line (identified by a line number), or by contextual search—and to bring in only those pages which need to be edited.

The computer mainframe may also be used to implement moves that cannot be effected within the buffer. The material to be moved can be sent back to the computer memory or disk and recalled when the desired page to be inserted at the indicated location is on the terminal.

Finally, even with a bit-serial interface, it may be possible to scroll quite rapidly through an entire file by paging a line at a time. Even at 2400 baud, a line of 80 characters may be filed away, and another line fetched, in less than a second. Then text within certain limits

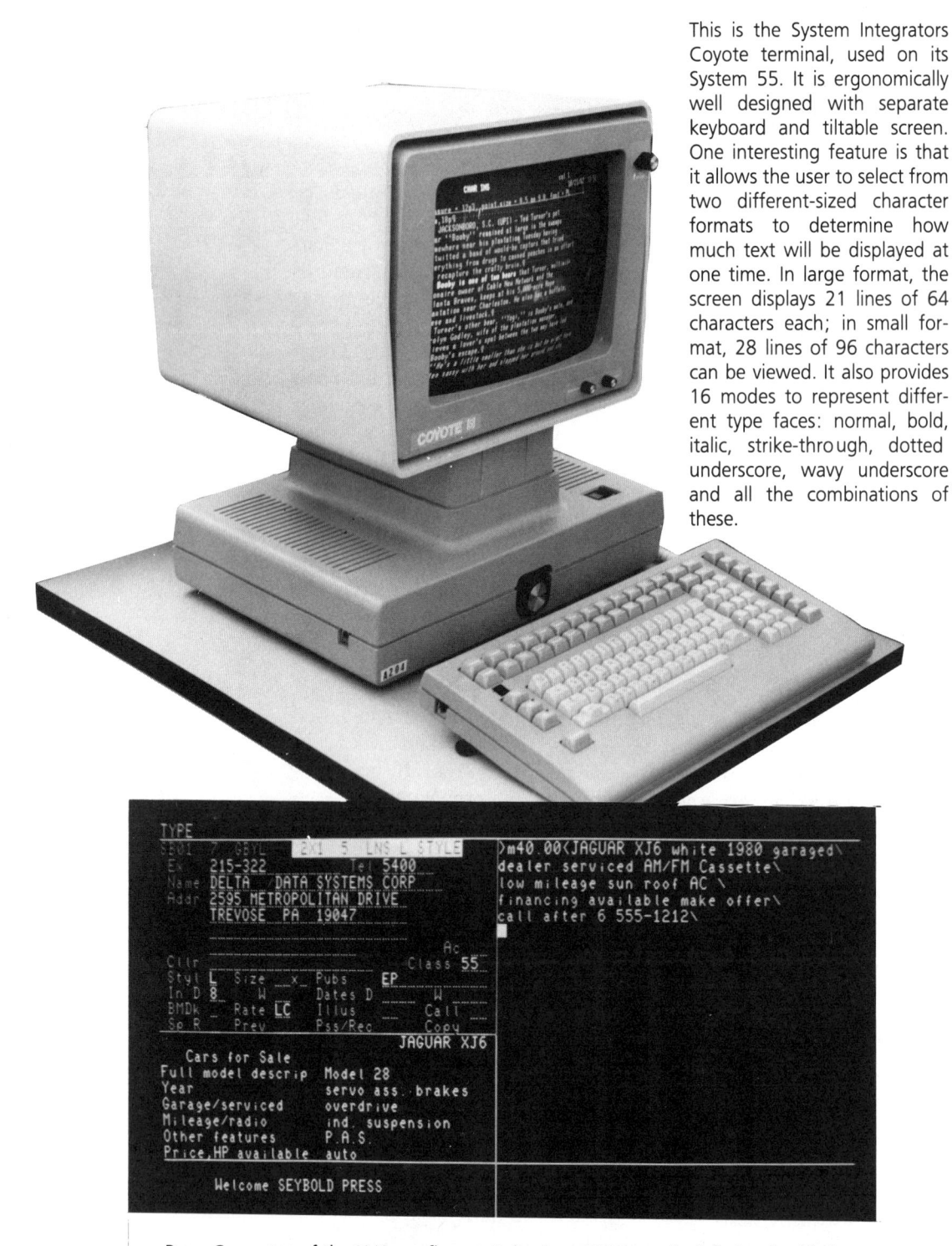

This is the System Integrators Coyote terminal, used on its System 55. It is ergonomically well designed with separate keyboard and tiltable screen. One interesting feature is that it allows the user to select from two different-sized character formats to determine how much text will be displayed at one time. In large format, the screen displays 21 lines of 64 characters each; in small format, 28 lines of 96 characters can be viewed. It also provides 16 modes to represent different type faces: normal, bold, italic, strike-through, dotted underscore, wavy underscore and all the combinations of these.

Press Computer of the U.K. configures Delta Data 7303 terminals in its classified ad system. The screen is divided into five windows for various functions involved with handling classified ads as they are telephoned in. The second window on the left prompts the ad-taker to suggest additional items to be included in the ad.

Video Terminals for Composition

With AM Varityper's Epics system (below), the operator can elect to see four different representations of a composed file, with varying amounts of command codes and statistical reports included. This device uses a reverse video mode to report statistics regarding hyphenation and justification. The Epics screen uses braces to distinguish format definitions and format calls from text characters.

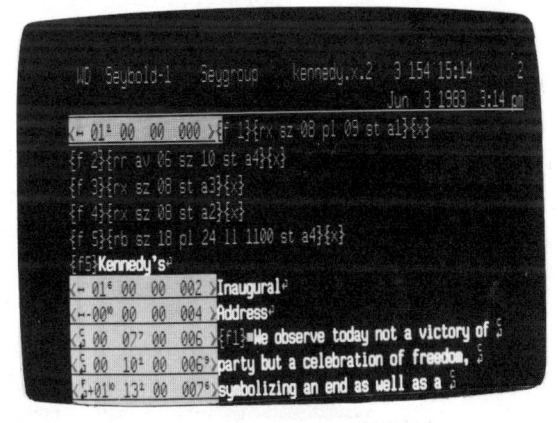

Autologic uses the Convergent Technologies workstation in its Microcomposer system for commercial typesetting. The display is on the left, with the controller in the box on the right, which also serves as a copy holder if desired.

Bedford Computer Corporation displays text in actual size and position on a page, using a variety of fonts. The Bedford system also has a very large and comprehensive keyboard, supporting up to nine levels per key.

prescribed by the size of the buffer could be tucked away within the terminal and reinserted elsewhere, as a result of a forward or backward scroll.

Parallel interface. Another solution is to transmit characters in a "parallel" fashion rather than 'bit serially." This means that eight- or nine-bit bytes can be transferred at comparable bit transfer speeds. A 9600 baud parallel interface would make it possible to transfer perhaps as many as 9,600 characters per second, or to dispose of one 2,000-character screenful and to fetch another in less than a half second.

The DMA solution. A third approach is to interface the terminal in such fashion that the buffer does not reside in the VDT at all, but in a portion of computer memory. Under such circumstances, the character generation and refreshing may be done by direct memory access, and the VDT has no intelligence of its own. *All* editing logic is performed by the computer, and the VDT screen is merely a "window" into a section of computer memory. The keyboard, separately connected, can directly address computer memory on an "interrupt" basis, and response times are often at computer speeds, reflecting themselves in the implementation of the desired change in one refresh cycle. Infinite scrolling or "virtual" scrolling, as it is sometimes called[1] is usually a feature of such systems. The penalty you must pay is that, generally speaking, such VDTs cannot be located remotely, but must be within a thousand feet or so from the mainframe computer. The other "penalty" is that this more intimate—rather than arm's-length—relationship between VDT and computer requires more support from the computer itself, thus imposing more of a load, and, under some circumstances, bringing about a deterioration in computer response time or overall performance.

Other approaches

AT THE TIME of this writing we are still witnessing dramatic changes in computer technology and computer architecture. Several trends will certainly impact the way in which editing terminals are to be configured in the future, and how they will be used.

In the first place, with the advent of individual personal and professional computers there have been dramatic economies in their manufacturing cost, and there is every reason to try to incorporate the use of such devices into the composition environment. Not only are they likely to be less expensive, but they are so ubiquitous that it seems more sensible to try to use what you already have rather than to purchase something else.

In the second place, new kinds of networking architecture are being developed. One such approach is the "LAN" or local area network which makes it possible to connect within a given location, a group of terminals—conceivably a fairly large number of them—all of which can thus access one another and common data bases, as well as other peripherals. This approach also promises to introduce

---

1. Virtual scrolling is a term which means that the text on a VDT (or in a window occupying a part of the screen) may be moved rapidly, usually in either direction, from top to bottom of a file of some considerable length. Scrolling is not constrained by buffer size since the buffer within the terminal or allocated memory is reloaded from disk for use as necessary.

economies, but it militates in favor of the use of "distributed-intelligence" approaches. In other words, there tends not to be a powerful central computer which services all of these terminals. Each one uses its own intelligence, but is able to pass its information on to others. However, some sort of "file server" or central computer filing system is indicated. Whether this means that each such terminal should therefore be able to perform all composition functions (and many functions not even remotely related to editing technology), or whether there would be a tendency to develop some degree of specialization of function as between workstations, is not entirely clear. Perhaps there will be many different kinds of approaches taken, including recourse to a central computer for some processing steps involving heavy computations, which may be the case with certain aspects of interactive page make-up.

In the third place, users are increasingly interested in the "WYSIWYG" (what-you-see-is-what-you-get) approach, which imposes a more severe requirement as to computer display technology. They want to be able to see "true" type in different sizes, perhaps graphics as well, and to review and even to interact with fully composed pages before they are typeset.

We shall be considering the implications of some of these technologies in much of the remainder of this book.

17

Pagination and "Area Composition"

THE SUBJECT of page make-up, and some of the concepts of area composition are topics which have been alluded to but not specifically addressed so far in this book. The term page make-up is probably more familiar to the average reader than "area composition." The latter is used to refer to the problem of arranging text (and perhaps graphics as well) within the confines of a given amount of space—whether it be a page or some portion thereof. What happens during page make-up is, of course, an extension of area composition to a sequence of pages.

Sometimes the term pagination is used, although the dictionary definition refers to this process as assigning page numbers to a book. However, in the computer typesetting world it refers to the process of making up pages and outputting codes which, when they drive a typesetting unit, will cause the device to generate fully composed pages.

Many tasks are involved in the performance of computer-aided page make-up. These tasks naturally differ according to whether one is considering the problems of the newspaper world, the magazine world, or the book world. They differ again if one is concerned with the arrangement of text and graphics in a display advertisement. Nevertheless there are similarities between all of these assignments, and there can be some overlapping of hardware and software, and much overlapping in terms of conceptual matters.

At the very outset we suggested that composition had to do, among other things, with the art of arranging type within a page or frame of some kind. We have also suggested that the editing task has sometimes to concern itself with the form of the final printed product as well as its contents, and that sometimes material has to be copy edited in order to achieve the desired relationship between content and form.

The way in which this book is being written may be taken as an example of this relationship. In this particular case the author has taken upon himself the responsibility for the manner in which pages are broken and has actually rewritten text where necessary to try to mnimize the problems caused by the necessity of making page breaks. We have placed our footnotes on the side of the page so as to avoid the difficulty of fitting them into the text "window." We decided that we would not permit some pages to run longer or shorter than others even though in the United States some variation in page depth is generally allowed. Consequently we have written this book with the

Pagination and "Area Composition"

expectation that the text would run precisely 40 picas in depth on chapter opening pages, and 50 picas in depth on all other pages, except for chapter endings. On the whole the editing changes which have been necessary to achieve this have not been great, but we have observed certain other rules during the process:
- For example, we have not started a new paragraph on the last line of a page.
- Nor have we ended a paragraph on the first line of a page.
- We have been careful to allow at least two lines of text to follow a subhead at the bottom of a page.
- And what is most troublesome of all—we have avoided ending any page with a hyphenated word.

Fortunately, we have been able to use workstations which permit us to define elements of text for processing through composition, so that we can see how lines break and can measure the depth of text as we go along. Thus we have been able to make our own page-ending decisions as part of the writing process. It was not necessarily the best way to proceed because once we were well along within a chapter we were reluctant to go back (as we had second thoughts) to make changes which would have affected those page decisions. Perhaps it would have been better to have written the entire book first (as most authors do) and then to have submitted the entire work to batch pagination, hoping that the program would come up with acceptable decisions or that only a few pages would need modification. However, the system at our disposal does not—at least at the moment—offer what we would consider a satisfactory batch pagination program, and while such programs exist elsewhere, the convenience of being able to write and edit in one's own office seemed to us to outweigh the drawbacks of the process.

We were also able to integrate our illustrative material with the text in a relatively satisfactory manner, although the ideal would have been for us to be able to arrange both text and graphics on the page as we went along, rather than to leave space for the illustrations.

Why "computerize" page make-up?

AMONG THE SUBSTANTIAL costs of composition are those associated with the arrangement of type into pages. Paste-up of copy blocks is time-consuming, and it is not an easy task to do with precision. If it can be automated, appreciable cost savings may be realized. The quality of the product may also be improved. Moreover, it will be possible to "go directly" to film positive, or to film negative in some cases, or even, perhaps, directly to printing plate, bypassing film altogether, if one has the ability to compose material in pages in such fashion that it does not need to be altered or modified by hand.

Most newspaper production people are convinced that pagination is a logical step and that it is indeed possible to go "direct-to-plate" at least for certain sections of the paper. What is not so clear is how this capability will affect the flow of copy and the way in which paging decisions are implemented in a newspaper environment.

If page make-up can be made interactive—so that those who are involved with the process can look at provisional solutions, and alter not only the arrangement, the size and shape of text blocks, the measure, the type face and the positioning and scaling of the graphics, but even the content of the text as well—then there could be other significant advantages in terms of the timeliness and effectiveness of the product. Moreover, the same capability might be useful for the preparation of provisional material—for copy that the ad agency wishes to show the client, or for the art director's layouts of the double page spread for *Time's* feature on federal election results. In such cases, once the layout of provisional copy is approved, that portion of the input (whether text or positioning data) could be captured and retained to be concatenated with the rest of the material, when available. Thus the interactive capability serves two purposes—a tool for experimentation and a facilitator for final implementation.

But there are many other applications where interactivity is not required or desired—at least not to accomplish trial setting, or changing one's mind, or making last minute changes in basic material. Nevertheless it is not easy to position the relevant material in an attractive way because of such problems as associating footnotes with text, placing tables, charts and other graphics adjacent to the textual presentation, and organizing the whole so that it presents an attractive, consistent, and coherent appearance.

A bit of history

AT THIS TIME we would presume that perhaps 80 to 90 percent of all page make-up is still performed by hand, except for the production of certain quite standard items such as telephone directory pages, or pages in the official airline guide, or for other special-purpose applications. For the most part, when it comes to photocomposition, type is composed in galleys, usually on photographic paper, and it is then cut apart and reassembled on a carrier, with some spacing out where required, and some shifting of blocks of copy from one page to another to balance facing pages or achieve other desired effects.

Nevertheless, some typesetting vendors had developed general-purpose book page make-up programs as early as 1965 or 1966. The advent of highspeed photocomposing devices made the need for page make-up quite urgent since these typesetters could produce galleys at prodigious speeds—far faster than a crew of employees could arrange them into pages. Moreover, these machines sometimes had the capability of setting wide measure material, thus offering an opportunity for the user to provide multicolumn setting, and allowing the user to avoid the stripping or paste-up that the arrangement of side-by-side columns would require.

One of the problems addressed, then, was the task of setting multicolumn text. And the first efforts had to do with the arrangement of such text when it could be assumed that all "leading" would be of constant value. Even where heads were to be set in larger point sizes, the basic increment of "primary leading" would be maintained

Pagination and "Area Composition"

so that a line-counting program could be used, and if 60 lines per column were cast off, one could assume that when three, four or five columns were arranged side by side, all text material would align.

There are two ways to achieve this. One is to compose a line within one column (say, line 1), and then "tab out" to the beginning of the second column, where line 61 could be laid down, and thence to the third column, where line 121 would be composed.

1 belief that the rights of man come not from the generosity of the state but from the hand of God.
We dare not forget today that we are the heirs of that first revolution. **Let the word go forth** from this time and place, to friend and foe alike, that **the torch has been passed to a new generation of Americans,** born in this century, tempered by war, disciplined by a hard and bitter peace, proud of our ancient heritage, and unwilling to witness or permit the slow undoing of those human rights to which this nation has always been committed, and to which we are committed today at home and around the world.
Let every nation know, whether it wishes us well or ill, that we shall pay any price, bear any burden, meet any hardship, support any friend, oppose any foe to assure the survival and the success of liberty.
This much we pledge—and more.
To those old allies whose cultural and spiritual origins we share, we pledge the loyalty of faithful friends. 60 United, there is little we cannot do in

61 states, the United Nations, our last best hope in an age where the instruments of war have far outpaced the instruments of peace, we renew our pledge of support: to prevent it from becoming merely a forum for invective, to strengthen its shield of the new and the weak, and to enlarge the area in which its writ may run.
Finally, to those nations who would make themselves our adversary, we offer not a pledge but a request: that both **sides begin anew the quest for peace,** before the dark powers of a destruction unleashed by science engulf all humanity in planned or accidental self-destruction.
We dare not tempt them with weakness. For only when our arms are sufficient beyond doubt can we be certain beyond doubt that they will never be employed.
But neither can two great and powerful groups of nations take comfort from our present course—both sides overburdened by the cost of modern weapons, both rightly alarmed by the steady spread of the deadly atom, yet both racing to alter

121 finished in the first one thousand days, nor in the life of this Administration, nor even perhaps in our lifetime on this planet. **But let us begin.**
In your hands, my fellow citizens, more than mine, will rest the final success or failure of our course. Since this country was founded, each generation of Americans has been summoned to give testimony to its national loyalty. The graves of young Americans who answered the call to service surround the globe.
Now the trumpet summons us again—not as a call to bear arms, though arms we need; not as a call to battle, though embattled we are; but a call to bear the burden of a long twilight struggle, year in and year out, "rejoicing in hope, patient in tribulation," **a struggle against the common enemies of man:** tyranny, poverty, disease and war itself.
Can we forge against these enemies a grand and global alliance . . . that can assure a more fruitful life for all mankind? Will you join in that historic effort?

This was most readily accomplished on the ATF B-8[1] typesetter because this typewriter-like device had tab stops which could be set manually just as on a typewriter. Unfortunately, few machines with higher speed capability could claim this convenient facility, and it was necessary to devise a more elaborate solution. This required that every line be actually justified by the computer and not merely brought within justification range. All spacing involved in each line had to be calculated by the computer program, which would also add extra space (say two picas) between columns. Then the photo unit could simply lay down type and spaces across the page. Obviously short lines (as at the end of paragraphs) had to be quadded out with fixed space, and if any width value was short in the first column, the other two columns across that line would appear out of position.

A somewhat more sophisticated approach could be taken if the three columns of text in our example were considered in the same category as "tabular material." After all, a program to set tables performs in exactly the same way: it justifies or otherwise arranges the text within the columns and sets white space between columns.

This method of composing multicolumn material is still used today by computer programs that set across the page. A column merge program is all that is required. Text is first arranged in galleys. Lines are numbered or otherwise identified, and then the first line, the 61st and the 121st are arranged side by side by pulling them in an orderly fashion from magnetic tape, or, more likely, from disk. In the early days you might have written out the first 60 lines to magnetic tape station #1, the next 60 to tape station #2, and the next 60 to tape station #3, and then pulled off each line in order, providing for film advance after setting the right-hand column.

1. See page 77.

An additional degree of sophistication is required, however, if the material does not align. If you are moving from "10 on 12" for text, to "8 on 9" for extract, then the program which arranges the sequence in which lines are to be set and the amount of film advance, has to be quite a bit more complicated. You might, for example, set 10 on 12 text in column one, 8 on 9 extract in column two, and 10 on 12 in column three. Then you would have to drop down nine points, move to the second column, set the second line of 8 on 9, and advance three points, moving back to the first column in order to set that and the third column. Then you would advance the film six points, set the next line in the second column, *etc.*

Column 1	*Column 2*	*Column 3*
Set first	Set second	Set third
Set fifth	Set fourth	Set sixth
Set eighth	Set seventh	Set ninth
	Set tenth	
Set eleventh	Set twelfth	Set thirteenth

But one no sooner grasps the solution to the challenge of multi-column setting then he or she is beset by unforeseen complications. When the program pulls lines from the various tapes (or from disk), it loses the precedence code information which the typesetting unit requires. Consider, for example, the possibility that the first 55 lines of text are to be set in roman, and the next 20 or so in italic, and then the balance returns to roman. Line one should be set in roman, therefore, but line 61 should be in italic and line 121 should be back in roman. But the instruction to enter italic will not be encountered until farther down the page. However, such information must nevertheless be incorporated with each line for this kind of setting, and the instruction which says, "stay in this type face and size until you are told to come out of it," simply does not work. The program that chops the text into columns must also "put out" at the beginning of each column line what the photo unit needs to know about that line. This is what programmers sometimes call "lineinf" or "line information."

One resolves this kind of problem by doing what is in essence a "leading sort" which subtracts from the leading normally assigned to each line (since it was previously laid down) the amount which has already been used up by leading associated with other lines.

An alternate solution

ANOTHER WAY—which requires less programming effort to accomplish—is simply to set column one, instruct the typesetting device to "reverse lead" back to the beginning of the page and set the second column, and then to reverse lead a third time to lay down the third column, making certain that if the columns are not all of equal depth, the depth of the longest column should be reinstated before going on to set other text or another page. In this case the only "lineinf" required would be concerned with the displacement of the various columns across the page and the necessary parameters at the top of each column to determine its type face and measure.

Pagination and "Area Composition"

A similar solution is possible when you output to a "full face" CRT typesetter which does not need to reverse the film, but simply the writing beam.

Problems of definition

THE READER might have been better served if we had not plunged into a rather complicated discussion of a particular problem of page make-up before providing some theoretical groundwork. However, the fact is that historically this is pretty much the way it happened—that is, one of the first pagination problems the industry tried to solve was multicolumn setting, and the price it was prepared to pay at the time was to remain on uniform leading increments throughout the entire page. It was not long, however, before programmers and their mentors began to yearn for the ability to provide for more intricate solutions to the page make-up problem. Not all requirements were met by the simple capacity to lay down three or four columns across the page. In fact, the business of composing even a single-column page proved to be surprisingly complex. Gradually it became possible to identify many of the problems and to come up with acceptable solutions for some of them.

The not-so-merry widow

THE MOST notorious problem is the *widow*. Programmers who had never before read a book, let alone appreciated its typographic niceties, suddenly learned, to their consternation, that to begin a page with a widow was not allowed. Nobody was entirely clear where this convention originated. Theirs is not to reason why! Someone hazarded the explanation that if the first line on the page was short of the defined measure, as it would be in the case of most paragraph endings, then the page did not have a proper "frame." However, if the line at the top of the page consisted of a complete paragraph which was only a partial line ("Here she comes now," he cried.), somehow the "frame" argument was set aside.

It is not our privilege, the computer typesetters were told, to do away with these established conventions. Our challenge is to achieve the same solutions. Find out what it is that the hand make-up man has been doing. Once you know what goes through his head when he divides galleys into pages then you can write programs to accomplish the same thing.

A widow can therefore be defined as a quad-left line that is immediately preceded by a justified line. If the preceding line is also a quadded line, then the line under consideration must be a stand-alone line which need not necessarily be rejected from a position at the top of a page.

Now that we can recognize the widow, we can avoid placing her at the top of a page or a column. Unfortunately we must then deal with the problem of having our pages or columns come out with unequal depths.

What is the rule about page depth? we ask. We learned that in the United States it is permissible for pages to be a line long or a line short, so long as facing pages balance and so long as facing pages which were short are not followed by facing pages which run long (*or vice versa*). In Great Britain, oddly enough, it seemed, at least at that time, that all pages, except chapter endings, had to come out precisely the same. When we asked an old-line typographer how this was achieved, he said he couldn't rightly remember. It was jolly well done, but it had been so long since he had had to perform the operation himself that he had jolly well forgotten. He thought for a while longer and then recalled that it must have been done by resetting some of the bloody lines, making them tighter or looser so that the "little lady" (the widow) got swallowed up. At that point the olive in his American martini also got swallowed up and he lost interest in the subject at hand.

It turns out, however, that precise page depths are often achievable if there are elements of vertical spacing in the page. An odd amount of space separates text from extract and extract from text. This can be stretched or shrunk a bit. There is room for a little "fiddle" (an anglicism again!) above and below the heads or around illustrations. Usually this does the trick. But woe unto you if they are not present to provide needed flexibility for vertical justification.

That term became very popular, for one suddenly saw that the problem of coming out to a fixed depth vertically was precisely the same kind of problem as coming out to a given width horizontally. There are fixed spaces (the lines themselves) and justifying spaces (the extra white space around heads and elsewhere). And just as compositors sometimes "cheated" by indulging in letterspacing (space between the letters) so they were tempted to cheat by "carding"—adding strips between metal type slugs—so that 41 lines took up as much space as 42, and the final line was pushed over to the top of the next page, to drive the widow down.

Could the photo unit card discretely? Some could and some could not. Increments of an additional half point between some lines (starting down from the top or up from the bottom) provide too crass a differentiation, even if the typesetting machine could advance its photographic film only in such increments. Later, machines came along that could lead in increments as small as a tenth of a point, which means that a deviation between two lines of this amount can hardly be observed. However, as can be seen from the illustration on the next page, where multicolumn material is involved, the presentation of nonaligning text may or may not be considered acceptable. Here we show a difference of one-fourth point between the leading in the left-hand column and that on the right. Across-page multicolumn alignment is not generally expected in newspapers, and it need not be mandated in text where there are frequent interruptions in the flow of the basic text size due to the interposition of heads, illustrations and extract material. On the whole it is indeed helpful to have the ability to space out vertically in fine increments just as one needs to do this to achieve aesthetically acceptable horizontal justification.

Illustration of vertical justification

"Carding" is not a sufficient (if acceptable) answer, however. Some pages simply can't be carded out, and even if there is additional white space for vertical justification, too much space might be required to bring the page to the proper depth. Why does this problem come to light? It is because there are certain situations, within the text stream, where it is not permissible to break the page even in the absence of a widow. What are some of these conditions?

When a head or subhead occurs it is customary (indeed, it would look odd otherwise!) for two or more lines of text to follow before the page can be broken. If a table appears, the table must be kept as one unit and not split over two pages unless it is in fact longer than one page. If the author turns poetic and makes his point by a stanza of verse:

> *Our author would surely explode in a rage*
> *If* this *line broke to the following page!*

One assignment we encountered fairly early in the game was a listing of lawyers, with title, birthplace, birth date and legal pedigree:

> **Jonah W. Jones**
> *Senior Partner*
> Hickory Rock, Pa., 1878.
> Admitted to practice before the Supreme Court of Pennsylvania in 1905.

It was not permissible to disassociate Mr. Jones from his title, nor from his birthplace. You could put his legal pedigree in the following column on the same page, or on the following facing page, but not on the obverse side of the same sheet.

It becomes evident, therefore, that there are certain "no-break" areas of composition. Two problems arise: one is to recognize these areas (how to tell a "head" from text or a rhymed couplet from parlor conversation), and the other is to make pages come out even despite the lumpiness of the elements one has to contend with.

Tables and illustrations have to be recognized as coming within one of two classifications: either the table (or the white space for illustrations) has to be positioned precisely where the text requires it to be (in which case it becomes a "non-floatable no-break area") or else it can be "floated" to another position if it will not fit directly beneath the text that is referenced.

Floatable no-break material may in some cases be permitted to move to a point earlier in the text, but in other cases it may only be floated to follow somewhat behind the point of reference.

Footnote callout references and the accompanying footnotes also pose very serious problems. If the reference occurs on the page, generally speaking the footnote must also be placed in the same column. And there are times when the footnote is so long that without it (and the line which references it) the page will be impossibly short, while with both the relevant text and the note itself the page becomes too long and the footnote, which could even be longer than the entire allotted page size, must be carried over to the bottom of one or several sequential pages.

Our discussion of these difficulties, which began with allusions to past experiences, is not intended to suggest that these matters have now all been solved. Far from it! But the major decisions have now at least been identified, and some program solutions have been developed.

Conceptual solutions

The problem of book page make-up can be approached in a number of different ways. Perhaps the most ambitious solution is what might be called "automatic page make-up" wherein the computer program presumably solves all pagination problems and produces acceptable results without intervention or further editing.[1] A second approach would be one in which the computer arranges solutions where it can, and identifies problem areas where a solution cannot be determined on the basis of the parameters which the system has specified. The user can decide whether to deviate from those parameters, modify the text, or provide an answer which the program was not "bright" enough to discover—for example, by backing up to an earlier point, which is beyond the programmatic purview of the software. Whereas this kind of information and opportunity for user involvement might be done by means of a printout which identifies problem pages, it is evident that users or potential users in the market place would prefer to implement their decisions on a screen and get immediate feedback as to the consequences of these decisions.

-----

1. The RCA "Page 1" program was illustrative of this approach.

A third, and somewhat similar, approach would take the form of an automated "cast-off" program, wherein the program suggests or indicates page breaks, but leaves it up to the user to accept or reject them. Presumably this would be done on a page-by-page or column-by-column basis, with the user scrolling the text material on a video tube and inspecting the locations where the program suggests that pages be terminated. Here, too, although the user might be satisfied with monospaced representations on the screen, one would prefer to see true type or a simulation thereof for a more realistic representation of the page's appearance.

A fourth approach would be an automated paste-up program. Here the user would tell the computer precisely what he wants on each page and in what position, and the program would merely translate those instructions into output commands to the typesetter. However, a review of the appearance of the page, at least as a preview of final output, would be highly desirable.

In all of these cases, the software would be armed with a vertical justification capability, so that it would space out (or in) to the extent allowable, once it, or the user, had determined the page or column break locations.

Totally automated solutions.

If a satisfactory solution can be totally automated there is no need for user interaction, and the program can be run in a batch mode. For certain kinds of material this is a satisfactory way to proceed, and in these cases it may be possible to accept text which has been carefully edited, and run it through typesetting and page make-up without further review. Certain work does indeed lend itself to this approach. And within this category there seem to be two alternate ways to proceed. One is to take the page depth as given and invariable, and to pour text into that page, regarding it as an area, and attempting to fill it up while hyphenating and justifying. A "trial setting" mode can be specified, and if a widow should appear at the top of the next page, or a copy block emerges which cannot be broken, then the program will make an effort to resolve the problem first by vertical justification, including carding, if it is permissible, and second by rehyphenating and rejustifying, if necessary, over and over again, until a fortuitous solution is determined. One such program sought to achieve appropriate fit by rerunning the h&j program to constantly varying parameters of interword space expansion, hoping that (sometime between then and infinity) a solution could be reached. Oddly enough, after some 40 or 50 iterations the answer was generally achieved, although the appearance of these pages, in terms of consistency of spacing, left something to be desired.

An alternate way to proceed is to assume that all lines which have been hyphenated and justified are, in effect, slugs of type. They are not to be reset. The problem is to array them logically and attractively. But if problems arise which cannot be resolved within a defined area or boundary, then the boundaries can be altered on facing pages—by going long or short. This approach implies that the program does not need to know what the text is all about. All it needs to work with is the facts about the text, and it can manipulate these statistics to try to get the best possible solution not just on a page-by-page basis, but on a chapter-by-chapter basis, again shuffling back and forth the obstinate elements, spacing in or out wherever allowed. Perhaps some combination of these two concepts is also possible.

Totally automated page make-up programs were popular in the days when batch processing was the rule and interactive intervention by means of video terminals was not available. As we have indicated, there is still some significant need for such programs, especially for relatively routine assignments. But one difficulty which arises is that if the program cannot in fact resolve the problem posed at a particular point in the manuscript, some change has to be introduced and at least the balance of the job—if not the entire job—must be rerun. And it may be that the second time the program is only able to advance another page or so before it again runs into a problem area. Consequently, some degree of interaction is clearly indicated, whether on a page-by-page basis or on an exception basis.

At this point it is necessary to determine whether the person who then makes the paging decisions is given the discretion to modify the text to fit the space, or must work with the space to accommodate text which may not, in fact, be altered. (One could not rewrite a verse in the Bible to avoid a widow, but many living authors would not object if a modification were made here and there in the interest of copy fitting.)

Editor's Note. In order to balance these two columns we have sacrificed column alignment. Although the text at the top of this page aligns across the page, this condition is altered in mid-page. Also, the space above this footnote gives us extra flexibility for vertical justification.

Consequently, in the "ultimate" interactive system one usually presumes that there should be the capability of addressing, editing, and reprocessing some portion of the text as well as merely spacing it, or reprocessing it without editing.

Embedding make-up parameters

TYPOGRAPHIC COMMANDS are at present sufficiently powerful that some elements of make-up (less ambitious than the "totally automated" schemes) can be incorporated into the text stream. You can, for example, insert a "mark" so that later you can issue a command to "reverse to mark" in order to lay down a second column alongside the first. There are even commands to permit you to cause a certain block of text to be divided into three columns of equal length. But the problem still usually exists of how to visualize what it is that you wish to achieve. Here is where a "soft copy display" or an interactive display device is especially helpful. If, on the other hand, copy is written (and rewritten) to fit a designated space—as with a news magazine or many catalogs—an interactive solution may not be required.

The video tube for typographic display

TURNING, THEN, to interactive page make-up possibilities and making use of video display technology, we find that the first significant work in this area had to do with display ad layout rather than page make-up. Perhaps this is because the task may be simpler. But more likely it is because the most promising market appeared to be with newspapers, and newspapers were not then ready for full-page composition, lacking, at the time, systems to handle news material with sufficient speed and efficiency. On the other hand, they were ready for some improvement in the method of composing display ads. Now they are ready for both—or nearly so.

The first interactive solution was again proposed by the Harris Corporation. This time it was the Harris 2200 ad layout terminal, and for several years Harris occupied a unique position as the only vendor of a device with functional characteristics sufficient to handle the problems of display ad composition.

Originally, the 2200 accepted input from paper tape keyed on noncounting keyboards. Subsequent models have been able to receive input from Harris' front-end newspaper systems (such as the 2500 "editorial" system) or from those of other vendors, or text keyed onto floppy disks by word-processing-like devices. Such input has consisted of the various text elements which will go to make up the ad. These did not need to contain any command codes signalling type faces, line lengths, type sizes or other similar characteristics. Thus the person doing the initial keyboarding did not need to have any knowledge of layout or typesetting coding conventions.

The 2200 operator would then read in this text based upon default parameters as presented in the columns on the left-hand side of the screen.

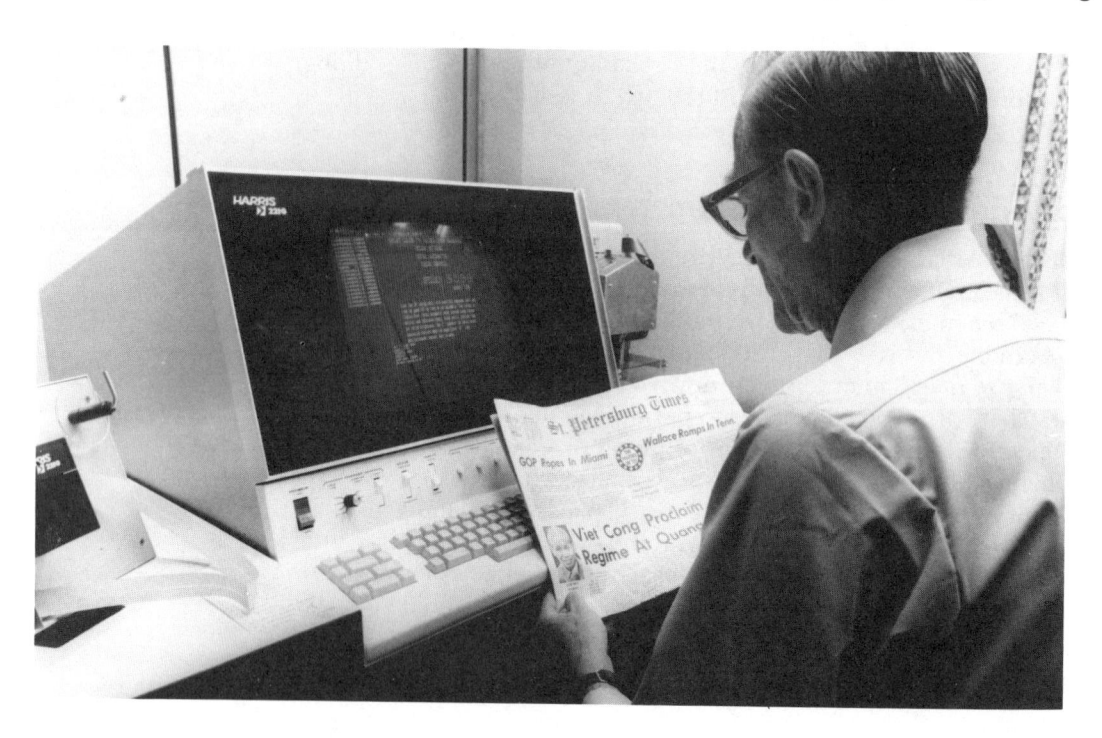

The Harris 2200 was the first display ad composition terminal to be introduced and marketed. It is used primarily among newspapers although some commercial typesetters have also installed 2200's for ad work. **Above:** The 2200 display with attached keyboard. **Below:** Ad copy on the screen of the 2200.

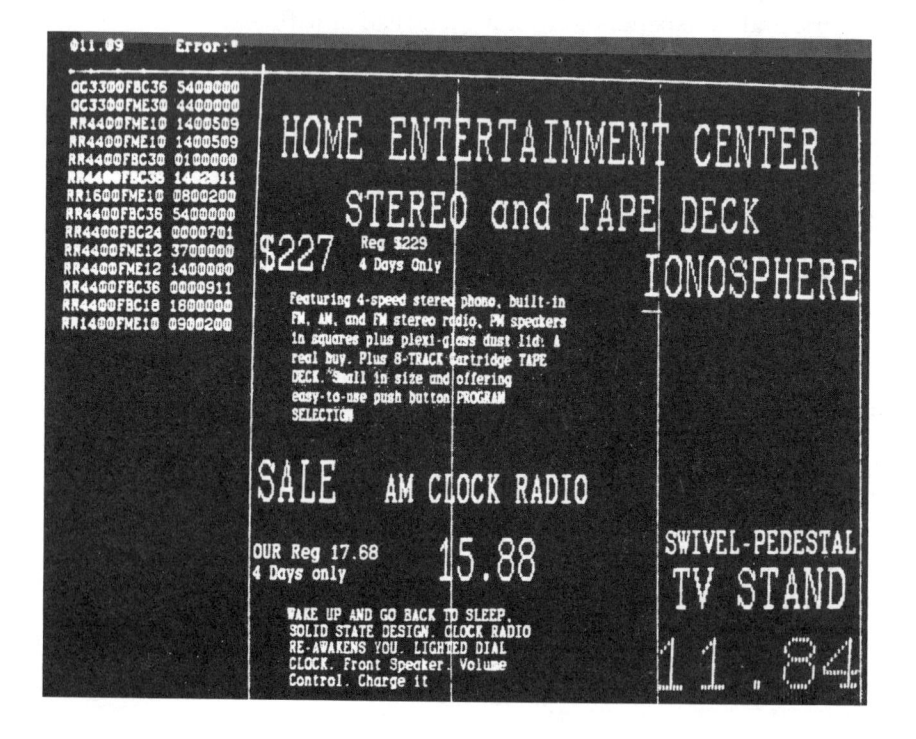

Pagination and "Area Composition"

The operator can then change these parameters. This could be done in one of two different ways. He or she could place the cursor on the parameters themselves and modify them by inputting the appropriate designators for a different type face, or line length, or point size, or leading, or positioning within the text area. And while this method must be used to define the desired type face style, the more likely approach for handling the other parameters would be to move to another pad of keys which permit him or her to "bump up" the size of the type, or to "bump" it down, one available size at a time, and to see how it fits and looks under those circumstances. The block of type could also be moved up or down, left or right. As various sizes are chosen and various lcoations are selected, the parameters on the left-hand side of the screen modify themselves accordingly. When the operator is satisfied with the appearance of that portion of the ad he or she would turn to the next block of copy and handle it in the same manner.

Thus the operator can get what he or she sees, subject to certain limitations. One does not truly see the actual shape of the type characters, but rather an abstract representation of the average shape of such characters, without the weight or appearance of the true type selected. Nor does the operator truly see the space that the character takes up, and he does not see precisely the amount of space that the block of text would fill. The word or phrase of type in question is "stretched" vertically and horizontally so that it fills the space the true type could in fact require.

Another limitation to this approach was that, in moving one block of copy, other blocks would not automatically be repositioned unless they were linked together in some hierarchical arrangement. One block of copy could be superimposed upon another and then moved up or down, left or right, and thus positioned experimentally at various locations. But once the operator has decided to link certain blocks together in a defined relationship, that entire structure can be moved about as one entity unless it is "disassembled" again. Moreover, once a given ad has been produced in this fashion, and output, these same parameters can be preserved and another series of text blocks can be read in, and this time they can be instructed to assume the characteristics of the previous group of elements, so that repetitive ads, or repetitive elements within a given ad can be handled quite expeditiously.

This kind of ad mark-up terminal was designed to simplify the mark up and composition of display ads that had already been sketched out in rough by the ad designer. First the text is keyed in, and then the terminal operator endeavors to imitate the appearance of the ad, approximating the size and position of the various elements. The ad designer would not have had to know precisely what would fit in a given space, but would deal roughly with sizes and relationships. He or she might have determined that a certain block of copy should be set in Trade Gothic Bold and might have imagined that 24-point type would have been about right. A second line, perhaps in the same type face, but perhaps around 18 points in size might then be centered within the same block at a sufficient distance below the first line so that the ascenders and descenders would not overstrike.

There were some limits as to the size of characters which could be displayed and the size of the ad which could be composed. Harris overcame these limitations somewhat in later models, such as the 2250, which permitted some reduction or enlargement of image (from "true size") and some sidewise scrolling to represent material which otherwise would exceed the width of the display.

Perhaps the point needs to be made that especially for the composition of display ads—even when the function is not to create the ad in the first place, but to reproduce what the original sketch intended, with whatever degree of precision the artist or agency layout man specified—the operator needs to see a fairly precise representation of the type to be composed. The only alternatives would have been to resort to character counting—which was the manner in which ads were originally designed and specified—or to repeat runs through a batch composition program, or by using some kind of computer-assisted character counting algorithm which permitted you to key characters experimentally and to see whether or not they would fit within the specified measure.

Camex, Raytheon and others

TWO OTHER VENDORS subsequently developed interactive ad layout and mark-up terminals, and a few years thereafter still others produced devices with similar capabilities. These vendors made use not only of a keyboard, but also of a tablet with which the operator could draw shapes and contours within which text could be "poured"—and hyphenated and justified to fit. In addition, Raytheon offered a "menu" of certain standard shapes—elipses, circles, squares and the like, to assist the mark-up man in the composition of text within such areas.

Both Camex and Raytheon[1] went well beyond Harris in that they came closer to being able to represent the actual position of each individual character as well as the general size and shape of the block itself. Their terminals were also perhaps more interactive in the way in which it was possible to move material from one place to another on the screen, and to link or de-couple blocks of text. It was easier to locate type with reference to the positioning of graphic elements with these two products than was the case with Harris, since the 2200 and the 2250 did not set type to contours or permit the outline representations of artwork on the screen.

The Camex technology was subsequently made available to Compugraphic: a low-cost, microcomputer version, operating much along the same lines was developed. A British company called Xenotron developed an approach much like that of the Harris 2200, but used an "area cursor" to indicate the size and position of a text block prior to its recomposition and display. Mergenthaler introduced the Linoscreen Composer and Mycro-Tex developed the AdComp.

1. The Raytheon product was subsequently taken over by Autologic when the former company decided to offer products for the graphic arts market.

Interactive page layout

DISPLAY AD TERMINALS whetted the appetite for still more powerful and flexible tools to permit the user to interact with blocks of text, and also with graphic images. Despite their apparent flexibility, such terminals were generally fairly limited in terms of their capabilities. They handled running text poorly. They wanted text to be presented in relatively small blocks. Such blocks could be linked together, but each block carried with it its own identifying information. In fact, in some instances the information so carried was expressed in terms of the combinations of codes and text which the output typesetter expected. In other instances there were two outputs: one for the typesetter and another which could be read back into the system for subsequent modification. When such terminals were interfaced to front-end systems—and this came about in due course—the information stored on the disk of the front-end system was not reprocessible by the composition program of that system. It was true that the input (*i.e.*, raw text) could be created on the front-end system, but it could not be formatted there. Nevertheless, it could be passed on to the output typesetter, along with other text so that if the front-end system had any kind of page make-up capability it could make allowance for the location of display ads, and when they were to be typeset it could simply direct a stream of information bits to the typesetting machine which the latter would respond to by composing type for that particular space location.

The next step was to adapt these display ad devices so that they were more flexible. Some of them were enhanced so that they could be used to create and prepare ruled business forms, including many interesting features having to do with the drawing of rules and boxes (even boxes with round corners). They could generate tints and reverses as well. There was also a need to be able to handle logotypes and other artifacts which typesetting devices had learned to set. In some cases these consisted of digitized artwork which could be output in the same manner as individual type characters.

It became clear that cursor-like devices limited the operator's ability to move quickly from one area within an ad or within a page to another, and tablets with some kind of pointing device (a joystick or a mouse) became common. Thus, by the early 1980s display ad terminals began to handle problems which went beyond area composition of display ads and business forms. They began to address the problems of page composition as well.

In the latter connection, it seems possible for an operator who is concerned with interactive page make-up, to work at a somewhat higher level of abstraction. He or she does not always need to see the type—or all of it, in all sizes—but may be satisfied with some indication of what items are to be positioned at various locations, and how much space they take up. Crude stick images of type for headlines, and straight or squiggly lines to represent text may be sufficient. However, the layout person would nevertheless like the capability of

1. See Chapter 21.

A newspaper ad department often receives a layout looking like the sample on the left, and is expected to produce an ad looking like the sample on the right.

Tools for positioning and sizing of text include graphic tablets as well as cursor controls. In the lower left photo is a system formerly produced by Raytheon. In the lower right photo is a terminal from Xenotron.

Pagination and "Area Composition"

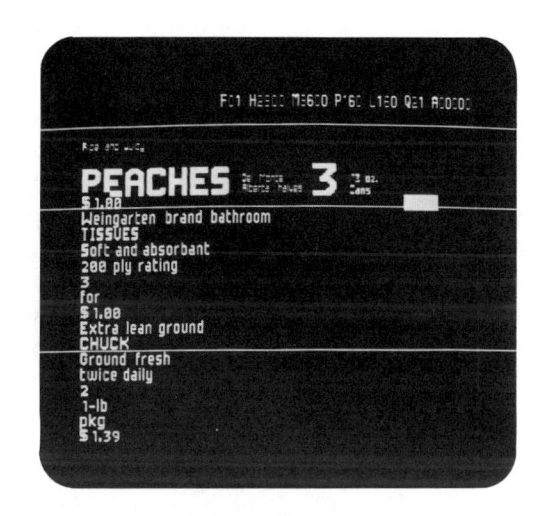

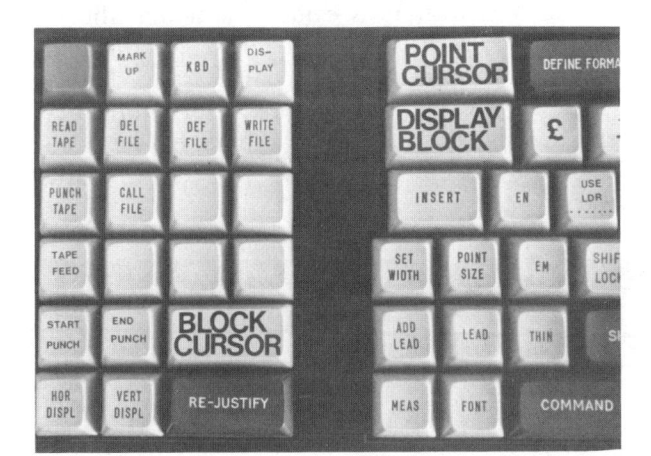

Top right: Blocks of text are read or keyed into the system with little or no mark-up and are then manipulated by sizing and moving about.

Bottom right: The newest of such devices can even display type set at an angle, or as reverse images, and can include other special effects. A raster image processor such as Camex's SuperSetter would be necessary to handle the output of such a page.

being able to zoom in on certain features of the page and to have these lines or squiggles magically converted into type characters so that they can be read in context, and even edited, if necessary, so that they will fit.

"Soft copy" displays versus interactive displays

ONE APPROACH which has been used since the mid-1970s is the "soft copy typesetter." This consists of a visual display which simulates a typeset page or some other typographic presentation which needs to be critically examined, such as a display ad. The display can consist of a representation of that typographic element on a storage tube—such as a Tektronix 4014—or a refresh-raster scan TV monitor. Another method whereby such an image can be created is a "flat glass" plasma display device, or a random-stroking VDT. In most cases the representations are not precise; they do not show the actual type, or perhaps even the actual weights and styles of type, but the approximate sizes of the individual characters is evident, although the x-heights and ascender/descender relationships are only approximated. However, several vendors have been able to show the actual characters which would be typeset.[1] By diverting the image (or, more precisely, the character stroking signals) from a CRT typesetter to a video storage tube or raster scan device, one can then see precisely what the effect would be if it were typeset.

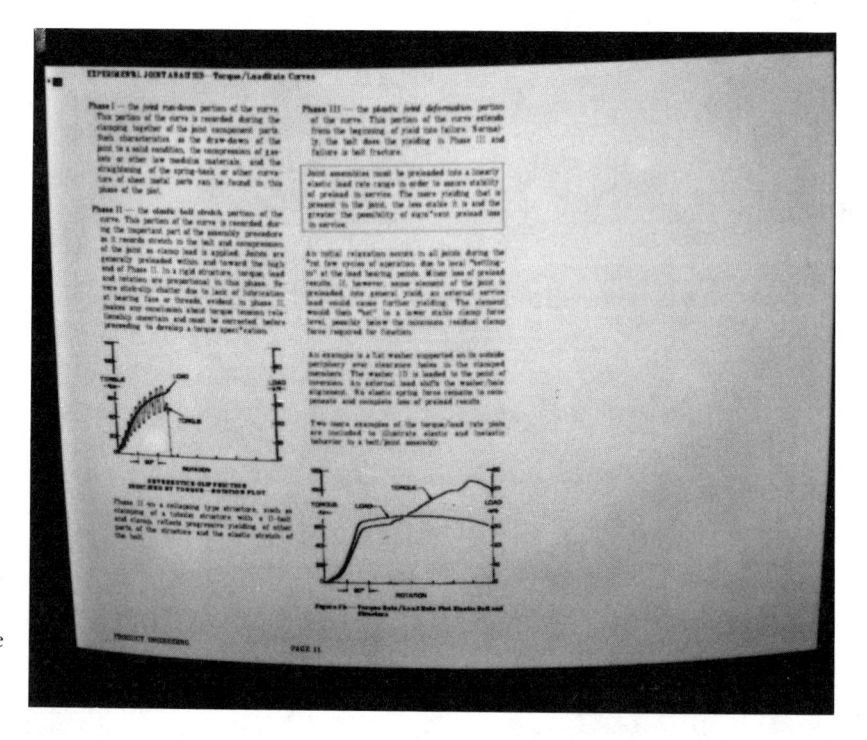

1. Information International and Compugraphic both have offered preview screens with fonts actually derived from the digital character representations stored on the typesetter itself.

A preview screen offered by Datalogics can also display digitized line art. The 8020 shown here is offered as an alternative to a storage tube.

Pagination and "Area Composition"

But such a soft copy display, convenient as it may be to help visualize the appearance of the page before typesetting, does not provide an interactive solution. If you are not satisfied with the results you must correct the typesetting parameters by calling the file onto a conventional VDT for editing.

More useful, therefore, are interactive, parameter-generating terminals which permit you to compose copy, move it around on the screen, recompose it if necessary, and then release it for typesetting. Display ad terminals are devices of this kind since, as you reposition the copy or change its boundaries and the size and fonts of type, the resulting parameters are incorporated into the text stream or otherwise directly associated with it. In other words, you are creating what you see, and not merely displaying it.

An in-between solution is one which will permit you to move blocks of copy about on a screen, but not to recompose them. Such a device might be used for "automated paste-up." You call up a file which contains a representation of the composed text and which links to the text file, but is not, in fact the same file. You then decide how much text will fit on the page, indicating where columns should break and where various blocks of copy should sit. You do this directly at the terminal display device. It records the position parameters, passes them on to an assembly file and concatenates them with the relevant portions of the text file. This information is then forwarded to the output typesetter. While reviewing the displayed text you cannot edit or recompose it. It would be necessary for you to cease the activity you were engaged in and return to the text file itself for such a modification.

Perhaps you could work simultaneously with two terminals, one of which would represent the blocks you were pasting up while the other provides access to the original files to permit their modification. Indeed, workstations consisting of two such terminals have been built for this purpose.

Hastech's PagePro workstation incorporates two screens. One, in landscape mode, is used for text files, while the other, in portrait mode, is used for making up a newspaper page. It can display a full page in reduced format, or part of a page in actual size.

Pagination of newspaper pages

PART OF THE DIFFICULTY in developing appropriate hardware and software for pagination lies in the problem of determining what the appropriate work flow arrangements should be. For example, is there in fact a need for editorial involvement during the pagination process? If so, can it be assumed that those who would be so involved are to be expected to be available as an integral part of the pagination process or merely to be on hand in case their judgment or approval is occasionally required? Will the decisions which need to be made also affect overall page design and the treatment of illustrative material? If so, do artists also need to be on line or on hand?

Perhaps it will be necessary to develop special systems or subsets of systems to deal with different kinds of publishing situations, but even within any one branch of the industry there are important differences in the way people work or would prefer to work.

Newspapers provide one such example. There is a great deal of interest in pagination in this field. This is especially so because there is some prospect that some time in the near future it will be possible to go "direct to plate" and thus, in a sense, do away with the typesetting device as such, and, more important, eliminate the cost of film necessary to transfer images from camera-ready copy to printing plate. If this indeed comes to pass it will be necessary for the system to be able to handle all aspects of page make-up including the incorporation of graphics. Consequently many newspapers are studying the prospects of electronic page make-up and several of them are actually performing it.

But even within this relatively specialized area of editorial/production copy flow, differences of opinion exist as to the manner in which procedures should be automated. Perhaps these differences will be resolved by the development of a technology which is compellingly superior to proposed alternatives, but to the extent that such technologies evolve from perceived needs, it appears that to some extent, at least, rival application solutions may emerge.

One approach to newspaper pagination might be for editors of various sections of the paper (news, sports, women's pages, real estate, business, *etc.*) to review a "budget" of articles in process, along with a copy depth estimate of what space these stories will require, and a layout which has already placed the display ads in position, thus leaving what is generally referred to as the "news hole."

This approach assumes that the editor will then assign story and picture locations, and that someone in a production capacity will sit at a terminal, call up the various stories, run them through h&j, and watch them form representational dashes and solid lines on a screen which represents actual type on a full broadsheet page at one-quarter normal size. Heads would be displayed, but rather than to seek to paint out the pictures, diagrams would indicate their allotted spaces. The text of the articles would also appear diagrammatically, as lines which show paragraph indents, paragraph endings and subheads, as

Pagination and "Area Composition"

well as running text. With some such systems it is possible for the workstation operator to zoom up to a full-sized or even double-sized scaling of a portion of the page in order to obtain legible text for possible copy-fit editing. This task might be performed on that screen or on an adjoining one.

Decisions must be made as to the termination or continuation of stories (as from the front page), and the assignment of "jump pages." In some instances column widths on jump pages will differ from those on the front page. With some systems the material which is run over to inside pages takes on a new file name, as it is assigned new parameters for column measure. In others it retains its identity as part of one file, bearing in mind that in subsequent editions of that daily paper (and there may be four or more), stories may be broken differently (as between pages) and may edited again, either to add new facts or to delete some portion of the story as later news tends to crowd it out.

At some point headlines must be written or rewritten. It will not do to wait until the last minute since there would be insufficient time to create all of the heads at once. This suggests that earlier in the day there decisions will have been taken as to the treatment and positioning of particular stories, with an assignment of head styles—banner, three column with kicker, two columns, double line, or one column, style #3 (which might be two lines in 24-point News Gothic).

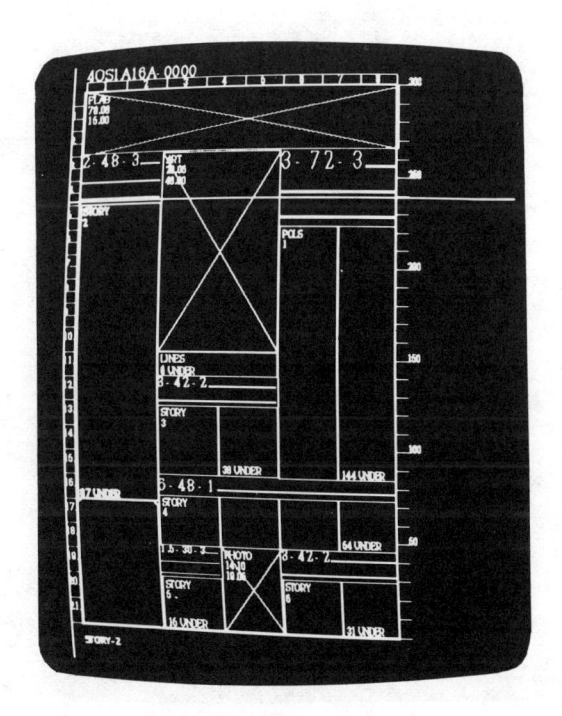

A page dummy on the screen of an Atex system. A rectangle with an "X" through it designates the location of a photo. Each story has an area for its headline (with numbers to indicate the point size and number of decks or lines the head will fill) and an area for the text, which is identified by the story's slug.

From dummy to typeset product. An alternative approach (and space does not allow us to explore all of the permutations and combinations of alternatives) would start with an editorial conference early in the day, where story assignments would be made, late-breaking news probabilities would be reviewed, and a dummy of the first page would be prepared, along with similar dummies of key section pages. Space allotments and general layout would be agreed upon, as well as head assignments.

From these dummy assignments, story slugs would be created, and each would carry with it relevant information as to the desired story length and placement. The "style file" for that particular story would be created, indicating headline treatment, column measure and other relevant factors. This information would serve as a guide for reporters and editors, and as the story progressed through composition it would look up its own parameters and be processed accordingly. When completed it would appear automatically on the desired page, as displayed on the editor's page layout terminal. It is then possible to review the story for news content and for length and general appearance. But best of all, there is available at all times a graphic representation of the newspaper's readiness to go to press. Holes still appear where stories are lacking, and the need for further trimming or jumping is also evident.

The new Atex GT68 page layout terminal works well for magazine pages such as this one, as well as newspaper pages. The user specifies the locations of stories on their repective pages, and the layout terminal shows the stories, headlines and photos in place. It can display halftones on the screen as well.

Pagination and "Area Composition"

There are yet even more automated concepts of newspaper page make-up, largely European in origin, which assign to the computer an even greater role in the decision-making process. Experimental programs have been developed which would have the editor merely assign degrees of importance to different news items and indicate the department of the paper where the stories should appear, as well as whether or not there are accompanying pictures. Based upon the length of the story and its importance, a program would actually lay out the paper according to the general design philosophy of that particular publisher (*e.g.*, use of rectangular boxes with all stories squared for presentation in the European style, or uneven single columns of text, with the more important stories floating to upper left or upper right, and display ads arranged in triangles or pyramids). The editor or editors would then review the proposed arrangement and make such modifications as seemed necessary.

These brief descriptions should serve to indicate that techniques necessary to automate pagination of a newspaper tend to be somewhat unique. While some of the technology being developed for this purpose may be relevant for other applications (magazines, books, technical papers and journals, documentation), much of it may not be.

Pagination of magazines

EVEN MAGAZINES vary considerably as to the manner in which they are put together. In general it may be helpful to think in terms of two extreme cases, with others falling somewhere in between.

On one hand there are news magazines where layout occurs at the same time the stories are assigned. Thus the writer knows precisely how long his story should be, and what areas of the page or pages will be devoted to illustrations. He also gradually learns what the illustrations will be—charts or graphs, photographs, or perhaps cartoons. It is therefore possible for him or her to write precisely to fit, but there will probably be a general policy that the story should be about ten percent oversized to permit tightening by editors in the interest of crispness and succinctness.

There is usually an advanced form which goes to the printers earlier in the week. Remaining pages are dispatched to the printer hour by hour toward the end of the week, and final pages will close as late as Sunday morning for Monday newsstand delivery throughout the United States. These magazines are printed at four or five different locations around the country, and even overseas, and text and graphics, in full-page format, are transmitted to various printing plants by satellite or microwave.

However, not all copies of each magazine are alike. There are regional and demographic editions, with varying advertising matter, and often there are also differences in editorial matter as well, so that the pages transmitted to one printer will differ from those transmitted to another. Even the same printer may receive and print more than one version of the weekly magazine.

Scitex has offered its Vista terminal (above) as a page designer's workstation, and its Response 300 system (below) for color separation, graphic manipulation and image enhancement.

Pagination and "Area Composition" 293

These magazines have placed more and more emphasis upon color in recent years, not only for advertising matter (which may be prepared in advance and shipped to the various printing plants ahead of time) but also for editorial treatment, where there may be extensive use of color for late-breaking news. (The football quarterback's successful pass into the end zone, resulting in the winning play of Sunday's game in Boston may appear in full color in the pages of a sports weekly delivered to homes and for sale on newsstands less than two days later in Los Angeles.)

It would seem that an appropriate system for such a magazine might well include layout terminals, so that designer and issue editor can first determine the amount of space to be devoted to a particular story, and then agree upon the general treatment of the piece. The designer would then submit a layout, or a series of layouts, of the pages in question, probably using dummy type to present a more realistic presentation of the appearance of the spread. Positions of blocks of copy would be indicated, along with varying levels of heads, captions, legends and the like.

The next stage would be to incorporate artwork or simulations of the artwork within the same pages. This might be done by calling up illustrations which have already been scanned and stored on a data base. Perhaps the designer's workstation will be capable of manipulating them, in terms of rotation, cropping, sizing, and conceivably even image enhancement. Such manipulation of graphics may serve to produce the actual linework and halftones, or they may merely serve to provide specifications for the printer or color separation house.

Writers would then undertake to prepare the various blocks of copy, and would receive immediate feedback on their terminals as to whether what they have written will indeed fill and fit the indicated space allocations. Typesetting parameters for such copy blocks would have been picked up by the system from the information derived from the page layout data already stored on the computer.

At the time of this writing, ingredients of such a system are already in place at Time, Inc., consisting of hardware and software from such vendors as Scitex and Crosfield, Atex, Systems Integrators and Information International. Other news magazines are taking similar steps. No information is as yet available as to the cost effectiveness of such approaches, but it is clear that they will provide powerful tools and could profoundly affect the manner in which type and graphics are blended together on such pages.

The reader will find more information on current developments bearing upon this subject in our chapter on the treatment of halftones and other illustrations.[1]

Other magazines. At another extreme are magazines which are not laid out until the various articles have already been set in type, more or less to a prescribed format. Then the editor, assisted by artists and layout men, do the best job they can in positioning text and artwork, trying to avoid the necessity of resetting type, and perhaps sizing the art and any illustrative matter to compensate for awkward paging

1. See p. 334.

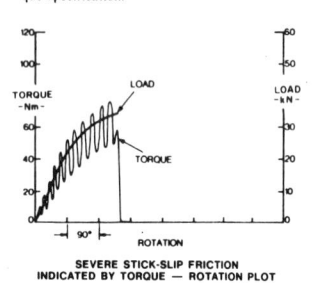

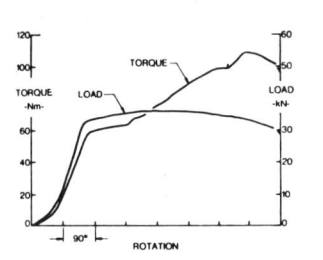

situations. In such a case what may be required would more likely represent an automated paste-up approach. Either an artist or someone in production, working under the supervision of an editor, would instruct the system as to the precise locations at which this pre-formatted and pre-composed text would be laid down.

Journals. Yet another approach might be taken for the pagination of journals. Such journals often resemble books in that the text is written by outside authors, and is not prepared with a specific layout in mind other than the house style for the publication in question. In such instances the system could attempt the automatic pagination of the entire magazine, just as this might also be the case for a book publisher.

Technical publications. One area receiving special attention at present has to do with the production of technical publications. Many of the approaches which are now being developed for this particular market may ultimately be applied to other markets as well. It is felt that this market offers early opportunities for software and system exploitation in those instances where text and graphics must be combined, but quality standards for presentation may tend to be low. Black and white illustrations will suffice rather than process color (*i.e.*, color halftones), and aesthetic composition features may not be required.

Systems proposed for this market would tend to be batch in nature. The program will seek to position graphics near the point of reference, will make end-of-page decisions, and will also cope with tables, footnotes, and the generation of running heads and folios (page numbering).

However, interactive review of pagination decisions is generally implied, and it affords the user an opportunity

Output of scanned graphics. This page reduced from 50% and output on an APS-5 is from a production run on Ford's Datalogics installation.

Pagination and "Area Composition"

to intervene whenever the batch program signals that it cannot resolve the problem within the allowed parameters.

Book composition. There are many kinds of books and it may well be that various programmatic solutions may be needed in order to resolve their pagination requirements. Books will vary according to the amount of illustrative material, the presence or absence of tabular matter, and whether such tables may be contained within the boundaries of a single page or may have to be composed in a landscape mode. Some books require the inclusion of multilevel mathematical formulae, the use of extensive and lengthy footnotes, and the generation of running heads derived from chapter subsections or other telltale heads. Books also vary in their requirements for tight setting according to stringent parameters, along with kerning and other artistic effects.

In general, solutions tend to be of two types: *one category of program* seeks to make end-of-page decisions at the same time that it makes its initial end-of-line (justification) decisions. As each line is composed the page depth is tallied. When the allowable depth has been encountered the page is terminated and a new page is begun. If, however, the point at which the page is to be terminated is impermissible due to the presence of a widow or orphan[1], various alternatives are explored on the basis of a set of "try tables."

One alternative looks for spacing-in or spacing-out areas within the page, represented by secondary leading[2] around subheads, or white space for illustrations, or between text and footnotes. A second seeks to add small amounts of white space between paragraphs of text. A third will attempt to "card" in very small increments between lines of running text. A fourth would be to go "short" or "long" on pairs of facing pages or related groups of columns. A fifth, and a much more complex solution, would be to back up and seek to find an alternate solution for the preceding pair of pages in the hope that doing so will present a different set of (more amenable) circumstances for the instant pair. A sixth would be to try to "float" non-text elements, consisting of illustrations or blocks of tabular material, forward (or in some instances backward) and thus to adjust the flow of running text.

A final effort might be to seek to reprocess some or all of the lines on the page, setting them tighter or looser in an effort to create a larger or smaller number of lines of text. For example, if the page cannot be broken because the first line at the top of the next page would be a widow, perhaps that paragraph could be set tighter to avoid this condition.

When the program reaches the end of the chapter it may discover that only one or two lines remain—lines which cannot be swallowed into the preceding body of text but which cannot be permitted to stand out like sore thumbs all alone on an otherwise blank page. Yet another variable which book pagination needs to take into account is whether new chapters must all begin on left pages, or right pages, or either page, or whether, under some circumstances, a succeeding chapter can begin on a page where the preceding chapter concludes.

---

1. A widow is the last line of a paragraph standing by itself at the top of a page. An orphan is a first line of a paragraph standing by itself at the bottom of a page.

2. Secondary leading is extra white space around a head or some other text element. Primary leading is the leading associated with a line of running text.

A *second category of program* presumes the preexistence of galley composition and applies its various alternative "tries" to the arrangement of existing lines of text and related matter. Again there is the possibility of expanding or reducing the amount of space (secondary leading) assigned above and below subheads, illustrations, footnotes and the like. This author happens to prefer this approach simply because it affords the opportunity for the pagination program to deal with the facts about the text rather than having to process the text itself. Thus a program can be written to create a descriptor file which indicates what it is that would be associated with each line of text. Is it a paragraph beginning? Is it a paragraph ending? Is it a subhead? Is it part of a designated "no-break" block? Does it contain a footnote call-out reference which implies that a footnote of a certain (to be ascertained) depth must be associated with that line on the same page?

These factors can be analyzed in pure mathematical or logical terms without the need to be burdened with the text itself. Then a set of commands can be generated that create an output file (in reality a file which still must be processed in output driver language) containing lines of type interspersed by spacing and positioning commands.

Reprocessability

THE READER should bear in mind that—especially for book work—the need generally exists to be able to make use of the same file to recompose the book according to different pagination parameters. The publisher may wish to produce two versions of the same work—perhaps a single-column paperback and a two-column hardbound version. Or he will most probably want to maintain a file to be revised and republished at a later date.

It will not be practical, therefore, to maintain a file in page format since paging will most likely be different the next time around. It will simply not do to have to reconstruct the various elements in order to disassociate text and running heads, footnotes and the like. Consequently a master file of a more generic nature should be maintained—not in paged format but in a prior-to-pagination condition.

Whatever the paging problem, however, it should always be possible to pick up the pieces without the need to back up to the very beginning of the process. Early composition and pagination programs (such as the RCA Page-1 and the later Page-2 version—both products of the 1960s, but which spawned subsequent approaches, especially to the problems of area composition) often made it necessary for the user to go back to the initial input file in order to introduce any corrections or modifications, and then to reinstitute all subsequent processing steps as though they had never been taken before. Nor was there any assurance that these processes might not have to be repeated many times over so that one could never foresee the happy occasion when a final solution had been achieved. In those days one often thought very fondly of the ease of the hot metal pagination experience. Slugs actually set were not conditional. They existed and could be seen and felt. Pages already paginated could be proofed and examined, and if one had to go back over what had already been done, one did not have to start at the beginning but could search for the place nearest to the location of the desired change or improvement.

This capability should still be preserved. Files should be reprocessible and this can only be assured if all relevant information about prior conditions is constantly maintained so that it is not necessary to go back to the beginning in order to trace sequentially all of the relevant bits of information which must be known at any one point. At least restart blocks should be generated periodically.

Other paginated-related products

ESPECIALLY in the area of book composition one needs to keep in mind the fact that there are other activities which are associated with book production which must be undertaken and can be handled at the same time, or at least related to that process. These have to do with the generation of indexes, or the extraction of data (including page references) from which such indexes may be created. In like manner, tables of contents and lists of illustrations may be created. Thus some program, somewhere, needs to be able to know what text is located on what page according to the most recent cast-off information.

Finally, pagination must also take into account the realities of book production in that, generally speaking, books are printed in signatures. Signatures are comprised of 4, 8, 16, 32 or 64 pages which need to be printed at the same time. Some of these signatures may require the use of more than one color. Others may not. Sometimes certain sections of a book (or magazine) are printed by different processes, such as offset and gravure, or letterpress and offset. Sometimes two or more forms need to be created from the same text, as with a red-letter edition of the Bible which requires a black printed form and a second which contains the words of Christ in red letters appropriately positioned and aligned with the black type. Or, more simply, dropped initials, running heads, or perhaps subheads and chapter openers may be printed in a second color and a smart computer program may be able to accomplish this by generating camera-ready copy consisting of only these lines in their correct locations, with register marks at top and bottom of pages to assist the printer in his press imposition.

There are, indeed, many challenges and many opportunities. And many problems are still crying for solutions. With each set of solutions new opportunities are created which, in turn, may give rise to new problems and opportunities. So, no doubt, shall it ever be.

18

File Management and Copy Flow

WHEN VIDEO DISPLAY TERMINALS are interfaced to a computer so that they can fetch text from computer storage—or create text and file it there—and so that operators of the terminals can engage in editing and other text processing activities, it is necessary to develop techniques to "manage" the textual material in question. These tasks are similar in many respects to those that computer systems analysts must cope with for any on-line and time-shared or real-time system involving multiprocessing or multitasking activities.

To understand how data files are managed it is necessary for us to know more about computer storage techniques.

Computer memory itself is not sufficient to offer room for the storage of large quantities of text. The core or "memory" is used for the temporary manipulation of this text—providing the programs, look-up tables, indexes and other necessary processing aids along with buffer areas within which portions of the text temporarily reside. The text itself—as long as it stays within the system—is generally stored on one or more moving head disks, although floppy diskettes and magnetic tapes or cartridges also occasionally serve the same or a similar purpose.

There are *fixed-head* disks—which are more expensive and generally offer less storage, but faster access times. *Moving-head* disks are more commonly used. In either case, the information is stored magnetically on tracks. It is written by a "write" head which moves over to an available track and records data as bytes or characters (really bit patterns). It is read by a "read" head which functions in the same manner. (In fact, the same head serves read/write functions.) A moving-head disk may consist of a single platter or of several platters. It is mounted on a disk drive, which is governed or directed by a disk controller. The controller, under a general operating system and a file management system, tells the write head where to record data and the read head where to find it. A multiple platter disk works in the same fashion, except that there are more read/write heads—one for each usable surface of the disk.

A certain amount of data can be written to each track of a disk. For example, a Digital Equipment RK05 disk and disk drive (with RK11 controller) provides a cartridge which holds something over 1.2 million 16-bit words (2.5 million characters). There are two surfaces, totaling 200 tracks (plus three spares), 12 sectors per track, with each sector recording 256 16-bit words. A one-track move requires 10

File Management and Copy Flow

A multiple platter, removable moving-head disk mounted on its disk drive. The plastic cover protects the rigid disk from being damaged by dust particles.

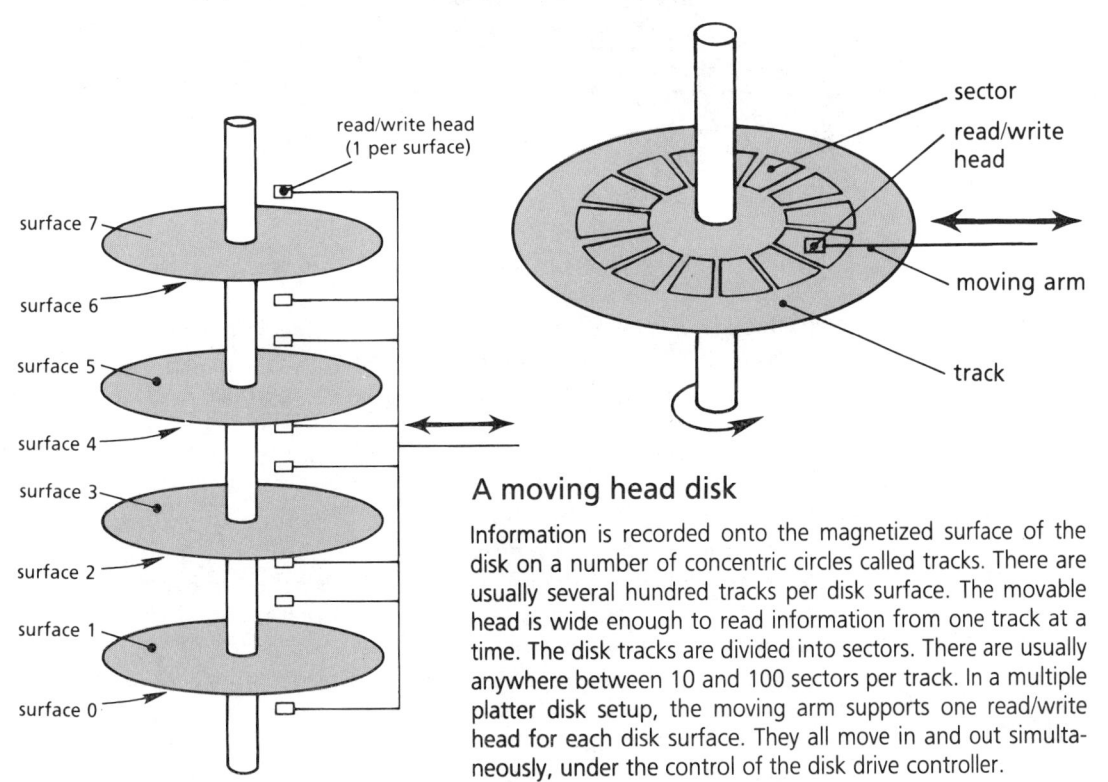

A moving head disk

Information is recorded onto the magnetized surface of the disk on a number of concentric circles called tracks. There are usually several hundred tracks per disk surface. The movable head is wide enough to read information from one track at a time. The disk tracks are divided into sectors. There are usually anywhere between 10 and 100 sectors per track. In a multiple platter disk setup, the moving arm supports one read/write head for each disk surface. They all move in and out simultaneously, under the control of the disk drive controller.

milliseconds, average track positioning time is 50 milliseconds, and maximum is 85 milliseconds. Data transfer speed is 11.1 microseconds per word; disk rotation speed is at 1500 rpm, and the time for a one-half revolution is 20 milliseconds.

We can see, then, that in this instance a track can be accessed, on the average in .005 seconds, and that an additional 20 milliseconds or so might be required before the desired sector is under the read head. At that time 512 characters can be brought into memory at a data transfer speed of 11.1 microseconds per word, or about 5 microseconds per character (.000005 seconds). A double-density disk might read or record twice that amount of information in the same time.

The read/write head does not come into physical contact with the disk (unless it is a floppy disk or diskette). The head floats over the track on a cushion of air created by the spinning motion of the disk. Consequently these rigid disks do not wear out, or are not damaged unless there is a disk crash when the head comes into physical contact and destroys data. Otherwise, when the system is shut down and the disk ceases to spin, the head retracts.

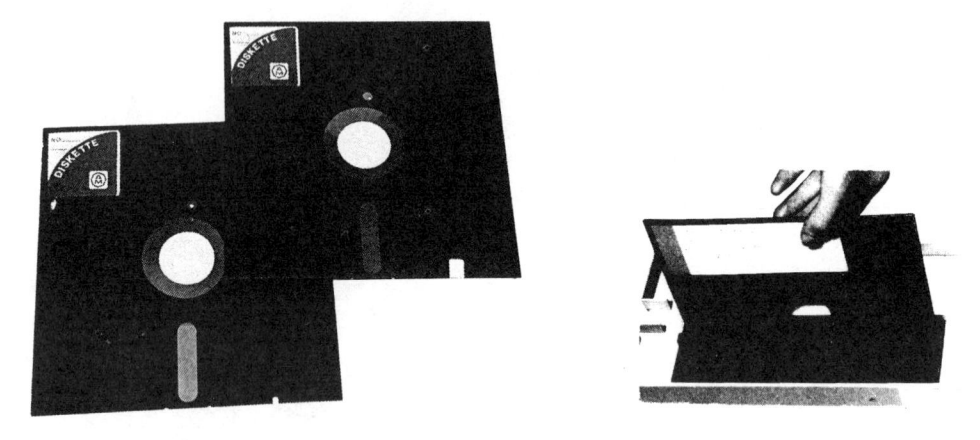

Left: Floppy disks. **Right:** A floppy being inserted into its disk drive.

Each track has an address, and within each track there is also a sector address. But the information on a given sector—say 512 characters—can only be read when that sector spins by the read head and when the head is positioned over the proper track.

The information stored on a disk is not generally written consecutively, but rather, randomly, in order to optimize retrieval time. Data may start out by being more or less consecutive, but if more information is added, then the text will overflow the allotted area and the extra (left over) data will be written elsewhere—any place that is available on the disk or disk pack, leaving behind an address indicating where to go next (what track and what sector or platter). The supervisory program and controller may also keep a record of where the previous batch of information was written, so that a file can be recovered by tracing it in either direction, once you know where to go to get an identifiable piece of that particular file. A bit map tells the

File Management and Copy Flow 301

disk controller where there are unused areas on the disk. An index—either in memrory or on a designated disk area—will indicate where the read head should go to pick up the beginning of the file. Consequently, a name must be associated with a particular file, and an index must be constructed, showing where that file's beginning may be found. If you want to retrieve the file, you need to tell the file management system the name of the file you wish to retrieve.

More simple-minded systems may place the burden of keeping track of files on the system operator or user, in which case the user would have to divide up a particular job into small takes and direct the system to go to a designated platter or even track (which he or she will have written down on a piece of paper) in order to get at the desired job. A higher degree of sophistication would keep an index as to the location of the beginning of the file, but the user would have to remember the name of the file. Other management systems permit the user to call up a directory of files, to point at the desired file, and order it to be fetched.

Disk-oriented file management systems can be—and are—very powerful. Without such systems it is not possible to command the computer to fetch a file, or to add to it, or to store it, without destroying other files. And without an index, and a trail which describes the current sequence of the file, it would not be possible to pull out the text in order to scroll backward or forward through the file by bringing it from disk to memory and from memory to terminal.

The use of directories

THE USER should not be expected to remember file names or to know where files are written, although if removable disk platters or packs are used (or, of course, floppies), he or she will have to know which disk or pack is required. Directories will be provided so that the user can ask to see the names of all files and their current status. He or she can usually access the desired file simply by pointing to it with the cursor or mouse.

But a large system will require the storage of many files, and a file directory—no matter how well organized—may be too long to peruse. So other techniques are developed. One is to search the directory to locate the file, if you happen to remember its name or certain of its attributes (such as that it was one you created). Another is to create subdirectories, associated with a particular user or a class of work, such as sports or wire service or jobs for customer "Jones." Newer systems offer cross directories so that it is possible to search several categories in order to find, say, all sports stories filed by local reporters between noon Monday and 7 a.m. Tuesday—or even just those within this category which have been accepted for publication and have already been typeset. Some systems will enable you, on demand, to construct a listing of all versions of the same file, indicating who worked on that file and in what sequence changes were made. Some of them can indicate, by means of an "audit trail," what specific changes were introduced at each phase in the editing process.

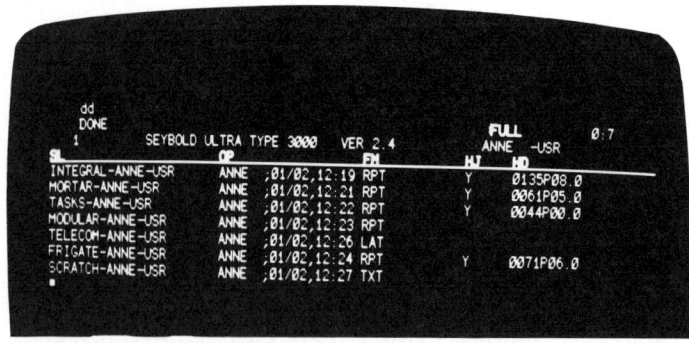

```
          dd
          DONE
                                                                   FULL            0:7
              1       SEYBOLD ULTRA TYPE 3000    VER 2.4            ANNE  -USR
          SL                     OP              FM                 HJ    HD
          INTEGRAL-ANNE-USR      ANNE     ;01/02,12:19 RPT          Y       0135P08.0
          MORTAR-ANNE-USR        ANNE     ;01/02,12:21 RPT          Y       0061P05.0
          TASKS-ANNE-USR         ANNE     ;01/02,12:22 RPT          Y       0044P00.0
          MODULAR-ANNE-USR       ANNE     ;01/02,12:23 RPT
          TELECOM-ANNE-USR       ANNE     ;01/02,12:26 LAT
          FRIGATE-ANNE-USR       ANNE     ;01/02,12:24 RPT          Y       0071P06.0
          SCRATCH-ANNE-USR       ANNE     ;01/02,12:27 TXT
```

This is the medium-length file directory common to systems of the Atex type. The first three lines are for commands, messages and functions. The files which are displayed are from a queue called Anne, which also happens to be the log-on name of the user. The fourth line indicates what is included in the columns in the directory. First is the slug name (with the queue and group in which the stories are located). Next is the operator who created the file (in this case all were created by Anne) and the date and time each was created. "FM" specifies the format which will be used when the job is composed for output to a printer or typesetter. "HJ" tells whether the file has been through hyphenation and justification or not. The last column gives the total depth of the file as of the last time it was composed, if it ever has been composed.

Routing files

IF THERE ARE many terminals on the system, it may be possible to send a story from one directory to another. Thus a reporter may file his story and direct it to his editor who, after reviewing it, will send it to the slot man and he, in turn, will assign it to a particular page. In each instance the story will be shifted, or copied, from one directory to another, although *there is no physical transfer of the information* unless the file is copied. It is the pointers to the file which are changed. Some systems will provide default routines which will automatically route stories in a certain sequence and stipulate whether the directory to which they are sent will rank them according to LIFO (last-in, first-out) which places the most recent stories at the top of the queue or pile of papers or FIFO (first-in, first-out), which puts all of the incoming stories at the bottom of the pile. Thus the directory serves as an "in basket" which is always maintained in a certain order.

In addition to the transfer of stories, messages can also be sent, and a "message waiting" indicator may flash on the operator's screen so that he or she will learn of some vital information, for example, that an awaited story is now in the in-basket, or a staff meeting has been called.

Stories may also be queued in a certain processing sequence, as for typesetting, or for use with the on-line printer. When a reporter completes a story and signs off on it the story name can be made to appear automatically in the editor's queue. When the editor finishes with it the story can be brought up instantaneously in the queue of the slot man who assigns the page positioning, and when the slot man has written a head and indicated the positioning and treatment of the

File Management and Copy Flow

```
R         CHAR INS                                           10/21/82  12:41
directory list for newsman (BA,    directory list for newsman (BA, SEYBOLD)
Slug       De Last Editor  Pb D    Slug       De Last Editor Pb Dt Part Pg  Edit
#9617         SEYBOLD              #15589        SEYBOLD
#2012         SEYBOLD              BC-Airline 3 London¶
#4374         SEYBOLD                There are rumors that Mrs. Thatcher will writ
#16234        SEYBOLD              off the debt if necessary to make the airline at
#9455         SEYBOLD              to private investors, sure to balk if British Ai
#11398        SEYBOLD              is saddled with over $170 million annually in de
#15589        SEYBOLD              charges.¶
#16836        SEYBOLD                Sir John confirmed that his board has asked t
#17375        SEYBOLD              
#17510        SEYBOLD              #16836        SEYBOLD
#18511        SEYBOLD              By Robert Woodward¦
#15993        SEYBOLD              ¶  BONN, Oct 21, Reuter -- ''Cable television w
#20104        SEYBOLD              become the most powerful stimulus for the econom
#17338        SEYBOLD              in the next few years,'' according to West Germa
#9079         SEYBOLD              new Post Minister, Christian Schwarz-Schilling.¶
#6534         SEYBOLD                He is planning for every household in the cou
#17445        SEYBOLD              to be wired for cable television by 1986 in a mo
#17703        SEYBOLD              
                                   #17375        SEYBOLD
                                   BC-Television 2 Bonn¶
                                     One area of controversy is the Post Minister'
                                   decision to use copper cable instead of the more
                                   glass fibre cable. His predecessor in the job, S
                                   Democrat Hans Matthoeffer, said this is a ''path
```

These are two System Integrators directories of wire service stories in the "newsman" queue. One the left-hand side of this split screen is a short directory of files which "Seybold" has been working on. Because they are wire service stories the slug or name is the wire service number. Local stories would most likely have a more meaningful alphabetic name. On the right is a long directory which enables the operator to see how each story in the directory begins. Note in both cases that the screen doesn't show the entire directory, since we are in split-screen mode. But we can scroll horizontally to view the entire screen.

```
DIRECTORY OF MORO (ALL)                          5-10-78  11:44

SLUG      GUIDE                        AUTHOR   ENTERED   LENGTH

MORO      REDMONT             RU A52  APA5820   5-10 11:36   33.98
MORO      S LETTERS 1ST LD-WRITETH     APA5770   5-10 10:06   19.04
MORO      S LETTERS BJT590 BY VICT    APA5680   5-10  9:35   18.17
MORO      642-48-1 W/K                 APA5250   5-10  7:08   33.92
MORO      RDP 2ND LD-WRITETHRU A48    APA4940   5-10  4:13   34.97
MORO      RDP 1ST LD-WRITETHRU A46    APA4870   5-10  3:13   33.48
MORO      REACTION570 WITH MORO BJ    APA4850   5-10  2:57   15.43
MORO      RDP BJT1000 RETRANSMITTI    APA4680   5-10  1:42   29.75
MORO      FAMILY BJT430 BY HILMI T    APA4640   5-10  1:11   12.32
MORO      RDP BJT1000 LASERPHOTOS     APA4630   5-10  1:03   29.50
```

This System Integrators directory shows all files with the slug "Moro," which a newsroom editor might use to plan coverage of a particular news event and its related stories. This directory gives the slug, each story's "guide" or identification, the author (in this case the wire service number), the date and time it entered the system, and the story length in inches.

story it can be directed through hyphenation and justification and on to the typesetter.

Obviously other arrangements can be customized not only by the vendor for a particular company, but by the system manager within that company for a particular department or individual.

In newspapers the use of disk storage, coupled with video terminals, has led to the development of all-electronic newsrooms which have automated (*i.e.*, eliminated) the copy boy, and which provide far more expeditious handling of editorial matter, offering better editorial control of the copy flow and production processes.

Relevance to commercial applications

SIMILAR PROCEDURES are also relevant for non-newspaper operations. For magazines, as well as newspapers, editorial or front-end systems may be utilized, enabling writers to record their preliminary drafts directly into computer files, to edit and update them, to compose them, and even to rewrite them for purposes of copy fitting.

In production shops, jobs may flow through the system (as from OCR input) according to designated job characteristics, and only those which raise questions or present problems may need to be queued for review on VDTs by operators who are skilled in diagnosing such difficulties.

And so the need to keep track of files, jobs or stories in order to process or revise them has opened the door to the development of techniques for the control of copy flow, the minimization of waiting time, the organization of like jobs for typesetting purposes, or the identification of problems, such as missing components (*e.g.*, legends or tables), or jobs which have exceeded their assigned deadlines.

On-lineness

THE MOST EFFICIENT method of operation is usually one where all of the functions and components are on line—from copy creation to typesetting, without the need to mount disks, paper tapes, magnetic tapes, filmstrips, or to feed in parameters of job specifications by manual means. Of course such systems may be too expensive or too complex for smaller users, but as a general rule, the less the manual intervention the more productive the system, and hence the entire operation.

For the most part, on-line editorial systems came into being during the primacy of the minicomputer. Large mainframe computers were too expensive for these applications, and neither software nor hardware was optimized for these purposes. Consequently, the minicomputers took over.

More recently, however, the microprocessor revolution has occurred and these new and very inexpensive computers have begun to play a larger role. Micros may provide the intelligence for workstations linked together under the aegis of minicomputers which operate as file servers or special-purpose boxes to perform the more compute-intensive tasks, such as hyphenation and justification or pagination. Microcomputers may also take over the file management functions, assuming the role of "file servers." The links which tie the various components together may be provided by local area networks rather than intercomputer busses or intermediate-speed parallel or serial interfaces. To the extent that distributed processing solutions are used, some of the advantages of the minicomputer systems, with their powerful file-management capabilities, may be lost, and more burden may be imposed upon the individual operator to keep track of his or her own files. For example, if each workstation has its own floppy disk, and if the operator can remove these files at will—assuming they do not reside elsewhere within the system—many of the logistical functions which are now performed so effectively may suffer. And to the extent that files must be physically transferred to a workstation—rather than using the workstation to address and modify centrally stored documents—then there is a greater burden on the system to support the transfer of larger volumes of data, and response times may suffer.

We must also remember that there are startling new possibilities for more massive and even more economical storage of data. Each year it seems that more information can be stored reliably in less and less space, and the cost of such storage continues to decline. As changes in costs and technologies occur, so new designs for system architecture may prove possible and advantageous. But whatever happens in the future, we will still benefit from the lessons and experiences that have been accruing over the past decade or so.

Definition of terms

SINCE WE HAVE referred to editorial systems, front-end systems and production systems, some more precise definition of concepts appears to be needed.

In all instances we are assuming the use of video terminals and some file management capabilities, but terminals are used somewhat differently in each such situation, and so are the demands for computational functions—not only for file management but for text processing and manipulation.

A front-end system is one which is used to capture writers' keystrokes so that their output does not have to be rekeyboarded and reproofed to check the errors introduced in the input process. It is also one in which directories and queues permit the routing of material from one person to another, and the subsequent review and revision of the initially created documents. But if it is only a front-end system, processing stops short of composition formatting, although it may include the insertion of codes for such formatting.

An editorial system starts with a front-end capability, as above, but it also offers writers (or some writers) and editors access to computer composition functions so that they can review the hyphenated and justified output and revise it for copy-fitting purposes. It implies, moreover, that they can revise the most recent version, as previously formatted, rather than to have to go back to the initial input. It also implies that it is editors (or some of them) who control the system, including the production into type of their material, by using appropriate commands from their VDTs. If page make-up is offered, it would also be editors who would determine and implement the page make-up functions.

A production system, on the other hand, implies either that a manuscript will be input in a production environment or brought in from external sources, as from OCR or office word processors or personal computers. Changes desired by editors are not reviewed on terminals, but are marked on hard copy, galleys or typeset pages, and the implementation of these changes is then done by production workers (computer composition craftsmen).

A back-end system is one which accepts unjustified input from a front-end system but performs composition and make-up functions without direct editorial intervention, although pursuant to editorial instructions. It is possible to have a front-end system strictly for editorial convenience, and a back-end system for composition formatting and typographic output. This configuration will differ only slightly from a production system, but it probably implies that the back-end activities are more streamlined than those which would be carried forward in a production system, because more of the functions being carried forward by writers and editors (but not all of them) reduce the level of responsibilities for those who are charged with the production of typographic output.

One recognizes that these distinctions are arbitrary and that relationships between writers, editors and production people are constantly in a state of flux, depending, of course, upon the nature of the applications and the extent to which uniformity of product (as opposed to variety of application) plays a part in the work cycle.

19

Composition and Word Processing

SIMILARITIES between the input and editing functions of editorial or front-end systems and those of word processors have already been mentioned. What are the differences? It may be that the term word processing implies control over the equipment by a secretary rather than by the writer or editor, but this seems too arbitrary a distinction to convey much meaning. Any front-end or even editorial system should seek to accommodate the requirements and needs of the particular installation. Some writers use typewriters and can use typewriter-like devices. Others cannot and do not. Some dictate, or think best when working with a pen and tablet, expecting a secretary to provide them with a subsequent clean script for further revisions.

But at some point in the manuscript preparation stage—somewhere "upstream" in the editorial process—it becomes advantageous to capture keystrokes and to avoid redundant retyping by merging in corrections and revisions. The objective may be simply to provide the printer or typesetter with a clean manuscript, or it may be that the manuscript is not destined for typesetting at all. A short-term objective may be to obtain clean copies in order to encourage further refinements in the manuscript and to secure the comments and contributions of others. But whatever the purpose, it is clearly facilitated by working—at some point in time—with a draft which can be modified and reproduced without the labor, cost and time-consuming aspects of retyping.

Word processing equipment was intended to serve this purpose, somewhat in the same manner as the front-end or editorial systems previously discussed do. The two applications are certainly not mutually exclusive, but at this point in the evolution of office technology word processing equipment is usually less sophisticated than the systems we have so far described. It usually does not offer directories and queues or control of copy flow. It is more likely to consist of stand-alone units or small cluster systems.

Originally, word processors were automated typewriters. Keystrokes were captured on paper tape or magnetic cartridges or cassettes. The material could be played back, the process interrupted, new material added, and a new version stored on tape. Hence a device for reading from tape and for writing to tape was required. To facilitate the retyping and correction procedure it was (and is) possible to instruct the typewriter "controller"—often hard-wired and with limited intelligence—to search for certain "file marks," perhaps

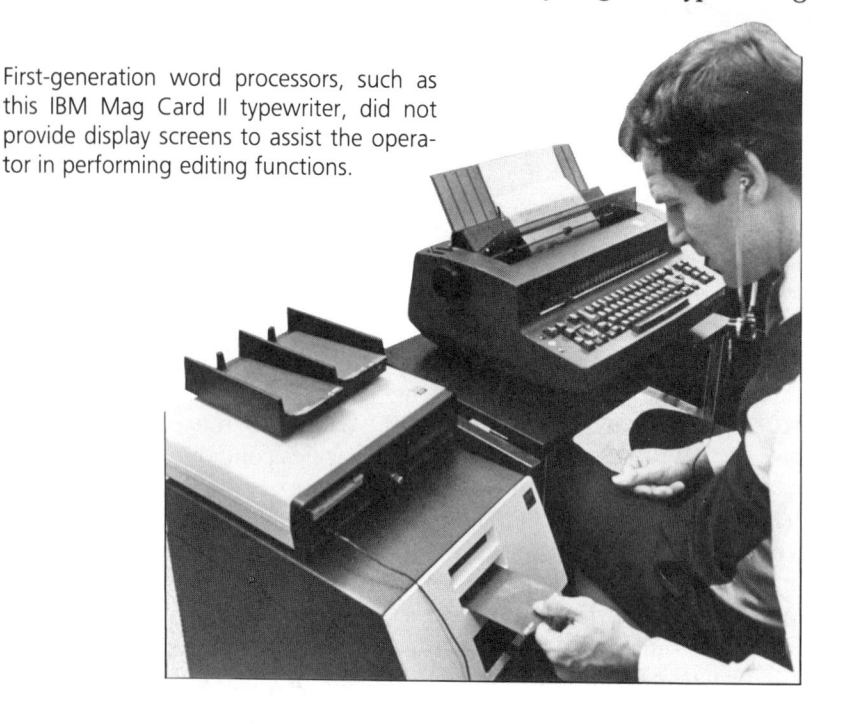

First-generation word processors, such as this IBM Mag Card II typewriter, did not provide display screens to assist the operator in performing editing functions.

performing straight copying to that point, and then permitting the operator to proceed on a line-by-line, word-by-word, or character-by-character basis until the point had been reached where a change was desired. Sometimes the new version was written back over the old, or more usually onto a new tape, cartridge or magnetic card. There were often stringent limitations as to the amount of new material which could be inserted, depending upon how the buffer within the typewriter was formatted. More recent versions provided a larger buffer within which material could be stored, and then written out, as to a mag card, but not to exceed the contents of the data which may be stored on such a card.

Such devices were clearly improvements which offered economies within the office environment, but they were generally less powerful than the cursor editing available on a VDT screen. More recent developments have substituted the VDT and keyboard for the conventional typewriter, and a Qume or Diablo daisy wheel printer for the typing element itself. Thus the printing function becomes output while input and editing are performed on the VDT.

Floppy disks were added to such systems to provide more interim storage, and shared-intelligence systems were also developed providing directories to help locate tracks on the floppy or small hard disk where text may be stored. Shared-logic systems have come into being, with several users having the ability to access the same programs and editing logic. For offices needing more than one or two individual stations, such shared-logic systems are often less expensive and more powerful. The systems which evolved began to look more and more like the front-end or editorial systems we have found to be so popular within the graphic arts industry. Word processing vendors began to offer directories, multitasking and queuing functions, messaging, electronic mail, and many other features which resemble the capabilities of editorial systems. They have moved into system-design architectures which are programmable, and they offer "sort" routines and other functions (such as column totaling or subtracting values of one column from those of another, to create a third set of figures, and even converting those into percentages). Thus word processors have become more powerful and more generalized tools which have tended to revolutionize many office procedures.

Then in the late 1970s and early 1980s personal computers began to appear, largely for home and hobby use. They, too, offered word processing packages, although these were often quite primitive compared to those available on systems intended for office use.

Gradually, however, the two products began to look more and more alike. Manufacturers of word processing equipment made it possible for their terminals to run some of the very useful programs that had been developed for personal computers—especially spreadsheets—and to handle more of the telecommunicating functions that could be added onto home computers. Home computers were moved into the office environment, and their word processing capabilities grew more sophisticated. Then it became possible to link the professional models of these home computers into a network, in order to share disks and output printers, and it was even more difficult to differentiate office systems from personal computers. Many new functions were conceived as value-added components, such as the ability to create and maintain appointment calendars and to use these to propose dates for conferences, thus analyzing the work schedules of those who might be involved. Similarly, by appropriate telephone links, calls could be placed automatically, redialed when lines were busy, and records could be kept of the cost of such calls for billing purposes. More versatility has been added to the functionality of both word processors and personal or professional computers, and we are obviously only beginning to appreciate the possibilities these ever-more-powerful and imaginatively programmed devices offer.

Just as home computers posed a threat to the word processing manufacturers, so such a challenge was issued to the lords who held sovereignty over the mainframe computers in the kingdom of "DP" (data processing). But gradually the data processing departments of private firms as well as those in the public sector began to realize some sort of accommodation was essential. As one astute observer commented:

> Much of the responsibility for developing computerized applications in business is moving away from centralized data processing departments down to the end user. As we see it, a large factor in this movement results from the use of professional computers to satisfy the so-called invisible demand for computing services. This large but diffuse demand is the sum of all applications not being developed by information systems departments. Such applications are non-recurring and time-intensive in nature. Most often they are useful only to a single person.

> A company's visible demand for software is simply its known demand. It's the collection of computer projects that are relatively large and sufficiently well understood to be organized into formal requests. That's why they are known: the projects are in the formal structure of the company. Most important, the projects are not critically time intensive. The known demand can be considered the "wholesale" component of total computer needs. Many companies still insist that the formal visible demand is the total of all their computer service needs. But the invisible demand—or "retail" component—cannot be ignored.
>
> Recent studies by the Center for Information Systems Research at MIT, Cambridge, Ma., suggests that in a typical large company the invisible demand is five times the size of the known demand, and the known demand itself is backlogged two to three years. Small wonder the professional computer is selling so well in large companies! And, we believe, the market is just starting to take off everywhere.
>
> For now and the foreseeable future, microelectronic technology favors development of desktop systems. The market pull of the invisible demand and the technical push of the professional desktop computer are unstoppable. But large systems will not go away. Actually, they will grow in importance. The micros and large systems will reach a complementary partnership providing a full range of wholesale and retail services in which each finds a niche based on inherent capabilities.[1]

This partnership became respectable when IBM announced its Personal Computer in July 1981.

> With IBM waving the white flag, an awkward peace has been made between today's PC users and DP management. Many of the key issues still haven't been solved: What about data security? How much is it going to cost to network these PC's together? How do we ensure compatibility? How do we make sure PC's aren't being wasted? What applications belong on PC's and which ones should stay on the mainframe? What about training? Who's responsible for technical support? What about software guidelines? Which machines should we buy? Lots of questions plague the corporate planners. The difference is that now PC's have become a corporate issue. Personal computing in the office has become a recognized phenomenon. It is now a company-wide issue. In fact, it is now a country-wide issue.[2]

So far as typesetting applications are concerned, attention soon began to focus on the problem of converting textual data files which were created on word processors or personal computers so that they could be processed for typesetting. Later on, typesetting programs began to be introduced which could be run on personal computers or on word processing devices. Personal computers were upgraded to become "professional" in nature.

The popularity of word processing applications has clearly given rise to a clearer understanding of what might be termed "composition" requirements—whether they have to do with the making of line-ending decisions or pagination. Many of the same issues present themselves in the word processing environment, and before

---

1. Column by Fritz R. S. Dressler in *The Seybold Report on Professional Computing*, Vol. 1, No. 6, p. 20.

2. This quotation from *The Seybold Report on Professional Computing*, Vol. 2, No. 1, pp. 4-5, has been included so that the reader will capture some of the flavor of the times.

Composition and Word Processing 311

proceeding to a discussion of ways in which word processing output may be converted into files to be processed by typesetting programs, it will perhaps be of some interest to look at the ways in which word processing software wrestles with the very same issues we have been discussing throughout this book.

Text formatting by word processors

MODERN WORD PROCESSORS have separated the output function of creating hard copy via some sort of printing device, from the input function of keystroking, and from the editing function of making insertions, deletions and moving text from one place to another. In many cases the word processing program assumes the existence of a particular output device (most often a Qume or Diablo daisy wheel printer), but this is no longer the case when one runs such programs on personal computers. A much wider range of output devices is available, with considerable variations in quality of output and product price. In either event, the word processing program has to know the line length limitations of the output device, whether or not it can change its "pitch"—as from ten to twelve characters per inch (or even, in some cases, fifteen), and how the output printer expects to receive signals commanding it to advance from one line to the next, to move the paper advance mechanism in order to print subscripted or superscripted characters, to underline, to embolden, or to create "shadow" characters.

Some such printers even permit the user to change sizes and styles of type (within relatively narrow limits), altering the distance between typed lines, and even laying down characters to proportionally adjusted widths. Moreover, many of these programs now offer the opportunity to compose justified lines, although few of them have as yet added automatic hyphenation to the bag of tricks.

Thus the front end—in this case the word processing device with its customized hardware and software—does indeed keep track of the number of characters which will fit on a line, how to end the line, to arrange type into tabular formats, to generate indents, to handle footnotes, to terminate pages and to generate running heads and folios. In many cases these problems have been solved without the benefit of prior knowledge of ways in which they had been addressed by programmers who were involved with typesetting. Yet the solutions have been quite similar, although quite a bit more primitive, in the word processing environment.

In general, two types of solutions seem to have emerged. In one instance all of the necessary formatting—both of line- and page-endings—is done as part of an output routine. The user is satisfied that his text is correct. He then inserts the various formatting commands, and the program drives the output printer—presenting the user with composed pages. If line and page endings are not satisfactory, the user has no other option than to go back to the text file (which served as input to the output driver program) and to make such modifications as he or she can to correct problem conditions.

Increasingly, word processing users have wanted the ability to see on the screen precisely what they "are going to get"—both with respect to line endings and page endings. They also would like to be able to see the entire page on the face of the screen, and not just a portion of it.

Various solutions have evolved. There is, for example, the softcopy approach which enables the user to review a paginated version on the screen, even though it is necessary to call up the original file to make adjustments or corrections. And there is also the more interactive approach, whereby each line ending is terminated at the time of input precisely as it will appear in print, and if modifications are made to the text, the lines and characters must be recounted and readjusted by the program—obviously involving quite a bit more in terms of real-time computation. Even in such cases, the treatment of footnotes introduces a complication, and in some cases they are not shown in position at the bottom of the page, although they will appear on the screen as close as possible to the relevant call-out reference. (They may be moved to the bottom of the page only at time of output.)

Out of increasing familiarity with these kinds of problems, the industry generally has now been obliged to come to grips with some of the intricacies of the composition process and has no doubt acquired some greater appreciation not only of the complexity of its tasks but also of the aesthetic values of its solutions.

However, even in those instances in which attractively paginated output may be produced on word processing equipment and personal or professional computers, the need still arises to be able to move that same file to another computer or system which will reformat it for final output of graphic arts quality by a phototypesetting device (or some other of the various image engines now emerging, which will be discussed in Chapters 21 and 23).

Interfacing to the composition system

THREE PRINCIPAL PROBLEMS present themselves when it comes to the interfacing of word processors to typesetting systems. One is a hardware problem of putting a device onto the typesetter or computer system which is able to read the word processing output—assuming that we are only interested in going one way—that is, from the word processor or personal computer to the typesetting system. Or, conversely, the problem could be resolved by putting a device onto the word processor to enable it to convert data into a physical format intelligible to the typesetting system.

The second problem is to translate data into a coding system or language which the typesetter expects.

The third problem is to incorporate into the translated data stream the typesetting commands which the typesetting system requires for it to do its own processing.

These problems are all interrelated. For example, many word processors do not record their characters as six-, seven- or eight-level bytes written in a "parallel" fashion onto magnetic tape or disk. They are likely to record these codes serially. For example, if the word processor used a Philips-type cassette such as you would find on the small audio tape recorders (although this signal is digital rather than analog), the coding will be "strung out" serially, and there will be extra bits written (sometimes) to signal the beginning or end of a particular character. There may also be some parity checking information. The writing process, moreover, will often not take place "incrementally"—that is, character by character, but it may take place by writing out a block of data at one time, with a gap between one block and the next, and so it is necessary for the interface translator to know how the bit stream is blocked.

Even if floppy disk technology is used rather than cassette, the interfacing problems persist. Floppies differ according to manufacturer. There are single-density, double-density, single-sided, two-sided, hard- and soft-sectored, and mini-floppies. Diskettes even from a given manufacturer may be encoded, blocked and formatted differently by the word processing vendor or by the typesetting system vendor.

It may not be too difficult to solve the problem of data transfer from a particular word processor to a particular typesetting system, although this would require the assistance of a hardware expert to accomplish it. But this does not afford a general solution. Output from other word processors could not be accepted by the typesetter and the word processor user would not be able to send data to other typesetters. Consequently, the more common approach is to try to connect the two devices together by means of telecommunications. This means that the word processor must contain a telecommunications capability, as must the typesetting system. This solution is more and more common, but there are still some compatibility issues to be resolved to be certain that both sender and receiver are able to transmit data (reaching agreement on such matters as baud rate, parity checking, and other protocol conventions).

Once this has been accomplished there is still the problem of translation. Even if it is agreed that the information is to be exchanged as seven-level ASCII characters there is still a great deal of interpretation to be done. Word processors generally put out one or two codes at the end of each line. These codes need to be stripped out if line endings are to differ (as they surely must), and in their place other codes (perhaps only an interword space) need to be inserted. But how can one distinguish between those situations where such a space is to be generated and those where it is not to be? Does the word processing program put out a special code to signal the end of a paragraph or the beginning of a new paragraph? Does the program write out its data in fixed blocks (*e.g.*, 80 characters) stuffing all lines that are not completely filled by meaningful characters with blanks? Does the word processor arbitrarily combine strings of data into blocks of 256 characters, including special signals at the beginning and ending of each such block? A study of these peculiarities will reveal that each word processor requires its own unique codes which must somehow be discovered and eliminated from the text stream since they convey no meaning to another program. On the other hand, the other program—for composition formatting—requires its own codes and signals which must somehow be introduced.

Consider, for example, the problem of text which the word processor has centered within a line. Some such devices use a centering code (which can be converted to a quad center code on a typesetter), but it may occur at the beginning of the line of text on the word processor and have to be moved to the end of the line during conversion. Other word processors merely space over to a point which causes the text to be centered, thus outputting a string of spaces which may be of no use to the typesetter. Some IBM word processors center text by counting over to the middle of a line, then inserting a backspace for every two characters of text, thus resulting in a centered line, but with a lot of backspace codes as well.

Different codes may be used to represent ordinary word spaces, underlined word spaces, spaces which fill to margins, spaces used in tab columns, and spaces used to justify a line. Subscript and superscript characters are handled in different ways by different word processors: some move the paper up or down for a single character only, while others move it up or down and leave it there until another command moves it again.

Text which is underscored may be represented by codes which first print a character, then backspace once, and underscore the character before moving on to the next one. These machines are actually using three codes to describe each underscored character which might eventually need to be reduced (for the typesetting program) to a single character, perhaps in an italic font. Another way of underscoring is used by IBM with its Displaywriter, which waits until it finishes a word and then puts out a signal which causes the device to back up and underscore the entire word. Still other programs do the same thing on a line-by-line basis.

Such formatting problems are generally tackled through the use of global search and replace operations, using string-for-string as well as character-for-character translations. (In a character-for-character translation, one character read from the source is translated into another character on the output end. Similarly, in string-for-string translations, a specified string of characters located in the original file is replaced by another string of characters, not necessarily of the same length, when output.) Some of these problems of translation are similar to those encountered in the OCR scanning of manuscripts,[1] and some of the lessons learned in developing translation programs for that application are relevant here.

There are also problems of character repertoire: how to access and typeset characters that could not be created by the word processor with its more limited symbol set. And obviously there are problems in signaling the use of different sizes and faces of type.

Where a proper, ongoing relationship is established between those who create the initial manuscripts and those who accept the input for typesetting, many—if indeed not most—of these problems

---

1. See pp. 245-246.

Composition and Word Processing

can be resolved. It becomes possible for the word processor to use emboldened characters to signal a particular type face, underlined to signal yet a second, underlined and emboldened to signal a third. Certain letter combinations (mu, delta, sigma, pi) could be translated into Greek characters. Relatively unobtrusive coding ($H1 for first-level head letters) may be incorporated into the manuscript at the time it is initially input on the word processor. Generally, however, other codes need to be added by an editing process after the text has been converted into a composition input text stream.

To facilitate the transfer of information for purposes of typesetting, a great deal of interest has focused recently upon generic coding, which involves the use in initial manuscripts of identifiers which can assist not only in the composition process, but which are also relevant for purposes of indexing and abstracting. To some extent flags signaling typesetting codes can be derived from the structure of the document itself.

An alternative to the use of telecommunications is the possibility of purchasing a black box which has been programmed to read various kinds of floppy disks, perhaps writing a different format of output onto another floppy disk which can in turn be read by the typesetting system (or piping such input directly on line to the typesetting system). Such boxes also contain quite sophisticated software to handle a number of the translation problems we have been describing.

Black boxes are rarely black anymore, but they still serve as interfaces between two different devices. One of the oldest and most prolific is the Shaffstall Media-Com, shown here. It originally served mainly as a telecommunications device, receiving data from one system and sending it on line to another. But it later became one of the dominant "media conversion" devices on the market, capable of reading 8" or 5¼" floppy disks and converting the data to the correct format and coding for another device, or even writing a floppy disk which could be inserted into the second device and used as if it had been created on that device. Here we see the interface box with its two floppy disk drives, as well as the terminal which serves as a "user interface" for issuing commands and selecting items from menus.

```
       aaa¹          $25.33           123.123            This is running
       H₂O           $370.80            3.987            text to be
       e=mc²         $12.43           2540.9             justified in the
                                                         fourth column

     aaa<HSU>1<HSD><DTB>$25.33<DTB>123.123<TAB>This is running <RLB>
     H<HSD>2<HSU>0<DTB>$370.80<DTB>3.987<TAB>text to be <RLB>
     e=mc<HSU>2<HSD><DTB>$12.43<DTB>2540.9<SIN>justified in the
     fourth column<RLB>
```

Converting data from a word processor to a typesetter can be a complicated procedure. Here we see part of what an Antares conversion device can do. Above is a sample tabular job printed out on a word processor. Next is what the Antares device saw when it read that job on a Wang disk, inserting Antares codes where the Wang disk specified such functions as "half space up" ("HSU") and "half space down" ("HSD") and to cause a word processing printer to print a superscript or subscript character. ("DTB" indicates a decimal tab which will cause the decimal points to line up when the job is output.) The last sample shows how Antares automatically translates the same job into Penta codes so that it can actually be output by the Penta system without requiring an operator to insert the codes needed by the typesetting system.

```
[ctXX]
[J9][cmaaa[sv1,5s][vd0,2,1][cb-1v]1[sv1,5s][vd0,2,1][cb1v][cm$25.33[cm123.123[cmThis
is running[cm
[J9][cmH[sv1,5s][vd0,2,1][cb1v]2[sv1,5s][vd0,2,1][cb-1v]0[cm$370.80[cm3.987[cmtext
to be[cm
[J9][cme=mc[sv1,5s][vd0,2,1][cb-1v]2[sv1,5s][vd0,2,1][cb1v][cm$12.43[cm2540.9[ipX]justifi
in the[cm
```

For the future, we look for the evolution of better and more powerful word processing devices which offer more editing power—similar, in other words, to the better devices now available for use with graphic arts. Ultimately, we look for a complete fusion of the two technologies. This trend has, indeed, already begun. And the printout techniques which are being used threaten to supplant typesetting in certain markets or applications. High quality, proportionally spaced printout devices are available, such as the Xerox 9700, 5700 and 2700, the IBM 6670 and the Canon LP-10,[1] using electrostatic or ink-jet imaging.

---

1. See Chapter 23.

20

Data Base Typesetting

OF COURSE any form of computer manipulation for typesetting, such as hyphenation and justification, is a form of data processing, but in the typesetting field a distinction is generally drawn between typesetting per se and the typesetting of data base material—sometimes referred to as *textual data bases*.

However, it is not always easy to determine whether a file which is created initially for typesetting purposes may not also constitute a data base. For example, one might suppose that the most ephemeral data of all would be that created for the publication of a daily newspaper, and yet there is a great deal of interest in preserving these files so that they can be converted into a kind of electronic library. Indeed, such electronic libraries exist and are gaining in popularity. An appropriate version of each story which appeared in the paper (the latest or the most complete account of the event) is selected by the newspaper librarians, the story may be enhanced by the addition of certain keywords or subject headings such as *U.S. Government* or *Economy* or *Nuclear Energy*, and then the file is transferred to a large mainframe computer data base, an inverted file structure is created, and free text searches can then be conducted not only by reporters and editors researching background information, but by remote terminals on the part of the public generally. Such a data base is potentially an important source of revenue for the newspaper and it can also eliminate the cost of maintaining large files of clippings and back issues and all of the work that such an effort entails.

The possibility of creating such data bases exists because text has been made machine-readable for the purpose of typesetting. Since it is machine-readable it can be stored and searched and used in a variety of ways. For example, newsletters produced by the company founded by this author are regularly cleaned-up by a computer program (and some manual assistance) and then transmitted to *NewsNet*, an on-line data base service. Those who are researching information in the various fields of our special interests (publishing systems, office systems and professional computing) can easily gain access to these files by paying only for "connect time," which includes a return to the computer data base service or publisher, and the data base provider.

Publishers are following very carefully the entire subject of "alternative publishing" opportunities. Secondary publishing activities do indeed exist whereby such on-line data bases serve, in a sense, as reference libraries. But the possibility also exists that some information which is now prepared primarily for print may never in fact be printed in the conventional sense (although the data base user may command his remote printer to output whatever information he has retrieved on a particular subject).

There are areas where the actual typesetting and printing of a document serves mainly as a means of affording recognition to the author and to the status of the document (*i.e.*, that it deserved publication), whereas the primary value of the publication lies in the fact that it exists within a data base where it may be retrieved for "SDI" purposes. SDI means the Selected Dissemination of Information. This is a service provided by some information publishers which alerts its members or subscribers to the fact that certain literature has been published (or stored in a data bank) which meets the individual reader's "profile of interests." Consequently, a scientist whose specialty consists, perhaps, of molecular biology, can rest assured that all papers which bear upon his field (whether published in certain respected journals or elsewhere) will be brought to his attention, and he will be able to access them (at a cost) but relatively painlessly the instant he is so notified. This can save him a tremendous amount of wasted effort in monitoring vast quantities of published material, and it can perhaps also assure him that he will not miss some important development or contribution.[1]

It appears that there is a data base potential for virtually every typeset document, and in some instances the potential exists not only because of its value for purposes of "alternative publishing"—that is, nonprint use—but also for typographic presentation in alternative formats.

For example, when the author first became involved in computer typesetting in 1963, he decided to have his keyboarders input the King James version of the Bible when there was no other work to be done. The decision was made to prepare the text in the most complete fashion possible—with pronunciation features, two levels of footnotes, special flagging of verses and chapters, editorially generated chapter titles (not part of the Bible as such), and special conventions to flag the words spoken by Jesus. All proper names were also identified so that they could be extracted and sorted to assure correct spelling, hyphenation, and pronunciation breaks and features, and then these names, inclusive of these identifiers, were "put back into the file." We had ascertained that if a Bible publisher wished to prepare a new printing he required several years and paid a cost of more than $50,000 for the setting. We were able to offer delivery in less than a month, for a fraction of the cost, of a Bible set in virtually any typeface and format the publisher desired. This soon became one of the most important sources of revenue for the company.

While the Bible is never updated (although many new translations are available), text books in many fields require frequent updating. In years past such books were revised infrequently, and such revisions were as minimal as possible if the hot metal type was in fact kept standing at all. (And the cost of storing standing type was a significant consideration in its own right.) Now it is possible to store the contents of such a text on magnetic tape, load it back onto the

---

1. In some cases involving technical material, techniques do not yet exist to retrieve scientific data meaningfully via video terminals or computer printouts because of the limitations of character repertoire and problems associated with the display of multi-level mathematical expressions and tabular material. Nevertheless abstracts of such articles can be provided.

Data Base Typesetting

typesetting or front-end editorial system, and make minor or major changes quite quickly and relatively inexpensively. This tends, one supposes, to keep the contents of such books more current and it is obviously less costly to produce new revised editions than was formerly the case.

The typesetting service bureau

WHEN COMPUTERIZED photocomposition technology was first developed it was not specifically conceived of in relation to the value of creating textual data bases. On the other hand, one of the compelling motivations for the invention of the early third-generation high-speed typesetters was to be able to typeset material which was already in machine-readable format. For example, the original Linotron 1010 was built by Mergenthaler in fulfillment of a contract with the U.S. Government Printing Office so that the latter could "dump" computer data files to a photocomposition device and thus significantly reduce the amount of paper required for the printing of documents then being reproduced by using computer printouts as camera copy for offset printing.[1] Similarly the Photon ZIP or 900 was developed in response to a similar need from the National Library of Medicine, and all of the major telephone subsidiaries needed a quicker and better way to typeset subscriber directories from information which was already stored in computer data files.

In fact, when computer typesetting first came into existence it soon became evident that the equipment was too expensive to be used for the ordinary one-time typesetting of books, newspapers and magazines.

Over the years, as the cost of computers and photocomposition device reduced steadily, computer programs became more effective and acceptance more widespread. The emphasis has shifted, and one-time typesetting by these techniques is of course cost-effective. Computerized composition has indeed become virtually the only kind of composition that is used, and there is an appropriate system for virtually any kind of typesetting requirement.

But those who were early in the game of computer typesetting soon found that they needed not only programs for typesetting and pagination, but programs for the creation of data bases, and programs for the conversion of computer data into input files for typesetting purposes.

In other words, various kinds of applications emerged, and a careful identification of these situations became necessary.

General categories of activities

THE LISTING below may serve to indicate the variety of ways in which typesetting and data processing activities can become intertwined:

1. *The typesetting company merely provides the output device, accepting input from his customer's computer.* This implies the customer has

1. Computer printouts use nonproportional characters. The use of proportional type saves approximately 40% in terms of space and pages, assuming the same-sized image. A 40% savings in printing plates, paper, handling, storage costs and mailing may easily justify the cost of "going to type"—especially if this can be done without having to rekey the data. Savings realized by the installation of the Linotron 1010 were sufficient to pay for this expensive equipment in a few years' time.

the programs and the capability to provide output in a form which can be accepted directly by the photo unit. The ones who have developed this capability are customers whose volume is so substantial, and where the economy of this method is so great, that they have taken the time and trouble to create the special-purpose software which their jobs require. The customer would have to know what code structure a particular typetting device requires, what commands it needs to make it go through its paces, what fonts and characters are available, and the set widths of those fonts. The customer might also have to write his own "h&j" program, and even a page make-up program suitable to handle his needs. In some cases this might be relatively easy. If the data base consisted of a telephone directory or an airline guide it might be possible to avoid some of the major composition programming challenges.

2. *The typesetting company accepts as input a tape or data stream formatted for the line printer, and processes it through a special program which prepares a tape for his output device.* In this instance the customer does not need to know fonts and width values, nor must he have his own composition program. The typesetting company must have the capability of converting this tape into a format which is acceptable as input into some special-purpose streamlined composition program. The probability is that new end-of-line decisions and end-of-page decisions must be made.

3. *The typesetting company accepts from his customer as input a tape or data stream containing data in the proper sequence, with the necessary generalized codes embedded at appropriate places in the text stream. This input is then reformatted, translated or interpreted, and processed through the vendor's composition program.* This implies that a special pre-processor composition program will need to be written or customized for this particular application. Thereafter the composition program will take over.

4. *The typesetting company accepts as input a tape or data stream which contains only the data to be typeset, but which requires all codes to be inserted by a program. The vendor prepares this program and processes the input through his composition system.* This implies more effort to recognize the places where special typesetting codes need to be inserted, since there are no special flags provided.

5. *The same as the previous point except that the typesetting vendor develops a special-purpose composition program which can be cost-justified due to the size of the job or its repetitive nature.* This special program will run more economically than the use of his own more generalized composition software.

6. *The input supplied to the typesetting company contains irrelevant information. The company must devise a program which pulls off only the data required, and then processes it in points four or five above.*

7. *The same as point six except that the typesetting company's program must also be capable of resequencing the data selected from the supplied input.*

8. *The typesetting company creates the original input for typesetting, but pulls from this file a subset of data to be returned to the customer for use by*

Data Base Typesetting

the latter's computer in computer manipulations other than typesetting.
9. The typesetting company creates the original file for typesetting and for other purposes. It is a structured file, which permits him to perform such operations as extraction, explosion, sorting, abridging, abstracting, and indexing.
10. The file created by the typesetting company is heavily encoded, but it is not structured. It consists merely of a running stream of text. Nevertheless, the company is able to extract certain data from the file, manipulate it, and either feed the results back into the composition program or generate other non-typesetting by-products, such as mailing lists or computer printouts. By means of post-processing routines the typesetting company in effect becomes the customer's computer center for all purposes related to the data base which has been created for the customer.

Obviously this listing is only illustrative and there are many combinations and permutations of the points enumerated. For example, from a text stream the typesetting company may be able to generate an index for an unabridged edition. It may then create an abridged version and generate an index from this. Or it may create an index each month from a certain publication that is typeset, and then cumulate that index quarterly, annually, *etc.* It may even cumulate the articles in the publication, especially if they are brief abstracts which are most conveniently gathered together in a more logical fashion than the manner in which they first appeared.

Moreover, in all of the examples listed above (except the last two) we have assumed that when data is supplied to the typesetting company it will first have been processed by another computer. It is entirely possible, on the other hand, that the typesetting company is provided with the initial input which may or may not have served some other purpose. For example, the customer may have a price list which has been maintained on punched cards or the customer has keyed his data directly onto a magnetic medium by some sort of key-to-tape device or word processor, but there has been no data manipulation such as would be performed by a prior computer program.

Characteristics of data processing activity

THE SINGLE MOST relevant aspect of conventional data processing (as opposed to text processing) is the existence of *structure* to the data. In other words, the information is *fielded*, and the usual arrangement is for the data to be structured in *fixed fields*. In the ensuing discussion we shall assume that the reader knows nothing about data processing. The best way to begin his education is to consider the punched or Hollerith card, since historically this has been the way most structured data (and some unstructured input as well) comes into being in the data processing world. The usual punched card contains 80 columns. These columns may be arbitrarily divided into fields. In each column one character may be written. Twelve positions are available in each vertical column. The 10 bottom rows represent the numbers 0-9. One punched hole per column is thus used to indicate figures. When a

1. See illustrations on p. 324.

hole is also punched in one of the top two rows (or in the zero row), and also in one of the rows 1-9, a non-numeric character is indicated.

Two significant factors emerge. One is that the character repertoire of conventional data processing, especially from punched card input, is extremely limited. The other is that the position of the data in fixed fields across the card enables the program (either the wired circuit board of the ancient unit-record equipment or the software of the computer) to identify each element.

A case study

LET US SUPPOSE, for example, that we wish to prepare a listing for a college alumni register, and we wish to present the following information: name, address, class, and department of specialization. We want to be able to produce one listing in alphabetical order irrespective of class and department. Another listing is desired alphabetically by year of graduation. A geographic listing is also sought, again arranged alphabetically, but by city and by state. Finally, a listing by department of specialization, irrespective of geographical considerations, may be useful. For some listings only the name and class will appear (not the individual's address).

We will keep our example simple by presuming a male college (if one exists anymore), so that women's married names (if such exist) do not complicate the picture (since this would imply a great deal of cross-referencing or duplicate listings), and we will not differentiate between the dropouts (who were nevertheless enrolled in the Class of '74) and those who graduated. Let's even forget about those who repeated a year or came back later to finish their education. But these and other problems cannot in fact be disregarded, and often are sufficient to make the system as initially conceived worthless.

Since we are going to sort on names, we must consider how this is done. We must have a field designated for the last name, and another for the first and second names. (If there are "Jr.'s" or a presumptuous "III," this will become part of the given name rather than of the surname.)

How long should the field be for the last name? If it is not long enough, it would be necessary to "truncate" someone's name, and if the list is ever published or used for a mailing list, this would alienate him and lose his contribution to the alumni fund.

If we already had all the names on a computer we could search for the longest name. But we are just starting to create the file. So we ask around and try to learn what others have done. We also scan the printed lists available to us. Finally we determine that the longest name of a graduate is Allenby-Whittall (and now we know that we need a hyphen in our character repertoire and perhaps in our sort routine.) Hence we decide to allocate 18 columns for the last name field. Although we keypunch only the characters required, from left to right, our program will fill up the remainder of the field with "trailing zeroes" in order to create a uniform sort field, which would look as follows:

```
                    AARON0000000000000
                    AARON0000000000000
                    ABBOTT000000000000
                    ALLENBY—WHITTALL00
                    BEAUCHAMP000000000
```

and so forth.

We decide, then, to allocate twelve columns for the rest of the name. Hence the first name will begin in the nineteenth column:

```
                    AARON0000000000000JONATHAN R00
                    AARON0000000000000LEONARD S JR
                    ABBOTT000000000000ARTHUR W III
                    ALLENBY-WHITTALL00PERCIVAL0000
                    BEAUCHAMP000000000BRODERICK L0
```

Now, turning to the problem of addresses, we visualize that we will want to arrange our information by state and city. What do we do about suburbs? Should Shaker Heights be listed as a part of Cleveland? Perhaps we are better off sorting by zip code, and then playing the file against a zip code identification file supplied by the government. But let us ignore this possibility and try to solve the problem ourselves. We shall take the lazy way out and sequence the geographic file by state and then town, without making any effort to group adjacent towns. Hence we field the address portion of the entry as follows:

> House number and street
> Town
> State
> Zip Code

Let us consider the problem of state first: the easiest way to represent the state is by a two digit alpha field: *MA* for Massachusetts, *CA* for California, *NJ* for New Jersey, *etc.* However, if we are going to sort on these abbreviations we will get the states out of order. *NC*, for North Carolina, will sort ahead of *NJ* for New Jersey. Or, we could number the states sequentially. If the file is only to be used for typesetting, these numbers could be stored in a table lookup and the name of the state could be generated. We can do the same thing for the computer printout run for mailing labels. It is only if we want a hard copy print that the initials or abbreviations need to be used. On the other hand, it is easier to use to alpha abbreviations than to have the input operator perform a look-up operation in order to assign state code numbers. So we settle for a two-digit alpha representation and we assign to our computer program the task of sorting these in proper order at a later stage of the game.

So far as town or city goes, we can truncate the town if we like, in case it is too long, and again use a computer program to genrate the full and complete name, if this is desirable for reasons of clarity or taste. It might reduce keyboarding if we told the operator to input only the consonants and use a table lookup for all names. On the other hand, it might result in creating some redundancies and ambiguities. Moreover, a listing of many hundreds of towns would be necessary to interpret the possible wide variety of mnemonics. So we conclude that we had better keyboard the town's entire name to

The IBM or Hollerith card is still widely used for data entry purposes. In its current version it usually contains 80 columns with 12 positions available in each vertical column. These cards are prepared by key punch operators.

Data Base Typesetting

the extent that it can be represented by 15 columns. We tell the keypunch operator that if it cannot be so represented, to truncate at 15 and write down these names so we can expand them in our computer program. This will reduce appreciably the number of exceptions we shall have to contend with. We do not anticipate having to do anything special with the house number and street field other than to print or typeset it, but we must allow room for it.

Three other fields remain. We must designate the graduating class for each person listed, and we can do this by two numbers, such as 60. (We can assume that all numbers referring to years yet to come actually represent those years in the preceding century, such as 1895.) The next field will indicate the major subject area field of the alumnus. One digit will suffice since we are pressed for space and we can indicate 36 different possibilities by using a letter or a number in this column. Finally, we wish to indicate whether the degree conferred is an A.B., a B.S., or perhaps a Ph.D., D.Litt., or M.D. Each degree can be given a number, and *1* may stand for the A.B.

By careful planning we have just reached the allowable 80 columns, and we can avoid the necessity of having to overflow onto a second card. Here are the allocations:

```
1-18    last name
19-30   first name
31-54   street address
55-69   city
70-71   state
72-76   zip code
77-78   class
79      field of specialization
80      degree
```

It will now be possible for the punched card itself to serve as input to a print format program which would generate labels. Additional programs can provide geographic and class listings, or could produce a sort by kind of degree or major subject area.

The master file could be kept on punched cards, and when addresses are changed the cards can be physically removed and new ones put into place. Or, the file can be maintained on magnetic tape or disk, in which case a file update program will need to be written or adapted. Our typical entry will read as follows:

```
AARON000000000000000JONATHAN R00APTC 1769
MACARTHUR AVWINSTON SALEM000NC6031075Z1
```

Going into type

IN ORDER TO TYPESET this file and to produce an alumni directory from these punched cards or from a tape image of the cards, it will first be necessary to create a master list in the alphabetic sequence in which the file is maintained. The program would work something like this:

1. Read in a dummy entry which will set up the job, defining the line length and giving the program other data it may require.
2. Read in the first regular entry and store it in memory.

3. Take the first field and move it to a new location, dropping the trailing zeros and inserting in front of it a flag which will subsequently identify the type face. Follow the field with a comma.
4. Read in the second field, dropping trailing zeros. Insert another typographic flag if the type face is to be different. Follow the field with a period.
5. Next go to positions 77 and 78. Put in a flag to indicate the desired type face, then an apostrophe (as in '90) and follow the two digits with a comma.
6. Go to position 79. Do a compare or table lookup which indicates that because the value in this column is 3 the letters *Econ* should be substituted with a flag to designate italic.
7. From column 80, the number *1* will be translated into A.B. followed by a quad left.
8. Then go back to position 31 and pick up the string from 31 to 54, dropping any trailing zeros and preceding the entry by an em space, forcing the address to indent. A typographic flag may also be added. Note there is no punctuation in this field. We may wish to interrogate this field for certain conditions. We will return to this point later.
9. Follow directly with the name of the city, beginning with position 55. We may require a routine to check first to see if there are any trailing zeros in the field. If not, the name may have been truncated. The name would then have to be compared against a list of truncations, and, if found, the full string of characters would be picked up. Preceding the city name would be a flag for the desired type face, if different. A comma is added following the end of the field.
10. Proceed to columns 70 and 71. Let's make it easy and assume we are merely going to pick up the two letters we find there. We decide that we will not try to insert punctuation between the N and the C in NC for North Carolina lest we have the problem of recognizing the difference in treatment for CA in California. So all we do is to add a comma after the two letters and then follow with field 72-76, where we pick up the zip code and end with a quad left. Then we insert a blank line before going to the next entry.
11. We write this information to magnetic tape or disk, and it is now, hopefully, in the format required to enter our composition program. Perhaps we have also inserted other flags to indicate the beginning and ending of an entry so that our pagination program will not break entries when it divides the material into columns and pages.

Although this description seems complicated, the task has been a relatively simple one. Since we also are required to produce a listing by state and town, we might have considered creating the information we needed for this purpose at the same time that we prepared the composition input tape for our main listing.

Returning to the initial file we recognize that we must create a sort field. We wish to sort by state and then town. We know that the number of states (fortunately there are no foreign countries) is less than 99. We call in the state field and assign a number. A translate table tells us that CA is California, and that California is the fifth state in the alphabetic sequence. And so we write out *05*. We follow this with the name of the town, allowing fifteen places, and then pick up the last name of the alumnus since we also wish to sort alphabetically by last name where there are several persons residing in one city. We must also consider the possibility that two persons with the same last name may live in the same town, and thus we need to pick up the first name of the alumnus as well. Now we have created a sort field as follows:

05WHITTIER0000000ALLENBY-WHITTALL00PERCIVAL0000

In addition to creating this sort field we will need to develop a trailer field which will contain the information we wish to typeset. In this case all we wish is the name and class of the individual. Let us suppose, although this is unlikely, that we decide to list the first name first, so that under California, and under Whittier, we will find:

PERCIVAL ALLENBY-WHITTALL, '59

There is no problem in doing this. The sequencing will be by last name, but the listing will begin with the first name. The only difficulty we will encounter is that we may have instances like this:

LEONARD S JR AARON
ARTHUR W III ABBOTT

because we did not field these post-surname characteristics. If we had, we would not have been able to "run in" this information in the same field, and more space on the fixed field card would have been needed.

In any event, after we had sequenced our entries by the use of the sort field, the program would drop that field and pick up only the trailer which contains those lines of text we require for typesetting in the sequence in which they have been arranged, and with the appropriate "before" and "after" information around them. By "before" and "after" information we mean such things as flags to indicate type faces or format instructions, and repetitive information, such as commas or dashes to separate one element from another, as well as to separate one entry from another.

That is all there is to it. One thing should be clear: it is easier to develop such a program if there has been communication from the very beginning about the typesetting possibilities of the input, rather than to try to improvise from a file which was created without such uses in mind. Consider, for example, the problem of setting the same file in upper and lower case. The customer proposes that this be done since it will be more legible and will take up less space. The solution is not to simply pull off the first letter of the last name so that it will remain a capital, and then to covert all of the other letters in the name to lower case. We encounter *McAdoo* and *MacDonald*, but we also find *Mackey*. There is a *Dupuy* in the class of '42 and a *duPont* in the class of '98. The latter, by the way, is a substantial contributor! Some of these problems can be solved by special routines, but now we are obliged to carry on a different level of data processing. Until now all we have been concerned with is to place characters at the beginning or the ending of identifiable fields (or in some cases to translate a field from one thing to another). Now, unfortunately, we have to make an analysis of the contents of the field itself. We can write a program to compare for *Mc* and can probably get away with the capitalization of the next letter. We can gamble with *Mac*, although the consequences will be somewhat more treacherous. We'd better give up on the *du* and *de* problem. An editing pass may be necessary to get the file into shape for typesetting. But if we do this, can the file be used again for other purposes, such as the generation of a mailing list? Or will it be necessary to edit the file each time a typesetting application is planned? These are difficult system questions to answer. Again, prior communication is indicated. If a dollar sign could have been placed ahead of the exceptions the problem could have been resolved nicely:

```
MAC$DONALD
$DU$PONT
```

which tells us to reverse the normal capitalization rule, but this takes up more room in our fixed field areas, and these irrelevant marks may interfere with the use of the file for mailing lists or for sorting, unless we incorporate into these programs some procedure which causes the routine to ignore them.

If it is difficult to infer the proper position of upper-case letters in the name field, it is all the more perplexing in the address field. The rule that the first letter in the word should be capitalized would, for example, produce *Afb* rather than *AFB* (for Air Force Base).

Creating a typesetting file

JUST AS the computer typesetting company often works with fixed field data supplied by the customer, so the company may be asked to assist in the development of the initial file. If so, a better method of fielding the information could be selected. The vendor would quite possibly elect to use variable-length fields, and the decision might be made to place these in random order, or even merely as a part of a text stream. But let us take a case where the sequence of elements would be prescribed. In this instance let us consider a library book catalog. It might be developed according to a procedure which constituted the order of the initial entries:

```
$aCooper$bJames Fenimore$cThe Last of the Mohicans
$dMacmillan$e1896, 395 p.$f12.95$gF$h$i$j$z
```

We have flagged the author's last name between *$a* and *$b*. We have flagged his given names between *$b* and *$c*. Thus we can find

Data Base Typesetting

these elements and create sort fields when necessary. We can also find them when we wish to pull them out for typesetting.

The title of the book appears between $c and $d, and a program can be written to drop off the articles (*The, A, An*) when a title sort is indicated, in which case the next word should begin with a capital if it does not already do so.

The publisher appears between $d and $e. Miscellaneous information which we shall typeset but not use for sorting, and which, when typeset, will always appear together, is found between $e and $f. The identification of the price of the book appears between $f and $g. The book is classified (between $g and $h) as F for *fiction*. Thus we can sort all fiction together, or identify the book for the reader by Dewey number or LC number and can sort on these fields. Finally, we have indicated that this book can be found in three libraries in the system, which we have chosen to identify individually by the codes $i, $j and $k. The entry ends with the flag $z, which is added in case certain preceding flags are missing (since one or more of the three libraries might not have the book in its collection and it's probably better to have a definitive signal to end the record).

This is a simple application. Library catalogs are of course much more complicated than this because they also deal with subject indexes, but the example suffices for the purpose of illustration. It is now necessary to create a program which responds to commands to create sort fields and trailer fields, generates information before and after the fields in the trailer, and otherwise manipulates the entry much as in the case of the preceding illustration of the alumni directory. But since the file was initially input for typesetting, upper- and lower-case codes, and other internal flags to extend the character repertorie, *etc.* can be widely used, so long as they do not interfere with the sorting rules.

Sorting rules themselves can be made more sophisticated by intermixing "file as if" commands where normal sorting sequences do not produce desired results. This is sometimes done by including in a particular field information which could be used for sorting but not for typesetting. Thus *Bible***1**,*O.T.* could be made to sort before *Bible***2**, *N.T.*, where the number shown in bold would be ignored for typesetting. In this fashion we can position the Old Testament before the New Testament, and *Albany***1**,*NY* will sort before *Albany***2**,*NC*.

Other opportunities and problems

FOR SORTING PURPOSES, variable length fields must be converted into fixed fields so that apples can be compared with apples. But for other purposes variable or random-length fields are much more convenient. It is not necessary to structure the input in a rigid fashion. Structure may be imputed by the presence or absence of flags and the sequence in which various items appear.

Flags can be placed around names which occur in random order in the text stream so that they can be recognized for the purpose of creating an index. Material to be omitted in an abridged version can also be identified. First lines of poetry can be tagged so that an index of such lines can be generated. These are only a few illustrations which come to mind. Space does not permit a further elaboration of this topic, which is obviously deserving of an entire book in its own right. But perhaps enough has been said to stimulate the reader into thinking about the ways in which typesetting and data processing can be interrelated. Since publishing need no longer be considered exclusively a function of typesetting and printing, it is obvious that many publishers will wish to store their products in such a way that they can provide information through a number of media, including a magnetic tape file which others can search or manipulate for their own purposes. Information retrieval and the selective dissemination of information is also possible from files which have been input with these applications in mind. The more thought that goes into the development of the original input, the greater the potential for by-products and alternate uses.

The reader should not conclude, however, that these by-products can be realized by trivial programming effort. Files not yet formatted for typesetting can perhaps be manipulated more readily than those which have already gone through a hyphenation and justification (or pagination) pass. Yet it is possible to develop software capable of processing the latter files (and thus deriving information such as pagination, for indexing purposes). And rather than having to write special software for each job, it is possible to develop some fairly general and widely applicable data base programs. Much will depend upon whether or not the user (*e.g.,* the typesetting firm) has access to the source code of the composition program, and whether or not the composition program runs under an operating system which also supports a popular programming language.

While it is true that the use of the file for purposes other than typesetting makes computer typesetting much more viable economically (and everyone these days wants to find himself a unique data bank which he can exploit on the marketplace!), programming and systems design are often complex and far from troublefree. Computer typesetters who have forsaken straight one-time setting for data bank applications on the ground that they cannot make a profit in competition with "Mom and Pop" shops and other low-end equipment, also find that the data processing *cum* typesetting path can be a thorny one. Programming ingenuity is obviously necessary, plus the ability to ancitipate the customer's requirements and to be able to identify the pitfalls before they are encountered. This insightfulness is rare, and its absence keeps the typesetter from profiting from the opportunities he is able to uncover. Neither he nor his traditional publisher customers may possess the imagination to discover the wealth of applications which lie around them.

New opportunities have suddenly sprung into being with the advent of personal and professional computers. This recent development suggests that there will be less emphasis upon the creation of data bases from files initially prepared for typesetting purposes, and more attention will need to be devoted to ways of moving such files

Data Base Typesetting

(already manipulated through sort routines and the like) into the typesetting environment.

Definitions of data-manipulation terms

SOME FORMS of data manipulation often used in typesetting applications include:
- **Extraction**—Selecting only certain elements from the text, such as the name of an author, a citation or title.
- **Explosion**—Generating the same information in different arrangements from the same initial input. For example, the name of a company followed by the products it manufactures, and then creating a list of products with the company name restated under each product (a product guide).
- **Abridging**—Eliminating certain material from the text stream.
- **Abstracting**—Summarizing the essence of an entry or article, as by selecting only flagged portions thereof.
- **Key words**—Flagging certain words for extraction and sorting, to help identify the contents of a document or the location of a place where a certain topic is treated. Sometimes these key words are assembled to form a *thesaurus* or are flagged because they already appear in an agreed-upon thesaurus.
- **Automatic indexing**—Generating a listing of index terms in alphabetic sequence, with reference to the page numbers where the items occur. The index terms are selected by computer program, such as to pick out all words in the text stream of five letters or more in length, and to assume that the words so used will frequently represent key words in the text (after certain common words are eliminated).
- **Redundancy elimination**—Dropping a portion of an entry when it already appears in a listing which immediately precedes it (after sorting). For example:

> U.S. History—Colonial Period—Early Settlers, p. 67
> Handicrafts, p. 14
> —Revolutionary War—Anecdotes & Satires, p. 4

Illustrations of data bases

SOME OF THE OBVIOUS data bases are listed below:
1. Telephone directories, especially including automatic updating, cumulating, reverse directories (by street address) and recombinations of elements within the directory, such as by exchange, or businesses, or types of businesses. Especially interesting are applications where the input can be derived from business files, such as service orders.
2. Airline schedules, where information is computerized in any event, and points of interconnection must be retrieved because of their effects on the operation of the total scheduling system.
3. Library catalogs, especially where the information can be derived from computerized book ordering systems within the library.

4. Publishers' book catalogs, especially where various combinations (*e.g.*, series) are published, and the same listings may be needed for inventory control.
5. Product guides and industrial directories, especially where information can be elicited from computer-generated questionnaires.
6. Price lists and parts lists, especially where information is maintained for inventory or billing purposes.
7. Abstracts and bibliographic citations, especially where cumulations, sorts and explosions are relevant and where information can be input during the process of intellectual abstracting.
8. Tariff listings, stock market transactions, bond holdings and other collections of data which require widespread dissemination and constant revision.

From a typesetting standpoint, there are certain unique features to the above classifications:

    a) Input costs are not usually relevant. The information has to be created and maintained in any event.
    b) Updating, cumulation and other data manipulation processes are common.
    c) The information is usually quite massive and repetitive.
    d) Typographic or composition demands are often quite simple. Formats, once evolved, do not vary. Special-purpose, high-speed composition packages are logical.

The editorial interface

MOST OF THE DATA BASES we have so far alluded to are structured either in a fixed-field or a variable-length record fashion. But there are also data bases which are not structured at all. The *Holy Bible*, referred to earlier in this chapter, is such an instance. An encyclopaedia or dictionary would be another. In the latter case, words are often indexed according to the field of specialization implied, and lists of such words are sent to different editors for the creation of definitions, synonymns and the like. Then these individual contributions are later compiled and combined.

Insurance forms and contracts, as well as "boiler plate" for employee booklets, can be stored. Programs can be written to extract the relevant paragraphs or provisions and put them together in order to meet the requirements of different policies and the laws of different states.

Statutes for various states need to be typeset. The same data base could provide a source for annotation. And legislative bill drafting programs can be offered whereby anyone wishing to submit a bill for legislative consideration can call up the existing law and indicate the manner in which it is proposed to amend or revise it. The drafts, as revised by the House and Senate committees, can be changed as required, and a trail can be provided showing what revisions were indicated and at what stage in the process they occurred. The final bill, as passed and "engrossed" by the Governor, can then be reinserted in the new revised statutes.

Data Base Typesetting

These are merely a few illustrations to suggest that the computer may be called upon to perform certain editorial functions—that is, tasks which were formerly done by people who worked tediously, usually reading and copying portions of text onto file cards, inserting or deleting from earlier versions, and searching for other occurrences of the same conditions, and then finally resequencing the results.

More and more attention is now being focused on the development of large data bases, where relevant portions can be retrieved upon demand. Often the text to be searched by the computer is unstructured. A newspaper, creating text for its news stories, may wish to store the text for future reference in an electronic library. Programs may be required to search these files for names, or places, or phrases. Or an abbreviated version of the text may be stored simply for the purpose of permitting the kind of computer search which would lead the user to the appropriate issue of the paper and perhaps automatically retrieve the microfilm display of the page or pages in question.

As the cost of data storage is reduced and as computers become faster and cheaper, there is more and more interest in text-searching techniques as an aid to research and scholarship. Ph.D. dissertations have been prepared involving the use of computer programs to gather together all phrases in Shakespeare's plays involving the use of particular words. The same has been done for Calvin and other writers. Published theses contain listings of "key words in context" (a so-called KWIC index).

In the future, the distinction between textual material and data bases will become less and less significant. All text that is input will be regarded as a potential data base, and all data that is stored and manipulated will be available for output by a typesetting device merely as another form of presentation. Alternate (nonprint) publishing methods of distribution will become more and more common. Classified ads collected for publication in newspapers will also be stored in data bases to be accessed by remote terminals so that seekers of jobs, second-hand cars or houses for rent will be able to elicit those listings that meet certain user-established criteria.

Thus the typesetting/data processing relationship will someday become so intimate that present disciplinary, programmatic and structural barriers will seem never to have existed.

21

The "Typesetting" of Art

IF AND WHEN the problems of page layout and interactive make-up are resolved, and if error-free pages can be composed effectively, attention will shift with even greater urgency to the "composition" of artwork and illustrative material along with text, making stripping and all subsequent camera work unnecessary.

Interest in this subject has already become strong as more and more typesetting systems are able to cope successfully with the arrangement of text within the page, thus avoiding the need for hands-on make-up. But if holes or windows must be left for the insertion of illustrations, some handwork remains, along with the possibility of error, and thus a failure to achieve optimal editorial control over the final product results.

There is also an urgent need to be able to output artwork from digital data in order to bypass the typesetter completely and go direct to plate, thus saving a great deal of time and significant amounts of money in terms of the utilization of photographic materials. The same urgency exists if illustrations are to be included in output generated in response to the needs of demand printing, where individual copies of books, manuals and brochures may be produced on request. Naturally some of these applications require the inclusion of graphics, especially in the area of technical manuals and documentation.

Yet another aspect of editorial control is the convenience and value of providing editorial people not only with the option of placing the correct picture in the correct location, but also of selecting and sizing pictures and other illustrative matter—*interactively*—as judgment is applied to the consideration of the total impact upon the reader of a happy arrangement of pictures and text.

Moreover, as we look about us and consider the evolution of "the book," we realize that the differentiation which presently exists between type and art is indeed arbitrary. It was foisted upon us by the requirements of hot metal typesetting with its limited supply of type fonts and matrices. While there are obvious advantages to be derived from this specialized treatment of "characters" as opposed to graphic images, there are also disadvantages. Those who are knowledgeable about calligraphic languages such as Chinese, Japanese and Korean are aware of how difficult it is to assemble a sufficient number of characters to set type. On the other hand, one cannot help but be impressed by the beauty of the calligraphy and the manner in which

The "Typesetting" of Art

illustrative matter can be intimately related to text in those languages. This was also true of literature written in Latin and Cyrillic alphabets until the time of Gutenberg. It is possible that new techniques for inputting, storing and recording text and graphics may once again provide the kind of fluidity and flexibility which once existed, and which has been represented in more modern times by such products as those of William Blake.[1]

Lest one suppose that increased editorial involvement and the urge to achieve a greater degree of interaction between text and graphics implies an unnecessary luxury or a frivolous convenience, we may point to experimental work done in this area in the early 1970s, when *Life* magazine had a special-purpose device built to permit the projection of 35mm slides onto "pages," the sizing and cropping of such pictures, and the inclusion of dummy text. A color Polaroid photograph of the resulting layout was to be referenced for subsequent review and to provide instructions to the printers and color houses charged with the task of performing final make-up and page-assembly functions. Later, in 1983, Time Inc. became the first magazine publisher to install a Scitex Vista system for a related, but much more ambitious, purpose.

Some publishers (whether commercial or in-plant) have the need not merely to set illustrations, but also to store them, retrieve them on demand, and manipulate them. There may also be a requirement to compose or recompose such pages at remote locations.

Even in the absence of such interactive manipulation there are benefits to be derived. Composition of telephone book yellow pages, for example, requires the extensive use of logotypes. And who is to say where a logotype ends and an illustration begins? Whenever the same picture or design needs to be used frequently—for subsequent issues or alternate versions—a method which composes the desired art on demand has high utility.

A similar example, involving the use of halftones rather than line art, is found in the composition of home owners' buying guides (multiple-listing directories). In these two instances (yellow pages and multiple listings) an interactive relationship between editor or layout man and his equipment is hardly necessary. But for the composition of a newpaper, magazine or book page (using the term "composition" in its broadest sense) the ability to interact and modify the various elements surely would offer a powerful and rewarding opportunity.

It may be that soon the distinction between art and type will become arbitrary and ambiguous. For example, in the composition of display ads for newspapers a significant amount of handwork is involved in preparing special-effect type elements, such as the word "SALE!" reversed as white on black and positioned at an angle incapable of being laid down by a traditional typesetting machine. Rules, borders and tints must often be added by artists. One may also wish to align type along a curve or other non-horizontal or non-vertical orientation. When Camex introduced its Supersetter in 1983[2] it made the point that until then all typesetting devices could only produce a subset of what was required.

1. William Blake (1757-1827) was an English poet and engraver who originated a method of engraving text and illustrations on the same plate. This method established an intimate, single-plate relationship between illustrations, text, and illuminated colors. The *Songs of Innocence* (1789) and *Songs of Experience* (1794) are considered by many to be the best examples of this method.

2. See Chapter 23.

In this chapter we will attempt to describe some of the trends of this new technology and perhaps to assess, to some degree, their implications. The relationship between the elements we shall be discussing here may not be entirely clear to the reader, but they may be taken as "straws in the wind"—indications of a new explosion of approaches possibly even more profound than those we witnessed in the 1960s and 1970s. The subject matter must be divided in an arbitrary manner since there is so much overlapping of the elements involved.

What are pictures?

IN A SENSE, a picture or illustration is anything to be reproduced that cannot be set in type. During the medieval period when manuscripts were created by hand it was, of course, possible that one scribe could produce an entire book, including the illuminated features and perhaps some drawings as well.

As a practical matter, there was indeed specialization among the monks, and some devoted their artistic endeavors entirely to the preparation of colorful dropped initials at chapter beginnings. Similar graceful decorations were often included in the margins.

After Gutenberg's time, there had to be a clear differentiation between what was done by type or by hand, and although some illustrative handwork persisted, it was natural to try to develop techniques for printing the illustrations. Hence wood blocks were used, along with other kinds of tooled or etched metal engravings. Illustrations became "cuts" which were locked into the forms for printing.

Some color was also used, as different portions of an illustration were carved or etched and then brought together by the application of colored inks, with careful "registration" of the pages and printing forms. It became apparent that printing presses handled large areas of solid color very badly—even solid black. Moreover, it was impossible to provide any shading effects with the use of a solid black pigment which could be applied only at one consistent depth or thickness. Various techniques were developed to create the impression of shades of gray, by the use of cross-hatching or methods of combining areas of print (black) with areas of non-print (white).

In the nineteenth century, after photography became a commercial practicality, efforts were directed to discovering ways of reproducing photographs by printing processes, and by 1881 the halftone technique was developed. This is a process of converting continuous tone images with varying shades of black and gray into a pattern of very small halftone dots which, if viewed from a distance, give the appearance of the original continuous tone picture. Such dots vary in size, and especially in their density. For a normal reading distance of fifteen inches or so, such dots must generally be small and grouped closely together. If the picture is to be viewed at a greater distance, as with a billboard, the dots can be larger and spaced farther apart. Techniques were developed which created a screened image and then prepared a metal printing plate which would carry more or less ink according to the density of these dots and thus transfer it to paper.[1]

1. The methods of doing this differ according to whether the printing process is letterpress or offset. In gravure, which is an intaglio process, the technique is still different since the ink-carrying cells can vary in their depth.

The "Typesetting" of Art

The new challenge of creating illustrations by digital means must take into account the ways in which such pictures can be input and stored, as well as how they can be output. And in our discussion we must bear in mind the distinction between what we will call a "line drawing"—which is any kind of artwork made up of lines and blocks of solid color—and halftones, composed of dots.

Getting the picture into the system

IN MOST INSTANCES, in order to input the picture, scanning is required, and you have a choice of scanning techniques, just as you do with OCR.[1]

- *Scanning with a vidicon tube or a TV-type camera.* The image picked up by the camera lens is brought into focus on the face of the tube, where a raster scan directed by an electron beam sweeps the tube in a predetermined pattern and "reads" what it sees, reporting signals which carry varying degrees of light, and hence electrical, intensity. Initially, these signals are of an analog nature. The electron beam within the vidicon camera senses and conveys not merely black or white observations, but a wide range of tonal values. If these values

1. See Chapter 15, p.239*ff*.

are retained in the analog form in which they are received, stored and output, then the entire system will remain analog in nature.

This was the principle behind the design of the Linotron 1010—a "Lexical-Graphical" CRT typesetter produced under a contract issued in March 1964 by the U.S. Government Printing Office. In addition to the two 1010s to be designed and built by Mergenthaler in conjunction with the Columbia Broadcasting System Laboratories for the GPO, the companies undertook to deliver two units to the Wright-Patterson Air Force Base with the capability of outputting line drawings (and even halftones), using the CRT in the typesetter for the display and exposure of images from data recorded and stored on a video tape deck as analog information. This feature was not, in fact, operative until 1971. It was still being used in 1979, and while a few halftones were created for military publications, line drawings were composed quite commonly.

But if these analog values (such as might be written to video tape) were subjected to analysis in an "a-to-d" (analog-to-digital) converter, they could be transformed into digital information, either as black and white "observations"—in which case they could be recorded as bits (0 or 1) or as shades of gray. In the latter instance they would be written as bytes with perhaps up to 256 different tonal variations, from "all white" to "all black."

In either case, the values read (as by a vidicon tube) are subjected to a "threshold" test. In a two-tone system, if the intensity of the signal fails to reach a certain level, it is recorded as white—or zero. If it reaches or exceeds that level, it is recorded as black—or one.

However, levels of intensity can also be translated into a graduated scale of steps, each determined by its own threshold value in a linear relationship or according to some preferred curve. Gray-scale levels—as from 0 to 3, 0 to 15, or 0 to 255—can thus be registered. Moreover, these threshold values can be altered from time to time to enhance or reduce the contrast scale (the slope of the line) or the mid-tone values (the shape of the curve) or both.

- *Scanning with a flying spot scanner or some other method of focusing a light beam on a specified location.* More precisely, the light focuses upon a series of locations which can be "tracked," usually in a raster pattern. Then this spot of light (probably as reflected and sensed) can be read by one or more photo-diodes or CCDs[1], and its intensity, in like manner, can be recorded as analog information or translated into digital form, either as black and white or as shades of gray.
- *Scanning an entire line of some minute depth simultaneously by an array of photo-diodes or CCDs.*

Getting light on the subject

THERE ARE, of course, various methods of directing a spot of light onto the subject (picture). You could use a flatbed scanner, where a beam tracks across the image a "line" at a time—and these "lines" can be very fine indeed, such as 1/1000 of an inch apart. Or a drum scanner could be used, where a reflected beam is read from a fixed

---

1. A CCD or charged-coupled device is an integrated circuit that is light sensitive. A charge builds up on a photo-sensitive site on a circuit in proportion to the length of the exposure.

The "Typesetting" of Art

location as the drum revolves, and then either the drum moves to permit the recording of another series of observations, or the beam advances. The beam can be a coherent light source, such as a laser, or it can be a relatively tiny spot of light played across the picture by means of a series of holes in an otherwise opaque revolving disk. It can also be a revolving mirror which sprays spots of coherent light across a surface. The sensing of the observations is usually performed by one or more photo-diodes or CCDs.

The scanning resolution

BY WHATEVER MEANS the process takes place, and whatever technique may be used to record the data (whether in analog or digital fashion) the resolution of the information is a function of the number of discrete observations made or "samples" taken. On a vidicon tube the maximum resolution is determined by the raster sweep of the scanning beam, and the granularity of the phosphor which is excited by experiencing the light rays of the image and the "play" of the electronic beam. For a coarser resolution, some of the observations, such as each alternate one, could be "thrown away," or fewer observations could be taken by altering the timing of the mechanism which triggers the scanning/recording process.

When a flying spot scanner, a flatbed or a drum scanner is used, maximum resolution is determined by the mechanics of the movement of beam, bed or drum, and the size of the spot produced by the light beam.

Thus one significant difference between existing systems or techniques has to do with the number of observations taken over a given area. It might be useful, for example, to take such observations in both horizontal and vertical directions every 1/1000 of an inch, but

The Optronics Pagitron drum scanner/writer could be used to input and store data on its scanning pass and to output data on its writing pass. In between storage and writing, text could be added and pictures positioned.

some systems, seeking to scan a continuous tone image and to generate a halftone, may make their observations only according to the screening resolution desired. (More about this later.) But if we do assume the 1/1000 inch scanning pattern, then presumably the spot to be read and recorded will also not be larger than 1/1000 of an inch (a "mil") and, indeed, may be somewhat smaller. Thus we shall assume, for the moment, that on the input side there will be 1,000 × 1,000 (which equals one million) observations for each square inch of surface scanned.

The simplest way to deal with this vast quantity of information would be to pass it on directly to the output device in "real time" as the scanning process takes place. If the output device or "writer" offers the same resolution as the input device or "reader" then each spot reported—with whatever intensity—could be written out, as by a laser beam, and recorded on a sheet of photographic film or paper or onto a treated printing plate. But, as we shall see, it would also be possible to read at one resolution and to write at another. (This might be the case if we wanted to enlarge or reduce the output relative to the input.) The output resolution would thus differ from the input resolution, being finer or coarser, as the case may be. For example, if we were to scan on the basis of one million observations per square inch with the expectation of outputting an image that was 50% smaller in both dimensions, we would now have one million bits of information for an area one-fourth of an inch square, or four million bits of information per square inch.[1] On the other hand, if the picture were to be enlarged so that it is 200% of the original (twice the original size), then the dot resolution would be only one-fourth of a million bits of information per square inch.

If the scanning device has been "told" what the size of the final picture is to be, it can sometimes determine how many observations it needs to make in its data collection mission. For example, if an 8 × 10 photograph is to be reproduced at a size of 4 × 5, perhaps it will read the original by taking only one-fourth as many observations in the vertical and horizontal directions if the object is to end up with one million pixels per square inch for the creation of the final output resolution. On the other hand, if the picture were to be doubled in size, and if you wanted a constant amount of data per square inch regardless of size, then the number of scanning observations would need to be 2,000 × 2,000 pixels or 4 million pixels per square inch to provide the data needed.

It is common to use the word pixels (for picture elements) to describe the number of such observations—read, stored or laid down. (An alternate term is "pels" which also means picture elements.) Each pixel could be recorded as either black or white or it could be recorded as one of perhaps 256 shades of gray. In the first case we would need one million bits to describe one million pixels. In the second case we would need one million *bytes* or eight million bits to describe one million pixels.

We have no particular knowledge of the "setting" of graphic images on second-generation phototypesetters, although there was

1. A 50% reduction means producing an image with only 25% of the area of the original.

The "Typesetting" of Art

always the possibility of creating a photographic master of a logotype and substituting it as a "pi" character where some other character photomat would have been located. There was also the possibility of directing a typesetting machine to lay down a series of dots, dashes or other characters in order to generate some kind of crude outline illustration or bar diagram. But as soon as third-generation CRT typesetters were developed, the interest in handling graphics quickened. The product of an effort to produce halftones from input generated on an IBM scanning device and output on a Fototronic CRT typesetter was circulated by Harris as early as 1969. And by 1974 Hell, the German manufacturer of the Digiset, had developed the Digigraph 40A20, a desk-sized drum scanner to be used for the creation of logotypes as well as line drawings. The finest resolution it could cope with was 420 lines per inch, but the image so produced could be electronically reduced (as was the case with any other "characters"). We witnessed the digitizing of drawings as large as A4 size, which took about 20 minutes to scan and store as "slices" of the final picture. Such an illustration, as digitized, required about two million bytes of storage. It was initially punched out on paper tape and then read onto the Digiset font disk. The setting of the A4-sized image required approximately 20 minutes.

Autologic also offered a relatively low-cost digitizer, primarily aimed at the creation of logotypes that were expected to be set as if they were type characters. Most manufacturers of CRT typesetting equipment offered the service of digitizing special characters for users of their equipment. In such instances they employed whatever scanner they used in their font design process, coupled with whatever font editing programs and hardware they had developed for this purpose.

The ECRM Autokon camera

PERHAPS THE MOST INTERESTING and most far-reaching product related to the creation of graphic images in the context of everyday use was the ECRM Autokon camera, which was first introduced by that company in 1975.

ECRM was known at that time as a manufacturer of OCR scanners for converting copy from typewritten manuscripts into machine-readable form for text processing. But it applied the same mechanism: a flying spot scanner from a rotating mirror deflecting the triggered coherent light beam from a helium-neon laser was used to convert the images from photographs and line drawings. In the first instance, however, the product was not a file of digital information, but direct output on photo-sensitive stabilization paper. In other words, the Autokon was intended merely as an electronic camera.

You laid down a copy of the picture to scan and dialed the reduction or enlargement size needed, along with other features having to do with screening, contrasts and similar effects. Then the same beam that scanned the image almost simultaneously laid down the exposed output onto the photographic paper. In fact, however, there was a

The ECRM Autokon electronic camera scans an image as delineated by cropping bars, outputting it at the desired size on photographic paper.

momentary, temporary storage of the data in digital form. Screening, especially, was handled in this fashion.

Sizing was provided in steps of one percent, from 20% to 199% of the original. Screening was accomplished through the use of a small digital memory and was limited to 65, 85 and 100 line screens. Cropping was done by the setting of adjustable frames to limit the area of the picture to be scanned. Mode selection permitted the production of negatives or positives. Tone controls were devised to create the same effects as those generally produced by a cameraman with the use of *main, flash* and *bump* exposures on a process camera. Mid-tone controls were provided by dials which could lighten or darken intermediate areas of the picture without affecting the end points. Each step on the mid-tone setting corresponded to a shift of about .15 density units in the portion of the scale which would translate to 50% dots.

It may be seen that the Autokon was intended primarily as a device to de-skill the camera operation, just as computerized typesetters were supposed to de-skill type composition. In fact, many cameras were purchased for this purpose, especially by newsrooms. However, ECRM modified the product so that the Autokon was able both to output the image and to store it in digital form so that it could be processed by a computer associated with another device, such as an output typesetter. For some years the Autokon became the standard, relatively inexpensive means of capturing and of digitizing graphics for output onto third- and fourth-generation typesetting devices.

The original concept of ECRM was that this same device would also be used for facsimile transmission of images from one location to another. One camera could be set up in an editorial office. Another might be installed remotely, perhaps in a printing plant or production facility, and signals from the first could drive the second. Unfortunately, financial problems prevented the implementation of this concept.

Facsimile devices

LOW-QUALITY facsimile scanning and reproducing devices were and are widely used within the business community. Some of them have functioned by generating and transmitting analog signals. Most of them contain an analog-to-digital converter. Whether or not they need to recognize gray scale factors and to cope with continuous tone images (called "contone") is related to the capabilities of the writing device. If they are likely to output onto a photo-sensitive material, contone imaging would appear to be logical. If they output by means of a device which can only lay down solid blacks (a method which is quite sufficient for reproducing manuscript copy), then some sort of threshold-setting electronics will determine whether a particular spot should be reproduced as black or white. It is possible, of course, to scan material which has already been screened, on the assumption that the gray scale features produced by the screening process can be transmitted reliably to the writing unit.

Facsimile processes have been widely used in the graphic arts industry, not only to transmit copy (manuscript and proofs) but also pictures (wire service photos) which in fact are not screened, but reproduced photographically as contone images, generally on stabilization or dry-silver paper. Facsimile technology is also used extensively for the transmission of signals from camera-ready paste-ups (including both text and screened halftones) to remote printing sites. There the writing medium may be either printing plates or positive or negative film from which printing plates may be burned.

Plate-making devices

INTEREST HAS LONG BEEN MANIFEST for machines to scan paste-ups and to write the images directly to printing plate without the need to use conventional photography. Normally plate making involves taking a picture of a paste-up (camera-ready copy), thus obtaining a negative, and then using that carrier as a mask through which a photo-sensitive printing plate is exposed. If one can scan the camera copy instead and write the image directly onto the plate, the step of producing the intermediate film image is saved, as well as the cost of the film and the necessary opaquing of the film to assure a better plate image. Moreover, the electronic processes involved in scanning permit adjustment of tolerances which can eliminate the need for opaquing, since cut marks (the worst offenders) can be disregarded by successful illumination of the camera copy plus threshold adjustments and other electronic manipulations during the scanning process.

There have been problems associated with electronic plate-making processes having to do with the amount of light required to burn the plate, the quality of that light (*e.g.*, whether it is sensitive to ultra-violet, infra-red or other kinds of rays within the light spectrum), and whether the laser writing device can generate enough power to provide a plate image to expose a plate capable of offering a sufficient run length. There are also problems having to do with whether it is possible to produce duplicate printing plates for longer press runs as expeditiously as the conventional plate-making processes. Nevertheless, significant progress has been made in the development of electronic plate-making equipment. For some applications it has been highly advantageous. For example, as early as 1975 Norway's largest newspaper, *Aftenposten*, signed a contract with Eocom Corporation,[1] of Irvine, California to purchase a Laserite Facsimile Network made up of five systems. This was the second such sale for Eocom, the first being to the *Los Angeles Times*. With the new system, *Aftenposten* was able to scan paste-ups in its downtown Oslo office and simultaneously expose laser plates or film in its new offset printing plant eight kilometers away. If the amount of coherent light generated by the laser system was insufficient to provide plates directly, it was at least possible to produce the film from which the plates were to be exposed, to avoid the need for opaquing, to achieve quick delivery, or to obtain duplicate plates at different sites.

The ability to go direct to plate thus raised the question as to whether or not it would also be possible to bypass the typesetter process altogether and to eliminate paste-up process as well. This development has indeed come to pass. The first live system of this kind was installed in Utica, New York, in 1983 at the *Observer-Dispatch*, using a Hastech front-end system for composition and page make-up, Autokon cameras for digitizing illustrative matter, and a raster image processor developed by Eocom to send signals to a Laserite plate maker. The problem of how to handle advertising matter not composed by the newspaper was resolved through the use of a "coincident imaging" technique. This permits the Laserite writing unit to be used as a scanner as well, and to lay down text and graphics from paste-ups on the same plate which is otherwise imaged in a raster-image mode from text and graphics stored on the Hastech system.

The typesetting of graphics

BUT WE ARE AHEAD of our story. The first successful production use of a third-generation phototypesetter to output graphics was developed by Information International, Inc. (often called Triple-I) in conjunction with *U. S. News & World Report*.

The Information International Videocomp 500 (and its later 570 model) were logical typesetters to be used for this purpose since these machines were capable of operating in a "full-face" mode. In other words, an entire magazine-sized image can be exposed without the

[1]. In late April 1984 Eocom was acquired by Gerber Scientific Instrument Company, a merge sure to broaden GSI's graphic arts market.

The "Typesetting" of Art

need to move film backward and forward across an exposure aperture on the CRT tube. Thus "reverse leading" can be avoided, and pictures and text can be exposed randomly at any point on the page simply by positioning the electron beam and not requiring the movement of photographic materials, since the latter can not be manipulated as precisely as an electron beam. Moreover, Triple-I developed what is known as the 3600 Continuous Tone Scanner.

U. S. News had been producing full-page output on an Atex copy processing system as early as 1973, leaving holes for illustrations. While it had its own Videocomp 500 in its Washington D.C. editorial offices, final output was transmitted by telephone line, microwave and satellite, at a 9600-baud transmission speed, to remote printing plants, each of which was equipped with its own Videocomp 500 or 570. The text stream so transmitted consisted of ASCII codes (or their equivalent in the Triple-I basic BAL format). Text was written to magnetic tape at the receiving end and these tapes were then mounted on a tape station which fed its input directly to the Videocomp. Pages were produced on photographic ("RC") paper and taken to a copy camera to provide either negative or positive film. The film transparencies were then assembled for plate making. The same process could be taking place simultaneously at each of the three or four printing locations, selected not only because the facilities were appropriate, but the geographical distribution, from a mailing and newsstand point of view, was optimal.

The problem was that the last-minute illustrations of an editorial nature had to be flown to each of the plants, at considerable expense, and stripped into the film transparencies prior to plate making. This not only cost a great deal of money, but it tended to reduce the timeliness of the illustrative matter associated with late-breaking news. It also imposed somewhat less demanding constraints with respect to other portions of the "book" where timeliness was perhaps not so critical.

After exploring the possibility and the economics of producing complete pages, including graphics, at one location and then transmitting high-resolution facsimiles of those pages to other printing sites, *U.S. News* decided to use the Videocomp as a total output device. Accordingly, it installed a 3600 scanner in its own editorial environment, digitized all of its editorial artwork, first writing the product to magnetic tape and then transmitting it to disk. Within the Atex system graphic files could be stored in the same manner as text files, except of course that they were not editable. The Atex pagination program, which positions stories according to the upper left-hand corner of any text block, is able to direct a typesetting output device to dump graphics in precisely the same manner. And, as it turned out, files conveying graphic information were not significantly different within the system than files of textual matter.

The 3600 continuous tone scanner does not use a laser reader or writer. In fact, it does not act as an imaging engine, but merely as an input recorder. The picture to be scanned is mounted on an easel. Cropping bars surround the picture to indicate the area of the picture

346 — The World of Digital Typesetting

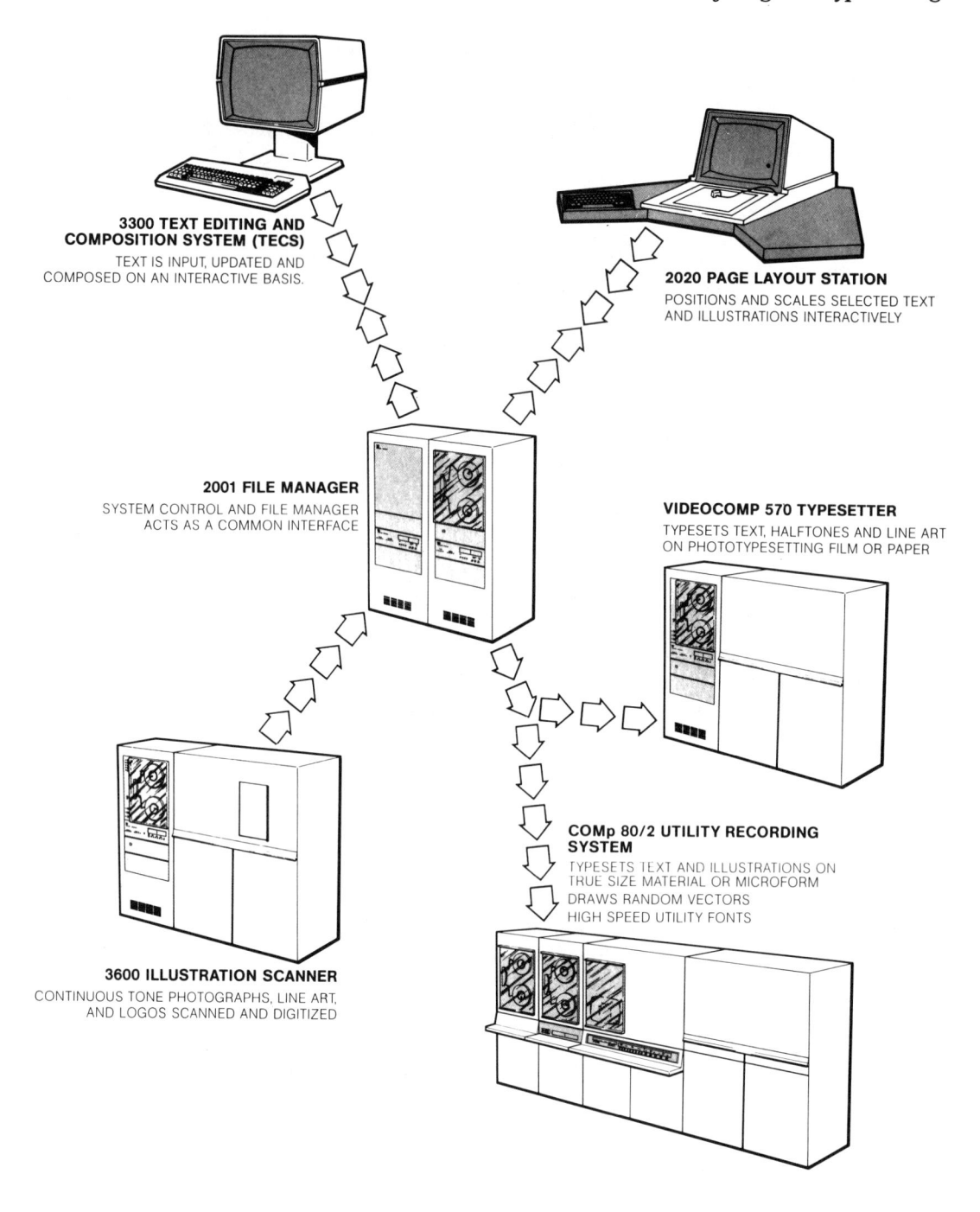

3300 TEXT EDITING AND COMPOSITION SYSTEM (TECS)
TEXT IS INPUT, UPDATED AND COMPOSED ON AN INTERACTIVE BASIS.

2020 PAGE LAYOUT STATION
POSITIONS AND SCALES SELECTED TEXT AND ILLUSTRATIONS INTERACTIVELY

2001 FILE MANAGER
SYSTEM CONTROL AND FILE MANAGER ACTS AS A COMMON INTERFACE

VIDEOCOMP 570 TYPESETTER
TYPESETS TEXT, HALFTONES AND LINE ART ON PHOTOTYPESETTING FILM OR PAPER

COMp 80/2 UTILITY RECORDING SYSTEM
TYPESETS TEXT AND ILLUSTRATIONS ON TRUE SIZE MATERIAL OR MICROFORM
DRAWS RANDOM VECTORS
HIGH SPEED UTILITY FONTS

3600 ILLUSTRATION SCANNER
CONTINUOUS TONE PHOTOGRAPHS, LINE ART, AND LOGOS SCANNED AND DIGITIZED

Information International incorporates the 3600 Scanner and Videocomp into a document processing system by adding a front-end editing system and page layout and makeup capability. But it also interfaces to other systems which offer their own text editing, composition and pagination capabilities.

The "Typesetting" of Art 347

to be scanned. A CRT tube, which strongly resembles that used by the Videocomp typesetter itself, traverses its electron beam across the picture and two photo-diodes catch the reflected light which is bounced off the image. (Transparencies are not used. The device scans opaque copy.)

Readings of the amount of light reflected from the area scanned detected by the photo-diodes are averaged and recorded directly onto disk or onto magnetic tape. All that is recorded is an eight-bit digital signal which represents an intensity or gray scale level from 0 to 255.

The scanner has been "told" what the size of the final illustration is to be and what the "mesh" is, so that it knows how far to move the beam during the scanning process. In general, it takes one observation to correspond with each halftone cell, or screen mesh element, whether it be 65 or 110 cells per inch. The resolution presently used is 110 cells per inch, although 133 line screens would be possible if the printing process can support it.

It is to be noted, therefore, that there is only one observation for each cell, and that the observation is represented by one eight-bit byte. Subsequently the value of that hexadecimal code is interpreted according to the desired halftone values. This is done by the output Videocomp typesetter, which is told what kind of photographic character representation to output for each code recorded.

At the time of output the minimum and maximum gray scale values are indicated, as well as the shape of the curve along which all mid-tone values will be interpreted. The Videocomp then decides which of 300 characters it should output at a particular location. The present system provides 64 gray levels along a linear curve, but in fact something more than 64 could be generated. On a 65-line screen the gray scale would require a repertoire of 100 photographic characters or less, we are told, but at 133 it could be as high as 220. What this means is that for a 65-line screen the program selects one set of characters. For 110 lines it could select another out of a total of 300 photographic characters. It is noted that each Videocomp can be adjusted to provide the characteristics desired for a particular printing operation, depending upon the nature of the printing process and the kind of plate material used.

The software produces a dot pattern which arrays the halftone cells for a black and white image at the conventional 45° angle. There is also software which is capable of enhancing the sharpness of the image. This is done by comparing the density of a given dot against that of the density of adjoining dots. If the program senses that a series of contiguous dots are producing gray scale values of 40% to be followed by another series at 80%, it would reduce the last 40% dot to a lesser value, perhaps 20%, and the first 80% dot to a higher value, perhaps 90%, to enhance the contrast.

Note, however, that the halftone dots which are typeset are truly photographic characters which can be stored and accessed just as if they were typeset characters. They are arrayed in a more dense fashion, however. For example, on the basis of a 110-line screen, a halftone illustration one inch square would consist of 110 × 110 characters or a total of 12,100 photographic images. Each character, represented by a certain gray scale value, would presumably be made of up to 99 pixels, generated, as with all Videocomp characters, as a series of vertical strokes. The Videocomp does not function as if it were a raster image processor.

Typesetting color. Information International also offers the ability to typeset process color images. In such a case the 3600 scanner would need to scan each of four unscreened color separations. The separations would be produced by a conventional electronic color separation scanner, such as one made by Hell or Crosfield. When pages are transmitted, the black printer version would include all type and the black printer image of the scanned illustrations. Other (color) pages would include only the color printer version (cyan, magenta, and yellow) of the scanned pictures. Line art can be scanned in the same manner as continuous tones, and two- or three-color line art rendition overlays can be handled as separate overlays. The color process just described is known as "Infocolor." It is used for editorial color illustrations by *Newsweek* and by other Information International customers. A considerable amount of experimentation and research had to be devoted to determining the screen angle for the various process colors, as well as the ideal dot shapes.

The Crosfield Magnascan 640 IS Quadracolour scanner comprising, from left to right, scanning data terminal, input unit and output unit.

The "Typesetting" of Art

We have discussed this process at some length because it is indeed the first successful application of its kind, but it is likely that this technology will be replaced or surpassed at some point by the use of an imaging device based upon raster image processor technology. One factor that makes it particularly attractive, however, is the amount of data compression implied by the technique of typesetting photographic characters. Note that *only one* eight bit byte is necessary to describe all of the information in one halftone cell. If each *pixel* within an equivalent contone area needed to be described and its gray scale level indicated within a range of 0 to 255, then there could be as many as perhaps 100 bytes of information to cover the same (black and white) area.

Contour information. The halftone dot which has conveyed gray scale information in the reproduction of continuous tone images has also, in the past, conveyed some contour information as well. It is generally not possible to reproduce the details of a picture simply by printing out cells of varying shades of gray.

There are actually some images within the cell itself which, when taken in conjunction with adjacent cells, provide the kind of detail one expects to see. For example, suppose a photograph of a building included a telephone pole carrying a wire to the house, and this wire is silhouetted against the sky. One expects to see this wire as a line and not as a grayish smudge. How is this achieved, normally, through the process of conventional photoengraving?

Usually it is done by a mysterious process which is sometimes called "dot migration." You start with the original continuous tone picture which is sharp and clear. In front of the film negative you expect to shoot, you interpose a screen. The manner in which the reflected light passes through the screen, the chemical properties of the film itself, and the action of the liquid developer all tend to concentrate dark areas within the halftone cell so that some contour or shape data are retained.

This is perhaps enhanced even further during the plate-making process. These effects are more difficult to achieve when using photographic characters whose only property is a relatively symmetrical or eliptical area of gray. The larger the halftone dot—that is, the coarser the resolution of the screen—the more important it is for the cell to contain some contour data. It may not be sufficient to use the kind of sharpness enhancement described above.

One way to seek to achieve such contour information is to scan the original with more than one observation for the equivalent halftone cell area. In fact, the ideal way would be to take as many observations as possible (perhaps as many as a million per square inch) each of which is recorded not to a black/white threshold, but on the basis of a full range of 256 gray scale levels, records one million bytes of data for an area which, let us suppose, represents a square inch based upon the size of the original. In fact, if the original were a 35-mm slide that was to be enlarged, this number of observations might be too few, but there is, of course, some question as to the smallest spot size that can be illuminated and detected. Spots below one mil in size may be difficult to create or detect.

Once this information has been collected, the electronic screening process may take over, and a software program may therefore be written to "look at" the values represented by these million bytes of varying gray scales and to seek to determine where the concentration of values should be, what the overall tone of the cell should be, and what kind of shape will best convey the contour information it contains. One cannot lose sight of the fact that the ultimate shape of the dot must be determined by the properties and requirements of the printing plate and the printing press technology. In this connection, Professor Willam F. Schreiber of M.I.T. has made the following comment in an unpublished article entitled *Production of Images on Printing Presses*:

> Obviously, if it were possible, we would choose a very fine screen in all cases since that would give imagery visually most like the original. Since we depend on the eye to average the array of dots to produce a similar effect to viewing the original, the finer the screen, the more closely the image could be examined without the dot structure becoming obtrusive. Of course, the image cannot be whiter than the paper or blacker than the ink. But within this range, the dynamic range is limited by the smallest black and white dots which can be printed reliably. This in turn depends on the ink, press, paper, and skill of the operator. Using the best coated paper with all other factors optimized, printing press results can be about as good as photographs on glossy paper—100 to 1 (2 log units) or slightly better. Newspapers, however, barely achieve 10 to 1 (1 log unit). In letterpress printing, an additional problem occurs with isolated highlight dots, which are bound to occur if dots are allowed to drop out in any light area. Such isolated dots tend to accumulate globules of ink and print very large. For this reason, letterpress printers usually try to keep a minimum dot everywhere. Lithographic printers, both offset and direct, may or may not keep dots everywhere, but in both cases, there is a smallest reliable dot. To achieve a given dynamic range with a given minimum dot requires a minimum dot spacing.

For some time the major concern of those who sought to be able to reproduce pictures in conjunction with type was limited to the question of how one could best use a third-generation CRT typesetter to produce such images. Obviously one thought in terms of photographic characters stored on disk like any other characters, which might consist of a finite and, hence limited, character repertoire. Each character represented a halftone cell.

If, however, one dispenses with the typesettter, as such, and intends to create images by laying down individual pixels on a raster-imaging basis, the opportunities for halftone reproduction may tend to improve, although these pixels still must contrive to arrange themselves into a cellular structure in accordance with the constraints of the printing process. Moreoever, the problem of data compression for data transmission and data storage remains a critical and troublesome factor.

The "Typesetting" of Art

Other imaging problems. It may be helpful to broaden our perspective and to consider other ways in which typesetting machines have been used to create pictures, and then to look briefly at ways in which pictures have been created from analog or digital information by other kinds of electronic non-typesetting devices.

One common problem has been how to typeset images which already exist in a computer data form. For the most part these images are generated by CAD/CAM systems. A CAD/CAM terminal is a device for "computer-aided design" and "computer-aided manufacturing." These exist for the purpose of creating engineering and architectural drawings, and they are not artists' tools but have been built to keep track of image structures. One can store in such a computer an instruction to draw a circle (as for a wheel) perhaps with spokes from the circumference to a smaller circle in the center. Then one might wish to size this image—making it larger or smaller—and to rotate it so that it stands vertically or horizontally or at some particular angle.

In each such instance the perspective and the relationship of the lines will change. One might then wish to superimpose another drawing (say a gear box), in order to indicate its relationship to the wheel, and then to instruct the program which of the two objects should take priority from the standpoint of viewing. Does the wheel obscure a portion of the gear box, or does the gear box obscure a portion of the wheel? (And when this is rotated those portions obscured or revealed will change.)

In the past, the hard copy of the final image has been reproduced on a device called a printer plotter. Such a machine might consist of inked pens capable of being moved about on a platen by means of mechanical arms. Occasionally some sort of rasterized dot matrix representation has been used. But if one wished to combine the artwork generated from the CAD terminal with the text stored on the text processing system it became relevant to explore the issue of whether or not the device which sets type could also be taught to draw lines and other shapes.

This generally was not possible in the past. The closest one could come would be to equip the typesetting machine with a repertoire of various kinds of shapes—line or curve segments—and to write a program which would then analyze the vector properties of the CAD output and seek to interpret it by laying down characters whenever possible to best represent the picture.

Examples of the geometrical kinds of output obtained in this fashion are shown on the next page. These samples display the intimate text/artwork relationship which CAD/CAM technology has made possible. This output was typeset on an Autologic APS-5, using software developed by Amgraf of Kansas City.

Another related problem arises when business graphics or artwork created on a digitizing tablet (as from a personal computer) is processed to be output on a typesetting device. The problems are substantially the same. As we shall see, these problems are more effectively resolved by means of a raster image processor.

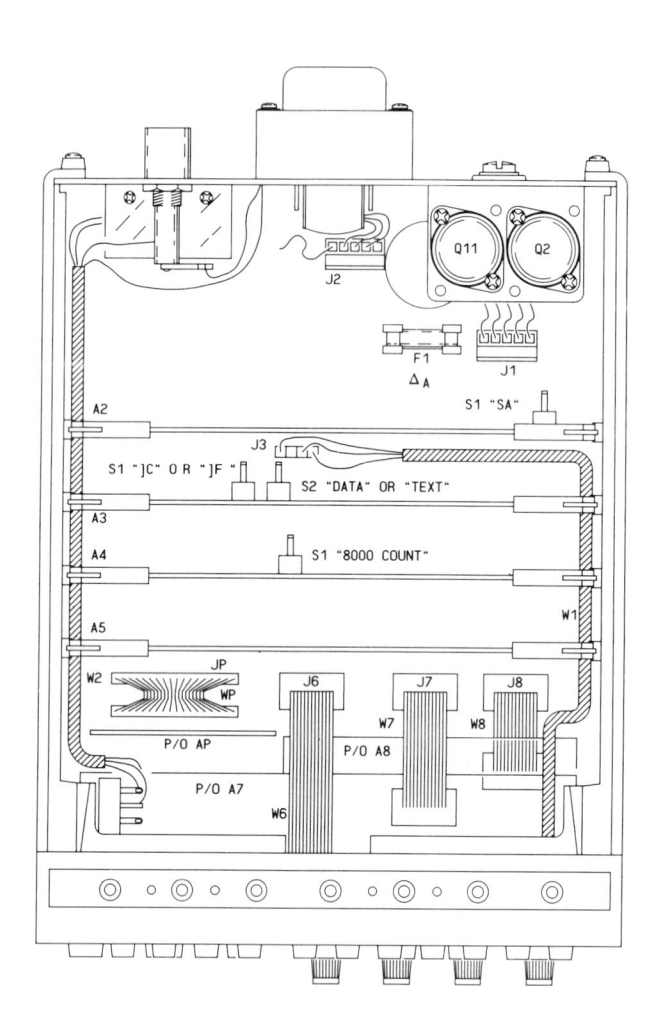

To produce these illustrations, CAD/CAM art has been processed against a program that generates various character shapes which are assembled to "typeset" the image. Amgraf offers such a program. The character shapes are designed by Autologic.

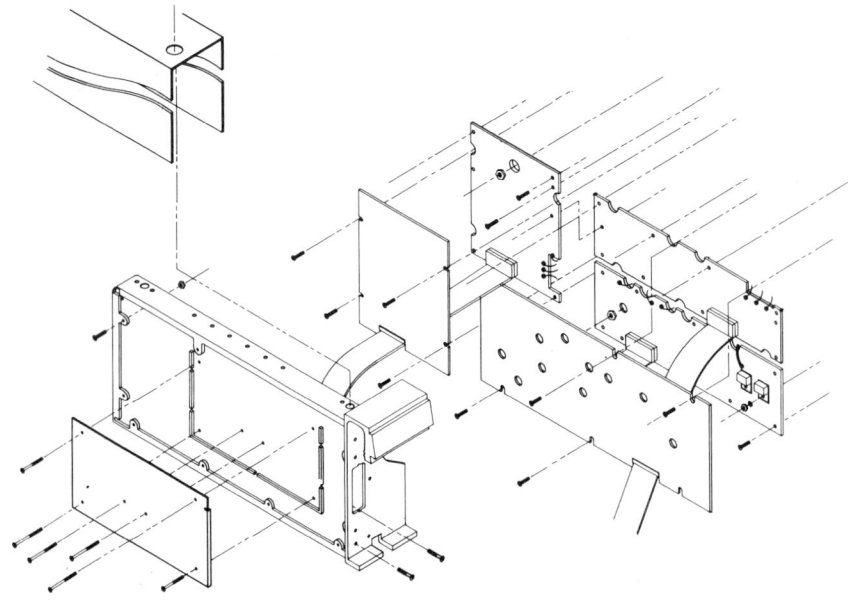

Color separation and image enhancement

ANOTHER ASPECT OF GRAPHICS which must be included in this discussion has to do with the development of color separation technologies for the graphic arts industry. The earliest color separation halftones were made with color filters over the lens of a process camera. Such filters suppressed those colors which were not within the range desired for a particular printer, such as yellow, cyan or magenta. Screening might be accomplished at the same time (with an appropriate angle for each color printer) or performed separately.

Eastman Kodak started research on electronic color scanners in 1934, but its patents and research were sold to Time Inc. in the late 1940s, and that company formed a new venture, Printing Developments, Inc., to experiment with the production of electronic color scanners and scanned separations. By the early 1960s it was possible for PDI to begin to produce quality products. This did not occur until it became possible to replace vacuum tubes with high-quality transistors.

In the late 1950s Dr. Rudolph Hell, a German manufacturer of wire-photo devices, developed a color scanner and gradually other vendors tackled the same problem. By the 1970s it became apparent that electronic color scanning was capable of producing high-quality images suitable for press reproduction. The processes involved were ordinarily analog in nature, although beginning in the 1980s digital circuitry was added, especially for purposes of edge enhancement.

Several new firms entered the marketplace, most notably Crosfield, a British firm, and Dainippon Screen, a Japanese company doing business in the United States as DS America.

Initially, the processes of scanning and writing took place concurrently, although there were electronic functions that could be performed while these processes occurred, such as color correction, unsharp masking and sizing.

An important part of the color separation process has always been color correction, since printing presses are unable to reproduce the full tonal range of color photographs and various compromises have to be made. Moreover, when tonal ranges are compressed this must be accomplished with a minimum loss of important detail. Until electronic color separation techniques were devised, these adjustments had to be made manually by varying the length of the exposure, the chemistry and the use of other photographic tricks, for example dodging and selective application of chemistry. Other manual processes required edge enhancement (also known as unsharp masking) and undercolor removal to help alleviate ink-related press problems.

The introduction of electronic processes made it possible to substitute electronic skills for manual and mechanical ones, and to obtain more precise information as to the ranges of tonal values and other properties, but the images scanned and written out were not stored in digital form for subsequent manipulation.

It was Scitex, an Israeli firm with an American subsidiary, which first introduced a technique for electronically altering, combining and outputting very high-resolution color images in an interactive manner, automating the labor-intensive processes of retouching, color separation and stripping. The input into the Scitex system was from scanners manufactured by other vendors, such as Hell, but Scitex added a color workstation, which permits the operator not only to make a variety of color adjustments (highlights, shadows and midtones are adjustable for each color separately or for all colors simultaneously) and also to manipulate individual areas, by the use of electronic airbrushing to remove unwanted objects, by outlining areas to combine various foregrounds and backgrounds, to change the proportions of selected objects, to introduce various shapes and rules, to rotate portions of pictures, and to superimpose one picture upon another.

The final output is then written to film by means of a laser plotting device. The laser plotter can use its special circuits to generate halftone dots "on the fly" and it can also produce continuous-tone separations for use in producing gravure cylinders via chemical etching.

Hell, Crosfield and Dainippon have followed suit, offering similar but not identical capabilities. Hell offers a "Combiskop" for page assembly, color correction and retouching.

Just as the Scitex workstation permits the operator to view the image in color or to look at the properties of any of the separations, so the Combiskop and other similar products permit the operator to view an entire picture at reduced resolution or a portion of it at full resolution. Two versions of the picture are kept on disk: a full-resolution version and a coarse representation which is derived from it. The final size of the piece of art needs to be determined upon initial input scanning because that is when the two disk-stored versions are created. There is also a "zoom" feature which permits apparent enlargement of an image by pixel replication. Zoom is provided for operator convenience and has no effect on the underlying data.

It is possible to throw a mask around any portion of a picture, thus isolating this segment from the rest of the picture, and to pick up this area and move it about or change its properties. Foreground and background masking can locate any object in front or back of any other.

After all operations at the color workstation have been completed and before a page can be output, there is a step called "final page processing" through which the image data must pass. Since the instructions are implemented on the coarse resolution version, the program must interpolate these instructions so that they take place on the final output version in fine resolution.

Space does not permit a more detailed discussion of these and other similar products, but some reference should also be made to the fact that other companies are entering the same field, and some are addressing the same problems or a subset of these problems, perhaps only for black and white reproduction, as with a company called

The "Typesetting" of Art

ImagiTex. One early entrant (in the early 1970s) was Optronics International, a company which had extensive experience with the interpretation of data transmitted from NASA satellites and had developed hardware and software to interpret this information and to output it onto photographic film via a drum scanner. The company also tried its hand at inputting, processing and outputting illustrative material and conceived the notion that it would also generate (rather than scan) text images for inclusion in what was to be a newspaper system. However, the task proved to be too ambitious for the company's available resources.

Eikonix is another company which has tended to specialize in the input, output and manipulation of color images, offering with its Designmaster the ability to enter local-area corrections.

ImagiTex introduced a subsystem which can be interfaced to a front-end system. This subsystem digitizes black and white line drawings and contones. It also produces a coarse resolution picture which can be manipulated for a variety of gray scale effects as well as for scaling, rotating and merging of images.

The decisions implemented on the coarse version are then applied against a full-resolution scan of the same data, and, since no halftone screening is performed, the continuous tone data are passed on to the front-end system. This data can, in turn, be relayed to an output device, such as a Monotype Lasercomp, which contains its own screening logic.

A less expensive scan-and-store facility is also offered, with a scanner which provides no storage capability of its own. The full-blown subsystem (level 3) offers a workstation with a color screen with 640 × 512 pixels. The color capability can be used to generate false-color images from monochrome scans. The system can output monochrome data (either binary for line art or 8-bit for continuous tone), or the false-color image can be output as 24-bit color or as individual 8-bit separations. The same subsystem can directly drive a video camera with Polaroid film for video-resolution color proofs.

It is interesting to observe, however, that at least one such company, Scitex, has been addressing the problem of setting type as well as imaging pictures. Rather than to include text along with the illustrations, by treating the text as if it were artwork and scanning it in as part of the picture to be digitized and output, Scitex has been working on a capability which permits it to accept typographic information as a string of ASCII characters, and to instruct the laser output writer to set type (from its store of digital masters) whenever type is called for, and to include such type on the same film.

Scitex has developed a designer's console, called "Vista," for the capture of page layout information. Text from a front-end system can be routed back to Vista for display. Like the Scitex Imager Console from which it was derived, Vista features 40-bit planes of memory, so that text and graphics may be held in separate memory areas and combined on the screen. Continuous zoom of both text and pictures is supported. Monochrome output for approval purposes can be produced on an Autokon camera.

What does all this mean?

IT SHOULD BE EVIDENT that there are two parallel developments at work: typesetting devices which are learning to produce pictures, and picture-imaging devices which are learning to compose type. These technologies are rapidly beginning to blend into one process. Products will differ according to the complexities of the tasks they undertake, but they will increasingly be based upon the same general solutions. These imply the ability to manipulate both type and other images at the pixel level—whether that manipulation be conducted on a video screen for manipulation and editing, on a proofing device for hard copy review, or by plain paper printing at relatively low resolutions for demand applications, or directly to film or plate for final high-quality reproduction.

There are many options which are open, and no doubt a wide variety of solutions will emerge. For example, there will continue to be CAD/CAM workstations used for the creation of engineering and architectural drawings. There will be a need to typeset these images, as part of a documentation process, along with explanatory text. Some of the text will be in the image areas. Some of it will be in non-related text blocks.

There will be a need to typeset other forms of graphics which will be generated on graphic workstations or on personal and professional computer terminals programmed to function as if they were graphic workstations. In some instances these illustrations will be composed of stored icons and other images which can be manipulated. In others they will be created by vector-related manipulations, in the CAD/CAM manner, but with less complexity. In yet others they will be able to capture information generated from free-hand drawings, as on a tablet, with the aid of a mouse. Some of these stations will offer several of these enumerated capabilities. In addition, there are and will continue to be programs that will generate graphics automatically from numerical data, as with pi charts and other kinds of business graphs, where the information may be taken from a spreadsheet such as Lotus 1-2-3.

There will also be inexpensive devices for the scanning of digitized art, and once the art has been input it will be possible (as indeed it is now) to edit the input, even at the pixel level. For example, the inexpensive Apple Macintosh which does not presently work with scanned input, but nevertheless has a "fat bits" routine which permits the user to erase or add pixels to any image that he or she may have created. More complex workstations with high resolution color will permit the user to modify color values, to overlay and merge pictures, to size, crop and rotate them, to cut holes in them for the insertion of text, and to determine orders of priority for the representation of overlaid images.

Many workstations permit the simultaneous viewing of text and graphics. They may also permit the editing and reprocessing of text and some manipulation of the graphics themselves—not only the

The "Typesetting" of Art

positioning of such graphics but also sizing, cropping, rotation and conceivably some image enhancement. It is obvious, therefore, that the workstation will either have to be extremely powerful in its own right, or have the ability to farm out certain tasks to a larger system of which it is a component.

There remains the problem of how the graphics (and the text) are to be output, and whether data for output can be stored in such fashion that the user can have a choice of output devices without the need for extensive reprocessing of the information itself. Where will the screening of images take place? For different output devices (and, indeed, for different printing processes) will it be necessary to re-screen images, and does this mean that they must be retained in their contone version until the output decision is made? Would one expect the output device to take data in continuous tone format and to perform the screening on the fly as it sets the type and the images?

What forms of data compression can be used? What will be the storage demands, and at what point should graphics be entered into the system?

For example, we are familiar with one yearbook publisher, producing thousands of high school and college yearbooks each spring, containing literally millions of "mugshot" photographs of students and faculty, scenes of the campus and of campus events, and the like. It would be highly desirable to be able to output text and illustrations direct to plate, after producing a lower-resolution plain-paper proof of the proposed pages. But would it be economical to provide sufficient storage to do this? It may be more advantageous to use this technology only where the illustrations are used reiteratively or need to be transmitted from one remote printing site to another (although even here the case of data transmission may prove to be a significant factor).

We are clearly only beginning to see the light with respect to the manner in which the new technology will evolve. Much may depend upon the time it takes to develop inexpensive mass-memory storage devices, and perhaps major improvements in methods of data compression and data transfer. But one thing that we can be certain of is that those who are developing new output devices and new systems to prepare text for output, must no longer ignore the challenge of graphics. The systems adopted must surely encompass solutions sufficiently broad to deal with images of many kinds. And of course this is already beginning to happen.

22

Looking Forward and Back

BY THE END of the 1970s computerized photocomposition was the prevailing method of typesetting throughout the western world. Except for the limited production of Monotype keyboards and casting devices for certain third-world countries, and some use of metal type and typesetting equipment which was obsolete but still extant in specialized applications such as check imprinting or the molding of rubber plates for flexographic printing, the world had shifted to phototypesetting, with computers of one kind or another playing an essential role.

But as early as 1980, new and profound changes were beginning to appear on the horizon. These are the changes that led us to entitle this book *The World of Digital Typesetting*. The title is intended to suggest that the use of digital computers for the creation of text and graphics will introduce yet another round of institutional changes within the printing and publishing industry and indeed throughout the entire world with respect to those activities which rely upon the written word for communication and information interchange.

The remaining chapters in this book will attempt to describe what is happening now and to predict the course of future events, at least in the near term. But in order to do this it will be necessary to establish some sort of frame of reference. Consequently, this chapter will undertake to characterize the state of the art as it existed around the year 1980, or perhaps in the period 1980 through early 1984.

Looking backward

AS WE HAVE SEEN, the first phototypesetting devices were developed immediately after World War II and began to find their way into production in the late 1950s and early 1960s. Initially, these machines were operated by keyboarders who required training in the use of codes and in the making of line-ending decisions. This activity was carried on for the most part by trade or commercial typesetting houses in a production environment, although similar, "captive" establishments were also in operation in some private printing plants and generally throughout the newspaper industry.

In the 1960s computers began to be applied to the front-end activity associated with typesetting. These computers accepted coded input (usually from paper tape) and massaged the data in order to produce a string of codes and text in hyphenated and justified format to drive one or more varieties of typesetting devices. Sometimes this output stream was so formatted that fully composed pages could be generated with "windows" for illustrative material. More often than not the output consisted of galleys which were cut and pasted into pages.

The typesetting devices driven by these computers acted as if they were "slaves," although many of them were not truly slaves. Most of them expected code and text streams containing end-of-line decisions, but had the ability on their own initiative to handle the distribution of white space within the line (as between words and letters) in order to assure that the lines did indeed justify. Some of the faster, higher-speed devices were true slaves. Some manufacturers even provided logic programs with varying degrees of sophistication which would run on the computer controllers within the typesetters themselves so that these devices could also make their own end-of-line decisions.

Initially, the typesetting programs were written for mainframe computers, but usually not for the largest and most expensive ones. However, it very soon became evident that those who wished to use such computer programs desired or were willing to do so in a dedicated environment. Moreover, manufacturers of the larger and more expensive computers, such as IBM, Control Data and Sperry-Univac, were on the whole not successful in developing efficient composition programs capable of being run under a time-shared or multi-processing environment along with other tasks, such as payroll, accounts receivable or even text-management systems. However, some proprietary software packages of this sort were in fact developed, often for specialized applications, but occasionally for commercial use by a particular service bureau typesetting company.

Thus, by the late 1960s, and into the 1970s, most composition systems were written for minicomputers—especially the Digital Equipment PDP-8 and the Data General Nova. Later, the DEC PDP-11 series of minicomputers came into widespread use for this purpose.

On the whole, typesetting machine manufacturers were themselves not able to develop or market such composition software packages and contented themselves by selling the output devices. However, they did begin to introduce direct-entry typesetters for smaller trade shops and in-plant users. Keyboarders on these machines usually made their own end-of-line decisions or ran them in a semiautomatic mode, although some of these devices could justify lines without hyphenation or could perform relatively crude logic hyphenation.

Attention soon focused on the need to handle corrections, and multiple-pass systems were developed to permit proofreading of computer printouts and to incorporate corrections and updates. These processes were awkward and time-consuming, whether they were performed by computers which accepted correction messages and merged them into stored text or whether they involved the merging of a "correction tape" with an existing paper-tape text and code stream.

The newspaper application. In the early 1970s video terminals came into use, first as paper-tape merging devices, next as production keyboard workstations for initial input and on-line corrections, and then finally as editorial (or writers') terminals. By the middle of the 1970s it became very clear that virtually all of the significant systems development activity in the graphic arts industry was driven by the demands of North American newspapers. Problems with unions had been resolved. Initial writer keystrokes could be captured. Stories could be routed from reporter to editor, composed within the system so that copy fitting could be performed, and then sent along to the typesetting machine for final (usually galley) output.

Other special application programs of considerable significance were developed, the most important of which was to capture the input of the classified ad-taker. Answering the telephone, the ad-taker on his or her terminal could call up relevant forms and prompts, enter the necessary information as it was dictated by the advertiser, actually compose the ad so that its length (and cost) could be ascertained and instructions could be placed in the file to permit the ad to sort in its proper sequence and appear only on the days and within the editions authorized. Billing information could be extracted and passed along to a "business" computer for processing.

The magazine market. The second market of particular interest had to do with news magazines and other periodicals with the same general requirements. (In fact, one of the most popular newspaper publishing systems—Atex—was initially developed to meet the specifications of *U.S. News & World Report*, a news magazine.) In the instance of such magazines, attention focused not only upon editorial input and copy fitting, but also pagination and remote transmission to satellite printing plants. Here began the experimentation which resulted in the ability to incorporate line drawings and halftones along with the text so that the final page could be output with these ingredients in place. (These developments will be discussed in the next chapter.)

Commercial typesetting. The third market addressed the needs of commercial typesetters. Production systems, provided by such companies as Penta, Datalogic, CCI in the U.S., and Mergenthaler Linotype in England and West Germany, sometimes included a capability to perform automatic pagination of running text. Gradually these systems were adapted so that they could accept raw input from word-processing systems. Some of these systems also offered specialized programs to address problems involving the conversion of textual data bases.

The "low-end" market. The fourth market consisted of lower-cost direct-entry typesetters and small systems based upon the same architecture. Thus, one could install a Compugraphic EditWriter, a CRTronic or an AM Varityper CompEdit, add supplementary workstations so that floppy disks could be formatted (even with line-ending decisions) and then run off on the back end of a complete unit machine (while the operator might also be inputting or editing another file in the foreground). Such systems were and are used by smaller commercial typesetting shops and in-plant publishers and printers. Increasingly, they began to make their appearance in the office environment.

Area composition. Display ad composition presented yet other kinds of problems. While this work was often performed in the trade shops of advertising typographers, the largest volume was and is produced by the newspapers themselves, usually on a separate system, for the resulting ads could be pasted into position during the hand make-up process. Stimulated by the creation of an industry-financed Newspaper Systems Development Group, interactive terminal workstations were developed to enable skilled operators to follow the carefully prepared layouts (as well as those not so carefully prepared) of layout men and ad designers. Relatively unskilled keyboarders simply typed the copy itself as unlabeled blocks of information, and these blocks were then moved about on a video screen by more highly trained operators. The text elements thus assumed the shapes and positions dictated by the mark-up commands imputed to them. Once a type face selection was made for a particular block, the text could be manipulated by means of cursor keys or a stylus/tablet arrangement, and sizing could be effectuated merely by "bumping" type sizes up or down until the desired fit was obtained. Offerings by Harris, Raytheon, Camex, Xenotron and others soon filled this need, and ultimately many of these terminals were integrated into front-end systems so that the initial input could be created on less expensive workstations, and the display ads themselves could be stored on the main system until it was time to dump them to the typesetter. The relationship between the display ad terminal and the front-end system was only concerned with input, storage and output. The area composition workstations themselves provided their own logic for all of the composition and data manipulation tasks.

The advent of these area composition terminals in the mid-1970s attracted a great deal of attention. Although they were quite limited in their functionality in the sense that the amount of copy that could be formatted in one "take" tended to be relatively small (equivalent to that of a "busy" full-page newspaper grocery ad), the operator functioned in an interactive environment.

He or she saw immediately what happened to the particular copy block as it assumed the characteristics of a particular type face, size and location. Such representations, crude (stick figures made of vectored segments or broadly generic font designs), nevertheless were adequate to determine whether the various elements which made up the ads did in fact take on their intended attributes, and some vendors provided a means of printing out representations of these ads on plain paper, using printer-plotting devices for this purpose.

In a sense, then, the area composition or display ad workstation was a WYSIWYG (what you see is what you get) workstation, and it no doubt contributed to the realization that productivity would be enhanced if terminals and composition systems were not only interactive but provided you with information which would enable you to evaluate what it was that you were doing and what the product would look like if it were composed on the typesetter.

These same tools were enhanced so that they could tackle some of the challenges of business-forms composition and even book work. (Camex introduced a "Page Master" which permitted interactive page-at-a-time composition of running text.)

Other developments. But there were other straws in the wind. One was the development of soft-copy display screens for previewing output. The first of these was a flat glass or plasma display which Dymo Graphic Systems introduced in the mid-70s for review of formatted text blocks. Again, using generic or representational type, text could be composed (by means of an output program much like that which drives a typesetter) to write pseudo-typeset images on a display. Since this was not interactive you would need to go back to the original file to correct errors in formatting or content, but the tool clearly offered the prospect of considerable time saving, especially when debugging new stored formats.

Other preview terminals were introduced, and one supplier (Automix Keyboards) put two screens side by side, one of which provided a preview of blocks of text while the other displayed the reprocessible text file, and cursor movements on the one display could be tracked on the other to permit easy location of text or command areas for modification.

Some preview terminals could actually display true type or at least a more precise representation of the typeset image. Information International and Compugraphic developed methods of actually calling up type characters from the font store on a CRT typesetter and generating the same images (at a somewhat lower resolution) on the screen of a storage tube. Autologic offered the same capability, and gradually other vendors followed with what first consisted of a preview representation and then gradually became more interactive in character. And, as we shall see, some of them also began to demonstrate the ability to combine graphics with the text on such a previewing screen, calling from disk storage graphic images that had been digitized for output by the typesetting machine.

Bedford's "Real-time Composition System." Again, in the mid-to-late 1970s one relatively small, New Hampshire-based company, Bedford Computer Company, introduced "the first truly interactive" composition system. Some degree of interactivity had already been offered by others. Even in the early 1970s a company by the name of Imlac introduced systems which used video terminals that permitted the use of proportionally spaced fonts of several sizes to simulate a justified display of text and made it possible for the user to make corrections and to reprocess only portions of the file (more accurately, from a given point on) rather than to make it necessary to handle all changes in a batch mode. Atex, although it used only a single-sized monospaced display, let the user define and reprocess selected blocks of copy provided all of the necessary command parameters were present or could be presumed to be imputed by the use of display modes (underlined, emboldened, etc.) on the screen. It was clear that many users wanted interactivity and wanted to use terminals that would enable you to see what it was that you were going to get.

However, it was difficult to create the complex software which would permit users to move about randomly within a story file, to make changes and to see the results played out immediately, much as they might appear when finally composed. Composition was still pretty much a sequential process. What happened next depended to a large measure upon codes and commands embedded in the text earlier in the file, which (as with an indent or a change into another type face) might still be presumed to govern even though such commands were not restated on every line or within every paragraph. To some extent, then, the problem of interactivity and the problem of partial processing (that is, not having to process the entire file from the beginning) represented a problem in file management (how to keep track of the various segments of the file, to tie them together, and to know all of the conditions which were to be operative at any particular location).

But aside from the matter of the software, the other problem was the hardware itself and the cost of it. Workstations offering proportional character displays, with characters assuming the width values of true type faces and perhaps possessing other characteristics, such as the presence or absence of serifs, differentiation of roman from italic and bold from light faces, and, especially, the ability to represent type characters at their true size, are expensive to build. Moreover, to build them to operate efficiently in a multi-terminal environment added significantly to the cost and the complexity of the task. It might be one thing to provide a single terminal capable of offering a preview of the composed text or, better yet, a presentation which could be modified interactively in real time. It would be quite another to provide many terminals with this capability on a multi-user system.

And who would need this capability? Does the writer or editor need a WYSIWYG representation? Is this a requirement only for people who are engaged in a production process, having to do with formatting and page make up? And if so, what should the relationship be between editorial people and production people? And how, precisely, would the artists and designers relate to such a system?

A redefinition of function

IT HAS BEEN CLEAR for some time that for newspapers editorial control is very important. It is not that editors want to take over production tasks, but rather that they would like to preserve the flexibility of making changes until the very last moment, all the while keeping track of the ingredients which comprise the paper. Time does not permit the delegation of production chores under such circumstances, and it is necessary for those who are concerned with editorial content to have all the facts and possibilities before them. The demand for editorial control becomes more urgent as newspapers must compete for public acceptance with other news media, especially television.

This requirement is also present when it comes to the production of news and other timely magazines. It is perhaps less urgent in the writing and assembly of books. Nevertheless, at the time that users or potential users began to develop the perception that writers, editors, artists and designers could become more intimately involved in the production process (or, to state it another way, that production decisions would automatically flow from editorial and artistic ones) the tools to achieve this restructuring of functions began to become available—not merely within the graphic arts industry, but from other sources as well.

To some extent the impetus came from the office environment. But it also came from an entirely new source and was brought on by the advent of the personal computer.

Enter the personal computer

PERSONAL COMPUTERS made their appearance in the mid-1970s. Perhaps the first such computer to be developed was the Altair 8800, a product of a company named Micro-Instruments Telemetry Systems (MITS) in New Mexico. That was in the year 1974, and within three years Apple, Tandy/Radio Shack and Commodore began to manufacture and sell literally hundreds of thousands of baby computers to the hobbyist market. In 1979, with the introduction of a software program called VisiCalc, it became apparent that there was a broader use for personal or "professional" computers within the business community. Even IBM observed the trend and announced its own IBM PC on August 12, 1981.

Although the early, low-cost, personal computers were relatively crude devices, often presenting a limited character repertoire in an all upper-case font across 40 columns, it soon became apparent that tasks which had been carried on within the nation's offices on dedicated word processors could also be performed on personal computers. But if there was to be widespread use of such computers by the uninitiated, computers had to become "user-friendly" and easy to operate.

The "Star" out of "Alto." The trend toward user-friendliness was accelerated by the introduction from the Xerox Corporation of a professional workstation called the "Star." And in a sense that product began to foreshadow the convergence of word processing and typesetting.

Researchers at the Palo Alto Research Center of the Xerox Corporation (PARC) had developed an experimental workstation for their own use as early as 1973. The purpose of the experiment was to explore how a self-contained, low-cost personal computer could be used to perform functions normally done on much larger time-shared

Looking Forward and Back

machines. This was certainly the most important unannounced computer product of the 1970s. Machines were used widely within the Xerox organization and experimental installations were set up in various universities as well as the White House.

Alto was conceived as a completely self-contained single-user computer which would communicate with other devices over a 3 Mbaud Ethernet local area network.[1] It was built around a microprogrammed minicomputer and contained a 2.5 Mb removable cartridge disk, a keyboard, a video display screen, and an interface to Ethernet. But because the designers had in mind applications which required graphic capabilities, it was given a high-resolution bit-map display screen and a mouse pointing device. It was these last two elements which gave Alto its distinctive character and which ultimately led to most of the unusual features of the Star.

The Star[2], derived from Alto, was officially introduced in April 1981. It offered a 10½ x 13½ bit-mapped monitor capable of displaying the print area of two typical 8½″ × 11″ pages side-by-side at 96% of true size. It could display typographic type fonts in the exact type face and point size on the screen—not as a "soft typesetter" presentation which could not be edited, but as the normal working mode for the machine. The software also included the ability to handle basic composition and page make-up, to incorporate graphics, and to leave space for illustrations, as well as to generate bar charts, forms and line graphics which could be merged into text files and edited in the same fashion as other elements in the file.

Part of the impact of the Xerox announcement was due to the fact that several years earlier (late 1978) Xerox had released its model 9700 electronic xerographic printer, capable of serving as a typesetter, printing press and collating machine. It cooperated in the installation of the first all-9700 publishing center for the production of manuals and documentation material at Mitel in Canada in the summer of 1980, and began an active program of font development to maximize the utility of type based upon a 300-dot-per-inch resolution. In the fall of 1980 it released a less expensive model, the 5700. Then, in January 1981, it announced the Xerox Integrated Composition System (XICS), a composition and page make-up package which could run on a wide variety of host computers and which was able to compose fully made-up pages to run on the 9700 and 5700 printers.

The Star, unfortunately, could drive neither the 9700 nor the 5700, but it was able to drive a 12-page-per-minute 8044 Print Server offered as an Ethernet peripheral.

Actually, although the Star made a profound impact upon the industry since it offered a preview of new technologies which were clearly to emerge in the near future, the product itself did not sell very well. Yet its concepts were far-reaching. They included the mouse, the use of icons to describe functions and options available to be performed, and the notion of "progressive disclosure" which brings to the screen (via a window) whatever functions or choices may be available to an operator at the moment, in terms of his desired work cycle.

---

1. The LAN was subsequently increased in speed to 10 Mb.

2. The name "Star" was subsequently challenged by another vendor. The official name of the product is the Xerox 8010. However the term continues to be associated with the product in a historical sense.

The impact of Star became even more obvious when the Apple Computer Company introduced Lisa in January 1983 and Macintosh in January 1984. Both of these products lean heavily upon the concepts pioneered by Alto and Star, and several key PARC engineers and system architects had in the meantime transferred their loyalty to Apple.

Text and graphics information created on the screen of the Xerox 8010 Star can be reproduced on the 8044 print server. Note the use of "icons" shown here on the right-hand side of the screen, the mouse in the foreground, and the intermixture text and graphics.

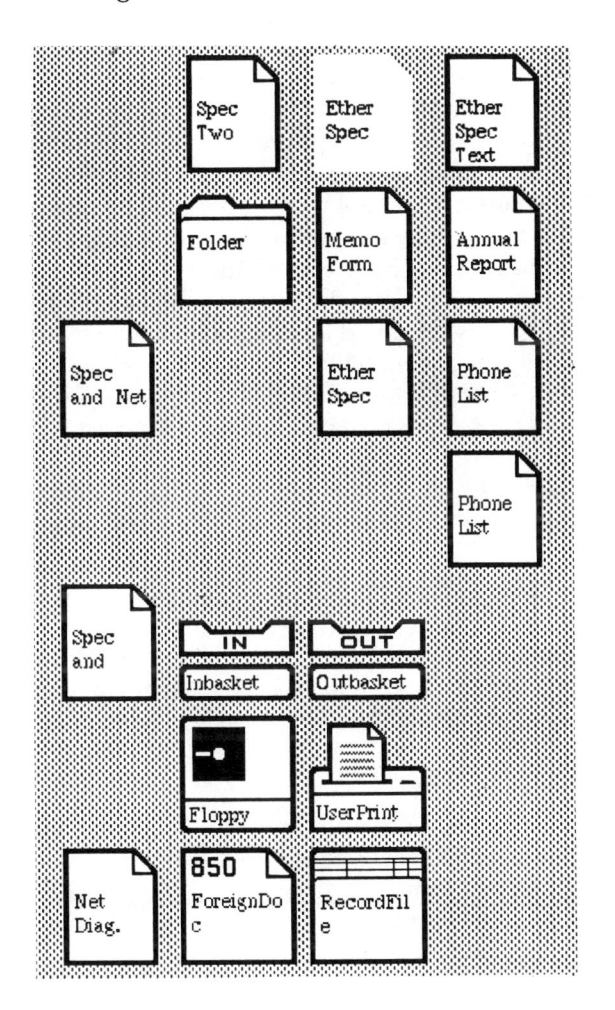

Looking Forward and Back

The Xerox Star pioneered the use of icons to simplify the activities of the user at the workstation. By moving a mouse so that a cursor points to the desired icon, the computer is instructed to perform a function. Hence, a manuscript such as "Annual Report" can be moved over to a "folder" or could be transferred to the out basket or to the printer.

A sample of output generated on the Xerox 9700 printer is also shown. Note the use of graphics and multilevel math.

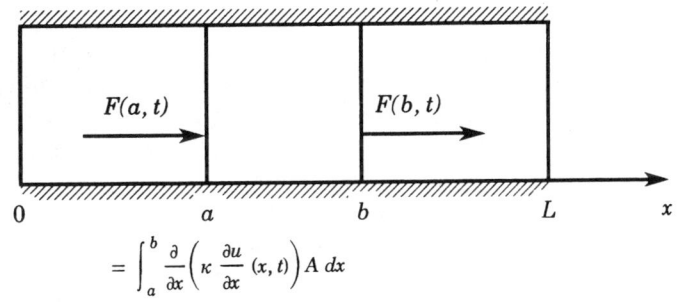

$$= \int_a^b \frac{\partial}{\partial x}\left(\kappa \frac{\partial u}{\partial x}(x, t)\right) A \, dx$$

Using this formula and computing dQ/dt from (3.1.1) the conservation law (3.1.2) becomes

$$(3.1.4) \qquad \int_a^b \left[c\rho \frac{\partial u}{\partial t}(x, t) - \frac{\partial}{\partial x}\left(\kappa \frac{\partial u}{\partial x}(x, t)\right)\right] A \, dx = source \, term$$

If there are no heat sources present in the rod, then the source term is zero and the integral in Equation (3.1.4) is zero. In this discussion, the interval $[a, b]$ is any subinterval of $[0, L]$. We assume that the integrand in (3.1.4) is a continuous function of x. It then follows that the integrand is zero throughout $[0, L]$. For if the

The Seybold predictions. Within the graphic arts industry it is possible that the course of development was influenced to some extent by some "Fearless Projections About the Next Generation of Systems" published in *The Seybold Report on Publishing Systems* in July 1980 (*see Vol. 9, No. 2*). In this article the author, Jonathan Seybold, took a look at some of the emerging computer technology and tried to anticipate what this might mean for the next generation of text processing systems. "We do not intend to romanticize the latest marvel in a chip," he wrote, "nor do we wish to suggest that the system you just bought yesterday is about to be instantly rendered obsolete. However, we do think that the new technology now coming into the market will have a profound impact on the shape of systems which will emerge in the next few years—and, indeed, on our whole perception of what we can expect such systems to do for us."[1]

Also in this article he predicted that the 1980s would be a decade of profound change in communication technologies and their usage patterns:

> There is widespread agreement that we are now laying the foundation for new digital means of storing, retrieving, transmitting, manipulating and combining sound pictures (both still and moving) and the written word. We believe there is also a growing perception that the new technology will bring a convergence of (and competition between) applications which we have thus far been able to fit into relatively neat market cubbyholes.

He cited, as illustrative of these applications, office word processing, graphics, voice communication, data processing, text and image processing for printing and publishing, television and radio broadcasting, video publishing, phone services, business and scientific data processing, and home computers.

He predicted that the next generation of computers to impact the graphic arts industry would be based upon 16-bit micros, especially the Motorola 68000 as well as the DEC LSI-11 series. Future systems would be able to use a large amount of computing power and lots of memory, to adopt system architectures which would place computer processing power and memory as close to the user as possible, and to dedicate computer processors to particular functions. Thus computer-intensive applications which have been expensive would become dramatically cheaper, especially extensive image processing, high-resolution interactive graphic displays for editing, page layout and image manipulation.

There would also be a movement away from assembler language programming to higher level languages, especially Pascal and "C" under the Unix operating environment. There would be extensive use of the Winchester (sealed disk) technology as well as RAM disks, with thin film and optical disks not very far in the future. Display screens for text processing would move away from the monospaced cathode ray tube monitor. "Fortunately, the same advances in processors and memory which make it possible to bring large amounts of computing power down to the user level will also make it far more

1. See "Systems for the '80s: Fearless Projections About the Next Generation of Systems," *The Seybold Report on Publishing Systems*, Vol.9, No. 22, pp.1-14.

Looking Forward and Back

IBM PC-XT

Hewlett-Packard

Apple Macintosh

The variety of approaches proffered to the potential user of personal and professional computers is illustrated by these three examples. The IBM PC-XT is the "big brother" of the IBM PC and shares with it the universality of available software written for the *de facto* standard which the latter has come to signify. The Apple Macintosh, on the other hand, is less intimidating, offering to the user the utmost in "friendliness" or simplicity of operation. For sheer convenience, the nine pound 13 x 10 x 3" Hewlett-Packard portable ranks high and exemplifies the itinerant portable computing power busy professionals have come to rely upon.

economical to provide individual users with high-resolution graphic display screens at comparatively modest (less than $10,000 per workstation) costs."

One of the most explosive areas of the 1980s would be in the area of digital communication.

> We have already seen this in the newspaper field with the movement of both major wire services into satellite communication to small local receive antennas, and with the growing trend toward transmission of facsimile pages between central plants and remote printing operations via microwave links. We have seen it in the magazine publishing field with the satellite transmission systems used by the national news magazines and others. We have even seen it in the growing tendency of commercial typesetting shops to receive customer input over phone lines and/or to return proofs via inexpensive facsimile units.

Although there would be a battle for jurisdiction over the performance of these common carrier functions, some winners would emerge. In the meantime certain de facto local communication channels would develop along the lines of Ethernet.

In terms of human factors, certain principles should emerge: anybody with rudimentary typing skills should be able to use the system. The system should be transparent to the user. It should not fatigue him or her or endanger the user's health. It must be completely dependable. It must provide instant response times and should not degrade under heavy loads.

It was predicted that there would be highly interactive workstations, with high-speed communication links to tie together multiple computers, a greater use of high-resolution graphic display screens, an integration of text and graphics, the ability to drive virtually any output device from typesetters to electronic printers, from laser platemakers to displays of the viewdata/teletext variety, and there would be a convergence of office and graphic arts systems and functions.

The trend begins

ALMOST IMMEDIATELY AFTER the publication of this *Report*, no doubt because many others were clearly perceiving the same trends, a rash of new firms sprang up, financed quite generously by venture capitalists.

For the most part these firms were founded by persons who had extensive prior experience as leaders of other companies in the graphic arts industry. Among them were such names as XyVision and Texet, Interleaf and Qubix, ImagiTex, Imteks, Intran, Impres, Data Retrieval Systems, and others. Older line companies, such as Intergraph, began to develop new products or to make deals to incorporate the ideas of some of the new vendors. Other companies crossed boundaries they had previously drawn in defining their areas of interest, and this included Crosfield and Hell, Scitex, Camex, Eocom, Autologic, Xenotron, and others.

Thus, by the spring of 1983, Tom Hagan, president of Camex, reported: "In the 1950s, '60s, and '70s the thrust of development in pre-press systems was to 'get the lead out.' In the 1980s it will be to 'get the silver out.' We are now striving to eliminate mechanicals and paste-ups as part of the printing and publishing process. It is taking longer than people had expected, but things are now happening very rapidly. Nineteen eighty-three will be a turning point. I cannot imagine a more exciting time to be involved in this industry."[1]

It is interesting to observe that the impetus for new developments lay primarily within the technology itself and the challenge to those familiar with the industry to apply it to the solution of perceived problems. There was no clear and present pressure by potential users for specific new products or solutions. In fact, one witnessed a fair amount of confusion on the part of users as to where they might want to go next and what remained to be done. Perhaps the news magazines were clearest in visualizing their needs. They wanted to be able to produce process color illustrations with late-breaking editorial content. They also wanted to capture the layout information created by the artist or page designer and pass this on as parameters so that text could be positioned and formatted automatically without the need to reintroduce these parameters. They also wanted to be able to produce "what-if" pages, permitting the review of alternative layouts for during editorial conferences.

Newspapers felt that it would be "nice" to go directly to plate, and that this would save a great deal of time and money. But they recognized that solutions would first need to be found bearing upon the storage and manipulation of graphic elements. Even more perplexing, however, was the problem of how to incorporate display ad matter which came from outside sources, without the need to scan it into the "system." They did not perceive that in the short run, at least, such material would be transmitted from ad agency to newspaper in digital form.

Newspapers began to experiment with systems for pagination, with and without the inclusion of graphics. The *Minneapolis Star & Tribune* cooperated with Atex in the devopment of an automated page make-up system which began with the page dummying process and story assignments. Completed stories thus arranged themselves into their respective niches, with the insufficient story lengths flagged, and "oversets" identified or automatically jumped to designated pages. As previously mentioned, the Utica *Observer-Dispatch* installed a direct-to-plate capability provided by the cooperative efforts of Hastech and Eocom. The Pasadena *Star-Times* installed a system by Information International which placed responsibility for both text and graphics in editorial hands.

And yet there was general agreement that newspapers were no longer the driving force in pre-press systems development. By 1984 the emphasis had clearly shifted to the technical documentation, in-plant marketplace. Virtually all of the entrepreneurial start-up companies were counting on sales to this market, and most of the new development work was now focused on this market.

1. See "Report from Santa Monica, Part I: '1983 Will Be a Turning Point'," *The Seybold Report on Publishing Systems*, Vol. 12, No. 15, p. 1.

Jonathan Seybold commented upon this trend in the April 9, 1984 issue of *The Seybold Report on Publishing Systems*:

> We believe . . . that this market will "drive" the industry in the '80s much as newspapers did in the '70s. Even products which are developed for or sold to other markets will be derived from or influenced by products which have been developed with the needs of documentation users in mind. This is a profound shift, and one which newspapers and magazines in particular are going to have some trouble adjusting to. . . . we expect that this shift will provide substantial impetus for more rapid development of systems which integrate text and graphics (especially line graphics), for continued emphasis on page make-up of long, structured documents which involve extensive uise of both text and illustrations, and for more emphasis on writers' and editors' tools.[1]

The underlying motivation for the changes which he forecast was

> . . . not the promise of directly measurable labor or materials savings, but rather a desire to change the nature of the publications production process. . . . People perceive present processes as messy, time-consuming, fraught with aggravation and difficult to control. They are beginning to realize that they do not have to live like this anymore. They are anxious to streamline and simplify the entire process, to shorten deadlines, to gain control.

There was, he reported, a strong desire "to get on with it." Integration had become the major thrust. And it is related not only to the integration of text and graphics, but also to the integration of all editorial and production functions. Whether the application involved newspapers, magazines, in-plant proposals, documentation groups, an insurance company or a commercial printer/typesetter, the common thread had become "how to tie together all of the steps and procedures required to produce a document."

Almost no one now disputes the contention that future output technology will be built around general-purpose raster image processors (RIPs) which generate both text and graphic output at virtually any arbitrary resolution to drive any raster output imaging device. Everyone appears to agree that this is what they really want to be able to do. They may want to output a page on an electronic printer for proof or demand-printing applications, on a high-resolution typesetter for use as a high-quality master, direct to plate, or direct to a facsimile receiver.

This does not mean that the output device necessarily has to be a laser imaging machine. Autologic and Information International both argue that cathode ray tube technology will continue to be appropriate for many applications. But the new generation of CRT typesetters will be raster output devices driven by the same RIP which can also drive electonic printers and other output devices.

Other possible output technologies include LED arrays (as in the Agfa P-400 printer), electro-erosion (as in the IBM 4250), direct electron beam recording, ion deposition (as in the Delphax electronic printer), and so forth. But all are basically raster output technologies, and all can be driven by a good general-purpose RIP.

---

1. See "Seybold Seminar '84: Integration of Text and Graphics," *The Seybold Report on Publishing Systems*, Vol. 13, No. 14, p. 5.

Looking Forward and Back

The raster image processor is therefore central to the implementation of the new technology. A consensus has emerged as to what such a RIP should be able to do, but the design and production of the RIP has proven to be more difficult than many had imagined. In general, these functions are seen to be:

- To produce good quality type in a wide variety of sizes and with a wide variety of faces, without any perceptible delay in accessing the fonts and faces in question.
- To be able to rotate type, even individual characters or blocks, to any angle.
- To be able to generate screen tints, patterns and reverses to any arbitrary geometric area, including the ability to have type cross boundaries from one area to the next, so that a word might begin as black on a white background and end up as white on a black background.
- To perform drawing and plotting functions, including the generation of boxes, shapes with rounded corners, as well as ovals and circles to plot arbitrary lines and curves and to store and access a library of geometric shapes.
- To be able to incorporate illustrative material and to output it, whether a line drawing or a contone image, at any size and any output resolution, including the screening of halftones on the fly.

Oddly enough, while these developments might suggest less interest in hard copy and more reliance upon WYSIWYG terminals, it is presumed that proof copy at lower resolutions will be conveniently available, and it, too, should resemble the final output as closely as possible, whether that output is intended to be direct-to-photographic material or to printing plate. To accomplish this, it is expected that there will need to be a closer integration of the hard-copy output, of whatever quality, with other system functions.

As Jonathan Seybold observes:

> As long as it simply had to supply character strings and command codes a system could be expected to drive a wide variety of "third-party" output typesetters. Now, however, output of full pages of text and graphics becomes far more intimately tied into the system. The more closely a system tries to approximate the true output type fonts on a display screen, and the more manipulation of line art and pictures which it permits, the more difficult it will be to support a variety of output image processors. In the end, we believe that system vendors will either have to supply the RIP or to specify that a particular RIP be used with their system.

In the next chapter, specific products will be discussed which fit into the pattern we have just outlined. The reader must understand, of course, that in a field which is changing very rapidly, no book can remain up to date. A discussion of the capabilities and systems covered in the next chapter is therefore not intended to be definitive, but rather to be indicative of trends and capabilities which happened to prevail at the time when this book was finally brought to a conclusion (May 1984).

23

Raster Image Processing

IN THIS CHAPTER we shall take a closer look at the technology which underlies new solutions to the problems of pagination, the treatment and manipulation of graphics, and the production of interim proofs as well as the final product. We shall begin with a discussion of raster image processors since these devices have now become a critical component of any new system. Thus it is appropriate to begin with a definition of the term.

Once we have arrived at an understanding of the term and the concepts behind it, we will proceed with a brief review of the evolution of various kinds of raster image processors and imaging devices. We cannot provide a comprehensive review in a field which is changing so dramatically, but we shall select a few products to illustrate these evolutionary trends.

What is a RIP? To develop such a definition turns out to be difficult. When we began to write this chapter we suddenly realized that the term raster image processor does not in fact have common currency and was probably invented by "the Seybolds." If it is true that we invented it, then it should mean whatever we choose to have it mean. But it is not certain that we have invariably used it in a consistent and precise manner. Now it seems essential for our own benefit as students of the technology, and for that of the industry as well, to try to give the concept a more precise definition.

The principal function of a raster image processor is to produce an image which can be output for visual inspection, either on paper (plain or photographic), on some sort of visual display such as a VDT, or to film or plate. The image so displayed is made up of picture elements (pels or pixels) at a resolution sufficient to permit inspection and review or even to suffice in some cases for final representation. The quality of the image depends upon its resolution (that is, the number of pixels laid down per inch or millimeter), as well as the size of the pixel itself. (It may vary from less than one mil in diameter to perhaps several mils.) A pixel is not the same thing as a halftone dot, although halftone dots may be constructed out of a combination of pixels.

A pixel usually consists of a tiny black spot on a white background, although it could just as well be a tiny white spot on a black background, or it could be a spot of one color on a background of another color. For text or line art, the spot or color is usually represented by a bit (that is, an "on" signal), and the background by an

Raster Image Processing

off-bit or an off-signal. To change the relationship between background and image you have only to reverse the on and off signals.

However, it is possible that pixels could vary in intensity. Should this be true it would be necessary to describe each pixel by a series of bits (such as a byte) and the number of bits so required would depend upon the number of gray scale levels desired. (Eight bits would get you 256 levels of gray.) The problem with producing pixels of varying levels of gray is that most output devices do not have the ability to vary the intensity of their output. Ink, for example, at least on a single-color press, is usually black. However, it would be possible to create colors and shades by superimposing one color upon another, and there are printing devices (ink jet or matrix ribbon printers) capable of accessing different colors more or less simultaneously, rather than as overlays, the general way a printing press reproduces color.

For purposes of the present discussion, however, it will be assumed that we are dealing only with black or white pixels, and that any gray scale effects desired will be created by the frequency and the distribution of such pixels.[1]

Across-the-page imaging. We shall also assume that the raster output device lays down pixels at whatever resolution selected or that it is capable of, *across* the page, although the page could consist either of a "portrait" orientation or a "landscape" orientation—that is, the contents of the page could be generated from top to bottom or from one side to another, and the top could itself be any one of the four edges of the image.

The resolution in the horizontal sweep direction is determined by the mechanism for producing the pixels. It may be based upon how close the nozzles of a comb of ink jets can be an assembled (although two rows could be staggered to enhance this effect), or how close metal styluses can be positioned. (They heat up to burn off a coating in the electro-erosion process.) Or, the proximity of one dot to the next may be a function of an electro-optical system involving the minute incremental motions of a revolving mirror which deflects a laser or electron beam. Or, it may be determined by the precision and discreteness of the control of a stepping motor that pulls a tiny CRT pixel generator across a page. Finally, the timing of the electronic dot-generating hardware (turning the beam on and off) is vital to the resolution process.

The resolution in the vertical direction is often determined by the distance the paper or film is advanced in front of the imaging area. Often the "carrier" (which could be a drum or belt transfering the image to paper, or a drum or platen carrying the paper or film itself) moves in such fashion that the resolution in the vertical direction is the same as that which occurs horizontally. But this need not be the case. One could lay down dots at a resolution of 480 per inch horizontally and only 240 per inch vertically—which is the case with certain versions of the Canon LBP-10. The "jaggies" or apparent irregularities associated with image shapes would be more conspicuous in that dimension with the coarsest resolution.

1. However, on a video screen additional bit planes can be used to supplement the basic image with an intermediate intensity representation, to improve the apparent smoothness of curves, thus minimizing the "jaggy" effect of the raster image. The shifting of pixel locations can also sometimes be used. These techniques are known as "anti-aliasing."

The "anonymity" of the pixel image. The relationship between the individual pixel and the image it is intended to convey is ambiguous or remote since the pixels are laid down in a sequence which disassociates them from the character or image in question. When you lay down strokes to form a character on the face of a CRT tube, those strokes comprise a slice of that character. In a sense, the program which calls for the stroke to be generated "knows" that it is creating a portion of a particular character. But with raster imaging, the device which forms the image pattern must "look at" a section of a page, and at the time the process takes place it will not need to "know" anything about the symbolism or "meaning" of the representation being created—not even whether it is laying down pictures or characters.

Other elements in the definition. But there is more to the definition of a raster image processor than the mere laying down of pixels. A facsimile device can read an image on one station and write out pixels to reproduce or reconstruct that image on another station. (Or, it can even store its observations and then write them to the same device used to scan them.) It can even alter the tonal values of the image by changing the threshold of its observations as it converts, for example, from analog to digital signals.

But our definition does not include the scanner-writer in the category of a raster image processor when its task is simply to record pixels more or less in the form in which they have already been detected. Our concept of a raster image processor is that it produces a raster sequence of pixels based upon input data which are not organized or presented in the same fashion. In a sense, then, a raster image processor, as we conceive it, converts a page descriptor file or an algorithmic listing of shapes and coordinates them into an image.

Perhaps the best illustration is to describe the way in which a vector diagram can be imaged by a raster output device. Computer hardware or software (or a likely combination of the two) studies a programmed instruction which would normally direct an imaging device to draw, say, a diagonal line from point A to point B. But the program knows that it may only do this by ascertaining the position of point A in terms of its x/y coordinates (rounding off the calculation to take into account the nearest available x/y position which the output device is capable of addressing). Having done this and then advanced the recording paper infinitesimally, it computes where the next dot should be positioned. This can only be determined by performing a mathematical calculation along these lines:

> Let point A be described as 42/74 where 42 represents the number of units from a theoretical base point in the y position, and 74 represents the number of units from a theoretical base point in the x position. And if point B is described as 142/3, and if we know that the vector is to be a straight line, with 100 steps possible in the vertical direction, then each x/y step must move down by one unit and over toward the left by a value which represents the addressable location closest to 1/100 of the difference between 74 and 3. That location is remembered and a pixel is deposited there at the appropriate time.

Raster Image Processing

If we suppose that we were dealing not with vectors, but with spline[1] curves or combinations of curves and lines, all of which abut to form the outline of a character, the mathematical calculations become somewhat more complex. Moreover, if we assume that the outline shapes represented by this assembly of spline curves and line segments can be enlarged, reduced or changed in their proportions, the complexities multiply.

In addition, we must generally assume that there will be many images to be produced across the page, that the paper probably advances inexorably at a constant speed, and that all calculations must be made with sufficient rapidity to keep up with the writing speed of the device.

Now, if we assume further that the input information from which all of these calculations must be made does not reside within the raster image processor all at once, but only (to save buffer memory) enough of it to provide the data for perhaps the first 10 or 20 passes of the writing instrument across the paper, then we appreciate all the more the magnitude of the task assigned to even the simplest raster image processor.

The dedicated RIP vs. the generalized RIP. The easiest raster image processor to build is one which is destined to produce output only for a particular device, with a known resolution and a limited number of variables so far as its calculations are concerned. For example, character shapes will not be sized at all, but merely laid down from existing outlines or even from predefined bits or run-length codes which can be stored on ROMs.

We might also assume that no images are to be rotated from the shape or configuration in which they have been input. And we might imagine that there will be only one (limited) set of alphanumeric characters. Perhaps there would be no graphics to include within the output.

Would we then use the term raster image processor to describe the activity of a device which simply converts a stream of ASCII characters into dot matrix representations?

Perhaps the term might be so used, and it thus becomes apparent that there can be different levels of RIPS, some of which are general-purpose in nature and some of which are built into particular devices to perform functions only relevant to the context in which they operate. To clarify this point, it will be helpful to take one particular case study and to follow the development of a single product. For this purpose, we will take a close look at the Camex Corporation.

The Camex evolution

WHEN CAMEX first developed its Model 135 display ad make-up terminal the characters of varying sizes and shapes, which were arranged on the screen of the workstation in accordance with operator decisions as to font, size and position selections, were all "stick" or vector figures. A raster image display could have been chosen (whereby each character was made up of individual pixels) and indeed

[1]. A type of mathematically defined curve which smooothly links a series of points. In typography, these points constitute the outline of a character.

this was the course chosen by Harris on its 2200, or Raytheon on the Raycomp.

Camex chose the vector approach (or calligraphic as Camex terms it) for the following reasons:

> A raster unit must generate the image on the screen in a fixed sequence, say from left to right or from top to bottom. For that reason the material to be viewed on the screen must first be sorted into proper sequence before it can be sprayed across the screen. A calligraphic display, on the other hand, uses an electron beam that moves randomly from place to place, thus painting strokes of characters or lines in any order.
>
> Because of the sorting required before an image can be generated onto the screen with a raster tube (or a storage tube, for that matter), all operator commands affecting the material displayed must invite software interpretation. With a calligraphic tube, since the implementation on the display of operator commands does not have to pass through this software sorting phase, changes are effected more rapidly—instantaneously, in fact.
>
> Apart from copy block movement, there are other parameter changes whose results can be displayed instantaneously on the Camex screen—*e.g.*, changes in point size, set size, interword spacing, letterspacing, leading, quading and indentations, as well as the scaling and rotation of graphics. Moreover, there is no limit to the amount of text which can be entered and edited in place within the ad.
>
> What you gain in opting for a calligraphic display is mobility and responsiveness. What you sacrifice is *density*. With a 40-frame-per-second refresh rate, no more than 2000 characters (or their equivalent in graphic outlines) can appear on the screen at any one time. A raster or storage tube can display 5000 or 6000 characters.
>
> Camex compensates for the relatively low density of its display unit in several ways. When the character capacity of the screen has been reached (in terms of character density) the material which was entered first will automatically be represented diagrammatically. In that situation, the user might choose that a particular region or item of previously-composed material be represented as lines, in order to allow him to work with a section of uncomposed text while still retaining a feel for the overall balance of the page. Moreover, the operator can zoom in on that portion of the text which has been represented diagrammatically whenever he wishes, and the lines will then become words and sentences, ready for editing, revision, or composition.
>
> The company feels that until someone comes along with the "perfect" CAM terminal—*i.e.*, one which could display a full-sized newspaper page filled with characters, graphics and halftones, all faithfully and stably rendered, and which could also be instantaneously responsive to operator commands, a trade-off must be made.
>
> So Camex has chosen *responsiveness over density*.[1]

The year was 1976, and economical hardware then precluded any other solution. However, Camex did offer a unique hard-copy proofing device. It used an electrostatic printer by Versatec, with an

---

1. See *The Seybold Report*, Vol. 5, No. 15, pp. 4-5.

Raster Image Processing

imaging resolution of 200 dots per inch. And Camex developed a raster image processor in the form of software to run on its host 32K PDP-11/35 that was capable of driving the Versatec. Camex did not attempt to use the Versatec to provide a "dump" of what was created by vectors on the workstation screen. Instead, it sent a stream of data to the Versatec that instructed the device to lay down pixels that emulated the vector diagrams previously shown on the screen. By modern terminology, then, the PDP-11/35 software program functioned as a raster image processor.

In the year 1983, Camex introduced a completely new workstation, which it called "Breeze." This terminal no longer used calligraphic or vector-generated stick figures. It didn't even use generic type constructed of pixels painted in rasterized format on the screen of the workstation. It used true type images, constructed of rasterized pixels. These characters can be manipulated and sized, moved about on the screen, and even rotated. Characters are generated from outline forms that are called into memory, as required, and stored on a Winchester disk associated with one million bytes of random access memory under the control of a Motorola 68000 microprocessor, along with additional hardware.[1]

> [The computer] really contains two separate processors. The first is a Motorola 68000 on an Intel Multibus. The second is Camex's own bit-slice image processor with a changeable micro-code instruction set and two data buses (the Multibus plus a separate high-speed internal communication bus). The RAM memory associated with the bit-slice image processor is dual-ported so that it can be accessed via both buses.
>
> Between the time that a data stream enters [the computer] and the time that it is output as a raster stream of black-and-white bits, it is passed through several processing operations, all of which can proceed in parallel. Because there are two separate processors, it is easiest to look at the functions performed by each of the processors: Input data is first processed by programs running in the 68000. These perform pre-processing housekeeping functions, including interpreting input command codes, ordering data, loading digitized character masters, and the sizing, expanding, condensing, obliquing and rotating of character masters. It passes to the actual bit-generation logic of the machine-sized character masters in the proper aspect ratio and angle of rotation.
>
> The data prepared by the 68000 may be passed directly to the image processor for explosion into raster image data. Or, if the second processor is busy setting another job or has not yet caught up with the previous data fed by the 68000, the intermediate data may be temporarily stored on disk.
>
> In either event, the second processor will read data passed to it from the 68000, generate the output bit patterns, and pass these on to the output device. Functions performed at this step include screening of continuous-tone pictures and decompression of compressed line art data.

The raster image processor we have just described is used not only to generate characters for hard copy output, but also to create character and graphic images on the display screen. In fact, at this

1. Extracted from comments which appear in *The Seybold Report on Publishing Systems*, Vol. 12, No. 18, pp. 10-11.

The Camex Breeze terminal can manipulate both text and graphics. The workstation is shown on this page as well as a close-up of the screen. The RIP which services the Breeze also feeds rasterized images to the BitPrinter and SuperSetter. The Camex SuperSetter, like the Sim-X typesetter, uses the back end of the Monotype Lasercomp. Output from the SuperSetter is shown on the facing page.

SuperSetter

RACCOON IN BLACK & WHITE

writing the RIP rasterizes output for the interactive workstation and for a product known as a BitCaster, which is a Canon LBP-10 electrostatic printer capable of outputting at a resolution of 480 dots per inch in both horizontal and vertical directions. It also outputs to the BitSetter, which consists of the optical bed and film transport portion of a Monotype Lasercomp,[1] with a resolution of 1,000 dots per inch. It is further capable of driving a laser platemaker (Chemco) at a 1,000-line-per-inch resolution. In fact, the RIP is intended to generate raster image output for virtually any size image area at virtually any resolution. The specifications claim a character size range of four points to six inches, a maximum output line length of at least 24 inches, a minimum width counting increment of 4320 units per em, and a minimum horizontal and vertical positioning increment so fine that the BitCaster can execute hundreds of horizontal and vertical positioning commands without having to worry about round-off errors. Characters may be drawn to any combination of height and width and may be obliqued or rotated at any angle from 0° to 360° in .006° increments. Lines, paragraphs or an entire job may be rotated as well as individual characters, not only making it possible to set type at odd angles, but also to reorient entire pages to optimize the width/length constraints of a particular output device.

Scanned line graphics may be input to the machine either as full bit maps or as compressed bit maps, using a fairly conventional run-length encoding scheme. The compressed data are decompressed on the fly by the bit-generator logic of the machine. The RIP can also generate reverses over any area, as well as a wide variety of screen patterns, tints, borders and rules. Plans include converting CAD/CAM images into raster format as well.

Continuous tone picture information can be sized and screened on the fly, but image enhancement capabilities are not presently offered. It is generally expected that such functions would be performed on another system, such as that offered by ImagiTex.

Camex had completed its raster image processor and applied it to the output task of driving its BitPrinter and BitSetter before it had completed its Breeze terminal. When outputting to a hard-copy device the RIP clearly functions in a batch environment, but when outputting to the Breeze terminal it may be said to be interactive in character.

However, there is no significant difference in the functionality of the RIP, whether it outputs to the Breeze or to the BitSetter. It does precisely the same thing in basically the same time intervals, except that data recorded on the Breeze is likely to be manipulated, zoomed, moved about on the screen, sized and rotated, etc., until the operator is satisfied with the results. Thus these functions take place in real time, and except for the few seconds that might be required to paint out a large image representing a continuous tone picture, the response on the Breeze is virtually instantaneous. The terminal viewing area is 19″ diagonal, the screen resolution is 1024 x 800 pixels and this means that, for screen viewing of either type or pictures, the RIP actually ignores a large portion of the data it has stored, but it

---

1. See Chapter 9, p. 137.

Raster Image Processing

nevertheless manipulates all of the information at once. For type it of course generates from stored outlines only the pixel information needed for a particular device. Other similar devices work with a subset of the data (sufficient for screen resolution) and then go back and reprocess the larger data set required for the finest resolution on the highest-quality output device.

It is to be noted that the same RIP can drive the BitPrinter, BitSetter and Breeze terminal. As a practical matter, however, it is likely that each Breeze terminal would have its own RIP, and a second RIP would be used to drive (alternately, but not simultaneously) either the BitPrinter or the BitCaster.

It does not follow that the Camex RIP is necessarily the "ultimate" RIP, but if one seeks a definition of precisely what a raster image processor consists of, one might wish to decide for himself just where the line should be drawn to differentiate a raster image processor from a more specialized and dedicated engine.

Below are the features, listed from the least demanding to the most complex and powerful, that might be included:

- To convert a stream of ASCII-like commands and character codes, already arranged in line and page format, into rasterized pixels to drive an output printer, displaying one type font with a limited character set and one type size.
- To perform the same function but to respond to the commands within the input stream which would size the characters, not by altering the bit maps of the individual characters, but by spacing them (closer together or farther apart) to change character size and density.
- To perform the same functions but to enhance the number of fonts available, from one to perhaps a half dozen (including script, Old English, serif, sans serif, etc.).
- To size type by outputting characters of a constant resolution—in other words, working generally from an outline font master, filling in that outline with the number of pixels which would be required to keep all type weights at maximum resolution such as 200 or 300 dots per inch.
- To be able to use true fonts, rather than generic ones. While the fonts will not contain as many pixels as would be generated on a high-quality output device, they would offer as much detail as one would find on a high-quality proof printer and would, of course, correspond precisely in the width values, weights and shapes of individual characters.
- To be able to reverse areas which are black and white, not only universally for a given page, but by command within selected areas of a page.
- To be able to include, along with text, graphic output which has been generated by a "pixel-fill" technique.
- To be able to go through a vector-to-raster conversion so that the RIP will rasterize vectors and even more sophisticated shapes made up of spline curves along with images created by the linking together of line segment elements.

- To be able to fill any areas defined by boundaries, either with solids or with numerous varieties of screened patterns.
- To be able to assign priorities to various overlapping areas so that one set of images (*e.g.*, type) might supersede another (which might represent a tinted background).
- To be able to use the same RIP to create output for various devices, including those with different resolution capabilities and representing different size and shape characteristics.
- To be able to enlarge or reduce an image or a picture for viewing purposes and either to add more dots (which were suppressed in the initial representation) or to interpolate additional dots to provide more detail to a picture (if enlarged) or to eliminate detail (if necessary, even at the expense of legibility) if sizing downward.
- To be able to use the same RIP for the creation or positioning of the input as for the creation of the output, and to be able to do this in real time, again taking into account different resolution capabilities of screen versus output units.
- To be able to define a particular shape by its inherent properties (such as a character, word or picture) and to move that shape from one place to another (perhaps displacing other data), to change the proportions of that defined element and also to change its orientation (*i.e.*, rotation).
- To be able to do the same thing with pixel information which has no inherent identity (that is, it is not a character or a word or a picture) but may represent only an arbitrary area of pixels with no particular distinguishing feature other than the initial location of the pixels and their proximity to one another.
- To be able to screen defined areas of an image or an entire image to meet predetermined requirements for reproduction as a halftone image.
- To be able to change the tonal values (degree of contrast, mid-tone values, etc.) of any such screened areas or of selected areas.
- To be able to manipulate color values as well and to handle such features as airbrushing and retouching.

It should be noted that as we broaden our definition of a RIP by adding more and more capabilities, we begin to move away from a *raster image processor* to a more generalized kind of *image processor*. But the functions we have described do not go so far as to embrace many of the CAD/CAM functions, such as to be able to change the perspective from which one might view an object and thus to rotate it in a three-dimensional context.

A brief overview of approaches

NOW IT IS TIME to step back and look at subsets of the generalized RIP we have described and to concentrate first upon those applications which bear directly upon the production of hard-copy output.

For the most part these new output devices will be of the raster image variety, but this does not necessarily mean that they will all be driven by lasers or will necessarily expose photographic materials.

Raster Image Processing

To begin with, there are certain transitional solutions. One of these has been adopted by Autologic. In 1983 that company built a Graphic Converter Interface in order to facilitate the reproduction of vector or raster input data. Until that time, the effort to use an Autologic APS typesetter as a film plotter was accomplished by converting vector or raster images into typesetting commands which would cause the APS to draw (*i.e.*, stroke) output pictures using type fonts consisting of minute line segments of differing weights and angles. This placed a considerable processing burden on the host system and produced output which was not as smooth or as finely detailed as it could have been if one were able to drive the machine in a more "native" mode. The GCI is a processor which sits between a host system and an Autologic typesetter. It accepts raster formatted graphics data, compressed graphics data, pre-screened halftone data, compressed pre-screened halftones, and normal Autologic typesetter input commands all intermixed in the same file. The typesetter text commands are passed through to the APS. The graphics data are converted into Autologic Graphics Mode 2 input data format. This instructs the APS typesetter to write raster image output as a series of 15-pixel-high swaths of data. The information is still stroked vertically, rather than in the characteristic horizontal format of a raster processor, but the vertical swaths are made up of an assembly of 15 rasterized sweeps reconstructed for vertically stroked output.

Output from an Autologic APS-5. The picture was scanned from a prescreened 85-line halftone, stored on disk, called from disk and then run through the GCI processor in order to cause the typesetting machine to "set" this illustration in a raster mode.

The GCI will also accept input in a Versatec plotter data format as commonly used by CAD systems. The GCI converts data at a rate of one million pixels per second, which is sufficient to keep up with the writing rate of an APS-5 typesetter which can image a square inch of data at a writing resolution of 723 spots per inch in one-half to one second. However, to achieve this speed it is necessary to install a high-speed parallel input interface.

But not only can a CRT typesetter "fake" the functionality of a raster image processor. It can be built to lay down pixels in a true raster mode, and there would appear to be certain advantages in doing so. One such advantage is that most other raster image processors present only the option of laying down a dot of a constant size and blackness, or of not laying it down. Since a CRT device can modulate the strength of its beam, it is theoretically possible for the dots generated in a raster scan mode by a CRT typesetter to vary in size and degree of blackness by changing the intensity of the electron beam. However, this would be difficult to do on a pixel-by-pixel basis, although it could be achieved with respect to certain areas of a page. Information International is presently in the process of building such an engine.

Another technology is the use of LEDs (light emitting diodes) This approach was been taken by Itek's Digitek, which was discussed briefly on page 138. It is also used by the Agfa P-400 printer.

The Monotype Lasercomp

FROM THE STANDPOINT of historical accuracy, we must make it clear that the British-developed Monotype Lasercomp was the first high-quality output device based upon the principle of raster imaging, and utilizing a raster image processor.

The Monotype Corporation made its entry into photocomposition with a first-generation machine (*see especially pages 74 and 75*). Subsequently it introduced a series of second-generation typesetters, each capable of producing type of extremely good quality, but limited speed.

When it became obvious that the company would need to enter the high-speed typesetting market, the decision was evidently made to skip third-generation products and to introduce an entry based upon bold new concepts. It is probable that the machine was not developed with the expectation that it would be useful for the outputting of graphics, as opposed to text. It is more likely that the principal design motive was simply to seek to provide a device which would be capable of producing output of typographic quality at speeds comparable to CRT typesetters, but at lower prices.

However, Monotype's Lasercomp was not the first laser typesetter. The first such machine was known as DLC-1000, and it was developed by Dymo Graphic Systems, following up on work already begun by the predecessor company, Photon. The product was first shown in June 1976 at the American Newspaper Publishers Association Research Institute meeting and exhibition in Las Vegas.

Raster Image Processing

Normally laser beams are deflected (if at all) in one direction only. A rotating mirror can be used to direct the coherent light beam across a film plane. But what the inventors of this DLC-1000 accomplished was to make the beam behave exactly as if it were generated by a cathode ray tube. A rotating mirror was used to provide beam motion in a horizontal direction for the Argon laser. But this beam also passed through an acoustic optical coupler which deflected it in a vertical direction as well. In this fashion, the beam could be turned on and off to write out the line segments necessary to draw characters. Consequently the effect was very much like that of stroking characters within the window of a CRT tube.

The DLC-1000 was marketed only for a very short period of time. The supplier of one essential component—the device that induced the vertical stroking pattern—went out of business. Moreover, there seemed to be no particular advantage in this approach as compared with the use of a conventional cathode ray tube.

Yet another effort to create a fourth-generation typesetter was launched at about the same time. As early as November 1976, *The Seybold Report* carried the news that Optronics had moved into the third phase of its project to build its Pagitron system, based upon a laser-driven drum scanner/writer. The first phase consisted of the ability to scan in artwork, photos and type, and to put all of these ingredients together in one piece as a film positive or negative. The second phase added the ability to enlarge, reduce, anamorphize, enhance, screen, reverse, mask and perform other similar tasks on type and photos. The third phase involved the setting of type. *The Seybold Report* at that time maintained that with the Pagitron system the type looked pretty bad, but it was only because the artwork used left everything to be desired. "Once Optronics is able to get hold of some good type masters the output should be impressive. Coupled to a good front-end system, Optronics could conceivably start a new revolution in graphic technology." However, as it developed, Optronics was unable to finance the necessary research to complete the project.

At approximately the same time British Monotype developed a true laser typesetter—perhaps it might also be called a fourth-generation typesetter. Not only did this machine utilize a laser instead of a cathode ray tube, but instead of stroking characters it laid down dots across the film plane. And it may be said to have introduced to the graphic arts world the basic principles of raster imaging.

Raster image typesetting (or printing) devices are those which involve the laying down of dots or pixels across a page without actually writing out characters as such. Instead of writing a character or a word at a time, a line of type or a horizontal slice of a page consisting of portions of characters, which may comprise many contiguous columns, appears as successive dots are positioned, each one of which helps to build the shape of a succession of individual characters. Perhaps the best way to explain the process would be to imagine that one were sitting at a typewriter which had only one key—the period. The operator would attempt to build letters using only this period, but could not build a single letter at a time. Rather, he would move the platen across in front of the striking bar, or move the typing element across the paper, producing periods wherever they were needed to contribute to the shape of whatever images (both text and artwork) were required. One would have to know precisely where to put down each period. After moving across one row, the paper would advance infinitesimally—perhaps only by one-thousandth of an inch, and the next horizontal line of periods would be produced.

One has no trouble grasping this concept if one thinks of a facsimile machine which scans across a picture or printed page. Assume that the page is wrapped around a drum. A light source sweeps across the drum, sensing the presence or absence of black areas, and turns a light beam on the writing unit whenever it records the presence of an infinitely small non-white area. Gradually, then, an image of the picture being scanned would appear on the output device.

By extension, one can imagine the same process taking place in two parts: first the scanning and recording of the image data, and second, the subsequent writing out of the stored data.

But the idea is even more difficult to grasp if there is no image to be scanned. The page in question has never actually been output in any visible form. Instead, a computer program undertakes to arrange in computer memory a map of what would have been typeset, thus assembling an entire page so that it is then possible to peel off a succession of pixels in a horizontal line, exposing them or printing them out at very high speeds.

A dot matrix printer used for output on a personal computer does exactly the same thing, except at a much lower resolution, and there is usually no laser involved. The software (or firmware) within the dot matrix printer (which represents a kind of RIP) accepts a string of ASCII characters which make up one line of text—perhaps a letter or memo to be typed onto an 8½" × 11" sheet of paper. These characters are arranged in a line, just as if they were displayed on a video screen. This following crude diagram illustrates in a general way how the process occurs:

This is a raster

Here periods were typed across the page on a Selectric typewriter to simulate the effect of a raster scan output device.

Raster Image Processing

The individual pixels shown are presumed to be laid down horizontally, from the top to the bottom of the page. Whether the pixels are laid down horizontally or vertically, from left to right or from right to left matters little to the image engine, although formatting the page to permit vertical imaging might be more demanding on the raster image processor.

The Monotype Lasercomp was first introduced at the Newstec Exhibition held in the U.K., at Brighton in November 1976. The initial output length was 58 picas, although a 100-pica version was brought to the United States to be shown at the St. Louis ANPA show in June 1978.

The Lasercomp uses a helium-neon laser beam which is deflected across the film plane by means of a multifaceted mirror which is in constant rotation. The beam is then transmitted through an optical lens system which performs the field flattening necessary to compensate for distortion as the laser beam reaches the extremities of the flat film plane. Characters are exposed onto high-speed emulsion panchromatic film or paper which advances continuously. The typesetter's only internal moving parts are the paper feed mechanism and the rotating mirror. The initial Lasercomp also contained the intelligence necessary to perform such functions as automatic flush and leader routines, automatic hyphenation and justification, an exception word dictionary, and offered room for the storage of up to 99 formats, each of 36 codes. However, for the most part the machine was purchased by those who used it as a slave, and the Ferranti computer was programmed in Britain to provide a useful and relatively powerful front end. From the very beginning, the unusual features of the machine attracted a great deal of attention: the ability to set white type on a black background, to lay down tints and to output graphic images.

The Lasercomp proved to be premature. While the market may have been ready for output devices capable of handling text and graphics, there was no integrated system yet available which could provide an effective production or editorial environment to take advantage of these features. And, in fact, the wide measure of the machine (especially the 100-pica version) proved to be a liability if one wished to use the machine only for the setting of galleys. Another drawback had to do with the fact that the machine was incapable of producing varying sizes of type from a given font master. Initially, those sizes specifically required for a given job were loaded into the typesetter from one of the unit's two floppy disk drives, and then read into rigid disk storage onto a 5-Mb hard disk.

As we shall see, however, the Lasercomp has had a long life, has undergone successive enhancements, and appears to be a much more relevant output device for the 1980s than it was in the 1970s.

Sim-X

IN THE FALL of 1979 a Norwegian company called Sim-X (comprised principally of former employees from a prominent Norse computer manufacturer called Nortext, announced that it was in the process of developing a new terminal for ad and page make-up, and that it would be a highly interactive product based upon raster scan technology.

The first public showing of this product occurred in June 1982 at DRUPA, a worldwide graphic arts show which is held every five years. The company was able to demostrate the construction of a display ad, including sizing and rotating of type as well as generation of screen tint backgrounds and reverses. It also exhibited a rudimentary newspaper page make-up capability. A Versatec proof printer was connected directly to the microprocessor-based SIM-X terminal, sharing the same logic as the terminal. The output shown on the screen was recomputed for the resolution of the proof printer. Final output was typeset on the Sim-X PAGEscan typesetter, which consisted of the imaging portion of the Lasercomp driven by Sim-X logic.

It is interesting that the developments which occurred in Oslo initiated by SIM-X, and those in Boston initiated by Camex, represented the same fundamental approach to the problem of raster imaging, and both chose to produce final quality output on the back-end portion of the Monotype Lasercomp.

Similar development work was being carried forward during the same time period by a Japanese firm, NIC (Nihon Electronics Company), but in that instance the quality output engine consisted of the Autokon camera, driven by external raster image signals generated from the NIC microprocessor-based RIP.

The Mergenthaler Omnitech 2000

ANOTHER EXTREMELY interesting product was the Mergenthaler Omnitech 2000, which was first introduced in late November 1979.

Raster Image Processing

The Omnitech was a revolutionary machine not only because it used the raster image processing technology, but also because it set its type on non-photographic material. The product consisted of three pieces housed in two cabinets. The front end of the system was made up of a keyboard, a video terminal display, two double-density Shugart floppy disk drives, and an Intel 8080 8-bit 96K microprocessor. It functioned very much as would any other direct-entry typesetting device, offering the ability to accept input keystrokes, to store its text on disk, to permit modifications and revisions of existing text, to format the text by performing the normal processes of hyphenation and justification, with some limited page make-up capability. It was possible to process two jobs simultaneously—one in the foreground and one in the background—although when so doing the result was so painfully slow that one fared better by working on such jobs *seriatim*.

In the same cabinet was located an electronic output subsystem, which was, in essence, a raster image processor based upon a Z-80 microprocessor along with some special-purpose hard-wired logic boards. The Intel 8080, which had processed the text in ASCII codes arranged in hyphenated, justified and paginated format, passed this information along to the Z-80, which then checked for the required fonts, pulled them from the program floppy disk and transferred them to RAM memory. Here, aided by yet another microprocessor, called an 8X300, and other special logic, the text was transformed into rows of dots or pixels ready to be passed along to the output recorder unit.

The output recorder consisted of a helium-neon laser. Its beam was displaced across an 11-inch surface by the usual galvo-driven mirror. The dot size generated was one-tenth of a point in diameter or, more precisely, 723 dotes per inch. Its function was to lay down electromagnetic charges upon a special zinc-oxide coated paper which was wrapped around a revolving drum.

This paper came in a roll, 430 feet in length. When the recorder was activated the paper was fed onto the roll, held in place by a vacuum which sucked the paper tightly against the external circumference of the drum. When enough paper had been wrapped so that the drum was completely surrounded, it was cut from the supply roll, and after a second revolution of the drum, the zinc-oxide coating was charged. Then a third revolution exposed the paper to the laser beam so that a toner or imager would adhere. During a fourth revolution a clearing solution was applied, followed by the liquid toner imager. The paper was then mechanically peeled from the drum, dried and deposited into a container or bin built into the lower front of the cabinet.

All of this took quite some time to achieve. The four rotations of the drum (which was about 21 inches in diameter) required almost nine minutes. The scan time took more than five minutes, but during this period it was able to write onto the surface of the drum on the basis of 512,729 dots per square inch.

(Continued on page 394)

The Monotype Lasercomp was the first typesetter to "set" type a pixel at a time across a page, rather than a character at a time. A helium-neon laser beam is deflected by a rotating polygon and then brought into focus across the film plane.

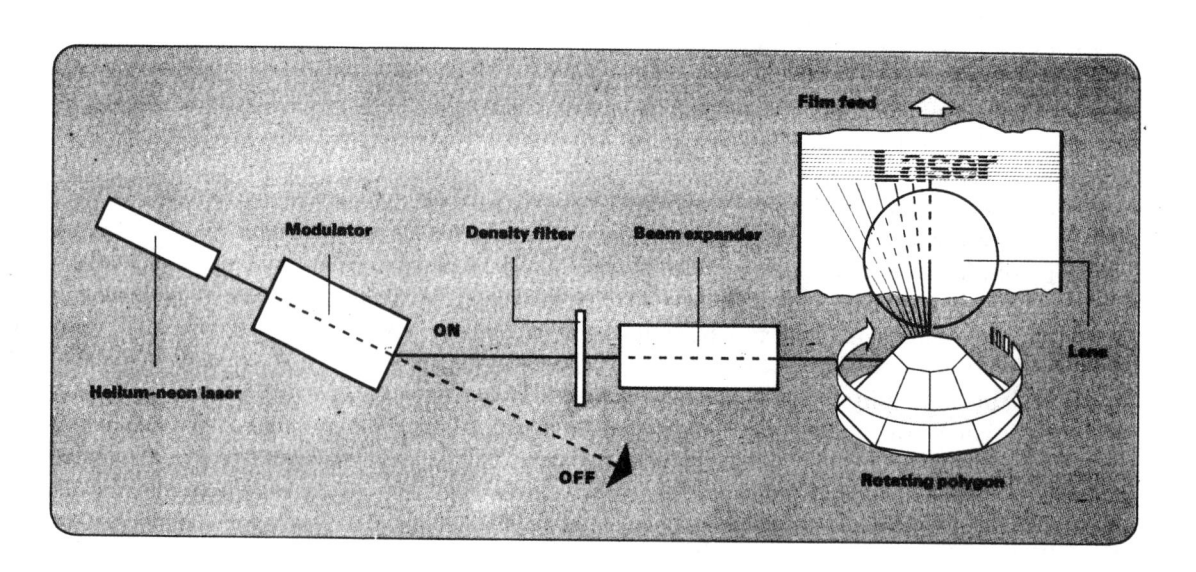

Raster Image Processing

Sim-X, a Norwegian company that has the capability of producing rasterized output using its own raster image processor and an output engine from the Monotype Lasercomp. A digitized image is shown here.

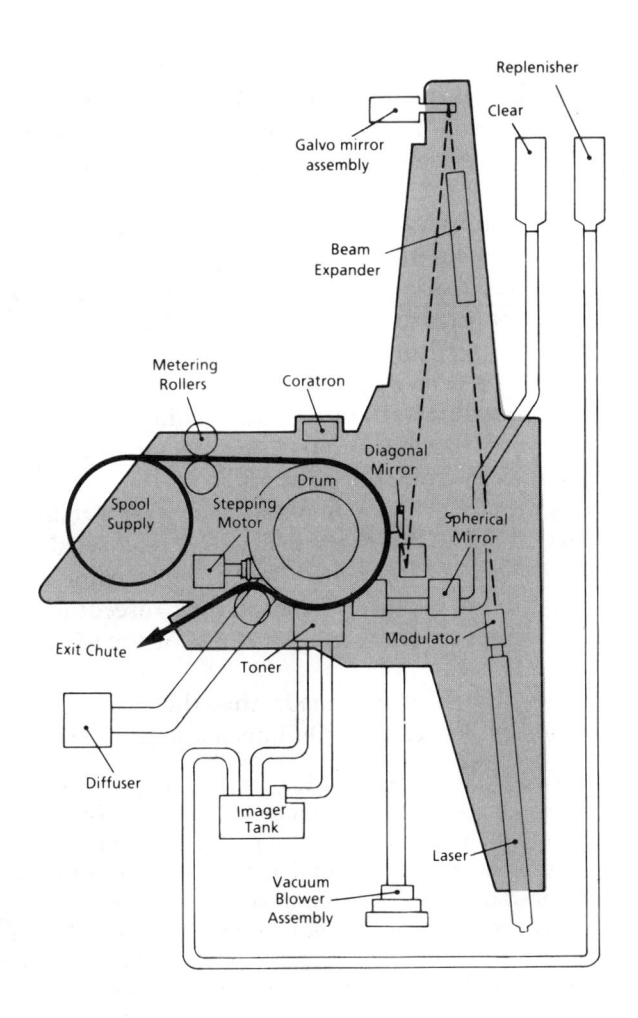

LILY OF FRANCE

The Mergenthaler Omnitext 2000 also uses HeNe laser beams modulated to interrupt its transmission, expanded to enhance the beam size, deflected by a galvo mirror to cause the image to step across the surface of the paper, and brought into focus by a spherical mirror. A charged mirror diverts the image to the charged paper which is wrapped around a drum as shown here.

During the third of these rotations, as noted, the laser beam swept across the 11-inch line at the rate of 37 scans per second for a total of approximately 12,000 scan sweeps as the drum revolved. A buffer held the information required for only two raster lines, representing approximately 16,000 bits of data. Obviously the RIP within the front-end box had to keep up with the rotation speed of the drum itself.

The speed of the machine. While the process seemed painfully slow, the machine was nevertheless capable of composing more than 120 lines per minute, even allowing for the time it required for the paper to be wrapped around the cylinder and charged. The company described the output in terms of a rate of 35 square inches of type per minute and argued that, in calculating throughput speed, one would normally have to take into account the time it takes to process the photographic material after it had been exposed in a conventional typesetter. It also pointed out that the so-called plain paper being used was significantly less expensive than photographic material, that the machine could be run in an office environment, and that the image was exceptionally sharp and crisp.

This was indeed the case, except for some tendency for the image to smudge, especially if the user attempted to wax or otherwise paste the paper into position on some sort of carrier, in the event that he could not achieve satisfactory page make-up with the aid of the supplied software.

Another interesting feature of the machine was its ability to size type from outline rasters, thus avoiding the limitation on the Lasercomp which required that a different font master be loaded for each variation in point or set size. Thus one could obtain, from the same master, a range of sizes from 4½ to 127½ points, capable of being expanded or condensed through point and set sizes in half-point increments and obliqued forward or backward either 7 or 14 degrees.

It was, of course, possible to set white type on a solid black background as well as to generate tint patterns.

There was only one major limitation with respect to this machine—it didn't work! At least it failed to set type reliably in user environments. *The Seybold Report* had hailed the machine as a "landmark" product. It did so because it believed that "direct-to-paper electrographics could replace many or even most of today's typesetting technology."[1]

Nevertheless, the point was made that there was a significant difference in concept between the Omnitech and the Xerox 9700.

> The Xerox 9700 . . . produces two-sided output at the rate of two pages per second. The Omnitech 2000 produces single-sided output at the rate of one (larger) page every nine minutes. The Xerox machine is fast enough that it can serve as both typesetter and "printing press." The Omnitech clearly is not.
>
> Of course there are also significant differences in quality and flexibility. The Xerox machine writes ouput at a dot spacing of 300 dots per inch (90,000 dots per square inch). Mergenthaler

---

1. See *The Seybold Report,* Vol. 9, No. 6, p. 6.

Raster Image Processing

uses a spacing of 723 dots per inch (512,729 dots per square inch— and the Omnitech achieves much sharper, cleaner edges and deeper blacks. However, we are not convinced that this is a generic difference. Technically, we can see no reason why a machine like the 9700 could not be built to achieve output quality equivalent to the Omnitech—although it would probably have to be both slower and more expensive than the present Xerox printer . . . A machine with medium speed and medium quality could conceivably serve as both an "electronic printer" for short runs and/or proof copies, [and] a "master maker" or "typesetter" for longer runs which are to be reproduced on conventional presses or duplicating machines.[1]

The Omnitech 2000 was delicately withdrawn from the market, but prior to that time a different model, the Omnitech 2100, was announced (April 1981). Mergenthaler had discontinued the electrographic approach and had substituted conventional photographic material. Modifications were also made in the product (as they had subsequently been made in the 2000) to permit the setting of type at one-half resolution, or 360 dots per inch, to increase output speed for proof-copy purposes.

It developed, however, that this product competed with the German-built CRTronic line of direct-entry typesetters, and eventually the 2100 was also phased out. However, the engine of the Omnitech appeared again, in a typesetter known as the 101, which was first introduced in June 1983, and in a wider-measure model, the 101S, which has become an output engine for certain models of the CRTronic. This replaces the small, travelling CRT tube which was built into the typesetter portion of that offering. Mergenthaler has also made the same raster image processor available to Hell to be used in conjunction with an imaging device on a direct-to-film product.

Other non-photographic imagers

OF COURSE THERE HAVE BEEN many varieties of imaging engines which have never been considered typesetters. The definition of a typesetter becomes more and more illusive as time passes. At one time a typesetting device was something which cast metal type and arranged it in justified lines. Then it also included machines which exposed type images on photographic material, again in justified format. The U.S. Government Printing Office at one time was obliged to consider the IBM Selectric Composer a typesetter even though it was a strike-on machine, because it set proportionally spaced characters. On the whole, however, until the Omnitech made its appearance, the use of photographic material, perhaps along with proportionally spaced type which required some sort of justification provided the essence of a definition. Then we began to move to the dry-silver photographic process and finally to plain paper (although a zinc-oxide coating which required the application of heat to fuse the toner wasn't exactly plain paper).

Nevertheless there were other kinds of devices, including such raster imaging engines as the Versatec, which used a dot matrix (200

1. See *The Seybold Report*, Vol. 9, No. 6, p. 2.

dot per inch) resolution, the IBM 4250 Electro-Erosion Printer, the Agfa P-400 LED imaging device, the Itek Digitek LED, and a number of printing devices that were developed initially for use in conjunction with word processors or personal computers but may have migrated into other fields.

Some of these office-oriented machines contain their own character imaging logic and fonts. Others are slaves that can only be driven by an external RIP of some sort, whether it is strictly a software program or includes special-purpose hardware as well. Whether or not these devices presently provide output with relatively crude resolutions (*e.g.*, under 200 dots per inch) and exaggerated dot sizes (*e.g.*, over 2 mils), it is clear that there is a distinct trend toward higher resolutions and finer dot sizes and, hence, the potential of significant enhancements in the quality of the output. Nevertheless there are certain inherent limitations having to do with the trade-off between speed, on the one hand, and the quality of the output on the other. An increase in resolution means an exponential increase in the number of dots to be generated and laid down, and presses insistently against such constraints as the amount of data storage required, the rate at which bits can be pushed along some sort of electronic bus, and especially the number and rapidity of calculations which can be computed on the fly.

In general, however, we can visualize two types of plain-paper raster image output devices: one will produce high-quality output and will run slowly. The other will produce lower quality output and will be able to function in a reprographic mode—that is, be capable of printing final pages in the manner of an office copying machine—for end-user consumption.

It is possible that this first type of device (high-quality) might provide an option of imaging on printing plates (especially paper plates) or low run-length coating lithographic plates of the office duplicator variety. It is also possible that such a device might be able to offer options with respect to speed versus resolution so that it might function both as a reprographic printer and as a camera-ready copy or direct-to-plate device. It is even possible that the same raster image output device might be able to change its resolution from page to page or even within a page (for example, if there were halftones on some pages and within pages) in an effort to optimize the speed/quality equation.

But the issue still remains as to whether, in general, the all-important RIP will be considered a part of the output device, the front-end composition device, or as a peripheral to a front-end system. We can even conceive of a system which offers or which accesses several different types of RIPS depending upon the functions to be performed.

WYSIWYGgery

IT APPEARS that raster image processors serve two basic purposes or functions:

Raster Image Processing

(1) They drive hard-copy output devices (for interim proofing output or for final output), whether directly to plain paper or indirectly via plate or film.

(2) They provide an interim soft-copy version, which more frequently is interactive.

There are still some "soft typesetter" devices which are used for viewing but not for editing, and there are also some quasi-soft typesetter devices which permit intervention, but only by erasing the entire screen image and repainting it, (albeit, fairly rapidly). But the most exciting and rewarding application is a screen representation which permits a high degree of interaction, modifying (in real time) only those portions of the page affected by the indicated change, permitting the user to examine not just one alternative solution at a time (such as, what if I move that picture *there* rather than *here*?), but rather, to display the effects of a series of changes such as, what happens to the appearance and arrangement of the page while I move the picture in this direction?

If one is concerned, however, about whether what you see as you make such changes is truly what you get if you approve those changes, one may require the highest possible fidelity of rendition that a video screen is capable of producing, thus increasing the price of the device significantly and also perhaps slowing down the response time.

Despite claims to the contrary, one will never truly see what one will get. The tag WYSITWYG, as opposed to WYSIMOLWYG (what you see is more or less what you get), thus overstates the options. The appearance of type on paper is inevitably different from the appearance of type on a screen. The resolution of an image to be printed on paper is greater than one can produce on a screen, and hence one will lose the graceful shapes of type characters (even if tricks like "anti-aliasing" are played or a second bit plane is introduced to add grayscale effects to fool the eye where "jaggies" appear).

What you come down to, therefore, is WYSITWYNTS (what you see is truly what you need to see) perhaps coupled with a bit of WYSIWYCATS (what you see is what you can afford to see).

While everyone would certainly agree with this principle, there are practical problems relating to the fact that different people need to see different things for different purposes, and it may not be economically feasible to manufacture special devices in an effort to meet (at lowest cost) the requirements of the different players in the publication process.

Presumably the writer is most concerned with *words*. As one gets involved with the publishing-related production process one is increasingly concerned with *fit* and *appearance* including the flavor and eye-catching attractiveness of the page. But even here there are several types of issues. One person will need to use a device for provisional design and final sign-off of the design concept. Another will need to assure himself that the final result is indeed precisely what the designer intended. And yet a third person may then need to see if there may have to be second thoughts, perhaps taking into consideration the limitations of the reproduction process.

Raster image processors may not be required to meet all of these needs. The author may be perfectly happy with a conventional monospaced screen display and a correspondence-quality printer. Some persons involved in the design process (especially when it comes to a CAD/CAM application) will prefer vectors, offering fast response times and three-dimensional renditions with varying orientations and perspectives. The person worried about the quality of a halftone, and perhaps its color values, will certainly want the best possible color renditions affordable and the most powerful capability for manipulation of pixel data. Presumably one would work with whatever subset of continuous tone information can be handled on the video display, with halftone screening to be applied in a batch mode "on the way" to the film recorder or platemaker.

24

Computer-Aided Editing

LOOKING BACK over the past twenty years or so, we find, on the whole, that the impetus for technological change in the printing and publishing industry has arisen because of the need to increase the efficiency of production techniques. The context in which this need has arisen relates not principally to the problem of creating a single book, pamphlet or other document, but rather to the problem of efficient replication and distribution. It may well have taken longer for the hand compositor of Gutenberg's time to assemble individual pieces of type than it would have to draw out neat letters upon a piece of parchment. But the objective was to assemble letters in such a way that they could be replicated in quantity to fulfill the need for the dissemination of information, which of course made possible the Renaissance and our entry into modern times.

Hence we must look at the automation of typesetting in relationship to the printing process and its ultimate objective—the distribution of the book, journal or treatise in question.

We find, for example, that it was the increased popularity of offset printing (essentially a photographic process) that provided the milieu within which photocomposition could flourish. And offset printing was itself encouraged by the increasing demand for illustrative material, the creation of which represented an expensive and time-consuming procedure when accomplished with either letterpress or gravure technology.

The typewriter satisfied the need for the production of individual documents, and the office copying machine bridged the gap between the printing process and the typing out of single copies.

Editorial benefits. It is true that some editorial benefits emerged from the automation of the typesetting process—none flowed specifically from photocomposition as such since this process was perhaps even less flexible than the setting of type by hot metal—but there were many which came into being when the computer was joined with photocomposition. Then text could be stored economically, revised quickly, and recomposed in different type faces and measures. Additional benefits were forthcoming, especially in the newspaper and magazine environments where initial keystroke capture first began to take place. Copy routing procedures then gave the editorial department the coveted control which previously had been assigned only to production people. Computer-related data base publishing opportunities opened up as well, with the capability of sorting, sequencing and exploding entries or listings. Other specific products and applications emerged which could only have been performed economically or in a timely fashion with the aid of computers.

But it was not until the advent of the personal computer (or at least the word processor) that a more general appreciation began to develop to the effect that other kinds of benefits could be gained from the use of computers within the publication process.

These benefits extend beyond the pay-offs in terms of economy and speed which are possible by virtue of keystroke capture. Increasingly, the publishing community has come to realize that the computer can assist in the writing and editing process as such. Computers can be helpful not only for producing clean manuscripts, but they also serve as an aid to supplying good copy.

Spelling assists. The "spelling checker" is the first, most obvious such application, and it gained its acceptance not from the typesetting world (although such things did exist there, too) but from the experiences of word processing and personal computing. Other approaches are now beginning to emerge: style-critiquing programs, on-line reference materials, and even grammar-checking programs.

The editing process. Editing tasks tend to fall into two categories: developmental editing and copy editing. In large publishing operations, particularly in the book publishing industry, these tasks are assigned to different people.[1]

An element of this process involves an outline drawn up by the author before a work is written. Also included in this process are the suggestions from the editor to the author about the order in which such topics are introduced or the way in which a subject is presented.

Copy editing, on the other hand, has to do with the details of the manuscript. Are the grammar and punctuation correct? Are there misspelled words? Does each sentence convey its intended meaning? Are there clichés or wordy passages that need to be improved? Have certain words been overused? Does the manuscript conform to house style—the set of conventions which the publisher has adopted to resolve arguments and facilitate expeditious decision-making when there are several acceptable ways in which material may be presented?

There are now computer application programs which address these issues, and there are even some which might be considered to be helpful during the less structured and structurable processes of developmental editing.

There are also some very specific benefits to be derived when it comes to the tedious tasks of indexing, table of contents generation, and the creation of lists of illustrations as well as compilations of citations and bibliographical references.

In fact there is every indication that the benefits to be derived from the use of such application programs may in themselves be sufficiently compelling to justify the installation of a computer editorial system (which might also happen to set type) even when no

---

[1]. Much of the material in this chapter has been paraphrased from *The Seybold Report on Publishing Systems,* "Computer Aids for Authors and Editors," *Vol. 13, No. 10,* February 13, 1984. This article was researched and written by staff member George A. Alexander.

such justification could exist simply from the standpoint of the costs of the production processes.

Writing and developmental editing. First of all, let us consider the possibility of using computer techniques during the very early stages of manuscript preparation, bearing in mind that many publishers (of books and encyclopaedias as well as magazines) employ large numbers of "captive writers "—in much the same way as is true with newspapers. Two examples of pre-writing aids come to mind in this connection. There is a program called "ThinkTank," which runs on the IBM PC and is designed to help an author develop an outline.[1] It has several special outline-related features. Two of the most basic are "expand" and "collapse." Collapse makes everything subordinate to the hierarchical position of the line the cursor is on disappear. Expand causes the lines which are subordinate to the cursor line to be displayed. ThinkTank also has an outline-adapted block move function; if you move a line, everything subordinate to the line moves too. This is often very handy.

The main advantage of such a program is that it enables you to start with the "big picture" and then to add detail as it occurs to you without obfuscating the major thrust of the paper. And, of course, to be able to rearrange the argument, in the interest of a more effective presentation, again without being distracted by the subsidiary or ancillary elaborations.

Another interesting program is called "The Idea Processor."[2] It is very handy for note taking and for note organizing. This offering contains normal text input and editing features, but permits you to associate with each entry a list of key words. Each entry can contain up to 8,000 characters, and the entry may then be placed in a "drawer" which in turn is part of a larger category, called a "cabinet."

Each cabinet has its own name. You can ask the program to show cabinets, unlock a cabinet, make a new cabinet, or lock a cabinet. You are allowed up to ten key words to describe the categories that will be found in any drawer within a given cabinet. Each key word can be up to 14 characters in length. A cabinet can contain up to 512 key words. You can call up cards from drawers within a particular cabinet by entering the key word you wish to find. You can also use "or" and "not." Under some circumstances it is also possible to store graphs and pictures as if they were ideas, and you can also pull data from spreadsheets.

We are certain that other similar packages will be offered in the near future for the benefit of writers and developmental editors.

For the copy editor. Obviously there is a great deal more available for the copy editor, and it is in this area that we expect to see some dramatic benefits in the near future. This does not mean that the publisher will institute computers and computer programs for the sake of reducing his editorial or copy-editing staffs. Our own research leads us to believe that the thrust will rather be to obtain better results and to get them more quickly. Our view is that these programs will be

1. *ThinkTank* is a product of Living Videotext, Inc., 1000 Elwell Court, Suite 232, Palo Alto, CA 94303.

2. *The Idea Processor* was developed by IdeaWare, Inc., 225 Lafayette Street, New York, NY 10012.

deeply appreciated by those whose responsibility it is to perform such editing tasks and will soon be considered such indispensable tools that one would wonder, "how we have gotten along without them."

Spelling checkers. As has been suggested, spelling check routines are widely used in conjunction with the preparation of manuscripts, either by authors working on their personal or professional computers, or by secretaries and typists using word processing devices. These routines address two kinds of problems. One has to do with the detection (and perhaps the correction) of errors which arise because the author of a manuscript simply didn't know how to spell a word and his typist or secretary, if one is involved in the process, did not rectify the mistake.

The second type of error, perhaps equally as or even common, occurs when the person doing the input (whether author or typist) simply strikes the wrong keys and is unaware of this fact at the time and then overlooks the error when checking back over the manuscript, either on the screen or in printout form.

It is interesting to note that the circumstances which give rise to these two kinds of errors are not identical, nor are their programmatic solutions the same. For example, an author or typist may suspect a word is misspelled. He or she then verifies the correct spelling by requesting correction or verification. This might suggest that an interactive solution would be most helpful. Keyboard errors, on the other hand, are made inadvertently, and they are best detected by a batch program which runs against the manuscript after it, or some portion of it, has been created.

It is also probable that the kinds of "deliberate" misspellings that occur when one doesn't know any better differ from the kinds of errors introduced by miskeying. Transpositions may be more common in the latter instance, and there are also certain unique bad habits which many typists seem to cultivate. For example, this writer will frequently add the letter *j* to any *ion* letter sequence, producing *iojn*, as in *conventiojn*. This happens because the index finger of the left hand strikes the *j* en route to the *n*. Note that when this occurs it adds an extra letter to any such word. On the other hand, in typing *ont he whole* a transposition of a space and the letter *t* occurs. Indeed, these typing errors happen so regularly that it would be possible for us to apply a program specifically designed to detect and correct such mistakes. The program could be general in nature, but our own peculiar bad habits could represent the specific data it contains.

We know that those firms offering spelling checks often boast in their literature about the number of words provided in the spelling dictionary. Our own experience indicates that such a dictionary should be relatively small—possibly somewhere between 20,000 and 30,000 words, and certainly not 80,000 or more. We would be inclined to leave out such words as *yea*, *vane* and perhaps even *vein*, as well as *boarder* and *coarse*. *The dictionary wood search in vane for wards that ire spelled wring as a matter of coarse.* (Although some of the *farmer* could *boarder* on *topographical errs*.) Our impression is that no one has really studied the problem with the attention it deserves, even though there is indeed a listing of words that are frequently misspelled. Some words (*ukulele, minuscule, braggadocio*) would be fun to add to our spelling dictionary and would probably cause no harm.

The reader may have the impression that we have a relatively low opinion of spelling checkers. In fact we like the idea very much and use checkers whenever we can manage to do so. We are always impressed at how rapidly they do their job, how small our vocabulary turns out to be, and how they do indeed discover mistakes we had not found in several careful readings of a manuscript, simply because we see what we want to see rather than what is truly there.

In some instances vendors will combine a spelling checker list with a hyphenation listing. This may be useful from a space-saving standpoint, but the tasks are not truly related. For example, one needs to be able to hyphenate words that are misspelled. And some misspellings may be deliberate, as for example, "Remember that *alright* is not a word but *already* is."

How spelling checkers work. In order to optimize speed, some spelling checker dictionaries are divided into three parts. The first part generally consists of about 150 words which are used so frequently that they may comprise from 25% to 40% of the text of an article and consequently can be stored in memory. They would include such words as:

> *all, and, are, as, at, be, before, but, by, can, could, did, do, each, every, for, give, gave, go, good, had, has, have, him, his, her, hers, i, if, is, it, its, left, like, look, may, me, mine, much, my, never, no, none, not, of, on, one, over, put, right, saw, see, show, some, than, that, the, their, theirs, them, there, these, those, time, true, truly, usual, usually, use, used, very, were, what, when, where, who, why, you, your,* and *yours.*

We have deliberately left out some of the words which probably should be included. The reader may wish to write a program analyzing a substantial block of text to see what he or she can learn about word usage.

The second category of words, representing perhaps another 10,000 entries, are those not listed above but used with such frequency that after these words have been counted the average document will probably contain only about five percent more. In other words, if you sort all words in a document of some length (say 10,000 words), you would probably only find about 500 words (and probably much less) that have not been included.

The third category of entries would be made up of words which are common in a given field or in documents used for a given purpose. They may well relate to a particular discipline. For this document, for example, such words would include *computer, typesetter, typesetting, hyphenation, justification,* and perhaps *serif, interword,* and *CRT* as well as such proper names as *Mergenthaler, Autologic, Camex* and *Xenotron.*

There are some very important system problems associated with the manner in which words to be accessed quickly should be represented and stored. Obviously some method of data compression is indicated, such as to sort all words (including all of the possible variants of the word) and perhaps to indicate only the manner in which one differs from the next. For example:

a,1ardvark,7s,4wolf,7ves,3on,5s,5ic would stand for: *a, aardvark, aardvarks, aardwolf, aardwolves, aaron, aarons, aaronic.*

Note that in this discussion we have made no distinction between upper- and lower-case characters, so presumably the spelling checker would not be able to determine whether *Constantinople* should be capitalized or NATO should be set in small caps, or whether *I'm, isn't* and *couldn't* should be included. Or, what to do about *re-do* versus *redo*.

Often the first task of a spelling checker is to sort all words in the manuscript (keeping track of their location) and then to make one pass through a dictionary. You will get almost immediately a count indicating that the manuscript contained 10,250 words, of which 2,333 were unique and 152 were not found in the dictionary. It would then probably proceed to list these words, alphabetically, one by one, giving you a chance to indicate whether the word is spelled correctly and should be left alone, spelled correctly and should be added to the dictionary, or is spelled incorrectly and should be flagged, or viewed in context, perhaps corrected and perhaps added to the dictionary in its corrected form.

Hashing. Another approach is to "hash" the dictionary. This means that you don't actually store the word at all. You compute an address from the combination of letters the program analyzes. The computer goes to that address, which is usually merely a bit within a storage area which is either turned on or turned off. If it is turned on, that combination of characters exists and the word is presumably spelled correctly. Because such computations produce errors or collisions, usually several different mathematical formulae are applied to each word producing, say, three different addresses. Also bits would need to be turned on at all three such addresses, in three separate memory locations, before you were assured that the word did indeed exist.

It is somewhat more complex, but not impossible, to update a hashed dictionary. Usually words not in the hashed dictionary are added in an unhashed fashion, however, a periodic rehashing of the data base updates the dictionary.

Words that can be stored in a compressed form in memory and especially words that can be handled by hashing may permit the program to avoid the necessity of going through a sorting pass. It may be faster to look up the same word many times rather than to sort all words, or to look up the word only once and then write it out in a special scratch area to be checked the next time it occurs, rather than to take time for the sort. On the other hand, the sort can produce some interesting statistics and information which will be useful for editorial purposes, soon to be discussed.

There are other methods of storing words in a condensed fashion, and there are other techniques for accessing such words. To save time, words should be stored ideally in memory rather than on disk, but this would require a very large memory especially if the words are stored on an individual workstation.

There is another nice problem, which is whether and how it is possible to guess what the misspelled word is that the writer (or typist) intended and to propose to substitute the desired word. This calls into play a series of tests (usually of a wild-card nature) which try to find the word that was probably intended, perhaps by leaving out certain letters, or adding certain letters, or looking for the words in an alphabetical list that approximates the spelling given and presents the user with a choice in the hope that one word so selected will indeed be the one desired.

There is also the question of whether each user should have his own dictionary or whether there should be a collective dictionary, and whether or not that dictionary can, somehow, incorporate certain elements of house style. Often a "keeper of the dictionary" is appointed.

Stylistic considerations

PERHAPS EVEN MORE INTERESTING than spelling checking programs are programs concerned with the kind of editing which helps to produce more lucid, succinct and cogent writing. But before considering programs devised to assist in this task we should take time out to consider programs that attempt to make some kind of overall analysis of whether the manuscript is likely to meet certain tests of lucidity or comprehensibility. *Readability scoring* has become increasingly popular in recent years, and indeed certain readability standards have now been incorporated into law. In certain states, insurance contracts must be written so that they are deemed understandable by the mass of contract purchasers, and this is presumed to be determinable by an analysis of various elements within the document. The so-called Flesch test is one such approach that has been incorporated into computer programs by various vendors.

In essence this test looks at two important variables: the length of the sentences used in the document, and the length of the words themselves (that is, the number of syllables). Presumably the longer the sentence the more difficult it is to understand. The more syllables in a word, the more difficulty the average reader encounters in understanding the meaning of the term. These standards are admittedly arbitrary, and yet they are widely used, not only in the preparation of legal documents, but also for instruction manuals in certain fields.

Grade level testing. In the preparation of texts for the elementary school grades, it is quite common to assure that new terms are systematically introduced and defined when introduced, or used in a comprehensible context. Thus one needs to be assured that such words are not inadvertently used prior to their formal introduction. One also needs to keep in mind that words which fall outside of the "grade level" do not appear in the text. While to our knowledge no general programs have been developed as yet for this purpose, special application programs have indeed been written by certain publishers for their own proprietary purposes. In addition, there are in more common use two lists of frequently used words presumed to be well understood: the Dale list contains about 3,000 words, and the Spache list has 1,014 words. These present only root words, but some inflections and plurals are considered familiar also, so the effective size of the lists is several times larger.

There is also a Dale-Chall test which is computed from average sentence length and a calculation of the percentage of non-Dale-list words in a passage. The Spache test is computed in much the same way except that a different list is used. There is also a "degrees of reading power" test which has been developed by Educational Testing Service. It is based on a calculation derived from the following statistics about a text passage: number of characters, words and sentences, and the percentage of words not on the Dale list.

Stylistic considerations

THERE ARE ALSO programs which have been devised to be applied to the first draft of a manuscript. They presume that matters of organization and content selection have not been dealt with. Their goal is to assist in the revising and rewriting process with proper word choice and stylistic consistency.

Such programs fall into two groups. One consists of *Writer's Workbench* from Bell Labs, and two similar (but more limited programs). The second group consists of more ambitious programs which seek to detect grammatical errors. Catching such errors can be an extremely difficult problem. Programs in this category are still under development, although some such programs are now beginning to appear.

Writer's Workbench has played a key role in making us aware of the potential which computers offer for improving clarity and achieving stylistic consistency. It had its origin in dealing with two problems which Bell faced a few years ago. One had to do with the development of a speech synthesizer that sounded as much as possible like human speech. To achieve better results an effort was made to analyze sentence structure in order to provide needed inflection. The other application developed a program to assist in critiquing papers prepared by the Bell Labs staff for submission to technical journals, assessing such papers for style, reading level and organization.

Writer's Workbench is primarily a tool for writers wishing to obtain a critique of a document. It does not check grammar. There are searching programs that look for specific strings of words and characters and offer suggestions for improvement, seeking out doubled words (the the) or wordy phrases and faulty punctuation, as well as split infinitives. The only part of speech this latter program considers is the use of an adverb to separate the parts of an infinitive.

Punctuation and Style, a product of Oasis Systems, was probably inspired by Writer's Workbench. It primarily ferrets out pompous or redundant phrases and questions them. This program also hunts down and notes clichés and awkward or erroneous phrases. Below are a few examples of word usage that are flagged by the program. The items on the left reflect the writer's word choice and the items on the right are the alternatives suggested by Punctuation and Style:

> a preference for = prefer
> accentuate = stress
> accommodate = fit
> accomplish = do
> accordingly = so
> acquire = get
> activate = start, begin
> adhere = stick
> advent = coming, arrival
> affirmative = yes
> aggregate = total
> anticipate = expect
> approximately = about
> assist = help or aid
> arrive at a decision = decide
> as a method of = for
> as regards = about, regarding
> as related to = for, about
> at present = now
> at the present time = now
> cognizant = aware, know
> commence = begin
> communicate = tell

Another somewhat similar program is *Grammatik*, originated by Aspen Systems, acquired by Dictronics, which was subsequently merged into Wang's Electronic Publishing division.

This program also looks for phrases, suggests substitutions of one expression for another, and generates statistics as to the number of sentences and words, the average length of words and sentences, the number of question marks and exclamation points, the longest and shortest sentence, the number of sentences longer than 30 words and those less than 14, the number of occurrences of forms of "to be," and the number of prepositions. The latter information is considered to be relevant in determining whether the writing style uses too many passive sentence structures instead of active ones. ("The problem may be looked at in this light," as opposed to, "You can look at the problem in this light.")

Grammar checking

THE PROGRAMS we have described so far, while extremely helpful, are relatively naive. IBM has attempted a much more ambitious

WordProof, a program offered by IBM for its PC, provides both a spelling checker and a list of synonyms. In the top picture the program has found that "different" does not exist in its dictionary. It offers a choice of alternatives in the dictionary (the user can let the word stand or correct it). Here "different" is clearly intended and the user indicates this.

In the second picture the user could ask the program to substitute a synonym (perhaps "entity") for the "system."

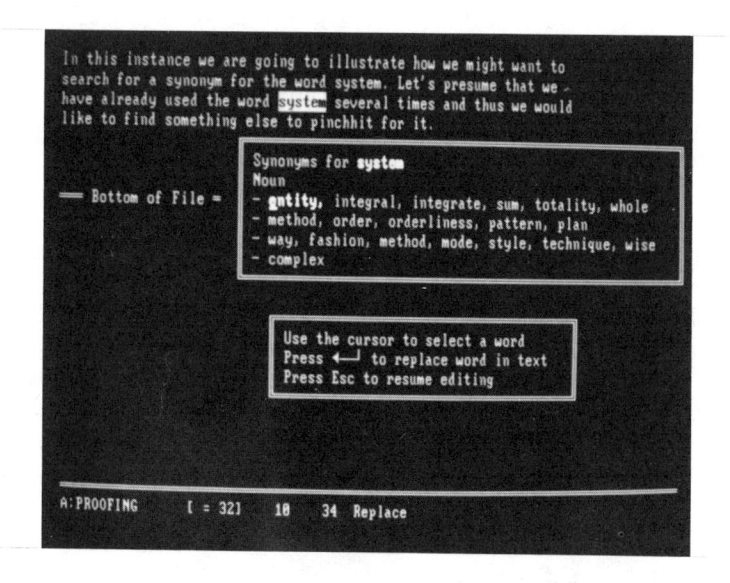

Computer-Aided Editing

undertaking in its development of *Epistle*. The underlying mechanism of Epistle's grammar-checking facility is a large dictionary (130,000 words), a set of 400 rules of grammar, and a rule-processing program. For example, when the program was asked, "Show me some rule processing," it first brought up from its dictionary the following information:

ME(PRON SING PERS1 OBJ ANIM HUM)

indicating that "me" is a pronoun, it is singular, first person, objective, animate and human. All of these attributes of the word "me" are used in checking its role in sentences. The word "show" had two definitions—as a noun and as a verb. In the verb form it had 12 attributes, including indications that it is plural, transitive, present tense and that it involves communication.

It appears that Epistle will set the standard for text editing programs, but it is also evident that there are many things it cannot and will not be able to do. It is hoped that it will also be useful in handling problems of machine translation from one language to another. Such programs do exist at the present time to provide the translator with a "rough cut" from, for example, Russian to English, but a great deal of human involvement is necessary to make sense of the end result or at least to make it reasonably literate. One classic story of such activities describes the translation of "The flesh is willing, but the spirit is weak," first into Russian and then back into English again, where it is alleged to have appeared as, "The whiskey is good but the meat is spoiled."

Some practical approaches

SOME PUBLISHERS have already found some very specific practical uses for computers to assist in the copy-editing process, while, at the same time they are experimenting with programs such as those we have just described. Already the spelling checkers are widely used and are said to save time and to help detect mistakes. There are other special-purpose programs which could be devised with trivial effort and which could serve useful purposes. In fact, some of them could be incorporated in an input-translate routine. For example, if an author transmits his manuscript from his IBM PC or his Apple to the publisher's computer, certain string substitutions can be made automatically at that time. If the author is known to misspell certain words they can be corrected automatically during the translation process, or at least flagged. For example, we would want to flag every occurrence of "effect" versus "affect" and "principle" as compared with "principal." For one of our writers, whose spelling has been influenced profoundly by a stay in a British-speaking country, we would find no difficulty modifying the spellings of "honour" and "colour" and "analyse" at the same time we translate every underlined phrase into italic and every emboldened phrase into our "Number 1 head."

The other editing applications which are beginning to put in their appearance relate to the generation of running heads which pick up subheads from the text material, the extraction of possible index terms, and the creation of tables of contents and lists of illustrations.

Generic coding

MANY OF THESE elements (heads, citations, figure captions, abstracts and the like) can be derived from flags that are automatically inserted by writers who follow quite stringent, but powerful, coding conventions of a generic variety. This grouping includes those coding rules which have been developed and promulgated by special committees formulatedsome years ago to work under the leadership of the Graphic Communications Association.[1] More recently the Association of American Publishers has extended these same development efforts.

It is our conviction that there are many things that can be done to improve the editing cycle. We believe that many of these ideas will be developed to meet the needs of specific publishing situations. One of these is illustrated by the work performed by the American Chemical Society. For example, no reference may be made, in any of its publications, to any chemical or chemical compound unless that term has been checked against the Society's extensive computer data base. All variant terms of the same compound will be immediately identified, and the molecular structure of the compound is immediately brought onto the screen so that the editor can be assured that the chemical referred to is truly the one intended.

Many professional societies have developed their own thesauri and listings of key words to assist in the indexing, abstracting and data retrieval processes. At the same time, more and more publishers are exploring the use of programs for full text search and information retrieval, as an aid to authors' research and as a commercial electronic publishing service offered to the public.

---

[1] In this connection see especially *GCA Standard 101-1983 Document Markup Metalanguage, GenCode and the Standard Generalized Markup Language (SGML)*. For further information write to the Graphic Communications Association, 1730 North Lynn Street, Suite 604, Arlington, VA 22209.

The first requirement for generic coding is a symbol
to mark the beginning and ending of an element of
text. The GENCODE book calls these ESMO for {q}Element
Star, Markup Open{/q} and ESMC for {q}Element Start,
Markup Close.{/q} {/p}
{p}The user can chose his symbols and in this instance
we have chosen to use { for EXMO and } for ESMC. To
obtain these unique symbols we have selected the
OCR-A type element.{/p}

{p}This is a code to signal the beginning of a
paragraph and within the paragraph added information,
called {q}markup{/} serves two purposes:
{ol}
{li}Separating the logic elements of the document; and
{li}Specifying the processing functions to be
performed on those elements.{/ol}
{/p}
{p}There are no quotation marks in the text; the
processing for the quotation element generates them
and will distinguish between the opening and closing
marks. Processing a document becomes a function of
its attributes. Note that a code has been used to
signal the beginning of a list and another for the
end of a list and yet a third for an item within the
list. Other kinds of coding could be used. For
example see the following.
{story}
{h1}This is a first-level heading{/h1}
{p}Now the story begins with the first paragraph
and there could be a list within the story.
{list}
{li} Item 1 of the list could be here.
{li} Item 2 of the list could be here.
{/list}
{h2}This could be a second-level head which
if one so defined could be a run-in heading.{/h2}
{p}And then the story would continue. Now the
story ends.{/p}
{/story}

25

Managing the Technology

THE READER, if he or she has patiently read the contents of this book, should surely be impressed by the wide variety of demands, requirements and expectations which the public brings to the publishing process. For many centuries techniques have been developed in response to these demands and expectations. Now, more than ever, there are prospects for increased economy and even better solutions to many diverse problems.

These needs are widely varied. Some have to do with timeliness: information must be collected and disseminated with unusual speed. Then there are problems associated with distance: those who create the manuscripts may be remote from those who edit and arrange the pages, from the artists who create the illustrations, from the compositors and the printers, and from the distribution centers.

There are, of course, problems of scale, having to do with the sheer size (or absence thereof) associated with the material to be typeset and distributed. There are variations in the number of copies required, from a mere handful to millions.

The question of how complicated the typeset product may need to be is certainly not trivial—whether it contains extensive tabular matter and multilevel mathematical and other scientific expressions. Must it be set simultaneously in several languages, reading from left to right, right to left, or vertically? Does it need to be impeccably presented, or can the presentation tolerate a significant error factor? May it appear only in black and white, or does it require a faithful process-color rendition? These are only a few of the variables that come to mind and must be dealt with, somehow, within the rigid constraints of available technology and financial resources.

It is not surprising, therefore, that many approaches, systems and organizational arrangements have been developed to address these needs and that all of these arrangements are generally in a constant state of flux—more so nowadays because of the rapid rate at which all aspects of technology are changing.

There is, nevertheless, an appropriate solution to a given problem or requirement at any point in time. It may not be, and probably never will be, an ideal solution. Compromises with respect to timeliness, form and manner of presentation are inevitably required. But choices and options must be exercised with knowledge of what is available now, what is about to become available, and what these choices imply in terms of the entire institutional structure surrounding the creative and production processes.

Managing the Technology

Should one install one's own equipment or instead rely upon a commercial or trade house? Should one generate one's own input? Should one look at a particular task as an isolated event or consider it in the light of an ongoing undertaking—to continue to publish the same kind of material or to keep a particular product up to date?

In making these judgments it may be helpful to consider the methods which are commonly used, along with the reasons why they have been selected.

It is also advantageous to identify others whose needs are similar, and to determine whether the compromises which they have had to make appear reasonable and offer practical guidance for one's own situation.

At this point we shall look at the problem only from the standpoint of the publisher, although our first consideration would certainly be to determine whether or not there is not a commercial service, manned with experienced people, ready and anxious to tackle our specific requirements.

Assuming that relevant commercial services do in fact exist, one needs to know whether these operations can meet identified needs in terms of service (time, volume, availability, capability) and cost. Similar decisions, perhaps made some years ago, must now be reviewed based upon new facts.

Has my situation changed because I now need computer or word processing equipment to perform related functions, especially those of an editorial nature? If so, surely I should explore the possibility of providing my input into my vendor's system, or the option of doing the entire job myself.

Has my situation changed because the new equipment available is simpler and more straightforward to operate than before, being more suitable for an office environment and involving less skill? Perhaps that equipment is now so inexpensive that it does not need to be used intensively and can be considered as a convenience item rather than as a production tool.

Is it now possible that I need to develop my own expertise in working with computers—and perhaps even typesetting—in order to gain a better appreciation of what the publishing process is all about? Is there a chance that new products will occur to me (and my associates) as we gain insights into these new processes? Or perhaps new and more attractive ways of presenting the same product? Or new markets may suggest themselves, such as electronic, on-demand publishing?

How intimately do I need to be involved with this new technology to gain an appreciation of these considerations?

Am I relying too extensively upon skills which are becoming impossible to find and increasingly expensive to obtain? Will I always be able to recruit and retain a good copy editor or a good indexer? Are there new alternatives which did not previously exist, or is it likely that such alternatives may exist in the near future? If these alternatives involve new skills of their own, should I take steps to acquire such skills?

What insights can I learn about my situation by looking at what my competitors (or others similarly situated) are doing? Can I profit by knowing more about their successes and failures?

What business am I in? Is my principal task to distribute information or to publish books? If publishing is incidental to my principal thrust (for example, if I must provide documentation for aerospace products), can I jeopardize my major activity by failing to support it in a timely and cost-effective fashion?

It may indeed be time for each of us to make an agonizing reappraisal of our companies, our roles, our capabilities, and our aspirations. Such questions are particularly appropriate during periods of rapid technological change.

Looking at what exists

TO PROVIDE THE READER with some positive and specific suggestions, we include, along with this bound volume, a supplement which we intend to update periodically in order to reflect the "real world" of the equipment available for use. Reference to that document will indicate approximate price ranges, modularity and application areas. The products included cannot be all-inclusive, but they will be suggestive and illustrative. No effort is made to evaluate the relevance of one product as opposed to another for a specific application. The various issues of *The Seybold Report on Publishing Systems* provide much more detail and timeliness, but the reader will be able to gather many insights into the range of solutions by an examination of this supplement, *A Classification of Typesetting System Solutions*.

But this supplement should be studied with the following comments in mind, and these comments, we believe, will provide a suitable conclusion for this book.

It was about ten years ago that most firms in the printing and publishing industry came to the conclusion that their requirements were so unique that general-purpose computer solutions could not deal with them satisfactorily. They had started, of course, with the opposite presumption. They had assumed that general-purpose mainframe computers could and would deal with their production needs as well as with their business requirements. They learned that this was not the case, not only because such systems were often too expensive, but also because they were too inefficient from the standpoint of the supporting software and the systems environment. Consequently they found minicomputers with special hardware and system features to be extraordinarily effective for input, for editing and for composition. By extension, some of these systems have also developed the power and flexibility to handle such tasks as page make-up and the manipulation of graphics, or to interface successfully to appropriate subsystems and peripherals.

Now, however, we are beginning to believe that demands at the workstation level are more varied. Workstation users want the best of all worlds: command over input, editing and composition functions

Managing the Technology

communication with the rest of the world, access to graphics and spreadsheets, and a host of office support activities, from time scheduling to the management of personal data bases. They want to be able to browse through relevant literature and to be alerted when information surfaces that meets their special interest profiles. They even want transportability so that resources available to them at the office are also at their fingertips at home and elsewhere.

We seem to be moving, again, toward a more general-purpose support environment, although neither the software nor the hardware has as yet fully evolved. It does appear, nevertheless, that with powerful, semi-independent but linked workstations at our disposal will function differently in the late 80s and the early 90s than was the case in the 70s and early 80s.

The modular approach. What we all clearly want and require now is a modular solution. We would like to be able to start out with a single, powerful terminal, adequately equipped with software, data storage and communications support. We want to be able to link that workstation to other similar stations, either a few or a large number. We expect that communication between these workstations will be transparent and instantaneous. We want all of the copy flow features of a large newspaper system, but none of the constraints. Our linkage to the larger (perhaps even infinitely larger) world must be fluid and yet efficient. We expect to make demands upon our support system that will bring to bear the most powerful of resources, but we do not want such demands to impose any particular discipline or response characteristics upon us. Can we have such an arragement?

The answer is that we are evolving in that direction. We are not there yet. But in our choice of systems we should look for as much modularity as we can contrive to find.

This may imply patching systems together, especially if sophisticated graphic manipulation is desired. If it does indeed mean dealing with more than one vendor, we may be compelled to take more responsibility ourselves for the integration of the entire solution. We may not be able to rely upon anyone else to network an entire system for us.

Since this may prove to be the case, our discussion in this final chapter may seem a bit unrealistic. We shall be holding out the promise of what ought to be, and hoping that somehow the building blocks—most of which are presently in existence—will somehow fall into place. We are confident, however, that this will ultimately take place.

There is presently no assured modularity between these elements, but we are moving there. Even those offerings which lay claim to modularity, such as the Compugraphic Modular Composition System, must admit that present functionality limits their scope to a relatively small number of workstations, thus confining their effectiveness to a limited set of circumstances. But we should keep in mind a more demanding set of criteria, and evaluate existing offerings against what we know or believe to be possible.

1. A general-purpose workstation is now available, providing excellent input and editing and communications capabilities. Given sufficient disk storage at the workstation level, a great deal of flexibility in the use of a variety of application software packages should be possible.

The manner in which such workstations will be linked together to permit editorial copy flow presents, in principle, no particular problems. A local area network (LAN) would contain a file server which would serve as the custodian of those files and directories which may be shared, either by specific routing or from a depository, and access to which is determined by conventions over which the file server itself will preside. Among programs which can be downloaded would be copies of application software packages, so that the workstation will be able to perform many tasks, including those associated with composition.

It does not follow that all workstations need to be equal in their capabilities. It is to be presumed that some workstations will be intended primarily for input and editing rather than for copy fitting and pagination. In the interest of economy (at least in the near future), the screen resolution or WYSIWIG characteristics of terminals will vary. Relatively expensive workstations, with gray scale or even color features will be assigned to those who need to see precisely what the final page will look like. Lower resolution monitors or even monospaced terminals will be sufficient for those mainly concerned with textual content.

2. The file server will provide control over the available software and access to files. It will also monitor job status, providing relevant queues and directories to link associated story ingredients (legends, pictures, heads, boxes and other components) and will provide tracking information and status information, while assuring security, confidentiality and back-up.

3. The local area network will handle internal communication and will link to appropriate communication nodes to transfer files as necessary from one such network to another over public or shared private communication facilities.

4. Location of data will, of course, be of critical concern. In the interest of minimizing communications traffic, reducing communication costs and optimizing response times, the underlying principle would involve data storage as close as possible to those who need it, and would work with subsets of data (especially abstractions or subsets of graphics) wherever possible. In many cases it may be sufficient to consider the facts about the text or the illustrative matter rather than the actual matter itself.

5. Tapping the required skill resources will bring persons and tools into the loop to perform the functions for which they are best qualified—whether as copy editors, writers and researchers, page layout and design artists, or creative artists and technicians concerned with the processes of image enhancement.

6. Housekeeping, record keeping, financial transactions and other support functions will be integrated as necessary.

7. Output devices appropriate for the particular application and the stage of the process will be available and located conveniently to permit those who need to interact to do so, whether with hard or soft copy.

But what is truly ready?

THEN, JUDGING AVAILABLE products against these standards, we must also consider the virtue of the established solutions, presumably more bug-free, probably developed over many years by persons who have learned the intricacies of the applications they are addressing rather than brashly rushing into a field armed only with ignorance and presumption. One is tempted to conclude, therefore, that since the things that truly work are already out of date, and the things that are consonant with contemporary technology do not yet function reliably, we should bide our time. But, this condition will continue to prevail, for so long as technology advances rapidly, that which works best is probably already obsolete. And that which holds forth the greatest promise is also that which will involve the most profound institutional adaptation—a process which is both upsetting and cannot be achieved quickly since its ramifications are seldom appreciated or totally identifiable.

Because of the changing nature of the industry, we include with this book a supplement, separately bound, which summarizes some of the solutions which are available at this time, and which addresses specific needs. It is our intention to revise this supplement yearly and to provide it as a guide for those who need to know what specific products and approaches are available for various kinds of problems and situations.

Our role as students and practitioners

THE END RESULT of study must be action: the making of decisions, the shaping of policy, meeting the exigencies of the day with the best that we can offer. That is what education is all about. And we cannot afford the luxury of pursuing knowledge simply for is own sake. We must indeed move forward, then, with all deliberate speed. We must all be pioneers and innovators, risking only what we can afford to risk and managing only what we can cope with at one time.

This point of view suggests that we should be hesitant to embrace total solutions, and that we should learn to crawl before we walk and walk before we fly. Thus we should not only prefer modular approaches but incremental steps, to allow time for institutional accommodation and verification.

And yet there are times when this is not sufficient and a more profound break with tradition is the only viable solution. The art is to know when this may and should be risked and when it must be avoided.

It is usually best to begin with one product, one application, one department, one publication, one plant, and when success has been demonstrated to move forward from that base, parlaying and extrapolating the experience thus gained.

One other philosophical observation may be hazarded: we began with a world in which "necessity" was "the mother of invention." That is no longer true. Today invention creates its own necessities. And we are launched upon a course which implies a kind of exponential imperative. In the future we will be able to anticipate, through the miracle of silicon, smaller and smaller processors of greater speed and power, and more storage capacity both for programs and data. The imperative is to find productive and useful ways for harnessing this technology in a constructive manner, without corrupting our values and our social institutions. There has always been a cultural lag. Given the rate of change we must deal with this laggard accommodation and help move it forward into constructive channels.

Happily, these technological advantages are occuring in precisely the most significant areas—those having to do with the exchange of information, with communication, with the acquisition of knowledge, and with techniques for making these innovations both more accessible and better organized. Thus the revolution which has launched us into this mad race in a changing world also gives us the tools to deal with the problems it presents and to maximize the promises it proffers.

Those of us who are fortunate enough to work closely with the technology, and especially to help to channel its potential for practical purposes which promote the horizontal and vertical growth of knowledge and civilization, are offered a rare opportunity and an exceptionally privileged position. Let us hope we make the most of it.

Index

A

AM International
    Varityper 77, *135*
    Comp/Set *94*
AP (Associated Press)
    60
ASCII
    (USASCII) *154, 227*
Ada, Augusta
    Countess of Lovelace *140*
Aftenposten, *344*
Agate
    definition of, *46n*
Agfa
    P-400 *386, 396*
Aiken, Howard H., *142*
Alexander, George A.
    "Computer Aids for Authors and Editors" *400n*
Allied Corporation, *50*
Alphanumeric Photocomposition System (APS)
    129
    APS-2 *127, 129, 131*
    APS-3 *129, 130, 131*
    APS-4 *130, 131*
    APS-5 *130*
    Manber patent *129n*
    Schwartz patent *129n*
    See also Autologic
Alphatype
    AlphaSette *93*
    CRS typesetter *134*
American Chemical Society, *411*
American Newspaper Publishers' Association
    Research Institute (RI) *253*
American Point System, *34*
American Type Founders (ATF), *76, 77*
    B-8 *77, 86, 89, 96, 273*
Apple
    Lisa *366*
    Macintosh *356, 366*
Area composition
    concept of, *270, 271*
Atex, *362, 363*
Autologic, Inc.
    APS typesetters *385, 386*
    APS-5 *131, 132*
    APS-5/100 *131*
    APS-5U *131*

APS-Micro-5 *134*
Graphic Converter Interface *385, 386*
Graphics Mode 2 *385*
Photon 7000 *130, 131*
See also Alphanumeric Photocomposition System
Automatic Sequence Controlled Calculator, *142*
Avisa Relation oder Zeitung, *10*

B

Babbage, Charles, *140*
Back-end system
    definition of, *306*
Bardeen, John, *142*
Barker, Christopher, *12*
Baud
    origin of term *65*
Baudot, Emile, *65*
Bell Labs
    Writer's Workbench *406*
Binary notation, *150, 151, 152*
Bishop's War of 1452, *9*
Bit, *148*
    definition of, *102n*
Black box, *233*
Blake, William, *335n*
Blind keyboards, *232, 233*
Bliven, Bruce Jr., *13, 14, 15*
Bobst, *238*
Boole, George, *143*
Booth, A. C., *65*
Brattain, Walter H., *142*
Brightype, *72*
Burt, William Austin, *14*
Byte
    concept of, *148*

C

CAD/CAM systems, *351*
CCD, *338n*
CRT typesetters, *114*
Camex Corporation, *382*
    BitCaster *382, 383*
    BitPrinter *382, 383*
    BitSetter *382, 383*
    Breeze *379, 382, 383*
    Model 135 *377*

420   *Index*

    SuperSetter *335*
Campbell, John, *10*
Canon
    LBP-10 *375*
    LP-10 *316*
Carlson, Jerry A., *171*
Cathode ray tube, *113, 114*
CCD, *338n*
CRT typesetters, *114*
Camex Corporation, *382*
    BitCaster *382, 383*
    BitPrinter *382, 383*
    BitSetter *382, 383*
    Breeze *379, 382, 383*
    Model *135* 377
    SuperSetter *335*
Campbell, John, *10*
Canon
    LBP-10 *375*
    LP-10 *316*
Carlson, Jerry A., *171*
Cathode ray tube, *113, 114*
Caxton, William, *9*
Center for Information Research, *310*
Central Processing Unit (CPU)
    components of, *147, 148*
Chappell, Warren, *7, 8, 9, 11*
Character repertoire
    character store *24, 25*
Chase
    definition of, *9*
Church, Dr. William, *40*
Code readers, *239*
Cognitronics, *238*
Coherent light
    definition of, *240n*
Columbian Exposition, *51*
Compgraphic, *238*
Composition process
    character sets *223, 224, 225*
    input programs *222, 223*
    keyboard *223*
Composition software
    programs *178, 179, 180, 181, 182, 183,*
    programs *184*
CompuScan, *236, 238, 250*
Compugraphic
    238, 282, 286n
    2961 *89, 92*
    4961 *92*
    8400 *134*
    8600 *134*
    ACM *9000 96*
    CompuWriter *93*
    CompuWriter Jr. *101*
    ExecuWriter *101*
    Modular Composition System *415*
    VideoComp *133*
    VideoComp *570 134*
    Videosetter *119,120, 121, 122*
    Videosetter Universal *133*
Computer languages

    ALGOL *167*
    BASIC *167, 177*
    C *167, 168, 177*
    COBOL *167*
    FORTRAN *167*
    Pascal *167, 168*
Computer structure, *145, 146, 147*
    instruction sets *157, 158*
    output devices *159*
    registers *158*
    speed *156*
Computer systems
    peripherals *158, 159*
Computer-stored files
    directories of, *301*
    routing of, *302, 304*
Contour information, *349, 350*
Control Data
    use of OCR *236*
Copy editing, *401, 402*
Correction of input errors, *217, 218*
    global substitution *218*
Counting keyboard, *233*
Counting logic, *52, 53*
Coxhead Composing Machine DS-J, *77*
Crosfield, *353*
    Magnaset *123*

D

Dainippon Screen (DS), *353*
Dale list, *406*
Dale-Chall list, *406*
Data General
    Nova *359*
Data bases
    examples *331, 332*
Data manipulation
    abridging *331*
    abstracting *331*
    automatic indexing *331*
    explosion *331*
    extraction *331*
    key words *331*
    redundancy elimination *331*
Data processing, *309, 310*
    characteristics of, *321, 322, 323, 325*
    fixed field *321*
    sort field *327*
    trailer field *327*
    typesetting from punched cards *325, 326, 327,*
    328
De Morgan, Augustus, *143*
Decimal numbering sets, *151, 152*
Delimiter
    definition of, *201*
Dest, *238*
Developmental editing, *401*
Diablo
    printer *380, 311*

Index

printer *308, 311*
Diagraphs, *30*
Didot system (Didot-Berthold), *34*
Digital Equipment Corporation (DEC)
    LSI-11 *368*
    PDP-11 *147*
    PDP-8 *359*
    RK505 *298*
    VAX *177*
Digital character representation, *123, 124, 126, 127*
Direct-entry machine
    concept of, *16*
Donnelly, R. R., *61*
Dressler, Fritz R. S., *309, 310*
DuPont
    Dycril *72*
Duenne, Hans, *6*
Duplexed fonts
    definition of, *77n*
Durer, Albrecht, *8*
Dvorak keytop assignments, *225*
Dymo Graphic Systems
    DLC-1000 *137n, 386, 387*
    soft copy display screen *362*

E

EBCDIC, *154, 227*
ECRM, *238, 242, 244, 250*
    Autokon *341, 342, 343*
    autofunctions and autostrings *245*
ENIAC
    Electronic Numerical Integrator & Calculator *142*
Earl of Dunraven, *51*
Eastman Kodak, *81, 353*
Eckert, J. P., *141*
Editorial systems
    definition of, *305, 306*
    magazines *175, 176*
    newspapers *174, 175*
Educational Testing Service, *406*
Ege, Otto F., *1, 2, 6*
Eikonix
    Designmaster *355*
Eltra Corporation, *50*
Em space
    definition of, *39n*
En space
    definition of, *39n*
Eocom, *344*
Ethernet, *365, 370*
Exception word dictionary, *210, 211*

F

FIFO
    definition of, *302*
Fairchild Lithotype Composer, *77*
Fiber optic face plate, *121*
File management systems, *298, 300, 301*
File server, *416*
Fixed-head disks, *298*
Flesch test, *405*

Floppy disks, *300*
Flow charting, *162, 164, 165, 166, 167*
Franklin, Benjamin, *10*
Franklin, James, *10*
Friden Justowriter, *77, 101, 109*
    Recorder and Reproducer *76*
Front-end system
    definition of, *305*
Full-screen display, *232*
Furniture
    definition of, *9*
Fust and Schoffer, *8, 9*

G

Gannett, Frank, *60*
Garamond, Claude, *10*
Goldberg, Hiram, *235*
Granjon, Robert, *10*
Graphic Communications Association, *411*
Graphic Systems, *238*
Great Britian regulations for page depth, *276*
Gutenberg, Johann (Johann Gensfleisch), *5, 6, 7, 8, 9, 30, 83*

H

Hagen, Tom
    The Seybold Report on Publishing Systems 371
Halftones, *336*
Hard-wired logic
    definition of, *261*
Harris Corporation
    (Harris-Intertype Company) *73*
    Fotosetter *96, 105, 111*
    Fototronic *92, 341*
    Fototronic CRT *130*
    Fototronic 1200 *103*
    Fototronic 7400 *134*
    Fototronic 7500 *134*
    Fototronic 7600 *134*
    1100 *253*
    2200 *279, 282*
    2250 *282*
Hashing, *404, 405*
Hell, Dr.-Ing. Rudolf, *127, 353*
Hell
    CRTronic *395*
    Combiskop *354*
    Digigraph *4020 341*
    Digiset *127, 128*
    Digiset 20T2 *128*
    Digiset 40T1 *128*
    Digiset 40T2 *128*
    Digiset 40T3 *128*
    Digiset 50T1 *127*
    Digiset 800 series *128*
Hendrix Electronics
    238,254
    5102 *254*
    5200 *254*

Hexadecimal notation, *152, 153, 154, 155*
Higonnet, Rene, *72, 78*
Hollerith Tabulator, *51*
Hollerith card
   141, 321
Hollerith, Herman, *140, 141*
Hollingdale, S.H.
   electronic computers *139, 139n*
Huss, Richard E., *41n*
Hyphenation, *200*
   British vs. American *208*
   exception word dictionary *209, 210, 211*
   fall-off point *201*
   logic algorithm *204, 205, 206*
   verification *214*
   with prefixes and suffixes *207, 208*
   word identification *201, 202, 203, 204*
Hyphenless justification, *200, 201*

I

IBM
   1130 FDP composition program *193*
   4250 Electro-Erosion Printer *396*
   6670 *316*
   Correcting Selectric *16*
   Courier 12 *243*
   Datatext *218*
   Displaywriter *314*
   Epistle *410*
   PC *177, 364*
   Printext commands *193, 194, 195, 196, 197*
   Selectric *15, 17, 18, 19, 25, 70, 95, 223, 250*
   Selectric Composer *395*
   use of OCR *236*
Idiot tape, *106n, 177*
Image dissector tube, *120*
Imlac, *362*
Incunabula, The, *9*
Indention, *191, 192*
Inferiors (subscripts), *18*
Information International (Triple-I)
   128, 133, 286n
   3600 Continuous Tone *345*
   Infocolor *348*
   InfoSet 400 *128n*
   Videocomp 500 *344, 345, 347, 348*
   VideoComp 570 *134, 135, 344, 345, 347, 348*
Intelligent Machines Corporation, *235*
Interactive page layout, *283, 286*
International Typographical Union, *76*
Intertype
   Fotosetter *72, 73*
   Monarch *64*
   linecasters *40, 41*
Itek
   Digitek *138, 386*

J

Jacquard, Joseph Marie, *140, 141*

Jenson, Nicholas, *9*
Jessell, Walter
   Composition definitions *225, 226*
Justification logic
   concept of, *105*
Justification
   concept of *32, 33, 186, 187*

K

KWIC index, *333*
Kerning, *31n*
Key-to-tape (key-to-disk) systems, *215, 216*
King Frederick III
   Elector of Bradenburg *10*
Koenig, Friedrich, *11*
Kurzweil, *251*

L

LIFO
   definition of, *302*
Lanston Monotype Company, *40, 51, 55*
Lanston, Albert, *11*
Lanston, Tolbert, *51, 279*
Leading
   definition of, *35*
Leibnitz, Gottfried Wilhelm, *140*
Letterpress, *72*
Letterspacing
   concept of, *33, 74*
Life, *335*
Ligatures, *30, 228*
Line drawing, *337*
Line information
   (lineinf) *274*
Line-ending decisions
   concept of, *26*
Linecasting process, *49, 50*
Linofilm, *89*
Linofilm Quick, *89*
Linotype GmbH, *50*
Linotype
   Electron *64*
Lithography, *11n, 72*
Lithomat (Photon), *78*
Lithomat Company, *72*
Local area network (LAN), *268*
Logotypes, *30*
Los Angeles Times, *344*
Lotus
   1-2-3 *356*
Ludlow process, *73*

M

Machine language programming, *167, 168*
Makeready
   definition of, *9*
Mauchly, J. W., *141*
McIntosh, Ronald, *114*
McMurtrie, Douglas C., *1, 3, 4, 5, 6*

Index

Mergenthaler, *115*
Mergenthaler Linotype Company, *40, 50*
Mergenthaler
    "Comet" *41*
Mergenthaler, Ottomar, *11, 50*
Mergenthaler
    CRTronic *135, 136*
    CorRecTerm *254*
    Linofilm *81, 82, 84, 85, 93*
    Linoscreen Composer *282*
    Linotron 1010 *114, 123, 319, 338*
    Linotron 202 *134*
    Linotron 303 *119, 136*
    Linotron 505 *114*-119,123,130
    Linotron 606 *134*
    Linotype *40, 50*
    Linotype Machine Principles *42*
    Omnitech 2000 *390, 391, 394, 395*
    Omnitech 2100 *395*
    V-I-P *89, 93, 94, 108*
    Wide-Range Super Quick *89*
Micro-Instruments Telemetry Systems
    Altair 8800 *364*
Miehle-Goss Dexter (MGD)
    Metro-set *133*
Mill, Henry, *13*
Mill, John Stuart, *143*
Minneapolis Star & Tribune, *371*
Mnemonic commands, *198*
Mohrtext, *254*
Monotype, *52*
    Lasercomp *137, 382, 389, 390*
    Monophoto *74, 75, 85, 92, 111*
    character repertoire *57*
    mat case layout *54*
Morey, Walter, *60, 64*
Morison, Stanley, *52*
Motorola
    58000 *368*
    68000 *167, 379*
Moving-head disks, *298*
Moyroud, Louis, *72, 78*
Multiple platter disk, *298*
Multiprogramming, *169*
Murray code, *65*
Murray-Baudot coding, *69*
Mycro-Tex
    AdComp *282*

N

National Geographic Society
    keyboard layout *229, 230, 231*
National Library of Medicine, *319*
NewsNet, *317*
Newspaper Systems Development Group, *361*
Newsweek, *348*
Nihon Electronics Company (NIC), *390*
Nipkow disk, *240*

O

OCR, *158, 159, 235*-252
    as a scanning device *237, 238*
    character identification *243*
    character recognition *243*
    data capture *240*
    definition of *239*
    editing and correcting routines *247, 248, 249*
    flying spot scanner *240*
    laser scanners *240*
    manual intervention *244*
    paper transport *239, 240*
    post-recognition logic *244*
    recognition logic *243, 244*
    scanner *240*
Oasis Systems
    Punctuation and Style *407*
Observer-Dispatch, *344, 371*
Octal numbering sets, *151, 152, 154*
Omnifont readers, *237*
Omnitext
    1500 *254*
Optronics International, *355*
Orphan
    definition of, *295*n
Overlay
    definition of, *9*

P

Page make-up
    vertical justification *277, 278, 279*
    widows *275, 276*
Page-ending decisions
    concept of, *26*
Pagination
    book composition *295, 296*
    journals *294*
    magazines *291, 293*
    newspaper pages *288, 289*
    related considerations *297*
    technical Publications *294*
Palo Alto Research Center, *364*
Paper
    orgin of, *3, 4*
Papyrus, *2, 3*
Parity
    concept of, *150*
Pascal, Blaise, *140*
Paul, K. S., *114*
Perry Publications, *210*
Perry typewriter font, *236*
Perry, John, *236*
Phoenician alphabet, *2*
Photon
    200 *78, 80, 81, 84,85, 111*
    260 *80*
    513 *80, 89*
    540 *80*
    560 *80*
    713 *86, 87, 103*
    900 (ZIP) *87, 88, 89, 114, 319*
    Pacesetter *99, 99*n
Pixel
    340, 374, 375, 376

Plantin, Christophe, *10*
Plate making, *343*, *344*
Post-recognition logic
    function of translate routines *246*, *247*
    string translator *245*
    translate routines *244*, *245*
Printing Developments, Inc., *353*
Production system
    definition of, *306*
Programming
    coding *167*, *168*
    documentation *169*
    loading the program *168*, *169*
Punched cards
    general concept of, *215*
Purdy, Peter, *114*

Q

Quadding, *187*, *190*, *191*
Qume
    printer *308*, *311*
Quoins
    definition of, *9*

R

RCA, *81*
    1600 *127*
    301 *177*, *210*
    822X *130*n
    Page-1 *296*
    Page-2 *296*
    VideoComp *127*
    VideoComp 830 *128*, *129*
REI
    use of OCR *236*
Ragged settings, *192*, *193*
Randolph, Woodruff, *76*
Raster image processors, *372*
    373, *374*, *375*, *376*, *377*
Raster scanning, *258*
Raytheon, *282*
Recognition Equipment, Inc., *236*
Remington, Philo, *14*
Rotophoto, *74*
Russell, Lord Bertrand, *143*

S

Saspoch, *9*
Scan Data
    use of OCR *236*
Scanner
    drum *338*, *339*
    flatbed *338*
    flying spot *338*, *339*
Scanning techniques, *337*, *338*
Scanning
    principles of, *340*, *341*
Schoffer, Peter, *6*

Schreiber, Prof. William F.
    Production of Images on Printing Presses *350*
Scitex, *354*
    Imager Console *355*
    Vista *335*
    Vista *355*
Seaco, *133*
Second-generation typesetters
    character escapement *95*, *96*, *97*, *98*, *99*, *100*, *101*, *102*
    character exposure *92*
    character selection *85*, *86*, *87*, *88*, *89*, *90*
    character sizing *92*, *93*, *94*, *95*
    character storage *85*
    justification *104*, *105*, *106*
Secondary leading
    definition of, *295*n
Selected Dissemination of Information (SDI) *318*
Sellers & Co., *51*
Senefelder, Aloys, *11*
Seybold, Jonathan
    The Seybold Report on Publishing Systems *368*, *370*, *371*, *372*, *373*
Shared-logic systems, *308*
Shockley, William, *142*
Sholes, Christopher Latham, *14*
Signature
    definition of, *47*n
Sim-X
    PAGEscan *390*
Singer Company
    8400 *254*
Slave typesetter
    definition of, *103*
Soft copy keyboard, *232*
Soft copy typesetter, *286*, *287*
Spache list, *406*
Spelling checkers, *400*, *402*, *403*, *404*
Stand-alone computer
    concept of, *177*
Standard signset (pseudofont), *226*
Star Parts
    CompStar 190 *101*
Star-Times, *371*
Stephen Day press, *10*
Stored formats, *198*, *199*
Straddle words, *201*
String substitution, *198*
Strobe
    definition of, *78*n
Superiors (superscripts), *18*

T

TEX, *185*n
TTS Standard Perforator
    keyboard *61*, *62*, *63*
TTS
    concept of, *60*, *61*
    paper-tape coding *64*, *65*, *68*, *69*, *70*, *71*
    precedence codes *69*, *70*

Index

Taft-Hartley Act, 76
Taplin, 238
Tektronix
 4014 286
The Chicago Manual of Style
 hyphenation rules 208
The Farm Journal, 171, 172
The Idea Processor, 401
The Seybold Report, 387, 394, 395
The Seybold Report on Publishing Systems, 414
ThinkTank, 401
Third-generation typesetter
 definition of, 112
Time, Inc., 61, 293, 335, 353
 Time magazine 130n
Time-sharing, 169
Toothill, G. C.
 Electronic Computers 139, 139n
Transistors
 computer applications of 142, 143
True type editing, 218, 219, 221
Turing, Alan, 141
Tympan
 definition of, 9
Typesetting/data processing fusion, 319, 320, 321

U

U.S. Government Printing Office, 122, 319, 338, 395
U.S. News and World Report, 175, 344, 345, 360
U.S. regulations for page depth, 276
UPI (United Press International), 60
USASCII
 154, 227
Underlay
 definition of, 9
Unibus
 concept of, 147
Unit-count fonts, 101
Unitized fonts, 101

V

Vacuum tube technology, 142
Von Neumann, John, 42
Video display terminals (VDT), 174
 buffers 258
 components and functions 257, 258
 composition applications 253
 display ad composition 279, 281, 282
 editing capabilities 258, 259, 260, 261, 263, 264
 peripheral hookup 264, 265, 268
 TV-type 258, 258n
VideoComp 820, 114
VisiCalc, 364

W

WYSIWYG
 definition of, 178
Wang Electronic Publishing

Grammatik 407
Westover, George, 74
Wheatstone Automatic Telegraph, 65
Wheatstone, Prof. Charles, 65
Whitehead, Alfred North, 143
Widows
 defintion of, 275
Width tables, 185, 186
Wiener, Norbert, 142
Winchester disks
 definition of, 261n
Word processing
 composition functions 307, 308, 309, 310
 text formatting 311, 312
Word processors/typsetter interfacing, 312, 313, 314, 315, 316

X

X-height, 34
Xenotron, 282
Xerox Corporation
 Star (Xerox 8010) 364, 365, 366
 Xerox Integrated Composition System 365
 2700 316
 5700 316
 9700 316

Z

Z-height, 34n.

Index of Illustrations

A

AM Varityper
  Epics system *267*
ATF B-8
  recorder and reproducing Units *77*
Access table for basic typographic
  command codes *246*
Ad composition screens, *285*
Analysis of TTS code assignments, *68*
Antares
  word processor/typesetter conversion *316*
Apple
  llc, *256*
  Macintosh *369*
Atex
  GT68 page layout terminal *290*
  page dummy *289*
  terminal keyboard layout *229*
Autologic
  APS-5 output with GCI inteface *385*
  APS-5 output of scanned graphics *294*
  Convergent Technologies workstation *267*
Automix Keyboards, Inc. (AKI)
  keyboard and VDT *256*
  PRO series terminal *256*
  Ultra series editing terminal *256*
Autostrings and autofunctions, *245*

B

Bedford Computer Corporation
  keyboard and VDT *267*
Binary and hexadecimal conversions, *153*
Binary and decimal conversion, *151*
Binary, octal and decimal conversions, *152*

C

CAD/CAM output from Amgraf, *352*
CRTronic preview screen, *220*
Camex
  Breeze *380*
  SuperSetter *285*
  SuperSetter output *381*
Cathode ray tube, *113*
Character spacing through kerning, *31*
Clay tablet and stylus, *3*
Comp/Set screen
  mid-typesetting *179*
Compugraphic
  Videosetter character generation *120*
  Videosetter character grid *121*
Computer circuitry
  And-gates, or-gates and flip-flops *144*
Computer instruction set commands, *157*
Counter for hand-set type, *31*
Crosfield Magnascan 540, *348*

D

Data line samples, *242*
Decimal and Hexadecimal conversions, *153*
Digitized letters, *128*

E

EBCDIC and USASCII coding, *155*
ECRM Autokon camera, *342*
Early computer output, *216*
Electric striking bar typewriter, *20*

F

Fiber optics bundle
  means of displacement *98*
Floppy disks, *300*
Flow chart samples, *163*, *164*, *165*
Flying spot scanner, *241*
Fotosetter's principle of escapement, *74*
Full-page ad composition, *284*

G

Greek letters and their Phoenician
  sources *2*
Grid basket, *80*

Index

H

Harris 1100 terminal, *255*
Harris 2200, *280*
Hastech
  PagePro workstation *287*
Hendrix 5200 terminal, *255*
Hewlett-Packard Portable, *369*
Hexadecimal translate table, *154*
Hot metal type in a chase, *32*

I

IBM
  Executive Boldface I typewriter, *22*
  Mag Card II typewriter *308*
  PC-XT, *369*
  1130 FDP composition program *194, 195, 196, 197*
IBM Selectric
  add-on characters available *22*
  examples from AIP publications *23*
  special character fan *23*
IBM Selectric II
  examples of available type faces *21*
  keyboard *27*
  typing element, ribbon and erasing tape *27*
Indention and measure changes, *191, 192*
Information International
  3500 Scanner and Videocomp *346*
Itek
  Digitek *138*

J

Justification routine
  sample flow chart *188*
Justification
  examples *193*

L

Laser scanning system, *241*
Leading samples, *37*
Lens turret
  focusing and sizing activity *100*
Letterspacing examples, *183*
Linecasting machine
  internal view *44*
  view of delivery channel and matrices *45*
Linend routine
  sample flow chart *189*
Linofilm 15-level tape, *82*
Linofilm Quick
  internal view *91*
  character storage and scanning *116*
  internal view of printout end *117*
Linotype
  linecaster *42*
  matrix *42*
  spacebands *42*
  view of assembling mechanism *45*
Lozenges to mark editing tasks, *248*

M

Mergenthaler
  CorRecTerm terminal, *255*
  Linotype CRTronic *136*
  MVP editing system *256*
  Omnitext *2000 393*
Monophoto
  diagram of, *75*
Monotype
  justifying scale *55*
  Lasercomp *392*
  Lasercomp output *389*
  matrix case *54*
  matrix positioning and caster *58*
  punched-paper tape *54*
Morey (TTS) Adaptation of Murray-Baudot Coding *66*
Morey adaption of Murray-Baudot Coding, *66*
Moving head disk
  diagrams *299*
  photo of multiple platter type *299*
Multilength file directory, *302*
Multicolumn text, *273*
Multiface Perforator, *63*

O

OCR fonts, *251*
Octal and decimal conversions, *151*
Omnitext 1500
  partial keyboard layout *257*
Optronics Pagitron drum scanner, *339*
Output from an IBM Executive Typewriter, *18*
Overflow routine
  sample flow chart *189*

P

PDP-11/34 system, *147*
Paper tape from a TTS keyboard, *65*
Paper tape fed into linecasting machine, *65*
Paper-tape perforating keyboards, *234*
Paper-tape punch, *67, 67*
Parity bits, *150*
Perry font
  sample of *236*
Photon
  200 Admaster *79*
  200 optical leverage *97*
  optical principles *79*
  ZIP *88*
Point size samples, *38*
Point-size variations
  illustrations of *94, 95*

optical principles of the *200* 79
ZIP *88*
Point size samples, *38*
Point-size variations
    illustrations of *94, 95*
Press Computer
    Delta Data *7303 266*
Punch housing mold for type casting, *7*

Q

Quadding
    Examples *187, 191, 190*
Qubix terminal, *256*

R

Raytheon
    composing system *284*
Remington typewriter, *20*
Rotating mirrors
    means of displacement *98, 99*

S

Screen of composed text, *220*
Screen of uncomposed text, *220*
Second-generation photosetters
    Compugraphic's method of escapement *96*
    imaging mechanism *96*
Second-generation typesetters
    rotating drum and film disk *90*
Shaffstall MediaCom
    black boxes *315*
Sim-X output, *393*
Six-bit configurations, *149*
Six-level TTS code, *67, 67*
Spelling checker
    WordProof *408*
System Integrators
    Coyote terminal for System 55 *266*
    directories, *303*

T

TTS Standard Perforator scale, *62*
TTS keyboard, *63*
Table-lookup procedure, *184*
Tally Model 525 Paper-Tape Reader, *67*
Third-generation typesetters
    table of font storage in memory *132*

Three-bit configurations, *148*
Type face used for typesetting by hand, *30*
Valid and invalid cross-outs and deletions, *249*
Vertical justification
    sample *277, 278*

V

Vidicon scanner, *241*

W

WYSIWYG file, *221*
Wooden tablets coated with wax, *3*
WordProof
    spelling checker and thesaurus *408*

X

Xenotron
    composing system *284*
Xerox "Star" (8010), *366*
    output *367*

Z

Zentec ZMS 70, *256*